The M&E BECBOOK Series

The Organisation in its Environment

JOHN BEARDSHAW
BSc (Econ.)
*Senior Tutor in Banking Studies
and Lecturer in charge of Economics
at Southgate Technical College*

DAVID PALFREMAN
BA
*Co-ordinator
Directed Private Study Unit
St John's College, Manchester*

SECOND EDITION

Macdonald and Evans

Macdonald & Evans Ltd
Estover, Plymouth PL6 7PZ

First published 1979
Reprinted 1980
Reprinted 1981
Second edition 1982
Reprinted 1983

© John Beardshaw and
David Palfreman 1982

ISBN 0 7121 1541 2

Made and printed in Great Britain by
Richard Clay (The Chaucer Press) Ltd,
Bungay, Suffolk

Preface

This book embodies the integrative approach of the BEC double module "The Organisation in its Environment", the pivot of the BEC national level courses. The modern business organisation is subject to an amalgam of social, economic, legal and political forces which no longer should be studied as isolated disciplines. Thus, this book integrates these disciplines and thereby escapes from the strait-jacket of traditional textbooks. It provides a more realistic examination of all the different influences and constraints which affect business organisations. However, it does so without sacrificing traditional academic rigour.

The five parts of the text follow the general objectives of the double module, and the book has been written specifically with the particular study needs of the student in mind. However, the arrangement of the material makes it possible for lecturers to approach the modules in the way which they consider best. Great care has been taken to ensure that all learning objectives in the double module have been fully considered.

Each chapter is followed by self-assessment questions. These are arranged as follows:

A = recall of material in the chapter;
B = understanding of material in the chapter;
C = application of the contents of the chapter and its integration with the rest of the double module.

There are also assignments following the questions. Lecturers will find these assignments a useful source of ideas for devising their own cross-modular assignments.

Whilst the book was specifically written for modules 3 and 4, its contents and approach make it a valuable text for all BEC conversion courses and business studies GCE "A" Level. It is also a useful first-year text for students on business studies and management courses at BEC higher or degree level.

The authors wish to acknowledge the valuable assistance of their colleagues at Southgate Technical College. Specific thanks must go to June Wildman, Don Payne and John Rowley, and to Denise and Hellen, two very patient and understanding wives.

J.B.
D.P.

July 1979

Preface to the Second Edition

BEC national level courses are now in their third year of operation in most colleges. Much has been learned both by students and staff. Without a doubt, the concentration on "skills" and "understanding" through student-centred courses is to be welcomed. Nevertheless, BEC imposes strains on the resources of many colleges and this is where, we hope, this book can help. In addition to the resource problems, the emphasis on student-centred and integrated study means that students need a structure to which they can easily relate. We have endeavoured to provide both the resources and the structure in this book.

For this second edition the entire text has been thoroughly revised and updated, Chapters 1 and 5 have been rewritten and a new chapter on the nationalised industries has been added. Much of the new material is a product of our work with the Directed Private Study Unit at St John's College, Manchester, where we have attempted to turn the basic text of this book into a student-centred self-study programme. We would be happy to give whatever help we can to any colleagues who would like suggestions for ideas on assignments and assessment techniques.

Our thanks must go to the others involved in the project, particularly to Sue Nicholson, David Fidler and Bill Orchard, all of whom have, in effect, contributed to this new edition. Thanks too to Jill Barber for typing. Not least our thanks must also go to the many students at Southgate and St John's whose comments and criticisms have helped in the preparation of this edition. Finally our thanks, once again, to Denise and Hellen for putting up with our somewhat idiosyncratic working methods and for providing the organisation in our environment.

J.B.

February 1982   D.P.

Contents

PART TWO: DEMOGRAPHY

PART THREE:
THE ORGANISATION AND ITS RESOURCES

PART FOUR:
THE ORGANISATION, ITS MARKETS, CUSTOMERS AND CLIENTS

PART FIVE:
THE ORGANISATION, THE STATE AND THE COMMUNITY

List of Illustrations

List of Tables

PART ONE
THE ORGANISATION

Organisations

CHAPTER OBJECTIVES

After studying this chapter you should be able to:
* define formal and informal organisations;
* describe the emergence of the modern economy;
* list the characteristics of organisations;
* state the objectives of different organisations;
* define public and private sector organisations.

We live in a world of organisations. Consider any aspect of our lives and you will find it is bound up with organisations. We are usually born in a hospital, spend a number of years in school and go on to work for a company or the government. If we misbehave we may end up in prison. These are all organisations. At the end of this life one is likely to be buried by another organisation—the church. Where did all these organisations come from?

Most organisations are surprisingly new. Consider the college you are working in. It is doubtful whether it was in existence more than twenty years ago. Consider the local authority which controls it—it is doubtful whether it existed in its present form before 1965. Go back beyond the Second World War and you will find only traces of the now vast apparatus of the welfare state. Even the most well-established business organisation will seldom have a history of more than a century. Thus, although we shall trace the origins of organisation we should realise that the "organisational" society is essentially a twentieth-century phenomenon.

THE EMERGENCE OF THE MODERN ORGANISATION

Feudal organisation and its legacy

Society has always been organised, but for most of man's history the organisation has been that of tradition and command. The feudal system provided a highly organised society, but one which was almost devoid of organisations. The most sophisticated organisation of feudal times was the church. Much of the tradition and custom on which feudal society functioned became embodied in the emergent *common law*. Whilst most other aspects of this society have vanished, it is interesting that some modern legal rights and duties and principles can be traced directly to this era and show, comparatively, little modification from their original form. When we come to consider the law of property and of land we should remember that some of its most fundamental principles are derived from a society which was totally different from the one in which we now live.

The beginnings of a market economy
In a feudal society the local community was virtually self-sufficient; it traded only for those things which it could not produce itself. In a process which lasted several hundred years, society evolved from a locally self-sufficient one to a large complex society based upon exchange. Thus *labour* became something divorced from social position and was made into an abstract quantity offered for sale. *Land* had become important because it bestowed power and status—what came to be important was its value. *Capital* had been a static concept of wealth but what became important was its yield. Thus, everything was a commodity to be bought and sold. This meant that society began to evolve into a market economy. Whilst we might dispute that we are still in a market economy today, it was undoubtedly the mechanisms of the market which gave rise to many of our organisations.

Economics, law and the organisation
When we examine the behaviour and structure of organisations, we will find that they are primarily economic and legal. Economic forces determine the ways in which man goes about making his living and law acts as a *regulatory medium* to further his economic activities and *resolve the conflicts* which inevitably arise. Thus, when we study organisations we shall be primarily concerned with these economic and legal aspects.

However, we cannot evaluate the organisations' activities purely in economic or legal terms; such questions as the siting of a new factory, the raising of old age pensions, the compulsory wearing of crash helmets and the siting of a new motorway will also have political, social, environmental and even religious aspects. Whilst we shall concentrate on the economic or legal aspects, the study of organisations in their entirety will present a fuller and more complete picture than any of the individual disciplines.

CLASSIFICATION OF ORGANISATIONS
Faced with the multiplicity of organisations, it is useful to classify them. There are several ways in which this can be done and one organisation might fit into several classifications.

Formal and informal

Formal organisations may be defined as those which have been established for the express purpose of achieving certain goals, aims or *objectives*, and which possess clearly defined *rules* to help them achieve these goals. This type of organisation includes all businesses, governments and international institutions. *Informal* (or social) organisations, on the other hand, are those in which social activities are carried on, usually without clearly defined goals or rules. Examples of such organisations include families, friendships and communities.

Formal organisations form the subject of this module and therefore of this book. You can see that the distinguishing feature of formal organisations is that they have *stated rules and objectives*, i.e. *characteristics*, which are common to all such organisations.

Productive and non-productive organisations

In the UK today there are many different forms of formal organisation and they could be classified in several ways. One of the simplest is to divide them into *productive* and *non-productive organisations*.

Productive organisations are all those which are in any way concerned with the production of goods and services. These can be *privately* owned, as is the case with the chemical industry, or *publicly* owned, as is the case with electricity. Do not make the mistake of thinking that only those industries which produce physical products such as cars or chemicals are productive; indeed, banking, which is a service industry, is one of the UK's biggest export earners.

All the industries mentioned so far *sell* goods and services to the community. However, publicly owned services such as health and education can also be considered as productive organisations, although they do not *trade* with the public in the usual meaning of the word. We might therefore also divide organisations into *trading* and *non-trading* categories.

Many organisations do not produce any goods and services and may be termed *non-productive*. However, they should not be considered unimportant. The legal institutions (courts of law, etc.) of the nation, the trade unions and churches are all examples of non-productive organisations which play an important role directly or indirectly in our lives.

The public sector and the private sector

The organisations which make up the economy may also be divided between the *public sector* and the *private sector*. *Public-sector* organisations are all those which are *owned* and *directed* either directly by the government (central or local) or indirectly through government-created bodies. Examples of public-sector organisations are Departments of State, nationalised industries and the armed forces. In 1980 total expenditure by the public sector accounted for 44 per cent of the *gross national product*.

The *private sector* of the economy includes all those organisations which are *owned* and *operated* by private citizens. This may range in size from huge organisations such as ICI to small local businesses. Organisations in the private sector take a variety of legal forms such as partnerships, joint-stock companies and co-operatives. There are some organisations which are counted as part of the private sector of the economy even though they may be wholly or partly government owned, e.g. BL.

Problems of definition

Having studied these classifications of organisations, it is apparent that there are no rigid divisions—BL for example, poses a distinct problem of classification. To cope with this problem we intend to use the term *trading organisations* to describe all the organisations which exist principally by *selling* goods and services, be they in the private or public sector. The next chapter will discuss the various legal forms which trading organisations take. This will include private-sector trading organisations, such as limited companies, which are normally termed *business organisations*, and public-sector trading organisations such as the nationalised industries.

Types of industry

All productive organisations, whether publicly or privately owned, form part of industry. It is often thought that industry just comprises those organisations which manufacture goods or produce raw materials, but banking, insurance and retailing are also parts of industry. In government statistics the Standard Industrial Classification (SIC) lists twenty-seven groups of industries, of which there are a further 184 sub-divisions. However, industries can be broadly categorised under three headings.

(*a*) *Primary*. These are industries concerned with the *extraction of raw materials*, and include agriculture, forestry, fishing and mining.

(*b*) *Secondary*. These are industries which are in any way concerned with the *processing* and *manufacturing* of products, and include such industries as iron and steel, motor vehicles and food processing.

(*c*) *Tertiary*. These are industries which do not produce goods but supply and sell a *service*. For this reason they are often termed "service industries". Included in this category are banking, education, tourism and the distributive trades.

In 1980 primary industries accounted for about 2.7 per cent of the national product, secondary industries about 40 per cent and tertiary industries the rest.

CHARACTERISTICS OF ORGANISATIONS

Rules and objectives have already been mentioned as characteristics which all formal organisations have in common. Seven such characteristics (including rules and objectives) are considered below.

(*a*) *Names.* All organisations have a name by which they are known. Mr Jones, the local grocer, may trade under his own name, but in many cases we shall see that the name and legal personality of an organisation may be quite separate from the people who own it.

(*b*) *Rules.* All organisations are governed by rules and regulations. These can be written, verbal or assumed to be known. Generally speaking the larger the size of the organisation the more formal will be the expression of the rules. An organisation may both develop its own rules and have rules imposed on it from outside, e.g. by the government. It is laid down by law, for instance, that all public joint-stock companies must hold an annual general meeting.

(*c*) *Objectives.* We have already seen that all organisations have objectives—in the case of businesses it is the pursuit of profit. Do not confuse the objective with the method of achieving it. For example, the objective of Ford UK is to make a profit; its method of doing so is to produce and sell cars.

(*d*) *Positions.* Within an organisation everyone has a role (or position) to fulfil. In a small organisation one person may fill several positions. In a large organisation roles tend to become more specialised, e.g. one might expect to find positions such as "marketing manager" in a large business.

(*e*) *Chain of authority.* All organisations have a chain of authority. This enables decisions to be made and jobs and functions to be carried out. The sophistication of a chain of authority will tend to increase with the size of an organisation. If the complexity is too great, however, this may damage the organisation's efficiency and performance.

(*f*) *Power.* The power in an organisation is usually said to rest with those who have the legal right to take decisions. In the case of a business organisation this is usually the owners, e.g. the shareholders of a company. On the other hand public corporations such as the National Coal Board are ultimately controlled by Parliament. The power to take decisions is often *delegated* via the chain of authority. For example, the shareholders will appoint a board of directors, they in turn will appoint managers, and so on.

(*g*) *Records*. All organisations have some method of recording their activities. These may range from the minutes of the local Women's Institute to *Hansard* (the publication which records every word spoken in Parliament). There are usually legal requirements to maintain certain forms of record, e.g. for tax-collection purposes.

THE OBJECTIVES OF ORGANISATIONS

We have said that one of the characteristics of all formal organisations is that they exist to pursue objectives or goals. The objectives which organisations pursue give us another way in which we might classify them. Firstly there are those which exist primarily to make a *profit*, secondly there are those which exist to direct or administer sectors of the community so as to attempt to *maximise national welfare*, and thirdly there are those which exist to *promote the interests of their members*. The list of organisations given below contains most of the types of organisations which we shall be concerned with in this book. As you work through the list, you should be aware that the distinction between them lies in their chief objectives. For example (*a*) *Business Organisations* are of very different shapes and sizes but all have the same objective.

Organisations classified by their objectives

(*a*) *Business organisations*. These are organisations with a variety of legal forms, e.g. sole traders, partnerships and companies, whose object is to make profit. We might distinguish between *industrial* organisations which are concerned with the production of goods, *commercial* organisations such as retailers, and *financial* organisations such as banks and insurance companies.

(*b*) *Governmental organisations*. Those concerned with the running of the country, either at national or local level, which are controlled by elected representatives.

(*c*) *Public corporations*. State-owned industries such as gas and steel are run by public corporations. Like business organisations they may exist by selling goods and services to the community.

However they do not exist primarily to make a profit but rather to run the industry in the national interest.

(*d*) *Quangos* (quasi-autonomous non-governmental organisations). These are organisations run by nominated boards, such as regional health authorities, the industry training boards (ITBs) and the Civil Aviation Authority. Almost any public body which is not elected could be described as a quango.

(*e*) *Economic interest groups.* People or organisations with common objectives may band together; for example the Confederation of British Industry (CBI) promotes the interests of employers, whilst the Consumers' Association tries to promote the interests of consumers.

(*f*) *Trade unions.* Although an economic interest group, they are certainly important enough to be considered separately.

(*g*) *Legal.* The administration of justice presents us with a set of complex organisations and institutions exercising specialised judicial and quasi-judicial functions.

(*h*) *Political.* The organisation of political parties is quite distinct from that of government in a democracy. This would not be true in communist or fascist states.

(*i*) *Charities.* These organisations are normally considered to exist to dispense goods and services to the needy. By and large this is true, but the legal form and status of a charity may be adopted to help the not-so-needy—most public schools, for example, are (legally) charities.

(*j*) *Mutual help.* Some trading organisations, such as co-operatives, are set up with the objective of helping their members rather than making a profit.

(*k*) *International organisations.* Internationally constituted bodies such as the IMF, the EEC or even FIFA are now extremely numerous and varied.

(*l*) *Multinational organisations.* These are business organisations which operate in many countries, e.g. Unilever, BP or ICI.

You can see that all the objectives of these organisations would fit into the three broad categories stated at the beginning of this section. Other types of organisation, such as religious or sporting, might be added to the list but they lie outside the scope of this book.

Objectives of private-sector organisations
It is often assumed that all organisations in the private sector are out to make a profit. A moment's reflection will show us that this is not so; obviously Oxfam is not out to make a profit and nor is a trade union, although they will both have a great interest in

remaining solvent. If you examine the private-sector non-business organisations in the list given above you will realise that most of them are concerned with mutual help or the advancement of the interests of their members.

Business organisations

A great deal of this double module is, however, concerned with the behaviour of business organisations and we will now consider briefly their objectives and their strategies for achieving them. A detailed consideration of their behaviour forms a greater part of the rest of this book.

(*a*) *Profit maximisation.* It is usually assumed that business organisations will always try to maximise their profits. This means that not only will they try to make a profit but they will also try to make as much profit as possible. There are well-established policies to achieve and maintain profit maximisation.

(*i*) Concentration on producing and supplying those goods and services where demand is increasing.

(*ii*) Minimisation of the cost of production by selecting the cheapest possible combination of premises, machinery and labour to use. Thus, if substituting machines for labour is cheaper, this will be done despite the social consequences associated with the redundancies which may follow.

(*iii*) Maintaining output at the level at which profits are maximised.

(*iv*) Where a single organisation is dominant in its own area of activity it can affect the price of the goods it produces by varying the amount it supplies to the market. It is therefore able to adjust either price or output to suit its own profit maximisation objective.

These strategies are considered in much more detail in Parts 3 and 4 of this book.

It is often thought that this pursuit of profit is a unifying characteristic of all business organisations. However, it is possible in very large organisations, where there is a divorce of ownership from management, that there are alternative objectives. There is a divorce of ownership from management when the directors (managers) of a company have little or no stake in the shareholding (ownership) of a company. Thus, the managers may be able to pursue policies more in line with their own self-interests so long as they are able to make enough profit to keep the shareholders happy. Three such objectives are now considered.

(b) *Market domination.* This may be pursued for the purposes of profit maximisation, but this need not be so—domination of a market may also give stability and security to the organisation, which might be viewed by the managers as more attractive than profit maximisation. Pursuit of market domination may lead a business to pursue a policy of sales maximisation. For example a business might cut prices and accept losses, for a time, with the object of driving its rivals out of business. Having achieved this it could then exploit the market.

(c) *Corporate growth.* Growth means increasing power and responsibility for managers, often reflected in higher salaries. Hence, this objective is obviously attractive. However, growth may be achieved at the expense of profit maximisation, and therefore may not be in the interests of the owners of the organisation. For example, new and less profitable goods may be produced.

Growth can be achieved by:

(i) *expanding* existing markets, e.g. through new products and advertising;

(ii) *diversifying,* i.e. extending the product range or activity of the organisation into new areas;

(iii) *takeover* (purchasing control) of other business organisations, for either of the two previous purposes.

(d) *Managerial utility function.* At the extreme a business organisation (or more correctly its managers) may have as one of its objectives the satisfaction (utility) of its managers. Providing that *sufficient* profit is made, managers may seek to expand, for example, their right to exercise personal discretion and obtain "perks" such as company cars. To achieve this objective part of the organisation's profit, which could be paid out to shareholders, must be diverted and used to pay for such managerial satisfaction. Since managerial satisfaction pushes up the costs of production, and hence the price charged, it is usually associated with organisations which do not operate in highly competitive industries.

It should be stated that these latter three objectives are of a controversial nature and are not accepted by all observers of organisations. It is argued by some that they can all be incorporated into the single objective of profit maximisation, while others go so far as to say that, although attractive, the ideas have little or no evidence to support them.

Objectives of public-sector organisations

There are a vast range of public sector organisations with an almost equally vast range of objectives. However, we might examine the objectives in terms of what is wanted by:

(*a*) the Government;
(*b*) those who operate and work in public sector organisations; and
(*c*) the public.

When we consider the relationship between the Government and the managers of public sector organisations, we may find the conflict we identified above between the managers and the owners of business organisations. That is to say, the Government may have one set of objectives, e.g. holding down costs, while the managers may be interested in expanding their jobs and power. Thus, we might also discover a *managerial utility function* in public sector organisations.

The government will usually state its objectives for public sector organisations in terms of the "maximisation of public welfare". It might be thought that governments and the electorate would be as one on this. This is, however, usually not so. A government may see it as its job to restrain public spending whilst sections of the public may wish to increase it, or vice versa. Governments also have political objectives which affect these organisations, not least amongst which will be its desire to be re-elected. It is not unknown for a government to prefer its own survival to the maximisation of public welfare.

When we examine business organisations it usually is apparent that employers and employees alike have an interest in the well-being of the business. Thus, there is at least some mutuality of purpose. However, for public-sector organisations this is often not so, e.g. their managers may be trying to expand them whilst a government is trying to restrain their growth. It is not surprising, therefore, that when we consider public sector organisations we shall find much uncertainty about their objectives.

CONCLUSION

It should not be thought that there exists an ideal form of organisation, a best way of doing things. Some people may advocate that everything would be best provided by private enterprise, or conversely, that everything should be nationalised. It should be obvious from the variety of objectives we have mentioned that no one organisational form could be expected to pursue them all successfully. *Thus, different objectives demand different forms of organisation.* In addition to this, technology takes a hand. Consider, for example, farming and coal mining; although they are both primary industries they are very different, and the form of organisation which is useful for supplying one is not for the other.

Thus, there exists a wide variety of organisations pursuing many different objectives. All of these form the subject of the book.

SELF-ASSESSMENT QUESTIONS

A. 1. Define: (*a*) a formal organisation; (*b*) the public sector; (*c*) a quango; (*d*) a primary industry.

2. List the different types of organisations.

B. 3. True or false?
   (*a*) Feudal society was not organised.
   (*b*) All public-sector organisations are non-productive.
   (*c*) Mining is a tertiary industry.
   (*d*) All formal organisations have rules.
   (*e*) The Business Education Council is a quango.

C. 4. True or false?
   (*a*) The public sector in the UK is larger than that of West Germany in percentage terms.
   (*b*) BL (British Leyland) is a public corporation.
   (*c*) All nationalised industries are public corporations.
   (*d*) The World Bank is a multinational organisation.
   (*e*) Political parties are governmental organisations.

5. Make a list of those goods which you consider are best supplied by public-sector organisations rather than by business organisations.

ASSIGNMENTS

1. Make a list of twenty-five organisations in your local area and for each one state whether it is: (*a*) productive or non-productive; (*b*) public sector or private sector; and (*c*) which sector of industry it belongs to.

2. Construct a simple organisation chart to show how the organisation for which you work or with which you study is organised. Show your own position in the organisation and state what it is.

3. List as many of the objectives of the organisation you work for or study in as you are able. Contrast these with the objectives of an organisation in another sector of the economy.

CHAPTER TWO

Trading Organisations

CHAPTER OBJECTIVES

After studying this chapter you should be able to:
* identify ways of classifying trading organisations;
* explain the concept of legal personality;
* distinguish between corporations and unincorporated associations;
* list and describe the six main forms of trading organisations;
* list and evaluate the comparative advantages of different forms of trading organisations.

INTRODUCTION

You have probably seldom stopped to consider how, and from what, the goods you consume and the services you use are produced and provided. It is even less likely that you have considered the type of organisation which made, sold or provided them. Manufacturing companies, shops, service agencies and the like are largely taken for granted, for they are an accepted part of everyone's life. Behind each, however, is an organisation, be it the state (Public Corporations), a large company, or a single person running a corner shop.

The organisations which trade with the public vary greatly—from ICI to the corner shop, from the National Coal Board to the local plumber. It may appear that ICI and the NCB have more in common with each other than they have with the local tradesman. However, in Chapter 1 we saw that ICI and the local plumber have a common interest in that they are both *business organisations*, i.e. they both basically attempt to maximise their profits. The NCB, on the other hand, is a public corporation and is supposed to operate the coal industry in the public interest. Co-operatives were founded on the idea of self-help by and for their members, while the trading activities of local authorities are primarily intended to provide a service to the community where breaking even is usually more important than profit. We have thus distinguished between trading organisations on the grounds of their *objectives*.

In this chapter we are principally concerned with the various *legal forms* which trading organisations adopt but we briefly consider other classifications.

Type of industry

You have seen in Chapter 1 that industries can be classified into primary, secondary and tertiary industries. This is an obvious criterion for classifying trading organisations but it is not, however, particularly useful. For example, manufacturing takes innumerable forms and a single large organisation such as BP may pursue activities in all three fields.

Size

Again this is an obvious criterion to use. However, what do we mean by "size"? Is it the number of retail outlets, the number of employees, the turnover, the share of the market, or profits? Despite the problems this means of classification is worth pursuing since it can give a good idea of the power, wealth and importance of the largest trading organisations.

In Tables I and II you can see lists of the largest organisations, ranked by number of employees and turnover respectively. Table I well illustrates the truly mixed character of the British economy in that six of the organisations on it are public corporations (often referred to as nationalised industries). The largest car company, BL, although nominally private, is almost entirely owned by the government through the National Enterprise Board. Public corporations have been excluded from Table II so that what you see is the familiar "top ten" British organisations in the private sector. Notwithstanding this, the government appears in the list in that it is the major shareholder in both British Petroleum and BL. The presence of Shell Transport and Trading (60 per cent Dutch owned) BAT Industries and Esso (US owned) is indicative of the large numbers of foreign companies which operate in the UK. On the other hand, all the companies in the list have extensive overseas operations. Unilever, for example, operates in over eighty different countries.

Legal status

The most usual way of classifying trading organisations, however, is by their legal status and the way in which they raise capital, are owned and are controlled. These three things are vital to the operation of any trading organisation. On this basis by far the most numerous type of organisation is the sole trader, accounting for something like 80 per cent of the total. On the other hand, by

TABLE I. THE TEN LARGEST EMPLOYERS IN THE UK 1979

Rank	Organisation	No. of employees
1.	Post Office (N)	410,977*
2.	National Enterprise Board (N)	298,490†
3.	National Coal Board (N)	297,000
4.	British Railways Board (N)	244,084
5.	BAT Industries	185,000
6.	British Steel Corporation (N)	181,000
7.	Electricity Councils and Boards (N)	158,780
8.	General Electric	155,000
9.	Imperial Chemical Industries	148,200
10.	Lonrho	140,000

(N) Nationalised Industry.

* Including 247,000 British Telecom employees (1981 figures) separate from the Post Office as at October 1981.

† Including 176,790 BL and 56,600 Rolls Royce employees. The NEB is a state holding company.

Source: Times 1000, 1980–81. Pub. Times Newspapers

TABLE II. THE TEN LARGEST ORGANISATIONS IN THE PRIVATE SECTOR, RANKED BY TURNOVER 1979

Rank	Organisation	Turnover £000 (thousands)
1.	British Petroleum Co.	22,705,700*
2.	"Shell" Transport and Trading†	13,932,000*
3.	BAT Industries	6,877,000*
4.	Imperial Chemical Industries	5,368,000
5.	Unilever Ltd.	4,058,400
6.	Imperial Group	3,614,900
7.	Ford Motor Co.	3,193,000
8.	Esso Petroleum Co.	3,112,504*
9.	Shell UK	3,003,400
10.	BL Ltd	2,990,300

* Including sales taxes, excise duties and similar levies.

† Based on 40 per cent of Royal Dutch/Shell Group.

Source: Times 1000, 1980–81 Pub. Times Newspapers

far the greater amount of business is done by public joint stock companies and, of course, by public corporations.

It is clearly unrealistic, however, to divorce the legal status of a trading organisation from its commercial role and economic significance. Indeed, political and sociological perspectives often need to be considered, as nationalisation and regional policy are matters of considerable domestic political importance. Multinational corporations can sometimes significantly affect or influence a country's policies or actions and pure economic considerations often have to bow to government policy. Similarly, interactions within and between organisations cannot be ignored, and concepts of "power" and "status" will affect the structure of each individual unit. Specific aspects of the organisation's structure, such as the level of automation or the percentage of women employed, may have much more wide-ranging effects.

The choice between different types of organisations is often made, however, on the basis of the legal status each type enjoys and the consequences which flow from this. Therefore, a general explanation of the legal status of trading organisations is a firm foundation on which to build a more detailed analysis and comparison of the various types of business unit, in which economic, legal, social and political factors can be assessed, and their interaction discussed.

In Fig. 1 you have a diagram giving a visual indication of how the trading organisations discussed in this chapter relate to one another.

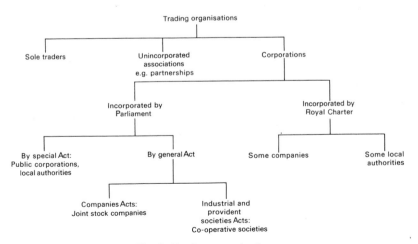

Fig. 1. *Trading organisations.*

LEGAL STATUS: CORPORATIONS AND UNINCORPORATED ASSOCIATIONS

Introduction: legal personality

To the man in the street a "person" means an individual human being, but at law the term has a wider and yet more precise meaning. Human personality and legal personality are not one and the same thing, and the term "person" means at law an individual, a group of individuals, or even a thing which the law recognises as being the subject of legal rights and duties.

At different times, various legal systems have accorded a degree of legal personality to things other than human beings, e.g. cats in ancient Egypt, church buildings and relics of saints in the Middle Ages and idols in modern India. Under early English law animals were tried for crimes, and even today Admiralty proceedings are taken directly against the ship. Conversely, some human beings have had either only limited legal personality or have been deprived of legal personality altogether. Under modern English law, women, particularly married women, did not enjoy legal equality with men until a variety of Acts of Parliament, passed this century, removed the remnants of inequality. Roman slaves had no directly enforceable rights and outlaws in Norman times were literally outside the law.

The common law, the basic judge-made law of the land, took as its norm the sane, sober, solvent, adult, male human individual, and anyone differing from this norm was the subject of special rules which either conferred privileges or imposed disabilities upon them. For example, a minor, a person under eighteen years of age, cannot vote in Parliamentary or local government elections, but is in a privileged position under both the criminal law and the law of contract.

Early in its development, the common law had to recognise the existence of "juristic persons"—the term used to denote persons recognised by law which are not human beings. It had become the practice for office-holders, most frequently church or borough dignitaries, to enter into legal transactions as officials and not as individuals and the common law gradually recognised their legal capacity to do this. The "corporation" eventually evolved, and this has resulted in a vital legal distinction between types of organisations; they may exist as either "corporations" or "unincorporated associations". Thus, a quite different theoretical concept is added to the socio-economic differences between types of business unit. However, you will see that commercial considerations and law cannot be realistically treated as separate matters in this context;

for example, the various methods of raising capital began as commercial practices, but have now become part of the law which is used to organise and control these practices.

What is a corporation?

A corporation is a group of individuals (a corporation aggregate) or one individual (a corporation sole) which is regarded at law as being a legal person quite distinct from the individuals or individual who compose it at any particular time. Hence, at law, any event affecting its members does not directly affect the corporation. A joint stock company is an example of the former; the Sovereign, bishops and trustees are examples of the latter. The corporation represents the furthest development of juristic personality in English law.

Methods of incorporation

The earliest corporations were created by Royal Charter, and, whilst one or two of the oldest existing trading companies were created in this way, e.g. the Hudson Bay Company, charters are now reserved for important non-commercial corporations such as universities and boroughs. They are sometimes known as "common law" corporations.

   All other corporations are created by statute. Sometimes a corporation is created by a special statute, for example the National Coal Board by the Coal Industry Act 1946, but most organisations acquire corporate status by registering as a company under the Companies Act 1948 after fulfilling the required statutory formalities. Corporations of this type are far more numerous than the other two and are today the most important type of trading organisation.

The importance of corporate status

As the joint stock company, incorporated with limited liability, is today the most important type of trading organisation, the consequences of incorporation are of crucial importance to modern commercial activity. Briefly, corporate status is important for five main reasons:

   (*a*) it is convenient for pursuing, managing and protecting the common interests of a large number of individuals;

   (*b*) any event affecting a member, e.g. death or bankruptcy, does not directly affect the corporation because it has its own separate and permanent existence;

   (*c*) corporations may pursue activities, within the limits of their powers, in the same way as an ordinary person, although to do this they will have to act through agents, as they themselves have no actual physical existence;

(*d*) land and other property can be owned, used and transferred by the organisation in the same way as an ordinary person;

(*e*) the organisation and not its members is liable for its debts and other legal obligations.

Unincorporated associations

This term refers to any group of people who pursue an activity in common without having the legal status of a corporation. Such associations may range from relatively informal organisations like local youth or tennis clubs, through trading or professional partnerships, to nationally influential bodies such as the Transport and General Workers' Union.

While these associations have no independent legal status, their existence cannot be ignored by the law. In particular, the partnership remains a business organisation of great importance and trade unions play an important role in the development of government economic policy in addition to their day-to-day involvement with industrial and employment law, wage bargaining and labour relations. Indeed, unincorporated associations are sometimes the subject of specific Acts of Parliament, and a compromise has been reached between legal disregard for their existence and the practical requirements of business activity and society in general. On the one hand:

(*a*) the association's property belongs to its members jointly and not the association itself;

(*b*) contracts made on its behalf can only be enforced by or against the individual members who make or authorise them, and;

(*c*) only those members who actually committed or authorised any wrongful act in the course of the association's activities will incur liability for it.

On the other hand, the law recognises their existence in four important ways.

(*a*) Legal proceedings may be taken by or against one or more members as representing all.

(*b*) In certain circumstances an unincorporated association such as a trade union may sue and be sued as though it were a legal person.

(*c*) Where property is owned by trustees (persons owning property on behalf of another) for the association, the law recognises and will enforce its right to have the property used for its benefit.

(A trustee would not, for example, be allowed to sell the property and use the proceeds for his own purpose even though the property is "legally" his.)

(*d*) Unincorporated associations may make and enforce rules for their own internal organisation. On a somewhat humble level, a local tennis club will have its own homely "dos and don'ts" while the relations between members of a partnership are governed by formal articles or a deed. Only where these rules are applied unfairly will the courts interfere.

THE DEVELOPMENT OF THE BUSINESS ORGANISATION

As society evolved from feudalism to *laissez-faire* and then to capitalism, so the forms of business organisations evolved. The earliest forms were the sole trader and the partnership. The joint stock company did not become common until the nineteenth century, although its origins are much earlier in the *commercial revolution* of the sixteenth and seventeenth centuries. During this period, the capitalist system of production became well established; that is to say a system where there was a separation of functions between the capital-providing employer on the one hand and the wage-earning workman on the other.

The joint stock form of organisation developed not from industry but from foreign trade. In order to raise the necessary capital and spread the risk of early trading ventures, a company form of organisation was adopted. These were called *chartered companies* because they needed a Royal Charter to establish them. Many businesses styled themselves companies without a charter but this did not constitute a legal form of organisation. At first they were *regulated companies*, such as the Muscovy Company (1553), which were established for one venture. However, the joint stock company which had a continuous existence and was run by a board of directors and controlled by its shareholders became much more popular. The most important of these early companies was the East India Company. This was founded in 1600 and became a joint stock company in 1660.

Limited liability was first introduced in 1662 but it was only granted to three companies. Dealings in shares took place from the beginning, but the first stock exchange was not established until 1778. By this time there was a flourishing capital and insurance market centred on a number of coffee houses in the city of London. The most famous of these was Lloyds. A great speculative boom known as the South Sea Bubble ruined many people and caused the passing of the Bubble Act 1720. This made it illegal to form a company without a charter and this effectively hindered the development of companies for many years.

The building of canals (1761 onwards) required vast amounts of capital and so the joint stock form of organisation had to be adopted. By this time companies were formed not by Royal Charter but by Act of Parliament. The building of railways involved hundreds of joint stock companies and by 1848 the quoted share capital was over £200 million. A few public utilities such as water supply had adopted the joint stock form of organisation but it was not until the mid-nineteenth century that industry began to adopt this form. The development of joint stock banking in England dates from 1826.

It was obviously inconvenient for Parliament to have to establish so many companies and so legislation was passed to enable companies to be set up more easily by *registration*. The most important acts were the Companies Act 1844, the Limited Liability Act 1855 and the Joint Stock Companies Act 1856. The Companies Act 1862 consolidated the previous legislation and was the basis of company organisation until well into the twentieth century.

Throughout the nineteenth century the family business remained the dominant form of organisation in industry. If such businesses sought company status it was usually for the protection afforded by limited liability and not for the purposes of raising capital. It is interesting to note that at this time, when industry and commerce were finding it necessary to adopt the joint stock form of organisation, the government was also finding it impossible *not* to interfere in the economy. That is to say, just as the sophistication of industry and commerce needed regulation through company legislation, so the increasingly complex urban world demanded government intervention to ensure adequate drainage, street lighting, education, etc. It was through the demands of these forces, which could only be satisfied through *legislative law-making*, that Acts of Parliament became the dominant form of laws.

Much of the organisation of institutions which evolved at this time, such as hospitals and schools, were modelled on factories. These forms have survived the *scientific revolution* of the twentieth century. We are now on the threshold of great changes in our economy which will be brought about by the *microprocessor revolution*. Perhaps if we are tempted to cling to the forms of organisation of the past we should recall that they originated in the need to exploit large steam engines as a source of power.

DIFFERENT TRADING ORGANISATIONS

When one looks at today's commercial and industrial world it is easy to see a structure dominated by a few giants, the ICIs and BPs of this world. This is, however, a rather misleading picture, for much of the country's wealth is generated by a vast number of small businesses, each often employing only a few people. This was even more true in the past and comments such as "Britain is a nation of shopkeepers" or "Britain is the workshop of the world", appeared almost literally to be true. Today Britain has a diverse economy, consisting of business units of all sizes organised locally, nationally and internationally.

The simplest and most basic trading organisation is the one-man business, i.e. the sole trader or sole proprietor. Commercial development originally started on this basis. However, the combination of a number of factors caused an evolution, markedly more rapid in the eighteenth and nineteenth centuries, from the one-man business to the corporate commercial giants of today. Principal among these factors were the greater capital resources and expertise available in larger units, business "enterprise", technical innovations, and the development of a framework of legal principles designed to aid the creation and operation of larger trading organisations.

Clearly one business unit can be distinguished from another in terms of size, organisation, area of activity, etc., but the basic practical distinction between different units is a consequence of the legal framework within which they are owned and operate. All businesses need capital, and its contributors take different risks according to the type of organisation in which they invest. You will see that this is a recurrent theme in this chapter.

The sole trader
What is a sole trader?
A sole trader is a business organisation where one person is in business on his own, providing the capital, taking the profits and standing the losses himself. Typical areas of commercial activity for the sole trader are retailing and building, i.e. activities which are not usually capital intensive.

Limits are placed on the growth of a sole trader's activities by two main constraints. Firstly, finance: economic growth largely depends on the availability of capital to invest in the business, and the sole trader is limited to what he can provide from his own resources and raise from a bank. Secondly, organisation: one man has only limited ability to exercise effective control over and take responsibility for an organisation. As a business grows, a larger and more complicated business organisation will generally replace the sole trader.

Legal status

A sole trader has no special legal status; he is treated in the same way as any other individual by the law. He alone is responsible for the contracts that he or his employees make in the course of his business and for his debts, while the business premises, stock and goodwill are solely his. Until the Companies Act 1981 the law laid down one special requirement: if he traded under a name other than his own surname (a business name) the name had to be registered under the Registration of Business Names Act 1916. The 1981 Act abolished the Register of Business Names because it was only partly effective, many firms failing to register at all or failing to re-register when changes in ownership occurred. The cost of enforcing the Register efficiently would have been too high. Instead, the Companies Act 1981 requires all organisations (not just sole traders) using a business name to make available details of their ownership by displaying the information both at their places of business and on their business letters and demands for payment.

Commercial considerations

The sole trader is in a potentially vulnerable financial position. The profits may all be his but so are the losses, and many sole traders are made bankrupt each year. His limited capital resources often make him particularly vulnerable, not only to sustained competition from large business units but also to bad capital investments, e.g. a grocer opening a delicatessen in an area which turns out to prefer more mundane food.

It can be argued, however, that a sole trader is able to weather a short reduction in consumer spending far better than a larger business unit. He can adapt quickly to the level of demand and, if necessary, can make personal economies until business improves.

The sole trader remains the most common business unit in the UK and he is the backbone of the business structure on which the country depends. Nevertheless, in terms of capital and manpower resources employed, sole traders are of limited importance. In recent years the number of sole traders has decreased. The main reasons for this are:

(*a*) lack of capital to invest in new premises, equipment and materials;

(*b*) lack of expertise in every aspect of the business resulting in inefficiency, e.g. the sole trader may be good at selling but bad at administration;

(c) lack of advice and guidance about the operation of the business—consultancy is usually too expensive to be considered;

(d) competition from chain stores and other larger business units which are able to benefit from various economies of scale;

(e) changes in shopping patterns caused by, for example, an increase in the number of married women working and an increase in car ownership;

(f) increased overheads resulting from bureaucratic functions such as VAT collection, imposed by law, which sole traders are often disinclined and ill-equipped to perform (this is less quantifiable as a reason but still important).

Yet sole traders survive. As a business organisation they offer attractive advantages when compared with others. The initial capital investment may only need to be very small and the legal formalities involved are minimal. In sharp contrast to joint stock companies, they offer financial secrecy, the "personal touch" (a subjective but often important factor), and the knowledge that a sole trader is his own boss and that the profit he makes will be his. Lastly, perhaps, a sole trader is able to alter his activities to adapt to the market without legal formality or major organisational problems. (*See* also page 150.)

The partnership
What is a partnership?
The Partnership Act 1890 defines a partnership as "the relation which subsists between persons carrying on a business in common with a view of profit". Many partnerships are very formal organisations, such as a large firm of solicitors or accountants, but two people running a stall in a local Sunday market would almost certainly be in partnership with one another and subject to the same legal rules as a firm of City solicitors with an annual turnover of several hundred thousand pounds.

Partnerships became common with the emergence of economic society, for they are better suited to cope with the demands of modern commercial activity than sole traders who must provide capital, labour and skill themselves. Two or more persons in partnership can combine their resources and in theory form an economically more efficient business unit producing a better return on the capital invested.

The maximum number of members possible in most partnerships is fixed by law at twenty. The professional partnerships that may exceed this number—solicitors, accountants and members of a recognised stock exchange—are often organisations of some size with considerable capital resources and offering economies of scale and the benefits of specialisation. It would be unusual, however, to find a trading partnership consisting of more than five or six partners, for corporate status as a company with limited liability is usually more attractive.

The organisation of a partnership

Partnerships are formed by contract and, within the general framework of the law, the partners may make whatever arrangements they like amongst themselves. It is usual to set out these arrangements in the Articles or Deed of Partnership for this should eliminate uncertainty and dispute between the partners. Where this is not done, the 1890 Act, in particular s.24 which sets out a miniature code, governs the relations between partners.

Membership

No new member may be admitted to the firm without the agreement of all the partners; similarly no partner may be expelled by the others unless the Articles permit this. If, however, the other partners have a good reason for wishing to expel one partner, for example because of personal deadlock between them, and no power of expulsion is given in the Articles, they may ask the Chancery Division of the High Court to dissolve the partnership, enabling them to establish a new firm without the unwanted member.

The retirement of partners is usually covered by express provisions in the articles or deed of partnership, e.g. as to notice and the continuation of the firm after a retirement.

Management

Every partner is entitled to take part in the management of the business but the rights of junior partners to participate in management are often restricted by the Articles. Some firms may have one or more "sleeping partners" who take no part in the management at all. Day-to-day decisions are taken by majority vote, but any change in the firm's business must be unanimously agreed.

Capital, profits and losses

Under the 1890 Act, all partners are entitled to share equally in the capital and profits of the business and they must contribute equally towards the losses. However, it is not always possible for the partners to provide capital equally, and senior partners will generally wish to receive a higher proportion of the profits than junior partners. Consequently, it is common for the Articles to vary the Act and deal with such matters in detail.

Legal status and liability

A partnership does not possess corporate status. Even where it trades under a "firm name" entirely different from the names of its members it has no separate legal existence. (Until 1981 the "firm name" had to be registered in the Register of Business Names, but this requirement was abolished by the Companies Act 1981.) Certain restrictions exist in practice upon the name which may be chosen. It must not, for example, deceive the public or represent the business of one firm to be that of another, and the word "Limited" must not be part of the title.

Each partner is the agent of the firm and of his co-partners for acts done in the course of the firm's business. As a consequence, the partners incur unlimited personal liability for the debts of the firm. Should the business fail, not only the partnership property but also the personal property of each partner will be sold to pay the firm's creditors. The concept of unlimited liability is a disadvantage common to partnerships and sole traders. It is possible, but uncommon in practice, to form a limited partnership under the Limited Partnership Act 1907, in which one or more, but not all, of the partners stands to lose only the capital he initially contributed if the firm fails. In return he is excluded from the management of the firm. The private joint stock company, incorporated with limited liability, is usually a far more attractive alternative to the limited partnership.

The commercial role of partnerships

Quite apart from the rules of professional bodies, which usually prohibit their members from forming a company, a partnership is a business organisation generally more suited to professional men in business together than to manufacturers or traders. In the former, the risk of financial failure is less and consequently unlimited liability is less of a disadvantage. For all but the small trading ventures, or where there are particular reasons for trading as a partnership, registration as a company with limited liability is usually to be preferred.

The joint stock company

A joint stock company may be described as an organisation consisting of persons who contribute money to a common stock, which is employed in some trade or business, and who share the profit or loss arising. This common stock is the capital of the company and the persons who contribute it are its members. The proportion of capital to which each member is entitled is his share.

The need for more capital accounts both for the development of partnerships and later for the development of joint stock companies. As soon as it became possible to do so (by the Limited Liability Act 1855, and the Joint Stock Companies Act 1856—repealed and consolidated by the Companies Act 1862), many partnerships chose to become registered joint stock companies with limited liability. Today, in terms of capital and manpower resources employed, the joint stock company is the dominant form of business organisation.

You may be forgiven for thinking that banks and insurance companies are rather different creatures from other companies. This is not so; they are ordinary joint stock companies. However, they are subject to specific legislation or certain sections of general Acts. For example, under the Insurance Companies Acts 1958–80 and the Companies Act 1967 no company may carry on any class of insurance business without the authority of the Board of Trade, and under the Banking Act 1979 no organisation other than a *recognised bank* (as defined by the Act) may use any name or in any other way so describe itself as to indicate it is a bank or carrying out banking business.

Legal status

At law a company is a corporation, which is, as you have seen, a collection of persons which has an existence, rights and duties at law quite separate and distinct from those of the persons who are, from time to time, its members. This fundamental concept was clarified in relation to companies by the House of Lords (the highest appeal court) in *Salomon* v. *Salomon & Co.* (1897). Salomon had incorporated his business as a limited company in which he held 20,000 shares. His wife, four sons and a daughter had one share each. He lent money to his company taking a charge (a right against property) on the assets of the company as security. The company eventually became insolvent and on liquidation the assets were found to be sufficient to satisfy the debt owed to Salomon but insufficient to pay off the unsecured creditors. Despite the commercial reality of Salomon and his company being one and the same, at law the House held them to be quite separate. Therefore, as Salomon was the only secured creditor, he was entitled to the assets of the company.

Hence the company's property belongs to the company and not to its members; in the same way its members are not liable for its debts, although they stand to lose the money that they have invested when the company is wound up with debts in excess of its assets (this is considered more fully in Chapter 12). A company can only act through human agents (its directors) but they only possess the authority given to them by the constitution of the company. Finally, the company is liable for torts (wrongful acts) and crimes committed by its servants and agents within the course of their employment or authority.

The registered company

The original method of incorporation was by Royal Charter, which was followed in the late eighteenth century by incorporation by special Act of Parliament. Both methods were expensive and elaborate, and a simpler method was required to cope with the rapid expansion of business enterprise associated with the industrial revolution. This need was met by the Joint Stock Companies Act 1844, which enabled a company to be formed by the registration of a memorandum of association and the payment of certain fees. The present law on registration is contained in the Companies Act 1948 as amended by the Companies Acts of 1967, 1976 and 1980.

Types of registered companies

Two main classifications are possible:

(a) according to the limit, if any, of the shareholders' liability to contribute towards payment of the company's debts;

(b) according to whether the company is a public company or a private company.

Companies limited by shares, companies limited by guarantee and unlimited companies. The liability of the members of a company *limited by shares* to contribute to the company's assets is limited to the amount, if any, unpaid on their shares. The vast majority of registered companies are of this type. In companies *limited by guarantee* each member's liability is limited to the amount that he has undertaken to contribute to the assets in the event of the company being wound up. Such companies are usually non-profit-making organisations, such as professional, trade and research associations or clubs supported by annual subscriptions. As the name suggests, the members of an *unlimited company* incur unlimited liability to contribute to the assets of the company if it is wound up. Unlimited companies are comparatively rare but there has been an increase in their numbers since 1967 because the Companies Act of that year exempts them from the statutory requirement to file accounts with the Registrar of Companies. Hence, they can keep their financial affairs private.

The principle of limited liability is of considerable economic importance and is fundamental to the financing of business ventures today. It encourages investment because it limits the risk an investor takes to the amount he has actually invested. Without limited liability it is likely that none but the safest business venture would ever attract large-scale investment. In particular, the institutional investors, such as life assurance companies and pension funds, would not hazard their vast funds in any speculative venture and would only invest in the gilt-edged market (government securities).

Public and private companies. The Companies Act 1980 completely altered the classification of public and private companies as it had existed since 1908. Previously, a private company was defined and a public company was any company which did not fall within this definition. The 1980 Act was passed as part of the harmonisation of law programmes within the EEC. By defining a public company for the first time it brings the UK into line with other member states.

A *public company* is a company limited by shares or guarantee, having a share capital, with a memorandum which states that it is to be a public company, and which has been registered or re-registered as a public company under the Companies Acts—Companies Act 1980, s.1(1). It has two or more members and can invite the general public to subscribe for its shares or debentures. It must have a minimum authorised and allotted share capital of (at present) £50,000. (No new company limited by guarantee can have a share capital and therefore must be a private company.)

A *private company* is any company which does not satisfy the requirements for a public company. In common with a public company it has two or more members.

Thus the essential *distinction* between a public and a private company is that the former may offer its shares or debentures to the public while the latter cannot. Restrictions on share transfers and the size of membership no longer constitute an essential part of private company status, but there is nothing to prevent private companies retaining such restrictions. It is a criminal offence to invite the general public to subscribe for shares or debentures in a private company.

The private company at present is in some respects a transitional step between the partnership and the public company; typically it is a family business. In common with a public limited company it possesses the advantage of limited liability, but in common with a partnership it has the disadvantage of only being able to call upon the capital resources of its members (supplemented by possible loans from its bank). Since public companies can offer their shares to the public—the shares of many (but certainly not all) public companies are quoted on the Stock Exchange—they are able to raise considerable sums of money to finance large-scale operations.

A private company may commence business as soon as its Certificate of Incorporation is granted; a public company may not do business or exercise any borrowing powers until the Registrar of Companies has issued it with a certificate under the Companies Act 1980, s.4, to the effect that the requirements as to share capital have been complied with. A private company is not under a statutory obligation to hold an annual meeting, although both public and private limited companies must submit annual accounts to the Registrar.

It remains to be seen what the nature of the typical private company will be following the Companies Act 1980. Under the now repealed s.28 of the Companies Act 1948, a private company was limited to a membership of fifty, was unable to invite the public to subscribe for its shares, and had by its articles to restrict the right to transfer its shares, e.g. only to existing shareholders.

The restrictions on membership and transfer of shares no longer exist. This means that private companies have the prospect of growth and development previously only open to public companies. If the articles of association of an existing private company are suitably amended, an increase in the value of its shares and the opportunity to increase its shareholder base would seem to follow. Non-public share offers, e.g. through business contacts or bankers, are now possible.

Nevertheless, in terms of capital, public companies dwarf private companies, and they have been responsible for the immense growth in investment this century. The typical public company manufactures cars, gives overdrafts and sells insurance—in other words, there is no such thing as a "typical" public company.

Forming a registered company

A registered company is formed by submitting to the Registrar of Companies the following documents.

(*a*) The memorandum of association.

(*b*) The articles of association.

(*c*) A statement of the names of the intended first director(s) and the first secretary, together with their written consents to act as such. The statement must also contain the intended address of the company's registered office.

(*d*) A statutory declaration of compliance with the Companies Act 1948 regarding registration.

(*e*) A statement of the company's capital unless it is to have no share capital.

The Registrar, when satisfied that the requirements have been complied with, issues a Certificate of Incorporation which brings the company into existence as a legal entity.

Of the documents submitted the memorandum of association and the articles of association are by far the most important.

The memorandum of association. This regulates the company's external affairs and enables a person who invests in, or deals with, the company to ascertain its name; its objects, and hence its powers; whether the liability of its members is limited; and its authorised share capital. At the heart of the memorandum is the "objects clause". This sets out the purposes for which the company was formed and serves two purposes. Firstly, it protects investors who can learn from it the purposes for which their money can be used; and secondly, it protects persons dealing with the company, who can discover from it the extent of the company's powers.

Any transaction which is not authorised by the objects clause or reasonably incidental to it is *ultra vires* (beyond the powers of) the company and void. The *ultra vires* doctrine was established by the House of Lords in *Ashbury Carriage Co.* v. *Riche* (1875), where it was held that the company, whose memorandum included only such objects as the construction of railway carriages, did not have power to contract to build a railway in Belgium, even though the shareholders had approved the project. Consequently, Joe Smith the sole trader may change his business activity whenever he likes; similarly Joe Smith & Co. the partnership; but Joe Smith & Co. Ltd may not. To change from sole activity X to sole activity Y requires a formal alteration of the objects.

As part of the harmonisation of law within the European Economic Community, the European Communities Act 1972 s.9(1) modifies the *ultra vires* doctrine to the extent that a person who enters into a contract with a company which is outside its objects but which was sanctioned by the directors of the company, will be able to enforce it against the company, providing he did not know that the contract was beyond the company's powers.

The name of the company must be given in the memorandum. If a private limited company, the name must end with the word "limited" (or Ltd); if a public limited company, the words "public limited company" (or PLC), or the Welsh equivalent for a company with its registered office in Wales, must be used. General restrictions exist preventing a name being registered which suggests, for example, a royal connection, or which might tend to mislead the public, e.g. a name which closely resembles that of an existing company.

The Articles of Association. These regulate the internal administration of the company, the relations between the company and its members, and between the members themselves. The articles cover such matters as the issue and transfer of shares, the rights of shareholders, meetings, the appointment and powers of directors, and accounts.

A company may adopt the model set of articles contained in Table A in Schedule 1 of the Companies Act 1948, or it may frame and register its own.

Operation and control of companies
Directors. A company acts through its directors, persons chosen by the shareholders to conduct and manage the company's affairs. Their powers are contained in the articles of association and so long as they do not exceed these, the shareholders cannot interfere in their conduct of the company's business. The directors will normally appoint one of their number as managing director and he will be given powers under the articles to take certain decisions without reference to the board of directors.

In respect of the company's money and property, and the powers given to them, directors owe duties to the company similar to those owed by trustees (persons who own property which they must use for the benefit of another) to beneficiaries. When approving share transfers or issuing and allotting shares, for example, they must act in complete good faith and they are liable to the company for any breaches of this duty.

Directors act as agents of the company in making contracts on its behalf and, as such, they are subject to the general rules of agency. They are, for example, personally liable on the contracts that they make if they exceed their authority or do not clearly indicate that they are acting as agents for the company, i.e. they make a contract in their own name.

The secretary. Every company must have a secretary. He is usually appointed by the directors.

In the nineteenth century the company secretary was regarded as a mere servant of the company and in 1902 a "law lord" in the House of Lords described his duties as being "of a limited and of a somewhat humble character". The modern position is different, for he is the chief administrative officer of the company with extensive duties and responsibilities. The law now recognises that the secretary has authority to make contracts on the company's behalf connected with the administrative side of its affairs.

Control by shareholders. In theory the company is a very democratic organisation, with ordinary shares giving the right to vote at the company's meetings. Thus the ordinary members should be able to decide matters of company policy and the composition of the board of directors. For two reasons, however, the reality of the situation is very different. It is common for a majority shareholding in a company to be held by a small number of investors or even by one, for example one family or a holding company (*see* below). In such companies the will of the numerical minority of the shareholders prevails over that of the numerical majority. This could be reflected in clashes of interest in such matters as takeover bids or choice of directors. More commonly, the vast majority of shareholders are either unable or insufficiently interested to attend company meetings, and are content to leave company management to the directors, provided the dividend paid to them is satisfactory.

Whilst in all probability there will always be "City scandals" involving mismanagement or fraud by directors, the trend of the law is towards greater disclosure of information by companies, which should make malpractice more difficult. Under the Companies Act 1980, directors must show in their report to shareholders, and usually in the company's accounts, details of any contracts with the company in which any director has a material interest. Furthermore, the Department of Trade may investigate any company following an allegation by a shareholder of mismanagement by the directors.

Control by a holding company. It is usually an advantage for companies with similar or complementary interests to group together. The individual companies will still retain their legal and commercial identities, and will function as separate units, but they will be controlled by a central organisation. Sometimes the grouping is not voluntary but is the result of fierce takeover battles involving millions of pounds.

This form of extended business unit can be created by forming a holding or parent company (a purely financial institution—it does not trade or manufacture itself) to purchase a majority, or sometimes all, of the shares in other companies. However, it does not necessarily follow that all the business interests of a holding company complement one another, as the following example shows. Sears Holdings Ltd (*see* Fig. 2) manufactures and sells shoes to most of the population, owns the largest gambling organisation in the country, builds ships, and has substantial automotive interests. Very little similarity can be found in such diverse activities and for this reason it is known as a "conglomerate" company.

By simple mathematical calculations based on Fig. 3 you can see that, through a system of subsidiaries, one holding company with a capital of £225,000 can control a commercial empire with a total capital of £1,465,000. Furthermore, a shareholding of £115,000 in the holding company gives effective control of the whole organisation. While £115,000 may represent a fortune to you or me, it is a small sum by the standards of the modern business world. Furthermore, this control of a large group of companies through the ownership of a relatively small part of its total capital is even more exaggerated when different types of shares, e.g. voting and non-voting shares, are considered (*see* Chapter 11).

Company reports and accounts
The main purpose of company legislation is to protect investors, for in practice they have little or no control over their money once it has been invested. Protection is afforded by opening the affairs of companies to public inspection at Companies House. You have already seen that perusal of the memorandum of association and the articles of association enables a potential investor to ascertain how, and for what purposes, his money will be used. In the same way, a person wishing to deal with the company, for example a bank which is contemplating lending money to the company, may make sure that the proposed transaction is *intra vires* (within its objects). In addition, further information can be gleaned from a variety of statutory books (required to be kept under the provisions of the Companies Act 1948) which contain, among other things, details of the company's membership, its directors, and mortgages and charges affecting the company's property.

The annual report. Each year, every company having a share capital must make a return in the prescribed form to the Registrar of Companies stating what has happened to the capital in the preceding year, for example the number of shares allotted and the cash received for them. The return must be accompanied by a copy of the audited balance sheet in the prescribed form, supported by a profit and loss account which is a true and fair representation of

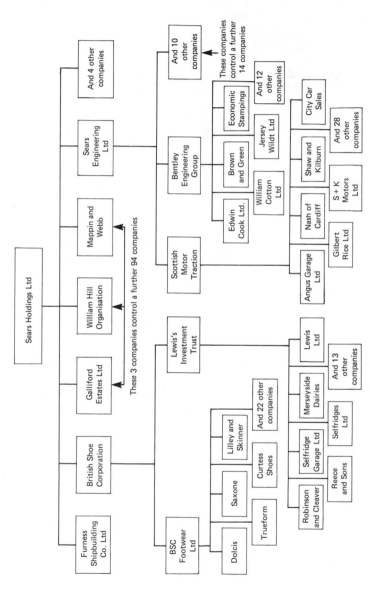

Fig. 2. *Sears Holdings Ltd. Altogether Sears Holdings Ltd controls 234 companies in the UK and a further fifty in twelve other countries. It also has large shareholdings in many other companies.*
Source: Who Owns Who, 1977.

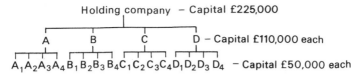

Total capital = £225,000 + (4 x £110,000) + (16 x £50,000) = £1,465,000

Fig. 3. *Controlling power of a holding company.*

the year's transactions. Unlimited companies, however, are exempt from this obligation to file annual accounts. These documents are available for public inspection on payment of a small fee.

In order to implement the EEC's fourth directive on company accounts, aimed at harmonising company accounting throughout the Community, the Companies Act 1981 introduced a new classification of companies for the purpose of accounts, and laid down new rules for the form and content of accounts.

A *small company*—one with a turnover of less than £1.4m or a balance sheet total of less than £0.7m or less than fifty employees—is permitted to file only an abridged balance sheet and it does not need to file a profit and loss account or a director's report.

A *medium-sized company*—one with a turnover of less than £5.75m or a balance sheet total of less than £2.8m or less than 250 employees—may omit details of its turnover and gross profit margin.

However, no public company or banking, insurance and certain shipping companies, or groups containing such companies, is treated as a small or medium-sized company. The changes are a recognition that on the basis of resources and organisation it is appropriate to apply different and less onerous requirements to small and medium-sized companies than to large companies.

Books of account. The directors of a company are under a duty to keep proper books of account showing, among other things, receipts and payments of cash, and details of assets and liabilities. The directors incur criminal liability if they fail in this duty.

Sole traders, partnerships and registered companies compared

Formation

Sole traders are not really formed, they just exist, for as soon as one person starts to manufacture, trade or provide a service by himself he is a sole trader. Partnerships and companies, on the other hand, are both commercial creations but differ considerably in their modes of creation. Partnerships are created by agreement and, whilst this agreement may be most formal, it may be just as informal. Indeed, there may be no express partnership agreement at all and an agreement can only be inferred from the circumstances. The vast majority of joint stock companies are formed by registration in accordance with the Companies Act 1948. This procedure is not necessarily complicated, but it is very formal. There is also more expense and publicity involved. Greater formality, expense and publicity are also involved in a company's operation in comparison with that of a partnership or a sole trader.

Legal status

A company exists as a separate legal entity distinct from its members (*Salomon* v. *Salomon & Co.* (1897)). In consequence, property belongs to the company and not to the members as individuals, and the company's debts and contracts are its own and not its members. Neither partnerships nor sole traders have separate legal identities as business organisations.

Legal status as a corporation facilitates dealings with a company's property and encourages investment. A corporation has perpetual succession and anything affecting its members does not affect its own legal position. The death, bankruptcy or retirement of a partner or of the sole trader, however, directly affects the organisation and may bring an end to its existence.

An important feature of modern commerce has been the increasing tendency for sole traders and partnerships to convert their businesses into private limited companies in order to obtain the legal and commercial advantages of corporate status.

Liability of members

Apart from limited partnerships, of which there are few, only registration as a limited company offers liability limited to the amount of his investment to a person who contributes capital to the business. This encourages investment, particularly in speculative ventures, and is the principal reason for the dominance of incorporated business organisations with limited liability in today's commercial world. Both a member of a partnership and a sole trader stand to lose virtually all their possessions if their enterprise fails (*see* Chapter 12).

Number of members

A sole trader is clearly one individual in business by himself. A partnership must consist of at least two members but, with certain exceptions, must not exceed twenty. A registered company must similarly have a minimum of two members but there is no maximum membership.

Two observations based on these figures can be made. Firstly, a small business unit can enjoy the legal and commercial benefits of corporate status as a limited company while still retaining most of the advantages of close co-operation and trust inherent in a partnership. Secondly, with some exceptions (*see* above), any business unit of more than twenty co-owners must be incorporated.

Transfer of interests
In this respect the greatest difference exists between a sole trader and a partnership. In the former the owner is completely free to sell, or otherwise transfer, his business, while in the latter no partner may transfer his share in the firm without the consent of his fellow partners. A member of a company may or may not be free to transfer his shares—it depends on the company's articles of association. It is very probable that most private companies will continue to include such restrictions in their articles in order to retain control within the family or small group and, since the Companies Act 1980, public companies are legally, if not commercially, free to do so.

Where interests are freely transferable, flexibility and free movement of capital are given to investors, but restrictions on transfer enable a strong common policy to be maintained within a business organisation, and encourage trust between its members.

Agency
A great deal of business activity is conducted through agents, i.e. persons who make contracts and dispose of property on behalf of others (their principals). A sole trader may employ an agent but, clearly, he cannot be an agent for himself. Each general partner is an agent of his firm and of his other partners. Therefore, provided the act is within the ordinary course of the firm's business, the act of one partner binds all the others. A shareholder of a company is neither an agent for the company nor for his fellow shareholders unless expressly appointed as such, for example as a director. Thus, the power to enter into transactions binding on the company lies in proportionally fewer hands.

Management
The management of a company similarly lies in fewer hands, for no shareholder, unless he is also a director, can take part in the management of the company. He can only attempt to influence management through his vote at company meetings. Under the

Partnership Act 1890 each general partner can take part in the management of the firm, and a sole trader's organisation is by definition controlled by one person. Management by directors accountable to the membership at company meetings is the only practicable solution for large (public) companies, but control of their activities by the many small shareholders is often more theoretical than real. Therefore, in recent years, "ownership" has been separated from "control" in larger public companies. However, removal of a director from office is a straightforward matter, while the desire to exclude a partner may result in the firm's dissolution.

In the future, greater worker participation in company management is a possibility, but it seems less likely that this step towards industrial/commercial democracy will affect partnerships.

Powers
The powers of a registered company are laid down in the "objects clause" of its memorandum of association. Any action in excess of these is *ultra vires* and void. Its internal affairs are governed by its articles of association. Any alteration of either must be in accordance with the Companies Act 1948. Both sole traders and partnerships are more adaptable business organisations. A sole trader is complete master of his organisation's business activities, and any alteration of a partnership's activities is effected by simple agreement between its members. The *ultra vires* rule applies to neither.

Publicity of affairs
The affairs of sole traders and partnerships are private. For example, no annual returns have to be made to any official registrar, and its accounts are not open to public inspection. In contrast, a company's affairs are public, its memorandum of association and articles of association are filed with the Registrar of Companies on registration and its accounts are filed annually. Unlimited companies, however, are exempt from the obligation to file accounts annually and in recent years increasing preference has been shown for partnerships and unlimited companies where financial privacy is of paramount importance. This is because there is a continuing trend towards greater public disclosure of the affairs of limited companies and greater government interest in their affairs generally.

Finance
Economic growth and commercial resilience depend largely on the availablity of capital. The sole trader must provide capital by himself and although a partnership is financed jointly, it too lacks the

financial advantages of a public limited company offering limited liability to investors and with access to the capital market. In particular, a company can offer security for long-term loan capital far more easily than can sole traders and partnerships. All three business organisations can create mortgages over their property, but only a registered company is able to create a "floating charge" over its property. This offers good security to the lender while still enabling the company to freely use and dispose of the property charged because it "hovers" over the company's assets and does not attach them specifically to the charge. Only when the charge "crystallises" (becomes fixed) does the lender acquire rights over specific assets. The ordinary mortgages that sole traders and partnerships can create over their property effectively prevent them from dealing with the property charged without the mortgagee's consent.

A bank will often accept the personal guarantees of directors as security for smaller loans to their companies. In similar situations, a bank is usually prepared to make occasional and seasonal unsecured advances to sole traders and partnerships, relying on the reputation of the firm and the financial standing of the parties concerned. In such situations the sole trader or partners are personally responsible for the advantage.

Taxation
All three types of organisation pay tax: sole traders and partners will pay income tax under Schedule D on the profits they receive from the business, and capital gains tax on gains from disposal of assets. Companies pay Corporation tax on both their income and capital profits. Tax liability may often be an important consideration when deciding whether to incorporate a business unit.

Comparative taxation is a specialist's subject and detailed discussion is outside the scope of this book. However, one typical consideration will serve as an example of the "tax factor". The tax liability of sole traders and partners is based on the profits made in the preceding financial year. Thus, with inflation or growing profits they will in effect pay tax on an income smaller than they are actually enjoying. A company pays corporation tax on the profits which it actually makes during its accounting period (its own financial year) and is charged at the rate for the financial year in which the profits arose. Therefore, the company's tax liability more realistically reflects the real profit made.

Public corporations
You saw in Table I that six out of the ten organisations employing

the greatest number of people were public corporations—trading organisations owned and controlled by the state. While their turnover is not listed in the "top ten" (*see* Table II), it is enormous.

Legal status

Public corporations are juristic persons created by either Royal Charter or, more usually, by special Act of Parliament. They are, therefore, the subject of legal rights and duties and must operate accordingly. Nevertheless, there is no one form of public corporation and the exact status, function, power and method of control of any particular public corporation can only be determined by reference to the statute which created it. However, their legal capacity will be more extensive than a registered company, the latter being constrained as it is by its memorandum of association and the *ultra vires* rule. Wide powers are usually granted to the corporation by the relevant creating statute and these in turn are widely interpreted by the courts.

Some public corporations are referred to as *nationalised industries* (*see* page 84). There is, however, no such form of legal entity as a nationalised industry. The name is a carry-over from the days when some industries such as coal mining and postal services were directly owned and operated by the government. The GPO, for example, used to be classed as a government department, its employees were civil servants and its head, the Postmaster General, was a minister who represented it in Parliament. This type of nationalised industry ceased to exist in 1969 when the GPO became the Post Office and adopted the public corporation type of organisation.

Ownership, finance and control

In the strict sense public corporations do not have shareholders but, as the government owns the whole of the organisation's capital, you and I—in fact the nation—"owns" the corporations and the government of the day acts as trustee of their assets on our behalf. Whatever profits the corporations make, if any, are ploughed back into the corporation for the benefit of the country as a whole. Our "dividend" could be said to be a relatively high standard of living and a tax rate lower than it might otherwise be.

Public corporations are mainly financed by the State—it is unlikely that the private sector by itself could or would raise the vast sums which are usually involved. Whilst being financed by the state, each corporation is controlled by a semi-autonomous *board of management* appointed by the government and is theoretically only accountable to Parliament through its annual report to the House of Commons' Select Committee on Nationalised Industries.

However, they must operate within a framework of policy laid down by Parliament, this being particularly true in respect to their financial objectives.

This method of control means that the Minister of State to whom the corporation is responsible can refuse to answer questions in Parliament about its day-to-day operations, although in practice Ministers frequently interfere in such matters on the grounds of the "national interest". We will return to this later.

While it may appear that the appropriate Minister controls the corporation, the recent case of the British Steel Corporation's accounts, when a Commons sub-committee demanded the appearance of the chairman of the board, demonstrates that it is ultimately Parliament which is the controlling force. In fact, as further funds from the public purse for public corporations require Parliamentary approval, they are frequently the subject of debate in the House of Commons.

The government also controls some businesses through its ownership of their shares, either directly, as in the case of BP, where it is the majority shareholder, or indirectly through the National Enterprise Board, as is the case with BL. These businesses, however, retain the legal form of registered companies.

You will find a more detailed account of public corporations, their role in the economy, their advantages and disadvantages and their future in Chapter 6.

Co-operative societies
Legal status and background
Co-operative societies date back to 1844 when the first co-operative society was founded in Toad Lane (actually T'Owd Lane), Rochdale. The object of the first co-operative was to provide cheap, unadulterated food for its members and to return any profit it made to them. Today there are around 190 co-operative societies in the UK and they constitute a quite distinct form of trading organisation.

Each retail co-operative society is registered and incorporated under the Industrial and Provident Societies Acts 1893–1961 (not under the Companies Acts), and exists as a juristic person, the subject of rights and duties in the same way as other corporations.

Additionally, they do not fall happily into the conventional division of the economy into the public and private sectors. They are neither nationalised nor state owned on the one hand, nor operated primarily for profit on the other. Their origin and continued existence lies in the notion of "self-help". As the profits are distributed to its customers, those that use the organisation the most benefit the most from its existence.

Traditionally profits were distributed as dividends (the "divi"). If for example a customer had done £120 worth of business with the society in a year and a dividend of 10p was declared, then that customer would receive a £12 dividend. Thus, most profits went to those who traded most with the society. In recent years many societies have replaced the "divi" with their own trading stamps which may be traded in at a better rate by members than by non-members.

Membership, finance and control
One becomes a member of a co-operative society by buying a share which provides part of the society's capital and entitles the holder to one vote at the society's annual meeting when its committee of management or board of directors, who control the society, is appointed. It is possible to buy more shares, but each shareholder is still only entitled to one vote. This is in sharp contrast to a joint stock company where each shareholder often has as many votes as he has shares. Thus, co-operatives are more democratically run than joint stock companies but, as their annual meetings are attended by very few members, their officers are elected and important decisions taken by a small minority of members. This lack of participation is, however, usually to be found in public joint stock companies as well.

Shares in co-operative societies differ from those in joint stock companies in a number of ways, for example:

(*a*) shares can be paid for by instalments;
(*b*) there is a maximum shareholding—at present £1,000, although the amount of loan capital that the society may raise and the size of the membership is unlimited;
(*c*) shares are not quoted on the Stock Exchange;
(*d*) shares cannot be sold, but members can join and leave at any time, i.e. shares can be redeemed at par value; consequently the amount of the society's capital constantly fluctuates.

Capital is also provided by loans, repayable at short notice, from its members. As its members are almost invariably its customers, its customers own the society and can influence its policy by voting in the election of its committee of management or board of directors.

The societies maintain their independence from one another but collectively they constitute the largest retailing group in Britain. In 1863 they founded the Co-operative Wholesale Society (CWS), which is also registered and incorporated under the Industrial and Provident Societies Acts. This organisation manufactures and supplies the member societies with produce for their shops. Today there is hardly a single retail commodity not sold by co-operative societies. In addition, there is the Co-operative Bank, now a member of the Clearing House, a Co-operative insurance service and a Co-operative building society (the Nationwide).

It is worth noting that the same concept of "self-help" responsible for the growth of co-operative societies was the origin of building societies in general. (Today they are incorporated under the Building Societies Acts and, as with co-operative societies, their activities come under the scrutiny of the office of the Chief Registrar of Friendly Societies.)

The co-operative movement
The co-operative movement as a whole has always taken an active interest in politics. At one time many people believed that the movement was a viable alternative to both capitalism and state socialism. The Co-operative Party was founded in 1917 and once achieved some success in returning members to Parliament. Today, the movement has close ties with the "grass roots" of the Labour Party and frequently sponsors candidates at elections. The Co-operative Union, the movement's spokesman and general advisor, represents its interests by lobbying at both national and local government level.

Other co-operative trading actitivities
Voluntary buying organisations, such as Spar and Wavyline in the grocery trade, are organised on a co-operative basis. Farmers' co-operatives exist in order that expensive farm machinery can be purchased and used collectively, and produce and supplies bought and sold in bulk. These organisations are not, however, owned and operated as true co-operative societies and are not registered as such under the Industrial and Provident Societies Act.

The same is true of a small number of workers' co-operatives, where the workers are the members and contribute their labour and not capital to the organisation. They receive in return a wage and a share in any surplus profits. Such co-operatives are, however, registered companies adapted to a co-operative form of organisation and structure.

Municipal enterprises
While local authorities are primarily concerned with government, they operate a range of trading ventures. Around 25 per cent of

dwelling houses and flats in the country are rented from local authorities, and this alone makes them important trading organisations. Other activities range from transport services, including docks and harbours, leisure facilities such as swimming pools and golf courses, to more mundane services such as public laundries and cemetries.

In common with public corporations, "profit" is not the driving force behind such activities and many (e.g. the provision of housing) are subsidised from the local rates. Local authority housing policy is a highly charged political issue in many areas, for while most people would agree that council houses satisfy a real social need, questions such as subsidies, further investment and development and the purchase of council houses by tenants are guaranteed to cause heated discussion at council meetings. Nor should it be forgotten that, while fulfilling a social need, council developments, particularly the now discredited high-rise flat blocks, have created their own serious social problems.

Local authorities are, of course, corporations, incorporated either by Royal Charter or by special Act of Parliament. They are able to finance their business activities by issuing municipal stock or by raising loans repayable over periods of time varying with the nature of the undertaking and the permanency of its capital assets. Both stock and loan are issued on security of the local rates and carry fixed (but often highly attractive) rates of dividend and interest. In addition, local authorities often receive government grants for their projects.

You and I are able to control the activities of our local authorities by voting at local elections. The elected councils are responsible for overseeing these activities on our behalf, although it is usual to employ professional managers to make all day-to-day business decisions.

SUMMARY

There are many hundreds of thousands of individual trading units in this country, and this chapter discusses the legal status and commercial role of the major types of organisations which exist, comparing in some detail sole traders, partnerships and joint stock companies. Each type of organisation has its own role to play in the economy and each is regulated by particular pieces of legislation and, to a lesser extent, case law. Law provides a framework in which these various organisations operate and in so far as they produce the nation's wealth, the economy can be considered as a structure of organisations. Figure 4 is a summary diagram of UK trading organisations.

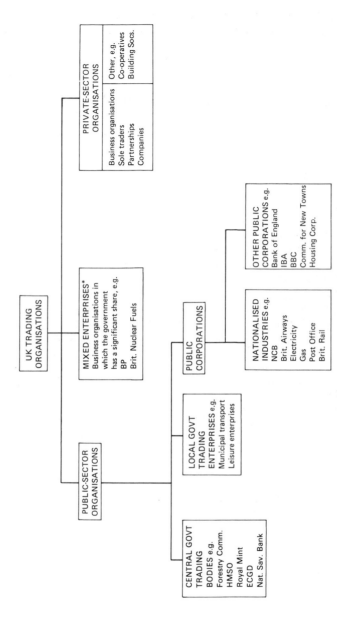

Fig. 4. *Types of trading organisation.* *Currently outside the public sector, as defined for statistical purposes.*

SELF-ASSESSMENT QUESTIONS

A. 1. Define the following: (*a*) a corporation; (*b*) a joint stock company; (*c*) a conglomerate; (*d*) the firm name.

2. List the main consequences of corporate status.

B. 3. True or false?

(*a*) The sole trader is the most significant form of business organisation in the UK today.

(*b*) A partner's liability for the debts of his firm is always unlimited.

(*c*) The public corporation with the largest turnover is the Post Office.

(*d*) Most companies are incorporated by Royal Charter.

(*e*) The memorandum of association govern a company's relations with other organisations.

C. 4. A group of friends wish to start a small business in the building industry. Advise them on the most desirable form of organisation to adopt.

ASSIGNMENTS

1. After studying Fig. 2 (Sears Holdings), assess to what extent the diagram illustrates the advantages of economies of scale.

2. How do individual trading organisations seek to influence government economic policy?

CHAPTER THREE

The Structure of a Business Organisation

CHAPTER OBJECTIVES

After studying this chapter you should be able to:
* identify and explain the main functions within a business organisation;
* outline the structural changes within a business organisation as it grows;
* explain the total systems approach to departmentalisation;
* identify different types of communication within an organisation.

The aim of this chapter is to give you a basic idea of:

(a) how the activity of a business organisation is controlled;

(b) the main functions within it,

(c) how its structure changes as it grows in size and complexity; and

(d) the importance of effective communication to the attainment of its objectives.

CONTROL OF ACTIVITY

The control of activity within a business organisation is achieved by management and administration. Activity within an organisation of any complexity needs careful planning, and this is the task of higher management. The plan produced is referred to as the organisation's policy.

The purpose of a business organisation's activity is the production of goods and services to satisfy demand from consumers. These may be consumers in the sense of you and I or other business organisations (producers). In so far as one section of a complex business organisation will often consume the goods and services of another, it partly generates its own demand.

The central feature of all business activity is the production unit which is often referred to as the plant. This could range from the factory of a manufacturing company, to the design studio of an advertising firm, to the shop of a trader. Its function is to produce *output* to satisfy anticipated demand. This requires the *input* of natural resources, materials, equipment and labour, as well as sufficient finance and entrepreneurial ability, all collectively referred to as the factors of production. One aim of the organisation's policy is to achieve the best mix of these factors and the role of higher management is to *co-ordinate* and *control* the different functions within the organisation and take the *decisions* necessary to do this. The control of activity is represented in Fig. 5.

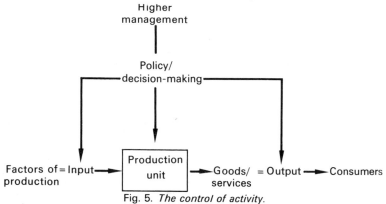

Fig. 5. *The control of activity.*

FUNCTIONS OF A BUSINESS ORGANISATION

Eight basic functions can be identified within a business organisation (*see* Fig. 6).

Buying of input (1)
This function consists of the acquisition of productive resources.

Production of output (2)
The conversion of productive resources into goods and services.

Sale of output (3)
The sale of goods and services:

   (*a*) to satisfy consumer demand; and
   (*b*) to make the profit necessary to the continued existence and growth of the organisation.

The production of output is a technical function dependent upon a combination of scientific and design development. The buying of

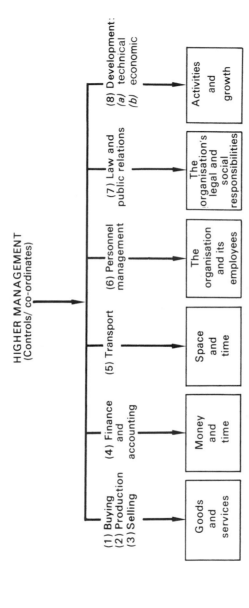

Fig. 6. *Functions of a business organisation.*

input and the sale of output are both commercial functions. All three functions are concerned with *goods and services.*

The six other basic functions are a response to the constantly changing socio-economic environment within which a business organisation pursues its activities. It is by efficiency in these functions that a business organisation is able to adapt to its changing environment.

Finance and accounting (4)
This function is necessary because the production of output takes time and there is an inevitable time lapse between the purchasing of *input* and the sale of *output*. Thus, this function is concerned with both money and time.

Transport (5)
As a business organisation's activities and markets expand, the transport of both input and output becomes increasingly important. Transport embraces constraints of both *time* and *space*, and will require expertise and specialisation in its management equal to that of the ostensibly more technical functions.

Personnel management (6)
All business organisations, no matter how small, must concern themselves with personnel management, and it becomes more important and its problems more complex as an organisation grows. Personnel management must be concerned with both the relationship between the organisation and its individual employees and its relationship with trade unions. It must endeavour to work with them and in some cases the organisation has a statutory obligation to do so, e.g. under the provisions of the Health and Safety at Work, etc., Act 1974.

Law and public relations (7)
This function is concerned with the business organisation's legal and social responsibilities to its employees, its customers, the state and the community in general. A business organisation pursues its activities in a complex socio-economic environment regulated and controlled by basic common law principles and a bewildering variety of Acts of Parliament and of orders made under them. It must appreciate its legal rights and duties and should consider social responsibility as a constraint upon profit maximisation. Without this specialist function it would be easy for a business organisation to unwittingly infringe the law and create a bad public image harmful to the sale of its output.

Development (8)

Development can be divided into two aspects: (*a*) technical and (*b*) economic, although in practice each are interdependent. Taking both aspects together, development is concerned with *growth* and the effect of complex and dynamic social, economic and political factors on the business organisation's activities.

All eight functions may be performed by one man in a small business unit but growth requires their careful balancing to achieve optimum efficiency. In particular, legal matters, public relations and development require more attention as the organisation grows in size. It is inevitable that the original owner–manager will have to delegate some areas of responsibility to his employees or outside organisations offering specialist services.

THE FIVE STAGES OF GROWTH

In this section of the chapter we trace the growth of a manufacturing company, although the principles involved are applicable to all business organisations.

In their growth most organisations pass through the highly idealised stages described and, as each stage is passed, the eight main functions described in the previous section will become more readily identifiable. The economic activity and policy of a particular organisation will determine the emphasis placed upon a particular function, and each organisation is likely to use its own terminology.

Stage one

At this stage the organisational structure is very simple (*see* Fig. 7)—the owner-manager (a sole trader) directly controls all functions.

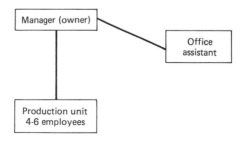

Fig. 7. *Stage one in the growth of an organisation.*

However, it is already necessary to delegate the actual production and he must decide, as the number of production employees increases, how far this direct delegation can be taken before it is necessary to employ a foreman to whom he can delegate immediate control of their work. It is also necessary to delegate routine administration to an office assistant.

Most business organisations in this country function along these lines. Primarily through lack of capital, many will have to fight continually for economic survival and many will fail. Evolution to a larger and economically more resilient business unit is a long process and for most an unattainable objective.

Stage two

Production has increased and the membership of the business organisation has grown, in our example, to thirty-eight. In consequence its organisational structure has become more complex (*see* Fig. 8). The owner–manager still has control over policy and management, but he has had to delegate the sales function to a sales assistant. Similarly, the office assistant will now deal with such matters as accounts and wages in addition to routine administration. He or she will be helped by two other employees, e.g. clerk/typists. The owner-manager will begin to rely on a secretary to attend to such administrative matters as correspondence and confidential records.

The *span of control*, i.e. the number of persons which one man can control, will begin to be an important consideration in the organisation's structure. The "span" will vary according to the nature of the activity involved but there is an inverse relationship

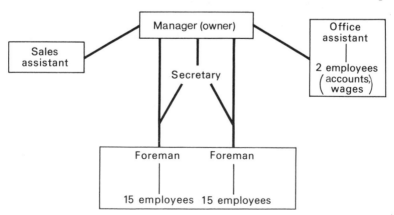

Fig. 8. *Stage two in the growth of an organisation.*

between the complexity of the activity and the number which can be controlled effectively.

Stage three

The business organisation now employs some 150 to 200 people, and its owner will probably be contemplating corporate status (*see* previous chapter). Many companies do of course have far fewer employees.

Whilst the owner–manager, now renamed the general manager, still retains overall personal control, increased output has made it necessary to delegate immediate control of both the production and sales functions. Higher management now numbers three (*see* Fig. 9). This delegation allows specialisation within functions and

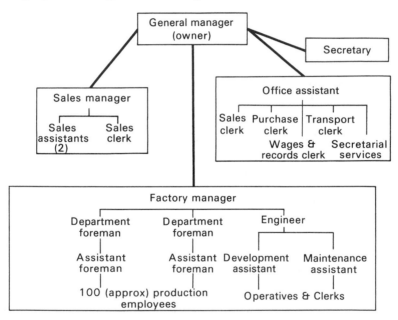

Fig. 9. *Stage three in the growth of an organisation.*

it should enable the organisation to operate more efficiently. If the delegation is successful, sub-delegation within functions will take place, e.g. a specialist engineer will be appointed to take charge of maintenance and technical development.

As the organisation continues to grow, proportionally greater importance will attach to the functions which are not directly concerned with goods and services (*see* Fig. 6).

Stage four

By stage four (*see* Fig. 10) the organisation has been registered as a limited liability company and its "owner" is now its managing director or chairman of the board of directors. It will probably employ between 500 and 1,000 people. The Companies Acts require the appointment of a company secretary to deal with statutory requirements, e.g. filing accounts with the Registrar of Companies. He must report to the board and not to the managing director. Control of policy has been relinquished by the organisation's original owner and it is now the responsibility of the board. However, if suitable restrictions on share transfer are included in the company's articles of association, it is possible that the original owner will continue to exercise effective control over it.

The remaining functions, formerly under the direct control of the owner–manager, will now be delegated to other directors or specialist managers.

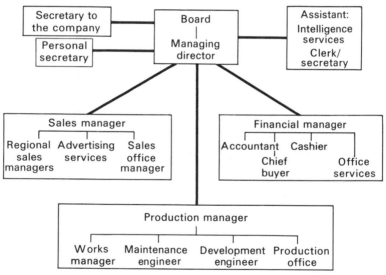

Fig. 10. *Stage four in the growth of an organisation.*

Stage five

The organisation now has over 1,000 employees and there is substantial delegation within each of the main functions as the limits of the *span of control* are reached (*see* Fig. 11). Few business organisations will evolve to this size.

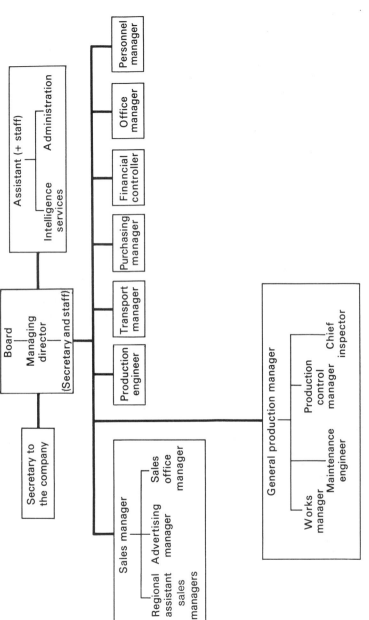

Fig. 11. *Stage five in the growth of an organisation.*

DEPARTMENTALISATION

Division of labour occurs within an organisation as soon as a sole trader employs additional staff. Immediately this happens thought must be given to the best way in which their separate contributions can be welded together to make a working unit. This process can be termed *organisation*.

As the business unit grows, two separate but interdependent relationships within it must be considered:

(*a*) structural relationships; and
(*b*) human relationships.

The latter is impossible to incorporate into the organisational process but the former can be shown in organisational charts (*see* the previous section of this chapter for examples). By illustrating the delegation of authority throughout the organisation and the responsibilities of the managerial and supervisory posts, they enable each employee to know to whom he is accountable and from whom he derives his delegated authority. They also enable him to appreciate his own role in the organisation. However, they tend to become quickly out of date because they are a static representation of the organisation's functional structure whilst the organisation itself is a dynamic entity.

Three separate tasks can be identified in constructing an organisational chart.

(*a*) Responsibilities must be established within the organisation and suitably grouped so that they may be assigned to individual employees.

(*b*) A decision must be taken as to who is to manage and be accountable for each area of responsibility.

(*c*) Formal relationships and lines of communication must be established between each area of responsibility.

The process of grouping areas of responsibility within an organisation is called *departmentalisation* and it is probably easiest to do this by using a functional criterion.

The total systems approach

A *system* within an organisation is a collection of interrelated and interdependent functions which together achieve an objective. However, when an organisation reaches a certain size there is a tendency for each of its functions to operate as separate activities in comparative isolation from one another. The essence of the *total systems approach* is that the organisation should be made to function as a whole, with systems designed to serve the whole rather than specialist departments. A simple comparison between a sole trader and a public company amply illustrates the problem. The sole trader is usually directly able to control his organisation's activity and he can easily acquire the data necessary to formulate his policy. The board of a public company, however, will usually rely on a number of specialist departments for the data they require, although each of these will probably collect data in the form which best serves their own specialist function rather than the needs of the organisation as a whole.

This division between functions will often foster interdepartmental rivalry and will usually be jealously guarded, partly as its own justification and partly to preserve the status of those in charge. Whatever the exact reasons may be the result is the same: higher priority is given to the separate departmental objectives than to those of the organisation as a whole.

Now that computer administration is often the norm rather than the exception, such factionalism within an organisation is likely to become more entrenched by the use of separate computer procedures. However, it is perhaps through a different technique of computer administration, one designed to serve the needs of the organisation rather than those of its separate functions, that something approaching the total systems concept may be attained.

By establishing a computerised central data bank, independent of traditional functional divisions and into which data is directly fed at source, the data required by the organisation as a whole would be provided whilst the efficiency of each of its functions would be unimpaired. This is because higher management would have immediate access to the information it requires to formulate policy, whilst each department could process the data further to satisfy their own individual requirements. Thus, the individual activities of each function and the work of all employees could be more easily directed towards achieving the organisation's objectives.

The introduction of a central data bank would strain traditional concepts and lines of authority within the organisation and may necessitate some structural reorganisation. This would entail three main steps.

(*a*) A complete reappraisal of the organisation's objectives in a concise policy statement. This would give each employee a clear idea of what he is trying to achieve and of his own part in the organisation's activities.

(*b*) An analysis of existing systems in order to assess their compatibility with the new concept and the feasibility of adapting them to meet its requirements.

(*c*) The standardisation of form design and the automation of compatible data input at source so that it can be used at a later date for different purposes by different people.

Perhaps the greatest obstacles to adopting a total systems approach are cost, time and inertia or positive opposition from management and staff. It is far easier, therefore, to adopt a total systems approach from the start. However, this assumes a level of expertise in organisational techniques that few entrepreneurs have when they start their business. Consequently, it is usually only possible where the new organisation has outside expertise available to it.

In the final analysis, any system is only as good as the people who operate it, and it must always serve the needs of the organisation. Consequently, it would seem impossible to achieve a perfect total systems concept in any dynamic organisation. At best a system which enables the organisation to function as a whole, and which facilitates change in its structure, can be achieved.

COMMUNICATION WITHIN AN ORGANISATION

Effective internal communication is absolutely vital to the success of an organisation, for it is by the transmission and reception of "messages" that the organisation's activity is controlled. In addition, a manager's effectiveness will directly depend upon his ability to develop two-way channels of communication between himself and those whose work he co-ordinates.

Two different forms of communication can be identified within an organisation:

(*a*) *vertical* communication; and
(*b*) *horizontal* communication.

Vertical communication

Vertical communication within an organisation can and should be both *upward* and *downward*. Downward communication originates in the boardroom and consists of instructions which are necessary to implement the organisation's policy. However, it is only through upward communication originating from the "grass roots" of the organisation that a manager can check the effectiveness of his own downward communication.

The methods of communication will vary according to the nature and purpose of the *message* to be transmitted, e.g. complex or "standing instructions" should be in writing, whilst verbal face-to-face communication is often more suitable for more informal or urgent instructions, particularly, in the latter case, where it is important to check the correct reception of the message. The method by which an instruction is communicated will have a considerable bearing on the way in which it is carried out. Two important factors to consider when deciding upon the method are:

(a) the possibility of the message being distorted, e.g. through lines of communication being too long;

(b) the personalities of those who will receive the message.

Horizontal communication
Horizontal communication is the term used to describe communication amongst people in different departments but on the same organisational level. Effective horizontal communication is essential if the organisation is to function as a whole and not as a series of separate departments.

The grouping of management offices close together and the setting-up of committees on which each department is represented are two basic ways in which horizontal communication can be encouraged.

SELF-ASSESSMENT QUESTIONS

A. 1. Define: (a) span of control; (b) delegation; (c) departmentalisation; (d) a system within an organisation; (e) vertical and horizontal communication.

2. List the main functions within a business organisation.

3. List the objectives of an organisational chart.

B. 4. True or false?

(a) Higher management's function is the co-ordination and control of "activity".

(b) Most business organisations pass through all the stages of development outlined in this chapter.

(c) Organisational charts quickly become out of date.

(d) Upward communication is just as important as downward communication.

C. 5. True or false?

(a) Trade unions play a part in the control of activity.

(b) The nature of the potential market is a factor of production.

(*c*) The sole trader is, in theory, the most efficient form of business organisation.

(*d*) A total systems approach prevents a rigid structure developing within an organisation.

6. List possible activities within each of the functions shown in Fig. 11.

ASSIGNMENTS

1. Identify and explain possible barriers to effective communication within an organisation. Discuss ways in which these could be overcome.

2. Construct an organisational chart for any one of the functions shown in Fig. 11.

CHAPTER FOUR

The Organisation in its Environment

CHAPTER OBJECTIVES

After studying this chapter you should be able to:
* define the law of diminishing marginal utility;
* state the principle of *ceteris paribus*;
* list the constraints imposed on an organisation by nature;
* identify the main constraints imposed by law upon organisations, and explain the reasons for their imposition;
* explain the law as an "enabling medium" for economic activity;
* identify possible effects of technological change;
* explain the economy as a structure of organisations.

In this chapter we will look at some of the constraints which act upon the organisation. In the market place it will be constrained by those principles which govern people's demands for its product. On the other hand, in producing goods and services the organisation will encounter those constraints which nature imposes upon the exploitation of resources. As well as the laws of demand and supply the organisation also has to work within the framework of the law itself.

CONSTRAINTS UPON THE ORGANISATION

Human behaviour
Later in the book we examine the markets and clients of the organisation in great detail. Here we wish to consider some of the assumptions we make about man's behaviour.

Firstly we assume that man is a *maximiser*: he tries to gain as much wealth or pleasure as possible. Those things for which man strives, be they goods, services or leisure, are said to give him utility. Perhaps in a true socialist state people would strive for the greatest good of all but this is not generally true of our society. In saying this we are implying that people are primarily economic creatures. If political, religious or aesthetic motives overcame man's acquisitive instincts then most of our theories on markets and production would begin to break down. By and large, however, the picture of acquisitive man seems to hold true. In addition to this we also assume that people are *rational*. That is to say they will stop to consider which course of action will give them the greatest utility for the least cost. This somewhat unlovely portrait of mankind is not a suggestion of how man should be but an observation of how he is!

We also assume that people are *competitive*. This is different from acquisitiveness for it implies that people want to do better than other people. We can also see from this that people are *individualistic*. In a competitive society such as ours not only are people forced to compete but also the good working of the system depends upon them doing so.

In addition to assuming that people generally compete to gain as much utility as they can, we also assume that they do not like work. Work is said to have *disutility* and therefore people have to be paid to encourage them to undertake it. There are people who do like work but in general if people were offered the same money for shorter hours of work they would accept it.

We may speak of the economic problem as being finite resources and infinite wants. Part of this problem comes from the fact that people's wants are insatiable. Most people seem to think that they would be satisfied if they had just a little more, but having attained a little more they discover more things that they want. It would seem that in satisfying one want we create another. For example, a person who does not have a car but wants one feels he would be happy with just any car; having acquired a car, however, he then finds he would like a better or bigger one and so on. He does not of course want more of everything: a person can rapidly reach the level of consumption of potatoes that he is happy with and not go beyond it.

If we consume more and more of a particular commodity in a stated period of time then the utility we derive from each successive unit becomes smaller and smaller. This is known as the law of *diminishing marginal utility* and is the principle which underlies the demand for any commodity. In Fig. 12 we can see that as more units of a commodity are consumed, in a specified period of time, so the utility given by each successive unit becomes smaller and smaller. People will only continue to buy the commodity so long as the utility they get from consuming it is higher than the price of the commodity. If, for example, the price were P then they would only consume three units. From this we can derive the general principal

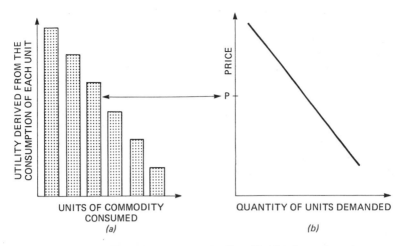

Fig. 12. (*a*) *Diminishing marginal utility.* (*b*) *The demand curve.*

of the *demand curve* illustrated in Fig. 12(*b*), showing that people will only buy more of a commodity if the price is lowered. This is often known as the *first law of demand.*

The nature of economic laws
We have mentioned two economic laws so far in this chapter. Let us digress for a moment to cover two important points.

Economic laws
The laws of economics are not immutable as the laws of physics are, but should be considered more as general principles and assumptions about human behaviour and the way the economic world works.

Ceteris paribus
This is the Latin expression for "all other things being equal". When we state something such as "more of a commodity will be demanded at a lower price" we should include the phrase *ceteris paribus*, for it may be that other things change at the same time as the price and then it will become impossible to reach any conclusion. In using this expression we are applying scientific method and isolating the one effect we wish to discuss. An inability to hold all other things equal when observing the real world is one of the factors which makes the study of the economy inexact.

Constraints imposed by nature

All organisations are constrained by fundamental principles which apply to the use of resources. These are considered briefly here. Their effect on the business organisation is considered in detail in Part Three.

The law of diminishing returns

Why can we not grow all the world's food in one garden? A silly question perhaps, but it illustrates a very important principle. We can get a greater output from a garden of fixed size by working longer hours or adding more seeds, etc., but the *extra* output we obtain will rapidly diminish. Indeed, if we just go on dumping more and more seeds in the garden total output may even go down. This is illustrated in Fig. 13. We can see that as we add more units of *variable factors* (seeds, labour, etc.) to the *fixed factor* (the garden) output increases rapidly, then slows down and finally declines.

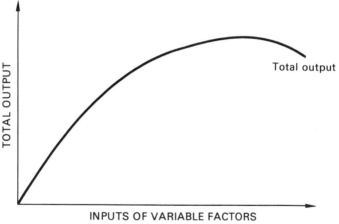

Fig. 13. *Diminishing returns.*

The law of diminishing returns will apply to any situation where there is one factor fixed in supply and successive units of other factors are added to it.

The law of increasing costs

The law of diminishing returns concerns what happens to output if one factor remains fixed: the law of increasing costs examines what happens to production, and therefore to costs, as all factors of production are increased.

Let us imagine we are faced with the choice which Hermann

Goering gave the German people in 1936: we can produce either guns or butter. Table III shows a list of alternative possibilities.

TABLE III. A PRODUCTION POSSIBILITY SCHEDULE

Possibility	Guns (thousands)	Butter (millions of kg)
A	15	0
B	14	5
C	10	10
D	5	14
E	0	15

If we start at possibility C, where we are producing 10,000 guns and 10 million kg of butter, and then try to produce more guns, this involves switching resources from farming to industry. To reach possibility B we have had to give up 5 million kg of butter to gain 4,000 guns. If we want still more guns, to reach possibility A we have to give up 5 million kg of butter to gain only 1,000 guns. Thus the cost of guns in terms of butter has risen sharply.

It would also work the other way; if we started from possibility C and tried to increase our output of butter, the cost in terms of guns not produced would become greater and greater. Figure 14 shows this graphically. As we move towards either end of the *production possibility curve* we can see that it is necessary to give up a greater distance on one axis to gain a smaller distance on the other axis. Why should this be? It is because as we concentrate more and more resources on the output of a particular commodity the resources we use become less and less suitable. For example, if we tried to produce more and more butter we must inevitably be forced to graze cows on land which is more and more unsuitable.

Increasing costs have been looked at here from the point of view of society as a whole but any trading organisation could easily become aware of it. If, for example, Fords tried to double the capacity of their plant at Dagenham they would immediately suffer from increasing costs as they would have to pay higher wages to attract labour in from greater distances and higher rents to attract land away from other uses. Increasing costs can therefore come about as a result of the competition for resources.

Opportunity cost
In the above example we looked at the cost of guns in terms of

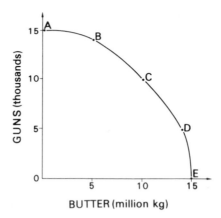

Fig. 14. *A production possibility curve.*

butter. This could be termed the *opportunity cost.* The opportunity cost of something is whatever we have to give up in order to produce that commodity. Any movement along the production possibility line AE of Fig. 14 will tell us the opportunity cost of guns in terms of butter and vice versa.

Economies of scale
There are some commodities it is better to produce on a large scale than a small scale. For example if a company only produced ten cars a year they would be very expensive, but by producing thousands a week the major manufacturers are able to make more cheaply. This is because they are able to take advantage of better technology and *division of labour.* In this case it will mean that as we produce more, costs instead of going up, will go down. A time will come however, when economies of scale are exhausted and costs begin to rise again.

Thus, on one hand an organisation has to deal with constraints which govern human behaviour, and on the other hand with the constraints placed by nature on production. In addition, there are also the legal constraints placed upon an organisation and the market which reflect contemporary political and social ideology and norms. We will now consider the legal framework within which an organisation functions.

The legal framework
We have seen how human behaviour and the natural world both *constrain* and *help* organisations. The legal framework within which

organisations operate also does this. Thus we have two apparently contradictory statements about this framework. On the one hand the law *constrains* organisations, preventing them from doing what they want to, e.g. the effect of consumer legislation, and forcing them to do what they might otherwise choose not to do, e.g. requirements laid down by health and safety legislation. On the other the law is an *enabling medium* helping organisations to pursue their activities and achieve their objectives, e.g. resources are acquired and products sold by making use of contract law, and patents and trademarks are protected by the law.

There is, however, no real contradiction between these two statements. We can explain this quite simply by making a comparison with a game of football. The rules of the game prevent players from doing certain things but they also help (enable) the game to take place.

This legal framework did not materialise overnight—quite the reverse in fact, it has developed over several centuries. As well as representing the social and economic norms of the present, it does, therefore, sometimes reflect the attitudes of the past.

The framework consists mainly of Acts of Parliament, although most of the law of contract—the basic law of the market place—is still to be found in the statements of law made by judges. In such spheres as consumer protection, health and safety at work, and job security, however, this traditional judge-made law (case law) is neither adequate nor appropriate and statutory law is far better able to formulate the necessarily detailed framework of regulations required. It can also more effectively take into account the important and often conflicting socio-economic and political considerations involved.

The framework produced since the Industrial Revolution is not just the work of lawyers. It has been shaped both by economic theory and practice, and by politics and pressure groups. The former have proved, for example, that a comprehensive framework of consumer protection and competition law is necessary to protect the individually weak consumer from the corporate economic might of organisations, while the latter have been instrumental in creating a protective framework of planning legislation and employment and labour law designed to encourage and enforce social responsibility in economic activity. Basic philosophical concepts of the law, such as justice and rights and duties, must be considered in these contexts. For example, until the Employment Act 1980 changed the law, an employee who was sacked for not joining a specific trade union where a closed-shop agreement was in operation could not sue for unfair dismissal. The Labour government's legislation of the mid-1970s—culminating in the Employment Protection (Consolidation) Act 1978—declared such a dismissal to be automatically fair. It was hard to accept that this was ever just in the philosophical sense but it arguably made economic and political (with a small "p") sense. A change of government has seen a change of belief which has been reflected in the law. Today, while closed-shops are not unlawful as such, the Employment Act 1980 does allow claims for compensation for unfair dismissal where a person is dismissed for not belonging to a specified trade union. This example clearly shows that the legal framework is the embodiment of a compromise among often conflicting social, economic and political perspectives affecting organisations and economic activity in general.

It is accepted today that business organisation owes responsibilities not only to its investors, members, creditors, etc., but also to the community in general, and must be accountable to both. Consequently, whilst the legal environment facilitates an organisation's activities, it somewhat paradoxically imposes constraints and obligations to do this. Without these it would be possible to pursue activities and employ methods which are socially, economically and politically unacceptable. Thus, the legal framework will restrain the minority to assist the majority. Some examples will illustrate this point.

Investment is vital to the activities of a public joint stock company and this can best be encouraged by effective legal safeguards against misuse of investments by business organisations. This is achieved through legislation requiring joint stock companies to file their memorandum of association and articles of association on formation, and information about their activities and financial position annually with the Registrar of Companies for public inspection. In addition the legal framework imposes sanctions for commercial malpractice, e.g. "insider trading"—the practice whereby persons such as directors are able to misuse confidential "inside" information likely to affect the price of the company's securities, for personal gain through dealings on a recognised stock exchange. Under the Companies Act 1980 insider trading is a criminal offence carrying a maximum sentence of two years' imprisonment.

It is in the interest of economic activity generally that certain limits are placed on the growth of business organisations, particularly through monopolistic practices and mergers which will reduce competition to the detriment of consumers and smaller business units. Private companies are essentially intended to be small businesses and this aim is achieved by allowing a company to restrict its membership and the transferability of its shares by appropriate clauses in its articles of association. On a quite different level the Monopolies and Mergers Commission can investigate monopolies or proposed mergers which would operate against the public interest. These constraints are also part of the legal framework, the simple principle being that since consumption of produced goods and services is vital to the existence of business organisations, the consumer should not be exploited by them. Thus the legal framework protects the consumers against unfair trade practices and strengthens their bargaining position relative to their suppliers.

Over the years the need to protect the natural environment and local community interests from unplanned or uncontrolled industrial development has become more pressing. The scars left on the landscape by the ravages of the Industrial Revolution are ample evidence of this. The legal framework consequently includes rules regulating land use and development, and attempts to achieve a satisfactory compromise between the legitimate interests of environmentalist and local community lobbies and the resources needed by modern business organisations to produce the wealth necessary to sustain a complex industrial society.

In a somewhat analogous way, the legal framework places constraints and imposes obligations on a business organisation's use of labour: maximisation of profits cannot be achieved at the expense of the environment or the employee. Thus, reciprocal rights and duties between employer and employee are part and parcel of the legal framework.

The government

You have just read above that the legal framework is far from being purely a lawyers' creation. It is formed by an amalgam of forces, one of these being the government and its politics. You will see later that the other constraints outlined in this chapter are, to a greater or lesser extent, affected directly or indirectly by the policy and activities of successive governments.

Since human nature tends to change only very slowly within a society, since fundamental economic principles remain unchanging, and since the legal framework is relatively constant and certain, a government's policy, therefore, is the least predictable constraint on an organisation's activities. It is true it will have its manifesto and other policy pronouncements, but these must be seen in the context of the practical demands and problems of government. Thus, whether because of external or internal pressures, governments tend to modify their policies during their period of office.

Because all modern governments intervene in the economy, organisations must therefore cope with a less than quantifiable constraint on their activities, and one which will possibly change course drastically every five years.

THE ORGANISATION'S USE OF THE LAW

All business activity involves uncertainty and each business unit poses a unique practical problem. Nevertheless discernible economic principles and a known legal framework enable an entrepreneur to narrow the area of uncertainty to an acceptable element of risk.

Here we are concerned with the latter, and in particular how organisations are able to use the regulatory nature and inherent certainty of the legal framework as an *enabling medium* with which to further and achieve their commercial objectives. It is argued by some that the economic might of large organisations enables them to use the law as a means of exploiting the consumer and society in general for the benefit of themselves and their owners. Undoubtedly this is sometimes true for, despite the considerable protection he now enjoys, the consumer faces an uphill struggle if it is he who must instigate civil proceedings against a business organisation. Against him will be arrayed not only its financial resources and purchased legal expertise but also the practical problems involved in taking even the simplest claim to law (*see* Chapter 25). However, acceptance of the "profit motive" as such is inherent in a mixed economy and the alternatives of extreme collectivism or economic anarchy are both socially and politically unacceptable to the vast majority of people.

Legal status
You have already seen in Chapter 2 that the law recognises various types of business organisation and in particular draws a distinction between corporations and unincorporated associations. Thus, the form of organisation most suitable to the specific business unit can be chosen, for each offers its own advantages, operates within its own framework of legal rules and has its own specific methods of creation and dissolution. Corporate status is sought in order to give the business unit an existence independent from its members. This enables it to own property, enter contracts and pursue legal action in its own right.

Agency
To cope with the increasingly specialised nature of modern com-

mercial activity, an organisation frequently needs the services of
outside specialists; or alternatively it is employed to use its own
specialised facilities or expertise on behalf of other individuals or
organisations. The relationship created is that of principal and
agent and the use of the law of agency is vital to economic activity
as we know it.

Contract

The rules of contract law are basic to the activities of organisations.
It is by making contracts that they are able to acquire raw materials
and sell their finished products and services. (The principles of contract law are considered in depth in Chapter 17.) In addition, specific aspects of contract law are used by organisations to regulate
their relationships with their employees, the methods by which they
pay and are paid for goods and services, e.g. by bill of exchange or
cheque, their responsibilities to those who provide their finance
and their rights as the creditors of others.

Property

By using the law, organisations can acquire property and protect
their interests in it. This may be land, premises, plant and machinery, or it may be industrial property such as copyrights and trade-
marks. The latter in particular need protection at law because by
their very nature they cannot be physically protected.

Conclusion

While the law regulates an organisation's activities according to
contemporary social, economic and political values, it remains first
and foremost an enabling medium which organisations can use to
pursue their commercial objectives. In later chapters we will consider the more specific regulatory role of the law in relation to the
organisation's use of its resources and the more general functions
of law within society.

MICROPROCESSORS

Improvements in technology are obviously of fundamental importance to the organisation. We shall learn that economics tells us
that the improved technology brings improved productivity and is
therefore beneficial. However, the impact of the *new technology* of
microprocessors is likely to be so massive that it is worthwhile considering this as a constraint upon the organisation.

  The chip has unleashed such power to process information and
control activity and functions of all kinds that it is virtually

impossible to foretell where it will lead. Let us consider a few examples: facsimile copiers can now transmit letters without the need for postmen; microprocessor-controlled lathes can undertake the most precise and complex of engineering tasks; robots can assemble electrical components; and still the possibilities of microprocessors have hardly been tapped. It could be argued that our technological knowledge has run ahead of our economic and financial understanding.

Many people view the new technology with alarm, seeing it purely as a method of making workers redundant. What will the future hold? Will microprocessors free us from the drudgery of work and create a new Utopia, or will they create vast wealth for those that are able to exploit them and unemployment for millions of others.

THE ECONOMY AS A VARIETY
OF ORGANISATIONS

Adam Smith saw the economy as made up of millions of individuals and small businesses guided by an invisible hand.

> Every individual endeavours to employ his capital so that its produce may be of greatest value. He generally neither intends to promote the public interest, nor knows how he is promoting it. He intends only his own security, only his own gain. And he is led in this by an invisible hand to promote an end which was no part of his intention. By pursuing his own interest he frequently promotes that of society more effectively than when he really intends to promote it.

To Smith, therefore, the economy was a self-regulating structure. For this to happen properly he believed that government should interfere in the economy as little as possible, for interference disturbed the mechanism of the market.

Today we do not believe that the economy is self-regulating and therefore the government directs and controls the economy. This is done by legislation which affects every aspect of an organisation's life—weights and measures, health and safety, fair competition, employment protection, and so on. It controls the direction of the economy through its fiscal and monetary policies. In addition to this the government takes a massive part in the economy directly through the welfare state and the nationalised industries. Thus, when we look at the economy we see a variety of structures rather than one single purposeful structure. Each works towards different objectives but the government intervenes to control their activities for the benefit of the nation as a whole.

It would be wrong, therefore, to take a hierarchical view of the economy; it should not be seen as one vast pyramid with the prime minister, the chairman of ICI or the general secretary of the TUC at the top. It is better to compare it to the cells and organs of a body. Cells may die but as long as they are replaced, the body is unaffected. However, if the organs (the institutions of the economy) fail in their function, or the cells are not replaced, the body as a whole will become less efficient and decline.

SELF-ASSESSMENT QUESTIONS

A. 1. Define: (a) the first law of demand; (b) opportunity cost; (c) the law of increasing costs; (d) insider trading.

2. List the constraints upon an organisation.

3. List five ways in which microprocessors have affected your own job.

B. 4. True or false?

(a) Economies of scale result in decreasing costs.

(b) Diminishing returns would cause costs to rise.

(c) The law of contract is mainly statutory law.

(d) Private companies can have an unlimited number of shareholders.

(e) The legal framework reduces an entrepreneur's risk.

(f) Industrial property can be physically protected.

C. 5. True or false?

(a) As more of a commodity is consumed the total utility derived diminishes.

(b) The demand curve illustrates an inverse relationship.

(c) The law of contract only applies to the selling of goods and services.

ASSIGNMENTS

1. Discover the ways in which the relationship of principal and agent arises.

2. Discover and describe in detail an example of division of labour.

CHAPTER FIVE

The Mixed Economy

```
CHAPTER OBJECTIVES
```

CHAPTER OBJECTIVES

After studying this chapter you should be able to:
* list the different types of economy;
* analyse the origins of the mixed economy;
* describe the different types of government activity;
* define fiscal and monetary policy;
* define a nationalised industry;
* state the problems facing the mixed economy.

TYPES OF ECONOMY

All societies in the world face the same problem: that of *scarcity*. That is to say there are not enough resources to satisfy all our wants. We do not have to be told that diamonds are scarce, but a moment's reflection will show us that potatoes, bread and clothes are also scarce, since there are millions of cold and hungry people in the world. Each society has only a limited amount of land, labour and capital (often referred to as *factors of production*) and it has to decide how to make the best use of them to satisfy the *infinite wants* of the population. This then is the *economic problem*—finite resources and infinite wants. Professor Samuelson says that every society has to answer three fundamental questions—"What?" "How?" and "For Whom?" What goods and services should be produced, how will they be produced, and to whom shall they be distributed once produced. How do countries attempt to solve this problem? We saw in Chapter 1 that an underdeveloped economy tends to function on tradition and command. In advanced economies we see three types of solution.

Free enterprise: capitalism

These are economies in which most of the economic decisions are taken through the workings of the *market mechanism*. Good examples of this type of economy are the USA, Canada and Japan. Often described as free enterprise economies, it might be better to describe them as capitalist for many markets are dominated by large monopolistic organisations.

Collectivism: communism

These are economies where production decisions are taken collectively, for example by state planning committees. Examples of this type of society are communist countries such as the USSR, China and Cuba. It should be stated, however, that a state does not have to be communist to be collectivist. In Nazi Germany many economic decisions were taken collectively, but it was most definitely not a communist state.

The mixed economy: the middle way

All economies are mixed in the sense that, even in the most aggressive free enterprise economies, the government usually intervenes to provide such things as defence and roads, whilst on the other hand, in rigorously collectivist economies such as Russia some decisions are still left to private enterprise. However, when we use the term "a mixed economy" we mean one which is fairly evenly divided between collectivist organisation and free enterprise. The most famous example of such an economy is the UK. The extent of government intervention in the economy may be measured by looking at the percentage of the gross domestic product (GDP) which the government disposes of. Table IV shows how government intervention has increased in most countries in recent years. Table IV also shows the UK with rather more government intervention than some of the other advanced industrialised nations such as Japan and the USA, but significantly less than others such as the Netherlands and Sweden.

TABLE IV. TOTAL GOVERNMENT EXPENDITURE
AS A PERCENTAGE OF GDP

Country	1960	1979
Switzerland	17.2	30.0
Japan	18.3	31.5
USA	27.7	33.4
Canada	28.9	39.3
UK	32.6	43.6
France	34.6	45.5
Germany	32.0	46.3
Belgium	30.7	50.9
Netherlands	33.7	59.5
Sweden	31.1	61.6

Source OECD: Economic Outlook, 1981

It is difficult to judge which is the best way to manage the economy. A Conservative, or right-wing, view would maintain that collectivism has gone too far already and the economy is being strangled by bureaucracy and state control. A left-wing person might argue that the free enterprise system has outlived its usefulness and that we can no longer leave important production decisions in the hands of capitalists and that, therefore, more state planning and control is needed. Little help can be given from the figures in Table IV for the two countries with the highest standard of living in the table, Sweden and Switzerland, lie at opposite ends of the spectrum.

Before going on to examine the components of Britain's mixed economy we will first trace its origins.

THE ORIGINS OF THE MIXED ECONOMY

The decline of the free market

The economy of the UK in the nineteenth century was one in which people and organisations were in a state of unfettered competition. It was believed that the economy would operate best if the government did not intervene in it. Such beliefs were based on the writings of Adam Smith (1723–90) who argued that *competition* was the best regulator of the economy. The belief that internal and external trade should be left to regulate itself became known by the French expression *laissez-faire*.

It is often thought that free competition is the "natural" state of the economy. This is not so: it is almost entirely a nineteenth century phenomenon. Before this time monarchs felt free to regulate the economy as they saw fit. On the other hand in the twentieth century the economy is dominated by the government and by giant business organisations. Only in a few sectors of the economy could free competition be said to exist today.

In his book *The Wealth of Nations* Smith argued that the many taxes and regulations which surrounded the commerce of the country hindered its growth. Business organisations should be free to pursue profit, restricted only by the competition of other business organisations. From about 1815 onwards government began to pursue this policy. Britain, already a wealthy country, grew wealthier still. The success of industries such as textiles and iron appeared to prove the wisdom of Adam Smith. Belief in the "free market" system became the dominant economic ideology.

However, as the nineteenth century progressed it became apparent that the free market system had two major defects.

(*a*) Although efficient at producing some products such as food and clothing the free market system failed to produce effectively things such as sanitation or education.

(b) Competition could easily disappear and give way to monopoly.

It was to combat these two problems that the state began to intervene in the economy. In the case of (a) the government did not take a conscious decision to depart from *laissez-faire* philosophy rather action was forced upon it by the severity of the problems. This is well illustrated by the *1848 Public Health Act*. In this case cholera epidemics forced the government to promote better drainage and sanitation. In the case of (b) there was a more conscious effort to regulate monopolies. This may be illustrated by the measures, which began as early as 1840, to regulate the activities of railway companies.

Thus, the nineteenth century presents a picture of governments believing in a free market economy but being forced to regulate its most serious excesses.

The effects of the First World War
The First World War thrust upon the government the control of the economy. Until this time wars had been fought on a free enterprise basis, if we can use the expression, with volunteer armies and little disruption of the domestic economy. Gradually the government had to assume control of more and more of the economy. The railways were taken over, agriculture was completely controlled, the iron and steel industry was directed and conscription was introduced. However, after 1918 the government immediately tried to return to a market economy. In 1921 a depression started in Britain and in 1929 it turned into a worldwide slump which the market economy seemed powerless to cure.

The Keynesian revolution
Between 1921 and 1939 the average level of unemployment was 14 per cent; it never fell below 10 per cent and in the worst years was over 20 per cent. Conventional economic theory concentrated on the demand for resources. This held that if there was unemployment it was because wages were too high. Thus, the way to cure unemployment was to cut wages and prices, thereby making people more willing to buy goods and employers more willing to employ people. *Say's Law* further maintained that if the market mechanism was allowed to work it would ensure the full employment of all resources and that this was the "natural" equilibrium for the economy.

The writings of John Maynard Keynes (1883–1946) are the most important contribution to economic thinking in the twentieth century. Keynes was English and worked for many years at Cambridge University. His views on the economy, however, were so radical that they were not accepted by governments in the 1930s. In his most famous book *The General Theory of Employment, Interest and Money* (1936) Keynes analysed the workings of the economy and put forward his solution to unemployment.

Keynes maintained that it was not the demand for resources which was important but the *level* of total (aggregate) demand in the economy. He said that a fall in the level of demand would lead to overproduction; this would lead to the accumulation of stocks (inventories) and as this happened people would be thrown out of work. The unemployed would lose their purchasing power and therefore the level of demand would sink still further, and so on. Cutting wages, therefore, would not cure unemployment: it would make it worse.

Since it would appear that the economy was no longer self-regulating there was a clear case for government intervention. Keynes' solution was that, if there was a shortfall in demand in the economy, the government should make it up by public spending. In order to do this the government would have to spend beyond its means (a budget deficit). In the 1930s this solution was not acceptable. As *Galbraith* has written: "to spend money to create jobs seemed profligate; to urge a budget deficit as a good thing seemed insane". It was, therefore, not until after the Second World War that Keynes' ideas were tried.

Socialism

Keynes was a "conservative revolutionary": his concern was to show not how the capitalist system could be abolished but how it could be modified. Thus, the post-Keynesian capitalist society has been even more successful than its predecessor. The fact that Keynes argued for government intervention in the economy does *not* make him a socialist. Socialists are those who believe that the means of production should be publicly owned. Socialism is therefore a different strand in the development of the mixed economy. Although much socialist thinking is based on the works of Marx, in Britain socialism has tended to be constitutional rather than revolutionary. Socialist thinking in Britain probably owes more to *Sidney and Beatrice Webb* and the other great *Fabian* socialists than to Marx and Lenin.

The effect of the Second World War

From the outset of the war the government took over the direction of the economy: industries were taken over, labour was directed, food was rationed. Britain could be said to have had a *centrally-planned economy*. The realisation spread that the government could intervene successfully in the economy. Keynes' ideas at last came to be accepted. Both the major political parties during the war committed themselves to the maintenance of a high and stable level of employment once peace was achieved. This was to be achieved by Keynesian techniques of the management of the level of aggregate demand. The fact that it was a Labour government which was elected in 1945 meant that an element of socialism was also introduced into the economy.

The welfare state
You do not have to be a socialist to believe that everyone is entitled to education, health services and social security. The origins of the welfare state might be traced back to *Lloyd George* and beyond, but its immediate progenitor was the *Beveridge Report* of 1942. This recommended a national health scheme for "every citizen without exception, without remuneration limit and without an economic barrier". Beveridge also stated that the basis for comprehensive social security must be the certainty of a continuing high level of employment. A White Paper, *Employment Policy*, was published in 1944 and accepted by both the major political parties. Subsequently, full employment was to become a first priority for all governments. The wheel had come full circle from the workhouses of 1834 which were designed to be so unpleasant that they would force people to find work. The age of *laissez-faire* had passed away.

The components of the mixed economy
What emerged from this period of Labour government was an economy which was a compound of socialist ideas, Keynesian management and capitalism. It was truly a mixed economy. Hence, we might summarise the main components of the mixed economy thus:

(*a*) a free enterprise sector, where economic decisions are taken through the workings of the market;

(*b*) government regulation of the economy through its budgets, etc.;

(*c*) public ownership of some industries;

(*d*) welfare services, either provided by the state or supplied through state administered schemes.

The remaining sections of this chapter consider the various ways in which the government intervenes in the UK economy.

MANAGEMENT OF THE ECONOMY

The objectives of economic policy

Whatever political party is in power, four main objectives of policy
are pursued:

(a) control of inflation;
(b) reduction of unemployment;
(c) promotion of economic growth;
(d) attainment of a favourable balance of payments.

These objectives are not in dispute, they are concerned with the
"good housekeeping" of the economy. Different governments may,
however, place different degrees of importance on individual objectives. Thus, for example, a Labour government might place a higher
priority on reducing unemployment than a Conservative one. In
addition to these generally-agreed objectives, more "political"
economic policies might be pursued such as the redistribution of
income. There are three areas of action in which the government
can pursue its economic policies: fiscal policy, monetary policy and
direct intervention.

Fiscal policy

This term is used to describe the regulation of the economy through
government taxes and spending. The most important aspect of this
is the overall relationship between taxes and spending. If the
government spends more money in a year than it collects in taxes,
this situation is referred to as a *budget deficit*. A deficit has an
expansionary, or inflationary, effect upon the economy. Conversely,
a situation where the government collects more in taxes than it
spends is referred to as a *budget surplus*. A surplus has a restraining,
or deflationary, effect upon the economy.

   If the government spends more money than it collects in taxes,
so that it is in deficit, the budget is financed by *borrowing*. The
amount of money which the government may be forced to borrow
in a year is referred to as the *public-sector borrowing requirement*
(PSBR). In recent years the PSBR has become very large and
governments have tried to restrain its growth.

Monetary policy

This is the regulation of the economy through the control of the
quantity of money available and through the *price of money* (that is
to say the rate of interest borrowers will have to pay). Expanding
the quantity of money and lowering the rate of interest should

stimulate spending in the economy and is thus expansionary, or inflationary. Conversely, restricting the quantity of money and raising the rate of interest should have a restraining, or deflationary, effect upon the economy.

It might be thought that, because the government controls the printing of banknotes, it is easy for it to control the quantity of money. This, however, is not so because most spending in the economy is not done with bank notes but with cheques. The amount of this "cheque money" is determined by the banking system and can only be affected indirectly by the government. The government does, however, have a great effect upon the rate of interest because all other interest rates in the economy tend to move in line with the rates of interest set by the Bank of England. In addition to this the government has a great effect upon interest rates since it is the biggest borrower in the economy.

Direct intervention

This expression is used to describe the many different ways in which the government, through legislation, spending or sanctions, tries to impose its economic policy directly upon the economy. Both fiscal and monetary policy are attempts to *create conditions* in the economy which will cause industry and people to react in a way which is in line with the government's wishes. Direct intervention, on the other hand, seeks to *impose the government's will* directly upon the economy leaving people no choice. A good example of this would be the imposition of a statutory prices and incomes policy.

PROVISION OF GOODS AND SERVICES

Many of the things which individuals use are provided either by *central* or *local government*. For example, most people's health care and education is provided by the state. These services are not, of course, free since we pay for them indirectly through taxes. The state also provides many goods and services to the public on a commercial or semi-commercial basis, i.e. they are *sold* to the public. These products, such as gas and electricity, are usually provided by public corporations. (These are considered in the subsequent section of this chapter.)

Many essential services are supplied by the government. These may be controlled directly by *central government*, e.g. social security benefits and motorway construction. Alternatively, the service may be decided upon by central government but administered by local government, e.g. education. Services such as street lighting and refuse collection may be entirely controlled by local authorities. On the other hand, services may be provided by bodies set up by the government but which are not regarded as either central or local government bodies. An example of these are health authorities. Those products and services which are provided to the community on a *non-commercial* basis, such as defence and education, are usually termed either *public goods* or *merit goods*.

Public goods and services

These are products the benefit of which is indivisible, i.e. the service which is supplied to the public is conferred on all equally well (or equally badly). The most obvious example of this is defence. Everyone in the country benefits equally from the activities of the army, the air force and the navy. Similarly roads and street lighting are available to all.

Merit goods and services

These are products which are allocated to the members of the public according to their merit (or need). Thus, for example, health services are not given to everyone, only to those who need (or merit) them because of ill-health. Similarly, education is not given to everyone equally. Educational opportunities are only made available to those between the ages of 5–16 and to those whose achievements in examinations qualify them for higher education.

PUBLIC CORPORATIONS

The legal form of a Public Corporation has already been examined in Chapter 2. Many of the public corporations are often referred to as nationalised industries. Strictly speaking this is a misnomer because, to be a true "nationalised industry", the undertaking would have to be run directly by the government and be headed by a minister. This, for example, was the case with the GPO up to 1969, but in 1969 the GPO was reconstituted as a public corporation, headed by a chairman, and renamed the Post Office.

Today, as you have already seen, there is no distinct legal form termed nationalised industry, but a group of public corporations are commonly referred to as such. Although termed nationalised industries for many years, an agreed definition was not worked out until 1976. The definition of a nationalised industry is that published in 1976 by the National Economic Development Office (NEDO). The nationalised industries are said to be those public corporations which exist mainly by *trading with the public*. The

NEDO definition said that nationalised industries were those public corporations:

(*a*) whose assets are in public ownership and vested in a public corporation;
(*b*) whose board members are *not* civil servants;
(*c*) whose boards are appointed by a Secretary of State;
(*d*) which are primarily engaged in industrial or other trading activities.

The NEDO study concentrated on the nine most important nationalised industries. These are listed in Table V according to the number of people which they employ. The list now contains ten corporations since the division of the Post Office in October 1981, although strictly speaking it ought to be reduced to nine as the government sold off the National Freight Corporation to its management and staff at the same time.

TABLE V. THE NATIONALISED INDUSTRIES

	Number employed in 1981 (*thousands*)
National Coal Board (NCB)	294
British Rail	227
British Telecommunications	248.5
British Steel Corporation (BSC)	109.6
Post Office	185
Electricity Boards (England and Wales)	154.9
British Gas	106
National Bus Company	58.4
British Airways	51
National Freight Corporation (NFC)	26

Source: The Sunday Times, 25th October 1981

The other nationalised industries, such as the British Waterways Board and the British Airports Authority, employ relatively few people.

In addition to these there are those public corporations which are not considered nationalised industries. These include the Bank of England, regional water authorities and port authorities. These you will note are not engaged in trading with the public, whilst organisations such as the Post Office clearly are. Thus we can conclude that *whilst all nationalised industries are public corporations* not all public corporations are nationalised industries.

A curiosity is the National Enterprise Board (NEB) which was set up by the Labour government in 1974. This public corporation owns and controls the shares acquired by the government in limited companies. Thus, for example, BL (British Leyland) is controlled by the NEB; it retains its legal form as a public joint stock company and is normally counted as part of the private sector of the economy, not the public. Organisations owned in this manner are sometimes referred to as *mixed enterprises*. The NEB grew very rapidly during the late 1970s, acquiring shares in dozens of companies, often those which were in financial difficulties. The Conservative government of 1979, however, decided to decrease the role of the NEB and sell many of the shares it owned. This was partly because they wished to raise money to reduce government borrowing and partly because they believed that the state should play a smaller part in the economy.

LEGISLATION

The government uses legislation to direct the economy less frequently than one might suppose. It cannot, for example, pass a law against inflation or to ensure economic growth. From time to time, for instance, it has a statutory prices and incomes policy, but it will not be able to pursue this very long if it is contrary to prevailing economic forces.

However, the government does legislate on such matters as monopolies and competition, so that certain commercial practices may become illegal. It may also impose planning legislation making it difficult for businesses to locate in certain areas. In recent years there has been an increasing amount of legislation on industrial relations and upon health and safety at work. However, in general the government hopes to *encourage* rather than coerce private enterprise to undertake the desired course. The role of legislation and its interpretation is considered in Chapter 24, whilst the legislation affecting the business organisation is discussed in Parts Three and Four.

THE PROSPECT FOR THE MIXED ECONOMY

We can look at the prospect for the mixed economy in political, economic or technological terms. Considering the economic point of view first, the central problem is the failure of Keynesian management of the economy. Keynes' analysis centred on the *macro-economy* and was based on the short-term management of demand.

This worked reasonably well until the 1960s, but since that time there has been a conspicuous failure to solve the twin problems of inflation and unemployment. In recent years governments here tried *micro-economic programmes*, trying to encourage potential growth wherever it can be found in the economy.

Economic policy, however, must function within the political framework. In practice this gives the consumers very little economic choice. However detailed the platform is on which a government is elected, it will only roughly approximate to the wishes of even its own supporters. In addition to this, experience has shown over recent years that governments are often forced into fundamental changes in their policy. This was well illustrated by the incomes policy of 1978 which the Labour government tried to enforce against the wishes of its own party, the opposition and parliament. Politics also places another constraint upon the mixed economy. At least once every five years the government must seek re-election. It is possible to argue that any major economic policy would take much longer than this and therefore the real welfare of the country is being subjugated to the government of the day's desire to ensure re-election. Thus, the politician is led to ask himself what most people want whilst the economist would maintain that the correct question should be "What do people want most?"

It is obvious that technology and, in particular, the revolution in microprocessing, is going to have a very profound effect upon our lives. There are many people, however, who believe that the revolution in technology has also brought about a revolution in economic order and created a new decision-making process. Foremost amongst the advocates of this point of view is Professor J. K. Galbraith. Galbraith maintains that power has passed from company directors, shareholders, trade unionists, voters and even the government to the *technostructure*. It is argued that in all advanced states power rests with those who have the high level of skill and information which is necessary to operate in a large corporation or government department. James Burnham in his book *The Managerial Revolution* (1941) argued that the new ruling class would not be capitalists or communists, but those who had expert technological skills. The argument is developed in Galbraith's books *The New Industrial State* and *The Age of Uncertainty*. Whilst this is probably an extreme point of view, it cannot be doubted that the new technology, particularly that of the silicon chip, is having a profound effect upon our lives.

Thus, the mixed economy stands poised between the two ideologies of capitalism and collectivism, pulled this way and that by differing political opinions. In addition to this, it has to cope with the rising power of the technocrat both in multi-national corporations and in government departments.

SELF-ASSESSMENT QUESTIONS

A. 1. Define: (a) public goods; (b) a nationalised industry; (c) technostructure; (d) *laissez-faire*.

2. List ten industrial economies in which total government expenditure exceeds 40 per cent of the GDP.

B. 3. True or false?

(a) Sidney and Beatrice Webb were revolutionary socialists.

(b) "Merit" goods are those whose benefit is indivisible.

(c) All nationalised industries are public corporations, but not all public corporations are nationalised industries.

(d) The five largest employers in the country are nationalised industries.

(e) Public goods are those which are freely distributed to everyone.

C. 4. True or false?

(a) Keynes believed that the economy was self-regulating.

(b) All public utilities are nationalised industries.

(c) It would be impossible for a nationalised industry to supply goods at a price which everyone could afford.

(d) There can be no such thing as a "technostructure" in a collectivist state.

(e) Keynes demonstrated that the equilibrium level of national income was fortuitous.

5. Make a case for regarding housing as a "merit" good.

ASSIGNMENTS

1. Compile a table of the nationalised industries showing their profits and losses over the last three years.

2. Economic activities can take place in (a) the public sector, (b) the private sector, or (c) both sectors of the economy. Coal mining, for example, is almost entirely a public-sector activity but shoe manufacture is entirely in the private sector, whilst armaments manufacture takes place in both sectors. Compile a table with three columns for possibilities (a), (b) and (c) respectively and in each column give three examples of economic activities which illustrate these categories.

3. Discuss the extent to which social justice can be achieved through legislation.

CHAPTER SIX

Nationalised Industries

CHAPTER OBJECTIVES

After studying this chapter you should be able to:
* assess the role of the nationalised industries in the UK economy;
* describe the growth of nationalised industries;
* list arguments for and against nationalisation;
* analyse the accountability of nationalised industries;
* describe the organisation of a nationalised industry;
* state the problems associated with evaluating the role of nationalised industries.

THE SCOPE OF NATIONALISATION

The importance of the nationalised industries

In the last chapter we considered the definition of a nationalised industry as a component of the mixed economy. Nationalised industries are an important topic of debate both in economic and political terms. In this chapter we will assess the role of nationalised industries and consider the problems they pose.

In 1980 the combined turnover of all public corporations amounted to £44 billion or 22.9 per cent of the gross domestic product; at the same time they employed 1,710,000 people and were responsible for 20 per cent of all investment in the economy. Thus by any measure nationalised industries play a key role in the economy.

The history of the nationalised industries

Nationalised industries are particularly associated with the Labour government of 1945, but there are examples of nationalisation before this. The oldest must surely be the Post Office, which has been "nationalised" since the time of Charles II. We can group nationalised industries under the following headings.

The early nationalised industries

Nationalisation can be truly said to have started in Britain with the establishment of the Port of London Authority in 1908. The inter-war period saw the creation of the Central Electricity Board (1926), the British Broadcasting Corporation (1926), the London Passenger Transport Board (1933) and the British Overseas Airways Corporation (1939).

The Labour Nationalisations of 1945–51

The major nationalisations of this period included coal, transport (road, railways and canals) and electricity generation in 1947, gas in 1948, and iron and steel in 1951. Road transport and iron and steel were subsequently denationalised by the Conservative government in 1953. The nationalisations of this period created the bulk of our present nationalised industries.

The later nationalisations

The scope of nationalisation has widened in recent years. Iron and steel was renationalised in 1967, and aircraft construction and shipbuilding were nationalised in 1977. Some of the nationalised industries have also been reorganised. The GPO ceased to be a government department in 1969 and became, as the Post Office, a public corporation. This was subsequently divided into the Post Office and British Telecommunications in 1981.

Conversely, in 1971, BOAC and BEA were merged to form British Airways. The Conservative government of 1979 tried to reverse the trend of nationalisation by selling off parts of nationalised industries to private enterprise. This process, referred to as *privatisation*, included the sale of some British Transport Hotels and the complete transfer of the National Freight Corporation to private ownership.

The mixed enterprise

So far we have seen that public ownership has been greatly extended as a result of nationalisation, but it may also be extended by a form of public ownership called the *mixed enterprise*. Business organisations in this category involve a partnership between private firms and the government, i.e. the industry or firm is not completely transferred into public hands. The mixed-enterprise form of business ownership is not common in the UK, and is largely a recent development. On the continent, in countries such as Italy and France, the mixed enterprise is a common business form. The most important mixed enterprise in the UK is British Petroleum, but other private sector organisations which have become mixed enterprises include Rolls Royce and BL (British Leyland).

In 1975 the Labour government introduced the Industry Act, which set up the *National Enterprise Board* (NEB) with powers to extend public ownership into manufacturing industries. The result has been an increase in the number of mixed enterprises. By 1979 the NEB held shares in a wide variety of companies inculding Ferranti, ICL and Sinclair Radionics. The Conservative government, however, then decided to reduce the role of the NEB.

THE NATIONALISATION DEBATE

Many arguments, both of an economic and a political nature, are advanced for and against nationalisation. These arguments often contradict each other. It should also be remembered that the arguments will not apply equally to each industry. We will consider both sides of the case.

Arguments in favour of nationalisation
Economies of scale
There are many industries which are best organised on a very large scale. A good example of this would be electricity. To have several electricity companies supplying electricity to one town would be very inefficient. The nationalisation of an industry should enable it to benefit from all the possible economies of scale and avoid *the duplication of resources.*

Capital expenditure
Some industries demand such major investment that only the government is capable of providing the funds. Such an argument was advanced to support the nationalisation of iron and steel in 1967. It might also apply to coal, railways and atomic energy. In addition to capital expenditure some industries demand large spending on *research and development.* In the case of atomic energy and aircraft it was decided that this could only adequately be met by the government.

Preventing the abuse of monopoly power
Where many economies of scale are obtainable it is quite possible that, if private organisations were left to themselves, they would become monopolies. This could well be true with industries such as gas, electricity and telephones. Nationalisation can ensure that they are administered in the public interest and not just for private profit, thus gaining the benefits of large-scale production without the abuses of monopoly.

Control of the economy
The nationalisation of industries may enable a government to pursue its economic policies on investment, employment and prices

through the operation of the industries concerned. For example, it might hold down prices in the nationalised industries as a counter-inflationary measure or, alternatively, invest to create employment in depressed areas of the economy.

Special pricing policies
The fact that a nationalised industry is usually a monopoly may allow it to charge different prices to different customers. This may be for one of two reasons.

(*a*) *Maximising revenue.* In this it would be acting no differently from a private *discriminating monopolist* (*see* Chapter 16). Examples of this can be seen when British Rail offers special fares such as "Awaydays" to customers, or the Electricity Boards charge different tariffs for electricity consumed at different times of the day.

(*b*) *Socially needy customers may be preferred.* A nationalised industry may offer special low rates to customers such as old age pensioners. Free bus passes for old age pensioners might be seen as an example of this.

Social benefits
A profit or service may be supplied to the public below cost price where this is considered beneficial. An example of this might be postal services supplied to the remoter parts of the country. Another example is commuter rail fares; these are effectively subsidised because if these customers switched to the roads the inconvenience and cost would be unacceptable.

Strategic reasons
The government might find it necessary to nationalise an industry considered vital for the defence of the country. Thus, for example, the aerospace industry in Britain has been nationalised to keep it in existence. The defence implications of nuclear power were also a reason for ensuring that this was a nationalised industry. *Key industries* of less obvious strategic significance, such as iron and steel, coal and transport, might be seen as vital to the defence of the country in times of war.

Industrial relations
It is argued that nationalisation will improve industrial relations. This would seem a hard argument to substantiate. It should be remembered, however, that many of the nationalised industries are *declining industries* and, therefore, problems in industrial relations are to be expected.

Socialism

A major reason for nationalisation is not based on economic considerations but is political, and is based on a commitment by the Labour Party "to secure for the workers by hand or by brain the full fruits of their industry and the most equitable distribution thereof that may be possible, upon the basis of *common ownership* of the *means of production distribution and exchange*, and the best obtainable system of popular administration and control of each industry or service". Thus ran the famous Clause IV of the 1918 Labour Party Constitution.

Arguments against nationalisation

The abuse of monopoly power

Many nationalised industries are monopolies and it could be argued that a state monopoly is more disadvantageous to the consumer than a private one. This is because there is no higher authority to protect the consumer's interests. The consumer, therefore, has to tolerate the lack of choice and high prices associated with monopoly with little hope of redress.

Bureaucracy

It is argued that nationalisation creates over-large and over-bureaucratic organisations which, therefore, suffer from diseconomies of scale. Evidence of this is the frequent reorganisation of nationalised industries and, often, the splitting of administration into regional boards, etc.

Lack of incentive

Although it would not be desirable for nationalised industries to maximise their profits, it could be argued that the lack of the profit motive removes the spur to efficiency which private enterprises have.

The problem of declining industries

Those industries which are faced with contracting markets, such as the railways, have a particular problem. The shrinking market forces up their unit costs. A commercial organisation would get round this by diversification. Nationalised industries, however, are prevented from doing this by the terms of the Act which established them. Thus they have declining business but are not allowed to branch out into anything else. Indeed, the decision of the Conservative government of 1979 to sell off the profitable sections of some of the nationalised industries, e.g. British Transport Hotels, worsened the situation for such industries by leaving them only the unprofitable parts of the industry.

The corporate state

Many people are opposed to the spread of nationalisation on political grounds. It is thought that it moves the country towards communism. Free enterprise, it is argued, is more democratic since it leaves decisions in the hands of individuals. However, today we probably have a *corporate state* because most of the important economic decisions are taken either by government or by large business corporations.

Nevertheless it is difficult to find an example of an industry being nationalised in the UK on purely ideological grounds. Most nationalisations have either been of public utilities such as gas and electricity, where centralised planning was considered important, or of loss-making industries such as iron and steel and railways.

Political interference

The sound administration of nationalised industries is often undermined by politicians interfering in the industries' policies for short-term political gains. An example of this would be a ministerial order not to raise prices in an attempt to combat inflation. Ministers who have engaged in this type of activity are as widely varied as Edward Heath and Tony Benn.

Discussions of nationalised industries frequently decline into arguments about political ideals of the "free enterprise versus the red menace" type. It should be remembered that nationalised industries are just another type of organisation and should be judged on how well they deliver the goods.

CONTROL OF NATIONALISED INDUSTRIES

Accountability

Business organisations in the private sector are controlled, ultimately, by their owners—in the case of joint stock companies this would be the shareholders. With nationalised industries the ultimate owners are the whole population. We will now examine the manner in which nationalised industries are held accountable to their "owners".

Legal accountability

Public corporations are corporate bodies and thus stand in the same relation to their suppliers and customers under the law as do other corporate bodies such as joint stock companies.

Additional legal restrictions
Nationalised industries may only indulge in those activities which are specified in the Act of Parliament which established them.

The minister
The chairman and board of public corporations are appointed by a minister of state. The minister may also lay down the general policy directives which the board must follow. Ministers are not supposed to intervene in the day-to-day-running of public corporations.

Parliament
The accounts of nationalised industries are debated by Parliament each year. The accounts are also subject to scrutiny by a parliamentary select committee which may require the chairman of a nationalised industry to appear before it. An industry is also subject to scrutiny by the Public Accounts Committee and by questions from MPs to relevant ministers in question time.

Consumer councils
The postal, coal, electricity, gas and transport industries have consumers' councils. These usually consist of twenty to thirty people nominated by various organisations such as trade unions. They are unpaid bodies. The councils deal with suggestions and complaints from consumers and advise both the boards and the ministers of consumers' views. Either through ignorance or apathy, consumers have made little use of these councils. In industries where consumers' councils do not exist *consultative councils* are set up.
   The public accountability of nationalised industries is summarised in Fig. 15.

The organisation of nationalised industries
Each nationalised industry is operated by a public corporation. The chairman and board of the corporation are nominated by the department and minister responsible; for example the British Railways board is nominated by the Department of the Environment. The board is then supposed to operate along the broad lines of the policy laid down by the government but to have autonomy in the day-to-day running of the industry. The activities which any corporation may involve itself in are laid down in the Act of Parliament which established it.
   The actual organisation of each industry naturally differs because

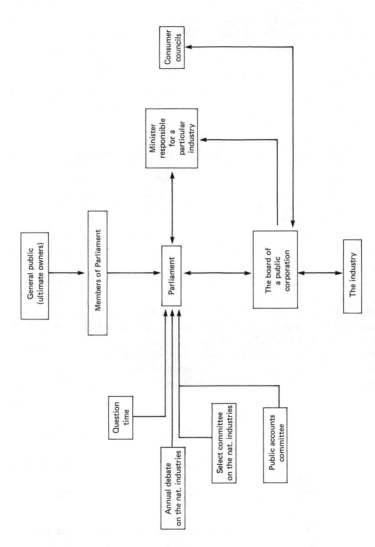

Fig. 15. *Public accountability and the nationalised industries.*

the technical conditions of supply vary greatly. It is common practice, however, for the corporation to subdivide its activities between a number of smaller boards, usually on a regional basis. Thus, for example, although electricity is generated centrally it is retailed to the public through twelve area boards.

Figure 16 shows how British Railways is organised. You will see that it is split into five regional operating groups. The other activities of the corporations are carried out through a number of subsidiary boards. These subsidiary boards, it will be noted, take the form of limited companies. Many of the other public corporations have limited companies under their control, a further variation on the "mixture" in the economy.

THE AIMS OF NATIONALISED INDUSTRIES

The overall policy direction of an industry must come from the government. In 1948 the government laid down that industries were to meet the demand for their product at a reasonable price which would allow them to break even over a number of years. This was extremely vague, and hopeless as a guide to practical management. There have been several subsequent attempts to refine policy direction. In 1961 a White Paper *The Financial and Economic Obligations of the Nationalised Industries* was published. Another White Paper in 1967 was entitled *Nationalised Industries—A Review of Economic and Financial Objectives*. Both these papers suggested that nationalised industries should break even after allowing for an 8 per cent return on capital.

In 1976 *A Study of UK Nationalised Industries* was published. This was a report made by the National Economic Development Office (NEDO). It was a detailed and searching analysis which concentrated on the nine major nationalised industries (*see* page 84). Some of its suggestions were:

(*a*) the operation of nationalised industries should be removed from politics;

(*b*) a policy council should be established to work out overall objectives for the industries;

(*c*) measurements for the efficiency of services provided should be developed.

Before any of these policies could be acted upon there was a change of government. Although the Conservative government of 1979 published no policy document on nationalised industries its actions towards the nationalised industries may be construed as a policy. It may be summarised as follows.

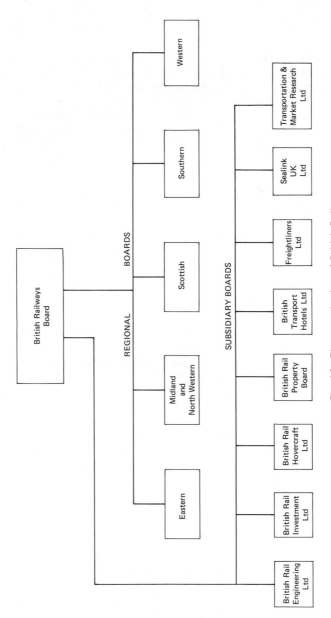

Fig. 16. *The organisation of British Rail.*

(a) Industries were to pay their way or at least break even. If this could not be achieved at the present level of service then sections of the industry were to be closed down until it did.

(b) Prices were to be increased. In particular British Gas was required to raise its prices to bring them into line with other sources of power, even though this would result in massive profits.

(c) Some of the profitable sectors of nationalised industries were to be sold off to private industry with the aim of reducing the role of the public sector, e.g. British Rail's Sealink operation was to be sold, whilst other industries were to be "privatised" altogether, e.g. road transport.

(d) Competition was to be encouraged both between different nationalised industries and private industry. To this end the government began to end some of the Post Office's monopolies.

(e) The Post Office was split into two. On the one side was the highly profitable telecommunications sector and on the other the less profitable postal services.

However, there was still no clear guidelines laid down on prices, output or investment.

Prices and output policy of nationalised industries
A business organisation usually sets out to *maximise its profits* and will orientate its prices and output policy accordingly. In doing this it is constrained not so much by the laws of the land but by the activities of its competitors. Usually a nationalised industry has no competitors and, as we have seen, its aims are not clearly defined by the government. This has the result that a nationalised industry could have several different objectives in mind when it sets the price and the output of its product. Some of these might well be contradictory. Below is a list of different price and output objectives all of which have, at some time, been pursued by a nationalised industry.

Profit maximisation
If a policy of profit maximisation were pursued then the be- haviour of a nationalised industry could be analysed like that of a business organisation. However, many people would see it as unreasonable that an industry should be given a legal monopoly and then be allowed to charge the public as much as possible. In 1977 the Post Office made a considerable profit on telecommuni- cations and was made to repay it to telephone users. On the other

hand, in 1980 the British Gas Corporation was forced to raise its prices to the level of other fuels, which resulted in enormous profits.

Social pricing
It could be argued that prices should be fixed at a level which everyone could afford. This would have two main effects: firstly the industry would probably make a huge loss; and secondly the price of the product would cease to have an allocating effect. This would mean that people would wish to consume much more of the product. If, for example, electricity were made free then many people might leave their lights and heating on all day. This would mean that electricity would have to be rationed in some manner. Electricity would in effect have become a public or merit good. No nationalised industry has supplied products free, but on occasions prices have been held down for social reasons, an example of this being commuter rail fares being held down.

Government economic policy
It could be argued that prices should be fixed to satisfy the government's economic strategy. An example of this might be prices restrained to assist a prices and incomes policy. Conversely it was argued that the large rise in gas prices in 1980 was part of the government's strategy to conserve fuel resources.

Cost pricing
A recurring argument has been that the prices of nationalised industries should be set so that the costs are recovered. Two such suggestions are that prices should be determined by marginal costs or average costs (*see* Chapter 14). However, in reality these are hard to determine for very large industries, in addition to which they vary rapidly with changes in output.

The reality
The result is that the prices and output policy of nationalised industries are a compromise, or perhaps a muddle, of all the different ideas, varying from industry to industry and time to time.

The profitability of nationalised industries
Having examined the prices and output policy of nationalised industries, let us turn to their actual performance. Table VI shows the performance of several of the major public corporations in 1980.

TABLE VI. PROFITS AND LOSSES IN THE NATIONALISED INDUSTRIES, 1980

Profit makers	(£m.)	Loss makers	(£m.)
British Gas	710	British Steel	665
British Telecom	181	NCB	181
Post Office	29	British Airways	141
CEGB	27	British Rail	78
		British Shipbuilders	37

The nationalised industries, like the rest of the economy, were in a state of depression. Thus even a corporation such as British Airways, which usually makes a profit, was heavily in the red. Table VII shows the overall figures for all public corporations for the last decade.

TABLE VII. NET PROFIT OR LOSS FOR PUBLIC CORPORATIONS, 1971–80

Year	Profit or loss (£m.)	Year	Profit or loss (£m.)
1971	+136	1976	+783
1972	+188	1977	+855
1973	+269	1978	+604
1974	+ 76	1979	−169
1975	−108	1980	−478

CONCLUSION

So long as nationalisation remains a political issue it will be hard to form objective judgements about the issues. It is widely believed for example that all nationalised industries lose money. The problem industries are railways, steel and shipbuilding, the other fifteen nationalised industries usually being in profit. The three problem industries mentioned are in fact in trouble worldwide; it would therefore be somewhat unrealistic to expect them to be booming in the UK. It is also commonly believed that nationalised industries are a peculiarly British phenomenon. This also is not so, as most Western European countries have nationalised industries and there are some novel variations; in Sweden, for example, distilling is nationalised and in France there is a government tobacco monopoly.

When evaluating nationalised industries it should also be remembered that nationalisation has usually concerned itself with either *public utilities*, such as gas and electricity, or with *loss-making industries*, such as steel. We do not have an example of a major profitable manufacturing industry being nationalised which we can examine, and furthermore, it remains difficult to judge existing nationalised industries so long as there are no commonly agreed aims.

The political issue remains as divisive as ever. The Conservative Party is committed to reducing the role of nationalised industry whilst the Labour Party has declared its intention of nationalising the banks and many of the major businesses of the nation, if it is returned to power.

SELF-ASSESSMENT QUESTIONS

A. 1. Define: (*a*) privatisation; (*b*) mixed enterprise; (*c*) the corporate state; (*d*) consumer council.

2. List the advantages and disadvantages of nationalisation.

B. 3. True or false?

(*a*) In 1980 the combined turnover of the nationalised industries was £44 billion.

(*b*) Nationalisation was first introduced into the UK in 1947.

(*c*) The largest single nationalised industry (by employment) is the Post Office.

(*d*) The National Enterprise Board is a mixed enterprise.

(*e*) All nationalised industries are supposed to break even.

C. 4. True or false?

(*a*) The nationalised industries are the largest employers of labour in the UK.

(*b*) If a nationalised industry were to equate its marginal revenue with its marginal costs it should maximise its profits.

(*c*) British Rail's commuter services subsidise the rest of its services.

(*d*) Nationalised industries may not be investigated by the Monopolies Commission.

(*e*) The borrowing of nationalised industries forms part of the public sector borrowing requirement.

5. Make out a case for subsidising rail fares.

ASSIGNMENTS

1. Select three of the major nationalised industries and compile a table to show: (*a*) the number of people employed; (*b*) the value

of the turnover; (c) the capital employed; (d) the profit or loss for each of the industries for the last two years.

2. Examine the organisation chart of British Railways (*see* Fig. 16) and construct a similar chart for one of the other major nationalised industries.

3. Re-read pages 97 to 101 dealing with the aims of nationalised industries, and then devise a policy document which the government could adopt.

PART TWO
DEMOGRAPHY

CHAPTER SEVEN

Demography

CHAPTER OBJECTIVES

After studying this chapter you should be able to:
* define and evaluate the concept of optimum population and explain its relevance to the government and the organisation;
* describe the present structure of UK population and explain how it came about;
* list and describe the main determinants of the structure of population;
* interpret and represent demographic data found in government and other statistics;
* state the relevance of the law of diminishing returns to world population growth.

WORLD POPULATION

The population explosion

Organisations have become complex in the context of rising world population. The impact of the population explosion on all aspects of human life, be they economic, legal, social or political, is so immense as to almost defy analysis. Population is the all-important backdrop against which all human activities are played. For the organisation it provides one of its essential resources, labour, and also the markets for its goods and services. Government organisations must also make their plans on their estimates of changes in the future population. Although it would appear that population growth has stabilised in many western countries, the continuing growth of world population poses some of the most imponderable questions for the future.

What is meant by the population explosion is demonstrated graphically by Fig. 17. It can be seen from this graph that estimated world population was 300 million in AD 1000 and that this slowly rose to around 728 million in AD 1750. Population then began to rise much more quickly, reaching 3,000 million by 1962. Estimates for the year 2000 envisage an increase to 6,200 million. This means that population will have risen over twenty-fold in the last 1,000 years, having been almost static for the previous 200,000 years of human history. Moreover, the majority of this growth will have

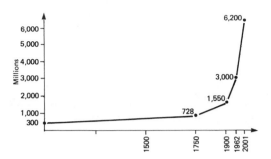

Fig. 17. *World population. Source: based on UN Department of Economic and Social Affairs, Population Division, Figures and Forecasts 1975.*

taken place in 100 years. At the moment estimates of world population are being revised downward. Dr Ravenholt, Director of USA Office of Population believes that world population may only be 5,500 million by 2001. It is unlikely that it will be this small, but it demonstrates how uncertain estimates are. Estimates for the year 2050 vary from 8 billion to 14 billion.

T. R. Malthus (1766–1834)

Accurate population figures for Britain start with the first census of 1801. Three years earlier Malthus published the first major work on population. This was entitled *An Essay on the Principle of Population as it affects the Future Improvement of Society*. Malthus had noted the quickening growth of British population and was also aware of the principle of *diminishing returns* as expounded by Adam Smith and other political economists. Malthus maintained that population would continue to grow in a geometric progression (1,2,4,8,16, etc.), whilst world food resources would grow in an arithmetic progression (1,2,3,4,5, etc.). Since the amount of land on the planet is fixed, this would mean that there would be less and less food to feed each person. This would continue until population growth was halted by "positive checks" of "war, pestilence and famine". This would give more food per person so that population would increase again, thus causing positive checks to set in again, and so on. Thus, the gloomy forecast of Malthus was that world population would forever fluctuate around the point when most of it is starving to death. This is termed a *subsistence equilibrium*.

For a number of reasons these pessimistic forecasts did not come true in Britain. Through technological improvements industry and agriculture became more productive, the New World and Australia provided room for expansion, and, towards the end of the century, parents in Britain began to limit the size of their families. Moreover, there is a debate in economic history as to whether population growth stimulated economic growth or vice versa.

You must note that the law of diminishing returns cannot be repealed, only offset. When one looks at much of the Third World today, one might be forgiven for thinking that Malthus was only too right.

The rich and the poor

There is a growing disparity between the rich areas of the world and the poor, both in proportional and aggregate terms. That is to say, the poor are poorer than they have ever been before. Population provides one of the major clues as to why this is so. It would appear that in some countries of the world, e.g., India, however fast the gross national product (GNP) grows, population grows faster, and therefore the country is poorer in terms of GNP per head.

Asia (excluding the USSR), South America and Africa together occupy about 55 per cent of the land surface of the Earth and have about 70 per cent of its population, whereas Europe, North America and Australasia occupy about 45 per cent of the Earth and have only 30 per cent of the population. By the end of the century it is likely that the first of these two areas will have 80 per cent of the population and the second only 20 per cent. Obviously the poorer areas will need enormous advances in agricultural and industrial techniques to cope with this rise, but most of the expertise and the capital is possessed by the richer countries. It is because of this that many people consider that a great fall in the birth-rate in the poor nations is the only way out of this cycle of poverty for them. It is possible, however, that continued population growth in poor countries will only increase the bargaining power of the richer nations in world markets, thereby making the problems even worse.

FACTORS INFLUENCING THE SIZE OF POPULATION

Population is affected by three main influences: the birth-rate; the death-rate; and by migration, i.e. the net figure derived from im-migration and emigration.

TABLE VIII. BIRTH-RATES

Year	Birth-rate (Great Britain)
1871	35.5
1911	24.5
1933	14.4

Birth-rates are normally expressed in this manner, that is to say, in 1871 for every 1,000 people in the country 35.5 births took place. This is sometimes called a crude birth-rate since it simply records the number of live births, no allowance being made for infant mortality or other circumstances.

TABLE IX. DEATH-RATES

Year	Death-rate (Great Britain)
1750	33.0
1851	22.7
1911	13.8

Death-rates are normally expressed as the number of people in the country that died in a year per 1,000 of the population. This is sometimes called the crude death-rate because it takes no account of the age of the person at death: they could be three months old or ninety years.

Net reproduction rate

By comparing the birth-rate with the death-rate an overall *rate of natural increase* or *decrease* in population is arrived at, excluding migration. One way to illustrate this is to superimpose one bar diagram on another (*see* McNamara, T., *Numeracy and Accounting*, Macdonald & Evans, 1979) as in Fig. 18. From Fig. 18 it can be seen that Britain had a rate of natural increase of 10.7 per 1,000 per year, or 1.07 per cent, in 1911. Today in the UK population growth is virtually static. However, if one did the same exercise for India today it would show a high rate of natural increase.

This, however, may be misleading, because the increase may be concentrated in the older age groups so that the future increase of society is threatened. To overcome this we can consider the *total period fertility rate* (TPFR). This measures the average number of children born per woman of child-bearing years (defined as aged

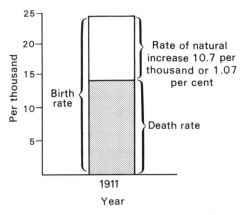

Fig. 18. *Rate of natural increase in population.*

fifteen to fifty) that would result if women survived to the end of
their reproductive period.

TABLE X. TOTAL PERIOD FERTILITY RATE

Year	*TPFR* (*Great Britain*)
1951	2.16
1966	2.78
1977	1.68
1979	1.86

Source: CSO, Social Trends

It is necessary for the rate to be 2.0 or above if society is to continue
to have the ability to reproduce itself. One might also consider the
fertility rate. This is births per 1,000 women aged between sixteen
and forty-four.

TABLE XI. FERTILITY RATE

Year	Fertility rate (*Great Britain*)
1900	115
1933	81
1951	72.5
1977	58.8
1979	64.0

(*Source: United Nations Department of Economic and Social Affairs*)

Thus, for every 1,000 women between the ages of sixteen and forty-four, 58.8 children were born in 1977. This was the lowest postwar rate. It rose to 64.0 by 1979 but this was still approximately 10 per cent below that necessary for the long-term replacement of the population. There has been a similar long-term decline in most Western European fertility rates.

Marriage and the size of family

As the vast majority of births are to married women, the number of marriages taking place obviously has an effect upon the number of births. However, the percentage of people marrying has remained fairly constant, around 88 per cent. The age at which people marry may also have an effect. In recent years the tendency has been for people to marry younger. Thus, there are more potential child-bearing years and, in addition to this, women tend to be biologically more fertile in their teens and twenties (these trends were significantly modified in the 1970s—*see* below). However, the most significant factor in British population over the last century has been the trend to smaller families. The reasons for this will be examined later, but we may note here the change from the five-to-six child family in 1870 to the present two-to-three child family. Today, there is also a social pattern to the size of family.

Social Class 1 (professional: doctors, lawyers, clerics, etc.) are most prone to have three-to-five children, but Social Class 5 (semi-skilled and unskilled employees) are most likely to have families of six and upwards. Overall, there is an inverse relation between social class and size of family. This is not only true for Britain but also for many other western countries. Ireland, however, continues to have a large average size of family.

Migration

If immigration is compared with emigration, a figure of net outflow or inflow of migrants is arrived at. Demographically, migration has not been a significant factor in Britain. On the other hand North America is an area where immigration has been very important, whereas emigration from Ireland has actually been responsible for a decline in its population. Only on two occasions has Britain been a net gainer by migration. This is illustrated by Fig. 19. The inflow after 1931 is explained by two factors: firstly, by people who had emigrated to the colonies returning because of the depression; secondly in the '30s there was a large flow of refugees coming from Nazi Europe. Successive waves of immigrants from the new Commonwealth countries account for the inflow in the '50s and early '60s. Although the net figure is not significant, the fact that many

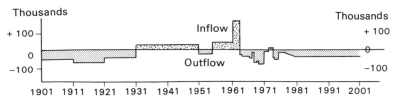

Fig. 19. *Net migration (by decade to 1964, then annually). Source: based on The Economist, 24 December 1977.*

of the immigrants were coloured has posed particular social and political problems. Economically the immigrants have filled a vital role in providing labour for the economy. One factor to be borne in mind is that immigrants are predominantly of working age and therefore swell the ranks of the productive part of society. Balanced against this is the fact that the emigrants which Britain has lost have often been highly trained and dynamic; this has sometimes been called the "brain drain".

THE GROWTH OF BRITISH POPULATION

The last census of the UK was conducted in April 1981. A census is usually followed by a more detailed census of 10 per cent of the population five years later. The first census was conducted in 1801 and one was held every ten years thereafter, with the exception of 1941. Calculations and estimates are few and unreliable before 1801 date and come from such things as the Domesday Book, 1086, the Poll Tax of Richard II, 1379, and the *Observations* of Gregory King, 1690.

British population grew rapidly up to the 1870s, at which time the rate of increase began to slow down. The First World War marked a great watershed, after which the growth of population came almost to a halt. Since 1945 the rate of population growth has fluctuated and is hovering around zero at present.

The period of rapid growth

The explanation of the rapid growth of population up to the 1870s is to be found in the decline of the death-rate (*see* Table IX). This is because the birth-rate remained almost constant up to the 1870s and Britain was a net loser by migration throughout this period. In 1750 the rate of natural increase was little over 0.2 per cent. The death-rate then began to drop dramatically, so that by 1851 the rate of natural increase was around 1.3 per cent, i.e. it had increased more than six-fold.

TABLE XII. POPULATION GROWTH 1801–2001

	Population of England, Wales and Scotland (000s)	Average percentage increase per decade
1801	10,501	13.9
1871	26,072	11.5
1911	40,891	4.5
1941 (estimate)	46,605	5.8
1971	53,720	0.8
1981	54,129	2.1
2001	57,193	

One of the main reasons advanced to explain this decline in the death-rate is the improvement in medical knowledge and provision, together with the elimination of many epidemic diseases such as plague, smallpox, typhus, typhoid and cholera in the nineteenth century. In addition to this there were improvements in diet, housing, clothing and water supply. It has even been argued that the reimposition of the gin tax in 1751 had a significant effect. However, these do not provide an adequate explanation. With the possible exception of the gin tax, none of these factors was effective early enough to account for the change in the death-rate. The origins of population growth therefore remain a controversial issue. It is worth bearing in mind that most people died before the age of five, and it was a decline in this *infant mortality*, for whatever reasons, that affected death-rate at least as significantly as increasing longevity. The growth of population certainly coincided with the quickening of economic activity in the industrial revolution either as cause or effect. This was also the time when the urbanisation of British population began. People flocked from the countryside to the towns, and from the south to the north of England. However, in the towns the conditions were so insanitary for the ordinary people that expectation of life was low.

The decline in the size of the family
After the 1870s the expectation of life continued to increase and therefore the reasons for the decrease in the rate of population growth are to be found in the birth-rate. It was from this time onwards that people began to limit the size of their families. It has been argued that up to this time people had seen children as a source of income, and when child labour was forbidden they were discouraged from bearing children. Whilst this argument is of dub-

ious value, it is certainly true that the new Education Acts of 1870 and 1876 increased the cost of bringing up children. Perhaps it was the decline in infant mortality that caused people to take a different economic attitude towards children, but certainly from this time parents began to want higher standards for their children and realised that limiting the size of their family would make this possible. The new age of Victorian prosperity presented many goods which competed for the income of households, and one way to have more income left to buy them was to have fewer children. Doubtless, many people had smaller families simply because this became the social norm. The emancipation of women and the availability of birth-control also played a part, as did the tendency for people to marry at a later age. It took time, however, for the knowledge and availability of contraception to filter down the social structure.

The First World War was a great watershed in demographic trends, as in all other aspects of society. After 1918 population growth became much slower. In addition to the influences discussed above the great economic depression in the 1930s also dissuaded people from having children. Although there has been some increase in the size of the family since the Second World War, it would appear that the smaller family is here to stay.

Population since 1945

Looked at in the long-term, the changes in population since 1945 may appear small and to be a continuation of previous trends. However, small aggregate changes may bring with them profound changes in the structure of population, with important consequences for all organisations in the economy. The war, for example, brought large numbers of women into industry and they have stayed there, thereby affecting both production and consumption. Similarly, the "baby boom" of the late 1940s brought changes in education and public services.

The rise in the birth-rate immediately after the war may be partly due to families being reunited. However, there were more significant longer-term reasons. One such reason was people getting married younger. This may be accounted for by increased prosperity and the improved opportunities for married women to work. With increased prosperity it was possible to afford both more consumer goods and children. A larger family became a smaller proportionate burden, especially when the benefits of the welfare state for example, family allowances (1946) and national health insurance (1948) are taken into account. Once again, one should not discount the importance of social fashion in parents' choice of the size of their family.

TABLE XIII. THE BIRTH-RATE SINCE
1945 (GREAT BRITAIN)

Year	Birth-rate
1947	20.5
1950	15.9
1955	15.0
1961	17.4
1963	19.2
1965	17.6
1970	16.1
1975	12.3
1977	11.6
1979	13.0

(*Source: COS and FPIS*)

As predicted, the high birth-rates of the late 1940s were followed by lower rates in the 1950s. However, in the 1960s the birth-rate began to rise more rapidly than predicted. This was followed by the fall in the birth-rate of the late 1970s to the all-time low of 11.6. This may have been partly due to the fact that child-rearing became a longer and more expensive task. The school leaving age was raised to sixteen in 1972, in addition to which the proportion of students continuing into further and higher education increased sharply. Despite the conditions of economic stagnation people still continued to expect a rising standard of living. This may have been a further motive for limiting the size of the family, or for having no children at all. In addition to this, the decline in the birth-rate was influenced by a decreasing proportion of people marrying (17.2 per 1,000 in 1972, 14.4 per 1,000 in 1977) and by an increase in the average age at which people married (twenty-five for men and twenty-two for women). It is difficult to assess the role of birth control and abortion in this but, certainly, the increased availability and efficacy of birth control most have had a depressing effect on the birth-rate. In 1979 there were 119,000 abortions. This compares with a total of 735,000 live births in 1979.

Death-rates have declined since 1945 as a result of long-term environmental improvements. In 1978 the death-rate was 11.9. Migration has varied as an influence on population. Immediately after the war there was a wave of emigration from the UK with many people going to Canada, Australia and New Zealand. The flow of immigrants from the Commonwealth made Britain a gainer by migration, the net inflow being 97,000 people in the period 1951–

61. This has been reversed since the early 1960s and Britain is once again a net loser by migration (*see* Fig. 19). The 1970s saw a net outflow of 358,000 people.

TABLE XIV. INFANT MORTALITY
(DEATHS PER 1,000 LIVE BIRTHS)

Year	Infant mortality
1951	31.1
1971	17.9
1975	16.0
1978	13.3

(*Source: CSO*)

The infant mortality rate has declined since the Second World War as a result of improved medical techniques and the introduction of the welfare state. Even so, it is still higher than in some countries such as Sweden (11.0), but it is unlikely that it will decline much over the next few years.

THE STRUCTURE OF BRITISH POPULATION

The age and sex distribution of the population
This refers to the number of people in each age group. The most important divisions are 0–15, 16–64 and 65 and over. The relative size of the 16–64 group is important because it is from here that the majority of the working population is drawn.

Both age and sex distribution in society can be presented as a pyramid. In a population where there was an even age and sex distribution a smooth pyramid would be the result. The population is divided between men and women and then between age groups at five-year intervals. This is a variant on a histogram (*see* McNamara, page 84). Figure 20 is a simplified diagrammatic representation of a population pyramid for the late nineteenth century in Great Britain. This smooth and even distribution is brought about because it was a period of population expansion and therefore each new generation was larger than the preceding one. Increasing mortality in the older age groups narrows the pyramid until at the age of ninety there is virtually no-one left. Decline in the birth rate would pinch in the bottom of the pyramid. This is well illustrated by Fig. 21.

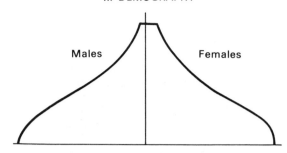

Fig. 20. *Simplified population pyramid typical of the late nineteenth century in the UK.*

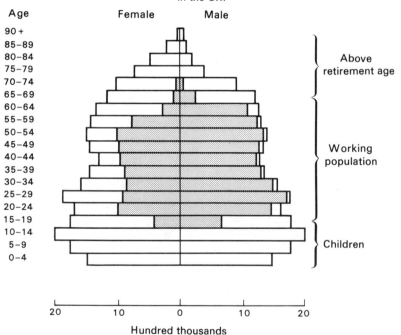

Fig. 21. *Age and sex distribution of the UK population, 1976. Shaded area indicates those who are economically active. Source: based on The Economist, 24 December 1977 and CSO information.*

The number of male births to female births does not usually vary much, with about 106 boys born for every 100 girls. Subsequently, mortality is greater for males in every age group, so that by the age of 85 there are 218 women for every 100 men. There are at present one and a half million more women in the country than men.

The expectation of life also varies. At present a man can expect

TABLE XV. THE AGE DISTRIBUTION OF THE POPULATION

Year	Under 15		15–64		Over 65	
	Population millions	*Percentage*	*Population millions*	*Percentage*	*Population millions*	*Percentage*
1939	10.0	21.4	32.4	69.7	4.2	8.9
1961	11.9	23.4	33.4	65.0	6.1	11.8
1971	13.4	24.2	34.8	62.8	7.2	12.9
1976	13.4	24.0	34.8	62.3	7.6	13.6
1981 (estimate)	13.0	23.2	34.9	62.5	7.9	14.1

(*Source: United Nations Department of Econ. and Social Affairs and Central Statistical Office.*) *Note: figures are still given as 15–64 rather than 16–64.*

to live 70.0 years, a woman 76.2. Life expectation has risen continuously since 1901 when men could expect 48.1 years and women
51.8. The discrepancy in the expectation of life of men and women
is explained by a number of factors; men work in more hazardous
occupations, more men are killed in wars, and men are more sus-
ceptible than women to a number of killing diseases such as lung
cancer and coronary illnesses.

Geographical distribution

The surface area of the UK is 244,104 km² with a population of
55.9 million. This gives a population density of 229 per km²—one
of the highest in the world. This population is spaced very unevenly
(*see* Fig. 22) and its distribution is not static. There have been
many changes during this century, some due to immigration but
most because of internal migration.

Fig. 22. *Areas of greatest density of population. The names of the major
conurbations are also shown.*

The population is predominantly urban. In England and Wales only 20 per cent of the people live in rural areas, in Scotland it is 28 per cent, and in Northern Ireland 45 per cent. The majority of the urban population is concentrated in the major conurbations, i.e. Greater London, the West Midlands, South East Lancashire, Merseyside, West Yorkshire, Tyneside and Clydeside. With the exception of London, the basis for these conurbations was the *old staple industries* of the nineteenth century, which were in turn dependent upon coal. The twentieth century has seen the relative decline of these industries and the emergence of new industries. The new industries, however, have mainly grown up in the Midlands and the south-east of England. This has meant that population has grown more rapidly in these areas. This is sometimes termed the "drift to the South-East". Another feature of recent years has been the decay of inner cities. Thus, although the South-East has gained population, London has lost people as they have moved out to the home counties such as Hertfordshire, Buckinghamshire and Berkshire. In these home counties population has grown more than 30 per cent in the last fifteen years. These people remain, however, to a great extent economically dependent on London.

A separate trend has been the depopulation of rural areas such as mid-Wales and northern Scotland. Here population has actually declined. As it is the young people who move away, the age structure of these areas is left most distorted. However, in the last five years North Sea oil has begun to attract people to north-east Scotland.

The occupational distribution of population
This describes the distribution of the *working population* between different occupations. The working population comprises all those people between the ages of sixteen and sixty-five who are working or available for work, and thus includes the registered unemployed. Also included in the figure are those over sixty-five who are still working. However, housewives not otherwise employed, those living off private means and those unable to work, e.g. the chronically sick, the insane and those in prison, are excluded from the working population.

The working population in the UK represents 48.6 per cent of the total population and 38.3 per cent of the working population are women. The percentage of women working is the highest figure for any developed country. The reason for this is that many married women entered the working population in the Second World War and this practice has continued and increased since then.

TABLE XVI. THE OCCUPATIONAL DISTRIBUTION OF THE UK WORKING
POPULATION, 1980

Occupation	Number employed (thousands)	Percentage
Agriculture, forestry and fishing	370	1.4
Mining and quarrying	344	1.3
Manufacturing	6,807	25.9
Construction	1,265	4.8
Gas, electricity and water	347	1.3
Transport and communication	1,500	5.7
Distributive trades	2,790	10.6
Financial, business and insurance services	1,258	4.8
Professional and scientific services	3,717	14.1
Catering, hotels, etc.	922	3.5
Miscellaneous services	1,597	6.1
National government service	621	2.4
Local government service	975	3.7
Other	1,536	5.8
Registered unemployed	2,244	8.5
Total working population	26,293	100.0

Occupations might be classified as:

(a) primary—extraction of raw materials, agriculture, fishing, etc;

(b) secondary—all manufacturing processes;

(c) tertiary—the provision of services, e.g. finance, education, the civil service and the armed forces.

As a rule an underdeveloped country would have a large percentage of its total population working and concentrated mainly in primary industries. An advanced economy would have a smaller percentage working population with a larger tertiary sector. In the UK the tertiary sector represents about 52 per cent of the working population. The proportion of the population which is available for work is affected by demographic factors such as the age structure of the population and by other factors such as society's attitude to women working, the school leaving age and the retirement age. These factors have meant that, while the number of people available for work has risen during the century from 32.4 million in 1911 to 34.8 million today, the percentage that are working has fallen.

Over the last hundred years there has been a sharp decrease in the percentage of people employed in agriculture, forestry and fishing. The UK now has one of the smallest percentages employed in these occupations of any country. Domestic service also used to be very important, but has now almost entirely disappeared. There have been large increases in those employed in commerce, the professional services, public administration, manufacturing and the armed forces. This has been caused by the industrialisation of society and rising real incomes which have given people money to spend on a wider range of goods and services. The growing complexity of society has increased the numbers of those engaged in administration. This is also associated with the rise of the influence of the state in economic and social life. Today the government disposes of over two-fifths of the national income; hence there is a growing army of civil servants and other state employees.

The labour available to a country is also affected by the number of hours worked. In 1979 the average working week for full-time male manual workers was 46.0 hours, whilst for non-manual male workers it was 38.8 hours. The comparable figures for female workers were 39.6 and 36.7 hours per week. This gives an average working week of 43.2 hours for men and 37.5 hours for women. The economy also had 1.5 million unemployed in 1979, in addition to which 29.5 million days were lost through industrial disputes and 166 million through illness. This latter figure represents 8 per cent of the working year lost because of illness. The working population is also decreased by 1,000 people killed each year in industrial accidents.

DEMOGRAPHIC CONSTRAINTS

Consequences of the changing structure of population

For the last two centuries UK population has been increasing in size and ageing. Most discussion has centred on the consequences of this, but now the future of British population seems less certain. It is therefore necessary to consider the consequences of the various alternatives.

If population is increasing in size then, other things being equal, there is less land and other resources available per head. In the short term this could lead to a tendency to import more goods, thus worsening the balance of payments. On the other hand there would be an increasing domestic market for goods which could lead to increasing economies of scale. In the nineteenth century Britain's population growth was accompanied by great technological improvements. Thus, increasing population was attended by increasing prosperity.

A declining population would, other things being equal, lead to more resources being available per head. It is possible, however, that, lacking the stimulus of population growth, there would be less incentive to improve technology. This could have an adverse effect on the long-term prospects of the economy.

If the population was becoming younger then there would be a smaller percentage dependence of the aged, and a changing pattern of consumption away from geriatric hospitals and the like to a greater demand for schools, pop records, etc. In addition, a younger population would be more flexible and dynamic and more able to take advantage of technological change. There would also be a greater mobility of labour, both occupational and geographical.

Throughout this century up to the 1970s the population of the UK has been ageing. There has also been a rising percentage of young people. Consequently the working population has had to provide for a growing dependent population. This has meant both more schools and more old age pensions. The ageing of the population has also made it less mobile and less able to take advantage of technological change. In addition there has been growing competition for resources such as houses and land. The growth of the tertiary sector has also meant that there is a smaller and smaller percentage of the working population involved in the manufacture of goods. The building of more schools and more senior citizens' homes both make demands on the nation's capital. Although education might be regarded as increasing society's productivity in the long run, services for the old do not do so. When these factors are considered together, they may partly account for the UK's depressing economic growth figures over the last thirty years.

The changing geographical distribution of the population also has economic and social consequences. In an area of declining population it is usually the young and active who move away, leaving a distorted population structure behind them with an even more intractable unemployment problem.

The future structure of population

Although current estimates are being revised downwards, world population continues to increase and there will still be several billion more mouths to feed in the next half-century. However, due to a combination of circumstances demography will actually be working in favour of Britain over the next twenty-five years. The dependency ratio (the ratio of dependent population to working population) reached a peak in 1974 and is now declining.

Since the mid 1960s the number of births has been declining and the fertility rate has dropped to 64.0. The number of children under fifteen has fallen since 1973. It remains to be seen whether the slight upturn in the birth-rate after 1978 will affect this. The fertility rate is likely to remain at this low level until the baby-boom of the early 1960s reaches child-bearing age. In addition to this, the number of people reaching retiring age will soon begin to decline. This is because there was a sharp fall in the birth-rate in the 1914–18 war and, although there was a rise in the rate immediately afterwards, the inter-war period as a whole was one of low birth-rates. Therefore, there are fewer people to retire in the 1980s and 1990s. Unless there are great breakthroughs in medicine, the death-rate will decline very little. There is also a trend to a unisex death-rate as women become more prone to fatal accidents, coronaries and lung cancer. This could also check the rise in the dependent population. As a result of these factors, dependence will decrease and the average age of the population is likely to fall from the present 33.7 years to 31.5 in 1995. The potential labour force will continue to grow so long as the number passing into it at 16 exceeds those leaving it at retiring age (see Fig. 21).

However, the dependency ratio could be misleading if a larger number of people go on to higher education or there is a rise in the number of the very old (since they make the greatest demand on welfare services). Recent work at the Office of Population Censuses and Surveys suggests this will not be so; educational activity, it suggests, has passed its peak and, although it may rise in the late 1980s, it will not reach the levels of the mid-1970s. Similarly, it is envisaged that hospital activity for the very old will decline continuously until the end of the century. It is possible to conclude, therefore, that Britain's dependency burden will decline until the end of the century. Beyond this it is difficult to make any forecasts.

The relationship of demography to government policy

For many centuries population was relatively stable and people lived in village communities which were mainly both economically and legally self-regulating. Such law as existed was mainly common law. However, under the twin pressures of population growth and industrialisation, the organisational complexity of society has increased and statute law is now the dominant form of law. Indeed, nearly all aspects of society are today regulated by legislation.

Education was once the prerogative of the few and was either provided privately or by the church. Today it is obligatory for everyone between the ages of five and sixteen. The raising of the school leaving age has decreased the relative size of the working population. In addition, many people have continued in education long after sixteen. Many employers today are obliged or persuaded to give day-release or block-release to their younger employees, thus, once again, reducing the working population and increasing the size of the vast educational industry. In a technologically-based society, however, it is increasingly important to have trained people. It is also becoming important to educate for leisure.

The *laissez-faire* State of nineteenth-century England believed that health was the individual's responsibility but, as population was crammed into an insanitary town life, the government was forced to introduce public health legislation. It became obvious that public health was indivisible and that disease was no respecter of social class. The state's involvement with health grew and now there exists a welfare state. Today it is considered important not only to provide medical services but to ensure a healthy environment in which prevention is as important as cure. The government's involvement stretches from the provision of hospitals to printing health warnings on packets of cigarettes. On the one hand these measures have increased the size of population, whilst the provision of free contraception and readily available abortion must have modified demographic trends.

Housing was once entirely the concern of the individual, but pressure on resources has meant that the government has interfered with the market mechanism through Rent Acts and the provision of council houses. The competition for houses has also led to changes in the private sector, with the growth of building societies as one of the most important financial institutions. The crowding together of people has also meant a multitude of planning regulations and controls on building. In an increasingly complex society, a government also has to intervene through such measures as the Health and Safety at Work, etc., Act 1974 and through legislation on prices and incomes. Migration was once a demographic influence but today it has become a social and political problem on which, once again, the government legislates.

Thus, it is possible to see that population is not just the backdrop against which economic and social life is played out but an all important influence upon individuals, organisations and the government.

The concept of the optimum population

The optimum population maybe defined as that size and structure of population which is most conducive to the betterment of the wealth and welfare of a society. If a population is too small in relation to resources, *underpopulation* exists; if it is too large, a country is suffering from *overpopulation*. However, it is very difficult to quantify these ideas. Singapore has turned the seeming disadvantage of overpopulation into an advantage by industrialisation. Conversely, New Zealand has turned the apparent disadvantage of underpopulation to its advantage through agriculture. The idea of optimum population must, therefore, also depend upon the level of technology, the amount of capital per head and the ability of a population to adapt to change. It is possible to conclude that if population is growing at a greater rate than gross national product (GNP) then it is overpopulated. The solution is far less obvious. From the above examples it can be seen that the country might industrialise or improve its agriculture. On the other hand it might attempt to limit population growth. Optimum levels of population are therefore not comparable from one country to another. What is right for an industrial country is not right for an agricultural one. Neither is the optimum level static. Two centuries ago. Britain would have been disastrously overpopulated with 55 million people, but technological change and capitalisation has proceeded at a rate sufficient to ensure that national income has gone up faster than population.

To date most concern has been with overpopulation, but in 1977 Britain experienced a decrease in population, probably for the first time since the Black Death. Many people fear that this may have an adverse effect on the economy, i.e. it might lose the spur to economic growth and the dynamism that population growth provides. On the other hand it might provide the breathing space in which Britain may solve the long-term structural problems of its economy.

SELF-ASSESSMENT QUESTIONS

A. 1. Define: (a) rate of natural increase; (b) overpopulation; (c) migration; (d) population pyramid.

2. List the factors which have influenced the average size of family in the UK since 1945.

B. 3. True or false?

(a) The main reason for rapid population growth in the UK in the nineteenth century was an increase in the birth-rate.

(b) Migration is not a major demographical influence in the UK.

(c) Dependency in the UK will increase over the next twenty years.

(d) A country with a TPFR of less that 2.0 would be losing the ability to reproduce itself.

(e) The size of family is related to social class.

4. True of false?

(*a*) There are more people in the UK over sixty-five than under fifteen.

(*b*) The birth-rate in 1977 was the lowest up to that date.

(*c*) Those engaged in primary industries represented 2.7 per cent of the working population in 1977.

(*d*) The total number of unemployed in 1980 was greater than the total of all those engaged in primary industries.

(*e*) There were more people coming to live in the UK in the 1970s than leaving it.

C. 5. In Singapore the birth-rate is 42.5 and the death-rate is 6; draw two composite bar graphs to compare Singapore's rate of natural increase with that of the UK.

ASSIGNMENTS

1. Present the information on page 109 (land areas and population) as pie-charts.

2. Present the information in Table XVI (occupational distribution) as a bar chart.

3. Having studied Table XVI, devise a different categorisation for occupational distribution and describe this and/or present it in tabular form.

PART THREE
THE ORGANISATION AND
ITS RESOURCES

CHAPTER EIGHT

The Organisation and its Use of Resources

CHAPTER OBJECTIVES

After studying this chapter you should be able to:
* explain the role of the law in relation to the use of resources;
* define the law of variable proportions;
* describe the cost structure of the organisation;
* list possible economies of scale;
* analyse the organisation's demand for a resource;
* state reasons for the continued existence of the small business.

In this part of the book we examine the organisation's demand for and exploitation of resources. Goods and services cannot be produced out of thin air and it is only by acquiring and combining resources that the organisation can produce them. Chapter 8 considers the mainly economic constraints that arise from combining resources and the regulatory role of the law in this context. Chapters 9–12 consider the economic and legal aspects of the four main categories of resources. The next part of the book deals with the sale of these goods and services both nationally and internationally, once they have been produced.

THE ROLE OF THE LAW

An organisation's use of resources to make maximum profit is determined by economic forces and not by the law, but the practical application of economic theory is regulated by the law. For example, the best use of labour might be maximum hours for minimum payment, i.e. wages just sufficient to provide adequate food and other essentials to enable the employee to work at maximum efficiency for the maximum possible hours. Clearly the law does not allow this today, although not so long ago it was precisely what happened.

The ruthless exploitation of economic resources is politically and socially unacceptable and the role of the law is to regulate their use to ensure it remains within acceptable limits. Thus the law imposes constraints on the exploitation of economic resources while remaining an enabling medium in relation to economic activity generally. Without suitable constraints it is arguable that business organisations would destroy the very society on which they depend.

The legal framework relating to the use of economic resources is practical and totally lacks any detailed theoretical basis comparable to the economist's Law of Variable Proportions. Such theory as there is originates in political and social philosophy and not in abstract theories of "justice" and "rights and duties". If there is an underlying principle in the law's approach to this subject, it is probably that economic resources should be exploited and economic activity furthered for the benefit of society generally and not for the benefit of the few.

In the following four chapters you will see the law's regulatory role in relation to each of the factors of production, and a brief introduction to this role will give you a general idea of the areas it covers.

The organisation's relationship with its employees was initially determined by individual contractual arrangements, but in recent years there has been a progressive superimposition of a statutory framework of rights and duties which are often quite independent of the contract of employment. Trade Unions are also regulated by the law and they enjoy important legal immunities which enable them to perform their functions and pursue their objectives effectively. The law's interest in land, its occupation and use is now determined as much if not more by the interests of the community as by the interests of landowners themselves. You will see in Chapter 10 how planning legislation, the Occupiers' Liability Act 1957 and the Health and Safety at Work, etc., Act 1974 embody this criterion. The raising, structure and use of finance by a business organisation also takes place within a regulatory framework which varies with the type of business organisation involved. The Partnership Act 1890 and the Companies Act 1948 in particular lay down guides or instructions which partnerships and registered companies must follow. Finally, you will see the importance of the law as a means of arriving at an equitable distribution of assets to creditors when a business organisation becomes insolvent and is forced into either bankruptcy or liquidation.

Taken together, the next four chapters should help you to appreciate that the reality of business activity does not conform to the neat textbook titles of "law", "economics", "accounts", etc., but is really an amalgam of many disciplines and the product of numerous influences.

THE ORGANISATION'S DEMAND FOR RESOURCES

The factors of production
The economic resources of the world have traditionally been divided by economists into four: *labour, land, capital* and *enterprise.* Some economists have been unwilling to classify enterprise as a separate factor of production, arguing either that it is inseparable from capital or that it is simply a special form of labour. Enterprise, being the organisational ability which combines the other factors together, is very properly a subject for discussion in this book. The factors of production can be separated one from the other by considering their special economic attributes or their legal attributes. The legal distinctions arise principally out of the law governing the payments made for factors of production, i.e. *wages, rent, interest* and *profit.* In this part of the book the economic and legal aspects of the factors of production and the payments for them are considered together. We will now examine some of the principles governing the exploitation of resources and their implications for the cost structures of the organisation.

The derived demand for factors of production
In order to produce goods and services the organisation must use the factors of production. Thus, to produce cars a company must demand land for the factory, capital to build the factory and labour to work in it. The demand for these factors of production, however, rests on consumers' demand for cars and therefore it is said to be *derived* from this demand. The demand for all factors of production is a *derived demand.*

The theory of distribution
In examining the organisation's demand for resources, we shall see what it is that determines the quantity of a factor a business will demand and also the price it is willing to pay for it. These are the principles which will determine how much of the national income will go to each factor of production. When we have done this for each factor it will show how income is distributed between the owners of the four factors, i.e. the labourers (or workers), landlords, capitalists and entrepreneurs. As we examine the factors of production and their returns we shall be covering the area of economics known as the *theory of distribution.*

THE LAW OF VARIABLE PROPORTIONS
Diminishing returns
In order to produce goods and services the organisation must combine the factors of production. At any particular time, however, the amount of certain of the factors which the firm can employ will be fixed whilst it will be able to vary others. For example, a firm will have a factory of a certain size or a farm of a certain area and to this *fixed factor* the businessman adds *variable factors* such as labour and power. Under these circumstances the firm will be affected by the law of *diminishing returns*. That is to say, as the firm adds more and more of the variable factor (e.g. labour) to a constant amount of fixed factor (e.g. land), the extra output that this creates must after a time become less. This means that the relationship between the amount of resources used (inputs) and the amount of goods produced (output) will vary. For this reason when considering the law of diminishing returns in relation to the business organisation it is often termed the *law of variable proportions*, or the *law of non-proportional returns*.

The short-run and the long-run
Economists often speak of *long-run* and *short-run* situations; these are not chronological periods of time but refer to the time over which factors of production can be varied. If, for example, we considered a business such as oil refining, the amount of capital equipment cannot easily be varied. If there were a large increase in the demand for oil it would take the oil company a considerable period of time to build a new refinery. In the meantime it can vary the other factors such as the amount of labour it uses but it is limited to its present amount of capital equipment. The period over which the fixed factors of production cannot be changed is referred to as the *short-run period*. The period in which the oil company can build a new refinery, i.e. vary the amount of *all* the factors of production, is known as the *long-run period*.

It is impossible to define these periods in terms of calendar time as they will vary from industry to industry. It may take ten years to build a new power station, whereas a farmer may be able to rent more land and therefore produce more food within twelve months.

As the firm moves into the long-run period it is able to vary all the factors of production and may therefore offset the law of diminishing returns. It may, however, still be subject to the principle of increasing costs.

TABLE XVII. MARGINAL AND AVERAGE PRODUCTS

Number of men employed	Output of wheat tonnes/week (Q)	Marginal physical product tonnes/week (MPP)	Average product tonnes/week (AP)
0	0		0
1	2	2	2.0
2	5	3	2.5
3	7	2	2.3
4	8	1	2.0
5	8	0	1.6

The marginal physical product

Because of the law of diminishing returns, as factors of production are combined, in the *short run* various cost structures for any firm will emerge. These are best illustrated by taking a simple example. In Table XVII a farmer whose land is fixed at 120 hectares, in the short-run adds more and more units of the variable factor, labour, in order to produce a greater output of wheat. Obviously if no labour is used then there will be no output. When one unit of labour is used the output of the farm works out at 2 tonnes of wheat per week (the year's crop divided by 52). If two men are used the output rises to 5 tonnes. The *average product* (AP) per man has risen from 2.0 tonnes to 2.5 tonnes. This does not mean that the second man was more industrious than the first but rather that an 120 hectare farm was too big for one man to work and it runs more efficiently with two. The higher average product therefore applies to both workers. It may have been achieved through specialisation and division of labour, impossible when there was only one worker.

Trying to obtain more output, the farmer employs a third worker, as a result of which the output rises to 7 tonnes per week. The total has indeed increased but when we consider the amount added to total output it is only 2 tonnes, whereas the second worker added 3 tonnes. The amount added to total output by each successive unit of labour is the *marginal physical product* (MPP). If we generalised this principle we could define the MPP as the change to total output resulting from the employment of one more unit of a variable factor.

These figures are illustrated graphically in Fig. 23. The MPP curve rises as the benefits of division of labour make the exploitation of land more efficient. Between one and two units of labour,

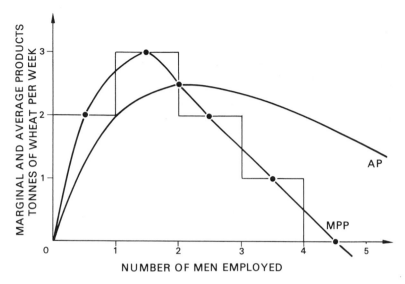

Fig. 23. *The marginal physical product and average product curves.*

the curve reached its highest and then begins to decline as diminishing returns set in. At two units of labour the farm is at its most technically efficient and after this its efficiency begins to decline. This is shown by the average product curve declining. When the AP curve is rising the firm is benefiting from *increasing returns*. When the AP curve is going downwards the firm is suffering from *decreasing returns*. The diminishing returns come about because as more labour is employed each successive unit of labour has less of the fixed factor, land, to work with. If it were not for the law of diminishing returns we could supply all the world's food from one farm simply by adding more and more labour to it. Obviously this is not possible.

You will see that the MPP curve goes through the top of the AP curve. This is always so. The intersection of AP with MPP, then, tells us when the organisation is at its optimum technical efficiency. Technical efficiency, however, is not the same as economic efficiency. If, for example, the product we were considering were gold then it might be worthwhile running a very inefficient gold-mine. Eventually, however, because of diminishing returns, MPP becomes negative when total output falls. No business would be willing to employ more resources to get less output.

You will note that MPP is plotted in a particular manner. In

Table XVII it is shown as halfway between the units of output. This is because the marginal product is the change in output involved in moving from one unit of a variable factor to another. All marginal figures are plotted in this manner. You will also note that in Fig. 23 the graph looks like a step-ladder. This is because a whole unit of labour was added. If we could divide up a unit of a factor of production infinitely and, instead of employing 1 man, employ 0.1 of a man, 0.2 of a man, etc., then we would derive a smooth curve for MPP. In Fig. 23 this is achieved by joining up the mid-points of the steps. It is usually more convenient to work with smooth continuous curves and this we shall do. Remember, however, the special incremental manner in which marginal curves are built up.

Production and productivity

Production is the total amount of a commodity produced whereas productivity is the amount of a commodity produced per unit of resources used. When a firm is improving its efficiency productivity will be rising. That is to say, if, by better management, more efficient equipment or better use of labour, the firm manages to produce the same, or a greater, amount of product with a smaller amount of resources then it has increased its productivity. If on the other hand the firm produces an increase in output but only at the expense of an even greater increase in resources then despite the increase in output its productivity has fallen.

Productivity may be difficult to measure. One of the most common methods is to take the total output and divide it by the number of workers. Another method, used in agriculture, is to express productivity as output per hectare. In the example we have been using productivity is rising whilst the AP is rising and falling when AP is falling. Productivity is vital to the economic welfare of both individual firms and the nation. It is only by becoming more efficient that we can hope to compete with other businesses or nations. We have only considered here two factors of production: other considerations, such as capital and the level of technology, are vital in productivity.

The marginal revenue product

The marginal physical product is measured in units of the commodity being produced—thus in our example it is tonnes of wheat. If this is expressed not in terms of the physical product but the money this product can be sold for, then we derive the marginal revenue product (MRP). Thus if the second man employed added 3 tonnes a week to output and each tonne could be sold for £20 then the marginal revenue product (MRP) would be £60. So marginal revenue can be calculated as:

$$MRP = MPP \times p$$

where p = the price of the commodity. This applies when the firm can sell more and more of its product at the same price. If, on the other hand, in order to sell more of its product the business organisation has to lower the price of its product then MRP will be calculated as

$$MRP = MPP \times MR$$

when MR = marginal revenue, i.e. the change to the firm's total revenue resulting from the sale of one more unit of the commodity.

If in our example we assumed that the firm could sell any quantity of wheat it wishes at £20 per tonne, then we could derive the MRP schedule shown in Table XVIII.

TABLE XVIII. THE MARGINAL REVENUE PRODUCT

Number of men employed	Marginal physical product (MPP) tonnes of wheat	Price of wheat per tonne (p) £	Marginal revenue product (MRP = MPP × p) £
0		20	
	2		40
1		20	
	3		60
2		20	
	2		40
3		20	
	1		20
4		20	
	0		0
5		20	

The MRP curve is drawn on the assumption that all other things remain equal; improvements in technology or an increase in the selling price of the commodity, for instance, would have the effect of moving the MRP curve rightwards.

The organisation's demand for a factor

The quantity of a factor of production which a firm will demand is determined by the marginal revenue product and the price of that

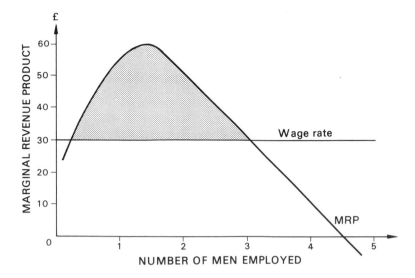

Fig. 24. *The marginal revenue product and wages. The business employs three men, which is where MRP equals wage rate.*

factor. If, for example, the marginal revenue product of a unit of labour were £40 and the cost of that unit of labour were £10 the business would obviously be £30 better off as a result of employing that unit of labour. If the MPP of the next unit of labour fell to £20 but the cost of it remained £10 the firm would still employ that unit of the factor since it would be a further £10 better off. In other words the business will go on demanding a factor of production whilst the MRP of that factor is greater than the cost of employing it. This is best understood graphically. In Fig. 24 if the wage rate were £30 per man, the best number of men for the firm to employ would be three. The cost of labour would be the area under the wage line, i.e. 3 × £30. The shaded area, above the wage line and below the MRP curve, would be the money the business would get back over and above the cost of employing the factor. The firm will always be best off by trying to obtain as much of this shaded area as possible. If, for example, the wage rate fell to £10 then the firm would employ four men, but if the wage rate rose to £50 it would be best off only employing two men. The MRP curve, therefore, shows us that the organisation's demand for a factor of production will vary in relation to the price of that factor. In other words the firm's MRP curve of a factor is its *demand curve* for that factor.

The shortcomings of marginal distribution theory

The theory of marginal productivity is a valuable guide in explaining the quantity of a factor which a firm will demand. The simple picture explained above is, however, complicated by the fact that selling a greater quantity of a product may require a firm to lower its prices, and also that demanding a greater quantity of a factor of production may increase the price of that factor. These problems, however, only make the theory more complicated. In addition to this the theory is subject to the following criticisms.

(*a*) *Non-homogeneity.* The theory assumes that all units of a factor are identical. This is not true either of the quality of a factor or the size of the units in which it is supplied.

(*b*) *Immobility.* The theory assumes that factors of production can move about freely both from industry to industry and area to area. In practice there are serious difficulties to the free movement of factors.

(*c*) *Inheritance.* Marginal distribution theory is also supposed to explain how the national income is distributed between the owners of the factors of production. However, much wealth in the UK is inherited and this is outside the operation of market forces.

(*d*) *Political–legal.* The value of factors such as land is often determined by planning regulations, etc.

(*e*) *Historical.* The value of factors such as land and labour is often affected by historical factors such as industrial inertia.

(*f*) *Inflation.* Today when the price of a factor such as labour increases instead of less of the factor being used it is often possible to pass on the higher costs to the consumer by way of higher prices.

These criticisms notwithstanding, marginal revenue theory is the best aid we have to understanding the cost structures of an organisation.

THE COST STRUCTURE OF THE ORGANISATION

So far in this chapter we have examined production in terms of units of factors of production. In this section we look at the costs of production.

Total cost

Total cost (TC) is the cost of all the resources which are necessary to produce any particular output. It is reasonable to assume that total cost will always rise with output since getting more output always involves increasing inputs. Total costs may be divided into two parts.

(*a*) *Fixed costs* (*FC*). These are the costs which do not vary directly with output in the short-run. Fixed costs are also known as *indirect costs*. They usually include such things as the cost of land, buildings and capital equipment. These costs will go on even if the firm produces nothing. In the long-run period the business can either increase or decrease its fixed costs.

(*b*) *Variable costs* (*VC*). As a firm produces more output so it needs to add more raw materials, more labour, more power, etc. These costs which vary directly with output are called variable or *direct costs*.

You will notice the correspondence between fixed and variable costs and fixed and variable factors of production. As total output increases more slowly once the firm passes its optimum capacity and diminishing returns set in, so total cost will increase more rapidly as a greater quantity of factors of production are required to produce each successive unit of output.

Average (or unit) cost (AC)

Average cost is the total cost divided by the output produced. This may be found by the formula:

$$AC = \frac{\text{total costs}}{\text{output}} = \frac{TC}{Q}$$

Since total cost can be divided into fixed costs and variable costs it would also follow that average cost may be treated in the same way:

$$\text{average fixed costs} = \frac{\text{fixed costs}}{\text{output}}$$

$$AFC = \frac{FC}{Q}$$

$$\text{average variable costs} = \frac{\text{variable costs}}{\text{output}}$$

$$AVC = \frac{VC}{Q}$$

It would therefore follow that:

$$AFC + AVC = ATC \text{ (average total cost)}$$

Marginal cost

Marginal cost may be defined as the addition to total cost from production of one more unit of a commodity. In practice, it may be impossible to calculate cost as finely as this so that we calculate marginal cost by the formula:

$$\text{marginal cost} = \frac{\text{increase in total costs}}{\text{increase in output}}$$

$$MC = \frac{\Delta TC}{\Delta Q}$$

Since costs arise from the employment of factors of production it will follow that average and marginal costs will be determined by the same principles which determine average and marginal product. This is illustrated in Table XIX. Here we use the same figures as earlier in the chapter and we assume that the farmers' fixed costs (land) are £40 whilst each unit of variable factor (labour) costs £30. Here you can see that marginal cost at first falls and then begins to increase. The same is true for average cost; the business is at optimum efficiency at an output of 7 tonnes of wheat where average costs are at a minimum. This is more clearly seen graphically in Fig. 25.

Here we see the short-run cost curves of the business. As the MPP curve went through the highest point of the AP curve, so you can see here that the MC curve goes through the lowest point of the AC curve. In the short run AFC declines continuously as the same amount of fixed costs are spread over a greater and greater output. The behaviour of the average variable cost curve depends upon the MC curve.

The relationship between marginal costs and average cost

The firm's average cost curve is always U-shaped in the short-run. This is because at an output of zero the firm still has to pay the fixed costs and therefore average cost is theoretically infinite. As output increases the fixed costs are spread over a greater and greater number of units of output and therefore average costs fall. This continues until the firm reaches optimum efficiency and then the extra variable costs needed to produce more output rise so rapidly that average cost begins to move upwards.

The average cost curve is always cut at its lowest point by the marginal cost curve. This is an important point and well worth repeating. This is because whilst the marginal figure is below the average it must be pulling the average down but as soon as it is

TABLE XIX. THE COSTS OF AN ORGANISATION IN THE SHORT TERM

Number of men employed	Total output of wheat (tonnes/week) (Q)	Marginal physical product (tonnes/week) (MPP)	Average product (tonnes/week) (AP)	Fixed costs (£) (FC)	Variable costs (£) (VC)	Total costs (FC + VC) (TC)	Average fixed costs (FC/Q) (AFC)	Average variable cost (VC/Q) (AVC)	Marginal cost (ΔTC/ΔQ) (MC)	Average cost (TC/Q) (AC)
0	0		—	£40	£0	£40	∞	—		∞
		2							£15	
1	2		2.0	40	30	70	£20	£15		£35
		3							10	
2	5		2.5	40	60	100	8	12		20
		2							15	
3	7		2.3	40	90	130	5.7	12.9		18.6
		1							30	
4	8		2.0	40	120	160	5.0	15.0		20.0
		0							—	
5	8		1.6	40	150	190	—	—		—

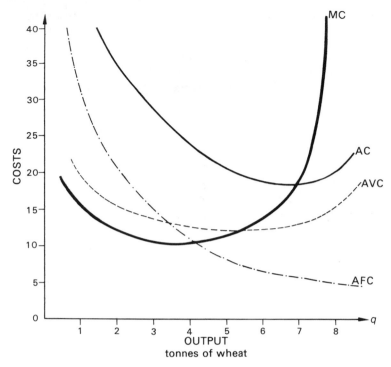

Fig. 25. *The average and marginal costs of the business organisation in the short run.*

higher it must be pulling the average up. The reasons for this are mathematical rather than economic. Consider a student who must obtain a certain course mark. So far his average is 50 per cent but his next mark (the marginal) is 30 per cent; this will obviously decrease his average. The succeeding mark (marginal) rises to 40 per cent which although it is higher than the previous mark it will still pull the average down because it is below it. In order to increase the average mark (50 per cent) the marginal mark must rise above it.

It is most important not to confuse marginal costs with average cost. Marginal cost relates to the *increase* in costs from producing one more unit whereas average cost relates to *total* cost which is divided by the *total* output to give the unit cost.

Average costs in the long run
It has already been stated that the average cost curve is U-shaped in the short term because of the law of diminishing returns. In the

long run however the fixed factors of production can be increased and so get round this problem. What effect does this have on costs? If the firm has already exploited all the possible economies of scale then all it can do is build an additional factory which will reproduce the cost structures of the first. However, if as the market grows the firm is able to build bigger plants which exploit more economies of scale then this will have a beneficial effect upon costs.

In Fig. 26 SAC^1 is the original short-run average cost curve of the firm. As demand expands the business finds it possible to build a large plant which is able to benefit from more economies of scale. This is shown by SAC^2; eventually, however, this passes the optimum point and SAC^2 also becomes U-shaped. SAC^3 represents a repeat of the process with an even larger plant. It is impossible, however, to go on producing more and more for less and less. This would violate the fundamental basis of economics—scarcity. SAC^4 represents a stage where all possible economies of scale have been achieved and the firm is now suffering from the long-run effects of diminishing returns and the principle of increasing costs. LAC therefore represents the long-run average cost curve for the firm, and you can see that this also is U-shaped. Such a curve is sometimes referred to as an *"envelope"* curve.

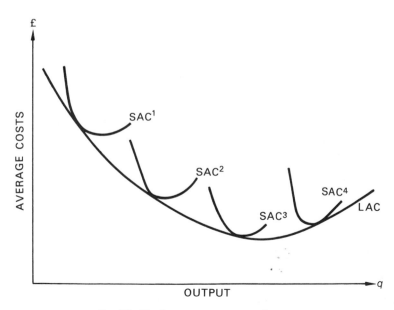

Fig. 26. *The long-run average cost curve.*

Marginal cost and price

So far we have said that the firm will try to equate the marginal revenue product of a factor with the cost of that factor. The MRP, however, depends upon the price at which the product can be sold. In Fig. 24 we assumed that the price of wheat was £20 per tonne and we therefore obtained an MRP curve by multiplying MPP by £20. It is now possible to see that the most important factor is marginal cost. While marginal cost is less than price the firm will find it worthwhile to go on producing. When marginal cost is greater than price the firm would do better to contract its output. The firm is therefore going to collect most profit by producing that output at which MC is equal to the price at which the commodity is sold.

The relevant information is collected together in Table XX. Here you can see that the firm will produce an output of 7 tonnes per week because, if the price is £20 per tonne, this is the only output at which it can make a profit. In Fig. 27 you see that this is the

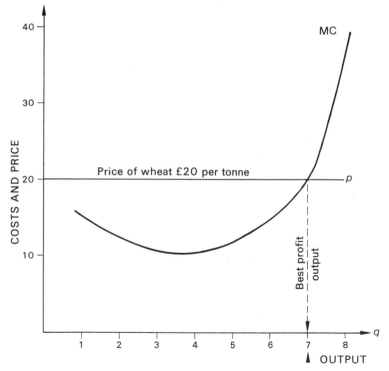

Fig. 27. *The best profit output for the business organisation. The business makes the most profit by producing the output at which MC equals p.*

TABLE XX. THE PROFITS OF THE ORGANISATION

Number of men employed	Output of wheat tonnes/week (Q)	Price of wheat £/tonne (p)	Marginal revenue product ($MPP \times Q$) (MRP)	Total revenue ($p \times Q$) (TR)	Total cost ($FC + VC$) (TC)	Total profit ($TR - TC$) (TP)	Marginal cost $\Delta TC/\Delta Q$ (MC)
0	0	£20		£0	£40	£−40	
			£40				£15
1	2	20		40	70	−30	
			60				10
2	5	20		100	100	0	
			40				15
3	7	20		140	130	10	
			20				30
4	8	20		160	160	0	
			0				—
5	8	20		160	190	−30	

output at which MC = p. You can also see from Table XX that to produce this output will require three units of labour. If you turn back to Fig. 24 you can confirm that this was the number of men at which the MRP of labour was equal to its cost.

COSTS AND THE SCALE OF PRODUCTION

Several times in this chapter reference has been made to economies of scale. These occur when, as a result of producing goods and services on a larger scale, the unit cost of production decreases. Not all industries benefit equally from economies of scale; in some the optimum size of a unit of production is small.

Some of the different types of economies of scale are listed below.

(*a*) *Technological.* These may occur when a large firm is able to take advantage of an industrial process which cannot be reproduced on a small scale. In some cases it may just be that "bigger is better", e.g. a double-decker bus is more cost effective than a single decker, so long as you can fill it with passengers. Technical economies are also sometimes gained by linking processes together, e.g. in the iron and steel industry where iron and steel production is carried out in the same plant, thus saving both transport and fuel costs.

(*b*) *Commercial.* A large-scale organisation may be able to make fuller use of sales and distribution facilities than a small-scale one. For example, a company with a large transport fleet will probably be able to ensure that they transport mainly full loads whereas a small business may have to hire transport or despatch part loads. A large firm may also be able to use its commercial power to obtain preferential rates of raw materials and transport. This is usually known as "bulk-buying".

(*c*) *Organisational.* As a firm becomes larger, the day-to-day organisation can be delegated to office staff, leaving managers free to concentrate on the important tasks. When a firm is large enough to have a management staff they will be able to specialise in different functions such as accounting, law and market research.

(*d*) *Financial.* Large organisations often find it cheaper and easier to borrow money than small ones.

(*e*) *Risk bearing.* All firms run risks but risks taken in large numbers become more predictable. In addition to this, if an organisation is so large as to be a monopoly this considerably reduces its commercial risks.

(*f*) *Diversification.* Most economies of scale are concerned with specialisation and concentration. However, as a firm becomes very large it may be able to safeguard its position by diversifying its products, its markets and the location of production.

As with division of labour the ability of a firm to benefit from economies of scale is not only limited by technology but by the size of the market.

Internal and external economies of scale

Internal economies of scale are those obtained within one organisation whilst external economies are those which are gained when a number of organisations group together in an area. Industries such as chemicals and cars provide good examples of internal economies, where the industry is dominated by a few large organisations. Historically, the most famous example of external economies of scale was the cotton industry in Lancashire, where many hundreds of businesses concentrated in a small area made up the industry.

Long-run average costs: an example

As a firm expands and takes advantage of more economies of scale so the average cost of a unit of output should fall. An example of this is shown in Fig. 28. Ethylene crackers are used in the petrochemical industry in breaking down oil to provide the raw materials for plastics, synthetic fibres, etc. The size of the average plant has grown from about 30,000 tonnes capacity in the 1950s to the present 500,000 tonnes capacity. However, beyond this point *diseconomies of scale* set in and unit costs begin to rise.

You will note that the AFC also turns upwards. This is because this is a *long-run* situation and the capital costs also increase disproportionately beyond the limits of technology. It is typical of an industry where there are lots of economies of scale to be gained that a high proportion of its costs are fixed costs.

Efficiency and economies of scale

Where an economy of scale leads to a fall in unit cost because less *resources* are used to produce a unit of a commodity then this is economically beneficial to society. If, for example, a large furnace uses less fuel per tonne of steel produced than a small one, then society benefits through a more efficient use of scarce fuel resources. It is possible, however, for a firm to achieve economies through such things as bulk-buying, where its buying power is used to bargain for a lower price. This benefits the firm because its costs will be lower, but it does not benefit society since there is no saving of resources involved.

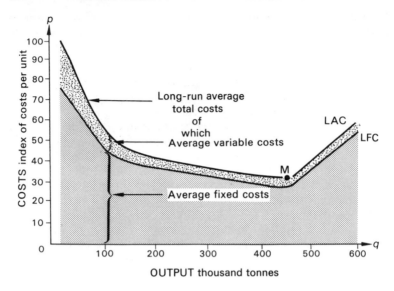

Fig. 28. *Long-run cost curve (ethylene cracker). Point M on LAC curve rep-resents the limit of economies of scale under present technology. Source: "The Uncommon market", The Economist.*

Diseconomies of scale

We saw earlier in the chapter that the short-run average costs curve of a firm will turn upwards because of the law of diminishing re-turns. When the long-run cost of an industry turns upwards it is because it is experiencing diseconomies of scale. The typical size of plant will vary greatly from industry to industry. In capital intensive industries such as chemicals the typical unit may be very large, but in an industry like agriculture the optimum size of firm is quickly reached and beyond this diseconomies set in.

The continuance of small businesses

There are over 620,000 registered companies in Britain today in addition to which there are several hundred thousand partnerships and sole traders. However, 44 per cent of total sales in the country are accounted for by the top 100 companies. Undoubtedly one of the reasons for this domination of large companies is economies of scale. It should be remembered, however, that many of these com-panies are *conglomerates* and may not therefore always be benefit-ing from economies of scale in the conventional sense. Nevertheless, despite a percentage decline in their importance in recent years, small businesses continue. This may be because there are only limited economies of scale to be gained as in industries such as agriculture and plumbing but small businesses also survive in industries where returns to scale are considerable. Some of the reasons for this are listed below.

(a) *"Being one's own boss"*. Entrepreneurs may accept smaller profit for the social prestige of working for themselves or the possibility of making a profit in the future.

(b) *Immobility in factor markets*. Labour and other factors may be unwilling or unable to move from one occupation or area to another. For example agricultural workers are often kept in their jobs by "tied cottages".

(c) *Goodwill*. A small business may survive on a fund of goodwill where its customers might tolerate higher prices for a more personal service.

(d) *Banding together*. Independent businesses may band together to gain the advantages of bulk-buying whilst still retaining their independence. This is so in the grocery chains such as "Spar" and "Wavy-Line".

(e) *Specialist services or products*. Businesses may provide small specialist services or products, e.g. many small car manufacturers exist making specialist sports cars.

(f) *Sub-contracting*. Many small businesses survive by sub-contracting to larger firms. This is very prevalent in the construction industry.

(g) *Monopoly*. A large organisation may tolerate the existence of small businesses in an industry as a cloak for its own monopolistic practices.

In recent years one of the effects of economies of scale has been to throw people out of work as men are replaced with machines. This has led to unions demanding shorter working weeks to create new jobs and to the government putting a new emphasis on small businesses as a possible source of employment. Whilst technology may cause redundancies in a stagnant economy, in an expanding economy new jobs would be being created. Many small businesses claim that it is having to cope with government regulations and complicated tax procedures which causes many of them to flounder.

SELF-ASSESSMENT QUESTIONS

A. 1. Define: (a) derived demand; (b) marginal revenue product; (c) short run; (d) increasing returns.

2. List five examples of economies of scale.

B. 3. True or false?

(*a*) The theory of distribution is so called because it is concerned with the distribution of goods and services in the economy.

(*b*) Improvements in technology can offset the effects of diminishing returns.

(*c*) The firm is at optimum efficiency when MPP is at a maximum.

(*d*) All units of labour are homogeneous.

(*e*) The benefits of division of labour may be limited by the size of the market.

C. 4. True or false?

(*a*) An improvement in technology would increase the demand for a variable factor.

(*b*) In Fig. 24, if the wage rate fell to £10 the business would employ four men.

(*c*) In Fig. 27, if the price of wheat rose to £40 per tonne the maximum possible profit would be £160.

(*d*) Any factor of production may be fixed in the short run.

(*e*) A small business cannot take advantage of economies of scale.

5. Redraft Fig. 27 assuming that the price of wheat rises to £40 per tonne; fixed costs rise to £100 and wages to £50. Determine the best output for the business and how much profit it will make.

ASSIGNMENTS

1. What are the legal limitations upon a business's ability to grow?

2. In the motor vehicle industry the five largest companies control 73 per cent of the market. Discover and list five other industries in which the leading five companies control over 50 per cent of sales.

3. Discuss the possible social consequences of increasing economies of scale.

The Organisation and its Employees

CHAPTER OBJECTIVES

After studying this chapter you should be able to:
* define labour as a factor of production;
* describe the structure of a trade union;
* define a contract of employment;
* list the contractual and statutory rights and duties which exist in employment;
* outline the law on job security;
* state the factors affecting the ability of trade unions to raise wages;
* analyse the effect of collective bargaining on wage rates.

INTRODUCTION

While both the traditional view of labour as a factor of production and the Marxist view of labour as the source of all wealth are relevant in the study of the economy, neither is of much direct relevance to individual employees and organisations. Of far greater relevance is the institutional and legal framework of employment and industrial relations. For this reason this chapter examines not only the conventional economic theory but also such things as trade union structure, employment law and wage bargaining.

Labour as a factor of production

Economically, labour may be defined as the exercise of human mental and physical effort in the production of goods and services. This means that to be classed as labour a person must be in some way concerned with the production of goods or services for sale. If, for example, a man works in his garden, this would not be counted as part of labour. If, however, he performs the same task but the produce is then sold then his efforts become part of labour. Usually, then, labourers are going to be employed for remuneration although they could, of course, be self-employed. The legal definitions of types of remuneration are considered later in the chapter.

Labour differs from the other factors of production in that it is human. Thus, we cannot just consider units of labour, we must also consider the personality of the workers. Likewise we cannot just talk about scrapping labour as we might an unwanted piece of capital equipment, for as well as being an economic waste the unemployment of workers brings social, psychological and political problems.

The supply of labour

The supply of labour in an economy is the *working population*. This will be determined by the age, sex and geographical distribution of the population. These are fully discussed in Part Two of this book. The supply of labour is also affected by a population's *leisure preference*. If a population has a very high leisure preference then as wages increase people will work less and take more time off.

Vocationalism also affects the supply of labour. In occupations like the clergy, nursing and teaching, people often work for a low wage because they consider the job worthwhile. People are also influenced by social prestige. Many people consider white collar jobs more "respectable" than manual work and will settle for lower wages. The supply of labour to some occupations is also affected by job security and prospects for promotion. A job might also be attractive for its fringe benefits such as long holidays, a car or cheap loans.

In considering the supply of labour it is also necessary to consider its quality, how well trained and educated people are, how healthy they are and how industrious. It is not enough just to hire a worker—it must be the right person with the right skill in the right place.

The mobility of labour

The UK is short of labour. This may seem strange when there are long "dole" queues, but it is true in that we lack people with the right skills in the right places. Unemployment and the shortage of labour could be eased simultaneously if there were greater mobility of labour. Labour mobility is of two main types, occupational and geographical. *Occupational mobility* is the ability of a person to move from job to job, e.g. from being a coal-miner to being an engineer. *Geographical mobility* is the ability of a worker to move from one area to another. Surprisingly in a country as small as the UK mobility is very low. Mobility also tends to be lower in times of heavy unemployment. People are reluctant to move from the places and people they know when the prospects are uncertain.

The government is making efforts to increase mobility with such things as Skillcentres and resettlement grants, but it seems fair to say that more is needed if the problem is going to be overcome.

TRADE UNIONS

What is a trade union?

Broadly speaking, a trade union is an organisation consisting wholly or mainly of workers, whose principal purposes include the regulation of relations between workers and employers or employers' associations (*Trade Union and Labour Relations Act 1974*). With a few exceptions trade unions are unincorporated associations but they resemble corporate bodies in certain important ways, i.e. they are allowed to make contracts and may be sued in their own names. In addition, simplified procedures exist for transferring the property of "listed" trade unions (*see* below) to new or continuing trustees (by which it must be held) when new trustees are appointed or a trustee retires.

There are nearly 500 trade unions with a total membership of about 11.6 million. Individual membership ranges from the 1.9 million of the giant Transport and General Workers' Union to the approximately seventy unions with less than 100 members. In 1982, 112 trade unions were affiliated to the TUC. Trade unions are collectively (and often individually) a very powerful pressure group to be consulted and considered in any political or economic decision taken by the government or business organisation.

It is likely that your experience of trade unions and your image of them will have been coloured by media coverage and family views. You must now be objective, consider the facts and then decide for yourself whether the trade union movement is the champion of the downtrodden worker or a confounded, legally-protected nuisance, interfering with damaging consequences in the economy. Whether this chapter will form, change or confirm your views, one thing is certain: trade unions are an integral part of our modern industrial society.

Types of union

Several different types of union may be discerned. These are not hard and fast distinctions; a union might belong to more than one category.

(*a*) *Craft or skill unions.* These occur where the members have a skill in common like the United Pattern Makers Association (UPA).

(*b*) *Industrial unions.* The members of these unions all work in the same industry although they may have very different jobs, e.g. the National Union of Railwaymen (NUR).

(*c*) *General unions.* The members of general unions may be in many different industries and occupations. They are often unskilled or semi-skilled workers. The largest union in Britain is a general union, the Transport and General Workers' Union (TGWU).

(d) *Company unions.* These occur when all the employees of one company form a union. These are practically unknown in the UK but common in the USA, where, for example, you would find a union of Ford workers. Probably the banks' staff associations are the nearest thing to them in the UK.

(e) *White collar unions.* Since the Second World War the white collar workers, who were previously almost completely un-unionised, have joined trade unions. For example the National Union of Teachers (NUT), the Association of Scientific, Technical and Managerial Staffs (ASTMS) and the National Union of Bank Employees (NUBE).

(f) *Professional associations.* Although they would strenuously deny that they are trade unions, some professional associations like the British Medical Association (BMA) and the Inns of Court exhibit many of the features of trade unions. Certainly the two mentioned above are successful in pay bargaining to an extent which would disgrace many trade unions.

It is certainly possible to argue that there are too many trade unions in Britain and that this is a case of endless demarcation disputes. On the other hand it is argued that some trade unions are too big and wield too much power.

THE STRUCTURE OF TRADE UNIONS

The organisation of trade unions

All trade unions are different; Fig. 29 summarises the features which are common to most. A union may not have all these layers of organisation—alternatively it may be even more complex. Many of the features described below often go under different names in different unions but most of these features can be discerned in the average trade union.

Branches

The basic unit of union organisation is the branch. This may have anything from a few members up to thousands and will be based on a factory or a town depending upon the circumstances. They will have an elected executive committee of chairman, treasurer, secretary, etc. Usually branch officers are volunteers and unpaid. A few of the largest branches have full-time secretaries. Branches are normally not well supported by the bulk of the membership so that some unions enforce quorums of around 10 per cent before deci-

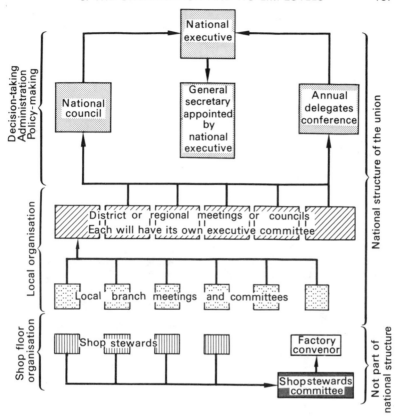

Fig. 29. *The structure of a trade union.*

sions may be taken at branch meetings. Delegates are appointed from the branches to the district councils.

Shop stewards

Shop stewards are elected by the members in a particular workplace and are the most misunderstood of union officials. Their functions include such things as enforcing agreements with the employers at shop-floor level, collecting union dues and representing workers' grievances to management. It is often very difficult to persuade people to become shop stewards although it is one of the most vital jobs in the union. The conventional picture of the shop steward as presented by the media is of a militant, bent on the destruction of British industry. Whilst this may be true of a few, the majority carry out vital tasks. As unions become more bureaucratic, workers feel alienated not only from employers but also from their own union hierarchy. This has led to the growth of unofficial bodies such as shop stewards committees headed by convenors. These committees are often more trusted and followed by the union membership than their official leaders.

District councils

In many of the larger unions the country is divided into districts or regions which have their own committees or councils elected by the branches. Such district organisations will usually have full-time employees whose job it will be to help and advise members.

Annual delegate conference

The branch or district organisations will appoint delegates to the union's annual conference. This is the supreme policy-making body of the union. It is at these conferences that the general outline of the union's policy will be decided. The delegate conference has little effect on the day-to-day running of the union because it is usually only an annual event.

The national executive and national council

Most unions are actually run by their national executive. It is they who not only take the day to day decisions but also negotiate with employers and government and formulate policy in the absence of direction from the annual conference. Also because of their experience most union memberships defer to their executives and seldom unseat them. Members of the national executive are frequently full-time officials and if they are not they will certainly require time off from their employers to carry out their jobs properly. Some unions also have a national council which may consist of around 100 members from the branches or regions who meet several times a year to advise and direct the national executive.

General secretaries

Most unions are led by their general secretary, although theoretically the secretary is the servant of the national executive, by whom he was appointed. Usually the general secretary holds the job for life or until he retires. Usually grossly overworked and underpaid, general secretaries are expected to be leader, chief negotiator, public relations officer, administrator and politician—it is their names and faces which are often best known by the general public. Hugh Scanlon, Jack Jones, Moss Evans and Len Murray all reached national attention as general secretaries.

External relations
The Trades Union Congress (TUC)
Founded in 1868, the Trades Union Congress is one of the oldest of trade union institutions. It is really just a talking shop as its decisions are only morally binding upon its members, although it has the power of expulsion. The TUC meets once a year to elect the general council of the TUC. The secretariat of the TUC is small and works on a shoe-string budget. It is headed by the general secretary, who at present is Len Murray. The TUC has always been overtly political, and in fact its first title back in 1868 was the "Parliamentary Committee". Its object was to try to influence government. In recent years, however, the mountain has had to go to Mohammed as governments have been forced to seek the TUC's co-operation in imposing pay policies.

The International Labour Organisation (ILO)
The ILO, set up in 1919, is just about the only survivor of the many institutions which were set up alongside the League of Nations in Geneva. Its task is to try to improve working conditions throughout the world. It has no power to compel governments and so it must proceed by persuasion. It is of valuable assistance to less developed countries who are trying to establish systems of industrial relations. One of the most important functions of the ILO is to publish economic statistics and reports. The *ILO Yearbook* is a valuable source of international statistics.

The European Economic Community (EEC)
Wide differences exist between unions in the EEC. In general, unions in the rest of the EEC tend to be fewer and larger than in Britain. In Germany the sixteen unions are based on industrial grouping. Ironically the highly stable system of industrial relations in Germany was designed, after 1945, mainly by British trade unionists, notably Ernest Bevin. Unions in Germany are apolitical whilst elsewhere unions may have a religious affiliation, e.g. Netherlands, or may be Communist-led, as some are in France and Italy. Therefore wide differences need to be overcome if European industrial relations are to be harmonised. Many of the European unions meet in the *European Confederation of Free Trade Unions*.

Not only do unions differ but the structure of wages also differs because of differences in taxation and social security payments.

Trade union finances
The bulk of a trade union's income comes from contributions from members. Most unions in Britain have very low subscriptions, often

as little as 10p per week. The unions also draw income from their investments. Investments make the unions dependent upon the well-being of the capitalist state, which may seem a strange state of affairs for overtly socialist organisations. The NUR is, perhaps, the most famous union investor with its purchases of fine art and antiques.

A union's expenditure falls under four main headings. Firstly there are *administration costs* and the salaries of its full-time officials. Another type of expenditure is *pensions and sickness benefits*. These were once one of the most important of the union functions but since the advent of the welfare state they are not so important. The pension fund is usually kept separate from the union's other finances. The *strike fund* is another aspect of union finance. It is a reserve of money kept to pay workers if there is a strike and, again, is usually kept separately. Finally there is the money the trade unions pay to support the Labour Party. Legally this must be raised by the unions as a separate *political levy* from which members may *contract out* if they wish. The levy is seldom more than 1p or 2p per week but is politically very contentious as some unions make it very difficult for people to contract out. Suffice it to say that if everyone who contributed to the financial support of the Labour Party in this way voted Labour we would always have a Labour government.

In 1981 the Conservative government proposed changing contracting out to contracting in. This would mean that trade union members would have to specifically request that they pay the political levy. A further suggestion was that members could say which political party they wished the levy to go to. Thus the political levy would be returned to the position it was in 1927.

THE FUNCTIONS OF TRADE UNIONS

It is widely believed that unions exist solely for the purpose of obtaining more pay for their members. Whilst this may be one of the most important functions they have many others.

(*a*) *Pay bargaining.* Unions are concerned to achieve a rise in the real wages of their members as well as the money wages. Actual earnings are not only determined by the wage rate but also by the hours worked, overtime rates and bonuses. Because of this, a 1 per cent rise in the wage rate tends to bring about a rise in earnings greater than 1 per cent. This tendency of earnings to rise faster than wage rates is known as *wages drift*.

(*b*) *Conditions of work*. It is important not only to have a safe and healthy workplace but also to have a good working environment. Many people believe that unions have not been sufficiently concerned with this aspect.

(*c*) *Financial benefits*. Unions frequently offer pensions, sickness benefits and insurance to their members. In the early days of trade unions this was one of their most important functions but most of this task has now been taken over by the state.

(*d*) *Training and conditions of entry*. Many unions regulate the supply of labour to an occupation by insisting on entry qualifications such as apprenticeships. Whilst this may ensure an adequately qualified work force it is also used to push up wages.

(*e*) *Security*. Everyone is familiar with the slogan "one out, all out". Unions will often fight strenuously for job security.

(*f*) *Participation in public bodies*. As representatives of labour, trade unions sit on many bodies such as the Monopolies Commission, the National Economic Development Council (Neddy) and the Food Hygiene Advisory Council.

It is unfortunate that industrial relations in the UK are still a "them and us" situation. In a mixed economy the management of economy and of industry should be a partnership. The 1974–9 Labour government brought in new legislation giving trade unions wider powers. The Health and Safety at Work, etc., Act 1974 obliges management to consult with unions on health, safety and welfare at work and to give union representatives adequate time to inspect the premises and carry out other duties connected with health and safety. The Employment Protection (Consolidation) Act 1978, as well as giving greater job security, obliges employers to give union officials time off for their duties. Under the Employment Protection Act 1975 employers are also obliged to consult with unions on redundancy.

It is still thought, however, that in some industries labour is so weak and badly organised that it is necessary to set up a wages council. Presently some 2.75 million workers are covered by wages councils such as the Agricultural Wages Board. If the Secretary of State considers a Council inadequate he has the power to abolish it and set up a *joint industrial council*. The Wages Councils Act 1979 consolidates previous legislation relating to wages councils and statutory joint industrial councils.

Many occupations have special institutionalised pay-bargaining procedures such as the *Whitley Councils* which determine Civil Service and local government salaries. Similarly teachers have the *Burnham Committees* which decide salaries and which are obliged to accepted compulsory arbitration.

ACAS (the Advisory Conciliation and Arbitration Service), set up by the Employment Protection Act 1975, is perhaps best known for its unsuccessful intervention in the Grunwick dispute in the mid-seventies. However, despite some failures, ACAS has had many successes in bringing peaceful conclusions to industrial disputes in the first few years of its existence.

The demands of trade unions, however, go beyond current legislation: many are looking for industrial democracy. This could mean worker directors, profit-sharing or co-ownership. The *Bullock Report* 1975 recommended worker directors but so far its proposals have not been acted upon. The participation of workers in the running of industry should not be looked on with horror; it can be very successful, as experience in Sweden has shown.

TRADE UNIONS AND THE LAW

The present legal framework within which trade unions operate is to be found in the provisions of the Trade Union and Labour Relations Act 1974, as amended by the Employment Protection Act 1975, the Trade Union and Labour Relations (Amendment) Act 1976 and the Employment Act 1980. The 1974 and 1976 Acts are together known as the Trade Union and Labour Relations Acts 1974 and 1976. Despite their name, certain important sections of the Acts apply equally to employers' associations, namely the provisions relating to legal status, accounting duties (all trade unions and employers' associations, whether listed or not, must keep proper accounts and submit an annual return about their activities, including their accounts, to the Certification Officer) and "listing" with the Certification Officer.

Under the 1974 and 1975 Acts the Certification Officer is responsible for maintaining a list of all trade unions within the legal definition (*see* page 155). Listing is essential if a trade union is to be granted a *certificate of independence* and it gives certain rights to tax relief. An independent union is one which is not under the domination or control of, or subject to financial or material support from, an employer. The Certification Officer determines any dispute as to independence. Recognition as independent is essential in connection with many collective and individual rights under current employment legislation.

The Employment Act 1980 was the Conservative government's counter to the increased power given to trade unions under the previous Labour government's employment legislation and policies. Amongst other things, the Act introduced totally new provisions concerning trade union ballots, and gives the Secretary of State wide-ranging powers to issue codes of practice "for the purpose of improving industrial relations". Assistance with the cost of secret ballots, for such purposes as electing officers, calling or ending a strike or amending rules, is now available. While it can be argued that this is likely to make union decisions more representative of the membership, the TUC view is that these provisions are intended to pave the way for compulsory secret ballots and greater government interference in the operation of trade unions. Perhaps, however, the true criterion on which the Act should be judged is whether or not it leads to an improvement in industrial relations and economic performance.

There are four main aspects of the legal framework which directly affects the relationships between trade unions and other organisations: collective agreements; the legal immunities and privileges enjoyed by trade unions; picketing; and closed shop agreements.

Collective agreements

Over two-thirds of all employees have their rates of pay and other terms of their employment decided by collective agreements between their unions and their employers. Under the Employment Protection Act 1975 an employer has a duty to disclose to a recognised trade union, on request, information for collective bargaining purposes. "Recognition" in this context means an agreement, between the employer concerned and the union, that the union has a certain status.

Collective agreements are vital both to the individual employee, whose bargaining power in such matters is negligible, and to industrial relations generally. However, under the Acts these agreements are not presumed to be legally enforceable unless they are in writing and expressly state that the parties to the agreement intend it, or a specific part of it, to be so. It follows that a union is not liable for strikes that occur in breach of a collective agreement.

It is arguable that with some 90 per cent of all strikes being unofficial, the legal framework of collective bargaining does not reflect the tremendous changes in the economy and industrial relations that have occurred over the last half century. The problem is not collective agreements themselves, but how to ensure that unions have sufficient control over their members to enforce a collective agreement once it is made. The problem has become more pressing in recent years, because a handful of workers taking unofficial strike action in an industry vital to the economy, e.g. the lorry drivers' strike (1979), can cause immense harm and disruption. In addition some people would argue that a small minority of trade unionists use trade disputes to further their own political ends. Should these activities increase they may seriously call into question not only the legal status of collective agreements but also the structure of union power and, conceivably, the legal immunities and privileges at present enjoyed by trade unions. The Employment Act 1980 can certainly be seen in this light, and further legislation is planned.

Legal immunities and privileges

The 1974 Act provides that in general no action in tort (*see* page 571) can be brought against a trade union (or employers' association). However, it further provides that a trade union (or employers' association) may be sued for negligence, nuisance or breach of duty resulting in personal injury, or for torts connected with the ownership, occupation, possession, control or use of any property real or personal, *provided* that these torts do not arise from an act done in contemplation or furtherance of a trade dispute.

On the premise that a trade union should have the right to call its members out on strike, this immunity is essential. Without it, a union could be sued for the loss a strike caused to the organisation(s) against which the strike was called, and union funds necessary to sustain striking members and finance its other activities would always be at risk.

The concept of a "trade dispute" is the key to the legal immunities and privileges of a trade union, its officers and its members. By the 1974 and 1976 Acts this concept covers disputes between workers and other workers, disputes concerning a worker's trade union membership, and disputes relating to matters occurring outside Great Britain.

No action in tort is possible against an individual union member acting "in contemplation or furtherance of a trade dispute" who induces or threatens a breach of a contract of employment, or any other contract, or who interferes with, induces or threatens interference with its performance, purely on the ground that his actions produce either of these effects. Actions which, solely because they are not resisted, do not result in a dispute are still actions in contemplation of a trade dispute. However, his conduct may be actionable on other grounds, e.g. he may be both sued and prosecuted for actions amounting to assault and battery or criminal damage. Thus he has immunity from legal actions for all loss and damage he causes purely because he was on strike, but he is not immune where his acts give rise to a cause of action quite independent of his strike action. For example, a line is drawn between damage to plant and machinery consequential to lack of maintenance during a strike and deliberate sabotage, and between reasonable argument and threats of physical violence made during a picket. However, no matter what the law says, attempts to regulate industrial relations by using the law have not been great successes.

Picketing

Picketing consists of communicating information or peacefully trying to persuade someone to work or not to work in the context of a possible dispute between management and workers or in support of a dispute already in progress. Before the Employment Act 1980 it was lawful to picket anywhere except at someone's home. The amended Trade Union and Labour Relations Act 1974 now states that it is only lawful for a person to picket at or near his own place of work or, if he is an official of a trade union, at or near the place of work of a member of that union whom he is accompanying. However, a person who does not have one fixed place of work, e.g. a supply teacher, or for whom it is impracticable to picket at his actual place of work, e.g. an oil-rig worker, may lawfully picket at the premises of his employer from which he works or from which his work is managed. If the trade dispute is caused by, or leads to, the dismissal of an employee, that ex-employee may picket his former workplace.

Since a person may only picket at his own workplace, an injunction can be issued against anyone who engages in *secondary picketing*, i.e. picketing at any workplace other than his own, e.g. his employer's supplier. Furthermore, an action for damages may be brought against him if he causes material loss by interfering with other peoples' contracts of employment. This provision against secondary picketing was introduced to prevent mass pickets, where hundreds, or even thousands, of people, most of whom would not be directly involved in the dispute, might join picket lines to support the workers in dispute.

The 1980 Act does not limit the number of pickets, although it was initially proposed that they should be limited to six. However, in theory the police can still control the number of pickets, in that picketing by large numbers may obstruct the highway or be likely to cause a breach of the peace, both criminal offences entitling the police to take action. Clearly, the law should not deny employees the right to picket peacefully but this right should (arguably) be regulated in the context of the social and economic cost to the community. The Employment Act 1980 represents the 1979 Conservative government's attempt to reconcile these sometimes potentially conflicting values. The Grunwick dispute of the mid-seventies is perhaps the best, and certainly the best known, example of these values colliding head-on. It remains to be seen, however, whether the current legislation will be more successful than previous attempts to regulate labour disputes by legislation. Undoubtedly, the police are still left in a very invidious position; whatever they do will anger one vociferous faction or another. But one thing is certain—it is very difficult to arrest several thousand people for obstructing the highway. Whatever future changes there may be in the law on picketing, the main problem will continue to be one of enforcement.

Closed shop agreements

Some of the most controversial aspects of present trade union law are the provisions relating to union membership agreements (closed shops), by which a person may be required to join a specified union, or one of a specified number of unions, in order to hold a particular job. Under the 1974 and 1976 Acts closed shops are legal but not compulsory, and the Acts give no statutory right to a closed shop nor do they outline any procedures for making such an agreement.

The Employment Act 1980 changes the law where a closed shop agreement exists. In such circumstances an employee is entitled not to be dismissed (or disciplined) for failing to join or remain a member of a union if he does so on the grounds of:

(*a*) conscience or other deeply held personal convictions;
(*b*) if the closed shop agreement was made after he joined his employer;
(*c*) or (in certain cases) if it has not been approved in secret ballot by at least 80 per cent of those entitled to vote in that ballot.

Also, if a closed shop agreement exists a union may not unreasonably exclude or expel a person from membership.

Trade union officials have argued that these changes are aimed at weakening trade union organisation. An opposing argument is that they merely restore freedom of choice to an employee. On the one hand, closed shop agreements have advantages in industrial relations generally, e.g. consultation is made easier and more effective, and the possibility of inter-union disputes is lessened. On the other, at least to some extent, an individual employee's freedom to choose whether or not to belong to a trade union is removed, sometimes in a situation where the job to which the closed shop agreement relates is the only suitable employment available.

Politics, history and the legal framework

Politics and law have always been closely linked in the evolution of the legal framework regulating trade union activities. Sometimes political influence or motivation is there for all to see, at other times it is far more covert and can only be surmised. At one extreme the legal prohibition on the police and members of the armed forces taking strike action is, in the widest sense, plainly political, while at the other the inherent conservatism of the judiciary is allegedly reflected in a number of judgments against trade unions in cases involving trade disputes and other trade union activities. It is certainly true that the evolution of the legislative framework has been influenced more than most branches of the law by party politics.

The ill-fated Industrial Relations Act 1971, for example, was introduced by a Conservative government and was broadly supported by pressure groups traditionally loyal to Conservative Party ideals. It was destroyed largely by trade union hostility and repealed by the following Labour government's Trade Union and Labour Relations Act 1974. In turn, some of the recent employment law, in particular the Employment Protection (Consolidation) Act 1978, in its original form, was said to favour employees unduly, and the original 1975 Employment Protection Act was certainly the product of far more consultation with the TUC, a traditional supporter of the Labour Party, than with the CBI and other employers' associations, traditional supporters of the Conservative Party. Now some say the Employment Act 1980, which amended the Trade Union and Labour Relations Act 1974 and the Employment Protection (Consolidation) Act 1978, swings the balance of the framework back against the unions. It is difficult to see how industrial relations can ever be improved so long as the two traditional major parties each seem to end up promoting confrontation by their legislation. However, the malady is far easier to diagnose than cure.

A detailed history of the present legal framework is beyond the scope of this book, but a brief survey of some of the legal landmarks of the last 150 years or so will show that a trade union's present immunities and privileges have been fought for rather than handed to them.

In the nineteenth century, trade unions were considered to be organisations in restraint of trade, on the basis that they inhibited a member's freedom to contract with whomsoever he wished on whatever terms he could successfully bargain for. As such, they were by their very nature contrary to public policy and regarded as illegal conspiracies. Before the repeal of the Combination Acts in 1824 a combination of workers was considered a criminal conspiracy, punishment for which included public whipping, imprisonment and transportation. Between 1824 and 1871, however, they were not recognised at civil law in any of their internal or external activities and dealings.

The Trade Union Act 1871 and the Conspiracy and Protection of Property Act 1875 together saw the successful end of one battle—

to remove the stigma of illegality from combinations of workers—and the beginning of another—to achieve total immunity from actions in tort for their activities in contemplation or furtherance of a trade dispute.

The 1871 Act provided that:

(a) a trade union was not illegal because it was "in restraint of trade";

(b) a trade union could register with the Registrar of Friendly Societies;

(c) a registered union could hold property and bring court actions in its registered name.

The 1875 Act legalised peaceful picketing, which had been made a criminal offence by the Criminal Law Amendment Act 1871, and declared that no action of a trade union was illegal unless it was also illegal if committed by an individual. Thus trade unions received legal recognition and a degree of legal protection for themselves and their activities.

The first great set-back to the trade union movement after the 1871 and 1875 Acts was the decision of the House of Lords in *Taff Vale Railway* v. *Amalgamated Society of Railway Servants* (1901). Damages of £23,000 and costs of nearly £20,000 were awarded against the union for the loss its strike action had caused to the Taff Vale Railway. In its effect the decision was tantamount to preventing strike action.

The Conservative government of the time was unwilling to take steps to mitigate the Taff Vale judgment, but in 1906 a Liberal government was elected and passed the Trade Disputes Act in the same year. The Act overruled the legal principle of the Taff Vale judgment and embodied principles still fundamental to the modern legal framework. It provided that:

(a) trade unions were to be completely immune from actions in tort (the immunity did not apply to its members as individuals);

(b) no legal action could be taken (against its members) for a "conspiracy to injure" in the context of trade disputes, provided unlawful means were not used, i.e. the commission of a tort; and

(c) inducements to break contracts of employment were not actionable.

Trade union political activity received legislative sanction by the Trade Union (Amendment) Act 1913, provided it was approved by a majority of members. A separate political fund had to be established, however, and members could contract out, i.e. they were given the right not to subscribe to their union's political funds. The

Act overruled the *Osborne Judgment* of 1909, in which the House of Lords had held that the Trade Union Act 1871 did not allow unions to use their funds for political purposes. The judgment had badly undermined the financial position of the Labour Party and its MPs. (In fact union funds had been donated for this purpose since 1900, when the Labour Representation Committee was formed, becoming the Labour Party in 1906.)

The General Strike in 1926 plainly demonstrated the extent of the privileges and immunities that trade unions had gained. While it soon collapsed, largely through poor leadership, the Trade Disputes and Trade Union Act 1927, an overtly political act by the Conservative government of the day supported by an economically panic-stricken public, was passed to control the collective power of the unions in the future. The act:

(*a*) provided for contracting in, i.e. if union members wished to subscribe to their union's political fund they had to expressly ask to do so (this harmed the Labour Party because fewer members contracted in than had not contracted out under the 1913 Act);

(*b*) prevented Civil Service unions affiliating to the TUC; and

(*c*) forbade general strikes and most sympathetic strikes.

The provisions of the Act were comparatively short-lived, however, for one of the first acts of the Labour government elected in 1945 was to pass legislation repealing the 1927 Act and restoring the privileges and immunities that trade unions had had in 1913.

The next serious set-back to trade union activity came with the decision of the House of Lords in *Rookes* v. *Barnard* (1964). The plaintiff was employed by the British Overseas Airways Corporation (BOAC, now part of British Airways) in their design office and had been, but was no longer, a member of the Association of Engineering and Shipbuilding Draughtsmen. The three defendants were officials of the union and two were also employed by BOAC. In order to preserve a 100 per cent union membership in the design office, they threatened to call a strike of their members unless BOAC dismissed Rookes. This would necessarily involve breaking their contracts of employment. Bowing to this threat, BOAC lawfully dismissed the plaintiff. The House held that the defendants had committed the tort of intimidation, ruling that the tort was not confined to threats of criminal or tortious conduct but included a threat to break a contract. Thus they had used unlawful means in their trade dispute with BOAC, and could not rely on the 1906 Act as a defence to the plaintiff's action against them. The decision meant that the trade union movement could be attacked through its officials when strike action was threatened.

The decision outraged the trade union movement and was generally considered politically unacceptable. The next year, the Trade Disputes Act 1965 excepted from the principle of *Rookes* v. *Barnard* a threat to break or induce the breach of a contract of employment in contemplation or furtherance of a trade dispute. Thus the Act gave personal immunity from actions in tort to union officials who made such threats. (The principle would still apply, however, in the unlikely event of a threat to break a contract where a trade dispute was not involved.)

The next landmark was the Conservative Party's Industrial Relations Act 1971. Its subsequent disastrous failure was mainly due to the trade union movement's hostility to it, and the controversy created by the Act was one reason for the Conservative government's defeat in the 1974 General Election. Many people would say that the electorate was presented with a straight choice by the government between their policies and those of the unions. The episode plainly illustrates the political power that the trade union movement can exert should it choose to do so. Additionally it illustrates the limitations of a law which hundreds of thousands of people refuse to obey. The Act repealed the 1906 and 1965 Acts and introduced a new statutory concept of "unfair industrial practices" to replace the law of tort as a way of regulating trade disputes. Registration under the Act was necessary in order to enjoy the benefits of the legal immunities and privileges.

The Labour government elected in 1974 repealed the 1971 Act by the Trade Union and Labour Relations Act 1974, subsequently amended by the Trade Union and Labour Relations (Amendment) Act 1976. Together these restored and extended the legal immunities of trade unions in their activities. These Acts, together with the Employment Protection Act 1975, were in part a product of the openly political "alliance"—the so-called "Social Contract"—between the trade union movement and the 1974–9 Labour government. As you have already seen, the Conservative government elected in 1979 has passed the Employment Act 1980 which, while leaving untouched the basic legal immunities, makes significant changes in the law relating to picketing and closed shops. Both these aspects are seen by many trade unionists as deliberate attempts to curb trade union power. In addition, the Secretary of State for Industry can issue codes of practice under the Act. Failure to observe the codes does not render a person liable to legal action but they are admissible in evidence before industrial tribunals, the central arbitration committee and the courts. Codes exist on closed shops and on picketing.

The conflicts remain unresolved. Will the relevant provisions of the Employment Act 1980 be repealed as and when the Labour Party is returned to power? What will be the policy of the Liberal/ Social Democrat alliance should its remarkable early success result in it holding the balance of power? Will *any* future government gradually change the basic framework on the grounds of public policy and economic necessity?

EMPLOYMENT LAW

Contracts of employment
The socio-economic background
There can be very few contracts in which such inequality in bargaining power exists between the parties to it as in a contract of employment (a general theme developed in Chapter 17). Only the superstars of the entertainment and sporting worlds, exceptionally able technicians, managers and the like are able to dictate the terms of their contracts of employment. However much unions and other organisations may negotiate national salaries, conditions of employment, pensions, etc., reality for the rest of us is ultimately a simple choice: accept the employers' terms or starve! Such a situation is the legacy of *laissez-faire* but it does not follow that an economy controlled entirely by the state would necessarily produce a better choice, or any choice at all. Indeed, it is arguable that while the basic social right to work might be better protected, conditions of service, pay, choice and variety of employment would be far worse.

The harshness of this stark choice is mitigated in reality of course by the power of the trade unions and by an elaborate system of national insurance and welfare benefits. Thus, no-one is actually likely to starve. However, it does justify the state intervening to lay down certain basic terms to be embodied in all contracts of employment.

In the late nineteenth and early twentieth centuries certain implied terms in employment contracts were established by judicial decisions, e.g. a mutual duty of care owed between employer and employee, but a comprehensive legislative framework of employment law is somewhat surprisingly a very recent creation, a product of the 1970s. Even so, there is such diversity in employment that only generally accepted rights and duties can be laid down; specific contractual terms are still (theoretically) the subject of negotiation between individual employers and their employees.

Employment law is far from being purely a lawyer's subject: many different influences affect its principles and practices. It is often a politically emotive subject; trade unions can exert tremendous influence in both particular and general issues, diverse pressure groups are active in furthering their causes at both grass-roots and policy-making levels and the media is guaranteed to get maximum mileage from a controversial or unusual "employment story". Remember, too, that while the right to work is a generally accepted social right, there is no corresponding legal right. Critics of the present welfare system might argue quite the reverse, i.e. that there is a legal right not to work in so far as a person is legally entitled to enough money from the state for a tolerable existence without working.

Today increasing numbers of people are becoming unemployed. Many traditional industries are contracting and even where there is expansion, the increasing use of computer-based technology means that not as many employees are needed as in the past. It is highly unlikely that we, as a country, will in the foreseeable future return to the full employment that existed in the 1960s. It would seem that in the future the necessary workforce may be much smaller than it is today. This will mean that accepted concepts of work and leisure will have to change.

These changes will almost certainly speed up the move towards employment in service jobs instead of in manufacturing and, per-haps, the introduction (even enforcement?) of maximum working hours. Indeed, it is highly likely that your (grand)children, working an average of twenty hours a week or less, will consider our hours and conditions of employment, and the whole recently created framework of employment protection, as outmoded and unaccept-able as we now consider the dreadful conditions endured by workers in the not so distant past. In our eyes the state failed to protect even the workers' basic social right to a dignified existence, but will our (grand)children view the monotony of the production line to be equally deplorable, and the work alienation it causes to be eco-nomically unacceptable?

What is a contract of employment?
A contract of employment is a *contract of service*, i.e. a contract under which a person puts his labour at the disposal of another in return for the payment of money or other remuneration. The rela-tionship created was traditionally called that of master and servant, but today employer and employee is a more realistic label. How-ever, the traditional term is still commonly used in cases, and the term contract of service is still used in modern statutes.

A contract of employment (service) must be distinguished from a contract for services, i.e. a contract where the relationship of em-ployer and independent contractor arises. For example, if a business organisation wished to paint its premises and arranged for a specialist decorating firm to do the work, a contract for services would exist. If, however, their own maintenance section did the work, the painters would be employed under a contract of employment (service). In a contract for services the employer is able to tell the independent contractor what to do but not how to do it, while in a contract of employment the employer (master) is theoretically able to do both.

In the olden days the test for a contract of employment was control of the employee, or perhaps more realistically the right to control, and this corresponded with the now rather outmoded terminology of master and servant. Today, however, the "control test" cannot realistically be applied to organisations employing thousands of people, particularly where many of the employees are highly skilled or professionally qualified. A number of tests have been put forward to replace the traditional control test, but it would seem that a simple common-sense appraisal of the facts of each individual case cannot be bettered. In fact it can only be in a very few situations that the nature of the contract is open to dispute.

However academic or legalistic the distinction between contracts of service and contracts for services may become, the distinction is fundamentally important. Two examples will illustrate this well. An employer is liable for the wrongful acts (torts) of his employee, enabling any person injured by the wrongful act to seek redress from the employer as well as the employee. (This is the principle of *vicarious liability* and it is discussed further on page 580.) Conversely, an employer is not generally liable for the wrongful acts of an independent contractor. The employee's statutory protection against unfair dismissal, his statutory right to redundancy payments and the statutory obligations imposed on employers, all contained in the provisions of the Employment Protection (Consolidation) Act 1978, only apply to persons employed under a contract of employment. These important provisions are all considered below.

It is worth noting, before we proceed further, that the relationship resulting from a contract of employment has changed a great deal over the years. In olden days the law allowed a master to sue anybody who injured his servant; in fact it recognised that the master had a kind of property right in his servants. Such a concept is quite unacceptable today and the relationship is now recognised to be essentially contractual. However, in an era of comprehensive employment legislation and collective agreements between powerful unions and vast organisations, you must remember that in real terms the scope of the individual employee's contract with his employer is very limited.

Terms of employment contracts
With a few exceptions a contract of employment requires no special form: it can be written, totally verbal or deduced from the conduct of the parties. One of the exceptions is a contract of apprenticeship: this must be in writing. Under the Employment Protection (Consolidation) Act 1978, however, employers are required to give detailed written information to their employees of the terms of their employment within thirteen weeks of their employment commencing. For an organisation with a great number of employees it would be unnecessarily onerous and expensive to give this information to each employee individually, and an employer fulfills his duty if he refers employees to a reasonably accessible document, e.g. a collective agreement, which contains the required information. Such documents are frequently displayed on works' notice boards.

The information which must be supplied relates to the parties to the contract, the date employment began, pay, hours of work, holidays, incapacity for work, pensions, the notice required by the employee to terminate the contract and the employee's job title. In addition, a statement must be included specifying any disciplinary rules, the person to whom application for redress of grievances may be made and the grievance procedure available to the employee. A written statement of any change in the terms must be provided within one month of the change.

Rights and duties in employment
The rights and duties which arise from and in connection with contracts of employment are a combination of the express terms of each individual contract, terms implied into them by the common law and by statute, collective agreements and a number of statutory rights enjoyed by an employee which exist quite independently of his contract.

Rights and duties arising from the contract
The employer's duties.

(*a*) To pay wages. The duty to pay wages is obvious but strictly speaking it only arises if there is an express or implied agreement to pay them. The amount paid again, strictly speaking, depends on the individual contract, but collective agreements on wages are now the norm.

(*b*) To provide work. You saw earlier in this chapter that there is no legal right to work as such, but following the decision in *Langston* v. *AUEW* (1974) (Court of Appeal), it may be that the law will recognise the principle that an employer is under a duty to provide work for his employees. If this were so, suspension on full pay could be a breach of contract.

(c) To take reasonable care of his employees at work. The common law recognised that an employer was under a duty to take reasonable care for the safety of his employees, but today all the important specific aspects of this duty are governed by statute. These will all eventually be regulated by Statutory Instruments made by the Secretary of State for Employment under the Health and Safety at Work, etc., Act 1974. The general duties imposed by this Act are discussed in the next chapter in the context of the responsibilities owed to employees and visitors through the occupancy of premises.

Should an employee suffer injury at work and wish to claim damages from his employer he may sue:

(i) on the principle of vicarious liability—an employer is liable if one employee injures another while acting in the course of his employment;

(ii) on the basis of his employer's own personal negligence in relation to the provision of adequate plant, premises and machinery, competent staff and a safe system of work with adequate supervision and instruction; or

(iii) because there has been a breach of statutory duty.

To succeed on this last ground the employee must show that he was one of the class of persons for whose benefit the duty was imposed and that he has suffered the type of injury which the Act was passed to prevent.

In any action for damages by an employee against his employer, the employee's own conduct will be taken into account. If he is found to have been partly to blame for his own injury the damages awarded will be reduced: Law Reform (Contributory Negligence) Act 1945. However the courts accept that the repetitive nature of modern industrial employment reduces an employee's awareness of his conduct. Furthermore, as the Employers' Liability (Compulsory Insurance) Act 1969 requires employers to insure against liability for injury to their employees, public policy dictates that it should be they who pay, even though the employee was partly to blame for his own injury.

(d) To indemnify employees. This duty is owed to all employees who incur expense and liability in the proper performance of their duties.

If the employer is in breach of any duty, an employee injured by it is entitled to claim damages at common law.

The employee's duties.

(*a*) To obey his employer. An employee is bound to obey the lawful instructions of his employer which are within the scope of his contract of employment.

(*b*) To exercise care and skill. An employee is expected to perform his contractual duties with reasonable care. Should his employer be held liable to a third party as a result of a breach of this duty, the employee can be made to indemnify his employer for the loss he incurs. In most cases, however, it is not worthwhile for an employer to seek this indemnity.

(*c*) To act reasonably. An employee's dishonesty or incompetence always justify his dismissal; whether disobedience, laziness, rudeness etc., also justify dismissal depends on the circumstances of each particular case.

(*d*) To act in good faith. An employee must not allow his own interests to conflict with those of his employer. There are two main aspects of this duty. Firstly, he must not disclose confidential information to third parties, e.g. trade secrets; secondly, he must not make a secret profit out of his appointment. An employee accepting a secret commission from suppliers with whom he places orders for his employer would be an example of a secret profit.

An employee's statutory rights. We mentioned earlier that an employee enjoys a number of rights in employment which exist independently of his contract of employment. Many of these rights were created or extended by the Employment Protection Act 1975 and are now found in the Employment Protection (Consolidation) Act 1978. They include:

(*a*) a right to guaranteed daily pay (£9.15 at present) for five days in any three month period when no work is available, e.g. through lay-offs caused by external strikes;

(*b*) a right to payment in periods of sickness when the health and safety legislation requires his suspension from work;

(In both (*a*) and (*b*) above many employees would not be entitled to payment under the terms of their contracts.)

(*c*) a right to paid maternity leave and a right to re-engagement within twenty-nine weeks of giving birth;

(*d*) a right to paid leave in order to fulfil certain trade union duties, and a right to unpaid leave to take part in trade union activities or public duties (this right is subject to certain limits regarding time and amount as the case may be.);

(*e*) a right to an itemised pay statement showing details of gross pay, deductions and net pay;

(*f*) a right to a written statement upon request giving the reason for his dismissal.

Termination of employment contracts and its consequences

In practice contracts of employment are nearly always ended by notice or by summary termination. At common law either side may lawfully terminate the contract by giving reasonable notice, or summarily (without notice) where the other side has committed a serious breach of contract. In particular, termination by notice used to put the employee in a very weak position—workers are usually more easily replaced than work—and the present situation must be considered in the light of the statutory protection from arbitrary dismissal that the employee is now given, and the wider political effect of exercising legal rights of dismissal to the letter. An employer would be very foolish to risk a confrontation with the might of the trade unions by unlawfully dismissing an employee (quite apart from the latter's legal rights) and it is a fact of life in industrial relations that it may in some cases be better not to legitimately sack an employee in order to avert the possibility of highly damaging unofficial strikes. In short, legal rights and duties must be seen in the light of the economic and political realities of each particular situation.

Termination by notice

At common law you have seen that the contract can be determined by giving reasonable notice: the more senior the employee and/or the longer the service, the longer being the period of notice required. By the Employment Protection (Consolidation) Act 1978, *minimum* periods of notice are laid down, but even here the concept of unfair dismissal (discussed below) must be considered, for a lawful dismissal may still be "unfair".

TABLE XXI. PERIODS OF NOTICE

After continuous employment for	*Period of notice*
4 weeks up to 2 years	1 week
2 years up to 12 years	1 week for each year
12 years or more	12 weeks

An employee who has been employed continuously for four weeks is required to give his employer one week's notice.

These periods can be increased by the contract but they cannot be decreased. Either side may, however, waive the right to notice or accept payment in lieu. If the contract specifies a longer period than the statutory minimum, the latter is irrelevant. Indeed at common law reasonable notice may be held to be longer than the statutory minimum, as in *Hill* v. *C. A. Parsons Ltd.* (1972), where the Court of Appeal thought that a chartered engineer, who had been employed continuously for 35 years, was entitled to at least six month's notice and possibly a year.

Summary termination
The contract may be terminated without notice in two cases: firstly, by either side where the contract gives an express right to do so; and secondly, by one party where the other has committed a serious breach of contract. It is always a question of fact, to be decided in the circumstances of each case, whether a breach is sufficiently serious to justify summary termination, but an employee's incompetence, dishonesty or wilful disobedience is usually considered sufficiently serious.

Statutory intervention
The common law provided little help to an employee who was wrongfully dismissed; he was not generally entitled to a hearing before dismissal and an award of damages was limited to his loss of earnings in the period of notice to which he was entitled. Dismissal by notice was generally lawful no matter how arbitrary, and no consideration of his future after dismissal was entertained.

Such a situation is no longer regarded as acceptable and Parliament has created a quite separate concept of *unfair dismissal* (applicable whether dismissal is lawful or unlawful) with its own system of remedies, and a system of *redundancy payments* following loss of employment. The systems recognise the weakness of the individual employee's position vis-à-vis his employer, and his right to financial compensation for his loss of employment. The compensation takes into account the disruption caused by the loss of the job and the possible difficulties in obtaining comparable employment.

Unfair dismissal. The concept of *unfair dismissal* was first created by the Industrial Relations Act 1971. The relevant provisions are now contained in the Employment Protection (Consolidation) Act 1978 as amended by the Employment Act 1980.

The concept is based upon the right to job security in which a person's employed status is more important than the terms of his contract. Under the Act an employee with at least 52 weeks continuous service (2 years if his employer employs less than twenty people) at a minimum of 16 hours a week can challenge his dismissal before an industrial tribunal, irrespective of whether or not he was in breach of contract and irrespective of whether he was dismissed summarily or by notice.

The burden of proving that the dismissal was fair used to be on the employer but since the Employment Act 1980 the tribunal looks at the facts presented by both sides in reaching its decision. In practice this will probably not make much difference because the Tribunal will still be looking to see that:

(a) the reason for the dismissal was fair; and
(b) that it was reasonable in the circumstances for that reason to cause dismissal.

To be fair, the reason must relate to the employee's capability or qualifications, his conduct, redundancy, a legal restriction which prevents the employment, e.g. a lorry driver who has lost his licence as a result of conviction for a motoring offence, or some other substantial reason, e.g. the employee had asked to be dismissed.

In cases involving the dismissed employee's conduct, a commonsense approach is adopted. Most people, for example, would agree that unpunctuality would be a reason for dismissal but would not expect to be dismissed the first time they were late. Where the employee's conduct would not justify a summary dismissal, the tribunal would expect that the employer had given verbal and then written warnings so that the employee was fully aware that his conduct would lead to a dismissal if it did not improve. How many warnings have to be given will depend on the circumstances. Someone who is persistently late may receive a verbal warning and then several written warnings before the final warning and dismissal. On the other hand, someone who has been caught fighting at work may receive a final written warning immediately. Many firms have a disciplinary procedure which states what warnings will be given before dismissal.

The statute declares certain reasons to be automatically unfair. These include dismissal for joining a trade union or taking part in its activities, and dismissal on grounds of pregnancy, unless the employee is incapable of doing her job or her continued employment would infringe the health and safety legislation. Conversely, certain reasons for dismissal are automatically considered to be fair, e.g. in order to safeguard national security and because the employee was on strike or locked out by his employer (unless only some employees were locked out or dismissed). This last reason is interesting in that it shows that the legislation is not intended to interfere with the legitimate exercise of economic sanctions by either side in a trade dispute. Before the Employment Act 1980 changed the law, dismissal for not joining a specified trade union where a closed shop agreement was in operation was also automatically considered to be fair. Today, if an employee's reasons for not joining are within the Act (*see* above), his dismissal would seem to be automatically unfair.

An employee's remedies for unfair dismissal are also contained in the 1978 Act, as amended. An industrial tribunal may order his *reinstatement* (he is given back his job and treated as if the dismissal had never taken place), or *re-engagement* (he is given a new job by the employer), or it may make an award of *compensation*. An award comprises two elements: a basic award made regardless of loss and calculated on a similar basis to redundancy payments based on age (with the difference that years of employment below the age of eighteen also count), length of service and rate of pay (*see* below); and a compensatory award based on the loss he has actually suffered through his unfair dismissal. This latter award is subject to a limit of £135 on weekly earnings and an overall limit of £7,000. The award can be reduced if the employee has unreasonably refused an offer of reinstatement or on account of his conduct before, and not necessarily cited or known at the time of, the dismissal.

Redundancy. Under the redundancy payments provisions of the Employment Protection (Consolidation) Act 1978, redundancy occurs when an employee is dismissed because his employer has discontinued or intends to discontinue the business for which he was employed, or because the need for his particular service has diminished or is expected to diminish. The payments are intended to compensate an employee for the loss of his job through no fault of his own. Thus, if a person is dismissed for a good reason, or unreasonably refuses a comparable job, he or she is not entitled to a redundancy payment.

To be entitled to a redundancy payment the employee must be under the age of sixty-five, if a man, or sixty, if a woman, and have worked continuously for the same employer for either:

(*a*) two years at not less than 16 hours a week; or
(*b*) five years at not less than 8 hours a week (in effect part-time employees).

The calculation of payments is based on age, length of service and final earnings.

For each year employed between

ages 18–21	half a week's pay
ages 22–40	one week's pay
ages 41–65	(men) } one-and-a-
ages 41–60	(women) } half weeks' pay

The maximum length of reckonable service is 20 years and the maximum reckonable weekly earning is £135. Thus, the maximum payment possible at present is £135 × 1.5 × 20 = £4,050. Some redundancy payments are higher than the maximum entitlement under the Employment Protection (Consolidation) Act 1978. These are, however, usually the result of negotiation between the employer and strong trade unions.

Every employer must make contributions to a redundancy fund operated by the Secretary of State for Employment, from which he will receive a 41 per cent rebate of any redundancy payments he makes provided he gives advance notice of the redundancy to the Secretary of State. The Employment Protection (Consolidation) Act 1978 requires an employer to consult the unions representing his employees about possible redundancies, and entitles individual employees who have been given redundancy notices to reasonable time off from work to look for new employment or to arrange for retraining before the dismissal takes place.

Other statutory protection of employees

Much has already been said about government intervention to regulate employment and protect employees. In particular we have discussed the terms implied in employment contracts, the protection against unfair dismissal and the right to compensation on redundancy contained in the Employment Protection (Consolidation) Act 1978. In addition, however, other statutes give important protection in more specific situations.

The dramatic increase in unemployment in recent years emphasises the fact that current employment and redundancy legislation is of little effect in preserving jobs in difficult economic times, particularly in the absence of positive government intervention. Therefore the effect of the legislation is only to ease the trauma of transition in the labour market and not to provide employees with any right to keep their jobs.

Discrimination

The Race Relations Act 1976 makes it unlawful to discriminate on the grounds of colour, race or ethnic or national origins generally, and Part II of the Act deals specifically with employment. It provides that it is unlawful to discriminate on these grounds in recruitment of employees, terms of employment, opportunities for promotion, training or other benefits, and dismissal. A complaint under Part II of the Act is dealt with by an industrial tribunal which may award compensation and order steps to be taken to stop the discrimination.

The Equal Pay Act 1970 and the Sex Discrimination Act 1975 taken together require that men and women (regardless of marital status) are treated equally as regards pay for equal or equivalent work, recruitment, training, promotion and dismissal.

The Rehabilitation of Offenders Act 1974, designed to enable offenders to make a fresh start, provides that after certain periods convictions become "spent" and need not be disclosed to an employer. Dismissal on discovery of a spent conviction would be "unfair" under the Employment Protection (Consolidation) Act 1978.

National insurance and industrial injuries
Both these important aspects of the welfare state are now regulated by the Social Security Acts 1975 and 1980. The national insurance scheme provides for contributions to be paid by both employer and employee, and for benefits to be paid on the occurrence of certain events, e.g. sickness, unemployment, maternity, retirement and death.

The industrial injuries provisions of the Acts entitle any person in insurable employment to benefits if he suffers personal injury caused by an accident in the course of his employment. Benefits are of three types: injury benefit, payable for a maximum of six months while the claimant is unable to work; disablement benefit, the amount and form of payment depending on the degree of disablement; and death benefits.

Employment law in perspective
Employment is vital to most people's economic existence and, whether we like it or not, we all spend a great deal of our lives working. Consequently, employment plays a vital socio-economic role in our existence. The legal framework of employment reflects this, and today there exists a comprehensive set of regulations designed to ensure that the employee's social rights and needs are equated with the economic forces which dictate the actions of his employer. Some of you may consider that the legal framework unduly favours the employee, others that the social cost of unemployment justifies even greater employee protection.

Employment is a subject which perfectly illustrates the need to arrive at a workable amalgam of social consciousness, economic reality and political possibility. Law as a concept has taken a back seat in the creation of the legal framework, but law as a social process is crucial to the operation and enforcement of the framework.

The organisation must concern itself with trade union and employment law: indeed, there are economic and legal penalties for not doing so. The average employee, however, knows little, if anything, about employment law and is generally apathetic about trade unions. He is, naturally, most concerned about the contents of his pay packet, but it is most likely that he is equally ignorant of the factors which determine the size of his wages. To obtain a full picture of the organisation and its employees, however, it is necessary that we discuss the factors which determine the level of wages.

THE DETERMINATION OF WAGES

The demand and supply of labour

The wage rate will be determined by the interaction of the organisation's demand for labour and the supply of labour forthcoming.

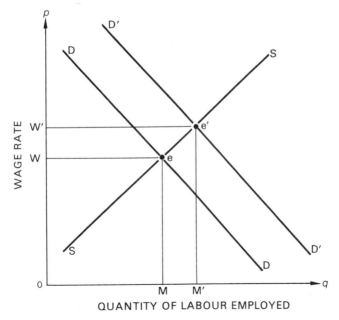

Fig. 30. *The determination of the wage rate.*

In the previous chapter we saw that an organisation's demand for a factor of production is the marginal revenue product (MRP) curve of that factor. The supply of labour, you will remember, is determined by such things as the size and age distribution of the population (*see* Part Two). Without interference from the government or trade unions the wage rate will be determined by these forces of demand and supply. This is illustrated in Fig. 30 (*see also* pages 291–3). Under these circumstances it is unlikely that the supply of labour will vary much from year to year. The wage rate in a business is therefore more likely to be the result of changes in demand. The movement of the demand curve from DD to D'D' could have been brought about by either an improvement in technology or a rise in the price of the product being produced. Although improving productivity is one of the most certain ways of increasing wages there is little that trade unions can do about it. They therefore tend to work by affecting the supply of labour. (Trade unions may, of course, be involved in agreements with employers to increase productivity.)

Restrictive labour practices

A most effective way for trade unions to increase their members' wages is to restrict the supply of labour to a particular occupation. This can be done by *closed shop* practices. These are not always aimed at increasing wages but have certainly been used for this purpose in some industries, e.g. printing and film-making. The supply of labour to an occupation could also be limited by the enforcement of long apprenticeships or training periods. Another method is *demarcation*, where particular tasks in a job may only be done by members of a particular union, for example plumbers not being allowed to do joiners' jobs in a particular factory. Demarcation or "who does what" disputes have been a frequent cause of unrest in British industrial relations, especially in the shipbuilding industry.

Figure 31 shows that the effect of restricting the supply of labour is to increase the wage rate from W to W' but it also means that the quantity of labour employed declines from OM to OL. Thus, while some workers are receiving higher wages other people are unable to obtain jobs. This kind of practice is not restricted to trade unions; the Inns of Court run a most effective closed shop which restricts the supply of labour to the Bar, thereby keeping out many young lawyers who might like to become practising barristers. This not only has the effect of driving up barrister's fees but also contributes to the delays which bedevil the administration of justice.

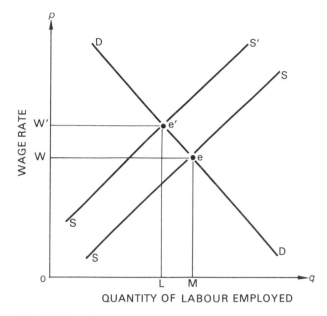

Fig. 31. *The effect of restrictive practices upon the wage rate.*

Collective bargaining

Working people learned long ago that to ask the employer individually for a wage rise was a good way to lose a job. Trade unions therefore negotiate on behalf of all their members and if agreement is not reached they may then take action collectively to enforce their demands. The collective bargaining strength of a trade union varies enormously from industry to industry. Bargaining strength is great in coal-mining, for here there is almost 100 per cent membership of the NUM, a strong community spirit and the possibility of bringing the country to a standstill. On the other hand the bargaining strength of $3\frac{3}{4}$ million workers in the country is so poor that the government has set up wages councils.

Figure 32 illustrates three possibilities. Which one occurs will depend upon the strength of the union. Here successful collective bargaining has raised the wage rate from OW to OW'. As a result of this the employer would like to employ less labour (OL instead of OM)—this is position *a*. However, the strength of the union may be such that it is able to insist that the organisation retains the same number of workers as before. This is position *b*, where the wage rate is higher but the quantity of labour employed remains OM. As a result of increasing the wage rate more people would like

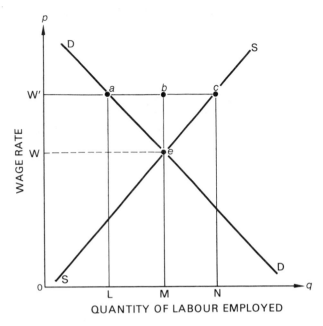

Fig. 32. *Collective bargaining and wages.*

to work for this organisation. In an extreme case the union may be able to insist that the organisation moves to position *c* where the wage rate is OW′ and the quantity of labour employed is ON. If the organisation is pushed into this position it may be forced to close down since *ac* represents a surplus of labour which it would not choose to employ if it were not forced to. Such *featherbedding* and *over manning* has occurred in a number of British industries. One of the most notorious industries for this is newspaper printing, where these practices have contributed to the demise of a number of newspapers.

Factors affecting bargaining strength

The ability of a trade union to raise wages will be influenced not only by its collective bargaining strength but also by several economic factors which are listed below.

(*a*) *The price of the final product.* If the demand for the product being made is such that it is not sensitive to changes in price (inelastic; *see* page 308) then the organisation will be able to pass the cost of increased wages on to the consumer. Conversely, if the demand for the product is sensitive to price changes (elastic) it will be difficult to pass on the cost of increased wages and consequently difficult for unions to gain wage rises.

(b) *The proportion of total costs which labour represents.* If labour costs make up a large proportion of total costs this will tend to make it more difficult for them to obtain pay rises. On the other hand, if the labour costs are only a small proportion of the organisation's other costs and more especially if the worker's task is vital this will tend to make it easier to secure a wage rise. This is referred to by Professor Samuelson as "the importance of being unimportant".

(c) *Factor substitution.* If it is relatively easy to substitute another factor of production for labour, e.g. capital. This will mean that as unions demand more wages the business will employ fewer workers. In Britain since the Second World War rising labour costs have encouraged employers to substitute capital for labour wherever possible, e.g. the microprocessor revolution.

(d) *The level of profits.* If an organisation is making little or no profit then the effect of a rise in wages could well be to put it out of business. Conversely, high profits would make it easier for unions to obtain higher wages and job security. In recent years high profits have often had the effect of stimulating wage claims.

(e) *Inflation.* Not only does inflation stimulate bigger wage claims but it may also make it easier for an organisation to pass on increases in wages to the consumer.

If trade union activity were successful in the national sense it would increase the proportion of the national income going to wages. Nevertheless, despite all the struggles of trade unions, this is not so. The portion of national income going to wages now is not significantly different to that of sixty years ago. The proportion fluctuates around 40–44 per cent depending upon the general level of economic activity. That is to say, when there is a slump it decreases and when there is a boom it increases.

Strikes

The withdrawal of labour is the ultimate weapon which unions possess. The word strike is very emotive and many people believe strikes are the cause of Britain's economic difficulties. It is more likely, however, that rather than being a cause, strikes are a symptom of Britain's industrial malaise. Rather than expressing opinions it is better to examine the facts. Statistics on strikes vary greatly from year to year but many countries often have a worse record than the UK, especially Italy and the USA. This is small comfort when we compare ourselves with the excellent industrial relations of the Germans. This section concentrates on general features, because of the wide variations in figures from year to year. Up-to-date figures on industrial disputes are published monthly in *The Department of Employment Gazette*. In the late 1970s strikes were certainly worse than for many years. A number of reasons might be found for this. The economy was stagnant and this made it very difficult for wage earners to obtain *real* increases in their earnings. On the other hand, inflation meant that unless large wage claims were made real income would decline and the rapid and continuing inflation encouraged unions to make exorbitant wage claims. The combined effects of inflation and incomes policy spread strikes to previously trouble-free groups such as hospital workers and firemen. There were also several protracted strikes for union recognition, notably the Grunwick dispute. It should be remembered, however, that good industrial relations do not make good television and that we always see the very worst side of industry's troubles on our television screens.

The vast majority of strikes are for increased wages. Sympathetic strikes, i.e. one union striking to support another, and political strikes are very uncommon in Britain. There was an exception to this in the years 1971–4 when many unions took action against the Industrial Relations Act 1971. In 1979, 28 million days were lost through strikes. This total was the highest since the General Strike of 1926, and it was partly as a result of opposition to the Labour government's pay policy in what became known as the "winter of discontent" (1978–9). However a far greater number of days were lost in the autumn of 1979 because of the series of weekly one-day and two-day strikes called in the entire engineering industry. In the early 1980s the number of days lost through strikes fell rapidly. This may be partly attributable at least to rising unemployment.

Most strikes are short lived, with 65 per cent of strikes lasting less than one week. Britain is, however, bedevilled by unofficial strikes. These outnumber official strikes by about twenty to one, but on the other hand official strikes tend to last about three or four times as long as unofficial ones. Unofficial strikes may be a symptom not only of bad relations between employer and worker but also between the union bureaucracy and its members.

Figure 33 shows that there is a definite correlation between the size of the workplace and strikes. Could it be that people strike as a reaction against the impersonal atmosphere of large companies, or against shop-floor boredom in large automated factories? Strikes are heavily concentrated in certain industries, with over 50 per cent of strikes regularly occurring in the same 100 companies. The engineering industry always heads the industrial strike table with over

Fig. 33. *Strikes and plant size.*

20 per cent of all strikes. The motor vehicle industry is perhaps the most notorious of all for strikes. There is also a geographical pattern to strikes, with the northern half of the country predominating. This is because many of the industries there, such as coalmining and shipbuilding, are declining whilst at the same time they are the most heavily unionised. Most people would agree that better industrial relations are essential if there is to be greater economic prosperity. This will take a great effort from employers, unions and government.

Before leaving the subject of the employee and his wages we must consider the law relating to their payment.

The payment of wages

You saw earlier in this chapter how the scope of the individual contracts between employers and their employees is very limited, for collective agreements and statutory regulations now determine the most important aspects and terms of most people's employment. This of course includes the method by which wages are paid, although the statutory rules, found in the Truck Acts 1831–1940 and the Payment of Wages Act 1960 only apply to manual workers. There has been considerable litigation on whether specific types of employment are or are not within the Acts, and in disputed cases the courts must decide whether the intellectual element predominates over the manual element in the employment or vice versa.

Payment in cash

The Truck Acts provide that a workman's entire wages must be paid in cash, and an agreement to the contrary contained in the contract of employment is "illegal, null and void". Also prohibited are provisions in the contract governing the place where, the manner in which or the person with whom the wages are to be spent. Contravention of the Truck Acts as a *criminal* offence and a workman can bring a *civil* action to recover any sums wrongfully deducted.

The original Act was passed to stop the practice of "trucking", whereby workmen were paid in kind or required to spend their wages in a "tommy shop" run by their employers where all the goods were sold at inflated prices. Today the Acts are often considered rather archaic and unnecessary. Indeed in one sense the very protection they provide discriminates against manual workers for it prevents the payment of fringe benefits (even luncheon vouchers) which are common in white collar employment and which become increasingly more important in periods of pay restraint. (Common fringe benefits include company cars, free life insurance and private medical care, and, in some cases, cheap loans and mortgages.)

As more and more people have opened bank accounts, payment in cash has become increasingly outmoded, inconvenient and risky, and the Payment of Wages Act 1960 amends the Truck Acts by allowing payment of wages in four other ways. These are:

(*a*) payment into the workman's bank account;
(*b*) payment by money order;
(*c*) payment by postal order; and
(*d*) payment by cheque.

However the workman must specifically ask for his wages to be paid by one of these alternative methods, and his employer is not allowed to make a deduction to cover any cost which may be involved in doing so.

Permitted deductions
As the Truck Acts require all a workman's wages to be paid in cash, only deductions specifically authorised by statute or exceptions established at common law are permitted. The 1831 Act itself allows an employer to make certain deductions from his employees' wages, e.g. for medicine, tools, materials, rent of a dwelling house and for the supply of food on the employer's premises. Other statutes require deductions to be made for income tax and social security contributions, and to comply with an order made under the Attachments of Earnings Act 1971, e.g. a maintenance order in favour of a former spouse. Among the common law exceptions is a deduction which is made and then paid to a third party at the

workman's request in satisfaction of a debt owed to the third party by the workman.

In the not so distant future the need to use cash may almost disappear; even today it is perfectly possible to pay for anything you need with a credit card. The technology already exists to take this a stage further and to debit a person's bank account, or perhaps some other monetary fund, at any point of payment. This would completely eliminate the transfer of cash and any intermediate accounting stage such as a credit card company or shop account. If the technology were to be exploited, the present methods of paying wages and the legal rules regulating them could become completely obsolete.

SELF-ASSESSMENT QUESTIONS

A. 1. Define: (a) the supply of labour; (b) a closed shop; (c) a wages council; (d) "trucking".
   2. List the possible criteria for establishing a contract of employment.
   3. Outline the legal privileges and immunities enjoyed by trade unions.

B. 4. True or false?
   (a) Under the Payment of Wages Act 1960, all workmen must be paid in cash.
   (b) Trade unions can register with the Registrar of Friendly Societies.
   (c) The Taff Vale case was a victory for the trade union movement.
   (d) Mobility of labour is greater when there is substantial unemployment in the economy.
   (e) Collective bargaining is when several unions combine to make a wage claim.

C. 5. True or false?
   (a) There are more work days lost through strikes than through illness.
   (b) There is a positive correlation between plant size and days lost through strikes.
   (c) Restrictive practices are always designed to decrease the supply of labour to a particular job.
   6. Explain the importance of the decision in *Rookes* v. *Barnard* (1964).

ASSIGNMENTS

1. Construct a bar graph showing the days lost through strikes in the last ten years.

2. Prepare arguments for and against, extending or reducing:
   (a) closed shop legislation;
   (b) union control of its members;
   (c) the legal privileges and immunities at present enjoyed by trade unions.

CHAPTER TEN

Land

CHAPTER OBJECTIVES

After studying this chapter you should be able to:
* define land in the legal and economic senses;
* state and explain the differences between freehold and leasehold estates in land;
* outline how title to land is transferred;
* list and evaluate the factors determining land use;
* describe the responsibilities arising from occupancy of land;
* analyse the concept of rent.

WHAT IS LAND?

All organisations use land. In this chapter we begin by considering the legal and economic meanings of land and later we consider the income derived from land and the factors which determine site value.

Definitions

Economically, land may be defined as the space in which to undertake economic activity. Although all economic activities do not use land in the way which, say, farming does, every activity must have a "space" in which it can take place. Included within the definition of land are whatever *natural resources* the land possesses. Land therefore includes mineral wealth, timber, climate, position and topography. Since fishing is an economic activity it is possible to regard the sea as "land".

At law the term land embraces not only the visible surface of the earth but also, in theory, everything above and below the surface and rights over land. When the term is used in Acts of Parliament it is defined by the Interpretation Act 1978 as including "buildings and other structures, land covered with water, and any estate, interest, easement, servitude or right in or over land". Hence we can say that land includes minerals, buildings, fixtures in buildings, reasonable rights in the airspace above the surface and rights over another person's land such as a right of way.

While a lawyer's definition of land may appear superficially similar to that of an economist, and indeed to some extent they are complementary, economists and lawyers view land from different perspectives. The economist views it as a resource, and is therefore interested in its utility; the lawyer is primarily concerned with its ownership, the transfer of ownership, restrictions upon its use and the legal obligations arising from its occupancy.

Practically, it may be difficult to separate land from other factors of production; theoretically, however, it possesses two attributes which distinguish it. Firstly, it is fixed in supply. Since we have already observed that the sea may be land it is obvious that there is only a finite amount of planet. However, although the total amount of land may be fixed, the *effective* area of land may be varied. In the nineteenth century, for example, the introduction of railways and steamships opened up the mid-west of America, thus effectively increasing the world's supply of grain-growing land. Similarly, the effective supply of land to any particular use may be altered by a change in price, e.g. the price of building land becomes higher so more land is switched from agriculture, thus increasing the effective supply of building land.

The second unique feature of land is that it has no cost of production. Although an individual may have to pay a great deal for land, and society may devote a lot of resources to its exploitation, the land itself has always existed and in that sense has no cost of production.

We mentioned earlier that, at law, land consists of more than the surface of the earth. Indeed, in so far as rights over water and its use are included in land law, "land" also includes water in a lawyer's definition. Ownership of land and rights over it have always been precious to English law, and an idea of the sophistication of the law's development can be gained by considering firstly the concept of fixtures and secondly rights in the airspace above one's property.

"Fixtures" are things which at law have become part of the land or building to which they are attached. Whether the objects are fixtures, however, may be a question of some nicety. For example in *Berkley* v. *Poulett* (1976) the Court of Appeal held that pictures fixed in the recesses of the panelling of rooms, a marble statue of a Greek athlete (weighing half a tonne and standing on a plinth) and a sundial resting on a stone baluster outside a house, were not fixtures which passed to the purchaser of the house. They were "chattels personal" (*see* below) and accordingly the seller of the house was entitled to remove them. In deciding such cases the courts look at the degree to which the object in question is attached to the building (the greater the annexation the more likely it is to be a fixture) and, more importantly, the purpose of the annexation. If the intention was to permanently improve the building, and not merely to enjoy the object, it is a fixture. Hence, fitted cupboards in a house and permanent installations in a factory are fixtures, while pictures hung on walls and moveable machinery are not.

Rights in airspace can be illustrated by two cases. In *Kelsen* v. *Imperial Tobacco Co. Ltd* (1957) an advertising sign which projected over the plaintiff's land was held to be an actionable trespass, while in *Bernstein of Leigh (Baron)* v. *Skyviews & General Ltd* (1977) the Court rejected the view that a landowner's rights in the airspace above his property extend to an unlimited height. In that case an action for trespass had been brought after an employee of the defendant had allegedly flown over the plaintiff's land in order to photograph his house. Normally, of course, legislation—the Civil Aviation Act 1949—prevents any action being brought in respect of aeroplanes flying over a person's land, and interference by space vehicles is verging on the realms of fantasy. However "space law"— in some ways the exact opposite of land law—must surely become important in the future.

Land and other property

Our legal system classifies property as either "real" or "personal", the former comprising only freehold interests in land and the latter everything else, including leasehold land (freehold and leasehold are explained below). In fact, however, freehold and leasehold interests in land are treated in much the same way and it is usual to refer to leaseholds as "chattels real" to distinguish them from "chattels personal", i.e. other forms of personal property (*see* Fig. 34).

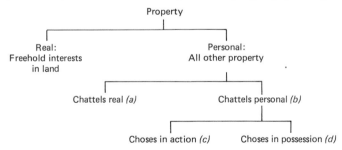

Fig. 34. *Types of property. (a) Leasehold interests in land. The word "chattel" is a linguistic corruption of "cattle", the ownership of which is still regarded as a measure of wealth in some societies. (b) All other personal property: "pure personality". (c) Property which does not physically exist and which consequently cannot be effectively protected by physical means, only by legal action, e.g. patents, copyrights, goodwill of a business. "Chose"—old French legal term for "thing". (d) Property with a physical existence. It can be physically possessed and protected, e.g. this book, clothes.*

These somewhat strange sounding categories are a legacy of the very rigid procedural rules which the common law courts (the Royal courts) developed early in our legal history. If a man's freehold land was wrongfully taken from him, not an infrequent occurrence in those days, he could recover the actual land by bringing a "real" action in the common law courts. If, however, he was dispossessed of anything else it was not possible for him to recover the actual property. He was only entitled to a "personal" action for money compensation against the person who had taken it. The concept of the leasehold interest developed later than the freehold, by which time legal procedure had become so rigid that the "real" action available to a freeholder could not be adapted to a leaseholder's claim. In time, however, a remedy developed which enabled a leaseholder to recover his land if he had been wrongfully dispossessed.

Already you can see that a knowledge of legal history is necessary to fully appreciate our system of land law and, in fact, the concept of ownership as applied to land is still based on ideas dating back to William the Conqueror and the Normans' own particular brand of feudalism! Fortunately, however, the present system can be described and explained in general terms without more than a few passing references to the past. Nevertheless, it is a remarkable fact that it was not until the Law of Property Act 1925 that our system of land law made any real concessions to complex industrial society, and even today land law may be criticised for being unnecessarily old-fashioned and complicated both in principle and practice. Law in practice often seems to presuppose the existence of lawyers and it can be argued that in land law they have created a system which in effect they alone can understand and from which comes a large proportion of their income.

Be this as it may, three main reasons can be put forward to account for land law's complexity.

(*a*) Land is permanent property and therefore a variety of interests, effective at the same time or consecutively, may exist over it. For example, A may "own" Number 1 High Road, but may let it to B who sub-lets to C, each of whom may have mortgaged it to different mortgagees. In addition there may be a variety of rights over the land on which Number 1 High Road stands (*see* below). In contrast, other forms of property, such as goods and shares, are normally the subject of absolute ownership only.

(*b*) History: land law has its origins in feudal society and no major attempt was made to reduce its accumulated complexities until the Law of Property Act 1925.

(*c*) Land is the one finite economic resource and its use is a subject of public concern. Thus, there are a variety of statutes, such as the Town and County Planning Act 1971, by which the State imposes restrictions on a person's use and exploitation of his land.

THE OWNERSHIP OF LAND

Since the Norman Conquest in 1066 all land in England has been theoretically owned by the Crown, and the same has been true of the rest of Great Britain for many centuries. The most that anyone else can own is one of the two legal estates which now exist: a freehold estate or a leasehold estate. An estate is a measure of a person's interest in a particular piece of land in terms of time. In the olden days it was held on a certain tenure, originally the provision of goods or services of some kind, and later the payment of a sum of money. We still have tenancies and rents, of course, but these are very different from the original feudal ideas of tenure which have now almost entirely disappeared.

A legal estate is an abstract idea and is quite separate from the land itself. It can be bought or sold, transferred by gift or by will, without affecting the actual land itself or the possession of it. It is possible, for example, to buy the freehold of a large block of flats without in any way affecting the rights of occupation of the many tenants in the flats.

When the property market is buoyant this divorce of the legal estate from the land itself is one factor which allows large profits to be made from the buying and selling of this purely abstract concept. Some people would argue that this is a quite proper benefit to be gained from the law's recognition of private property rights, while others would argue that this is a reason why land, a fundamental social and economic resource, should be nationalised. They would allow, perhaps, absolute ownership of houses and other buildings built upon it. In such a question political beliefs are all-important.

Freehold land

All land in this country is now held on freehold tenure (free as opposed to unfree in the olden days) which for all practical purposes amounts to absolute ownership. A freeholder may, for example, dispose of his estate to anyone he pleases. Nevertheless, there are important restrictions upon the rights of a freeholder to do as he pleases with his land. At common law the law of torts prevents him from using his land in a way which would cause an actionable nuisance to his neighbours, and his right to develop land is restricted by the Town and Country Planning Acts.

Before 1925 there were a variety of freehold estates which the common law recognised, but since the Law of Property Act 1925 only the "fee simple absolute in possession" is recognised as a legal freehold estate. All the former freehold estates can now only exist as equitable interests in land behind a trust—an arrangement whereby property is held by one person (a trustee) who must use it for the benefit of another (a beneficiary).

The words used in the term "fee simple absolute in possession" have the following meanings.

Fee—an estate of inheritance, i.e. one that may be inherited or which may pass by will.

Simple—the inheritance is not limited to a particular class of the estate owner's heirs, for example males only or the offspring from a particular marriage. (An estate where the inheritance was limited in this way was known as a "fee tail".)

Absolute—not subject to any conditions, as a "life estate" would be for example.

In possession—takes effect immediately. This includes not only the right to immediate possession but also the immediate right to rents and profits where the land is leased to a tenant.

Leasehold land

As you have seen, all land in this country is held on freehold tenure but the estate owner may create from his freehold an estate of limited duration: a leasehold. Technically a leasehold estate is a "term of years absolute", and it is the only other legal estate in land which can exist under the provisions of the Law of Property Act 1925. The words "terms of years" include not only leases for a specific number of years but also those for less than a year or from year to year, although short leases are commonly referred to as tenancies. "Absolute" means that the estate is not subject to any conditions.

To create a legal estate the Law of Property Act 1925 requires a lease for more than three years to be made by deed, but a lease which takes effect in possession (immediately) for a term not exceeding three years at the best rent which can be reasonably obtained may be created orally or in writing.

The essential features of a leasehold estate are that:

(*a*) it gives the right to exclusive possession;

(*b*) it is for a definite term, i.e. the start of the term and its duration are fixed or can be determined (This is the essential distinction between a lease and a freehold for the latter is of unlimited duration.);

(*c*) it creates the relationship of landlord and tenant.

At the end of the lease the land reverts to the freeholder. However the common law position is clearly socially and politically unacceptable, and varying degrees of protection have been given by statute to both domestic and commercial tenancies. A brief summary of the protection given to domestic tenancies is given here and commercial tenancies are considered more fully below.

The Leasehold Reform Act 1967 gives a leaseholder of a house, originally let for twenty-one years or more (a long tenancy) at a low rent and held for at least five years, the right to enforce a sale to him of the freehold in payment of the value of the freehold interest in the site. Alternatively he may ask for a fifty-year extension of the lease. This is known as leasehold enfranchisement. However the Act only applies to houses (not flats) of less than £200 rateable value (£400 in Greater London) as at March 1965.

A tenant under a long tenancy of a flat at a low rent is protected by the Landlord and Tenant Act 1954, and many other tenancies, of both furnished and unfurnished property, are protected by the Rent Acts. However, under these Acts the "statutory tenancy" that the tenant is given only protects the tenant's personal right of occupation, a much lesser right than that acquired under the Leasehold Reform Act 1967. A statutory tenant cannot, for example, pass his tenancy on to someone else, either during his lifetime or by will. In addition, the tenancy will end if the tenant ceases to occupy the premises as his home.

The 1979 Conservative government's Housing Act 1980 covers a "secure tenancy", i.e. that of a dwelling house let as a dwelling by a local authority, or other listed body, to an individual, or individuals jointly, who occupies it as his only or principal home. The Act codifies the rights and protections of a secure tenant, including the right to take in lodgers *without* the consent of the council, the right to sub-let part of the dwelling house *with* the landlord's consent, the right to carry out repairs and make improvements, and the right to be consulted by the landlord concerning matters of housing management.

The codification of these rights is only to be welcomed, but other rights conferred are controversial, to say the least. A secure ("council") tenant of at least three years' standing has the rights:

(*a*) to acquire the freehold (of the house) or a long lease (of the flat); and

(*b*) to a loan secured by a mortgage on the property to assist in its purchase.

This involves either leaving an amount to be paid to the landlord outstanding, or, where the landlord is a housing association, the right to have a loan from the Housing Corporation. Discounts on the property's value of between 33 per cent for a tenant of three years' standing and 50 per cent for a tenant of twenty years or more make these rights together a very attractive financial proposition.

It is most improbable, however, that these rights will long survive any change of government. They clearly seek to further a Conservative aim of a property-owning democracy, but to the Labour Party (and the Liberal/Social Democrat alliance?) they represent a wrongful selling-off of community assets, to the detriment of those who will be in need of public housing in the future. It is certainly likely to be the better houses and flats which will be bought first, and by the better-off tenants. Would you, however, deny somebody the right or chance to own his or her own home?

The 1980 Act introduced a new kind of Rent Act tenancy—a *protected shorthold tenancy*, lasting from one to five years. It is intended to encourage landlords to make property available for letting by allowing them to recover possession at the end of the tenancy if the statutory conditions are met. It also introduced the *assured tenancy* and provides that such a tenancy is not a protected tenancy under the Rent Act 1977, meaning that Rent Act protection and rent limits do not apply. This is intended to encourage certain "approved bodies" (landlords), e.g. housing associations, to build new homes for letting. An assured tenancy can only apply to homes built after the 1980 Act was passed and not occupied by any person as a residence before the tenant's occupation, except under an assured tenancy.

Whether these measures will substantially alleviate the often chronic shortage of decent private rented accommodation in large cities, itself partly an unfortunate (but perhaps inevitable) consequence of giving security of tenure to tenants of private rented accommodation in previous landlord and tenant legislation, remains to be seen. Clearly the 1979 Conservative government has sought to meet demand through the private and not the public sector (*see* also page 5).

Interests in land

Although there are, as you have seen, only two legal estates in land, there are a considerable number of "interests in land", the distinction between an estate and an interest being that the former is a right to the land itself while the latter only gives a right to some claim against the land of another.

Such interests are either legal or equitable. Legal interests are rights against the land itself and are therefore enforceable against the "whole world" but an equitable interest only gives a right against the person who granted it. Therefore, before the property legislation of 1925, a purchaser of a piece of land was bound by any legal interests which existed over it but was not bound by equitable interests unless he knew of them. If he did it was considered unfair for him to be allowed to disregard them.

A national system for the registration of many of the possible interests in land was established by the Land Charges Act 1925 (now replaced by the Land Charges Act 1972), and the old rules about notice no longer apply to registrable interests. Protection of such an interest now depends solely on its registration. The system applies mainly to equitable interests—these are the more vulnerable of the two types—but some important legal interests are also registrable, e.g. a legal mortgage of unregistered land (*see* below) which is not supported by a deposit of the title deeds with the mortgagee. Technically this is known as a puisne (pronounced "puny", meaning "lesser") mortgage and is a common security taken by a bank for an overdraft.

The most important legal interests are: easements (a bare right over the land of another), e.g. a right of way; profits (the right to take something from the land of another), e.g. fishing or shooting rights; a right of entry held by a landlord in respect of a lease, e.g. to inspect the property or to effect repairs; and legal mortgages.

The 1925 property legislation converted all the old legal estates and interests, except the "fee simple absolute in possession" and the "term of years absolute", into equitable interests and hence there is quite a variety of them, e.g. life tenancies and future freehold interests. The latter cannot be legal estates despite their freehold nature because they are not "in possession" as required by the Law of Property Act 1925. Equitable interests of this nature must be created behind a trust, but there are others, e.g. a restrictive covenant, which need not. A restrictive covenant is an agreement whereby one person promises to restrict the use of his land for the benefit of another's adjoining land. A typical covenant is that land shall not be used for the purpose of trade. If the covenant is registered it will bind any subsequent purchaser of that piece of land.

TITLE TO LAND AND ITS TRANSFER

Land, or more correctly, estates in land, can be bought and sold by contract in the same basic way as any other type of property. However, due to the way that our land law has developed and the miscellaneous interests which can exist over it, considerable formality and complexity is often encountered in the transaction.

Proof of title to land is evidenced in one of two ways, depending upon whether title to it is unregistered or registered. If the former, title is proved by a collection of deeds and documents (the title deeds) which show a good chain of title dating back fifteen years and concluding with the right of the present owner. If the latter, proof of title is an entry on the register at the appropriate Land Registry, as evidenced by a land certificate. A registered title is guaranteed by the state. The system of land registration now covers most of the country and with time unregistered land will become rare. As you can imagine, the system of registration of title greatly simplifies the whole process of proof of title and its transfer.

Title to unregistered land is transferred by an appropriately drafted deed of conveyance in the case of freehold land and by a deed of assignment in the case of leasehold land. Title to registered land is transferred by a short simple Land Registry form. The transaction is, however, in two stages. Firstly, the contract of sale which binds the parties to the transaction but does not actually transfer title to the land. (By s.40 of the Law of Property Act 1925, the contract must be in writing or evidenced in writing; in practice the buyer and seller each sign a copy of the contract which are then exchanged.) Secondly, the transfer of the legal estate in return for the balance of the purchase price (the completion). This must be by deed (a document which is signed, sealed and delivered) and usually takes place one month after contracts have been exchanged.

RESTRICTIONS ON THE USE OF LAND

There is an old saying that an "Englishman's home is his castle". Sociologically this may be true in so far as it reflects primitive territorial instincts, and legally it is true in that the protection of private property rights has always been a fundamental principle of the common law, but today a variety of direct legal restrictions are placed upon a man's use of his land. These may be grouped under three headings:

(a) restrictions imposed and enforced by the common law (the basic judge-made law which originated in custom);

(b) restrictions enforceable in equity (the body of rules which originated in the jurisdiction of the Lord Chancellor and the Court of Chancery);

(c) restrictions imposed by the state through government policy in the form of legislation.

Restrictions at common law

These may be further subdivided into those which result from an agreement and those which do not.

Restrictions arising from agreement

You have seen that title to land is transferred by deed and it may be that the purchaser of the freehold estate will make a covenant (a promise contained in a deed) not to use the land for a particular purpose. Similarly, on the grant of a lease, the lessee (the tenant) may accept restrictions on the use of the property, e.g. not to use it other than as a dwelling house. Reinforcement of existing covenants or imposition of further restrictions, e.g. not to grant leases without the mortgagee's (the lender's) consent, are usually to be found in mortgages.

Other restrictions

An important branch of the common law is the Law of Torts. A tort may be defined as a legal wrong against an individual which gives a right of action at civil law for damages (*see* Chapter 24).

The modern law of torts restricts a person's or an organisation's use of its land in three ways; firstly by the tort of trespass. You saw in *Kelsen* v. *Imperial Tobacco Co. Ltd* (1957) that it is possible to trespass in the airspace above a person's land, and a person or organisation must be sure that any structure on their land does not encroach on to adjoining land, either on the surface, or above or below it. The two other restrictions are imposed by the tort of nuisance and the rule in *Rylands* v. *Fletcher* (1865)—a development from the tort of nuisance. These are more important in practice.

Nuisance is usually defined as "an unlawful interference with a person's use or enjoyment of land or some right over, or in connection with it" (Professor Winfield), the essence of the action being, in the words of Lord Denning, the Master of the Rolls and head of the Court of Appeal (Civil Division), in *Miller* v. *Jackson & Another* (1977) (discussed below), "the unreasonable use by a man of his land to the detriment of his neighbour". Hence, in *Bland* v. *Yates* (1914) a landowner was liable for an unusual and excessive collection of manure which attracted flies and caused a smell, and in *Nicholls* v. *Ely Beet Sugar Factory Ltd* (1936) the defendant was liable for the interference with fishing rights caused by discharging factory waste into a river. Therefore any organisation must bear in mind the rights of neighbouring landowners. Ironically it is not so much large manufacturing organisations which may transgress the law in this respect—their activities are mainly confined to industrial estates where the law allows activities which would not be permissible elsewhere—but small units operating in predominantly residential areas, e.g. smells or heat from restaurants, fumes from dry-cleaners or noise from industrial out-working. In the London garment industry, for example, a considerable amount of production is in out-working homes.

From these examples you can see that the restrictions imposed on land use are not purely legal matters but encompass general environmental issues. A somewhat unusual case which illustrates these wider issues, albeit in a humble setting, is *Miller* v. *Jackson & Another* (1977). Mr Miller was a "newcomer" to the village of Burnopfield in Yorkshire. He bought a house on a new estate adjoining a cricket ground which had been used for the last seventy years by the village cricket club. He brought an action for damages for the interference with his use and enjoyment of his property caused by balls being hit for six on to his property, and for an injunction (a Court order) to prohibit cricket being played on the ground in the future. In the event an actionable nuisance was proved and damages were awarded. However an injunction was not granted and the village club was able to continue as before.

The case itself is perhaps the unfortunate consequences of, and least important issue involved in, a much wider problem. The village community had been disturbed by the planners and developers whose motives and interests were rather different from those of the villagers. The newcomers felt their property interests threatened by the village cricket club and the villagers felt their longstanding leisure activities threatened by the newcomers. Once created, such tension in a small community is slow to disappear. Even though damages were awarded but an injunction withheld—arguably a compromise—the law was still patently inadequate in solving the problem. Nor could it be expected to, for it had been presented with a clash of interests to which there was no real solution available to the Court. The situation was the work of neither the newcomers nor the villagers; the relevant decisions had been made elsewhere and it was arguably these which should have been on trial.

To an economist the case illustrates the economic truism that the value of land is largely dictated by the uses to which it can be put and the nature of the neighbouring land uses. The value of structures upon land is not merely a reflection of initial building costs. While the playing of cricket might not decrease the value of adjoining property, a less pleasant land use probably would.

So far we have considered the tort of nuisance in relation to individuals, but where it affects the public in general it may be the subject of criminal proceedings (a public nuisance) and some important examples are now the subject of legislation, e.g. the Clean Air Act 1956 and the Noise Abatement Act 1960.

The essence of the rule in *Rylands* v. *Fletcher* (1865) is that a landowner is strictly liable, i.e. whether at fault or not, for damage caused by the escape of "dangerous things", likely to do harm, which he brought or artificially stored on his land. The case itself concerned the escape of water from a reservoir.

"Non-natural use" of the land is an alternative but complementary explanation of the principle. This reasoning reconciles economic activity with the accumulation of "dangerous things", for the land use of the area is a major factor in determining liability under the rule. The criteria to be applied are perhaps "unreasonable risk to the community" and "public policy". In practice the rule is seldom invoked, for disasters of the magnitude of the Flixborough explosion some years ago are normally settled out of court (was it "non-natural use" anyway?), and lesser damage, potentially within the rule, is usually the subject of insurance claims.

Restrictions in equity
You have seen earlier in this chapter that a restrictive covenant is an equitable interest in land which restricts the use of the land of another. The concept originated purely as an agreement between the parties to the transfer of the legal estate of a particular parcel of land and enforcement of the covenant against subsequent purchasers of the land depended upon notice of it. However, since the late nineteenth century restrictive covenants have been considered as rights existing over one piece of land (the servient tenement) for the benefit of another piece of land (the dominant tenement). Thus they can now only be enforced against a purchaser of the land to which the covenant applies by a person who occupies land that benefits from the covenant. Additionally, it is a cardinal rule that a restrictive covenant will only be enforced if it is negative in nature. Any covenant which entails expense to perform properly is not negative, e.g. a covenant prohibiting industrial use is negative, but a covenant not to let premises get into disrepair is essentially positive, despite its wording. Restrictive covenants are far more likely to affect domestic land use or small business units than large organisations, the latter mainly having to concern themselves with statutory planning control. Indeed, state intervention in land use has reduced the importance of restrictive covenants because the amenities of an area may now be preserved by statute, and there may be little incentive to enforce private covenants. However the statutory system complements rather than supersedes them. Covenants entitle a landowner to take direct action to protect his interests rather than having to rely on his planning authority, and they can cover far more particular restraints than the more general curbs imposed by legislation. Clearly, organisations must ensure that they infringe neither the private system of restrictive covenants nor the

public system of planning control in any of their activities. It is to the public system of planning control that we now turn.

Restrictions imposed by the state

State planning controls do not affect the ownership of estates or interests in land, only the use and enjoyment of land. In this way the often opposing interests of the individual and the state are reconciled. Such controls are necessary for there are ample legacies of unplanned or ineffectively controlled urban development in most large cities. Sometimes entire developments appear as environmental scars on the landscape: Peacehaven, a speculative development right on the south coast, is commonly considered a prime example.

In the past under the common law any landowner could develop his land as he wished, provided he did not infringe his neighbour's common law rights (*see* above). The nineteenth-century *laissez-faire* philosophy in government, law and economics was conducive to speculative and profit-oriented development, and while there are important examples of social consciousness in urban and industrial development, e.g. Robert Owen's development at New Lanark, the concept of planned development essentially belongs to the twentieth century. Since the middle of this century the state has attempted to play an active role in planning, for land is now considered a far too scarce and valuable natural resource to be left purely in the hands of private interests.

The present statutory controls are to be found in the Town and Country Planning Acts 1971–4, under which local planning authorities are responsible for the routine administration and the Department of the Environment for overall control of the system of regulation. The Local Government, Planning and Land Act 1980 shifted some planning functions from county to district council level, e.g. applications for planning permission. The essence of planning legislation is *development*, defined by the 1971 Act as building, engineering, mining or other operation in, on, over or under the land, or any material change in the use of any building or other land.

Under the legislation the applicant must obtain planning permission to develop land from the local planning authority or from the Secretary of State for the Environment on appeal, having first notified his intentions to those owning interests in the property and advertised his application where the proposed development is likely to offend his neighbours. These provisions enable objections to the application to be lodged. Each local planning authority maintains a register of applications and their results. In 1981 a scale of fees was introduced for planning applications in an attempt by the government to recover some development control costs. Any individual or organisation contemplating the purchase of land in an area likely to be the subject of a development application should check the register before going ahead with the purchase.

A specific control directly relevant to organisations is that industrial development usually requires an Industrial Development Certificate before planning permission can be applied for. (Recent developments are discussed later in this chapter.) Such control is necessary if regional imbalance in the level and type of economic activity, with its attendant social problems, is to be ameliorated. Enforcement and stop notices, backed by possible criminal proceedings, are issued if development is carried out without the required permission.

In addition, there are a variety of other controls under the Town and Country Planning Acts, including: tree preservation orders, preventing the cutting of trees; regulation of advertising on land; and "listing" of buildings of special or historical interest, preventing their alteration or demolition. An interesting example of this last restriction, also illustrating the possible financial consequences of a preservation order, is *Amalgamated Investment* v. *John Walker & Sons Ltd* (1976). The parties had made a contract for the sale of land near the Thames on which stood a disused warehouse. The purchasers intended to redevelop the site for office use and had obtained an Office Development Permit (since abolished) to this end. The vendors were aware of this. Unknown to either party, a civil servant in the Department of the Environment had already decided to add the warehouse, somewhat arbitrarily as it happened, to a list of protected buildings which would prevent the proposed redevelopment. The building was actually listed the day after the contract was made. On the facts there were no grounds on which to set the contract aside even though the property as a protected building was only worth £200,000 while the contract price was £1,500,000! An amendment to the Town and Country Planning Act 1971 by the Local Government, Planning and Land Act 1980 enables an application to be made to the Secretary of State for a certificate guaranteeing that no listing will occur within a five year period when planning permission has already been granted for the extension, alteration or demolition of an existing building.

The development of land is also subject to other statutory controls designed to ensure that minimum standards of design and construction are adhered to. The Public Health Acts 1936–69 enable the Secretary of State for the Environment to make bye-laws regulating such matters as the construction, materials, sanitation and size of rooms of new buildings. The Health and Safety at Work, etc., Act 1974 (considered in more detail below) indirectly affects development by enacting regulations designed to maintain and improve existing standards of health, safety and welfare at work.

In the mid-1970s the then Labour government passed the Community Land Act 1975 and the Development Land Tax Act 1976. These introduced a new and more far-reaching form of government intervention in planning and development in general. The objectives, at least partly determined by political philosophy, were:

(a) to replace the existing "negative" approach to planning by a positive one in which the local authority rather than the traditional developer was to be the initiator; and

(b) to enable the local authority to benefit from the increase in land value which flowed from the granting of planning permission.

The aim of the legislation was to enable the community to control the development of land in accordance with its needs and priorities, and to restore to the community the increase in value of land arising from its efforts.

The subsequent Conservative government's Local Government, Planning and Land Act 1980 repealed the Community Land Act in an apparent attempt to delay the erosion of private land-ownership. It in fact created a new machinery for forcing public bodies to sell unused, or insufficiently used, land to the private sector on specified terms of sale. In these respects it is exactly opposite in its objectives to the Community Land Act 1975 for under it local authorities were eventually to be under an obligation to buy development land, using their powers of compulsory purchase if necessary. The 1980 Act also secured the surplus resources of the new town corporations for the benefit of the Treasury.

The Development Land Tax Act 1976 provides for a tax to be levied on the difference between the sum paid for development land and a figure based on its original purchase price or "current use value". In its original form the maximum rate levied was to be 80 per cent, and, indeed, local authorities were eventually to pay only the "current use value" for the land, i.e. a development land tax of 100 per cent. There is now, however, a fixed rate of tax of 60 per cent, with the first £50,000 of development value exempt. Charities and urban development corporations have total exemption and the tax on developments for the owner's own industrial use, begun before 1 April 1983, will be deferred until the property is sold or otherwise disposed of. In addition, development land tax is currently not charged on the disposal of land within an enterprise zone, provided the disposal takes place within ten years of the designation of the zone. Any existing building may be enlarged by up to one third of its existing cubic content without this constituting material development for development land tax purposes.

So, although development land tax survived a change in government, it is now being used in some respects to return resources to private enterprise, a very different purpose to that envisaged by the Labour government which introduced it in 1976.

A completely different form of restriction on land use is the activity of pressure groups (considered more fully in Chapter 26). The environmentalist lobby is becoming increasingly more vociferous and effective, and individual groups of protesters have scored resounding successes, both in persuading local authorities or the government to significantly change their plans and, in some cases, in preventing development altogether, the success of the opposition to plans to build the third London airport at either Wing in Buckinghamshire or Maplin in Essex being notable examples in recent years. Battle lines are currently drawn at Stanstead in Essex over the same issue. An interesting sociological fact is that it is usually what can be described as "middle class interests" which are most successfully protected, the simple reason being that "middle class" protesters have both the financial means and the necessary expertise to fight the "system".

Restrictions have been placed upon the use of land for centuries but, as you have seen, it was not until the second half of this century that the intervention of the government became the overriding influence on land use and development. For better or for worse we live in an era in which the state actively intervenes in most facets of the country's socio-economic structure.

Organisations are mainly concerned with statutory restrictions on land use and clearly these are here to stay, the only real argument being the extent to which these restrictions and the methods are employed. Land is a finite resource and while some may protest at the limits placed on private rights, it seems reasonable to argue that the socio-economic consequences of unplanned development or excessive private gain justify putting the community first.

FACTORS INFLUENCING THE ORGANISATION'S USE OF LAND

The location of industry

Land is not a homogeneous commodity. It differs greatly in its contents and its position. There are, therefore, many factors which affect the attractiveness of a site to an organisation. These are examined below in two groups: those occurring spontaneously in the economy; and those engineered by the government. We might imagine that organisations weigh all the possible advantages and disadvantages carefully and site their business so as to minimise their costs. It is doubtful whether this is ever really so. Historical accident might play a big part in location. For example, William Morris started car manufacture in Oxford because that is where his cycle shop was. Equally businessmen tend to be gregarious and will often site their organisation where there are lots of others. However, no-one will begin a business or site a new factory without considering some of the following factors.

Non-government influences upon site value.

(a) *Raw materials.* Extractive industries must locate where the raw materials are, and this may in turn attract other industries, e.g. the iron and steel industry being attracted to coalfields. Engineering industries were then often attracted to the same location. Thus, around Glasgow there is the Lanark coalfield, an iron and steel industry and shipbuilding. Today, when many raw materials are imported, industries frequently locate at ports.

(b) *Power.* The woollen industry moved to the West Riding of Yorkshire to utilise the water power from Pennine streams. In the nineteenth century most industries were dependent upon coal as a source of power. Since coal was expensive to transport, they tended to locate on coalfields. Today, most industries use electricity, which is readily available anywhere in the country. This means that the availability of power is not an important locational influence today. An exception to this is the aluminium smelting industry which uses vast quantities of electric power. The industry is therefore centred on countries where there is lots of cheap hydro-electric power, such as Canada and Norway. Recently the aluminium smelter which was constructed at Invergordon to utilize the power generated by the North of Scotland Hydro-Electricity Board.

(c) *Transport.* Historically transport was a vital locational influence. Water transport was the only cheap and reliable means of transporting heavy loads. Most industries, therefore, tended to locate near rivers or the coast. Canals and later railways allowed industry to spread to other locations. Today access to good transport facilities is still a locational influence. This is illustrated by the town of Warrington in Cheshire, which has experienced a renaissance in its industrial fortunes partly as a result of standing at the intersection of three main motorways.

Max Weber, a famous economic historian and sociologist, developed a theory on the location of industry. Weber maintained that industrialists would try to minimise their transport costs. This

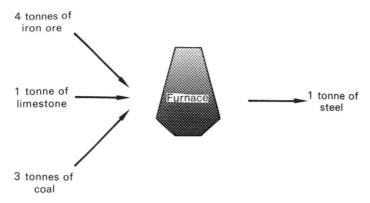

Fig. 35. *Weight loss.*

means that if a commodity *lost weight* during manufacture the industry would tend to locate near to the raw materials, whereas if it *gained weight* during manufacture it would tend to locate near to the market. Steel is an example of a commodity which loses weight during manufacture. To manufacture steel near to the market would mean transporting several tonnes of raw materials but only selling one tonne of finished product. This is illustrated in Fig. 35. Brewing is an industry in which the product gains weight during manufacture. It is therefore more economical to transport the hops, barley and sugar to near the market, where water is added and the brewing takes place. Traditionally, brewing was a widely dispersed industry although in recent years it has become more centralised. Weber's theory is modified by the value of the commodity. Whisky, for example, is so expensive that transport costs are only a small percentage of the price and are therefore not a locational influence.

(*d*) *Markets.* Service industries such as catering, entertainment and professional services have nearly always had to locate near their markets. In the twentieth century many more industries have located with respect to markets so that today it is one of the most important locational forces. Goods which are fragile and expensive to transport, such as furniture and electrical goods, are better produced near where they are to be sold. The ring of consumer-goods industries around London is adequate testimony to the power of the market.

(*e*) *Labour.* It might be thought that the availability of cheap labour would be an important locational influence. It does not appear to be so. The existence of a pool of highly skilled labour may be a locational influence but increasingly manual skills can be replaced by automated machinery. An exception to this may be "footloose" industries. These are industries which are not dependent upon other specific locational influences and are therefore attracted to cheap labour. An example of this is electronic component assembly, but organisations in this field have tended to locate in the suburbs to utilise cheap female labour rather than moving to areas of heavy unemployment.

(*f*) *Industrial inertia.* This is the tendency of an industry to continue to locate itself in an area when the factors which originally located the industry there have ceased to operate. An example of this would be the steel industry in Sheffield, although this may be partly explained by external economies of scale and the existence of skilled labour.

(*g*) *Special local circumstances.* Such things as climate or topography may affect the location of an industry. The oil terminal at Milford Haven is located there because of the deep-water anchorage available. A further example is provided by the market gardening industry in the Scilly Isles, located there to take advantage of the early spring.

Governmental influences on the location of industry

The old staple industries, such as iron and steel, shipbuilding and coalmining, have been in decline for most of this century. These tended to be heavily concentrated in the coalmining areas. The operation of free market economics seemed powerless to alleviate the economic distress of these areas. This has meant that since the 1930s the government has brought in more and more measures to try to attract industry to these areas. There are today so many legislative controls and financial inducements that the government must be considered the most important locational influence upon industry. It is possible to identify four main ways in which the government tries to influence the location of industry.

(*a*) *Financial incentives.* Financial incentives to encourage organisations to move to depressed areas have existed since the Special Areas Act of 1934. The Distribution of Industry Acts of 1945 and 1950 established *development areas* to replace the special areas and made Treasury assistance available for firms establishing there.

The present policy is based mainly upon the Industry Act of 1972. This designated three types of area which would be given assistance. These areas are termed special development areas (SDAs), development areas (DAs) and intermediate areas (IAs), to which may be added Northern Ireland. Collectively these areas are termed by the Department of Industry the "areas for expansion". The geographical definition of these areas (excluding N. Ireland)

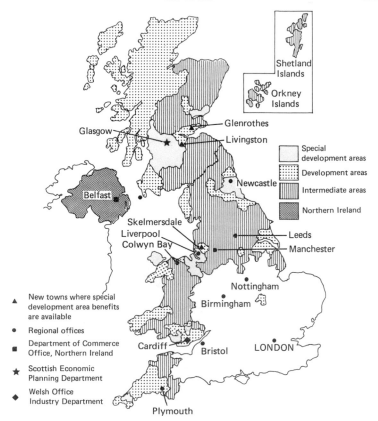

Fig. 36. *Government aid to the regions (the Isles of Scilly are a development area). Reproduced by permission of the Department of Industry.*

was changed in July 1979, when there was a general reduction in their size. Figure 36 shows the areas as they were at August 1980. The areas for expansion are to be further reduced by August 1982, these proposals being shown in Fig. 37. The reason for the reduction in the size of the areas for expansion was the government's desire to curtail public expenditure. The areas of the country which do not have any development status are referred to as non-assisted areas (NAAs).

A new development in 1980 was the introduction of *enterprise zones.* These are small areas of inner cities. By early 1982 eleven such zones had been designated:

1. Clydebank and Glasgow;
2. Belfast;

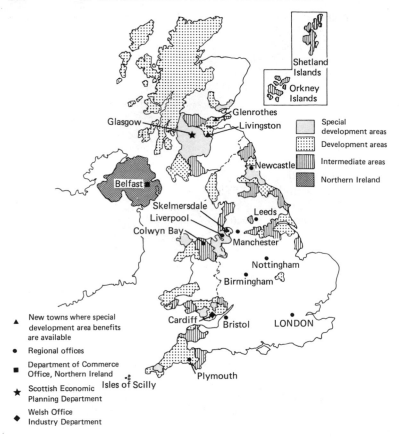

Fig. 37. *Proposals for aid to the regions, to come into effect in August 1982* (*subject to review*). (*The Isles of Scilly are a development area.*) *Reproduced by permission of the Department of Industry.*

   3. Newcastle and Gateshead;
   4. Hartlepool;
   5. Wakefield;
   6. Salford and Trafford;
   7. Speke;
   8. Dudley;
   9. Corby;
  10. Swansea;
  11. Isle of Dogs.

The average size of an enterprise zone is approximately 150 hectares.

Financial assistance is available to firms *moving into* the areas for expansion. Regional development grants (RDGs) of 22 per cent, in SDAs, and 15 per cent, in DAs, of the cost of new buildings and machinery are available. Regional selective assistance (RSA), usually in the form of a grant, is also available where projects would provide or safeguard jobs. RSA can also take the form of rent-free workshops and factories. Assistance for Northern Ireland is more generous and includes industrial development grants of 30 per cent and 50 per cent of the cost of new buildings and machinery. Financial incentives for intermediate areas were drastically reduced in July 1979. Firms setting up in enterprise zones, however, get a stream of incentives: no rates; 100 per cent capital allowances on all commercial and industrial property; no liability for development land tax; and generally less bureaucracy and fewer planning regulations. Investment assistance is available nationwide from the National Research Development Corporation, the National Enterprise Board and the European Investment Bank. There is also another type of area which may qualify for assistance and that is *derelict land and clearance areas.*

[*b*] *Legislative controls.* The government can influence the location of industry by the negative method of forbidding or discouraging new building where it does not want it.

The Town and Country Planning Act of 1947 required that all factory building in excess of 5,000 square feet (464.5 m^2) needed approval in the form of an industrial development certificate (IDC). The Office Development Act of 1965 applied similar controls to office building. After the 1974 Act (*see* page 206) the 5,000 square foot rule applied only to the South East Planning Region; in other non-assisted areas it was 10,000 sq ft (929 m^2) and in intermediate areas it was 15,000 sq ft (1,393.5 m^2). However, in 1979 the controls were significantly relaxed. The area of industrial space which could be created without an IDC was increased to 50,000 square feet (4645 m^2) and the need for an IDC in any of the Areas of Expansion was removed. In December 1981 the government suspended the regulations requiring organisations to obtain an IDC before development, in effect abolishing them. Similarly, all the provisions of the Town and Country Planning Act 1971 relating to the control of office development have been removed. These changes were partly due to the government's desire to reduce the role of government intervention in the economy and partly due to the need to facilitate development of all kinds in an effort to alleviate unemployment.

(*c*) *Direct intervention.* The government can place orders for goods and services in development areas or encourage nationalised industries to do so. In addition to this it could decentralise government developments such as it did when the Inland Revenue administration was moved to Middlesbrough. The Distribution of Industry Acts of 1945 and 1950 allowed the government to build factories in development areas and lease or sell them. Today the government may lease a factory to an organisation for two years, rent free, if it creates enough jobs (*see* above).

The New Towns Act 1946 and the *Town Development Act* 1952 brought a number of new towns into existence, the first of which was Stevenage in Hertfordshire. In August 1981 the government decided to curtail the activities of new towns and eight of the new town corporations were to dispose of £140m. of their assets (*see* page 208).

(*d*) *Persuasion.* Information about the regions is provided both centrally and regionally. *The Local Employment Act* of 1960 set up development councils in depressed regions. However, in 1965 the whole of the UK was covered by eleven regional economic planning councils. Each of these is responsible for devising an economic strategy for its region and for publicising opportunities in the region. Adverts placed by regional planning councils and by new town corporations are a familiar sight in our newspapers. The Department of Industry provides information and advice both from its headquarters in London and from its regional offices (*see* Fig. 36).

The effectiveness of government policy on the location of industry

There is little evidence to show that government policy had much success up until 1963. Since that date there has been a more aggressive regional policy. The discrepancies between regional rates of unemployment and the national rate have generally narrowed. This, however, is complicated by the overall rise in unemployment during the 1970s and 1980s.

There is also evidence to show that employment has been "diverted" from the Midlands and the South East to the development areas. However, large disparities still exist between incomes per head in the South East and those in the development areas. It is too early to evaluate the effect of enterprise zones, but in some cases they have had spectacular effects upon property values if not upon employment.

The costs and benefits of regional policy

In the financial year 1981–2 the government spent £4.9 billion on industrial and employment policies. However a large part of this was taken up with job creation schemes which, although heavily concentrated in the regions, were available nationwide. It is difficult to estimate the cost to the government of creating genuine jobs in the regions. A government inquiry in 1977 into the building of two petrochemical plants in Scotland revealed a cost to the government of £1 million per permanent job created. The De Lorean car plant in Northern Ireland had by 1982 cost the government £74 million and had created 2,500 jobs, thus giving a cost of approximately £30,000 for each job created. This is a wide variation, but both schemes seem costly. The reason for this is that government policy so far has tended to create capital intensive schemes rather than labour intensive ones. The government has stated that it wishes to stimulate more small firms but the owners of such firms frequently complain that the "red-tape" surrounding regional aid often prevents them from obtaining assistance.

Against the financial cost to the government of the creation of employment we must set social security benefits which will not have to be paid out, the income tax which the workers will pay and the extra jobs that are created via the employment multiplier (*see* page 489).

The most important criticism of regional policy is that it creates inefficient units of production. For example, Chrysler (now Talbot) were persuaded by the government to build a new factory at Linwood outside Glasgow rather than in Coventry where they would have preferred to build it. Car engines were made in Coventry, transported to Scotland to be put into car bodies and then transported south again to be sold. The closure of the Talbot Linwood plant in 1981 requires little further comment. Whilst the creation of inefficient plants may be tolerated within the economy as a way of coping with unemployment it has very bad consequences for our external trade because it destroys our comparative advantage (*see* page 398).

However, if we look at regional policy in the context of the whole economy there are several points to be borne in mind. Firstly, although organisations might choose to locate in the South East, they often ignore the very high social costs in these areas. Housing, for example, is in very short supply in the South East and is consequently extremely expensive, whilst elsewhere in the country houses stand empty. Furthermore, as aid is put into the regions it should regenerate the areas to such an extent that their recovery becomes self-sustaining. The lessons of the 1930s also teach us that there is a great danger in concentration. Diversification is a good safeguard against changes in demand, even if it is slightly less efficient.

OCCUPANCY OF LAND AND ITS RESPONSIBILITIES

An occupier or owner of land or premises owes important duties to anyone who comes on to his land: to visitors, under the Occupiers' Liability Act 1957; to trespassers, under a common law principle evolved by the House of Lords in "Herrington's Case"; and to employees, primarily under the Health and Safety at Work, etc., Act 1974.

Responsibilities to visitors

The Occupiers' Liability Act 1957 enacted that an occupant of land or premises owes a *common duty of care* to all his visitors. Premises are defined as including "any fixed or movable structure, including any vessel, vehicle or aircraft" and not just land and buildings. A visitor is anyone who enters on land with permission, and the common duty of care is defined in s.2(2) as ". . . a duty to take such care as in all the circumstances of the case is reasonable to see that the visitor will be reasonably safe in using the premises for the purposes for which he is invited or permitted to be there."

The meaning of an *occupier* under the Act has been interpreted as being the person in *control* of the structure. Therefore, an owner out of possession is not generally liable if the premises are occupied by someone else. However, exclusive possession is not necessary to establish *control*. This was illustrated in *Wheat* v. *Lacon & Co. Ltd* (1966), where the manager of the defendant's public house in Great Yarmouth was allowed to take paying guests in the upper part of the premises occupied by himself and his wife. This part was quite separate from the licensed premises. A guest was injured on the staircase leading to the upper floor. The facts posed the Court with an interesting problem. Physically the defendants did not *occupy* the upper part, but the whole premises were theirs and public policy would be best served by making them responsible for it all. Although, on the facts, it was decided that the common duty of care had not been broken, the defendants were held to have enough residuary control of the upper floor, particularly as it was occupied by a manager and not a tenant, for them to be occupiers within the meaning of the Act. As a result of this interpretation, organisations cannot escape the responsibilities of occupancy merely because they are not in actual physical occupation and control of the premises. The public interest is clearly best served by this.

If an organisation employs an independent contractor to undertake work on the premises, the organisation, as occupier, is not liable for any injury caused to visitors by the independent contractor's shoddy work, providing the organisation exercised reasonable care in choosing the contractor and checked the work (if that was possible) after it was finished.

In relation to the common duty of care, the Act provides that an occupier can expect children to be less careful than adults (therefore extra care is required), and a person to be aware of dangers normally associated with his work. An electrical contractor, for example, called in to repair faulty equipment, is expected to realise the dangers of and to take his own precautions against electric shocks and other injuries from the defective equipment.

Whenever an individual or organisation is in a position of potential legal liability, there is a natural tendency to try to limit, or preferably exclude, that liability altogether. This has been true of liability under the Act. Until recently it was possible for the occupier and visitor to make a contract which limited the former's liability under the Act for any kind of injury. In addition, it was possible to employ the simpler expedient of displaying a notice restricting or more usually excluding liability. (A straightforward warning notice, indicating danger, is just one *possible* way of satisfying the common duty of care.) Since the Unfair Contract Terms Act 1977, a person cannot by contract or by notice exclude or restrict his liability under the 1957 Act for death or personal injury arising from negligence in connection with the occupancy of premises used for the *business purposes* of the occupier. An exclusion of liability for other loss or damage must satisfy the requirement of reasonableness.

This important provision clearly strengthens an individual's rights against organisations without unjustly imposing a burden upon them. Any actual liability of this kind is almost invariably met through an insurance claim, and as insurance premiums are related to claims made, the financial burden is spread amongst the business community in general.

Very often organisations will lease or sub-let office or other commercial space on terms entitling their tenant to permit other people to enter and use the leased premises. The lease will usually limit the organisation's responsibilities towards the tenant under the Act. This is reasonable, as both the landlord and tenant have roughly equal bargaining power, but what, however, is the position of the organisation towards its tenant's visitors? Under the 1957 Act, the organisation cannot reduce its obligations to visitors who are not parties to the contract (the lease) to a level below that of the common duty of care. This is particularly applicable to common staircases, lifts and passages.

Under the Defective Premises Act 1972, a landlord under an obligation to repair or maintain the premises let owes a duty to all persons who might reasonably be expected to be affected by defects in the state of the premises, to take reasonable steps to ensure that such persons and their property are reasonably safe.

Responsibilities to trespassers

An occupier of premises, whether used for business purposes or otherwise, clearly cannot be expected to owe the same standard of care to a person who should not be there in the first place as he owes to a visitor. A trespasser must generally take the land or premises as he finds them.

Limited protection is afforded to trespassers under the House of Lords decision in *British Railways Board* v. *Herrington* (1972). It was decided by the Law Lords that where an occupier knows that there are trespassers on his land, or knows of circumstances which makes it very likely that trespassers might come on to his land, he owes a duty, assessed in terms of common sense and common humanity, to take reasonable steps to enable a trespasser to avoid dangers on his land of which he was aware but of which the trespasser was not.

In the actual case the British Railways Board were liable for injuries sustained by a six-year-old boy when he wandered through a gap in the guard fence and on to the live rail. The Board were aware both of the gap in the fence and of the frequent presence of children in the immediate vicinity of the gap.

Responsibilities to employees

Great Britain was the cradle of the industrial revolution, and it is all too easy to allow the technological and industrial achievements to obscure the harsh realities of working conditions in those not so distant days. A fourteen-hour day was commonplace and conditions were quite simply appalling. The social cost to the ordinary man of Great Britain's emergence as the world's foremost industrial nation in the nineteenth century was extremely high. Even today coalminers can justify their relatively high wages by the fearful conditions and accident rate that they still have to endure.

Over the years social consciousness about the plight of the usually exploited worker grew and with it began to develop the concept of the employer's responsibility to provide a minimum standard in working conditions for his employees. Today we largely take such ideas for granted, and via a whole range of statutes we have come a long way from the Factories Acts of 1802 and 1819, and the Coal Mines Act 1842, to the Health and Safety at Work, etc., Act 1974. The Acts of 1802 and 1819 forbad the employment of *children under nine* in cotton mills, and limited working hours to *twelve a day* for persons *under sixteen*; the 1842 Act prevented *women and girls and boys under ten* being employed underground. Fortunately, this is history to us and it is perhaps just as well that the physical strain, squalor and degradation endured by the early industrial worker is virtually unimaginable.

The Health and Safety at Work, etc., Act 1974 is the latest landmark in the evolution of the responsibilities owed by an employer/occupier to employees. At present the greater part of the previous relevant legislation, and subsidiary regulations made under it, remains in force but repeal, amendment, revision and updating by regulations made by the Secretary of State for Employment, under the enabling powers contained in the Act, will eventually see the effective disappearance of previous landmarks in health and safety at work legislation. Two such examples are The Factories Act 1961 and The Offices, Shops and Railway Premises Act 1963. The major requirement of the former is that dangerous parts of machinery must be securely fenced. The latter contains general requirements relating to cleanliness, overcrowding, heating, ventilation and lighting, the occupier of premises being responsible for ensuring that the Act is obeyed. However, the owner will be liable for those parts of the premises covered by the Act but not included in the occupier's leases, e.g. stairways. The 1963 Act does not apply, among other places, to premises where self-employed persons work.

Besides the subject matter inherent in the short title of the 1974 Act, the "etc." covers other aims such as protecting people from risks created by people at work, controlling dangerous substances and preventing their unlawful acquisition and use, and controlling the escape of fumes into the atmosphere.

The Act lays down a number of general duties with which employers, employees, controllers of premises and designers, manufacturers, importers and suppliers of articles for use at work must comply. It is an offence punishable by a maximum penalty of £400 fine to fail to discharge these duties. However, there is no civil liability under the Act for breach of the general duties. After consultation with the Health and Safety Commission (one of two corporate bodies established by the Act), the Secretary of State has power to make Health and Safety Regulations to achieve the Act's objectives. These may repeal, modify or give exemption from existing statutory provisions and may exclude or modify the general duties. Civil liability exists for breach of those health and safety regulations.

The five general duties are as follows.

(*a*) It is an employer's duty to ensure so far as is reasonably practicable the health, safety and welfare at work of all his employees. For example, the provision and maintenance of plant and systems of work that are safe and without risks to health, and, more generally, the provision of a working environment that is without risks to health.

(*b*) It is an employer's duty to conduct his undertaking in such a way that so far as is reasonably practicable, non-employees are not exposed to risk.

(*c*) A duty is imposed on a controller of premises made available to others, not his employees, to take measures to ensure so far as is reasonably practicable that the premises and the entrances and exits are safe for those using the premises.

(*d*) A duty is imposed on anyone who designs, manufactures, imports or supplies an article for use at work to ensure, so far is reasonably practicable, that the article is safe and that adequate information on its use is supplied.

(*e*) A duty is imposed on an employee to take reasonable care at work for the health and safety of himself and others who may be affected by his conduct at work, and to co-operate with his employer to enable his employer to carry out his duties.

In most cases the duties are absolute, i.e. the breach of the general duty itself is the offence, i.e. there need be no intent nor negligence, and no defence to the charge is available.

The duty of enforcing the Act and previous relevant legislation lies with the other corporate body established by the Act, The Health and Safety Executive. Failure to obey notices to comply with the provisions of the Act and regulations made under it is punishable with a maximum fine of £400 on summary conviction or by imprisonment for up to two years, or a fine, or both, on indictment (*see* page 602).

The importance of the Act can be judged by the fact that it applies to *all* persons at work; employers, the self-employed and employees alike (with the exception of domestic servants in private households), and about 5 million people have legislative protection for the first time, e.g. those employed in education, medicine and leisure industries. It also protects the health and safety of the general public who may be affected by work activities.

Restrictions: more or less?

In this section we have discussed the responsibilities which follow from the occupancy of land. Remember that employees are also visitors within the Occupiers' Liability Act 1957 and any specific responsibilities owed to them by their employers as occupiers of land and premises are in addition to their general responsibilities.

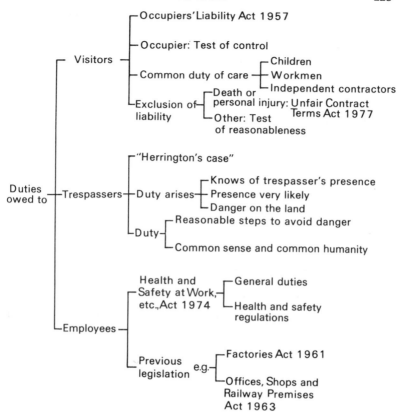

Fig. 38. *Occupancy of land and its responsibilities.*

Some of you may feel that the restrictions imposed by the state on the use of land, and the duties owed by occupiers are basically necessary in essence but grossly excessive in extent. Others may think that they strike a reasonable and workable compromise between the often opposing interests of the state and the individual. A small minority may believe in one of the two extremes; either complete freedom from any State imposed restrictions and duties, or complete nationalisation of land.

A summary diagram of this topic is to be found in Fig. 38.

RENT: ITS THEORY AND PRACTICE

Different types of rent

The term rent can be used in four different ways; it is important not to confuse these.

(*a*) *Commercial rent.* This is rent in the legal sense and is used to describe the payment made for the use of buildings or land.

(*b*) *Hire charge.* People often think of renting a TV or a car but actually this is really hiring or leasing.

(*c*) *Rent.* The payment made for the use of land as defined in the economic sense. In practice, however, land is frequently "mixed up" with other factors of production and it is difficult to ascertain precisely how much is being paid for the land and how much is being paid for the capital on it.

(*d*) *Economic rent.* This is the payment made to *any* factor of production over and above that which is necessary to keep the factor in its present use. For example, a soccer star may earn £500 a week because his special skills are in great demand. If his skills were not in great demand it is possible that he would be willing to work as a footballer for £100 a week, for there is little else he can do. In which case £400 of the £500 is a kind of *producer's surplus* or *rent of ability*, for it is not necessary to keep his skills in their present use. This payment can therefore be described as an *economic rent.*

Economic rent and transfer earnings

The concept of economic rent is derived from the ideas of David Ricardo, who was a political economist of the early nineteenth century. In developing the idea Ricardo made two assumptions. Firstly, that the supply of land is fixed; and secondly, that land has only one use and that is growing food. If this were the case, the supply curve for land would be a vertical straight line as in Fig. 39.

The demand for land, or any other factor, is a derived demand for it is demanded, not for itself, but for what can be produced with it. In Ricardo's time the demand for land was very high because Napoleon's continental system had cut off European grain from the British market. The result of this was that landlords were able to charge very high rents for the land on which to grow grain. Ricardo argued that this did not create more land, so that landlords were receiving more money but not supplying anything more. Conversely, the demand for land might fall, in which case the rents would decrease but the supply of land would not. From this Ricardo concluded that rent fulfilled no purpose and was a *producer's surplus*. Although Ricardo's assumptions were incorrect, he did manage to construct the theoretical extreme of the supply of a factor of production. In Fig. 39 you see that the supply curve is vertical and that, therefore, the factor earning is determined by the demand curve. The increase in demand from DD to D'D' increases the price but not the quantity of land. Theoretically demand could decrease until the price (rent) were zero without the quantity supplied decreasing. Thus all the earnings made by this factor are over and above that which is necessary to keep it in its present use and are therefore *economic rent*. (*See* pages 285–92 for demand and supply curves.)

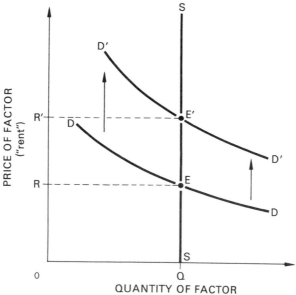

Fig. 39. *Economic rent. All factor earnings are economic rent because whatever happens to the price the quantity supplied remains the same.*

Ricardo also argued that rent was *barren* since, however high rent was, it produced no more of the factor. To some extent this is true, but high rents do have the function of making us exploit scarce resources more sensibly. For example, when land was very cheap in the USA it was ruthlessly exploited. This resulted in the "dust bowl". High rents for land mean that farmers are anxious to preserve the fertility of land and look after it carefully.

In practice, if a factor's earnings decline there comes a time when that factor will transfer to some other use. The payment which is necessary to keep a factor in its present use is described as a *transfer earning*. If we assume that a firm employs men at a fixed wage agreed with the trade union, then we could represent the supply of labour as a horizontal straight line. In other words, the firm must pay that amount or no-one will work for them. This would mean that in this case all the workers' earnings could be regarded as transfer earnings. This is illustrated in Fig. 40.

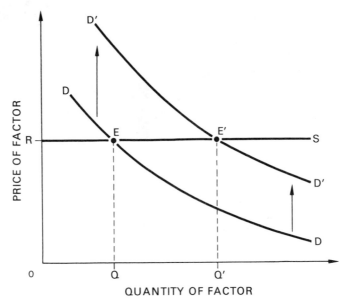

Fig. 40. *Transfer earnings. All factor earnings are transfer earnings because whatever the demand the same price must be paid for the factor of production.*

Most factor earnings are a composite of economic rent and transfer earnings. In Fig. 41 the firm requires a work-force of 500. In order to attract this many workers it must pay a wage of £20 a day. If we consider the 200th worker, however, it appears that he would have been willing to work for a wage of £9. He is, therefore, receiving £11 a day more than is necessary to keep him in his present employment. This is, therefore, economic rent. One could make a similar division of the earnings of the workers until one reaches the 500th worker where all of the £20 is necessary to attract him to the firm. Thus all the shaded area is economic rent whilst the area beneath it is transfer earnings.

It is possible to consider more than one transfer for a factor. For example, if one considered land in the centre of London, a site might earn £500 per square metre as an office but only £400 per square metre as a cinema, in which case the owner of the office site is earning an economic rent of £100 per square metre. If, however, the site reverted to agriculture it might only earn £20 per square metre, in which case the economic rent would be £480. The amount of economic rent and the amount of transfer earnings, therefore, depend upon the transfer considered.

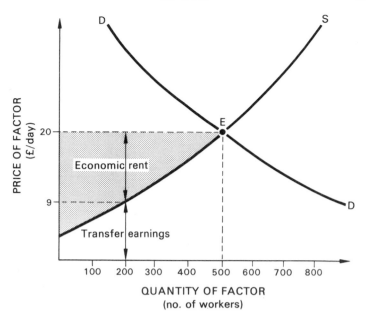

Fig. 41. *Factor earnings. A composite of economic rent and transfer earnings. The wage is £20; therefore the 200th worker's pay is £9 of transfer earnings and £11 of economic rent.*

Quasi-rent

If one considers a machine that is recovering £500 a year above its operating cost, then in the short run we could consider this as economic rent since it is £500 more than is necessary to keep capital in its present use. However, in the long run the machine must re-cover not only its operating cost but also its replacement cost if capital is going to remain in that use. If, for example, the replacement cost of this machine were £500 per year, then, in the long run, all the machine's earnings become transfer earnings. Those earnings which are economic rent in the short run but transfer earnings in the long run are correctly termed quasi-rent.

Rent and taxes

Henry George, a nineteenth-century economist, hit on the idea that if rent were a surplus which could be removed without affecting the distribution of resources, then all taxes could be raised from rent. This idea was very popular with those who did not derive their income from rent. The idea is not feasible, however, because George's argument only works for economic rent and we have seen how difficult this is to quantify.

From time to time governments have, however, tried to tax economic rent. In 1947 the government introduced *development charges* under the Town and Country Planning Act. This was soon repealed but the Land Commission Act of 1967 introduced a betterment levy of 40 per cent. This was abolished by the Conservative government in 1970. At present, local authorities are able to benefit from gains due to change in use of land under the Development Land Tax Act 1976.

The legal agreement under which rent is paid for the use of land and premises is called a "tenancy". Since many business organisations rent their premises, business tenancies, and the obligations imposed by them, are subjects of considerable practical importance to them.

Tenancies of business premises

A constantly recurring theme in this chapter has been the intervention of the state in land ownership, its use and the consequences of occupancy. This again is so with tenancies of business (commercial) premises. Until 1915 there was no intervention of any substance by the state in any kind of tenancy. In that year a "war economy" necessitated legislation restricting rises in rent and mortgage interest. Before 1915 landlords and tenants had been free to strike whatever bargain they wished.

The present law relating to rent and security of tenure of business premises is contained in Part II of the Landlord and Tenant Act 1954 as amended by the Law of Property Act 1969. The Act applies to all property occupied by a tenant for the purpose of any trade, profession or employment. There are, however, certain exceptions, e.g. tenancies of farmland, "controlled" tenancies under the Rent Act 1977 (this Act deals in the main with tenancies of dwelling houses but covers a house used for both domestic and business purposes—taking in paying guests would be a case in point), and mining leases, among others.

In any landlord and tenant situation, the tenant is the more likely to be in the weaker position at common law and to a greater or lesser extent needs the aid of legislation to redress the balance, the two key matters of concern being protection against eviction and control of rent. Thus the basic aim of the 1954 Act is to allow the tenant to conduct his business in the premises indefinitely, subject to the landlord's legitimate rights when the tenancy expires or the tenant abuses his tenancy. Initially commercial tenancies are unrestricted in their terms, but any renewal, as you will see, is controlled by the courts.

Security of tenure

A tenancy of business premises can only be terminated in accordance with the Act. While the tenant may give notice to quit or surrender the lease at any time, a landlord must give between six and twelve months notice, in the form prescribed in the Act, to expire not earlier than the date at which the tenancy would have ended but for the Act.

However, if the tenant does not wish to give up possession and he applies in the proper way, the Court is *bound* to grant him a new tenancy unless the landlord successfully objects on one of seven grounds specified in the Act. For example, failure by the tenant to fulfil his obligation to keep the premises in good repair; persistent delay in paying rent; because the premises are part of larger premises and the landlord could obtain a substantially greater rent if the property was let as a whole and not in parts; and because the landlord has the firm intention to occupy the premises for his own business or residential use.

A new tenancy granted by a court will be for a maximum of fourteen years, but there is no limit on the number of applications that a tenant can make under the Act.

Control of rent

A distinction is drawn between the original tenancy and any subsequent tenancy granted under the Act. As you have seen, the former is unrestricted in its terms, and hence there is no limit on the amount of rent that may be charged and no power to secure its revision. Under the latter, the rent is assessed on an "open market basis" and a rent revision clause can be included in the tenancy. Both the rent and the other terms of the tenancy can be decided by the Court in the event of a dispute between the parties.

Compensation for eviction and improvements

A tenant who is evicted in accordance with the Act is not entitled to any compensation unless the statutory ground on which the landlord successfully objected to a new tenancy being granted was for his own benefit, e.g. he intended to occupy the premises himself. In such cases, compensation equivalent to the rateable value of the premises is payable, doubled if the tenant had been in occupation for fourteen years or more.

A tenant must give his landlord three months notice of his intention to make improvements and he can only recover compensation for them, when the tenancy ends, if they add to the letting value. In addition he must claim at the right time and in the right way. Compensation is never payable if the landlord successfully objected to the improvements or effected them himself in return for a reasonable increase in rent.

CONCLUSION

Running through this chapter has been the theme of the organisation's ownership and use of land. However, the legal and economic concepts involved extend beyond land as a natural resource and can be applied to other property. It may seem that economic rent is an abstract concept, but it is interesting to note that when it is clearly discernible, as in the case of a soccer star, consequences more usually associated with land result. In the example, the soccer star becomes treated as though he were a chattel and he is the subject of personal and commercial restrictions and he may even be leased.

The organisation must use land as a resource. The law both facilitates and controls, even frustrating the organisation's exploitation of this resource. For example, government intervention, giving security of tenure to tenants of business premises, protects them from the unbridled workings of the market mechanism.

From the beginning of legal history, governments have always interfered in the use of land to a greater or lesser extent. Today, however, the interference has extended so far that it could be argued that the economist's theories and the lawyer's definitions have been to some extent superseded by the effects of government policy.

SELF-ASSESSMENT QUESTIONS

A. 1. Define the following: (*a*) freehold land; (*b*) transfer earnings; (*c*) an "occupier" under the Occupiers' Liability Act 1957; (*d*) a restrictive covenant.

2. List the main acts of Parliament affecting the use of land by business organisations.

B. 3. True or false?

(*a*) Freehold and leasehold estates are distinguishable in terms of their respective durations.

(*b*) The Health and Safety at Work, etc., Act 1974 replaces all previous legislation on the subject.

(*c*) In relation to injuries sustained on premises, the Unfair Contract Terms Act 1977 only applies to premises being used for business purposes.

(*d*) Quasi-rent is an earning of economic rent by a factor other than land.

(*e*) "Footloose" industries have mainly located in areas of heavy unemployment.

C. 4. Evaluate the factors present in your area which may attract new industry.

ASSIGNMENTS

1. Construct a diagram similar to Fig. 38 to illustrate restrictions on land use.

2. Find out what types of land development do not require planning permission.

3. Prepare arguments for and against taxing capital gains made on the transfer of land.

CHAPTER ELEVEN

The Financial Resources of the Organisation

CHAPTER OBJECTIVES

After studying this chapter you should be able to:
* define the different meanings of capital;
* describe the ways in which different organisations raise finance;
* state the ways in which a company issues shares and debentures;
* list the different forms of share and loan capital;
* calculate the return on invested and loaned finance;
* explain the factors which determine the rate of interest.

CAPITAL, WEALTH AND FINANCE

Types and forms of capital

The accumulated resources of the economy such as roads, houses, factories and the stocks of raw materials may be described as the country's *wealth* or *capital*. The definition of a *capital* or *producer good* arises not out of its intrinsic nature but out of the use to which it is put. For example, if we consider a commodity such as a potato, to the household it is a consumer good but if used by the farmer to plant for next year's crop then it is capital because it is being used in the production of further wealth. Similarly a can of beans is a consumer good once it reaches the shopping basket but it is a producer good whilst still on the shelves of the supermarket, since it is part of the capital of the business. There are some goods, such as oil tankers or tractors, which are invariably capital goods; this is because they are only used for the purpose of supplying other goods and services.

All organisations must use capital goods when they are producing goods and services. Capital goods can be classified under two main headings.

(*a*) *Fixed capital* which comprises such things as buildings and machines, i.e. items which continue through several rounds of production.

(b) *Working or circulating capital*, i.e. items which are used up in production such as raw materials.

The organisation can acquire capital goods either by buying them, often with the aid of hire-purchase or trade credit, or by leasing them. Leasing of capital is becoming much more widely used since it offers tax advantages to the business.

The term capital is used in two senses, either to describe capital goods or to describe financial resources. In this latter sense one may distinguish between invested finance (*share capital* in the case of a company) and the loaned finance (*loan capital*) of an organisation. This is the way most people think of capital. These two expressions are the legal forms of capital and they illustrate the way in which the organisation is owned and controlled (*see* below).

It is important to realise that capital goods represent *real wealth*, whilst shares, debentures, money, etc., are not wealth but a legal claim upon it. This distinction may not be important to the individual but it is vital to the economy as a whole. If these paper forms of capital were real wealth then the country could solve all its economic difficulties by printing more money.

Where does capital come from?

As we have already seen, capital goods are not necessarily different from consumer goods but are rather used for a different purpose. If, for example, we have a stock of potatoes then we can consume them all or consume some and plant some. In this way one hopes to have more potatoes next year. In the same way, an organisation is faced with the choice of distributing all its profits or *ploughing them back* in the business in the hope that this will enable them to make even more profit in the future. This is the old familiar idea of "no jam today for more jam tomorrow". In other words capital is *formed* by doing without now and using the resources so freed to create more wealth in the future.

The output of capital goods

Each year the economy produces new capital goods: roads, factories, machines, etc. However, each year some of the existing capital of the country wears out. It is necessary, therefore, for the economy to produce new capital goods to replace them. The sum total of all capital goods produced is referred to as the *gross output of capital*. When capital *depreciation* has been allowed for we arrive at a figure for the *net output of capital*. *The National Income and Expenditure Accounts* ("The Blue Book") records all the output of capital goods in one year. This output is termed *capital formation*, whilst the depreciation of capital is referred to as *capital consumption*. For an economy to become wealthier it is necessary for capital formation to exceed capital consumption.

Since capital is vital to the growth of an economy, the rate of capital formation is important if we are to improve our living standards. It is not the case, however, that any capital formation will produce more economic growth. It would be of little use today, for example, to produce more steam locomotives. Even if the capital equipment constructed is superb it can still be rendered useless by such things as bad labour relations. This has been illustrated in the coalmining industry where the opening of automated pits has been opposed by the miners.

The rich and the poor

The thing which separates the rich nations of the world from the poor is the possession of capital. Since capital is formed by going without now to produce more for the future, it is relatively easy for the richer nations to become even richer since they can forgo current consumption of some goods and still have a high standard of living. However, if a very poor country is living near to subsistence level, it is impossible for them to depress living standards to form capital since this would result in mass starvation. Imagine an economy which is so poor that everyone must spend all their time working in the fields to produce sufficient food just to keep them alive. Under these circumstances it will be impossible for the population to turn aside from agriculture to build roads or factories which might increase their living standards since they will have nothing to live on whilst they do so. It is very difficult indeed for poor nations to break out of this cycle of poverty.

Even for a country such as Britain it is important to realise that we cannot hope to keep pace with our competitors whilst we are devoting less than 20 per cent of the national income to capital formation and countries such as France and Germany are devoting 30 per cent.

FINANCING THE ORGANISATION

Sources of finance

If an organisation wishes to raise finance there are a number of sources from which this might come.

(*a*) *Ploughed-back profits.* An existing business might be able to finance new investment from retained profits. This is one of the most important sources of finance today.

(b) *The public.* Finance might be raised by selling shares to the public or by persuading them to make loans (debentures).

(c) *The government.* It is becoming more common for the government to make loans or give grants to organisations, especially in development areas.

(d) *Institutions.* The organisation might acquire the finance from banks, insurance companies and other financial institutions (*see* page 525).

Smaller businesses will usually have to raise finance through personal contact, be it with friends and colleagues or the bank manager. Banks are in fact the main external source of loan capital for the small business and to whom, of course, the interest must be paid. Security is nearly always required for the loan. Large companies will need to draw finance from a variety of sources.

The ownership of share capital has tended to become more and more centred on institutions such as insurance companies and pension funds. In 1981 financial institutions accounted for 43.2 per cent of the ownership of ordinary shares in the UK. This compares with 39 per cent owned by private persons. By putting his money into insurance or unit trusts the person with a small amount of money gains extra security as his "investment" is spread out over many different companies.

Different forms of finance

Different organisations obtain their finance in different ways, and different rules accordingly regulate the return to its contributors. We will now consider in turn the financial resources of the various types of trading organisations discussed in the second chapter of this book.

Sole traders

You have seen that a sole trader is a business organisation where one person is in business on his own. He alone is responsible for the organisation's financial capital and consequently he alone is entitled to any income from its use.

In common with the other forms of business organisation, a sole trader will need to raise loans when ploughed-back profits are insufficient to finance his future capital development. As you have seen, the principal sources of loan capital are banks. In nearly all cases the bank will require security for its advance and this will usually be provided by a mortgage over the sole trader's dwelling house or business premises. Alternative securities that he could offer would include a mortgage of stocks and shares or a life assurance policy, or a guarantee of the advance by a third person. Unsecured temporary overdrafts may sometimes by available to a reputable sole trader who is a trusted customer of the bank.

Partnerships

Contribution of capital by each partner is an essential feature of a conventional partnership, although the partners need not contribute capital equally. Therefore, in common with sole traders, partnerships basically generate the finance that they require from within their own organisation. The Partnership Act 1890 provides that, subject to an agreement to the contrary, a partner is not entitled to any interest on his capital contribution until the profits of the firm have been ascertained.

A partnership raises loan capital in much the same way as a sole trader with mortgages being possible over the partnership property in addition to the separate property of individual partners. In addition, a partner may make a loan to his firm quite separate from his capital contribution. The Partnership Act 1890 provides that, in the absence of an express agreement on the matter, he is entitled to interest at 5 per cent each year on such a loan.

Joint stock companies

Shares and debentures. Joint stock companies raise finance by issuing *shares* and *debentures*. While both result in the same thing, i.e. money which the company can use to pursue its economic activities, there are a number of differences between them. Primarily, debentures are loan capital which acknowledge and secure loans to the company while shares are evidence of part ownership of the company and investment in it. Thus, debenture-holders are a company's creditors while shareholders are its members. Debentures normally provide for repayment and they are usually secured by a mortgage over the property of the company; a shareholder's investment is only completely repaid if and when the company is wound up while solvent. Consequently, the latter involves greater *risk*. An important commercial difference is that dividends on shares can only be paid out of profits and therefore presuppose a profitable year's trading, but the interest on debentures may be paid out of capital. Hence, a debenture-holder receives payment for the loan he makes irrespective of whether the company makes a profit or a loss.

Debentures are usually issued to raise temporary finance up to the limit specified in the company's articles of association. Debentures may be either *redeemable* or *irredeemable*. The former are repayable at or after a specified date and they are usually issued when the need for finance is temporary or when interest rates are high and likely to fall. Conversely, the latter are not repayable until the company is wound up or it defaults in the payment of interest due. They will usually be issued when longer term finance is required or when interest rates are low and likely to rise.

Many companies will also have overdrafts with their banks and these accommodate fluctuations in their "cash flow". The amount and duration of the overdraft will depend largely upon the reputation of the company. The directors of small companies often give their personal guarantees as security for the debt to the bank.

Types of shares. There are three main types of shares and they are distinguishable according to the voting rights and rights to receive dividends and repayment of capital which their holders enjoy.

(*a*) *Preference shares.* The holders of preference shares receive a dividend in priority to other shareholders, but it is usually only a fixed rate dividend. Preference shares are presumed to be *cumulative*, i.e. if in any one year the dividend cannot be paid, it is carried forward and added to the dividend for the following year and so on. In many cases, preference shareholders are also entitled to repayment of capital in priority to other shareholders should the company be wound up.

(*b*) *Ordinary shares.* The precise rights of ordinary shareholders depend on a company's articles of association but normally they are entitled to attend and vote at meetings and to receive a variable dividend according to, and from, the profits remaining after the preference shareholders have received their dividend. If the company is wound up they are entitled to share in the surplus assets after all debts have been discharged and shareholders repaid. Ordinary shares are the *risk-bearing* shares because they have the greatest potential for either profit or loss.

Preference shares do not normally give voting rights and their holders are not entitled to share in the surplus profits of the company unless they hold *participating* preference shares. On liquidation they do not share in the company's surplus assets unless its articles expressly give them this right.

(*c*) *Deferred shares.* These are now rare but they are still sometimes issued to promoters (those persons who actually form and set the company going) or employees of the company. No dividend is paid to a holder of deferred shares until dividends have been paid to both preferential and ordinary shareholders. However, after these prior payments, all the surplus profit is distributed as dividend to the deferred shareholders.

Stock and debenture stock. Fully paid-up shares may be converted into *stock*. There is, however, no advantage in doing this today and the holder's investment in the company remains the same, merely being expressed in different terms. For example, 1,000 £1 shares can be converted into £1,000's worth of stock.

The essential difference between stock and shares is that the former is expressed in terms of money and can be transferred in fractional amounts, e.g. £51.25 worth (although the articles of the company usually provide that stock can only be transferred in round sums), while the latter are units, e.g. 10, 50 or 100 shares, and can only be transferred as such.

Debenture or *loan stock* is borrowed finance consolidated into one debt in the same way as shares may be consolidated and converted into stock. It is usually issued for short periods and it avoids the expense and formality involved in a public issue. Institutional investors such as banks, insurance companies and pension funds are the usual buyers. Debenture stock differs from debentures in the same way that stock differs from shares, i.e. it may be transferred in fractional amounts. Debenture stock may be convertible into ordinary shares. This gives the investor a choice between fixed but secure interest on the loan stock, and the possibly better but less certain return (dividend) paid to shareholders.

Authorised, issued and paid-up capital. The company's memorandum of association will state the amount of *authorised (or nominal) capital* which its directors may issue. However, the authorised capital need not all be issued and the shares need not be fully paid. Hence, in a company whose memorandum of association states that its authorised capital is £20,000, of which only £12,000 has been issued at 75p per £1 share, the *authorised* capital is £20,000, the *issued* capital is £12,000 and the *paid-up* capital is £9,000.

It is quite common for a company not to issue all its authorised capital at once, but to issue part at a later date either by direct invitation to the public or through an issuing house, or by a rights issue or bonus issue to its existing shareholders (*see* page 242).

Alteration of share capital. The members of a company may either *increase* or *alter* its share capital by resolution in a general meeting of the company. Increasing the share capital is self-explanatory, and alteration occurs where the company either: consolidates its shares, e.g. converts every four 25p nominal shares into a single £1 nominal share; or sub-divides its shares—the reverse process; or converts shares into stock; or cancels unissued shares. Any increase or alteration of the share capital must be notified to the Registrar of Companies.

Share capital can be *reduced* by a resolution of the company confirmed by the court. A reduction of the share capital might be used either to reduce the liability of its shareholders to contribute unpaid capital in respect of their shares, e.g. by reducing 50,000 £1 shares on which 50p per share has been paid to 50,000 50p shares, each fully paid, or to return paid-up capital in excess of its needs, e.g. where a company has issued 50,000 £1 shares fully paid and reduces its capital to 50,000 50p shares fully paid by repaying 50p per share.

Confirmation of the court is necessary because a reduction in share capital adversely affects the company's creditors, i.e. they are deprived of funds which otherwise would have been available to them in winding-up. Banks in particular would be affected where they had made a loan on the security of the company's shares because the value of their security would automatically be reduced. Consequently, before confirming the resolution the court must be satisfied that the creditors will not suffer through the proposed reduction in share capital.

Capital gearing. As you may have seen there are different types of both shares and loans. The make up of the company's financial resources we refer to as its *capital structure.* The proportion of loan capital to share capital in a company is referred to as the capital gearing of the company. If there is a small proportion of share capital to loan capital, the capital is said to be *high geared,* because a small number of ordinary shares (giving voting rights) controls a large amount of capital. Conversely, if the company's capital is mainly shares, with only a small proportion of loan capital, it is said to be *low geared.* Generally speaking it is to the company's advantage to have at least some of its capital as loan capital, since this gives two benefits.

(*a*) *Reduced tax burden.* Since debt interest can be claimed against corporation tax this will reduce the amount of tax the company has to pay.

(*b*) *Increased growth.* Because the company retains more of its earnings it will require a smaller cash sum to pay the *rate* of dividend on each share. This could result in more money being available for ploughing back into the company or it could be used to pay a higher dividend on each share.

Public corporations

The initial capital of a public corporation is provided by the government and authorised by Parliament, but once established it could raise loan capital on its own security in much the same way as other trading organisations if ploughed-back profits are insufficient to finance future development. However, as the sums involved will normally be too large to raise on the open market, public corporations will continue to look to the Exchequer for their loan capital.

The taxpayer receives no actual dividend from the government's investment on his behalf, but he may benefit by transfers to the Exchequer fund, lower prices and even the occasional cash refund, as happened with the rebate on telephone charges from the Post Office in 1977 and from British Telecom in 1982.

Co-operative societies
While there are basic differences in formation, economic objectives and organisation between co-operative societies and joint stock companies, they raise finance in similar ways, i.e. through issuing shares and from loans. However, as you have seen, shares in co-operative societies differ from shares in joint stock companies in important ways, and loans to companies are usually from banks and not from their members, as with co-operative societies.

Shareholders receive a dividend on their investment but it is paid and calculated in a different way from joint stock company dividends. Traditionally it took the form of a cash payment—the "divi"— directly calculated according to the amount of business that a member had done with the society. Today the return on investment is the greater value of co-operative societies' trading stamps to a shareholder than to a non-shareholder. The dividend is still, however, directly related to the amount of business the shareholder does with the society.

Municipal enterprises
The concept of financial capital seems somewhat out of place in the context of local authorities, but it is as necessary to their trading activities as it is to joint stock companies.

In relation to their finance, a distinction can be drawn between a local authority's trading services, e.g. public transport, and its other services. The former may be run on the principle that they should be financially self-supporting, the full cost being met by the charges made. The initial finance required for trading services comes from the issue of municipal stock and from loans. Both are issued on the security of the local rates and carry fixed rates of dividend and interest respectively. The latter, which may in fact involve an element of trading, e.g. a leisure centre, are financed from the rates and by central government through the rate support grant in some cases. Ratepayers and central government receive no direct financial return on their investment, but local authority loan stock usually offers the investor an attractive rate of interest.

Raising finance for companies

The public are invited to subscribe for shares or debentures through a document known as a *prospectus*, defined by the Companies Act 1948 as "any prospectus, notice, circular, advertisement or other invitation offering to the public for subscription or purchase any shares or debentures of the company". The prospectus will set out the objectives and past performance of the company, and other information designed to prevent investors from being misled. A copy of the prospectus must be delivered to the Registrar of Companies by the company or issuing house before the prospectus is issued.

The subscription can be handled in one of three ways.

(*a*) By the company directly inviting the public to subscribe for its shares or debentures through the issue of a prospectus and press advertisement. In contract law (*see* Chapter 17) this is an *invitation to treat* and not an offer to sell its shares. By his application for shares it is the prospective investor who makes the contractual offer. The applications are considered by the company's directors and the contract to take shares is complete when the letter of allotment is posted to the applicant.

(*b*) By an "offer for sale" made through an *issuing house* such as a merchant bank or firm of stockbrokers. In this method the issuing house will subscribe for the shares or debentures itself and then resell them at a higher price direct to the public. This method is usually preferred to a direct invitation to the public from the company, particularly for companies too small to be quoted on the Stock Exchange. In contrast to direct invitations by the company, the issue of a prospectus by an issuing house is a contractual offer to sell.

(*c*) "Placing", by which an issuing house may subscribe for the shares or debentures itself and then invite its clients, e.g. insurance companies and pension funds, to purchase from them at a higher price. Alternatively, without subscribing, they may act as the company's agents in selling the securities offered, receiving a commission called *brokerage* for their services. Placing is a popular method of raising finance for a small public company where the amount is too small to warrant either direct invitation to the public or an "offer for sale".

Underwriting
To guard against the possibility that not all the *shares* will be

bought, the issuing house may engage *underwriters,* e.g. banks, issuing houses or stockbrokers, who guarantee to buy any shares that the public do not take up. This is important, for if the minimum subscription is not received no shares may be allotted.

False statements
Should the prospectus contain false statements of fact which induce people to subscribe for shares, any investor misled may rescind the allotment of shares and reclaim any money paid to the company for them. He may also bring a civil action for damages against the person(s) responsible for the false statement. In addition, it is a criminal offence either to issue a form of application for shares which does not comply with the requirements of the Companies Act 1948 or to make a false statement in the prospectus, unless any person responsible for it had reasonable grounds to believe the statement to be true.

Special methods of issue
Shares are usually sold at a fixed price, which is the *par value* of the share. It is possible, however, for them to be *sold by tender* in which case the company may obtain more or less than the par value. In addition to these procedures for selling shares to the general public, there are two ways by which the company could issue shares to existing shareholders.

(*a*) *Bonus or scrip issues.* In this case the shares are *given* to existing shareholders and therefore no additional finance is involved. They are usually issued as special method of dealing with undistributed profits.

(*b*) *Rights issues.* These involve the sale of shares to existing shareholders at less than the market price. Therefore additional finance is raised.

Paying for the finance
Debentures have a fixed rate of interest. That is to say, in return for a loan of £100 the debenture holder will receive a guaranteed rate of interest. Some shares, for example, preference shares, may have a stated income on them but by and large their income will depend upon the *dividend* declared by the company. When the company has paid all its costs, including taxes, and after it has retained some profits to finance growth, it distributes the rest of its earnings as a dividend on the par (or face) value of each share. If a share is bought on the Stock Exchange it will almost certainly be at a price other than its par value, e.g. a £1 share may be bought for

£2. This, however, will not affect its earning capacity. If, for example, the company has declared a 10 per cent (or 10p) dividend per share then it is 10p that the owner of the share will receive. Since he paid £2 for it the effective return to him is not 10 per cent but 5 per cent. This principle also applies to the return on debentures.

The Stock Exchange

The Stock Exchange is not involved with the issue of shares, it is only concerned with the sale and transfer of "second-hand" shares. Thus, when shares are bought on the Stock Exchange they do not bring money to the company concerned but to the shareholder who has sold them. The Stock Exchange is important to the new issue market, however, since the ease with which shares can be resold encourages people to invest since they know they can easily turn their shares back to cash. In addition stock jobbers may be members of the Stock Exchange and may sell the new shares they have recently acquired to other brokers on the Exchange.

CALCULATING THE RETURN

Economists and accountants might disagree on the proportions of a share's earnings which might be called profit and that which might be called interest. To the owner of the share, however, the important thing will be how much the earning of the share is. A shareholder may obtain income from his shares in two ways; firstly, from the *dividend* declared by the company. This will be expressed as a percentage of the par value of the share. Secondly, he could gain income by selling the share for more than he paid for it. Since dividends vary from share to share and the price of a particular share may vary from day to day, various methods of expressing the shares earnings or potential earnings have been devised. This is so that the shares of one company may more easily be compared with the shares of a different company. The different ways of expressing this are listed below.

Yield

This gives a simple measure of the return to capital expressed as a percentage of the shares current market price. If, for example, a company declared that it would pay a dividend of 15 per cent on each £1 share in the company but the current market price of each £1 share is £2.50p then the yield is not 15 per cent but 6 per cent. This can be worked out in the following manner.

$$\text{yield} = \frac{\text{par value} \times \text{dividend}}{\text{market price of share}}$$

In our example:

$$\frac{1.00 \times 15}{2.50} = 6\%$$

Price/earnings (P/E) ratio

The yield of a share may not be a good guide to its earning capacity. The P/E ratio is the relationship between the market price of the share and total earnings, i.e. all profit, not just the declared dividend. The P/E ratio can be expressed as

$$\frac{\text{Market price of share}}{\text{Earnings}}$$

If the company has a share capital of £100,000 and its total profits or earnings are £50,000 then its earnings are 50 per cent or 0.50. If the market price of the shares is £2.50 then the P/E ratio will be

$$\frac{2.50}{0.50} = 5$$

This is a ratio, not a percentage.

Dividend cover

Since 1973 the complexities of corporation tax have made the calculation of the P/E ratio somewhat problematic. A new measure of the earnings of shares has arisen and that is dividend cover. This relates the net after-tax profits of the company to the declared dividend. If, for example, the profits of the company were £50,000 after tax had been paid, and £20,000 were distributed in dividends, then the dividend cover would be 2.5.

There are thus several ways of looking at the earnings of a company. Anyone contemplating the purchase of shares in a company should take care to look at the financial position of the company in as many different ways as possible.

THE NATURE OF INTEREST

What is interest?

Interest is the payment made for the use of capital. As far as the individual lender is concerned it is the *price* he receives for hiring out his money. All interest payments are expressed as a percentage per annum. It is important to distinguish between *lending* money and *investing* money. The main distinction is that money lent is repayable whereas money invested is not. If, for example, someone buys a share in a company, even if it is a fixed interest preference share, he is acting as an investor since his money is not repayable. If on the other hand he is a debenture holder or the money is placed on deposit in a bank he is a lender since it is repayable.

The payment made of the use of money is *pure interest* only when no risk is involved. If one lends money to a major bank or the government the risk is virtually non-existent and therefore we could regard all that payment as interest. If, on the other hand, money is lent to a less certain business organisation then, although the payment for it may be termed interest, it will in fact involve some consideration for the uncertainty involved. The rate of interest is also affected by the period of time for which the money is lent. Generally speaking, the longer money is lent for the greater the payment the lender will expect.

Why pay interest?
As with any other factors of production, an organisation employs capital for the product which it creates. Imagine that the owner of a barren hillside in Scotland invests £100,000 of capital in it by planting and growing trees on it. The trees take twenty-five years to grow, at the end of which time they are sold for £250,000. Thus in return for his investment the forester has received £150,000 or £6,000 per annum. This income resulting from the employment of capital is referred to as the *net productivity of capital* and is normally expressed as a percentage which, in our example, would be 6 per cent. Organisations are willing to pay for the use of capital, therefore, because it enables them to produce goods and services in the same way that the employment of labour does.

Ultimately the payment of all interest must rest upon the net productivity of capital since if capital did not produce enough to pay the rate of interest organisations would cease to employ it. (An organisation would not calculate the return on capital by the simple means illustrated above: *see* McNamara, page 84.)

Moral and political attitudes to interest
Since the time of Aristotle the taking of interest on money has been condemned. It was argued that the person who received interest was obtaining "something for nothing" and was living off the efforts of other people. The medieval church condemned the taking of interest as the sin of *usury*. The Marxist opposition to interest is based on the idea that since capital must have been created in the

first place by the efforts of workers, any income that accrues to it must belong to the workers and not to the capitalist.

It is apparent from the example we used above that interest is not "something for nothing". Capital produces a net product in the same way that labour produces a *marginal product*. The payment of interest is therefore necessary to compensate the owners of capital for the loss of the net product which they might otherwise have received themselves. Interest is also necessary to encourage people to forgo current consumption so making the formation of capital possible. The ownership of capital is a political question beyond the scope of this book. One should realise, however, that in Britain today, the state is the largest "capitalist". The ownership by the state of the means of production does not mean that economic principles can be ignored. For a nation, as for an organisation, if it is to prosper, capital must be directed towards those schemes which show the highest net productivity. An economy ignores this principle at its peril.

The rate of interest

Although the rate of interest is related to the level of net productivity, it is not the same thing. There are many different rates of interest in the economy, e.g. deposit rate, base rate, Treasury bill rate and so on. There are also short-term interest rates and long-term interest rates. There is, however, disagreement about how rates of interest are determined. Some of the more important ideas are discussed below.

The loanable funds theory

The classical view of the interest rate was that it was determined by the demand and supply for loanable funds. The interest rate was therefore an *equilibrium price* (*see* page 291). The rate of interest was thus more than just the cost of borrowing; it equated investment and saving in the economy. If, for example, there was a great demand for funds this would raise the rate of interest which would, in turn, encourage more people to save. The weakness of this argument is that it does not take into account the other uses to which people might put money other than saving and investing.

The liquidity preference theory

John Maynard Keynes argued that if we regarded the supply of money as being fixed at any particular time then the interest rate would be formed by the interaction of the supply of money with the economy's desire to hold cash. Keynes identified three motives in the demand for money.

(a) *The transaction motive.* This money held for carrying on everyday business. Receipts and payments of money do not coincide. If, for example, you receive a monthly salary then your income comes in twelve instalments but you have to spend money every day. Both the individual and the organisation, therefore, will have to hold money in hand or in current account deposits in banks to cope with these day-to-day payments. The proportion of income which is retained for the transactions motive will depend both upon the frequency with which income payments are received and upon the level of income.

(b) *The precautionary motive.* This refers to money retained to cope with unexpected eventualities. For example, an organisation might be faced with an unexpected rise in its costs or the individual might have to cope with something like a breakdown of his car. The amount of money retained for the precautionary motive is also closely linked to the level of income and for all practical purposes we may link the two motives together.

(c) *The speculative motive.* This is money held in expectation of a speculative gain. To understand this fully it is necessary to appreciate that the price of securities and the rate of interest vary inversely with one another. If, for example, a £100 bond has a guaranteed rate of interest of 5 per cent then should the interest rate rise to 10 per cent it will only be possible to sell that bond for £50 since it only generates a payment of £5 per year. Conversely, if the interest rate fell to 2.5 per cent the earning capacity of the bond would raise its price to £200. Keynes also believed that investors had a concept of *the normal rate of interest.* If the rate of interest were below this then people would retain cash since interest rates were low and bonds were expensive. They would also retain cash because they expected the interest rate to rise thus making bonds cheap and the interest on them greater. Conversely if the rate of interest were high then people would put their money into bonds because they were cheap and their earnings were high. They would also put money into bonds because they were cheap and their earnings were high. They would also put money into bonds because they expected the rate of interest to fall which would mean that they would then sell the bonds at a higher price.

For these reasons the liquidity preference curve (so called because it shows the community's demand for cash, or its *liquidity*) slopes downward showing that when the rate of interest is low there is a high liquidity preference, i.e. a large amount of assets are kept in cash form.

If we assume like Keynes that the supply of money is fixed then the rate of interest will be where the liquidity preference curve

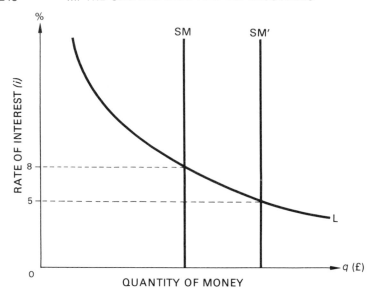

Fig. 42. *The determination of the rate of interest. The rate of interest is deter-mined by the interaction of liquidity preference (L) with the supply of money (SM). An increase in the supply of money (SM') leads to a fall in the rate of interest.*

intersects with the supply of money. This is illustrated in Fig. 42. Here L is the liquidity preference curve and SM the supply of money. If the supply of money increases to SM′ you can see that this has the effect of decreasing the rate of interest from 8 per cent to 5 per cent. Shifts may occur in the liquidity preference curve as a result of such things as changes in income, changes in consumers' tastes and expectations about the future.

A modern view of the rate of interest
Today we do not believe, as the classicists did, that the rate of interest entirely determines investment, neither do we believe as Keynes did that it has little effect upon investment. Keynes believed this because he was primarily concerned with short-term interest rates. If the rate of interest remained high for a long period, how-ever, one can see that it would depress consumption, for example by making hire-purchase expensive. It follows that if people were not consuming then business would have to cut back on investment.

Businessmen's expectations of the future are one of the prime determinants of investment. If they are optimistic they will tend to invest irrespective of the rate of interest. High rates of inflation may cause lenders of funds to look for higher rates of interest but constantly rising prices may also make it easier for organisations to pass these increased costs on to consumers. In recent years there has been great emphasis on the money supply and a neglect of the rate of interest. Changes in the money supply come about through government action. The government also has a great influence on interest rates through its borrowing and through the Bank of England's policies, so it would seem fair to conclude that government policy is one of the chief determinants of the rate of interest. Thus, we can conclude that the interest rate is the result of the interaction of several forces, i.e. government policy and the money supply, liquidity preference and business expectations.

CONCLUSION

This chapter has examined the organisation's demand for financial resources and the payments it will have to give for them. It is important to realise, however, that each organisation is one amongst many, and therefore investment and the demand for funds must be seen in the context of the whole economy. Thus the picture will only be complete when we have studied the determinants of savings and investment in the whole economy—this is done in Chapter 21.

SELF-ASSESSMENT QUESTIONS

A. 1. Define: (a) capital goods; (b) authorised and paid-up share capital; (c) a debenture; (d) a company prospectus; (e) the transaction's demand for money.

2. List the sources of finance available to business organisations.

B. 3. True or false?

(a) Debenture holders can vote at general meetings of the company.

(b) Capital is formed by forgoing current consumption.

(c) A rise in the rate of interest will usually cause an increased demand for securities.

(d) A bonus issue raises finance for a company.

4. Distinguish between ordinary and preference shares.

C. 5. True or false?

(a) The net productivity of capital would be higher in a developed economy than in an underdeveloped economy.

(b) A zero rate of interest is never possible.

(c) The fixed capital of an organisation will constitute its fixed costs.

6. Examine the balance sheet of the company for which you work, or a major company in your area, and discover or determine the P/E ratio, the yield and the dividend cover of its ordinary shares.

7. Discuss the likely effect of the government setting interest rates in the economy too low.

ASSIGNMENTS

1. Draw up a prospectus for a projected tin mine in Cornwall.

2. Prepare arguments for and against public ownership of the means of production.

CHAPTER TWELVE

The Risk Factor

Labour, capital and natural resources do not naturally form themselves into a wealth-making combination. Someone must make the decision, not only *what* to produce but also *how* and *when* to produce. The person who undertakes this task is providing a very special service because he must, in so doing, take a *risk*. In this chapter we discuss the nature of this risk and the consequence of taking it both successfully and unsuccessfully. Economists term this decision-taking and organisational factor *enterprise*, and the person who supplies it the *entrepreneur*.

THE IMPORTANCE OF RISK-TAKING

The role of the entrepreneur

The entrepreneur is the person who runs a business organisation; he is not necessarily the capitalist. The capitalist might be a group of people (stockholders) who have lent money to the business but may have never visited it, but the capital could also just have easily come from the banks, from the government or from the entrepreneur himself. The entrepreneur's function, however, is to *organise* the business. In order to produce goods and services it is necessary for someone to take a risk by producing in anticipation of demand. That is to say, since it takes time to produce goods the entrepreneur must predict what the demand is going to be when the goods are produced. The entrepreneur differs from the other people involved in the business in that the amount of money he makes is uncertain. The workers, the capitalists and the landlord will all have to be paid an agreed contractual amount if the business is not to go into liquidation. There is no way in which one can contract to make a profit and if the entrepreneur is unlucky or unwise he will be left with not a profit but a loss.

In organising production the entrepreneur carries out three main functions.

(a) He buys or hires the resources, labour, raw materials, etc., which the business requires.

(b) He combines the resources in such a way that goods are produced at the lowest cost.

(c) He sells the products of the business in the most advantageous way possible.

We assume that the entrepreneur will always try to maximise the profits of the business and also that he will act in a rational and sensible manner. These assumptions are discussed more fully in the next Part of the book.

The role of profit

Since goods must be produced in anticipation of demand it is essential that someone takes the risk of doing this. In a mixed economy many production decisions are taken by the government but there are still many more taken by private persons. Entrepreneurs do not act from a sense of public duty but out of a desire to make profit. Adam Smith argued that the "invisible hand" of self-interest guided the economy to the best possible use of its resources. This was because to produce profitably the business would not only have to produce the goods which people wanted but also the business would have to produce them at minimum cost in order to compete with its rivals. Profit acts not only as an incentive to encourage businessmen to produce but it also acts as an indicator. If, for example, profits are high in one particular line of business, this indicates that people want more of that good and encourages more firms to produce it. Also if one firm in an industry is making more profit than another this could indicate that its methods are more efficient, and the other firms will therefore have to emulate this greater efficiency or go out of business.

Thus profit acts as an incentive to firms to encourage them to take risks as a measure of efficiency and as a spur to the introduction of new products and processes.

Risks in the large firm

In a small firm it is easy to identify the entrepreneur; this may not be so in a large firm. Whilst the board of directors may be the most obvious risk-taker, many of the senior and middle management may have to take decisions which in a small firm would be considered the job of the entrepreneur. In a large firm therefore the *entrepreneurial function* may be spread amongst many people and be hard to identify. It may also be the case that when a large company is run entirely by managers and not by profit earners they may be less interested in maximising profits and more interested in such things as growth of the company and security. They may therefore act more as risk-avoiders than risk-takers.

When a company is in a monopoly position the profits it earns may be more a return to its power in the market than to any risk taken.

MIXING RESOURCES

The successful running of any business, be it a farm, a vehicle manufacturing company or a bank, depends upon using the right mix of resources. This is essentially an economic problem rather than a technological one. One can produce a technically superb product such as a Rolls Royce and still go bankrupt. It is an economic problem, because the supply, and hence the prices of resources, differ greatly from place to place. An English farmer who tried to grow wheat in a manner which is successful in Canada would rapidly come to grief, since in Canada land is plentiful and cheap, whereas farming in England depends upon getting as much as possible out of a limited area. This simple but fundamental point is commonly misunderstood. Many projects in less developed countries have come to grief because they have copied the techniques of advanced countries. If, for example, a heavily capitalised synthetic fibre plant were built in India this would throw many people in the textile industry out of work. If labour is cheap and plentiful it is better to use a process which exploits that. Many people laugh at pictures of the Chinese building reservoirs by moving earth in wicker baskets, but, if labour is cheap and plentiful and capital equipment expensive and imported, then wicker baskets are the better way. This will give work and wages to the workers whilst an imported earth-moving plant would make them unemployed.

The equal product curve
There is always more than one way to undertake any particular task. We could, for example, dig a ditch with six men with picks and shovels or employ one man with a mechanical digger. If we

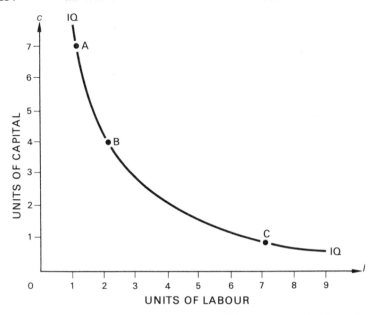

Fig. 43. *The equal product curve or isoquant. This shows combinations of two factors (capital and labour) which would produce the same output of goods.*

consider two resources such as capital and labour there will, there-fore, be several combinations of them which will produce the same output. This is illustrated in Fig. 43. At point A on the curve a *capital intensive* method of production is used employing seven units of capital but only one of labour. As we move down the curve labour is *substituted* for capital. Point C represents a *labour intensive* method of producing the same output—here seven units of labour are used but only one of capital. Other things being equal, poor countries will tend to use labour intensive methods whilst advanced countries will use capital intensive methods.

Achieving the best mix of resources
Achieving the best possible combination of resources for a firm is a case of balancing not just two factors but many. If the firm is to prosper and maximise its profits the mix must be precisely right. In Chapter 8 we saw how a business would go on employing more units of a variable factor up to the point where the marginal revenue product (MRP) of that factor was equal to its price. It would follow, therefore, that if the firm could do this for every one of the re-sources it employed it would be achieving the best combination of

factors of production. Thus, the best profit combination of resources for the firm would occur when

Marginal revenue product of labour = Price of labour

and

Marginal revenue product of capital = Price of capital

and so on for any number of factors. In this manner the firm will achieve the most output for the least cost and also maximise its profits.

These principles may seem a little abstract but they are only common sense. Most businessmen will know whether they wish to employ another man or another machine without bothering with MRPs and isoquants.

There is no blueprint for the running of a firm because each commercial situation is unique. Two farms side by side will have to be run differently, just as two chemist shops in the same High Street will have to be run differently. Therefore, in every situation the entrepreneur has to work out that combination of resources which is economically correct. If he does it successfully he will be rewarded with profit—unsuccessfully and he will make a loss. Since he is responsible for production decisions you can see that the entrepreneur is one of the most vital cogs in the economic system.

INDUSTRIAL PROPERTY

What is industrial property?

Great Britain has a record of significant "firsts" in the history of technology, from the Spinning Jenny to the hovercraft, and a talent for invention and development is a considerable economic resource. The exploitation of inventions (*innovation*) is a form of *enterprise* and the financial rewards from it can be considered as part of the "proceeds of enterprise"—in an economist's terms, a risk successfully taken. Such enterprise benefits the economy and is to be encouraged. Therefore, it deserves and requires protection at law.

An analogous situation arises if a business organisation earns a reputation for quality, service, etc., in its particular sphere of economic activity. The financial returns from this reputation are also "proceeds of enterprise", and the right to benefit from this reputation similarly deserves and requires protection.

Inventiveness and reputation are abstract concepts and cannot be physically possessed or protected. However, the right to benefit from them is protected through the ownership of *industrial property*, a generic term encompassing copyrights, patents, trade-marks and goodwill. Such intangible property is clearly very different from land, buildings, cars, etc., but, as you saw on page 195, "personal property" includes the intangible as well as the tangible, and both are capable of being owned. The various types of industrial property are known as "choses in action", i.e. property which does not physically exist, and which consequentially cannot be effectively protected by physical means, only by legal action.

Thus, through the concept of industrial property, individuals and business organisations are able to protect their right to benefit from inventiveness, business reputation and hard-work, i.e. their *enterprise*.

Protection of industrial property

As economic activity becomes increasingly more diverse and complex, the protection of business interests against unfair trade practices becomes increasingly more necessary. Basically a line must be drawn between fair competition, no matter how damaging, and business practices that can be considered unethical. Originally the common law adequately controlled trade practices through the tort of passing off (*see* page 260), but only goodwill and, to a lesser extent, trade-marks are now, in practice, protected by common law actions. In general industrial property has additional and more specific statutory protection today, and the role of the common law is of relatively little importance. The relevant statute usually makes interference with these forms of industrial property a tortious act. In addition, as the Trade Descriptions Act 1968 (*see* page 383) makes it a criminal offence to apply "a false trade description" to any goods, or to supply any goods to which such a false trade description has been applied, infringement of rights in certain types of industrial property can lead to prosecution. However, although the scope of the criminal law is wide, civil proceedings are usually preferred by a trader whose rights are infringed.

We will now consider the types of industrial property listed above and the protection afforded at law to the rights of their owners or proprietors.

Types of industrial property
Copyrights
The term "copyright" is used in legislation to mean:

(*a*) the exclusive right of an author, painter, composer, etc., to profit from the printing, selling or copying of his original work (the Copyright Act 1956); and

(*b*) the exclusive right of a proprietor of a registered industrial design to profit from the manufacture of articles to the design (the Registered Designs Act 1949).

We are concerned here with the latter meaning.

"Design", for the purposes of the 1949 Act, relates to those features of the article which appeal to the eye. The design of an article which is determined solely by its function or construction cannot be registered. This, however, is extremely rare, for the design of nearly all manufactured articles will contain some element which is determined by artistic and not functional or constructional criteria.

To receive legal protection, an industrial design must be registered by its proprietor at the Patent Office. To be registrable, the design must be new or original and an application for registration must state the features of the article which the proprietor considers to be novel. A search through the register of earlier designs is made before the claim to originality is accepted. Registration is for a period of five years, renewable for two further periods of five years.

Statutory protection of industrial designs. The 1949 Act gives the proprietor of a registered industrial design the right to a civil action in the High Court against any person who, without permission, makes or imports, or sells or hires, or offers for sale or hire, any article which infringes the design. Such an infringement entitles the proprietor to damages or an account of profits (compensation for the profits lost), the amount being assessed in terms of either his lost royalties or his lost orders, depending upon whether he licensed others to manufacture his design or he manufactured it himself. In addition, the court may grant an injunction preventing further infringement and order the delivering up or destruction of the articles which infringe the registered design.

Patents

A patent may be defined as the exclusive right to exploit an invention for commercial gain. Should anybody else wish to make or make use of the patented article they must either buy the patent from its proprietor or use it under licence and pay a royalty to him.

Under the Patents Act 1977 there are three types of patents.

(*a*) "Community patents", granted by the European Patent Office under the EEC Patent Convention and applying throughout the EEC. Domestic courts have jurisdiction over local infringements but not over questions of validity.

(*b*) "European patents (UK)", which can be granted for a transitional period (until about 1987) by the European Patent Office under the EEC Patent Convention, but applying only to the UK.

(*c*) "Patents under this Act"—patents granted by the Patent Office which apply to the UK. These are fully under the jurisdiction of the UK courts and the Patent Office.

Transitional provisions, preserving part of the old system, apply to patents registered under previous legislation.

Under the Patents Act 1977 an invention may only be patented if:

(*a*) the invention is new (formerly an invention known abroad but new in this country could be patented);

(*b*) it involves an inventive step, i.e. a step not obvious to a person skilled in the particular field to which the invention relates;

(*c*) it is capable of industrial application;

(*d*) it is not a scientific discovery or theory, an artistic creation, a mental process (including a computer program), a method of presenting information or an invention likely to lead to offensive, immoral or anti-social behaviour and does not relate to an animal or plant or a process for their production.

Applications for Patents under this Act are made to the Comptroller-General of Patents and he has jurisdiction to decide questions concerning the entitlement to a patent, although he may refer the matter to the court if he considers this to be more appropriate in the circumstances. Once granted, a patent continues in force for twenty years and can be renewed on payment of the prescribed fee.

An invention made by an employee of a business organisation in the course of his normal duties belongs to the business organisation but, on application to the Comptroller-General or to the High Court, he is entitled to compensation if the invention is of outstanding benefit to them.

Protection of patents. Patents are generally infringed by making, using, importing or disposing of a patented article, or using or offering for use a patented process for commercial use without the proprietor's consent. If a patent is infringed, the Act gives its proprietor: the right to bring civil proceedings in the High Court for an injunction against the defendant restraining him from any act of infringement; the delivering up or destruction of articles infringing the patent; damages or an account of profits derived by the defendant from the infringement and a declaration that the patent is valid and has been infringed by the defendant.

It is a criminal offence to falsify the register of patents or to make a document falsely representing to be a copy of an entry in the register, or to make an unauthorised claim of patent rights or that a patent has been applied for.

It may be that a business organisation uses a secret process or mode of manufacture insufficiently original to patent, or which they do not wish to patent. The term "trade secrets" can be applied to such things, and they will be accorded a certain degree of protection at law (*see* below).

Trade-marks

A basic sales technique is to encourage consumers to identify goods with a particular manufacturer. Sometimes this is done through an advertising slogan or distinctive packaging but usually a registered trade-mark is employed. Indeed, some names which are trade-marks have become so well-known that they are acceptable everyday English, e.g. Gramophone and Hoover.

There are three main types of trade-marks.

(*a*) the manufacturer's name (a trade name) written in a distinctive way, e.g. Coca-Cola;

(*b*) a specially made up trade name, e.g. St Michael, Kodak; or

(*c*) a brand symbol, e.g. the Levis jeans trade-mark depicts two horses trying to rend a pair of their jeans. Other well-known symbols include the Bass Charrington triangle and HMVs dog listening to an old-fashioned gramophone.

Trade-marks can be registered under the Trade Marks Act 1938 providing they satisfy certain criteria. In particular they must not suggest fictitious patronage, e.g. by using the word "royal" in their name, nor convey, nor suggest a particular meaning which can be identified with the goods, e.g. a trade name such as "Good Value" would not be registrable.

Protection of trade-marks. The Trade Marks Act 1938 entitles the proprietor of a registered trade-mark to bring a civil action for infringement of his monopoly right. He may: seek an injunction restraining further infringement; claim damages or an account of profits derived from the unlawful use of the trade-mark; and demand an order for the delivery up of the infringing articles or other action to prevent them constituting an infringement, e.g. obliteration of the offending trade-mark.

Injunctions are more readily granted to restrain infringement of trade-marks than damage to other industrial property, for the court accepts that "the very life of a trade-mark depends upon the promptitude with which it is vindicated."

In addition to the statutory right of action, the proprietor of a trade-mark may bring an action in tort for passing off. This is considered below.

Goodwill

Goodwill can be said to be the economic benefit which arises from a business organisation's connections or reputation. In business the term is well understood, but at law it is, according to Lord Macnaughten (in a 1901 case), "a thing very easy to describe, very difficult to define. It is the attractive force which brings in custom. It is the one thing which distinguishes an old-established business from a business at its start." As such, goodwill can be a very valuable business asset and it may be worth as much as the business premises and stock. Goodwill is usually associated with sole traders, partnerships and small private companies having personal contact with its customers, not with large public companies.

Protection of goodwill. Unlike the other forms of industrial property discussed above, goodwill does not receive specific statutory protection. This is mainly because its whole concept is rather subjective and very difficult to define. In this case the more flexible protection afforded by the common law (the tort of passing off and by an action for breach of contract) is more suitable.

Passing off. A business organisation commits the tort of *passing off* where, deliberately or innocently, i.e. with no intention to deceive, it falsely represents its goods or its services to be those of another. The plaintiff need only show that its goods or its services are known by their get-up, description or trade-mark, and that there is a probability of confusion between them and those of the defendant; he need neither show that any consumer has actually been deceived, although it clearly helps if he can, nor that he has suffered any actual damage.

If the court finds that the tort has been committed, the plaintiff is entitled to an award of damages or an account of profits to compensate him for the financial injury he has suffered through the defendant taking his customers, and through any loss to his business reputation or goodwill. As an addition or an alternative to damages, the court may award an injunction forbidding the continuance of the unfair trade practice or, in the case of an infringed trade-mark, the delivering up of infringing articles or the removal of the offending mark.

The tort of passing off now mainly protects the property right of a trader in the goodwill of his business rather than rights in the other forms of industrial property considered above. For example, it is committed by: marketing a product and claiming it is made by the plaintiff; using the plaintiff's trade name, although purely descriptive names such as "vacuum cleaner" are less likely to receive protection than purely fanciful names; imitating the appearance of the plaintiff's goods; and selling the plantiff's inferior goods, e.g. "seconds" or "rejects", as perfect goods—in one case an injunction was issued to stop used Gillette razor blades being sold as genuine blades. In addition, while a person can use his own name in business, despite injury to another business with the same or similar name, he may possibly commit passing off by doing so. However, in such a situation, the plaintiff must show that consumers have learnt to associate his name with particular goods and that the use of the defendant's own name on similar goods is very likely to mislead consumers into believing the defendant's goods are those of the plaintiff. (In the case of a limited company, the Companies Act 1948 provides additional protection because the Department of Trade can require a company to alter its name if it is too similar to that of an existing one.)

While passing off primarily protects goodwill, the Trade Marks Act 1938 expressly preserves the right to bring a common law action for passing off if a statutory action for infringement of a trademark is not available, e.g. through want of registration. Similarly, the common law would allow an action for passing off committed by infringing a patent in the unlikely event of the statutory action being unavailable or declined. Conceivably, an action for passing off could also be used to protect a copyright or patent if, by their infringement, the defendant falsely represented his goods or his services to be those of another in a manner likely to deceive the public.

Two other actions in tort also protect property rights in the goodwill of a business. Firstly, *slander of title* is committed where the defendant falsely asserts that the plaintiff's goods are either not his to sell or that he has no right to sell them, e.g. denying an auctioneer's authority to sell and thereby causing him to lose custom and damaging his reputation. Secondly, it may be possible to bring an action in tort for a breach of confidence or the unauthorised use of information given in confidence, e.g. trade secrets, which damage the goodwill of a business.

Breach of contract. An action for breach of contract arises where one party to a legally enforceable agreement does not fulfil the obligations imposed upon him by the contract. Through a suitably drafted contract both the goodwill and trade secrets of a business can be protected in certain circumstances.

When a well-established small business is sold it is usual to sell the goodwill along with the business premises and stock. In the absence of an agreement to the contrary, it will be implied in the contract of sale that:

(a) the seller may set up a similar business in competition with the purchaser, but he may not use the old name nor represent himself as carrying on the old business;

(b) the seller may not canvass his former customers but he may otherwise publicly advertise his new business.

A purchaser of the goodwill can further protect himself by expressly including a term in the contract preventing the seller setting up a competing business for a certain time and/or within a certain area. Goodwill can be similarly protected from possible damage by former employees through an analogous term in their contracts of employment preventing them working for a competing business for a certain time and/or within a certain area. They must, however, have been employed in a capacity in which they dealt with customers who in consequence might possibly follow the former employee to his new employment. Such restraints have been applied to a variety of employees, e.g. a solicitor's clerk, a tailor's cutter-fitter and a milkman.

Trade secrets can also be protected by suitable terms in a contract of employment which prevent an employee with knowledge of them working for a competitor for a certain time and/or within a certain area. If an employee disclosed his employer's trade secrets during his employment this would be a breach of his contract of employment and would almost certainly justify summary dismissal.

While contractual terms may be used to protect the goodwill and trade secrets of a business, any contract which unreasonably restricts a person's freedom to carry on his trade, business or profession as he chooses (a contract in restraint of trade) is presumed to be void on the grounds of public policy. To enforce any such restraint the purchaser of the goodwill or the owner of the trade secrets, as the case may be, must show the restraint to be reasonable and in the interests of both the parties themselves and those of the public in general. For example, the area and duration of the restraint must be no wider than is necessary for the proper protection of the property interest, and the community must not be deprived of a necessary and useful service or skill. Thus, a restraint on the vendor of the goodwill of a hairdressing salon in a small town which prevents him establishing a new business in the same town in competition with the purchaser of the goodwill would probably be upheld if the town were adequately served by other hairdressing salons. Also to be considered is the firmly established rule that a restraint on a former employee is far less likely to be upheld than that on a vendor of a business. The reason for this different treatment lies in the inequality in bargaining power which exists between the parties to a contract of employment, while the vendor and purchaser of a business are presumed to bargain from positions of roughly equal strength.

PROFITS
The accountant's profit
To the accountant profit is essentially a residual figure, i.e. the money which is left over after all the expenses have been paid. Even so one might talk of profits before tax or after tax, distributed or undistributed. Without a clear understanding of company taxation it is difficult to understand these figures properly. Accountancy is often regarded as an exact study but in arriving at a figure for profit the accountant will have to exercise his judgment in *estimating* many figures in the accounts. For example, estimates will have to be made in arriving at figures for the value of stock, debts and assets. These calculations are made all the more difficult today when the accountant must also estimate the effects of inflation. It is therefore possible for a company to have a healthy-looking balance sheet but be near to insolvency, or to appear to be making virtually no profit at all but be very sound.

It is possible that an organisation owns some of the resources it uses; for example, it may have the freehold on its premises. In these circumstances it is essential to its effective running that these are costed and accounted for as if they were rented. This point is developed below.

The economist's view of profit
It is possible for a business to make an accounting profit but an economic loss. This is perhaps best explained by taking a simple example. Imagine the case of a solicitor who works for himself in premises he owns. At the end of the year he finds he has made £10,000 above the running costs of the practice and he therefore regards this as profit. The economist, however, will always enquire about the *opportunity cost*, that is to say what else he could have done with his resources of capital and labour, etc. We may find on examination that he could have rented the building out for £2,000 p.a., that the capital involved would have earned £1,000 interest if invested elsewhere and that he could have earned £8,000 working as a solicitor for the local council. Under these circumstances he could be £1,000 p.a. better off as a result of closing down his practice and placing his resources elsewhere.

Economists also have a view of the *normal profit* for an organisation. Normal profit is that amount of profit which is just sufficient to keep a firm in an industry. That is to say even though a firm may be making a profit in accounting terms, if this is very small the entrepreneur will not consider it worthwhile and will close down. The amount of profit which is considered normal will vary from industry to industry and area to area. Since this profit is necessary to keep the firm in business economists regard this as a legitimate cost of the business. Once the cost of this profit has been met any profit remaining is described as *super-normal profit*.

Sources of profit

Profits might be regarded as simply the reward for running a business organisation well, but in fact there are several different ways in which profits might arise.

The returns to other factors

As we saw above, much of what is commonly called profit is in fact the *implicit cost* of other factors of production. Thus the owner of a corner shop might say he has made £15,000 profit but in fact £5,000 is payment for his own labour, £2,000 is rent for the shop which he owns, and so on. This principle can apply to any size of organisation.

The return to innovation

One way to look at profit is that it is the reward for bringing new products or processes to the market. This has a special name and that is *innovation*. Innovation is the application of invention to industry. It is often the innovators who are remembered rather than the inventors, for example, James Watt, George Stephenson and Guglielmo Marconi were all people who made a commercial success of already existing inventions. If someone is enterprising enough to bring in a new product or process and it is successful then they will for a time make a large profit. This will disappear after a while when competitors can copy the process. This is the view of profit put forward by the famous American economist *Joseph Schumpeter*.

Recognising the importance of innovation the state rewards the entrepreneur with a limited legal monopoly of it in the form of a patent. However, the Competition Act 1980 provides that if a report of the Monopolies Commission shows that an anti-competitive practice which operates against the public interest involves the use of a patented product or process, the Minister may apply to the Comptroller-General for variation of the patent rights.

There are of course many more unsuccessful inventors and in-novators than successful ones.

The return to risk

Frank H. Knight in his book *Risk, Uncertainty and Profit* said that profit is the reward for a risk successfully taken. Profits arise, therefore, because the future is uncertain. This would certainly in-clude the innovator's profit because this can be viewed as the reward for the risk of bringing in a new product.

To a certain extent all the factors of production may earn a profit from uncertainty. For example, when a young person decides to train as a lawyer he is taking a risk that society will later wish to buy his services. The man who trained as an engineer runs the risk that he might be replaced by an automated machine. We saw in the previous chapter how the payment made to a debenture in a risky business contained an element of profit. In all these cases if the risk is successfully taken then the person receives a reward, if un-successful a loss. In other words profit can be both positive and negative.

We might distinguish between:

(*a*) *a speculative risk*, where a broker or similar person buys shares, bonds or commodities in expectation of a favourable change in their price;

(*b*) *an economic risk*, where an entrepreneur anticipates the demand for goods and services and supplies the product to the market.

Businessmen do not, of course, go around looking for "risky" products. In fact they tend to try and avoid risk as much as possible. Indeed, many risks may be avoided by *insurance*, but so long as uncertainty remains in the world someone, be it the entrepreneur or the state, will have to assume the risk of supplying goods to the market.

The return to monopoly power

Where a company has reached a dominant position in the market it may reap a rich reward without taking very much risk. However, it is not only entrepreneurs who might benefit from monopoly power. A trade union might use its monopoly power in a wage market to obtain a greater reward for its members. Similarly, any factor which is earning an *economic rent* could be regarded as making a monopoly profit (*see* page 224).

We would distinguish, however, between the situation where a monopolist deliberately *contrives a scarcity* to drive up the price of his product and a situation where the scarcity occurs *naturally* (*see* Chapters 10 and 16).

The role of risk-taking and of the entrepreneur is fundamental to the working of a free enterprise economy. When one observes the mixed economy in which we now live the consequences of taking economic risks are now much modified by government action. In recent years such things as the rescue of BL (British Leyland) seem to call into doubt whether the government is willing to let large businesses go bust. This practice too might spread to small businesses since the *Roll Committee* recommended that the government guarantee bank loans made to small business. If these practices continue and grow it is doubtful if we can speak any longer of a truly private sector of the economy.

GOVERNMENT POLICY TOWARDS PROFITS

The problem

Profits present the government with social problems of taxation and control. Although profits represent a much smaller share of national income than wages, the government may have very special reasons for controlling them.

(*a*) *Fairness*: if the government is trying to impose an incomes policy on the economy then it cannot expect wage restraint if it is not willing also to restrict profits.

(*b*) *Monopoly profits*: when an organisation makes large profits as a result of its monopoly power the government will need to regulate the situation.

Methods of control

The government has two main options if it is trying to eliminate excess profit.

Price control

By forcibly holding down the price which a firm would wish to charge, the government can reduce or eliminate profit. There are two circumstances in which this might be the appropriate policy. Firstly, the government might wish to do this as part of an *incomes policy*. To enlist the co-operation of trade unions in any incomes policy it will be necessary to have price restraint. Secondly, irrespective of prevailing economic conditions, price control would be one of the best ways of dealing with monopoly profit. Taxing monopoly profits does not alleviate the misallocation of resources involved in prices and output policy of the monopolist (*see* page 342).

Taxation

The government has a number of fiscal weapons which it uses, depending upon how the profits arise and how they are paid. The earnings of a company are taxed by *corporation tax* and *advance corporation tax*. However, the firm will usually incur less tax if it ploughs profit back into the business rather than distributing it. On distribution the profit may also become subject to *personal income tax*. Profits which are made from the sale of shares, commodities, property, etc., are taxed by *capital gains tax*. The rate of tax is much higher if it is a short-term capital gain rather than a long-term gain.

It is only companies who pay corporation tax whereas anyone may be subject to capital gains tax.

The consequences of profit control

The control and taxation of profit presents problems to any government. Although price controls may be appropriate to a monopoly situation and may be politically expedient, elsewhere it runs the risk of forcing the firm into a loss and so driving it out of business. Since profits are the return to enterprise, high profits could be regarded as the reward to a very successful business. By removing this profit the government will take away the incentive for firms to seek new opportunities and to take new risks. Under these circumstances the removal of profits could have a disastrous effect upon the economy. Alternatively, the firm may find it possible to pass taxes on to consumers by way of higher prices, in which case the object of the government will have been defeated. If the business is an exporter, high taxation may have the effect of making its products uncompetitive abroad.

Another problem of company taxation is that it encourages what Keynes termed "the double-bluff of capitalism". This is where companies are not taxed on the profits which they plough back because capitalisation will be to the advantage of the economy. The ploughing back of profits will, however, lay the foundation for even larger profits in the future. Undistributed profits also improve the dividend cover, thus forcing up the price of shares and making capital gains for their owners.

Sharing the profits

In the previous chapter you saw that some form of capital is necessary for any economic activity to be possible, and also how interest is payment for the use of capital. In this chapter you have already seen that profit, from which this interest may be paid, is the return to enterprise. Thus, the different types of investment and loans which comprise an organisation's financial capital must now be considered in relation to profit and risk.

A sole trader takes all the profits from his enterprise and, under the Partnership Act 1890, the partners in a firm share profits (and losses) equally, unless there is an agreement to the contrary. The members of a company share its profits according to the nature of the shares that they hold and the dividend agreed by the board of directors. While public corporations and municipal enterprises do sometimes operate at a profit, the concept of profit in its accepted sense is not really applicable to these organisations and the proceeds of enterprise are better viewed in their cases as "community benefit", and not as cash returns to the taxpayer or ratepayer. Similarly, the profit made by members of co-operative societies must be viewed rather differently to profit derived from membership of joint stock companies because the profit obtained in the former case is less applicable to risk than to the amount of business done with the society.

The sole trader or partner might feel that his risk is greater than that taken by a member of a limited liability company since sole traders and partners are potentially liable for all the losses of their organisation. However, someone who had invested £50,000 in a company which became totally insolvent might not agree. Nevertheless, it is true to say that no matter how great the investment, the risk involved in membership of a limited liability company is finite and calculable. It is impossible to say which form of business organisation is potentially most profitable.

Within a joint stock company the risk factor varies according to the type of shares held by the members. The risk factor is greater for ordinary shares than for preference shares, particularly cumulative preference shares, because the latter are entitled to a lower but more certain dividend than the former. In addition they often have priority in the repayment of capital on liquidation.

A shareholding in a co-operative society involves a lower risk than investment in a joint stock company. The dividend paid to co-operative society members is in effect fixed but secure, and the shareholding can be redeemed from the society at any time. In real terms, however, the risk factor involved in holding shares in co-operative societies or joint stock companies, being a member of a partnership or a sole trader mainly depends on the individual enterprise. The risk factor is low in running an established corner shop, being a partner in an established firm of solicitors or buying shares in ICI or Marks and Spencer Ltd. Conversely, the risk factor is higher in opening a new shop or forming a partnership, and still higher in investing in a purely speculative company, e.g. a speculative mining operation. While they do not necessarily end up insolvent, over 75 per cent of new business units go out of business within three years.

So far we have discussed the risk factor in relation to the finance of an organisation which is generated by its members, but it also applies to loan capital. In theory the contributors of loan capital only receive interest, but the different returns they receive in different types of business units is determined largely by the risk factor involved, i.e. the higher the risk factor, the higher the rate of "interest". In addition, there is always the danger that they may lose their money and the contributors of loan capital will try to minimse this aspect of the risk factor. Some loan capital for business organisations is provided by banks and they will always take a mortgage over the organisation's property or other suitable security, e.g. a director's guarantee. A partner who advances money to his firm receives some security in so far as he will be repaid on the firm's dissolution before the partners are entitled to receive back the capital they contributed.

Finally, it must always be remembered that a significant proportion of "profit" goes to the state in the form of taxes. Whilst there will always be argument about their best form and rate, taxation is clearly necessary to the continued existence of our mixed economy and our society in general.

THE FAILURE OF A BUSINESS

Why businesses fail

Failure is always a possibility in any business enterprise and you have seen above that loss can be attributable to a risk unsuccessfully taken. Its consequences can be disastrous not only for the person or organisation involved but also for its creditors (those to whom it owes money), its employees and even other persons or organisations engaged in the same or complementary economic activity.

Business failure may be due to a variety of causes; at its simplest it could be the result of producing a good or providing a service which nobody wants or, alternatively, it could fall the innocent victim of a combination of more complex forces such as difficulty in obtaining raw materials from abroad, bad labour relations and/ or management, inexorable competition or general economic recession.

Terminology

The term "bankrupt" is commonly applied to any person or organisation which is insolvent, i.e. where liabilities exceed assets, but this blanket usage is in fact incorrect. Sole traders and partnerships are made *bankrupt*, but registered joint stock companies are *wound up*, i.e. go into *liquidation*. Public corporations do neither—the taxpayer meets any debts they cannot pay themselves. There is, in fact, an important distinction between bankruptcy and liquidation; the former always entails insolvency but the latter does not. Liquidation or winding-up is the process by which a registered company ends its legal existence and this need not be through business failure. For example, it is common for the members of a private company who wish to retire to wind up the company as a more practical alternative to its sale.

Insolvency legislation and its aims

Whatever the reason for the failure of a business, it is necessary to regulate its consequences by using the law. In 1980 there was a total of 10,860 company liquidations, of which, 2,935 were compulsory liquidations, 3,970 members' voluntary liquidations and 3,955 creditors' voluntary liquidations. Receiving orders in bankruptcy proceedings totalled 3,652 (these terms are explained below).

The primary aim of the insolvency legislation is to secure an equitable distribution of the available assets among creditors so that fraud or secret arrangements cannot prejudice some to the benefit of others. Additionally, bankruptcy law frees the debtor from a hopeless situation so that he can start afresh. However, as you will see, bankruptcy deprives a person of almost all his possessions so that no-one will resort to it merely to avoid the inconvenience of being in debt. In contrast, the failure of a company registered with limited liability does not usually mean total financial ruin for its members; they only lose their investment, and any further liability is limited to the amount unpaid, if any, on their shares.

The law of bankruptcy is found in the Bankruptcy Acts 1914 and 1926, and the Insolvency Act 1976. These Acts are supplemented by the Bankruptcy Rules which govern procedure in bankruptcy matters. The winding up of companies is regulated by the Companies Act 1948 as amended.

The bankruptcy process

The bankruptcy process begins with a person committing one of ten *Acts of bankruptcy*. These include:

(*a*) "deeds of arrangement", i.e. transferring all your property to a trustee for the benefit of your creditors generally;

(*b*) "keeping house", i.e. refusing to answer the door or communicate with creditors;

(*c*) "fraudulent preferences", where the debtor conveys property to a creditor or charges property to a creditor intending to give him preference over others; and

(*d*) criminal bankruptcy orders made by the Crown Court against a person convicted of causing loss or damage to property exceeding £15,000.

However, the most common act of bankruptcy is;

(*e*) a debtor's failure to comply with a bankruptcy notice served on him by a creditor, who has obtained final judgment against him, requiring him to pay or provide security for the judgment debt.

Within three months of the act of bankruptcy having been committed, a *bankruptcy petition* must be presented by the debtor himself, alleging inability to pay his debts, or by a creditor(s) who is owed at least £200. If satisfied with the petition, the court will make a *receiving order* which makes the Official Receiver the receiver of the debtor's property, e.g. he handles all income, and prevents the debtor disposing of his property and the creditors taking further proceedings against him. It does not, however, actually make the debtor bankrupt. The order is advertised in the *London Gazette* and a local newspaper.

A *statement of affairs* is prepared by the debtor which is submitted to a *meeting of creditors*. The creditors have two basic courses of action open to them: they may accept the debtor's own plans for partial repayment or they may agree to ask the court to adjudicate the debtor bankrupt. They would probably adopt the former course where the delay and cost of bankruptcy proceedings is likely to be greater than the value of the property which would be recovered for division (*see* below) if they proceeded to adjudication. This course would also save the debtor from the socio-economic stigma and legal disabilities of bankruptcy.

If the creditors decide to continue bankruptcy proceedings a *public examination* of the debtor is held in open court. Its purpose is to ascertain the cause of the debtor's failure, but if no useful purpose would be served by doing so, for example, where the failure does not affect a wide circle of trade creditors and is of little public interest, it may be dispensed with under the Insolvency Act 1976. On the conclusion of the examination, the court makes the *adjudication order*. This declares the debtor bankrupt and passes title to his property to his trustees in bankruptcy, a trustee normally having been appointed by the creditors at their meeting.

An *application for discharge* may be made by the bankrupt at any time after the adjudication order. It will be heard in open court after fourteen days notice has been given to the creditors. The trustee, creditors and the Official Receiver may all object to the application, but if a discharge is granted the debtor is freed (sometimes conditionally) from all debts incurred before his bankruptcy and restored to his former status. The Insolvency Act 1976 provides that the Official Receiver must apply to the court for a review of the adjudication if no application for discharge has been made after five years have elapsed from the date of the adjudication order.

The process of company liquidation

There are three possible methods of liquidation.

(*a*) *Compulsory winding up.* Under this method the company is wound up by the court and it most commonly occurs where the company is unable to pay its debts, e.g. where a creditor to whom at least £200 is owed presents a petition after having made a proper demand for repayment which remained unsatisfied for three weeks. In addition, the Secretary of State for Trade has certain powers under the Companies Act 1967 to present a winding-up petition in order to protect the public interest.

When the winding-up order is made the company ceases to be a going concern. Any disposal of property or any transfer of its shares after the order is void unless sanctioned by the court.

The court collects the assets of the company and asks all members whose shares are not fully paid up to contribute the amount they owe. The assets are then applied to discharge the company's liabilities.

(*b*) *Voluntary winding up.* In a voluntary winding up the process of liquidation begins at the company's own initiative after a resolution to this effect has been passed by its members. Whether they or its creditors control the liquidation is determined by the company's financial position. If it is insolvent, the liquidation is controlled by the creditors who are able, therefore, to appoint a liquidator of their choice. The liquidator's functions are to settle the list of contributories (those members whose shares are not fully paid-up), collect the company's assets, discharge its liabilities to creditors and, where the company is solvent, redistribute the surplus to its members according to the rights attaching to their share of the company's capital.

(*c*) *Winding up under supervision of the court.* This occurs where a voluntary winding-up subsequently becomes subject to supervision by the court following a court order or a creditor's petition. Supervision orders are rare today.

When winding up is complete the company will be dissolved: its legal existence ended. Following a compulsory winding up, an order may be made by the court to this effect but more usually it is dissolved by asking the Registrar of Companies to strike its name off the Register. In the case of a voluntary winding up, the liquidator submits his account to a final general meeting of the company— also a creditor's meeting if the company was insolvent—and within one week files a copy with the Registrar. Three months after this the company is regarded as dissolved.

The consequences of insolvency

In terms of immediate consequences, bankruptcy is more disastrous to an individual than liquidation (through insolvency) is to the members of a company. The latter lose only their investment but the former will lose virtually all his property. However, the failure of a large company can have far-reaching socio-economic and even political consequences, quite apart from the larger financial losses likely to be involved. It will almost invariably mean redundancy for its employees with perhaps limited prospects at best for their immediate re-employment (although much will depend on the area and the age and qualifications of those made redundant). This in turn will affect the social structure of the immediate locality, possibly even causing migration of the young and middle-aged to more prosperous areas in search of jobs. It will certainly damage morale both on the micro-level of the family units affected and on the macro-level of economic activity generally (*see* page 468). It may even result in the government taking political decisions to encourage and direct investment to the area in order to provide alternative employment. Increasingly, governments have intervened to rescue large business organisations from insolvency when their failure would have serious socio-economic consequences (perhaps political as well) for the community in general, e.g. Rolls Royce, British Leyland and Upper Clyde Shipbuilders.

Leaving aside both the rules relating to the payment of creditors, where in fact the law on bankruptcy and the liquidation of insolvent companies is similar, and the often unquantifiable economic effect on creditors, the consequences of bankruptcy fall under two main heads: firstly, the effects on the debtor's property; and secondly, the legal disabilities which he suffers.

As we have already said, bankruptcy deprives the debtor of nearly all his property, vesting title to it in his trustee for the ultimate purpose of its division among his creditors. *Divisible property* includes not only property owned by the bankrupt at the commencement of the bankruptcy and property acquired by him before his discharge, but also property within his *reputed ownership*. This is property in the debtor's possession for his business use with the consent of its owner, e.g. a hired delivery van. In addition, certain property formerly owned by the bankrupt can be recovered by the trustee and forms part of the debtor's divisible property. For example, property which is the subject of a *fraudulent preference*, or which belongs to the trustee by virtue of the doctrine of *relation back*. Under the Bankruptcy Act 1914, the trustee's title to the bankrupt's property relates back to the first available act of bankruptcy in the three months preceding the presentation of the bankruptcy petition. Hence, subject to certain important restrictions, any property transferred to other persons by the bankrupt in these three months may be recovered by the trustee. The doctrine is designed to ensure that the trustee is not left empty-handed, as he might well be if the commencement of the bankruptcy was the order of adjudication.

The bankrupt is allowed to keep tools of his trade and clothing and bedding for himself, his wife and his children not exceeding £250 in value, and personal earnings necessary to support himself and his family and benefits under the National Insurance Acts, e.g. old age pensions.

The three disqualifications imposed on a bankrupt are designed to protect society from the inept or imprudent businessman.

(*a*) He may not act as a director of, nor take part in the management of, any registered company without the court's permission. A similar disqualification is imposed by the Insolvency Act 1976 where a person has been a director of two insolvent companies which have been wound up within five years of each other.

(*b*) He commits a criminal offence if he obtains credit of more than £50 without disclosing his bankruptcy.

(*c*) He may not trade under an assumed name without disclosing the name under which he was made bankrupt.

It is perhaps worth noting in conclusion that bankruptcy involves a debtor in business and financial ruin but the liquidation of an insolvent company may have little personal effect on its directors. Indeed, it would be quite possible to shelter behind the veil of incorporation and use the process of voluntary liquidation as a device to end an unsuccessful business venture without involving its owners in great financial loss, particularly if the company's assets are few and its capital small. Furthermore, there is nothing to stop the same people buying an "off-the-peg" company and commencing the same or similar economic activity the very next day, conceivably from the same premises. Alternatively, equally unscrupulous businessmen could use voluntary liquidation as a means of avoiding future onerous and expensive obligations after having made a large initial profit, e.g. after-sales service or guarantees. However, as you have seen, the Insolvency Act 1976 in effect prevents this being done more than once in five years, and it does assume that sufficient numbers of people, perhaps even banks, will be taken in a second time. Nevertheless, it serves to illustrate that no matter how carefully a legal framework is constructed to facilitate the activities and protect the interests of the vast majority, there seem always to be a few people with the ability and inclination to exploit the framework's loopholes and deficiencies in principle and procedure for their own ends. Corporate personality is fundamental to modern economic activity, but it can be used unfairly by the few.

SELF-ASSESSMENT QUESTIONS

A. 1. Define: (*a*) isoquant; (*b*) normal profit; (*c*) innovation; (*d*) fraudulent preference; (*e*) a deed of arrangement.

2. List the legal disqualifications imposed on a bankrupt.

B. 3. True or false?

(*a*) The accountant's view of profit does not take account of the resources which the business owns.

(*b*) The business will always try to minimise the opportunity cost of a project.

(*c*) Public corporations do not make profits.

(*d*) A criminal bankruptcy order must involve the loss or damage of at least £15,000.

(*e*) Ordinary shareholders take a greater risk than preference shareholders.

C. 4. True or false?

(*a*) A rise in the MRP of capital would cause businesses to demand more capital and less labour, other things being equal.

(*b*) The best combination of resources for the business is the most profitable one.

(*c*) A business does not take a risk if it is a monopolist.

5. If Public corporations are not supposed to maximise their profits, how should they devise their market strategy?

6. Draft a restraint on an employee or the vendor of a business designed to protect trade secrets, goodwill, etc.

ASSIGNMENTS

1. Construct a bar chart to show the number of bankruptcies and company liquidations in each year for the last decade. Account for the observed variations.

2. Advance arguments for and against increasing the taxation of profits.

CHAPTER THIRTEEN

Responsibility, Accountability and Resources

CHAPTER OBJECTIVES

After studying this chapter you should be able to:
* explain the business organisation's responsibilities which arise from the use of resources;
* list the different groups to which a business organisation is accountable for its economic activites;
* identify and explain the basis on which business organisations are accountable.

In this part of the book we have discussed the use of resources by organisations, and you have seen how their use is determined by a combination of economic principles and social and political considerations embodied in a regulatory framework of law. Thus, the use of resources gives rise to economic and social responsibilities encouraged or enforced by legal or political accountability.

We have already dealt in detail with the accountability of public corporations in Chapter 6 and we intend, therefore, to concentrate in this chapter upon sole traders, partnerships and companies.

ECONOMIC RESPONSIBILITY

The primary economic responsibility owed by joint stock companies, partnerships and sole traders (the three main types of business organisations is to make a profit, for it is from this profit that contributors of their financial capital receive a return on their investment or loan. (Rather different economic criteria apply to municipal enterprises, public corporations and co-operative societies.) Profit is equally important to create and secure market confidence in their activities. Without this confidence invested finance would be endangered and economic recovery or growth would have to be financed by expensive loan capital. Ultimately the result could be takeover by another business organisation, or insolvency.

SOCIAL RESPONSIBILITY

The economic responsibility to make a profit cannot nowadays be considered in isolation from the wider social responsibilities that organisations owe to their employees, the community and the natural environment. The profit-motive may seem at odds with these responsibilities, and with the profit maximisation characteristic of owner-managers of yesteryear this would indeed be the case, but today business organisations are to a much greater extent legally and politically accountable for their activities.

Whilst control of resources is largely in the hands of a few, the partial reconciliation of economic and social responsibility has meant that profits from the use of resources are shared somewhat more fairly. In particular, investors receive a good return, employees are better paid and enjoy greater job security, and society as a whole benefits from the enormous tax payments made to the Exchequer by business organisations. To whatever extent the profit motive has been reconciled with social responsibility it is due to a combination of changes in socio-economic philosophy, the divorce of management from ownership in large business organisations, the power and influence of trade unions and the imposition of legal and political accountability upon business organisations.

It is now probably accepted by most people that a business organisation's economic activity should not profit its owners at the expense of the employees and the community in general. Thus, a framework of employment law (regulating methods of payment, stipulating minimum standards in working conditions and protecting a person's employed status) and planning law (protecting the natural environment and the community from unplanned and antisocial use of land) are accepted constraints upon a business organisation's activities in general and profit maximisation in particular.

The divorce of management from ownership in large business organisations (*the managerial revolution*) has come about as a result of their increased size, the emergence of the joint stock company as the dominant form of business organisations and the need for specialised technical skills in management. Gone are the days when the owner-manager reaped all the profit from his relatively small but profitable organisation. Today, the managers of large public companies do not usually own them and the profits made by small business units, where owner-management is still possible, must be shared more equitably among those responsible for its generation. Whilst small businesses vastly outnumber large, the latter have the greater effect on the socio-economic environment, and some people would argue that their managements, now divorced from ownership, are far more likely to consider social responsibility in decision-making, providing profits are sufficient to satisfy shareholders and to safeguard their own continued employment. The likely increase in worker participation in management will probably see further reconciliation between the profit motive and social responsibility.

In theory, business organisations are neither responsible nor accountable to trade unions, but responsibility to employees is in practice very largely responsibility to trade unions. The provisions of the Health and Safety at Work, etc., Act 1974 are a good example of this. Trade unions have tremendous influence both with business organisations and with the government over conditions of employment and wage rates. In some ways the "sanctions" which a powerful trade union can impose may be more effective than formal legal accountability should a union consider that a business organisation has acted against the best interests of its members.

ACCOUNTABILITY

Legal or political accountability cannot ensure that business organisations will fulfil their economic responsibilities to their members and other contributors of finance, but it can ensure that economic activity is pursued according to standards designed to protect the interests of investors, creditors, employees and the community in general.

Political accountability

Political accountability is associated mainly with public corporations and municipal enterprises, the former being accountable to Ministers of State and ultimately to Parliament, and the latter to the appropriate local authority or other local government organisation. Increasingly, however, an element of political accountability is being employed by the government to encourage private enterprise to abide by its policies. In recent years, for example, the government has attempted to enforce "voluntary pay codes" by threatening any business organisation which breaks them with the loss of its government contract—the "black list". In foreign affairs the legal penalties imposed for breaking the economic sanctions against Rhodesia (now Zimbabwe) were used by successive governments as a means of reinforcing what was essentially political accountability.

Legal accountability

In the private sector of the economy all organisations are legally accountable for their economic activities to: their contributors of finance, be it invested or loaned; to their employees; to the state; and ultimately to their consumers.

To investors and creditors

This is reflected in the Partnership Act 1890 by the duty to keep proper books of account and the right to inspect them, and the right to take part in the management of the firm. Public joint stock companies are accountable to their shareholders through the annual general meeting required by the Companies Act 1948 at which the shareholders can in theory exercise control over the running of the company. All creditors are able to take legal action to enforce payment of sums owing, and secured creditors, i.e. those whose loan is covered by a security such as a mortgage, can in addition realise that security if repayment of the loan is unforthcoming.

To employees

Accountability at law to employees is imposed by the law of contract and the law of torts at common law, and by the comprehensive statutory framework of rules regulating contracts of employment, job security and working conditions. Such accountability is necessary to ensure that social responsibilities are fulfilled.

To the state

Business organisations are legally accountable both directly and indirectly to the state. Direct legal accountability is found in the general duty to obey the law and in a number of specific obligations, e.g. the duty to pay taxes, to abide by planning legislation, to provide safe working conditions for employees and to supply information required by law to state officials such as the Registrar of Companies. In so far as the state imposes sanctions for all infringements of the law, whether these directly harm the state or solely an individual, all business organisations are indirectly accountable at law to the state for all their activities.

To consumers

The sale of goods and services to consumers for profit is the ultimate purpose for which business organisations acquire and use resources. The "law of the market place"—contract and consumer law—makes all business organisations legally accountable to consumers and to the state (primarily through the courts and the Office of Fair Trading) for failure to meet standards of quality and behaviour required by law, and for much of the damage that this failure may cause. The business organisation's markets and clients are the twin themes of the next Part of this book, and the law of the market place is considered in detail in that Part.

SELF-ASSESSMENT QUESTIONS

A. 1. Define the "managerial revolution".

2. List the reasons for the partial reconciliation of the profit motive with social responsibility.

B. 3. True or false?

(*a*) Profit is important solely in order to provide dividend and interest payments to the contributors of a business organisation's financial capital.

(*b*) Business organisations are legally accountable to trade unions for their activities.

(*c*) Business organisations are never politically accountable to the government.

ASSIGNMENT

1. Discuss whether the present forms of accountability are sufficient to ensure that business organisations pursue their economic activities in a socially responsible manner.

PART FOUR
THE ORGANISATION, ITS
MARKETS, CUSTOMERS
AND CLIENTS

CHAPTER FOURTEEN

The Price System

CHAPTER OBJECTIVES

After studying this chapter you should be able to:
* define and evaluate the concept of the optimum allocation of resources;
* state the defects of the price system as a method of allocating resources;
* define the basic laws of supply and demand;
* list the five main determinants of supply;
* describe the consequences of interfering with the price mechanism;
* analyse changes in the equilibrium price.

HOW THE MARKET FUNCTIONS

Allocating resources

In the first Part of the book we looked at different economic systems such as collectivism and capitalism. In Part Three we examined how organisations utilise resources in a mixed economy. In this chapter we examine the determination of the prices of consumer goods. If we put the two together, the demand and supply for consumer goods and the demand and supply for factors of production, we obtain a picture of the *price system*, i.e. a method of allocating resources based on free market prices. This is illustrated in Fig. 44. This shows the critical importance of prices as the connecting, or communicating, mechanism between households and business organisations.

Any economy is interested in achieving an *optimum allocation of resources*, i.e. the best possible use of scarce resources. This is not, however, simply a measure of technical efficiency. If we considered any commodity, for example shirts, it would be possible to envisage a much more efficient system of production in which we concentrated on one design and one colour. However, a best use of resources should also be judged by whether it gives people what they want and clearly, at the present time, people are not content to wear identical clothing. Therefore an acceptable economic system must take account of this.

Consumer sovereignty

It is often said that the "consumer is king", meaning that he decides

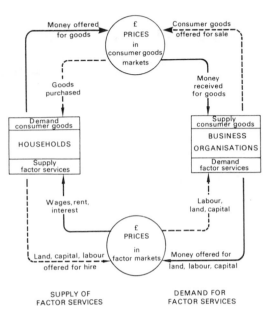

Fig. 44. *The price system.*

what is to be produced by being willing to spend his money on those particular goods. It is probably more accurate to say that there is a joint sovereignty between the consumer and the producer because the producer's behaviour and objectives will also have a great influence on the market.

The price system is also said, by some people, to be democratic in that every day consumers "vote" for what they want to be produced by spending their money. Although to some extent this is true it is considerably modified by the fact that money "votes" in the economy are unevenly distributed. Thus those with a high income have more "voting" power than those who are poor.

DEMAND

Market demand
The demand for a commodity is the quantity of the good which is purchased over a specific period of time at a certain price. Thus there are three elements to demand; price, quantity and time. This is the *effective demand* for a good, i.e. the desire to buy the good backed by the ability to do so. It is no use considering a

person's demand for the good if he does not have the money to realise it.

Other things being equal it is usually the case that as the price of a commodity is lowered so a greater quantity will be demanded. This is because of the *law of diminishing marginal utility*. The law states that over a specific period of time as more and more units of a commodity are consumed so the *additional* satisfaction, or *utility*, derived from their consumption will decrease, other things being equal (*see* page 64). For example, if one has had nothing to drink all day, the utility of a glass of water would be very high indeed and in consequence one would be willing to pay a high price for it. However, as one proceeded to drink a second, third and fourth glass of water the extra utility derived from each would become less. In this case, one might have been willing to pay a great deal for the first glass of water but as one continues to consume the price you would be willing to pay would decrease because you would be deriving a smaller utility from each successive glass. This helps to clear up the puzzle of why we are willing to pay so little for bread, which is a necessity, and so much for diamonds, which have little practical value. The answer is that we have so much bread that the extra utility derived from another loaf is small whereas we have so few diamonds that each one has a high marginal utility. Thus this principle helps to explain why more of a good is demanded at a lower price. The extra sales come from existing buyers who buy more and new buyers who could not afford, or who did not think the good was worth buying at, the higher price.

Price effects and income effects
As the price of one commodity falls relative to the price of other goods then usually people buy more of the cheaper good. If, for example, carrots become cheaper than cabbages, people will tend to eat more carrots and less cabbage. This is known as a *price* or *substitution* effect.

If the price of a commodity falls or the prices of commodities in general fall then the amount of money required to buy them will be less. This, therefore, leaves the consumer more of his income to spend. If he buys more of that or another commodity this is known as an *income effect*.

The demand curve
The following data is a hypothetical *demand schedule* for wheat. It illustrates the *first law of demand* which is, other things being equal, more of a good will be demanded at a lower price.

TABLE XXII. THE DEMAND SCHEDULE

	Price of wheat (£ per qtr. tonne)	Quantity of wheat demanded (qtr. tonnes per week)
A	5	10
B	4	17
C	3	25
D	2	35
E	1	50

Such information is usually expressed as a graph called a demand curve. As you can see in Fig. 45, the graph marked DD slopes downwards from left to right, and this is almost invariably the case. The relationship between price and the quantity demanded is an inverse relationship since as price *goes down* the quantity demanded *goes up*. If the price is lowered from £3 per qtr. to £2 per qtr. then the quantity demanded grows from 25 qtrs. to 35 qtrs. This can be shown as a movement down the existing demand curve from C to D. This is termed an *extension* of demand. Conversely, if

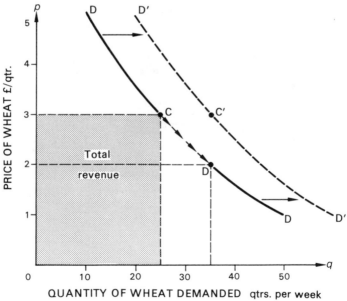

Fig. 45. *Changes in demand. The movement from C to D is an extension of demand. The movement from C to C' is an increase in demand. If the price is £3 and the quantity demanded is 25 qtrs. then the total revenue is £75.*

the price of the wheat were raised, then, this could be shown as a movement up the curve which is termed a *contraction* of demand. An extension or contraction of demand is brought about by a change in the price of the commodity under consideration and by nothing else.

If there were a failure of the potato crop then people would wish to buy more wheat but the price of wheat has not fallen. This is shown as a shift of the demand curve to the right. In Fig. 45 this is the move from DD to D′D′: as a result of this, at the price of £3, 35 qtrs. are demanded instead of 25; we have moved from point C to C′. A movement of the demand curve in this manner is termed an *increase* in demand. If the curve were to move leftwards, for example from D′D′ to DD this would be termed a *decrease*. An increase or decrease in demand is brought about by a factor other than a change in the price of the commodity under consideration.

Total revenue

The total revenue is the total sales receipts in a market at a particular price. In Fig. 45 you can see that if the price were £3 per qtr. then the quantity demanded would be 25 qtrs. per week. Consequently the total revenue would be £75.

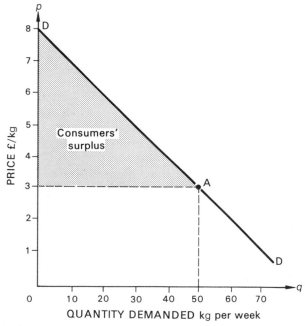

Fig. 46. *Consumers' surplus. Shaded area is the utility derived but not paid for by those who would have been willing to pay more than the market price.*

Total revenue = Price × Quantity

If the price were lowered to £2 per qtr. then the total revenue ($p \times q$) would be £70. You can see that, graphically, the total revenue can be represented as the area of a rectangle drawn under the demand curve.

Consumers' surplus

In Fig. 46 the price in the market is £3 per kg and at this price the quantity demanded is 50 kg. However, we can see from the demand curve that, had the price been £7, there would still have been a demand of 10 kg. Some people derive such a high utility from the consumption of this good that they would be willing to pay this high price. If we consider the market price of £3 we could then argue that the people who would have been willing to pay £7 are receiving £4 worth of utility for which they are not paying. A similar exercise would be carried out for a price £6 and £5 and so on. This excess utility is referred to as a *consumers' surplus*. It would be very good for the supplier if he could charge consumers different prices according to the different utilities they derived from the goods. This, of course, is not possible, so that if the supplier wishes to sell 50 kg. he must set his price to sell the 50th kg not the 1st one.

SUPPLY

Market supply

By supply we mean the quantity of a commodity that suppliers will wish to supply at a particular price. This is illustrated by Table XXIII. As you can see, the higher the price is, the greater the quantity which suppliers will wish to supply. If the price decreases there will come a price (£1) at which suppliers are not willing to supply because they cannot make a profit at this point.

TABLE XXIII. QUANTITY OF A COMMODITY SUPPLIED
AT A PARTICULAR PRICE

	Price of wheat (£ per qtr. tonne)	Quantity of wheat suppliers will be willing to supply (qtr. tonnes per week)
A	5	40
B	4	34
C	3	25
D	2	15
E	1	0

A greater quantity is supplied at a higher price because, as the price increases, organisations which could not produce profitably at the lower price find it possible to do so at a higher price. One way of looking at this is that as price goes up less and less efficient firms are brought into the industry. A good example of this is provided by North Sea oil. Britain's oil costs four or five times as much to extract as Arabian oil. The low prices of the 1950s and early 60s would certainly not have allowed Britain to extract the oil profitably but as the price rocketed in the 1970s it became a lucrative trade for Britain.

When asked why more is supplied at a higher price students frequently reply "because increased profits can be made". This you can now see is not so. The organisations which could make a profit at the lower prices do indeed make more profit but the extra supply comes from the marginal firms which are now brought into the industry. Thus we can conclude that more is supplied at a higher price because at a higher price increased costs can be incurred.

The supply curve
If we take the information from Table XXIII and plot it as a graph

Fig. 47. *Changes in supply. The movement from D to C is an extension of supply. The movement from B to B' is an increase in supply.*

we obtain a supply curve. This is illustrated in Fig. 47. As you can see the supply curve slopes upwards from left to right. This is a direct relationship, i.e. as price *goes up* the quantity supplied will *go up*. If the price increases from £2 per qtr. to £3 per qtr. then the quantity suppliers are willing to supply grows from 15 qtrs. to 25 qtrs. As with the demand curve, this movement along the supply curve from D to C is called an *extension* of supply. A movement down the curve would be called a contraction of supply. As with demand, an extension or contraction is brought about by a change of the price of the commodity under consideration and nothing else.

If the weather were very favourable then farmers would supply more wheat, not because the price had increased but because the harvest had been better than expected. This would have the effect of shifting the supply curve to the right. This is shown as the move from SS to S'S'. Previously, if the price was £4, 34 qtrs. would be supplied, after the shift, 44 qtrs. are supplied. This movement B to B' is called an *increase* in supply. Conversely, a shift of the curve to the left is termed a *decrease* in supply. An increase or decrease in supply is brought about by a change in a factor other than the price of the commodity under consideration.

Regressive supply curves

Supply curves usually slope upwards from left to right. Sometimes, however, they change direction, as in Fig. 48, and are said to become regressive. For example, this might be the case with the supply of

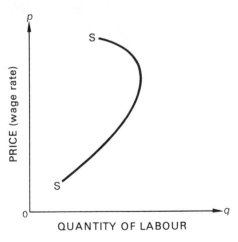

Fig. 48. *A regressive supply curve. As price continues to rise, less is supplied because suppliers are content with their level of income, and use the increased price to finance increased leisure.*

labour. In coalmining, where the job is extremely unpleasant, it has often been noticed that as wage rates have been increased miners have worked shorter hours. This is because instead of taking the increased wage rate in money the miners are taking it in increased leisure.

The determinants of supply

The behaviour of organisations in the market and the economy is the subject of the greater part of this book. More particularly the prices and output policy of organisations in the private sector is examined in Chapter 16. In this section of this chapter we simply note the factors which may influence the supply curve.

The most important determinant of supply is price. A change in the price of a commodity will cause a movement up or down the existing supply curve. A change in any of the other determinants of supply, which may be termed the *conditions of supply*, will cause a shift, left or right, to a new supply curve.

An important condition of supply is the price of the factors of production. A rise in the price of raw materials, for example, would have the effect of moving the supply curve leftwards. The large rise in oil prices in 1978 had this effect upon many industries. The supply of a commodity is also affected by the price of other commodities. If there is a rise in the price of barley then this will tend to decrease the supply of wheat as farmers plant more barley. It would be fairly easy for a farmer to do this but economic theory often assumes that businessmen in any field can alter production rapidly in this manner. This is obviously unrealistic; it would not be possible for an organisation producing shoes to change and produce cars simply because the price of cars is rising. It is the case, however, that there are often rapid transfers on the Stock Exchange in response to such changes.

Changes in the level of technology also affect supply. An improvement in technology allows us to produce more goods with less factors of production. This would, therefore, have the effect of shifting the supply curve to the right.

Some people would also maintain that the tastes of producers also affect supply. This is best illustrated in the case of the supply of labour, e.g. in nursing. There, because the suppliers of labour have a vocation they often tolerate low wages and poor working conditions.

EQUILIBRIUM PRICES

The formation of an equilibrium price

If we bring the demand and supply curve together we will see how a price is determined in the market situation (*see* Fig. 49). As you

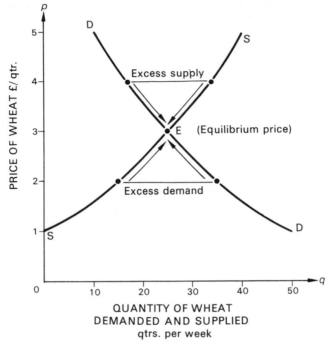

Fig. 49. *The equilibrium price. At the price of £3 per qtr. the quantity which is offered for sale is equal to the quantity people are willing to buy at that price.*

can see when the price is £3 per qtr. the effective demand for wheat is 25 qtrs. per week and this is also the quantity which suppliers will wish to supply. This price is termed *the equilibrium price* since, having arrived at it, there is no tendency for it to change. If the price was higher, for example £4, then suppliers would try to sell 34 qtrs. but buyers would only be willing to purchase 17 qtrs. There is an *excess supply* of 17 qtrs. In order to get rid of the surplus wheat suppliers will have to lower their prices. Conversely, if the price were £2 then buyers would like to purchase 35 qtrs. but suppliers would only be willing to sell 15 qtrs. There is an *excess demand* of 20 qtrs. Suppliers will therefore put up their prices to ration out the scarce wheat. The excess demand will have pushed up the price. Thus, there is only one equilibrium price. At any other price there is a tendency to move towards the equilibrium.

Equilibrium prices ration out the scarce supply of goods and services. There are no great queues of people demanding the best cuts of meat at the butchers. A price of £6 per kg of fillet steak ensures that only the rich or those who derive great utility from

beef steak buy the meat. It might appear iniquitous to some people
that even a small house in London costs £40,000, but if we do
away with price as a rationing mechanism we only have to put
something else, perhaps equally unacceptable, in its place.

In this section of the chapter we examine two examples of where
the government has interfered with the price mechanism in our
economy.

Price fixed above the equilibrium: the butter mountain

The common agricultural policy (CAP) of the EEC gives support
to farmers through guaranteed high prices. The EEC realises that
at the world price many European farmers could not produce and
so would go out of business. To keep farmers in business and encourage European food production the EEC therefore fixes an
intervention price. If the farmer cannot sell all of his output at or
above this price then the *intervention agency* steps in and buys the
rest. Consumers are prevented from buying food more cheaply from
non-EEC countries by the *variable import levy*. Thus, the price of
most agricultural products is fixed above the equilibrium price.

Probably the most notorious consequence of this was the "butter
mountain"—the surplus butter production which the EEC had to
buy up and store because it could not be sold at the *target price*. In
1976 this amounted to 260 thousand tonnes of butter. In addition
to this the EEC had bought and stored 1,100 thousand tonnes of
skimmed milk powder which is enough skimmed milk to keep the
whole of the EEC supplied for over five years. This is explained in
Fig. 50. Here the free market price is represented as OR. At this
price the quantity demanded and supplied is OM and there is,
therefore, no excess demand or supply. The target price fixed by
the EEC is OT (at some times the EEC price has been over three
times the world price). European housewives are not, however,
prepared to pay that price. Thus, the demand contracts to OL,
whereas, encouraged by the high price, European farmers supply
ON. This, therefore, leaves a quantity of LN to be bought by the
intervention agencies, thereby creating the butter mountain. The
proportions are greatly exaggerated in this diagram. The excess
supply is in the region of 20 per cent, but this still amounts to an
awful lot of butter.

This method of supporting agriculture is wasteful because it
creates surplus food. It is often sold outside the EEC at a loss, as in
1977 when a large tonnage was sold to the Russians at 36p per kg.
Thus the European consumer is paying higher prices in the shops
to subsidise Russian consumers. The system is also inequitable since
it is poorer families who spend a higher proportion of their budget

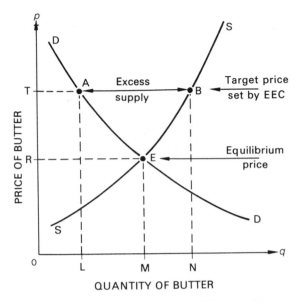

Fig. 50. *The butter mountain, created by the EEC setting the target price above the equilibrium price.*

on food. They are therefore giving a greater proportion of their income to support farmers' incomes and are getting less food as a result of it. In recent years the EEC has been more successful in eliminating these surpluses, but the tendency to overproduce because of guaranteed high prices remains. The previous British system of supporting agriculture was to give subsidies to farmers. This resulted in more being produced, but it was sold at a *lower price*. Although this was still inefficient, since the subsidies had to be paid for by taxes, it had the desired effect of supporting farmers, giving low prices to consumers and creating no excess supply of the good.

Price fixed below the equilibrium: rent control

Since the First World War there have been several Acts of Parliament (*see* page 228) which have tried to fix the price of accommodation. These have usually had the laudable motive of trying to ensure reasonably low rents for tenants. Through inflation the effect of fixing rents has meant that, in many cases, the rent is now way below the equilibrium price. As you can see from Fig. 51 the effect of this is to create excess demand. The supply of houses for rent has contracted as landlords sell their homes rather than lease them at low rents. The number of people who wish to rent has become

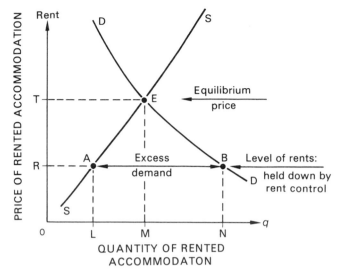

Fig. 51. *Rent control. Artificially low rents bring about less supply but a greater demand and therefore an excess demand for rented accommodation.*

greater. In the diagram, LN represents the amount of excess demand. Those who occupy rented accommodation are pleased with the low rent and are naturally very unwilling to move, thereby worsening the situation. The fact that landlords have not legally been able to put up prices has frequently led to black market payments such as "key money".

About a quarter of Britons live in council houses and the rents of most of these are also below the equilibrium price. Here another rationing mechanism comes into play: the housing lists of local authorities.

CHANGES IN THE EQUILIBRIUM PRICE

In the previous section we examined the consequences of interfering with an equilibrium price. Prices frequently change, however, as a result of market forces. In this section we examine the four basic changes that are possible in the equilibrium. It is important when considering these changes to stick to the rule of *ceteris paribus* (*see* page 65), i.e. we must keep all other things equal and only consider the effect of one change at a time.

Figure 52 demonstrates these four basic changes. This illustrates all the variations that are possible unless regressive demand and supply curves are considered. You will see that an increase in

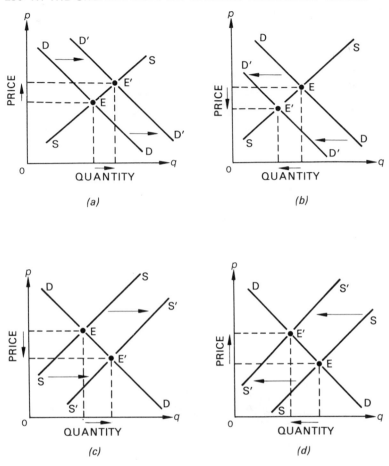

Fig. 52. *Changes in the equilibrium price.* (a) *Increase in demand results in more being bought at a higher price.* (b) *Decrease in demand results in a smaller quantity being bought at a lower price.* (c) *Increase in supply results in more being supplied at a lower price.* (d) *Decrease in supply results in less being supplied at a higher price.*

demand brings about an extension of supply, an increase in supply brings about an extension of demand, and so on. We have here considered the change from one equilibrium to another. This will take time to come about and there may be several transitional stages before the new equilibrium is arrived at. However, having reached a new equilibrium there is no further tendency to change.

ECONOMIC DEMAND AND SOCIAL NEED

In this chapter we have seen something of how demand and supply help us to deal with the economic problem. Prices are a method of rationing out the scarce goods and services in the economy. The price system provides one answer to the three vital economic questions; *what* shall be produced, *how* shall it be produced and *who* will receive the goods when they have been produced. In many ways the price system is a remarkably efficient mechanism: there are no unsold stocks of goods left rotting; there are no long queues waiting for goods that are in short supply.

There are some commodities, however, which the price system is not so good at producing; things like medical services, defence and education are usually better provided on a community basis. The state also usually intervenes to prohibit or control the sale of certain goods such as dangerous drugs and firearms. Today there is also a great deal of legislation surrounding process of manufacture, e.g. to prevent organisations from discharging toxic waste. Governments also often lay down minimum standards of manufacture. This may increase prices but it is considered better to have safer products made. The fact that income is unevenly distributed also means that the price system is inequitable. There may be no queues outside the foodshops, but nevertheless people may be hungry or starving and simply not have the money to buy food. This is not a problem which is confined to poor nations. Indeed, recent reports in Britain have suggested that many children suffer from malnutrition, and each year many old people die of hypothermia because they cannot afford to heat their homes. People of all political persuasions therefore agree that the state should intervene in the running of the economy to ensure social justice. The basic political argument is therefore between those who believe that the price system is basically sound and that the government should intervene by levying taxes to finance old age pensions, defence, etc., and on the other side those who wish to see the state taking a bigger part in the direct running of the economy.

SELF-ASSESSMENT QUESTIONS

A. 1. Define: (*a*) effective demand; (*b*) the law of diminishing marginal utility; (*c*) excess supply; (*d*) the equilibrium price.

    2. List the determinants of supply.

B. 3. True or false?

    (*a*) The "butter mountain" is the result of excess supply.

    (*b*) A fall in the price of a good causes demand to increase.

(*c*) The market mechanism is not capable of producing services such as education.

(*d*) The price mechanisim does not always take account of social costs.

(*e*) An improvement in the method of producing a commodity would move its supply curve to the right.

C. 4. True or false?

(*a*) In Fig. 49 if the price were £5 then the excess supply would be 30 qtrs. per week.

(*b*) Figure 45 illustrates that lowering the price of the commodity always decreases the total revenue.

(*c*) The EEC has a greater tonnage of butter stored than any other foodstuff.

(*d*) In Fig. 45 the move from DD to D'D' represents an increase in demand of 50 per cent at every price.

(*e*) An increase in the equilibrium price of a commodity must always reduce the size of the consumers' surplus.

5. Find out which other commodities being supported by the CAP are in excess supply and find out the size of this surplus.

ASSIGNMENTS

1. Present the information you have acquired for Question 5 in diagrammatic form.

2. Discover what restrictions there are upon the rents of privately let accommodation.

CHAPTER FIFTEEN

The Chain of Demand

CHAPTER OBJECTIVES

After studying this chapter you should be able to:
* define market demand and evaluate its importance to the business organisation;
* describe the channels of distribution;
* list and describe the determinants of demand;
* calculate the elasticities of demand;
* state the importance of market research and advertising to the organisation.

THE SCOPE OF THE MARKET

The market as a mechanism and the market as "demand"

In the last chapter we saw how the market functions as a mechanism for allocating goods and services in the economy. Left to itself the price mechanism can answer the three fundamental questions of economics: what shall be produced; how shall it be produced; and for whom? The price mechanism, then, is a means of communication between the very disparate organisations which make up the economy. Most organisations, however, are not interested in the market mechanism from this point of view. The thing which concerns trading organisations is the market for their particular product; how much of their output they can sell and for how much. In this chapter we examine markets from this point of view. Although the relationship is essentially between the producer and the consumer of the product, we shall see that there are many organisations and factors which make up the chain of demand between the two.

Channels of distribution

The most direct channel of distribution is if the manufacturer sells directly to the customer. This may be the case, for example, with very expensive equipment such as aircraft, or alternatively with individually customised items such as bespoke tailoring. There are often, however, one or more intermediate stages between the manufacturer and the customer.

There are, of course, many different ways in which finished products can reach the customer and the product may pass through

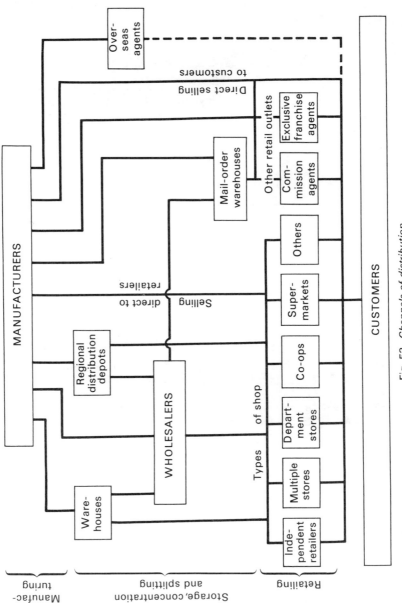

Fig. 53. Channels of distribution.

many different hands before being sold to its eventual owner. Figure 53 summarises some of the more common channels of distribution. The wholesaler frequently plays a key role in the *chain of distribution*. It is often said that the wholesaler does nothing for the money he receives and that, consequently, he makes the price of goods unnecessarily high. Wholesalers do, however, perform several useful functions. Firstly they *concentrate* stocks of different goods in one place; this allows manufacturers to make one bulk delivery instead of several small ones. The goods are then *split* as the wholesaler breaks them down into smaller consignments for the retailer. This is a more efficient use of transport since the manufacturer is able to send full loads of the same good to the wholesaler and the wholesaler is then able to send full loads, made up of many different products, to the retailer. It is also convenient for the retailer to be able to do his "shopping" in one place. The wholesaler is also able to develop an expert knowledge of the market and advise retailers on how demand is changing. Wholesalers also perform a valuable service in holding stock. He will, of course, charge for the risk involved. If the demand for products is regular and predictable, as for example in foodstuffs, the margin of the wholesaler is likely to be small. On the other hand, if the wholesaler holds very specialist stock which may not be demanded for months or years, for example specialist ironmongery, he is likely to look for a higher margin. If wholesalers do not demand immediate payment for goods they are also acting as suppliers of trade credit.

There have been, however, many successful examples of wholesalers being eliminated. On the other hand the customer should treat carefully offers of "straight from the manufacturer prices" and "discount warehouses"—these are frequently just alternative forms of retailing. It is not unrealistic to assume that wholesalers survive because they fulfil some useful function. There is a danger of course that a wholesaler might be able to "corner" the market in a product and reap monopoly profits.

There are many different types of shops. Some of the more common are shown in Fig. 53. They are not mutually exclusive categories. Co-ops operate supermarkets and there are multiple department stores such as the John Lewis Partnership. Over the past twenty years multiple stores and supermarkets have grown in importance whilst the independent retailers', department stores' and the co-op's share of the market has declined. The large retail groups frequently undertake their own wholesaling. This was pioneered by the co-ops when they set up the CWS, but today it is multiples like Marks and Spencer who have made a great success of it, frequently using their monopsonic buying power to dictate terms to manufacturers.

Retailers often enter into an agreement with manufacturers to become the exclusive agent for a particular product. This is often the case with car sales and sometimes with hi-fi equipment. The retailer acquires a monopoly of the product in his local area whilst the manufacturer secures a more energetic promotion of sales. This type of *franchise* should not be confused with franchise chains such as Wimpy or Kentucky Fried Chicken where the retailer pays considerable sums of money for the use of the franchise.

The mail-order business was pioneered in the USA where most of the people could not reach a city. In recent years the mail-order business has become more important in the UK although it still only accounts for just over 5 per cent of all retailing. The mail-order "house" usually acts like a department store, selling well-known brand names. The mail-order catalogue is often backed up by local commission agents. Sales have often been helped by the instant credit available to customers through the catalogue. The mail-order business in Britain has traditionally been strongest among the lower income groups. In recent years mail order has tended to move "up market", with many articles being sold through colour supplement advertisements and often being paid for by credit card.

Transport

The producer of a good must, almost invariably, use some form of transport to deliver the product to the consumer. The importance of the different forms of transport within Great Britain can be gauged by studying Table XXIV.

TABLE XXIV. TRANSPORT OF GOODS WITHIN GREAT BRITAIN

Mode of transport	Quantity of freight carried (million tonnes)		Share of total tonne kilometres (%)	
	1966	1979	1966	1979
Road	1,641	1,504	57.9	67.9
Rail	217	169	20.4	12.9
Coastal shipping	53	59	20.2	12.2*
British waterways	8	5	0.2	0.1
Pipelines	31	85	1.2	6.7
Air freight	0.1	0.1	0.1	0.2
Total	1,950.1	1,822.1	100.0	100.0

* estimated

Source: CSO

The picture is modified by the value of the goods which are transported. Air traffic ·for example looks to be of very little importance but many of the most valuable and important cargoes travel by air. In Britain the tendency is for an increasing proportion of goods to travel by road. The great advantage of road transport is its convenience and flexibility. The suppliers of goods must decide between owning their own transport and hiring transport from road hauliers. To some extent this is governed by the size of the company and by the type of transport required. A frozen food company, for example, would usually have its own fleet of refrigerated trucks. Business organisations frequently find road to be cheaper than other modes of transport. Society, however, may not find this so. In 1978–9 the direct cost of building and maintaining roads was £1,658 million. There are also indirect costs by way of damage to buildings through vibration and damage to the environment through air pollution. In addition to this, in 1978 6,831 people were killed in road accidents. It would take 66 years of rail accidents to equal one year of road fatalities. Rail transport in Britain is of course nationalised and frequently criticised for the losses it makes. It is, however, a quick and efficient means of transporting passengers. It is very efficient as a transporter of cheap bulky goods such as iron ore and is vital for the distribution of mail and newspapers. It has the disadvantage that it only operates between fixed points and goods nearly always require another form of transport to complete their journey.

In recent years two important developments in transport have been containerisation and pipelines. Containers are more important in overseas than in domestic trade. In 1978 Britain exported 80.9 million tonnes of goods by sea and imported 154.3 million tonnes. The importance of pipelines can be judged by studying Table XXIV. Their importance will further increase with the exportation of North Sea oil. Despite all our advances in technology water transport still remains the cheapest way of moving goods from A to B. Britain makes much less use of internal waterways than most of her European neighbours. The greatest expense in transport is often in loading and unloading and it is because of this that containers have been so successful. Producers will not always want the cheapest form of transport. Commodities such as diamonds are usually transported by air, while for perishable goods speed is all-important. In general, however, manufacturers will always want to minimise their transport costs. Society, however, must weigh the total advantages and disadvantages of one form of transport against another.

Finance

The availability of finance has an important effect on both sides of the market. As was pointed out in Chapter 12 organisations produce in anticipation of demand. During the process of manufacture they must therefore have the resources to finance their operations. This can either come from their own resources, from trade credit, or from outside sources.

Whilst it is always readily accepted that income is a major determinant of demand, it is not so obvious that credit may also have an important effect. Today many expensive consumer durables such as cars are bought with the aid of credit. The general availability and price of credit, therefore, can affect demand. Government legislation governing hire purchase and bank lending is also important. If the government alters the percentage of the purchase price which is required as a deposit, this can bring about large changes in demand for certain goods. For many years the motor trade complained that the government used the industry as an economic regulator by altering credit restrictions.

Thus we have seen that a market is not usually a producer selling directly to a consumer, between them are transport, shops, wholesalers, finance houses and so on. Despite this one should not lose sight of the fact that it is still a market controlled by the prices which people are willing to pay for goods. Any organisation which tries to sell goods or services will therefore have to consider the factors which will determine the demand for his product.

FACTORS DETERMINING DEMAND

Price

The relationship between the price of a good and the demand for it was fully discussed in the previous chapter. We may note here that price is the single most important factor in determining the demand for a good. It is interesting to note that there are a few exceptions to the *first law of demand,* i.e. where a rise in the price of a commodity *causes* more of that commodity to be demanded.

Goods demanded for their price (snob value)
With some expensive items, such as a Rolls Royce or Chanel perfume, the consumer may buy the commodity because it is expensive, i.e. the price is part of the attraction of the article and a rise in its price may render it more attractive.

An expectation of a further change in price
You may observe a *perverse demand* relationship on the Stock Ex-

change; a rise in the price of a share often renders it more attractive causing people to buy it and vice versa.

Giffen Goods

Robert Giffen, a nineteenth-century statistician, was studying the Irish economy and noticed that a rise in the price of potatoes caused more to be bought and vice versa. This was because potatoes are an *inferior good* (*see* below) and households were having to spend the major portion of the family budget on potatoes just to keep alive. As the price of potatoes declined this freed a portion of the family income (income effect) which was immediately spent on other foods to vary the diet. Thus, less potatoes were needed. As the price of potatoes increased again the family had to revert to living entirely on potatoes. Because of the peculiar combination of circumstances the income effect completely masked the price effect.

Income

Since *effective demand* is the desire to buy a good backed by the ability to do so it is obvious that there must be a relationship between the demand for an organisation's product and the consumer's purchasing power. Purchasing power is usually closely linked to income. The nature of the relationship between income and demand will depend upon the product. A rise in income is hardly likely to send most consumers out to buy more bread whereas it might cause them to buy a larger car. If the demand for a commodity increases as income increases it is said to be a *normal good.* Conversely if, as income rises, the demand for a product goes down then it is said to be an *inferior good.* There are some products, for example salt, which tend to have a constant demand whatever the level of income. These three possibilities are illustrated in Fig. 54.

You will note that the demand for the inferior good behaves like the demand for a normal good at low levels of income. All inferior goods start out as normal goods and only become inferior as income continues to rise. Cotton sheets might be considered an inferior good if, as you became very wealthy, you substitute silk sheets. In other words the goods are not intrinsically inferior, it is the commodity's relationship with income which is inferior. It is, however, commodities such as bread and potatoes which are usually termed inferior, since here the relationship of *market* demand with the community's income is inferior, whereas the demand for a product such as cotton sheets is not.

The price of other goods

In marketing its products any organisation is aware that it is

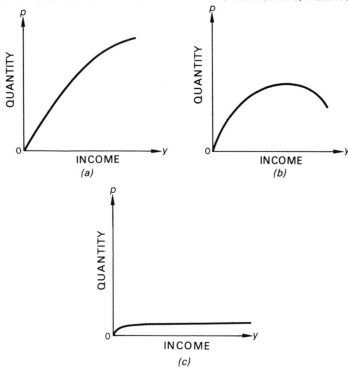

Fig. 54. *Income and demand.* (*a*) *Normal goods.* (*b*) *Inferior goods.*
(*c*) *Inexpensive foodstuffs, e.g. salt.*

competing for a share of a limited amount of households' incomes.
In this sense all demands are interrelated. However, there are two
particular interrelationships of demand which may be observed,
where goods are *substitutes* one for another or are *complementary.*
Examples of substitute commodities would be tea and coffee, or
butter and margarine, where one consumes one or the other. The
case of complementary or *joint demand* is illustrated by commodities
such as cars and petrol, or strawberries and cream. In all these
cases there is a relationship between the price of one commodity
and the demand for the other. If, for example, the price of cars
were decreased this would cause more cars to be bought and hence
an increase in the demand for petrol.

Other factors influencing demand
When discussing the factors influencing demand we must remember
the rule of *ceteris paribus.* That is to say, for example, we can only

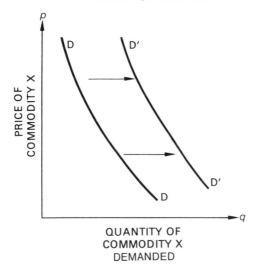

Fig. 55. *A shift in demand. An increase in demand brought about by a change in the conditions of demand, e.g. a fall in the price of a complement, a rise in the price of a substitute, a rise in income if commodity X is a "normal good", a fall in income if commodity X is an "inferior good", a change in taste in favour of commodity X, or a successful advertising campaign.*

conclude that a fall in the price of a complementary good such as cars would increase the demand for petrol if we state that all other things remain equal. If, for example, incomes decrease at the same time it would be impossible to come to any conclusion.

The factors we have discussed above, i.e. price, the price of other goods and income, is to a certain extent quantifiable. There are numerous factors which can influence demand, many of which it would be extremely difficult to quantify. However, as we stated in the last chapter, it is possible to conclude that if we change any of the determinants of demand other than price, i.e. any of the *conditions of demand*, we will cause an increase or decrease in demand (*see* Fig. 55). It will be remembered that the effect of this is to shift the demand curve rightwards or leftwards.

Some of the other factors which may influence demand are listed below.

(*a*) *Tastes, habits and customs.* This is extemely important as most people tend to continue their habits of eating, etc. A change in taste in favour of a commodity shifts the demand curve rightwards.

(*b*) *Changes in population.* Demand is obviously influenced by the number of people in the economy and the age, sex and geographical distribution of the population.

(c) *Seasonal factors.* The demand for many products, such as clothing, food and heating, is influenced by the season.

(d) *The distribution of income.* It is not only the level of income which influences demand but also the distribution of income. A more even distribution of income might increase the demand for hi-fi equipment but decrease the demand for luxury yachts.

(e) *Advertising.* A successful advertising campaign would obviously increase the demand for a product. Advertising might also be aimed at making the demand for a product less elastic (*see* below).

(f) *Government influences.* The government frequently influences demand; for example by making it compulsory to wear seat belts it increases the demand for them.

Students are often tempted to say that supply is a determinant of demand; this is *not* so. Supply influences affect demand only via the price of the commodity. Similarly, indirect taxes on commodities, e.g. VAT, or subsidies, are supply influences since they affect the costs of production.

MEASURING DEMAND

Price elasticity

So far we have said that if price is lowered, other things being equal, a greater quantity will be demanded. Thus, the demand curve slopes downward from left to right. If, however, an organisation is going to cut its prices then it would be most advantageous for it to know how much more was going to be demanded. A cut in price might cause a lot more to be demanded or not very much more. This is illustrated in Fig. 56.

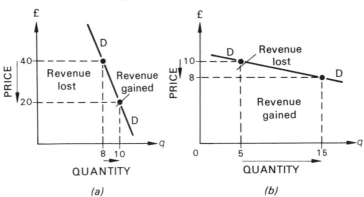

Fig. 56. *Elasticity of demand.* (a) *Inelastic demand.* (b) *Elastic demand.*

In Fig. 56(*a*) you can see that a relatively large drop in price from £40 to £20 results in demand growing by a relatively small amount from eight to ten units. Thus demand is not very *responsive* to changes in price and is termed an *inelastic demand*. However, in Fig. 56(*b*) you can see that a relatively small fall in price causes a proportionately much greater rise in demand. In this case demand is *responsive* to changes in price and the demand is said to be *elastic*.

The criteria we have discussed above are somewhat vague but elasticity can be categorised precisely by looking at total revenue. If the price of a commodity is lowered and the total revenue ($p \times q$) increases then demand is elastic. Conversely, if the price of the commodity is lowered and the total revenue ($p \times q$) decreases then demand is *inelastic*. There is also an inbetween case where if the price is lowered and this causes just enough more to be demanded so that total revenue ($p \times q$) remains unaltered then demand is unitary. These principles may be summarised:

(*a*) price decreases—total revenue increases ⎫
     price increases—total revenue decreases ⎬ demand is elastic

(*b*) price decreases—total revenue decreases ⎫
     price increases—total revenue increases ⎬ demand is inelastic

(*c*) price changes (+) or (−)—total revenue constant, demand is unitary (*see* Fig. 56).

You can see from this why elasticity of demand is of crucial importance to a business organisation. Recently three of the four major car manufacturers in the UK announced price increases whilst the fourth announced a price decrease. Can you determine from the above principles which categories of elasticity they thought existed for their products?

It might be thought that elasticity could be judged from the slope of the demand curve. In Fig. 56 the steep curve is inelastic demand and the one tending towards the horizontal is elastic. But the appearance of the curve is an unreliable guide. Here we find that with the exception of the extremes, where the demand curve is vertical, there is no elasticity at all and demand is said to be *perfectly or absolutely inelastic*. Conversely, where the demand curve is horizontal demand is *perfectly elastic*. A unitary demand curve must have the property that whatever the price the total revenue remains constant. This must mean that any rectangle drawn under the curve (TR) must have the same area. A curve with this property is known as a rectangular hyperbola. These possibilities are illustrated in Fig. 57.

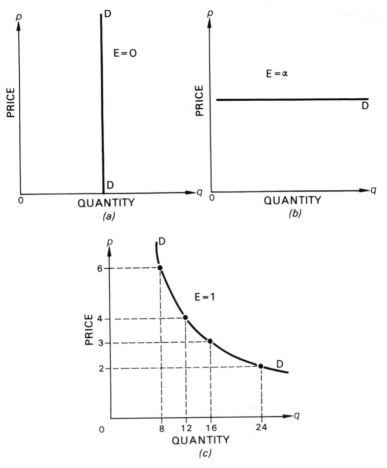

Fig. 57. *The limits of elasticity.* (*a*) *Totally inelastic demand.* (*b*) *Perfectly elastic demand.* (*c*) *Unitary demand.*

The extent to which demand will respond to a change in price may be *measured* by comparing the percentage change in quantity with the percentage change in price which brought it about. If, for example, a 1 per cent cut in price brings about a 3 per cent increase in quantity demanded, then we have a value for elasticity of three. The numerical value of elasticity is termed the *coefficient of elasticity*. The categories of elasticity can be allotted numerical limits. If the value of the coefficient is greater than one then demand is elastic, because there is a greater percentage change in demand than there is in price. If the value of the coefficient is less than one then demand is inelastic. Where the value of the coefficient is exactly one then elasticity is unitary, because the percentage change in quantity is equal to the percentage change in price so as to leave total revenue unchanged. The value of the coefficient is thus worked out as:

$$\text{the coefficient of elasticity } (E) = \frac{\% \text{ change in quantity}}{\% \text{ change in price}}$$

This can be illustrated by considering the demand schedule in Table XXV.

TABLE XXV. DEMAND SCHEDULE

Column	Price of commodity £/kg (1)	Quantity demanded kg/week (2)	Total revenue £s (3)	Category of elasticity (4)
A	10	0	0	
B	9	10	90	
C	8	20	160	Elastic
D	7	30	210	
E	6	40	240	
F	5	50	250	Unitary
G	4	60	240	
H	3	70	210	Inelastic
I	2	80	160	
J	1	90	90	

Suppose that the organisation which markets this commodity is selling it at £8 per kilo, then it might consider what the effect would be if it lowered the price to £7. You can see from column (2) that the quantity demanded would grow from twenty kg per week to thirty. Thus a 12.5 per cent cut in price has brought about a 50 per cent growth in demand. The percentages involved here are very simple to work out and you can probably calculate them in your head, but we need the formula if the figures are not so straightforward. Thus we can write out the above calculation as:

$$E = \frac{\% \text{ change in quantity}}{\% \text{ change in price}} = \frac{\dfrac{10}{20} \times \dfrac{100}{1}}{\dfrac{1}{8} \times \dfrac{100}{1}} = 4$$

Thus, in this case the coefficient is 4, which is greater than 1 and demand is therefore elastic. You can confirm this by checking the change in total revenue in column (3). Here a cut in price has resulted in an increase in total revenue so demand is, indeed, elastic.

From the above calculation we can derive the simple formula to calculate the coefficient of elasticity which is:

$$E = \frac{\dfrac{\Delta q}{q}}{\dfrac{\Delta p}{p}}$$

Where Δq is the change in quantity considered and q is the original quantity. Similarly Δp is the change in price and p is the original price (see McNamara, page 84).

This formula can be applied to other prices in the schedule. Thus, if the original price were £2 and we consider changing the price to £1

$$E = \frac{\dfrac{10}{80}}{\dfrac{1}{2}} = \frac{10}{80} \times \frac{2}{1} = \frac{1}{4}$$

Thus the coefficient is less than one and demand is inelastic. If the value of the coefficient is $1/4$ this tells the seller of the commodity that if he cuts his price by 1 per cent it will result in only a $1/4$ per cent more being bought.

The elasticity of demand should be unitary where total revenue is maximised in our example this is at a price of £5 per kg. This we can confirm by calculating the coefficient at that price:

$$E = \frac{\dfrac{10}{50}}{\dfrac{1}{5}} = \frac{10}{50} \times \frac{5}{1} = 1$$

The demand schedule of Table XXV is presented as a demand curve in Fig. 58. From this you can see that although the slope is constant the elasticity changes along its whole length. In fact at point A elasticity is infinite and at point K it is zero. Most demand curves tend to behave in this manner being elastic at the top and inelastic towards the bottom. The factors which determine the degree of price elasticity are as follows.

(a) *The number of substitutes available.* The greater the number of substitutes, the greater the elasticity will tend to be.

(b) *The percentage of income spent on the good.* If a purchase

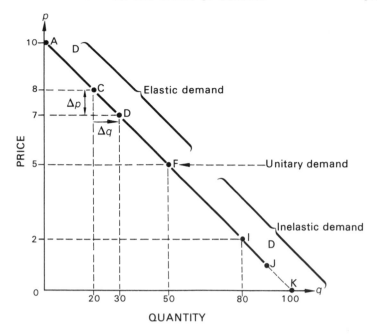

Fig. 58. *Elasticity of demand. One demand curve can have all three categories of elasticity.*

takes up a large percentage of income, for example buying a car, this tends to make the demand more elastic.

(*c*) *Durability*. Durable goods, for example cars and furniture, usually have a higher elasticity of demand than perishable goods, such as food.

(*d*) *The number of uses for the commodity*. If the same product can be put to many different uses this tends to increase the elasticity of demand for it.

Thus cigarettes, which have no substitute, occupy a relatively small proportion of a person's income, have no durability and only one use, therefore have a very low elasticity of demand. In addition to this cigarettes are addictive. You will also note here that the product does not have to be a necessity to have an inelastic demand.

Income elasticity
We said in the previous section that elasticity of demand measures the degree of responsiveness of quantity demanded to changes in

price. It has already been noted in this chapter that there is a measurable relationship between demand and income. It is possible, therefore, to calculate *income elasticity* which measures the relationship of changes in demand to changes in income.

The coefficient of income elasticity can be calculated as:

$$E_y = \frac{\%\ \text{change in quantity}}{\%\ \text{change in income}} = \frac{\dfrac{\Delta q}{q}}{\dfrac{\Delta y}{y}}$$

where y = income.

If an organisation is selling a normal good such as cars it might expect that as incomes rise so would the demand for cars. In this case an increase in income has brought about an increase in demand. The value of the coefficient is therefore positive. If, however, the organisation sells inferior goods such as potatoes, then as income rises demand will decrease. The value of the coefficient will therefore be negative. For some goods, such as salt, the demand may not vary at all with income, and in these cases there is zero income elasticity. These possibilities are illustrated in Fig. 59 (*see also* Fig. 54).

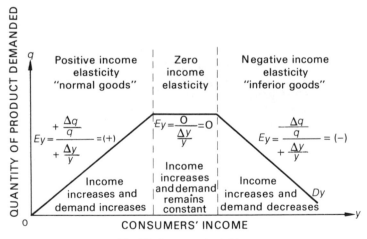

Fig. 59. *Income elasticities.*

Cross elasticity

Where there is a relationship between the price of one commodity and the demand for another and it is possible to measure this, it is termed the *cross elasticity of demand*. There is, therefore, a coefficient of cross elasticity, and this may be calculated as:

$$E_c = \frac{\% \text{ change in quantity of commodity B}}{\% \text{ change in price of commodity A}} = \frac{\frac{\Delta q\text{B}}{q\text{B}}}{\frac{\Delta p\text{A}}{p\text{A}}}$$

In the case of complementary commodities a fall in the price of one should increase the demand for the other. For example, an oil company might expect an increase in demand for petrol as the result of a fall in the price of cars. In this case the value of the coefficient would be negative since a decrease $(-)$ in the price of cars has brought about an increase $(+)$ in the demand for petrol (*see* Fig. 60).

Conversely, if an organisation were selling a commodity for which there were a substitute the opposite would be the case. For example, Stork margarine might expect a decrease in the demand for its product as a result of a fall in the price of butter. In this case a decrease $(-)$ in the price of one product has led to a decrease $(-)$ in the demand for the other, and the value of the coefficient is therefore positive (*see also* page 305).

Elasticity and tax revenues

It has already been explained that elasticity of demand is of great importance to a trading organisation. If an organisation knew that the demand for its products was inelastic it might be tempted to raise its prices, whereas it might be tempted to lower its prices if it believed the demand was elastic. (A simple observation of this is complicated by changes in the general price level brought about by inflation.) The Chancellor of the Exchequer is also concerned with the elasticity of demand for the products on which he levies *indirect taxes*, such as VAT and Customs and Excise duty.

In Fig. 61 a tax of £10 per unit is levied on the commodities. This raises the price to £30 per unit. In (*a*) this raises a tax revenue of £100,000 (£10 × 10,000), whereas in (*b*) the tax revenue is £30,000 (£10 × 3,000). If, instead of a £10 tax, the Chancellor were to impose a £20 tax you can see that where the demand is inelastic the tax revenue would now be £180,000 whereas where the demand is elastic tax revenue would only be £20,000. Thus, in the latter case, increasing the tax has decreased the tax revenue. This is because where demand is elastic increasing the price through higher taxation discourages sales to such an extent that less tax revenue is raised. When the Chancellor imposes an indirect tax on a commodity it can therefore be with the object of either raising more money *or* discouraging consumption: it cannot do both. This point is illustrated by excise duty on tobacco. Chancellors have frequently

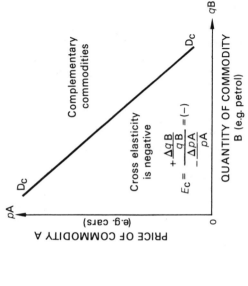

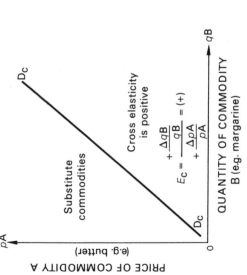

Fig. 60. *Cross elasticities of demand.*

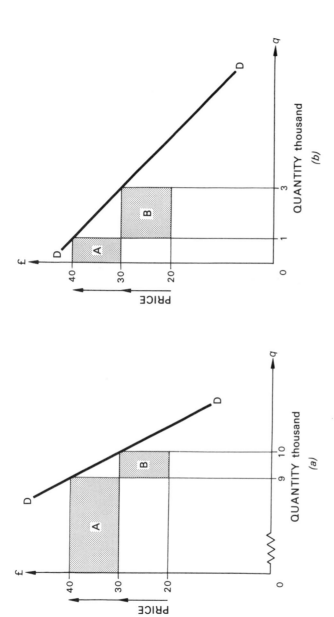

Fig. 61. *Revenue from an indirect tax.* (a) *Inelastic demand.* (b) *Elastic demand. A = revenue gained by raising the tax; B = revenue lost by raising the tax. Only if A is greater than B will raising the tax be worthwhile.*

said that they are raising the tax on tobacco to discourage smokers, but since the demand for tobacco is extremely inelastic it is to be doubted whether the government means this, but rather is using this argument to legitimise the increasing of an already very high tax.

It is commonly believed that it is only the consumer who pays indirect taxes but this is not always so. The *incidence of taxation* depends upon the elasticity of demand for the product. This is demonstrated in Fig. 62.

Indirect taxes have the effect of moving the supply curve of the commodity vertically upwards by the amount of the tax. In Fig. 62 this is the move from SS to S'S' where the amount of the tax is shown by the arrow. The equilibrium price increases from E to E'. The price does not go up by the full amount of the tax because part of the tax has been absorbed by the producer who is worried about the effect increased prices would have on his sales. The greater the elasticity of demand, the greater the percentage of the tax the producer will absorb. If, therefore, the tax on tobacco is increased, most of the increase is passed on to the consumer. This is because the demand is very inelastic. However, if the tax were increased on cars more of it would be absorbed by the motor trade because the demand is more elastic.

There are two ways of calculating an indirect tax. Firstly, it could be a *specific or unit* tax, where the tax is the same per unit of a

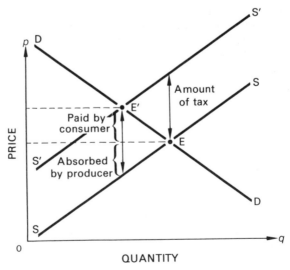

Fig. 62. *The incidence of an indirect tax.*

commodity irrespective of its price. In Britain, the most important unit taxes are the excise duties on tobacco, alcohol and petrol. The other method is to levy a tax by the value of the commodity, this being known as an *ad valorem* or percentage tax. In Britain the most significant *ad valorem* tax is VAT.

Market research and advertising

It has been said that if you have the right product "the world will beat a path to your door". In an increasingly complex business world it is doubtful whether this is ever true without a good deal of careful planning. It is necessary to discover the size and nature of the market for a product, and to design and produce the commodity accordingly. If one has the right product it is usually necessary to inform the world of this through advertising. Thus market research and advertising enter the demand chain.

The production of almost all goods and services involves risk as the producer, even if he is a monopolist, cannot be sure that consumers will demand a sufficient quantity of the commodity or be willing to pay the right price. Market research, which today is a considerable industry, tries to determine not only the size of the market but also the design of product. It is no good producing the right sort of product if it is the wrong size or colour. This is particularly true of overseas markets where customers may, for example, want products in metric sizes, will certainly want descriptions and product instructions in their own language, and will look for adequate after-sales service.

We saw in the previous section of this chapter that it is not just a case of how large the market is; the organisation will also be interested in the elasticity of demand, the cross elasticity and the income elasticity for its product. The simplest form of market research is historical, being based on past knowledge of the market and projection of past trends. For a small organisation, where the entrepreneur is in close contact with his customers, this may be the most effective form of market research. For a large organisation projection of historical trends is a tricky business. For example, it is obvious that people buy warmer clothes in the winter, but what style of warmer clothes? For large organisations with millions of pounds of capital equipment to commit, accurate knowledge of the market is essential.

Active market research consists of sampling public opinion in much the same way as political opinion polls. It is beset with problems from the statistical viewpoint and also because it is necessary to ask exactly the right questions. Some years ago Ford of America introduced a new car, the Edsel, which was designed, via extensive market research, to be the car everyone wanted. The project was a failure, and a glance at the streets will show that there is no *one* car that everyone wants.

New products require market research, and this is frequently done through pilot schemes where the product is tried out in one part of the country. This, however, can also be difficult as the national market is far from homogeneous. Market research also seeks to find out not only how much will be bought, but also who the customers are. This is very important for the design of the advertising campaign.

Advertising takes two main forms, *informative* and *persuasive*. An informative advertisement is one which uses only economic and technical criteria such as the price and the specification. A purely informative advertisement is hard to find, but such things as the ads for houses in local papers or advertisements for capital equipment are mainly informative. Persuasive advertising seeks to convince the consumers that one product is better than another using primarily non-economic criteria. Since, in the British economy, most people have satisfied the basic economic wants of food, clothing and shelter, many advertisements appeal to psychological motives, hence the consumers are promised that consumption of the product will make them sexually more attractive, more socially acceptable, emotionally more secure and so on.

Advertising does not only have the aim of increasing the sales of a commodity, it may also be designed to maintain brand loyalty. The object of advertising may also be to decrease the elasticity of demand for a product, i.e. to persuade the consumer that there is no real substitute for that particular brand and therefore make them willing to pay more for the commodity. *Product differentiation*, i.e. making essentially similar products appear different through advertising, packaging and design, is also partly aimed at exploiting different elasticities of demand in different parts of the market. An example of this would be detergents, where the same product is sold under one brand name at a high price for those who believe they are buying a quality product whilst the same detergent is sold under a different brand name at low price for those who are interested in economy. Product differentiation also helps advertising by allowing the same product to be promoted in different ways. The multiplication of brands also allows the producers' goods to occupy more space on supermarkets' shelves, etc.

Advertising is also used by some large companies as a means of political propaganda. Some of Britain's leading companies have placed advertisements in national newspapers not to sell their products but to defend free enterprise and/or to attack nationalisation.

It can also be argued that advertisements put out a more subtle form of propaganda through the way of life they show as desirable. In recent years legislation and the advertising industry's own efforts have tried to make advertisements more truthful. In some cases the government does intervene to prohibit some advertisements; for example, it is now forbidden to advertise cigarettes on television. (For a discussion of Consumer Legislation governing advertising *see* page 390.)

SUMMARY

The consumer may buy goods directly from the producer or his demand may become effective through a long chain of events. However demand becomes effective it is determined by the same factors of price and such things as income, the price of other goods and consumers tastes. Figure 63 summarises some of the main stages in the chain discussed in this chapter. The producer may try to assess and manipulate the demand himself but the goods are usually demanded through a chain of other institutions. The effect of consumer legislation on the chain is discussed in the next two chapters. Thus a large number of organisations are usually involved in the demand for a particular commodity. If you imagine the case of a car being imported into the country and sold, this will involve shipping companies, garages, HM Customs and Excise, banks and finance houses, road hauliers and advertising agencies. An organisation selling its product must be aware of all these factors, whereas the average consumer is usually just interested in the right product at the right price.

SELF-ASSESSMENT QUESTIONS

A. 1. Define: (*a*) market demand; (*b*) inferior goods; (*c*) cross-elasticity; (*d*) persuasive advertising.

B. 2. True or false?

(*a*) If price is lowered and this results in an increase in total revenue then demand is elastic.

(*b*) A substitute good is usually an inferior good.

(*c*) If the Chancellor increases the tax on a commodity with an elastic demand he will collect less revenue.

(*d*) All advertising has the object of selling more goods.

(*e*) An increase in the price of butter would extend the demand for margarine.

C. 3. True or false?

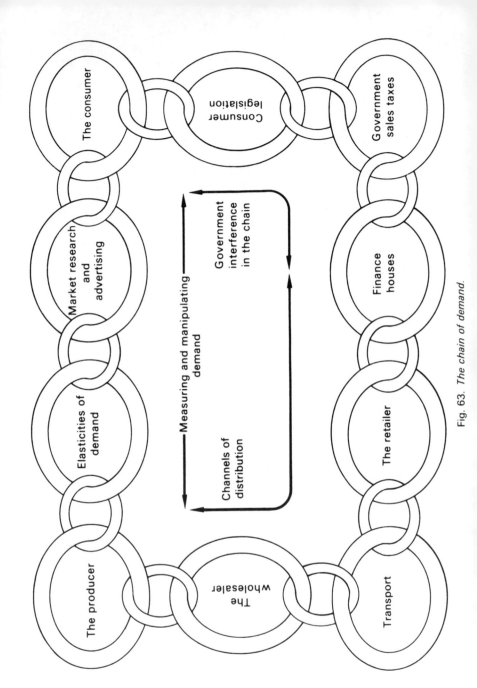

Fig. 63. *The chain of demand.*

(*a*) Road transport is more important in terms of tonne kilometres than in total tonnage carried (Table XXIV).

(*b*) In Fig. 56(*a*) the value of the coefficient of elasticity at the price of £40 is $\frac{1}{2}$.

(*c*) A rightward shift of the demand curve will always decrease its elasticity.

(*d*) If income elasticity of demand for a product is −2 then an increase in income of £100 will cause £2 more to be spent on it.

(*e*) At point H in the demand schedule in Table XXV the coefficient of elasticity is 0.4286.

4. Determine how you would calculate elasticity of supply and say how it differs from elasticity of demand.

5. Find out the shares of the retail trade enjoyed by the various types of retailers shown in Fig. 53.

ASSIGNMENTS

1. Design a market research questionnaire for a product of your own choice.

2. Write an article for a newspaper criticising the effects of advertising on society.

CHAPTER SIXTEEN

Market Structure and Supply

CHAPTER OBJECTIVES

After studying this chapter you should be able to:
* define and evaluate the profit maximising hypothesis;
* describe different market structures;
* list and describe different types of market;
* analyse the effect of market structure on the allocation of resources;
* state the different ways in which a government might deal with monopoly.

DIFFERENT TYPES OF MARKET

Maximising profits

In the previous chapter we examined the market for goods and services. In this chapter we examine how a business organisation's prices and output policy is determined. It is usually assumed that business organisations will always try to *maximise their profits*. This means not only will they try to make a profit, but they will always try to make as much profit as is possible. This assumption is given the somewhat grand title of *the profit maximising hypothesis*. In general, this is a realistic assumption. However, profits are often regarded as the return to a risk taken; a businessman may try to minimise the risks he takes and in doing so he could therefore be accepting lower profits. It is certainly true that many businessmen are interested in stability and will be willing to tolerate slightly less profit if that profit is stable and predictable. (For a full discussion of this *see* pages 9–11.)

Market places

We have previously discussed the market as a mechanism for allocating goods and services and a market as the demand for a particular commodity. The word market can also be used to describe a *market place*. In this sense a market is any means by which buyers and sellers are brought together. This may be directly as in a street-market such as Petticoat Lane, or indirectly, as for example, by telex in foreign exchange markets. A market can be local, national or international; this will depend upon the nature of the commodity, the state of communications and upon government restrictions. Some of the main types of market are listed below.

(a) *Retailing*. Goods and services are sold to the final consumers; usually through shops.

(b) *Wholesaling*. Commodities are sold to retailers for resale to consumers. As well as general wholesalers, there are specialist markets, such as Billingsgate for fish, and Smithfield for meat.

(c) *Commodity markets*. Since Sir Thomas Gresham built the Royal Exchange in 1571, London has had important commodity markets where raw materials are bought and sold both for use in the UK and abroad. Indeed, Britain remains the world centre for many of these trades. There are about forty commodity trade associations which make up the *British Federation of Commodity Associations*. The following are examples of these markets.

(i) The London Commodity Exchange at Plantation House: markets in rubber, cocoa, jute and sugar.

(ii) The Tea Auction Room in Plantation House: markets for both tea and coffee.

(iii) The Baltic Exchange: markets for coarse grains, oils and oil seeds.

(iv) Hatton Garden: market for gem stones and industrial diamonds.

(v) Beaver House: market for furs.

There have been commodity markets outside London such as the Manchester Royal Exchange and the Bradford Wool Exchange.

(d) *Shipping and insurance*. London remains a world centre for both shipping and insurance services, which are centred on Lloyds. Shipping services are also sold on the Baltic Exchange.

(e) *Financial Markets*. There are many national and international financial markets in London (*see* Chapter 22).

(i) The money market; loans made for very short periods—that is to say money "at call or short notice".

(ii) The discount market; dealing in bills of exchange, both Treasury bills and commercial bills.

(iii) The capital market; dealing with the provision of capital both to government and industry.

(iv) The new issue market; dealing with the raising of capital through the issue of new stocks and shares.

(v) The stock market, dealing in the sale and purchase of previously issued stocks and shares.

(*vi*) The foreign exchange market; dealing in the sale and purchase of foreign currencies.

Trading is carried on in the markets in very different manners, some of which are listed below.

(*a*) *Auctions.* Sales of easily standardised commodities such as tea or grain are carried out by auction. London is also a centre of the auction market for antiques and works of art.

(*b*) *Private deal.* This is where a broker concludes a deal with a trader on behalf of a client having approached several sellers to obtain the best terms. This is the practice, for example, on the Stock Exchange and the Baltic Exchange.

(*c*) *Ring trading.* This is the practice on the Metal Exchange where the forty members of the ring sit in a circle bidding for one consignment of metal at a time, until the five minute limit is announced by the ringing of a bell.

(*d*) *"Sights" market.* The seller shows his commodity, asks a certain price and if this is not met he withdraws it from the market. This is the case in the sale of diamonds. The sellers of diamonds have frequently acted as a *cartel* to restrict the flow of diamonds to the market and thereby raise their price.

(*e*) *"Spot" markets.* This is where the goods are sold for immediate delivery and could have been sold by any of the above methods.

(*j*) *"Futures" markets.* In this case the goods are purchased "forward", that is to say they will be supplied at the agreed price at some time in the future. This is often the case with commodities such as metals, grains and sugar. Foreign exchange is also often bought in a "futures" market.

Thus it can be seen that there are many different ways in which goods and services can be bought and sold. The business organisation is not, however, concerned with the physical attributes of the market so much as its economic characteristics. Economically, markets can be distinguished by the type of competition which exists in them, i.e. by the number of sellers who make up the industry and by the number of purchasers of the commodity. It is the state of competition in the industry which will be the most important determinant of the prices and output policy of the business organisation.

The perfect market

For a state of perfect competition to exist in an industry the following conditions would have to exist.

(*a*) A large number of buyers and sellers of the commodity, so that no one person could affect the market price through his own actions.

(*b*) Freedom of entry and exit to the market for both buyers and sellers.

(*c*) Homogeneity of product, i.e. all the goods being sold would have to be identical.

(*d*) Perfect knowledge of the market on the part of both the buyers and the sellers.

(*e*) It must be possible to buy or sell any amount of the commodity at the market price.

It is obvious that all these conditions cannot exist in one market at once. There are, however, close approximations to perfect competition, e.g. the sale of wheat on the commodity market in Canada. In this situation there are thousands of sellers and ultimately millions of buyers and it is relatively easy for farmers to enter or leave the market by switching crops, for, once graded, one tonne of wheat is regarded as identical with another. In addition to this, when wheat is sold on the commodity market, both sides have a good knowledge of the market and it appears to the farmer that he can sell all he wants at the market price but he is, individually, unable to influence it. The perfection of the market is, however, flawed by farmers banding together in co-operatives to control the supply, by widespread government intervention in agriculture and by some very large buyers in the market. For instance, in recent years the USSR has bought millions of tonnes of wheat on the North American market to make good the shortcomings in its own domestic output.

Although perfect competition does not exist, we continue to examine it because it represents the ideal functioning of the free market system. Thus, although we cannot eliminate all imperfections in the market, we may try to minimise them as an engineer may try to minimise friction in an engine. If there were perfect competition the individual firm would *appear* to face a horizontal demand curve for its product. If it raised the price of its product it would no longer be on the demand curve and would sell nothing. Conversely, it would have no incentive to lower its prices since it appears to be able to sell any amount it likes at the market price. The organisation is thus a *price taker* and its only decision, therefore, is how much to produce (*see* Fig. 64). The price may of course change from day to day, as it does in the case of wheat, but to the farmer the demand curve always appears horizontal. The industry demand curve will remain a formal downward sloping one; indeed the world demand curve for wheat is fairly inelastic,

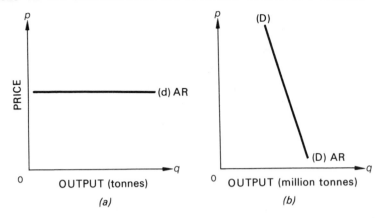

Fig. 64. *The demand curve under perfect competition. (a) The demand curve for the individual business organisation's product. (b) The industry demand curve.*

large changes in price bringing only relatively small changes in demand.

Imperfect competition

All markets are to a greater or lesser extent imperfect. This is not an ethical judgment upon the organisations which make up the markets. There is nothing morally reprehensible about being an imperfect competitor, indeed, this is the "normal" state of affairs. It could be the case, however, that firms contrive imperfections with the object of maximising their profits to the detriment of the consumer. This is discussed later in this chapter and also in the next chapter.

All imperfect competitors share the characteristic that the demand curve for their individual firm's product slopes downward. That is to say if the firm raises its prices it will not lose all its customers as it would under perfect competition. Conversely, it can sell more of the product by lowering its prices. In addition to this it can be affected by the action of its competitors. In Fig. 65, for example, the decrease in demand DD to D'D' could have been brought about by a competitor lowering his prices. If, for example, Ford were to drop the prices of their cars by 5 per cent it would probably bring about a substantial decrease in demand for BL cars. This would not be so in the case of perfect competition. If, for example, Farmer Jones were to cut the price of his wheat by 5 per cent it would scarcely affect the sales of the thousands of other farmers who make up the market.

It is possible to distinguish several types of imperfect competition.

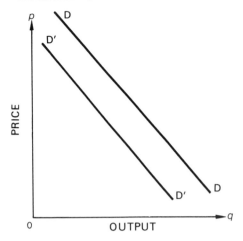

Fig. 65. *The demand curve for an individual organisation's product under imperfect competition. The firm has some choice over price or output but can also be affected by competitors. The decrease in demand from DD to D'D' could have been brought about by a fall in the price of a competitor's product.*

These distinctions arise, chiefly, out of the different numbers of firms which make up any particular industry and the consequent differences in market behaviour in the short run and the long run.

Monopoly
This, literally, means a situation where there is only one seller of a commodity. This is the case in the UK with Tate & Lyle, who have a virtual monopoly of cane sugar, and Joseph Lucas with an almost complete monopoly of electrical components for cars. Legally speaking an organisation may be treated as a monopoly under the Fair Trading Act 1973 if it has more than 25 per cent of the market.

There are, of course, many state monopolies in the UK such as the National Coal Board. Since, however, their economic behaviour is not usually governed by the profit making hypothesis, their behaviour is not discussed here (*see* Chapter 6).

Oligopoly
This word, like monopoly, is derived from the Greek and means a situation where there are only a few sellers of a commodity. There are several industries in the UK dominated by a few large firms, e.g. the production of detergent is almost entirely divided between Procter & Gamble and Unilever. In some cases these firms might *legally* be described as monopolists rather than oligopolists.

Oligopolists might produce virtually identical products and compete with each other through prices. It is more common, however, for them to compete through advertising and *product differentiation*. In the case of detergents, for example, although all the products are basically similar, there is a proliferation of brands and heavy advertising but very little price competition.

Monopolistic competition
When there are a large number of sellers producing a similar but differentiated product then a state of monopolistic competition is said to exist. This might be the case in the supply of a commodity like shirts, where essentially similar items are supplied by many different firms at widely differing prices with a lot of product differentiation by way of colour, style and material. Such an industry is also characterised by the frequent entry and exit of firms.

It is called monopolistic competition, because, due to imperfections in the market, each organisation has a small degree of monopoly power. If, for example, "Double 2" shirts can convince the public that their shirts are better than those of their competitors, then they have, as it were, created a small monopoly for their own product. The *branding* of goods is an attempt to break the *chain of substitution* by which one commodity can be substituted for another. When a consumer enters a shop and asks for a bar of chocolate, a shirt or a tube of toothpaste by its brand name, then the manufacturer has succeeded in his designs and may be able to reap the reward of his monopoly. Some advertising and branding is so successful that people use brand names without realising it, e.g. Thermos, Hoover and Vaseline (*see* 259).

It is paradoxical that under perfect competition very little competition is visible since there is no advertising and promotion of products, whereas under all types of imperfect competition rivalry between organisations is only too obvious. Even monopolies advertise. Tate and Lyle, for example not only promote their product but extol the virtues of free competition. It is a case, as Professor Galbraith wrote in *The Affluent Society*, of competition being advocated "by those who have most successfully eliminated it"!

MARKET BEHAVIOUR UNDER PERFECT COMPETITION

Marginal revenue
In Chapter 8 we examined the cost structures of organisations. Before considering how the prices and output policy of a firm is determined we need to consider only one more concept, that of

marginal revenue (MR). If, for example, a farmer can sell any amount of his product at £5 per kg then the demand schedule for his product would be like that in Table XXVI.

TABLE XXVI. DEMAND SCHEDULE

Demand for commodity X (kg per week)	Price of commodity X (£/kg)	Total revenue (£s)	Marginal revenue (£s)
0	5	0	
			5
1	5	5	
			5
2	5	10	
			5
3	5	15	
			5
4	5	20	

Thus, each time he sells another kg his total revenue increases by £5. This increase to his total revenue is termed the marginal revenue. Under perfect competition marginal revenue is the same as price because the producer can sell more of his output without lowering his price. Thus the demand curve and the marginal revenue curve are the same thing. This is not the case with imperfect competition. If the producer wishes to sell more of his output he must lower his price to do so. Thus under imperfect competition the marginal revenue curve slopes downwards beneath the demand curve. These two possibilities are illustrated in Fig. 66.

As the imperfect competitor continues to lower his prices there comes a time when it is no longer worthwhile. The extra demand he acquires is not sufficient to offset the drop in the price and so his total revenue decreases. At this point marginal revenue will become negative and the MR curve will cross the horizontal axis. (The reader might like to consider the relationship between MR and elasticity; what, for example, is the elasticity of demand when marginal revenue is zero?)

Since marginal revenue can be both positive and negative it is best to define it as the *change* to total revenue resulting from the sale of one more unit.

You will note that in Fig. 66 the demand curve is labelled AR. This stands for *average revenue*. This is the usual practice when considering the price and output policy of firms, as this brings it in

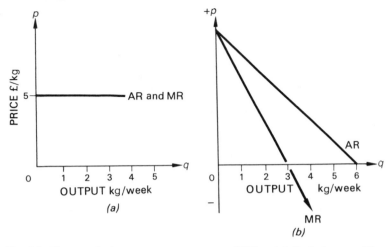

Fig. 66. *The marginal revenue curve: two possibilities. (a) Perfect competition. MR and AR curves are identical because price is constant. (b) Imperfect competition. The MR curve descends twice as quickly as the AR curve, bisecting the horizontal axis.*

line with the other terms being used such as average cost (AC) and marginal revenue (MR).

Output and profits in the short run
Under perfect competition the producer is a *price taker*, i.e. he has no control over the market price. He can only sell or not sell at that price. Therefore, in trying to maximise his profits the producer has no pricing decision to make, he can only choose the output which he thinks most advantageous. For example, in a freely competitive market a farmer could choose how much wheat he planted but could not control the price at which it would be sold when harvested.

The best profit position for any business organisation would be where it equated its marginal revenue (MR) with its marginal cost (MC). If the cost of producing one more unit (MC) is less than the revenue the producer obtains for selling it (MR), then he can obviously add to his profit by producing and selling that unit. Even when MC is rising, so long as it is less than MR the business organisation will go on producing because it is gaining *extra* profit. It does not matter if the *extra* profit is only small, it is nevertheless an *addition to profit*, and, if the producer is out to *maximise his profits*, he will wish to receive it. This is illustrated in Fig. 67 where the most profitable output is OM. If the business produced a smaller

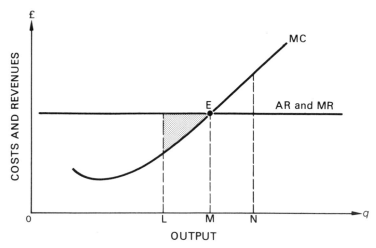

Fig. 67. *Perfect competition: the short run. The organisation maximises its profits by producing the output at which MC = MR.*

output (OL) then the cost of producing a unit (MC) is less than the revenue received from selling it (MR). The business could therefore increase its profits by expanding output. The shaded area represents the extra profit available to the producer as he expands output. At point E (output OM) there is no more extra profit to be gained. If the firm were to produce a larger output (ON) then the cost of producing *that* unit (MC) would be greater than revenue from selling it (MR) and the producer could increase his profits by contracting output back towards OM. Thus the output at which MC = MR is an *equilibrium position* for the producer, i.e. the one at which he will be happy to remain if he is allowed to (*see* page 336). Imagine that a farmer has produced a crop of apples. He now has to harvest them and send them to market. Since apples are highly perishable he will continue sending apples to market while the extra cost (MC) he incurs in doing so (labour, transport, etc.) is less than the money he can get for selling them (MR). As soon as the cost of getting them to market is greater than the money he receives for them he will cease to do so, even if it means leaving the apples to rot.

Shut-down in the short run

In the above example the cost of planting the apple trees and of renting the land for the orchard could be regarded as *fixed costs* (FC) since the farmer can only shed these costs by going out of business. That is to say, he cannot vary these costs in the short run.

His other costs, such as maintaining the trees, harvesting the crop and transporting it to market, can be varied in the short run and can therefore be described as *variable costs* (VC). This being the case, it is apparent that if the price of apples were so low that the farmer could not recover all his costs he would still continue to sell apples in the short run if he could cover his variable costs. In other words, if the money he is getting back from the sale is greater than the cost of picking and selling them, it would appear that in the short run he will produce, ignoring his fixed costs.

Conversely, if the cost of harvesting, transport, etc., were greater than his sales revenue, the farmer would obviously minimise his losses by closing down immediately and saving the expenditure on variable costs.

Thus, we can conclude that a firm will continue to produce and sell its product in the short run, even when it is making a loss, so long as it is covering its variable costs, because this way it is minimising its losses. In the long run, of course, all costs must be covered if the firm is to remain in the industry. This conclusion is true for all types of firm, not just for those operating under perfect competition.

Output and profits in the long run

In the short run the firm will choose to produce at the output where its marginal revenue is equal to its marginal cost. This is true whether the firm is making a profit or a loss, so long as it is covering its variable costs. However, in the long run all costs must be covered and it is therefore necessary to consider the total costs (TC) of the organisation. It is most convenient to consider total cost as average total cost (ATC). In this way it may be compared with AR and MC. The MC curve always cuts the ATC curve at the lowest point of the ATC curve (*see* page 144). When we consider the firm under perfect competition three possibilities exist, i.e. this intersection of MC and ATC must occur at a level higher, lower or equal to the price at which the commodity is being sold. These three possibilities are illustrated in Fig. 68. This demonstrates that only (*c*) can be a long-run situation. Before going any further with this explanation, the reader should recall the idea of *normal profit* (*see* page 264); that is, the minimum amount of profit a firm will require to remain in an industry. It will be remembered that since this is necessary to keep the firm producing it is considered as a legitimate cost of production and is therefore included within the ATC.

In all three diagrams in Fig. 68 you will see that the firm produces output OM, i.e. the output where MC = MR, because at this output it either maximises its profits or minimises its losses.

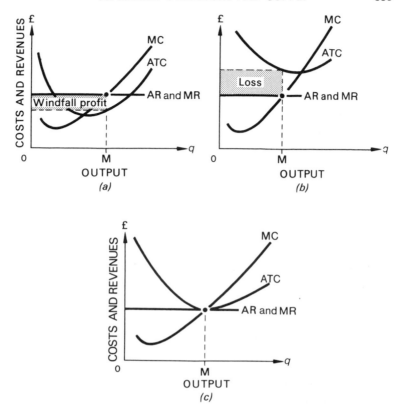

Fig. 68. *The long-run equilibrium of the firm under perfect competition.* (a) *Windfall profits attract new firms to the industry. This lowers the price and elim-inates the abnormal profit.* (b) *The firm is making a loss and in the long run will leave the industry.* (c) *The firm is just recovering "normal profits"; this is the long-run equilibrium of the firm, where MC = MR = AR = AC.*

In (*a*) the average revenue (price) is higher than average total cost. This means that the firm is making an above normal profit. Under perfect competition this is often described as *windfall profit* since it is not a profit which has been contrived by the firm; it arises because the price is unexpectedly higher than anticipated. However, this situation will not continue in the long run because, under perfect competition, there is freedom of entry and exit to the industry and these high profits will attract new competitors into the industry who will compete the profit away.

In (*b*) average total cost is at all times higher than average revenue. It is therefore impossible for the firm to make a profit.

Although the firm may produce in the short run (*see* above), it is impossible for it to continue in the long run and it must therefore close down unless there is a favourable change in the market.

Neither (*a*) nor (*b*) can be long-run situations, but in (*c*) we see that the ATC curve is just tangential to the AR curve. At a greater or lesser output the firm would make a loss, but at output OM it is just receiving normal profit. The situation represented in (*c*) can continue in the long run because the firm is just recovering enough profit to keep it in the industry, but not sufficient to attract other competitors to take that profit away.

Thus we can see that under perfect competition the *long-run equilibrium* for the organisation is one where:

$$MC = MR = AC = AR$$

The average businessman is hardly likely to look at the running of his business in this way. Profit maximisation is arrived at by his practical knowledge of his business and by trial and error. The concepts of marginal cost, average revenue, etc., allow us to rationalise the principles that are common to all businesses. Although the businessman may not be familiar with words like marginal revenue, he is nevertheless used to the practice of making small variations in output and price to achieve the best results; he is thus using a marginal technique to maximise his profits.

The supply curve

No matter how the *market price* changes, the demand curve always appears to be a horizontal line to the individual firm under perfect competition. Therefore as price goes up or down the firm always tries to equate price with marginal cost in order to maximise its profits. In Fig. 69 as price increases from OP to OP' to OP'' the firm expands output from OM to OM' to OM''. This, therefore, shows how the firm varies output in response to changes in price— in other words, it is a supply curve. Thus we may conclude that under perfect competition the firm's MC curve, above AVC, is its supply curve.

The optimum allocation of resources

The importance of the idea of perfect competition is that it represents the ideal working of the free market system. The fundamental problem of any economy, it will be remembered, is to make the best use of scarce resources. If we look at the model of perfect competition we will see how it relates to this. In its long-run equilibrium the firm is producing where MC = AC, i.e. at the bottom of the average cost curve. At this output, costs, that is to say the

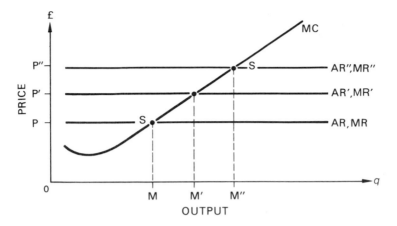

Fig. 69. *The supply curve under perfect competition.*

quantity of resources needed to produce a unit of the commodity, are minimised. Looking at Fig. 68 (*c*) you can see that if the firm produced a greater or a smaller output the cost of producing a unit would rise. In equilibrium, therefore, the firm is making an optimum use of resources. If every firm in the economy operated under these conditions it would follow that there was an optimum allocation of resources and every commodity would be produced at a minimum unit cost. Indeed all firms would be producing to consumers' demand curves and therefore not only would goods be produced at a minimum cost but they would also be the goods which people wanted.

It has already been seen that this view of the economy is subject to two major criticisms. Firstly, that the commodities which people are willing to pay for may not be the goods which are most useful to society, and secondly, that income in the economy may be unevenly distributed, meaning that an efficient system may not be socially just (*see* Chapter 14).

Competition is, however, also important as a political idea. When right-wing parties advocate increasing the amount of free competition in the economy it is in the belief that this would lead to a more efficient use of resources. Even trade unions have advocated "free competition" in wage bargaining. Free competition in our economy is something of a myth in that markets often tend to be dominated by large organisations with a great deal of monopoly power. In the same way, "free collective bargaining" is dominated by large powerful unions. It is imperfections of the market which are the rule rather than "free and unfettered competition".

MARKET BEHAVIOUR IN IMPERFECT MARKETS

Maximising profits in an imperfect market

Any organisation will obviously make most profit where there is the biggest possible difference between its costs and its revenues. This does not mean, however, that it will seek either to minimise its costs or to maximise its revenues; instead it will seek the best relationship between the two. Table XXVII illustrates the costs and revenues of a firm operating under conditions of imperfect competition. Here you can see that the best possible profit position is where the output is 4 units and the price is £48. At this point MC = MR. You will note that this is not the output at which revenues are maximised (this is 5 units where TR = £200), nor average cost minimised (this is also 5 units where AC = £24).

In the previous section we saw how a firm maximises its profits where MR = MC. If we construct the relevant graphs from the above figures we will see that this is so. The MR and MC curves do, indeed, cross at an output of 4 units. Under perfect competition the MR curve slopes down below the AR curve because the firm must lower its prices in order to sell more. This is illustrated in Fig. 70. In the same diagram we can see that when the output is 4 the price (AR) is £48 and that at this output the average cost (AC) is £25. This firm is therefore making £23 profit on each unit. Since the firm is selling 4 units, the area of the shaded rectangle represents the amount of profit that this business is making (£92).

You will recall from the previous section that normal profit is included in the costs of the firm, and therefore the profit discussed above is all *abnormal profit* (also called *excess profit or monopoly profit*), i.e. all of this profit could be eliminated without forcing the firm to leave the industry. How has this abnormal profit been made? The answer is by selling a restricted output at a higher price. Under imperfect competition, in order to sell more the firm must lower its prices. Therefore there must come a time when the price is so low that profit is eliminated. It is not so surprising then that a firm finds its best profit position before this point. This idea is often unintentionally illustrated by bad harvests where the lack of supply forces up prices and farmers find themselves much better off, even though they are selling less produce. Abnormal profit is usually, however, considered a *contrived profit*—a return to the *monopolistic power* of the organisation. Earlier in this chapter we referred to the diamond market, where supply is often deliberately restricted to increase the profits of diamond producers.

As a result of imperfect competition, then, consumers are paying more for products than they might and yet this is not the most

TABLE XXVII. COSTS AND REVENUES OF A FIRM UNDER CONDITIONS OF IMPERFECT COMPETITION

	Output units per week (q)	Average revenue £/unit (p)	Total revenue (p × q) (TR)	Total cost £ (TC)	Total profit (TR − TC) (TP)	Marginal cost ($TC^n - TC^{n-1}$) (MC)	Marginal revenue ($TR^n - TR^{n-1}$) (MR)	Average cost (TC/q) (AC)
A	0	80	0	58	−58			∞
B	1	72	72	70	+2	12	+72	70
C	2	64	128	80	+48	10	+56	40
D	3	56	168	88	+80	8	+40	29.3
E	4	48	192	100	+92	12	+24	25
						MC = MR		
F	5	40	200	120	+80	20	+8	24
G	6	32	192	148	+44	28	−8	24.6
H	7	24	168	184	−16	36	−24	26.3
I	8	16	128	228	−100	44	−40	28.5

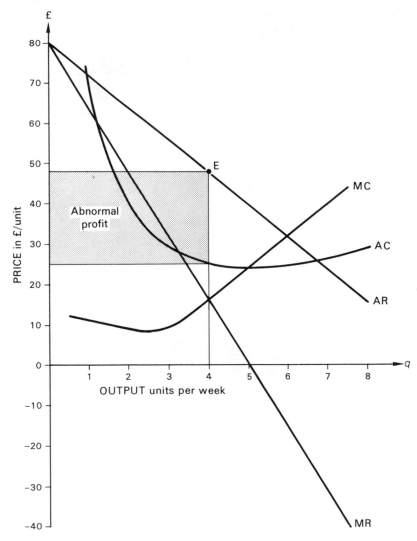

Fig. 70. *The equilibrium price and output of the firm under imperfect competition: the short run. Profit is maximised at an output of 4 units and a price of £48, where MR = MC. Profit = (AR − AC) × q = £92.*

serious consequence. You will also observe from Fig. 70 and Table XXVII that the product is produced at a higher average cost than it need be. In our example average cost is minimised at an output of 5 (where AC = £24). Thus it would seem that imperfect competition leads to an inefficient use of resources, and this is the most important criticism of it.

Thus we can conclude that in order to maximise its profits the firm restricts its output and thereby raises the price of its product. In so doing it moves backwards up its AC curve, producing fewer goods at a higher cost. This situation can only continue if other firms are prevented from entering the market and competing for this profit. In other words this is a short-run situation. What happens in the long run will depend upon the type of imperfect market we are considering.

Monopoly

A monopoly is a firm which, for one reason or another, enjoys freedom from competition. In the long run there is no-one, therefore, to come into the market and compete for the monopolist's abnormal profit. The long-run equilibrium of the monopolist is thus like the short run.

A monopolist may, however, choose not to maximise his profits as full as he might for:

(a) fear that the government may intervene;
(b) respect for the community's welfare;
(c) fear that he may attract competition from overseas.

Oligopoly

Oligopoly, the situation where the market is dominated by a few large firms, is hard to analyse. The most practical implication is, however, that oligopolists realise that if they were to co-operate and have a common prices and output policy they could treat the market like a monopolist and there would therefore be a greater total amount of profit to be made from the market. Such a policy would amount to setting up a *cartel* or price fixing ring. Since these are usually illegal some industries have resorted to *information agreements* or *market sharing*. For example, the construction companies in an area might get together and take it in turns to submit the lowest tenders for contracts. Virtually all such arrangements are now illegal and the law relating to them is discussed in the next chapter.

Although agreements between organisations to exploit the market may be illegal, it is possible to see that in many oligopolistic markets price competition is avoided. If, for example, we consider the detergent market, we can see that Procter & Gamble and Unilever prefer to compete by product differentiation and advertising rather than by price cutting wars with each other.

One consequence of oligopoly can be that a firm appears to face a "kink" in the demand curve for its product. This arises because, although its competitors will allow it to put up the price without interference, the moment it brings its prices down below the ruling market price, they will respond by lowering their prices. Thus the elasticity of demand for the firm's product is much greater above the ruling market price than below it.

Monopolistic competition

In situations where there are lots of competitors in an imperfect market, if one firm is seen to be making high profits, other businesses will be encouraged to enter that line of production and compete the profit away. The situation is thus similar to that of perfect competition. This is illustrated in Fig. 71. In (a) the average cost curve is below the average revenue curve and abnormal profits are being made. Since there is free entry to the market, other firms enter and compete this profit away. In (b), however, AC is above AR at all points and the firm is making a loss and will, in the long run, leave the industry. The long-run equilibrium is therefore (c) where the AC curve is tangential to the AR curve and the firm is only receiving normal profits.

For example, a company manufacturing shirts might accurately predict a new fashion trend and for a short while be able to exploit its monopoly of that design of shirt, but other companies will soon be able to copy this and price competition between the firms will compete the excess profit away.

You will note in (c) that, unlike perfect competition, the company does *not* produce at the lowest point of average cost. It is still the case, however, that it produces where MC = MR. Thus, even though the company is not making abnormal profits, it is still producing a restricted output at a higher unit cost. It follows that in all types of imperfect market the organisation, in following its own interest of profit maximisation, is likely to bring about an inefficient use of resources.

ASPECTS OF MONOPOLY

Mergers and amalgamations

Business organisations frequently acquire monopoly power through takeovers and amalgamations. A *takeover* is when one company

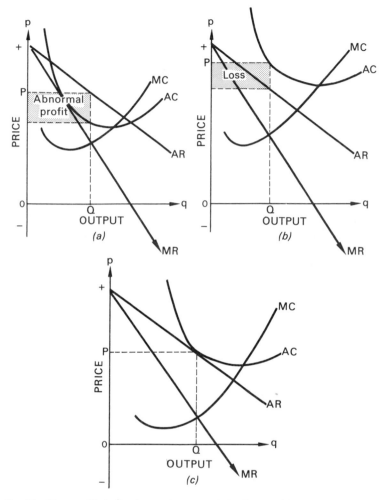

Fig. 71. *The equilibrium price and output of the firm under monopolistic competition: the long run. (a) The existence of abnormal profit attracts new firms to the industry which lowers the price and eliminates the profit. (b) The firm makes a loss at all levels of output and will in the long run leave the industry. (c) The long-run equilibrium where the firm just recovers normal profit.*

acquires a controlling interest in another company. In many cases takeovers happen with the co-operation of the company which is being taken over. A *merger* or amalgamation does not require that all the shares are taken over; usually a *holding company* is set up to control the original companies (*see* page 34). There are several types of merger.

(*a*) *Vertical merger.* In these the business expands "backwards" to its sources of supply and "forwards" to its markets. A good example would be an oil company which controlled everything from the oil well to the filling station.

(*b*) *Horizontal mergers.* In this the business expands and integrates with other businesses involved in the same activity. An example of this would be the large breweries taking over more and more of the small brewers.

(*c*) *Mergers of diversification.* Businesses frequently spread out into other fields to diversify their risks. One of the most famous examples is Unilever which produces a wide variety of products from soap to sausages.

There are several reasons for mergers, the two most important being as follows.

(*a*) *Economies of scale.* This is where the larger company is able to make a better use of resources. The Peugeot motor company is hoping to achieve more economies of scale by having taken over Chrysler Europe.

(*b*) *Market domination.* The object of the merger is to eliminate competition and so allow the company to maximise profits, no economies of scale need to be involved. It is this type of merger which frequently attracts the attention of the Monopolies and Mergers Commission.

Mergers sometimes come about because of government intervention, often with the object of trying to revive a flagging industry. This was the case with the creation of Upper Clyde Shipbuilders. In recent years there have been takeovers for the purpose of "asset-stripping".

Desirable economic consequences can frequently follow the creation of a larger company as a result of economies of scale and rationalisation. Whatever the reason for a merger, however, it has the effect of placing greater monopoly power in the hands of the larger company. For this reason there has been an increasing amount of government control in recent years (*see* below).

Discriminating monopolists

Every producer knows that there are some consumers who are willing to pay more than the market price for the good. The consumer

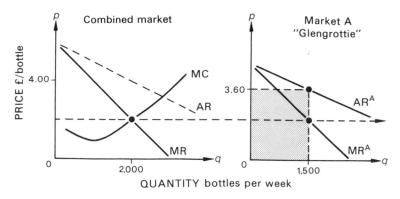

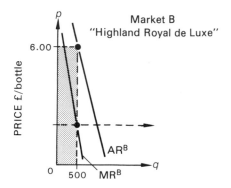

Fig. 72. *The discriminating monopolist divides output between two markets. (a) Combined market without price discrimination. Price = £4, quantity = 2,000, total revenue (p × q) = £8,000. (b) Separate market A with price discrimination. Price = £3.60, quantity = 1,500, total revenue = £5,400. (c) Separate market B with price discrimination. Price = £6.00, quantity = 500, total revenue = £3,000. Total revenue from markets A and B = £8,400. Profits £400 greater than in the combined market.*

is therefore in receipt of utility he is not paying for and this is known as a *consumer's surplus*. A monopolist may be able to eat into this surplus by charging some consumers higher prices than others. A monopolist with the ability to do this known as a discriminating monopolist. Two conditions must be present for this price discrimination to take place.

(*a*) The monopolist must be able to separate the two markets; this he may do geographically, by branding, or by time. The suppliers of personal services such as doctors and lawyers also often charge different prices for the same service.

(*b*) The two or more markets thus separated must have different elasticities of demand, otherwise the exercise could not be worthwhile.

Figure 72 shows how the monopolist might set about increasing his profits by price discrimination. The manufacturer, in this case of a drink, maximises his profits by equating MR with MC and would therefore sell 2,000 bottles a week at £4.00 each. However, he realises that many customers are willing to pay more than £4 for a bottle (market B). He therefore puts some of the drink in bottles labelled "Highland Royal de Luxe" and sells it as a high-class product. At the cheaper end of the market there is a great deal of elasticity of demand (market A). Here he drops the price to £3.60 and sells 1,500 bottles labelled "Glengrottie". The way in which he decides his marketing strategy is to take the MC for the combined market and equate it with the marginal revenues for the two separate markets. This tells him the output to sell in each market. By tracing that output up to the demand curves in the separate markets you can see the price which he would charge. In our example he collects £400 a week extra profit because he is able to convince his customers, by branding and advertising, that one bottle of drink is better than the other. Price discrimination is fairly widespread. The following are examples of some of the types of price discrimination.

(*a*) *Geographical*. Goods are sold at different prices in different countries. This was illustrated in 1977 when the Distillers Company were ordered by the EEC to cease selling the same brand of whisky at one price in the UK and at a higher price in the rest of Europe.

(*b*) *Branding*. Many manufacturers sell the identical product at one price under their own brand name and at a lower price branded with the name of a retailer. For example many famous manufacturers sell some of their output more cheaply under the "St Michael" label of Marks and Spencers.

(*c*) *Time*. Many public monopolies sell the same product at different prices at different times. Examples of this are off-peak electricity, weekend returns on British Rail and "stand-by" flights by British Airways.

(*d*) *Dumping*. This is a variation on geographical discrimination, but in this case the manufacturer "dumps" surplus output on a foreign market below cost price. This often has the object of damaging foreign competition. Examples of this in Britain are Russian cars and cameras and Korean shoes and clothes. The EEC has to resort to dumping to get rid of excess agriculture products.

Consultant doctors are often said to operate price discrimination by working in both private practice and the National Health Service. Patients might find, however, that they receive more prompt and personal service in the private sector and feel this is worth paying for.

Mark-up pricing and break-even charts

Although an organisation's behaviour may be governed by concepts such as marginal revenue and marginal cost, in practice they may be very difficult to determine, especially when a large organisation is marketing a variety of products. In these circumstances they often try to base their prices on average or unit cost. To do this they must make assumptions about the future volume of sales and likely average cost at that output. This having been done, a *mark-up* of, say, 10 per cent is then added for profit. This fascinatingly simple theory seems realistic but stops tantalisingly short of telling us why the average mark-up should be 40 per cent in one industry and 5 per cent in another.

The reader should take careful note that this is the way the organisation may try to determine the right price for *itself* but the consumers may or may not be willing to pay the right price or buy the right quantity. Prices in the market are still determined by the forces of supply and demand. The monopolist has greater power, of course, to impose his wishes on the market. If an organisation sets its prices in this manner then we can draw up a *break-even chart* to demonstrate its profits and losses. In Fig. 73 the TR curve is a straight line because price is constant. TC is a normal total cost curve; costs turn upwards very sharply after point C when the firm passes optimum capacity.

This way of looking at profits is much closer to the accountants' view than most of the economists' ways of looking at the market.

Governments and monopoly

In any free enterprise economy governments will usually have legislation concerned with monopolies, since the existence of monopolies is a negation of the free market ideal.

The next chapter includes a consideration of the legislation governing monopolies and consumer affairs. The last part of this chapter is devoted to a view of the economic considerations involved.

There are three basic policies the government can adopt towards monopolies.

(*a*) *Prohibition.* The formation of monopolies can be banned and existing monopolies broken up. This is basically the attitude in the

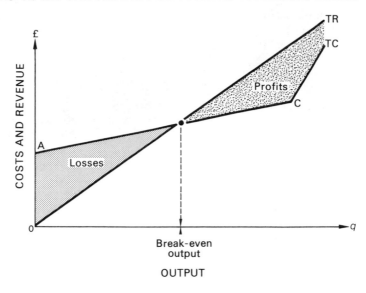

Fig. 73. *A break-even chart. If the price is fixed, TR is a straight line. Profits or losses are the vertical distance between the two curves. B is the break-even point at which losses turn into profits.*

USA. "Anti-trust" legislation, as it is called, in the States dates back to the Sherman Act of 1890. There are nevertheless a considerable number of monopolies in the USA. Legislation against actions "in restraint of trade" has been more vigorously prosecuted against unions than against big business.

(*b*) *Take-over.* The government can take over a monopoly and run it in the public interest. Although many industries and companies have been taken over by the government, it has not usually been done with the object of controlling a monopoly.

(*c*) *Regulation.* The government can allow a monopoly to continue but pass legislation to make sure that it does not act "against the public interest". This is basically the attitude of the British government.

The attitude of a government towards a monopoly will partly be influenced by the way in which the monopoly arose. Some monopolies are *spontaneous*: they arise naturally out of the conditions of supply. For example, Schweppes have a *natural* monopoly of Malvern Spa water because they control the spring from which it comes. Other monopolies are *contrived*, that is to say a business or group of businesses have deliberately set out to create a monopoly. Some of the origins of monopoly power are listed below.

(a) *Natural.* This arises out of the geographical conditions of supply. For example, South Africa has an almost complete monopoly of the western world's supply of diamonds.

(b) *Historical.* A business may have a monopoly because it was first in the field and no-one else has the necessary "know-how" or customer "goodwill". Lloyds of London's command of the insurance market is largely based on historical factors.

(c) *Capital size.* The supply of a commodity may involve the use of such a vast amount of capital equipment that new competitors are effectively excluded from entering the market. This is the case with the chemical industry.

(d) *Technological.* Where there are many economies of scale to be gained it may be natural and advantageous for the market to be supplied by one or a few large companies. This would apply to the motor vehicle industry.

(e) *Legal.* The government may confer a monopoly upon a company. This may be the case when a business is granted a patent or copyright. The right to sole exploitation is given to encourage people to bring forward new ideas.

(f) *Public.* Public corporations such as the Post Office and the Gas Council frequently have monopolies. Most public utilities are monopolies.

(g) *Contrived.* There is nothing much a government could or would wish to do about breaking up the monopolies discussed above. When people discuss the evils of monopoly, however, it is not usually the above forms of monopoly they are thinking about but rather those that are deliberately contrived. Business organisations can contrive to exploit the market either by taking over, or driving out of business, the other firms in the industry (*scale monopoly*) or by entering into agreements with other businesses to control prices and output (*complex monopoly*). It is this type of monopoly that most legislation is aimed at.

The government's regulation of monopoly will depend upon the technical conditions of supply pertaining in the industry. In the "normal" monopoly situation, illustrated in Fig. 74, monopoly legislation should be aimed at making the monopolist produce at point F where AC = AR. At this point the price is OS and the output ON. All monopoly profits have been eliminated and the public is obtaining the largest output for the lowest price that is compatible with the monopolist remaining in the industry. In this instance the government could also consider breaking up the monopoly into smaller units.

In some industries, however, especially those involving a great

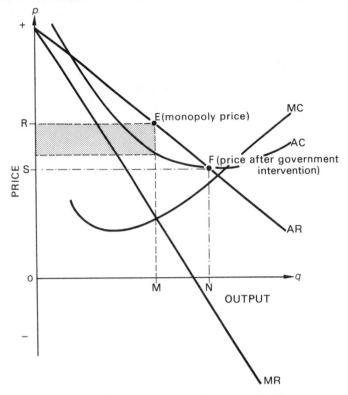

Fig. 74. *Government intervention in monopoly. The monopolist would choose to produce at point E making maximum profit. Government policy aims to compel the monopolist to produce where AC = AR thus eliminating abnormal profit (this is still not at the lowest point of AC).*

deal of capital equipment, such as chemicals and motor vehicles, it could be that the larger and more monopolistic a business organisation is the more it is able to take advantage of economies of scale. The industry is said to have a flat-bottomed average cost curve.

In Fig. 75 the national market for cars is 2 million per year. In our example production is divided between two companies, Kruks and Toymota. Toymota has a bigger share of the market (1.1 million) and, because of the economies of scale to be gained, the long-run average cost curve (LAC) of the industry is downward sloping. This means that Toymota's average costs (£2,000) are lower than Kruks (£2,400). In the price-conscious car market this means Toymota will sell even more cars, gaining a bigger share of the market

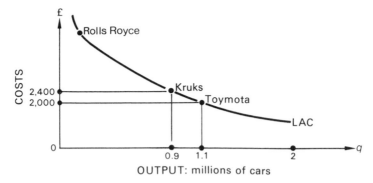

Fig. 75. *Long-run average cost curve.*

and leaving Kruks with a smaller share and even higher costs. In this situation Kruks will eventually go out of business and Toymota will have a complete monopoly. This could be to the public's benefit if continuing economies of scale mean even cheaper cars.

The end result of such a situation, then, is monopoly or some form of oligopoly. This is very much the case in the motor industry, which is dominated by a small number of very large firms. Most medium-sized firms have tended to disappear, but companies producing a very small output of specialist and expensive cars still exist, e.g. Rolls Royce and Lotus, because they are not very concerned about unit costs.

In such an industry it would not be economic sense to break up the monopoly. Indeed it has been observed that in the UK the government has often promoted the formation of monopolies in these sorts of industry. In these circumstances the government's options are limited either to taking over the industry or regulating its prices and output. Although the choices are very clear in theory, in practice it is often very difficult to acquire enough information to judge what is happening in an industry.

CONCLUSION

This chapter has attempted to show that however dissimilar markets may be in their physical attributes their market behaviour is governed by the same fundamental economic principles. The model of the market is modified by government intervention, by way of taxes, legislation and the government's own production of goods and services. In the next chapter the legal framework of the market place is considered.

SELF-ASSESSMENT QUESTIONS

A. 1. Define: (*a*) "spot" markets; (*b*) marginal revenue; (*c*) price discrimination; (*d*) oligopoly.

2. List six possible sources of monopoly power.

B. 3. True or false?

(*a*) Dealings in Hatton Garden are an example of ring trading.

(*b*) There is no "futures" market in foreign exchange.

(*c*) Business operating under conditions of perfect competition are "price-takers".

(*d*) Abnormal profits are those which are in excess of 30 per cent.

(*e*) Private companies are never granted monopolies by the government.

C. 4. True or false?

(*a*) A company operating under perfect competition will always produce where MC = AC.

(*b*) Under monopoly a firm will always choose to produce where demand is inelastic, since here it can raise its prices and therefore its profits.

(*c*) In Table XXVII, at point F, the coefficient of elasticity of demand is equal to 1.

(*d*) If in Table XXVII the firm's fixed costs were to increase by £92 it would cease trading.

(*e*) If the government forces a monopolist to produce where AC = AR then he must be producing as efficiently as under perfect competition.

5. Compare the economist's view of profit with that of the accountant.

6. Present a case study of one industry which has been investigated by the Monopolies and Mergers Commission.

ASSIGNMENTS

1. Devise a strategy for the revitalisation of the British motor industry.

2. Compile a table of the greatest profit earners in the private sector of the UK economy.

CHAPTER SEVENTEEN

Law and the Market Place

CHAPTER OBJECTIVES

After studying this chapter you should be able to:
* define a contract;
* state and explain the essentials of a valid contract;
* explain why inequality in bargaining power exists between business organisations and their customers;
* list the statutes by which this inequality is lessened;
* describe the roles of the administrative agencies of consumer protection;
* outline the legal remedies and sanctions, and the administrative action by which consumer and competition law is enforced.

THE LAW OF CONTRACT

The need for contract law

An organisation pursues its objectives by entering into agreements with other organisations and individuals. Resources are acquired and products sold, services provided and obtained by making agreements complying with a set of rules which must have the force of law in order to ensure the smooth operation of commercial activity. These rules constitute the law of contract. This is illustrated diagrammatically in Fig. 76.

Too often the law is viewed as a constraint upon a person's activities. Justifiably, this may be so in the case of the criminal law or the law of torts, where society prohibits a particular activity or protects a certain right, but the law of contract should be viewed as a facilitating medium enabling organisations to operate. It cannot be viewed realistically as a medium of constraint, automatically involving sanctions for anyone who becomes involved with it.

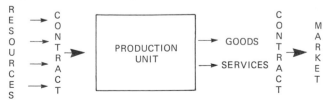

Fig. 76. *The role of contract law.*

However, unless society wishes to have a commercial world in which there are no rules and no protection for the weak, some constraints in the law of contract are clearly necessary, for example in employment and consumer contracts.

Contract law provides a framework around which an organisation can build its activities and with which it can regularise its operations, both externally in its relations with its clients, customers and other organisations, and internally with its own employees.

Before we start to look at what a contract is, it is important to realise that the vast majority of commercial and consumer transactions never result in any dispute or court action. Most run their course according to the contractual terms, and even where there has been a clear breach of these terms by one of the parties the other will frequently not take legal action. The breach of contract has to be seen in perspective; legal action frequently loses a firm goodwill, high costs are involved, with no certainty of recovering them, and at the very least time and trouble are involved. The advantages of taking legal action must be weighed against its disadvantages: a legal remedy versus financial and general business considerations.

What is a contract?

Contract law consists of legal rules governing the enforceability of obligations arising from agreements between individuals, and a contract is simply an agreement which the courts will enforce. The law in this sphere reflects its commercial origins and an agreement will only be enforced if it is also a bargain that is intended to create legal relations between the parties. Each side must give something of value for what they receive from the other; a mere agreement where one party receives without giving anything in return is not enforceable. To this there is one exception—an agreement made by deed. This is a historical legacy which is extremely unlikely to be found in normal business transactions.

When an organisation enters into a contract with another party it is the final step in a process of negotiation, which may have taken many weeks to conclude in the case of a large complicated transaction. Not only the organisation's legal department or its solicitors will have been involved but also its executives and economic advisers, for such a contract may involve important questions of policy, procedure and economic prediction. Alternatively, the contract may have been an ordinary retail sale or a contract for the provision of a simple service, in which case the customer and possibly the organisation's servants may have been only vaguely aware that they were entering into a legal relationship, involving well-defined and important rights and duties.

Freedom to bargain

Whatever the exact nature of the contract the parties are free to negotiate with each other and conclude a voluntary bargain, stipulating and agreeing the terms which they wish the contract to contain. The courts will uphold the bargain, good or bad, provided the essential elements required by the law exist.

However, in many cases this freedom to bargain is rather illusory for the seller may only be willing to sell his goods or services on his own standard terms of business. In such a situation the buyer's only real freedom is to accept the seller's terms or to buy elsewhere. In this country it is difficult to imagine the parties bargaining in an ordinary retail sale or a hire agreement. Most contracts of hire, for example, contain a list of standard terms, and the standard forms produced by banks when mortgages or guarantees are taken to secure overdrafts or loans are usually lengthy and complicated documents. Sometimes the roles are reversed and the buyer has the upper hand, e.g. where a leading chain store wants to purchase clothes made to its own specifications from outside contractors, or where processed food manufacturers buy in bulk from the producers of their raw materials.

Organisations design and use their own standard form contracts so that they can trade on the terms *they* want to. This, of course, usually means the terms which are most advantageous to them, both commercially and administratively. Indeed the use of standard form contracts is also to the advantage of the other party in so far as he knows in advance the terms of the contract and can plan accordingly. The disadvantage, if any, will lie in the terms themselves.

Most standard form contracts are perfectly proper and unobjectionable; even those which take away rights the other party would have had, e.g. bank guarantee forms, are only doing what the law allows and are well within accepted standards of commercial morality.

A few, however, do rather more than this and are morally questionable by any standards, although (usually) quite legal. These are the sorts of contracts which get publicity in a TV programme like *That's Life*. In one programme a firm had sold some very expensive bathroom suites, the various outlets from which did not comply with by-laws; in fact anybody fitting them would have committed a criminal offence. No mention (of course) was made of this in the showroom but the standard form contract made it the purchaser's responsibility to check whether the suites complied with the relevant regulations. Consequently, people who bought the suites had no right to a refund when they found they could not get the suites fitted.

In the public sector of the economy the provision of goods and services is almost invariably on standard terms, often including a term allowing for automatic price adjustments when raw materials or other costs rise in price, e.g. fuel cost adjustment (FCA) in electricity charges. Here the inequality in the bargaining power of the parties is even more marked, for the public corporation will often have a monopoly in its particular activity, the various electricity, gas and water boards being obvious examples.

While the courts have always been aware of such basic inequalities in bargaining power and have to some extent mitigated the harshness of their effect by their own singular process of evolving the common law, Parliament has only comparatively recently entered the arena of "consumerism" with a range of statutes designed to redress the balance in favour of the consumer. Before this invention, the *laissez-faire* rules of contract law were often exploited by the stronger party, most frequently by including a term in the contract comprehensively excluding his liability or limiting the other party's rights in the event of a breach of contract. "Guarantees" which in fact excluded a buyer's rights under the Sale of Goods Act 1893 (now the Sale of Goods Act 1979) in return for the seller's own less extensive promises to rectify faults, and blanket exclusions of liability for negligence were two of the most common.

Sellers occasionally would go further—possibly some still do— and would tacitly accept that they were in breach of contract but would refuse to do anything about it. As will be seen later, consumer legislation often requires the consumer to take the initiative against the seller and, while his task is now much easier, many consumers with a legitimate complaint may be unwilling to become involved with the law for the sake of a few pounds.

To some extent lawyers are to blame for creating a legal system which deters people from looking to the law for compensation. However, in recent years the state has increasingly intervened to help the consumer, both by protective legislation and by simplifying the legal process. This combination of state aid and individual initiative in consumer law will be discussed and assessed later in the chapter.

The essentials of a valid contract
Having discussed the central role the law of contract plays in the

legal framework within which an organisation operates, the essential elements of a valid contract can be outlined.

A valid contract has three essential features.

(*a*) The *agreement*, consisting of one party making an offer which is accepted by the other.

(*b*) The *bargain*; there must be an element of exchange, the law requiring what is called "consideration".

(*c*) The *intention to create legal relations.*

These features are represented diagrammatically in Fig. 77.

Fig. 77. The essentials of a contract.

The rest of this section discusses each of these in turn and we mention quite a few cases. Mentioning these cases has two purposes: firstly, the cases illustrate the situations we discuss, and secondly, and more importantly, the law is derived from the cases and any conflict arising between the contracting parties would be resolved in a court of law by reference to decisions in similar cases.

The cases we describe are all well known and their principles apply to all fields of business. Remember, however, that such well-known cases either laid down a principle which to us now seems self-evident and/or were clear-cut and often extreme situations. Unfortunately, many contractual problems encountered today are rather more involved although, ultimately, a simple rule of law will probably be applied to resolve the dispute once all the evidence and arguments have been heard.

The agreement
Offer. The law requires that one party must make a definite offer to the other, although it need not be express but may be made by implication. The presence of an automatic car park, for example, is an implied offer to any motorist that he may park his car inside in return for a specified payment.

Similarly, an offer does not have to be made to a specific person or group of people, it can be made to anyone—the world at large. In *Carlill* v. *Carbolic Smoke Ball Co.* (1892) the company offered to pay £100 to anybody who used their "smoke-ball" in the way described and still caught influenza. When sued by Carlill, who had used the "smoke-ball" and caught influenza, the company unsuccessfully pleaded, amongst other things, that they could not be held to their promise as they had not made the offer directly to Carlill.

An offer must be distinguished from an invitation to treat. This is an invitation to enter into negotiations or to make an offer which may or may not result in the conclusion of an agreement. Many organisations advertise or display their products and whilst these may be interpreted by the man in the street as "offers" to sell goods or provide services, at law no offer is made. Hence, in *Pharmaceutical Society of G.B.* v. *Boots Cash Chemists (Southern), Ltd* (1952) a prosecution under the Pharmacy and Poisons Act 1933, which made it an offence to sell any listed poison "unless the sale is effected under the supervision of a registered pharmacist", failed because it was held that selection of an item from a self-service display did not amount to a sale. The display was an invitation to treat; the customer had made the offer by selecting the article, the defendants had accepted it and completed the sale when a pharmacist approved the transaction near the cash-desk. At law, therefore, the sale took place according to the provisions of the Act. In the case of a sale by auction, the call for bids is an invitation to treat, the bid is the offer, and the acceptance the fall of the auctioneer's hammer.

The recent case of *Gibson* v. *Manchester City Council* (1979) is well worth mentioning at this point because it illustrates the idea put forward on several occasions already in this book that law should not be seen nor studied in a vacuum. In 1970 the Council had a policy of selling council houses to existing tenants. In February 1971 the plaintiff received a letter from the council stating that the Council "may be prepared to sell the house to you at the purchase price of £2,725 less 20% = £2,180 (freehold)" and inviting him to make a formal application. This he did. However, before formal contracts had been exchanged the local government elections in 1971 brought a Labour controlled council to power and the policy of selling council houses was reversed. The Council decided only to complete the sale of those homes on which formal contracts had been exchanged; this did not include the plaintiff's house. Nevertheless, Gibson maintained that he had a binding contract with the Council. The House of Lords decided, however, that the Council's original letter to him was an invitation to treat and that his application to purchase was the offer. This offer the Council had clearly rejected.

All organisations require "land" as a fundamental economic resource. It has already been seen that land became a complicated concept at law and considerable formality attaches to its sale and transfer as a consequence. A series of cases show that the courts are generally unwilling to acknowledge the existence of an offer to sell land unless the clearest evidence of this intention exists. In *Harvey* v. *Facey* (1893) a telegraphed reply giving the lowest cash price at which the defendant was willing to sell his property was held not to amount to a definite offer to sell and in *Clifton* v. *Palumbo* (1944) an "offer" to sell a large estate for £600,000 was held to be merely a statement of price. However, in *Bigg* v. *Boyd Gibbons Ltd* (1971) the Court of Appeal found that the parties had concluded a contract to sell the property in question, even though only the names of the parties, the property and the price were certain. These aspects, however, are the essential features of the agreement in a contract for the sale of land.

Termination of the offer. At any time after the offer is made it can be revoked (withdrawn) by the offeror (the person who makes the offer) provided the revocation is communicated to the offeree (the person to whom the offer is made) before the latter has accepted the offer. Although the offeree incurs the responsibility of deciding where the notice is reasonable, the decision in *Dickinson* v. *Dodds* (1876) clearly shows that it is not necessary for the offeror to communicate his revocation personally. In that case, an offer to sell a house to the plaintiff was held to have been effectively revoked after the defendant sold it to a third party and the plaintiff was informed of this by a fourth. He had received sufficient notice of the defendant's revocation.

Where the offeror revokes his offer the offer terminates through the positive act of one of the parties involved. This is also the case where the offeree accepts or rejects the offer that was made to him. However, an offer can terminate in other ways. The offeror may have specifically stated that his offer was to remain open for a limited period and it will automatically terminate if not accepted within that time limit. If no time limit is stated, it is a question of fact whether the offer still exists after a given time has passed.

Offers are sometimes made subject to a condition that must be fulfilled before any acceptance of the offer creates a binding agreement: a condition precedent. It is normal when buying a second-hand car to want a valid MOT certificate for the car and therefore X might say to Y: "I offer to buy your car for £600 provided it passes its MOT test." Should the car not pass, X's offer to buy terminates.

In *Financing Ltd* v. *Stimson* (1962) a more difficult situation arose. The defendant alleged the existence of an implied condition precedent. He had signed an "agreement" to buy a car, which he had seen at a dealer's premises, from the plaintiff on hire-purchase terms. The "agreement" stated that the plaintiffs were only to be bound when they signed it. The defendant paid the first instalment and took the car away but, being dissatisfied, returned it two days later. The car was then stolen from the dealer's premises and recovered badly damaged. In ignorance of all these events the plaintiffs signed the "agreement". On discovering what had happened they sold the car and sued the defendant for breach of the "agreement". The Court of Appeal held that the "agreement" was in fact an offer which had been made subject to an implied condition that, until it was accepted, the car would remain in substantially the same state as when the offer was made. The defendant's offer had therefore terminated before it was accepted by the plaintiffs.

The death of either party clearly affects any proposed transaction. If the offeree dies, the offer probably dies with him. Similarly, if he knows that the offeror has died, the offeree cannot accept the offer. The possibilities are a little more complicated when the death of the offeror is unknown to the offeree. If the offer involved personal services, for example performing in a play or painting a picture, the offer cannot possibly be accepted. However, an offer independent of personality, for example the guarantee of a friend's overdraft, can be accepted, for this type of obligation can easily be satisfied from the offeror's estate.

Acceptance. The agreement is made by the offeree accepting the offer which has been made to him, and, just as the offer must be firm and certain, so must the acceptance. No agreement results from "I'll think about it" or "I might buy that." Legal obligations must be definite and only a complete acceptance of the offer will result in an enforceable agreement.

The same is true where the offeree wishes to have a second opinion before committing himself to a contract. For example, when a second-hand car is offered for sale, a potential purchaser might say "I'll buy it providing it passes a garage inspection"; this is not a definite acceptance. Such conditional acceptances are also common when the offeree does not wish to be legally bound until a formal contract is drafted, and the phrase "subject to contract", which solicitors invariably include in preliminary correspondence relating to the sale of land, operates as an express denial of any binding agreement.

Should the offeree wish to try to vary the terms of the offer it is a question of fact whether his proposals amount to a counter-offer and a rejection of the original offer, or merely a request for information which would still allow him to accept the offer in its original form. In *Hyde* v. *Wrench* (1840) a reply to an offer, quoting a lower price for the land that the defendant wished to sell, was held to be a rejection of the original offer preventing the plaintiff subsequently accepting the offer at the original price.

In some agreements there is no express acceptance; the offeree does not say "I accept", but the existence of a firm acceptance can be gathered from the circumstances. In *Brogden* v. *Metropolitan Rail Co.* (1877), Brogden had supplied coal to the Company for a number of years without any formal agreement and at length the parties decided to put their dealings on a more formal footing. A draft agreement sent by the Company was amended and approved by Brogden and then returned. The Company's agent did not complete the formalities required but both sides began to deal with each other according to the terms of the draft. Brogden had not accepted the draft because he had added a new term by his amendment and it was up to the company to accept or reject this. However, the subsequent conduct of the parties could only be explained on the basis that the draft had been agreed by both sides. On the facts a binding contract existed.

Certainty in the agreement. There must be *certainty* in the agreement reached by the parties, for the law will not enforce vague agreements. In *Loftus* v. *Roberts* (1902), an agreement where an actress was engaged at "a West End salary to be mutually arranged between us" was held to be unenforceable because the salary, an important term in the agreement, was clearly too vague. Similarly, in *Scammel* v. *Ousten* (1941) an agreement to buy a motor van on the "usual hire-purchase terms" was too vague because at the time there were no usual hire-purchase terms which could have been implied into the contract.

The law recognises, however, that there are a number of ways in which vagueness can be rectified and will enforce agreements that can be made certain. For example:

(*a*) terms may be included in the agreement by Acts of Parliament, the courts or by trade custom to give it certainty;

(*b*) the parties to the agreement may have had dealings with each other before and it may be possible to rectify any uncertainty in the agreement by referring to these dealings;

(*c*) the agreement itself may provide a way to rectify the uncertainty. In *Foley* v. *Classique Coaches Ltd* (1934) a provision to submit disputes to arbitration overcame the uncertainty in an agreement to supply petrol "at a price to be agreed by the parties in writing from time to time". However, in *May* v. *Butcher* (1929) an arbitration clause did not rectify the uncertainty where the date of payment, the delivery period and the price had still to be agreed. In truth there was no concluded bargain and the law would not recognise an agreement to agree. An arbitration clause can only operate after a bargain has been concluded.

Communication of acceptance. It is not enough merely to accept the offer, the acceptance must be communicated. Usually this is done verbally or by letter.

In this context it has long been established that remaining silent in response to an offer is not an acceptance of it. If the law were otherwise, contractual liability could be imposed on an unwilling person by merely stating that his silence was acceptance of the offer. However, in his offer the offeror may expressly or by implication waive the need to communicate acceptance. In *Carlill* v. *Carbolic Smoke Ball Co.* (1892) the company argued that Carlill had not communicated her acceptance but it was held that the nature of the offer implied that it was unnecessary to do so. Her conduct was her acceptance.

The *post* is a basic form of communication in business and special rules relate to postal acceptance of offers. Normally an acceptance by post is complete as soon as it is posted, provided it is properly stamped and addressed. Once posted, the acceptance cannot be withdrawn, but an offeror will be bound by a postal acceptance even if it is never delivered. In contrast, a postal revocation of an offer is only effective when actually brought to the offeror's attention. The postal rule is an exception to the general rule and cannot apply where the terms of the offer specify actual communication or communication within a time limit. In *Holwell Securities Ltd* v. *Hughes* (1973) the proper construction of an option to purchase property "exercisable by notice in writing to intending vendor at any time within six months from the date thereof", was that the notice had to be delivered to him personally, and a properly posted letter which never arrived did not amount to an exercise of the option.

The offer may itself specify the way in which it is to be accepted and the method amounts to a term of the offer. The courts, however, allow some flexibility and where the requirement is not obligatory they will accept another method equally as good. In *Yates Building Co. Ltd* v. *R. J. Pulleyn & Sons (York) Ltd* (1975), a letter exercising an option was held to have been wrongly rejected even though it was sent neither by registered post nor recorded delivery as requested. The requirement was not obligatory and the letter sent was equally effective. Where the offeror does not stipulate any particular method of communication, the effectiveness of the method chosen depends upon the facts of the case. An offer by telegram, for example, implies a similar method of acceptance.

The bargain

The nature of consideration. A contract is a bargain and a bargain involves an element of exchange: each side must give and receive something of value. Goods in exchange for cash is a simple and perfect example. Therefore, the law will only enforce a promise when it has been bought by the person who wishes to enforce it. Consideration is the price of this promise. An agreement in which consideration is present is nearly always an enforceable bargain. More formal judicial definitions of consideration exist but they often serve merely to cloud the essential simplicity of the concept. Even so, over the years the law has evolved a series of requirements which must be fulfilled before the proposed consideration will be acceptable.

Consideration must move from the promisee. The consideration must be provided by the person to whom the promise was made and who wishes to enforce the promise.

Consideration must not be past. The consideration must not precede the promise that it supports. In *Re McArdle* (1951) a father's will left his house jointly to his children. One of the children and his wife still lived with the mother, and the wife had made substantial improvements to the house. The other children subsequently agreed to contribute towards the cost. An action to enforce the agreement failed because the improvements preceded the promise to contribute towards them.

Exceptions to the rule exist. If one person asks another to do something for him in a way which raises the presumption that he will be paid, a subsequent promise to pay will be enforceable. In *Re Casey's Patents, Stewart* v. *Casey* (1892) a promise to give a one-third share of the patent rights, in return for services which the plaintiff had already performed in working the patents, was enforced. The services had been requested and it was clearly understood that they were to be paid for. A statutory exception exists in the Bills of Exchange Act 1882 s.27. This states that in relation to bills of exchange, "an antecedent debt or liability", i.e. a previous or existing liability, is "valuable consideration". A bill of exchange contains a promise to pay a specific sum of money and many bills, particularly cheques (the most common type of bill of exchange), are drawn to settle existing (past) debts. Thus the consideration given for the promise contained in the bill is past, e.g. payment by cheque for goods delivered a week ago. In short, the consideration precedes the promise. Clearly, however, this exception is necessary in order for bills of exchange to fulfil their function as a method of payment. It is also a good example of the needs of commerce and industry affecting the rules of contract law. (If in *Re McArdle* (1951), for example, the other children had given the wife a cheque, she could have enforced the promise of payment contained in it.)

Consideration must be sufficient. The consideration must be of some legal value. It must be sufficient but it need not be commercially adequate. For example, a person could sell his car for £1.00 and the law would not question the bargain that the parties had struck, provided that the bargain was not defective in any other respect.

Consideration is said to be insufficient when the person providing it is merely fulfilling an existing legal duty. This may be either a public or a contractual duty. In *Collins* v. *Godefroy* (1831) the plaintiff was under a public duty to give evidence in court for the defendant but accepted the defendant's promise to pay him six guineas (£6.30) for doing so. The plaintiff could not recover the sum for he had provided no consideration, he had merely fulfilled his duty.

It follows, however, that where a person exceeds his duty he provides consideration for a promise of payment. This was the situation in *Hartley* v. *Ponsonby* (1857) where the extent of the contractual duty of a group of sailors was at issue. The sailors had been offered extra wages to continue working the ship because the crew had become so depleted that the continuation of the voyage was dangerous. On the facts, their original contractual obligation had been discharged by the change in circumstances, and they were free to enter into a new contract. The extra wages could therefore be recovered.

A somewhat different problem arises where a person pays or promises to pay part of a debt in return for the creditor promising to forgo the balance. Here it is a question of avoiding an existing duty, not enforcing extra payment. It is not uncommon for a business organisation to be in a position where it has to forgo the balance of a debt to avoid liquidity problems. By the time the full debt is recovered a crisis could have arisen. This means that a firm might be forced, indeed even willing, to accept £500 in payment for a debt of £750 in order to pay its own overheads and thereby stay in business. This economic truth, coupled with an almost traditional reluctance on the part of businessmen to resort to legal action, has resulted in a divergence of theory and practice. At law the balance can be recovered because the debtor has provided no consideration for the creditor's promise; he has not even fulfilled the legal obligation that he was already under. In *Foakes* v. *Beer* (1884) the House of Lords confirmed the rule when Beer sued Foakes for the interest owed to her on a judgment debt. The House rejected Foakes' argument that, in return for his payment of a lump sum and the balance of the judgment debt in instalments, she had agreed to take no further action on the matter.

To this rule a number of exceptions were laid down in *Pinnel's Case* as long ago as 1602. Payment of a lesser sum amounts to consideration where at the creditor's request it is paid at an earlier date or at a different place. The debt is similarly satisfied where the debtor gives or does something else which may be worth more or less with the creditor's consent. In each of these cases the debtor has introduced a new element into the transaction, giving the creditor something other than that to which he was entitled. The exceptions make commercial sense: an earlier payment of less might solve an acute cash-flow problem, while payment at a different place may be convenient (particularly so in olden days), and if the creditor wishes to take payment in kind, e.g. goods instead of money, a contract is after all a private bargain between two or more individuals.

A more modern exception exists where it would be unfair for the promisor who agrees to accept less to go back on his word. The exception emerged in the *High Trees Case* (1947) and is known as promissory or equitable estoppel. In 1939 the plaintiffs had leased a block of flats to the defendants. In January 1940 they agreed in writing, but without the defendants providing consideration, to accept only half of the rent due under the lease because the war had caused many of the flats to be unoccupied. From 1940 to 1945 the defendants paid the reduced rent. However, when the flats were again full in 1945 the plaintiffs brought an action claiming that they were entitled to the full rent not only for the future but also from 1940, thereby seeking to go back on the written agreement. To test their claim they sought payment of the full rent for the last two quarters of 1945. On the facts, the actual claim succeeded because the agreement was intended to be a temporary arrangement which would cease to operate when conditions changed, as they had by mid-1945. However the judge was of the opinion that had the claim been pursued right back to 1940 the plaintiffs would have failed because they would have been estopped (prevented) from going back on their promise, even though the defendants had given nothing in return.

The application of the principle of promissory estoppel, to prevent the promisor going back on his word, is at the discretion of the court and subsequent cases show that it can only be used as a defence against a person seeking to enforce his original contractual rights and never as the basis for a legal action. A promise can only be enforced where consideration was given for it. It is unresolved at present whether promissory estoppel merely suspends the promisor's original rights or whether it extinguishes them entirely. If the former is the case the promisor can reassert his rights by giving adequate notice of his intention to do so. For example, if a buyer has waived a contractual delivery date he would subsequently be able to take back his promise and exercise his right to reject delivery after giving the seller a reasonable ultimatum.

Another situation where payment of less is full satisfaction for a greater sum owed is to be found in bankruptcy law. A debtor may make composition (as it is called) with his creditors under which his creditors each agree to take a proportion of what they are owed. They are bound by the composition for any action to recover the balance would amount to fraud against their fellow creditors.

Finally the performance of an existing duty is sufficient consideration where the duty is owed to someone other than the promisor. This was illustrated in *The Eurymedon* (1974) where the defendants, who damaged goods whilst unloading them from a ship, were held to have provided sufficient consideration by unloading the goods, a duty that they already owed to the shippers, to take the benefit of a promise from the plaintiffs to treat them as exempt from any liability for damaging the goods.

The intention to create legal relations
The existence of a definite bargain between the parties still does not mean that an enforceable contract exists. The law requires that the parties must have intended their bargain to be legally binding. In effect this requirement is more apparent than real, for every commercial agreement is presumed to be legally binding unless the contrary is proved by the person who disputes the presumption. In the event of a dispute the question is decided by looking at the facts of the case. In *Carlill* v. *Carbolic Smoke Ball Co.* (1892), for example, the defendants had advertised that they had deposited £1,000 with their bankers as evidence of their good faith. This deposit was held to be sufficient indication that their promise was not intended to be a "mere puff" but a statement upon which they expected to incur legal liability. It is possible, however, to expressly exclude legal liability in a commercial agreement by including a suitably worded clause—an honour clause—in which the parties declare that their agreement is not to be binding at law.

In contrast, social and domestic agreements are not presumed to be legally binding, and if one of the parties wishes to enforce such an agreement he must prove the required intention. This is done by producing evidence to show that the social agreement is in reality a commercial arrangement or that the domestic relationship has ceased to exist. In *Merritt* v. *Merritt* (1970) an agreement between a wife and her husband, by which he promised to pay £40 a month to her and to transfer the matrimonial home into her sole name in return for her paying the outstanding mortgage payments, was legally binding because the domestic relationship had ended when the husband had left his wife to live with another woman.

Further requirements
The presence of an "agreement", a "bargain" and an "intention to create legal relations" are the essential requirements of a valid contract but four other factors have an important bearing on its validity and enforceability. These factors may be termed "form", "contractual capacity", "reality of consent" and "legality". They can best be considered, perhaps, as possible legal defects in the bargain the parties have struck.

Form. It is a common and understandable misconception that contracts have to be written, or at least recorded in writing, for in a great many transactions one or both of the parties signs a written contract or receives a written receipt. This practice is seldom based on legal requirement but on the practical needs of administration. Within an organisation records must be kept, accounts filed and sent, stock turnover monitored and generally a whole host of internal functions either directly depend on, or are fuelled by, written records of the organisation's transactions.

Legal requirements as to form are comparatively few and the most formal document known to English law, the deed—a document that must be signed, sealed and delivered—is only commonly required in the law of contract where a lease of land is granted for more than three years. Even here an agreement to grant a lease, as distinct from the grant itself, need only be evidenced in writing and for many purposes creates the same rights between the parties.

In recent years a requirement that certain contracts must be written has proved effective in consumer protection and all consumer credit agreements covered by the Consumer Credit Act 1974 are required to be in writing. A regulated agreement which fails to satisfy the statutory requirements can only be enforced against the debtor on the order of the court.

Finally, certain contracts cannot be enforced in a court unless they are evidenced in writing, although they may be perfectly valid in every other respect. The requirement was introduced by the Statute of Frauds 1677 to stop fraud being committed by perjury.

The original Act applies to contracts of guarantee (a promise to answer for the debt of another) and the Law of Property Act 1925 re-enacted a similar stipulation with regard to any contract for the sale of land or any interest in land.

Contractual capacity. Traditionally, the law took as its norm the sane, sober, adult human male and anyone or anything else either had to be protected from society or suffered disabilities within it. Today most of the disabilities have gone, but special rules exist concerning the contractual capacity of minors and corporations.

A minor, a person under eighteen years of age, can only be bound by contracts for "necessaries" (basically food, clothing, lodging and other things without which it would be unreasonable to expect him to live) and contracts of employment that are to his advantage, for example those containing an element of education or training such as articles of apprenticeship. Contracts of loan made with a minor are expressly declared to be void by the Infants' Relief Act 1874 and contracts involving continuing rights and duties, for example a partnership agreement, may be avoided by a minor during his minority or within a reasonable time after he becomes eighteen.

The contractual capacity of corporations is governed by the charter or statute which creates them. The vast majority of corporations are limited companies registered under the Companies Acts and their contractual capacity is governed by the "objects clause" of their memoranda of association. Any contract which is *ultra vires* (beyond the powers of) the "objects clause" will not, subject to certain important exceptions, bind the company.

Reality of consent. An agreement where one of the parties did not freely and fully consent to the terms will generally not be enforced. An agreement obtained by actual or threatened unlawful force (duress), or by the use of unfair pressure may be set aside by the party who was unable to exercise a free will. The former is highly unlikely but in the latter, more common, case, certain well-defined confidential or fiduciary relationships give rise to the presumption that unfair pressure or undue influence, as it is termed at law, has been exerted. This must be disproved by the stronger party if he wishes to enforce the contract. Such relationships include those between a solicitor and his client, a doctor and his patient and a parent and his child.

Similarly a contract is voidable (capable of being set aside) where one party has misled the other by misrepresenting, either fraudulently, negligently or innocently, the true facts.

Undue influence and misrepresentation both entitle the weaker party to rescind (to set aside or cancel) the contract but he will lose this right if he subsequently confirms the agreement after appreciating the true facts, delays too long before seeking to rescind, or, in certain circumstances, where other people have become involved.

Occasionally, where one or both parties to a contract makes a mistake, the contract will be void and a total nullity, but most types of mistake have no effect at all. For example, the law will not assist an organisation which mistakes the quantity of goods it requires or underestimates the time required to complete a project. Where, however, the mistake prevents any agreement being reached at all, or where an agreement is reached which lacks any foundation because of the mistake, the contract will be void. The former situation can possibly arise in a contract of sale where the seller mistakes the identity of the buyer or, more likely, where the buyer and seller are at cross-purposes as to the subject-matter of the sale, the seller wishing to sell X, but the buyer wishing to buy Y. In the latter situation the effect of a mistake is very limited. Only where the intended subject-matter of the contract has ceased to exist for the purposes of the contract, without the knowledge of either buyer or seller, before an agreement is reached, will the contract be void. This could happen where the seller's agent has already sold the goods to another buyer or where they have been physically destroyed.

Legality. All contracts must be within the law. Illegality is an umbrella term in the law of contract, covering contracts which involve actual criminal acts, e.g. an organisation allowing an employee to include his tax liability in his expense account, thus defrauding the state, through to contracts which merely offend public policy. A contract in which a person restricts his future freedom to carry on his trade, business or profession as he pleases comes into this latter category. An example of such a contract would be where a term in a person's contract of employment prevents him from working for a competitor of his employer for a certain period and/or within a certain area after leaving his job. You may, perhaps, have such a provision in your own contract of employment, but the point is that the restriction will be upheld if it can be proved to be reasonable and necessary for the protection of your employer's legitimate trade interests. A further example where such a restriction may be justified is where an established shop is sold with its goodwill and the vendor agrees not to open a similar shop within a certain area and/or time.

In all cases those aspects of the contract which are illegal or tainted with illegality are void but where the contract merely

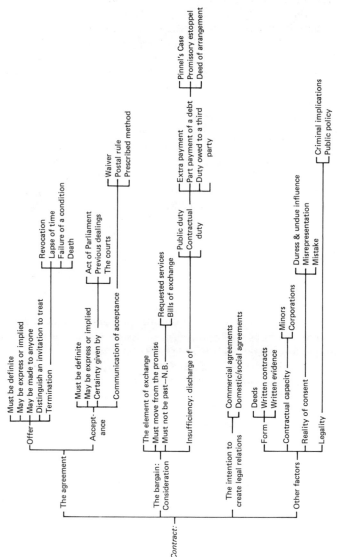

Fig. 78. *The structure of a contract.*

Contract:

- The agreement
  - Offer
    - Must be definite
    - May be express or implied
    - May be made to anyone
    - Distinguish an invitation to treat
    - Termination
      - Revocation
      - Lapse of time
      - Failure of a condition
      - Death
  - Acceptance
    - Must be definite
    - May be express or implied
    - Certainty given by
      - Act of Parliament
      - Previous dealings
      - The courts
    - Communication of acceptance
      - Waiver
      - Postal rule
      - Prescribed method
- The bargain: Consideration
  - The element of exchange
  - Must move from the promise
  - Must not be past—N.B.
    - Requested services
    - Bills of exchange
  - Insufficiency: discharge of
    - Public duty
    - Contractual duty
      - Extra payment
      - Part payment of a debt
      - Duty owed to a third party
        - Pinnel's Case
        - Promissory estoppel
        - Deed of arrangement
- The intention to create legal relations
  - Commercial agreements
  - Domestic/social agreements
- Other factors
  - Form
    - Deeds
    - Written contracts
    - Written evidence
  - Contractual capacity
    - Minors
    - Corporations
  - Reality of consent
    - Duress & undue influence
    - Misrepresentation
    - Mistake
  - Legality
    - Criminal implications
    - Public policy

offends public policy, the offending parts may be severed from the whole and the rest enforced. An employee whose contract contains an unlawful restraint of trade can still enforce the payment of wages owed to him although his employer cannot enforce the clauses in which the unreasonable restraint is contained.

Conclusion
Such then are the essentials of a valid contract (*see* Fig. 78). Its concepts underlie all aspects of business law and it exists as a medium through which an organisation can pursue its activities. The essential simplicity of the main concept should never be forgotten; it is a bargain struck between two parties who, as in all spheres of social activity, must observe certain rules so that commercial activity may continue with the minimum of disruption, dispute and uncertainty.

ORGANISATIONS, CONSUMERS AND THE LAW

Consumer law in context
You have already seen in this chapter that the concept of freedom to bargain is usually rather illusory when an individual consumer enters into a contract with a large organisation. A large organisation will usually conduct its business according to set procedures, prescribed terms of business and on standard form contracts. Ally this to the increased standardisation in methods of production and distribution, and the average consumer's lack of financial resources and unwillingness (often inability) to pursue a claim through the courts, and you have a compelling case for the law to recognise and to attempt to remedy the inequality in bargaining power between consumers and producers and distributors of goods and services. In particular, the consumer needs protection from misinformation, unfair influence and unfair limitations on his range of choice—economic exploitation in general. As you will see in the rest of this chapter, the principle of *caveat venditor* (let the seller beware) has now made significant inroads into the nineteenth century *laissez-faire* approach of *caveat emptor* (let the buyer beware).

In this context the framework of consumer law provides the corresponding responsibility and accountability of an organisation in relation to its products as that discussed in Chapter 13 in relation to its resources. Once again, responsibility is both economic and social: a trading organisation must make sufficient profit to continue in business and it cannot grossly exploit the market to the detriment of the community at large. Legal accountability to consumers is clearly inherent in the framework, but in recent years a comprehensive structure of administrative accountability has been created, primarily in the form of the Office of Fair Trading. However, administrative accountability is in truth an amalgam of legal, economic, political and social forms of accountability.

The common law has played only a limited role in consumer protection, concerning itself more with specific aspects of consumerism, for example the interpretation of clauses excluding a supplier's liability for supplying defective goods, rather than with general policy. Consumer law is therefore largely statutory and the product of government intervention in both the common law principle of "freedom of contract" and in the free working of the economy. This intervention can be considered as a political response to some of the socially unacceptable characteristics of a capitalist economy.

A consumer is defined for the purposes of the Fair Trading Act 1973 (the most important single piece of legislative consumer protection) as a person:

(*a*) to whom goods or services are supplied, or sought to be supplied, in the course of a business carried on by the supplier; and

(*b*) who does not receive or seek to receive them in the course of a business carried on by him.

However, while we are here concerned with the consumer as defined by the 1973 Act, you have already seen that organisations "consume" goods and services in a similar way to individual consumers. Therefore, the law is not based upon the nature of the goods or services supplied but upon the *status* of the recipient and the *use* to which the goods or services are put. Thus a distinction can be drawn between "consumer" goods and "producer" goods, the latter being goods that are used in the creation of further wealth. This corresponds to the legal distinction between persons dealing as consumers and those who do not. For example, a typewriter would be classed as a consumer good and the sale a consumer sale when sold to a private individual, but a producer good, sold in a non-consumer sale, when sold to a trading organisation of any kind. A formal definition of "dealing as a consumer" is given in the Unfair Contract Terms Act 1977. A person deals as a consumer if:

(*a*) he neither makes the contract in the course of a business nor holds himself out as doing so;

(*b*) the other party does make the contract in the course of a business; and

(*c*) the goods passing under or in pursuance of the contract are of a type ordinarily supplied for private use or consumption.

Governments have used the law to distinguish between what can be termed "domestic consumers" and "business consumers" primarily because the latter are considered better able to appreciate the law and to be in a position to enter contracts on more equal terms with suppliers of goods and services than the former. They do, of course, have the protection of the general law, but some specific statutory protection, e.g. relating to exclusion clauses, does not apply to business consumers. Continuing our example of the typewriter, you will see later in this chapter that the Sale of Goods Act 1979 implies into every contract for the sale of goods a condition that the goods must be of "merchantable quality", e.g. that the typewriter works properly. In a sale to a person dealing as consumer this implied condition cannot be excluded at all, but where a person deals other than as consumer, i.e. a sale to a trading organisation, an exclusion of the implied condition of merchantability will be legally effective if it is reasonable in the circumstances of that particular transaction (*see* the Unfair Contract Terms Act 1977).

On the face of it, organisations may seem to be unfairly treated in the realm of consumerism. On the one hand, their freedom to bargain with their customers has been greatly reduced, while on the other they do not receive the same protection as their own customers when they in turn enter into contracts for the supply of goods and services. However, experience has shown that positive discrimination in favour of consumers is necessary to counter-balance the control over prices, output and terms of business which large organisations can exert. As you saw in the previous chapter, organisations in an imperfect market are able to use their position in the market to maximise profits to the detriment of consumers. While consumer law cannot hope to make imperfect markets perfect, it can at least mitigate the worst excesses of unfettered economic might.

Consumerism is a field where pressure groups have been very active and very successful, both against individual firms and in a wider political role, two of the best known consumer lobbyists being Ralph Nader in the USA and the Consumer Association (publishers of *Which?*) in the UK. MPs frequently adopt consumer causes; for example, Jack Ashley MP has been prominent in furthering the interests of the disabled, perhaps his best known campaign being the battle with Distillers Co. Ltd to obtain realistic compensation for thalidomide victims.

The legal framework of consumer protection
The object of this section of the chapter is, as the heading suggests, to describe the legal framework of consumer protection, and only

general references will be made to the working of the actual law involved.

The law protecting consumers may be either civil law or criminal law, and the relevant rights, duties or liabilities may in turn be created or imposed by the common law or by statute. The nature of these different types of law is discussed in Chapter 24, but each may be briefly described as follows.

(*a*) *Civil law.* The body of law concerned with the rights and obligations of individuals (and organisations) towards each other. Unlike criminal law, the injured party, and not the state, must initiate legal proceedings, and compensation, not punishment, is the object of court action.

(*b*) *Criminal law.* This consists of rules protecting society which are enforced by the state on pain of punishment. A criminal conviction for a "consumer offence" does not necessarily mean that the injured consumer will receive compensation; he may have to bring a separate civil action to obtain this. He may, however, use the trader's criminal conviction as evidence in his civil action.

(*c*) *Common law.* The body of law consisting originally of customs but now consisting of case law.

(*d*) *Statute law.* This consists of Acts of Parliament and Orders and Regulations (Statutory Instruments) which have been made under them. Since the passing of the original Sale of Goods Act in 1893 there have been a considerable number of statutes passed to protect the consumer, giving him civil remedies where there has been misrepresentation, misleading advertisements and the like. Additionally, Parliament has employed the criminal law to stop such trade malpractices as the use of false trade descriptions and the sale of adulterated food.

In reality, of course, this strictly legal framework cannot be divorced from the administrative safeguards which exist to protect consumers. In particular, the Office of Fair Trading exercises a variety of quasi-judicial functions based upon the general legal framework of consumer protection (*see* below).

It is worth noting, before we begin a detailed look at the legal framework of consumer protection, that the aim of the law is prevention rather than the punishment of "consumer offences". In relation to the number of consumer transactions, the number of civil actions brought by consumers is very small, the vast majority of business organisations fulfilling their legal obligations. Similarly, prosecutions of traders are fairly rare, and trading standards officers will often prefer to warn rather than prosecute where the law is infringed.

The common law

The law of contract and the law of torts are the two most important branches of the common law. The former, as you have already seen in this chapter, regulates business agreements. If either party fails to perform his side of the bargain, the other can sue for breach of contract. The latter protects the rights of individuals (and organisations) by imposing duties on other individuals (and organisations). A breach of duty entitles the injured party to an action for damages (a payment of money). For example, if you take your car to a garage to be repaired—a service—you are entitled to a reasonable standard of workmanship. Similarly, if you hire tools or equipment to repair your car yourself they must be of reasonable quality and reasonably fit for the job. In both cases failure to measure up to the standard of "reasonableness" (a question of fact) amounts to a breach of contract. However, should you buy tools or equipment which injure you or somebody else, or damage property, their manufacturer could be sued for damages in the tort of negligence. (You, as purchaser, could of course also sue the retailer under the Sale of Goods Act 1979 for the injury *you* have suffered.)

The liability of manufacturers to the ultimate consumer for injury caused by their negligence was established in *Donoghue* v. *Stevenson* (1932), an extremely well-known House of Lords decision which is also the foundation of the modern tort of negligence. In that case the plaintiff's friend had bought her ginger beer in a dark opaque glass bottle. She drank some and when the remainder was poured, out flowed the remains of a decomposed snail. The plaintiff suffered shock and gastroenteritis as a result of the impure ginger beer.

The plaintiff had not bought the ginger beer herself and consequently could not sue the retailer under the Sale of Goods Act 1893. However, the House of Lords held that the manufacturer owed a duty of care to the plaintiff. In the words of Lord Atkin "A manufacturer of products, which he sells in such a form as to show that he intends them to reach the ultimate consumer in the form in which they left him with no reasonable possibility of intermediate examination, and with the knowledge that the absence of reasonable care in the preparation or putting up of the products will result in an injury to the consumer's life or property, owes a duty to the consumer to take reasonable care."

The liability of manufacturers to ultimate consumers is called the "narrow principle" of *Donoghue* v. *Stevenson*; there is also a "broad principle". This states that "You must take reasonable care to avoid acts or omissions which you can reasonably foresee would be likely to injure your neighbour" (Atkin). A "neighbour" is anyone whom it could reasonably have been foreseen would be affected by the act or omission in question. This "broad principle" is important in consumer law. For example, a repairer of goods owes a duty of care to their users and a provider of a service is liable if goods left with him are misappropriated by an employee, a fur coat left with a dry cleaners for cleaning being an example.

There has been much talk recently about "product liability", a system under which a manufacturer would have to compensate anybody who suffered personal injury or damage to property caused by his faulty product, even if the injured person was unable to prove negligence in its manufacture. From the consumer's point of view "product liability" would be a great boon because it is often extremely difficult to prove negligence on the part of a manufacturer, e.g. the thalidomide case. It would of course mean the virtual end of the tort of negligence in actions brought against manufacturers. It is argued by some that "product liability" would increase prices and that one large claim could force a small firm out of business. However, it is quite possible in the long run that insurance against claims would be less costly than fighting court actions.

At present, however, while the government has accepted the principle of strict liability (*see* page 578) under an EEC draft directive on product liability, planned further negotiations with the member states over such matters as the defence of development risk will mean that UK legislation is some years away. The government takes the view that a fair, just and proper balance must be struck between the interests of the community and the interests of the producer. For example, it argues that the defence of development risk, or "state of the art" as it is known, should cover defects beyond the control of the producer—defects unknown and unknowable and unforeseen and unforeseeable.

While the common law offers some general protection to consumers, it is not an adequate means of consumer protection. In particular, the basic "freedom of contract" approach of the common law allowed traders to exclude or limit both their duties and consumers' rights, and the common law's intervention was limited to interpreting such exclusions in favour of the consumer (where possible). The bulk of the law protecting consumers is therefore to be found in Acts of Parliament and Orders and Regulations made under them.

Statute law
Legislation on consumer protection unfortunately does not fall into neat categories for textbook purposes. A particular Act may cover more than one aspect of "consumerism", and may employ both the

criminal and civil law to achieve its objectives. Thus, it is best to list the legislation grouped according to general areas and then consider each alphabetically (*see* Tables XXVIII and XXIX).

Competition Act 1980. Under this Act the Director General of Fair Trading is able to investigate the trading practices of individual business organisations to see whether they are operating an *anti-competitive practice.* The Act defines this as "comprising a course of conduct which has, or is intended to have or is likely to have the effect of restricting, distorting, or preventing competition in the UK". If the DGFT makes enquiries and finds such a practice, he can try to obtain an undertaking from the trader concerned to stop it. If he will not give one, or will not abide by his undertaking, the DGFT can refer it to the Monopolies and Mergers Commission and the Secretary of State for Trade can then prohibit that person from operating that practice. The Act extends this possible action to monopoly situations arising in nationalised industries, as these organisations are not covered by the Fair Trading Act.

Consumer Credit Act 1974. The Act is a framework into which detail can be written by the Secretary of State for Trade by means of Statutory Instruments. Its basic aims are:

(*a*) to remedy the inequality in bargaining position in consumer credit transactions;
(*b*) to control trading malpractices;
(*c*) to regulate remedies for failure to comply with the Act.

It covers all credit agreements where no more than £5,000 (at present) is advanced to private individuals, sole traders and business partnerships; it does not apply to limited companies and other incorporated bodies, e.g. public corporations. Also covered are agreements for the hire of goods where the agreement may be for more than three months and no more than £5,000 will be involved.

This stricter control of the credit industry is achieved administratively by a system of licensing (licences can be withdrawn), and by law through the creation of several criminal offences and civil rights and duties. The Director General of Fair Trading is responsible for licensing credit organisations and administering the Act generally.

First and foremost, it is a *criminal* offence to trade as either a provider of credit or as a credit broker, e.g. shops that introduce customers to finance houses, without a licence, and an unlicensed trader is unable to enforce his credit agreements without the Director General's consent. Further offences include sending credit cards

TABLE XXVIII. LEGISLATION ON CONSUMER PROTECTION

Area involved	Main relevant legislation
Business practices against consumer interests	Restrictive Trade Practices Act 1976, Resale Prices Act 1974, Fair Trading Act 1973, Competition Act 1980
Compensation for injury suffered by consumers as a result of a criminal offence	Powers of the Criminal Courts Act 1973
Credit	Consumer Credit Act 1974
Dangerous goods	Consumer Safety Act 1978, Sale of Goods Act 1979
False or misleading descriptions	Trade Descriptions Act 1968, Misrepresentation Act 1967, Theft Act 1968, Food and Drugs Act 1955, Sale of Goods Act 1979
Faulty Goods	Sale of Goods Act 1979
Faulty services	Unfair Contract Terms Act 1977
Food	Food and Drugs Act 1955, Sale of Goods Act, 1979
Hygiene	Food and Drugs Act 1955
Prices: their display	Prices Act 1974, Trade Descriptions Act 1968
maximum prices	Prices Act 1974
Quantities for sale	Weights and Measures Act 1963
Short measure	Weights and Measures Acts 1963–79, Theft Act 1968, Trade Descriptions Act 1968, Sale of Goods Act 1979
Unordered goods and services	Unsolicited Goods and Services Act 1971

to people without being asked to do so and sending documents to minors (persons under eighteen) inviting them to borrow money or obtain other credit facilities. Prosecutions are brought by either the Office of Fair Trading or, more usually, by the trading standards departments of local authorities.

A variety of *civil* law rights are given to the consumer. He may complain to the court if he thinks that the terms of the credit

TABLE XXIX. LEGISLATION AND ENFORCEMENT AGENCIES

Legislation	Enforcement agency
Consumer Credit Act Consumer Safety Act Trade Descriptions Act Food and Drugs Act (composition and labelling of food) Prices Acts Weights and Measures Acts Fair Trading Act Unsolicited Goods and Services Act	County council, trading standards department (sometimes called consumer services or consumer protection)
Food and Drugs Act (unfit food and hygiene)	District council or metropolitan borough council, environmental health dept.
Theft Act	Police
Fair Trading Act Consumer Credit Act (licensing and information) Restrictive Trade Practices Act Competition Act Resale Prices Act	Director General of Fair Trading
Powers of the Criminal Courts Act	Criminal courts
Sale of Goods Act Misrepresentation Act Unfair Contract Terms Act Unsolicited Goods and Services Act Consumer Credit Act	Civil courts

agreement are extortionate and the court has the power to order repayment if it agrees with the complaint. He has the right to the name and address of any credit reference agency consulted about him and further rights to obtain a copy of the reference and have corrected any mistakes that it may contain. Another important provision is that a provider of finance other than the actual seller, e.g. a finance house or credit card company, is equally liable with the seller for any breach of contract or misrepresentation by the seller.

Consumer Safety Act 1978. This Act enables the Secretary of State for Prices and Consumer Protection to regulate the composition, design and construction of certain goods in order to prevent risk of death or personal injury caused by them. Examples include oil heaters, electric blankets and flexes on domestic appliances.

Infringement of the regulations is a *criminal* offence and a consumer who has suffered loss or injury caused by such infringements is given a right of action for damages at *civil* law. (In addition, actions under the Sale of Goods Act 1979 or at common law for negligence may be available.) The Secretary of State for Trade may also make "prohibition orders and notices" under the Act. These prevent the sale or supply of goods which he considers unsafe. It is a *criminal* offence to disregard "prohibition orders and notices".

Fair Trading Act 1973. This Act established the Office of Fair Trading, which is now the main institution of consumer protection, granting wide-ranging powers to its Director General. The Office of Fair Trading is considered in more detail below, but one of its powers is that traders who persist in breaking the *criminal* law or flout their *civil* obligations, can be asked to sign an undertaking promising to stop doing so. If they refuse to give such an undertaking or do not abide by an undertaking previously taken, the Director General can bring a *civil* action for an injunction against them in the Restrictive Practices Court.

The Act also gives the Secretary of State for Prices and Consumer Protection the power to make orders outlawing undesirable trade practices following the recommendation of the Director General or the Consumer Protection Advisory Committee. Two such orders are the Consumer Transactions (Restrictions on Statements) Order 1976 (considered below) and the Business Advertisements (Disclosure) Order 1977. The latter order seeks to ensure that consumers are not misled about the status of the seller of goods advertised for sale. It requires all advertisements by persons seeking to sell goods *in the course of a business* to make this fact clear. Failure to comply with either order is a *criminal* offence punishable by a maximum fine of £400 on summary conviction, i.e. conviction before a magistrates' court, or an unlimited fine or a term of imprisonment not exceeding two years, or both, on conviction on indictment, i.e. before judge and jury in the crown court.

Food and Drugs Act 1955. This empowers the government to make regulations governing the composition and nutritional quality of food, its labelling and advertising. Provisions concerning the misdescription of food and hygiene requirements for food shops are also given.

It is a *criminal* offence to have food or drink on sale which is unfit for human consumption, and local environmental health officers have the power to close down premises which infringe hygiene regulations.

Misrepresentation Act 1967. A consumer is able to bring a *civil* action for damages under the Act for any loss he suffers as a result of false statements of fact made by the seller or provider of goods or services which induces him to enter into a contract for those goods or services. An attempted exclusion of liability under the Act is ineffective unless it is fair and reasonable in the circumstances. This is for the court to decide.

Powers of Criminal Courts Act 1973. One provision of this Act enables courts to award compensation to anyone who has suffered loss as a result of a criminal act. At present the power of the magistrates' court to award compensation is limited to £1,000. While the Act is of general application, it has quite frequently been used to compensate consumers for loss suffered through offences under the Trade Descriptions Act 1968.

Prices Act 1974. The Act enables the government to make Orders and Regulations governing prices, particularly their display but also maximum price levels. For example, Orders have been made requiring that the price per weight of food is given, that pubs and other licensed premises must display the prices of their drinks and that garages must not display their petrol prices in a misleading way.

The Price Marking (Bargain Offers) Order 1979 only allows a price display stating that an article is worth, say, £100 but that the price charged is only £75 if the seller, or someone specified by him, has charged, or will charge at some future specified time, the higher price for the article.

Resale Prices Act 1976. This Act, which consolidates previous relevant legislation, prohibits "resale price maintenance" in order to encourage competition in the interests of consumers. Although "recommended" prices can still be laid down by manufacturers, any pressure on retailers to sell at a minimum price, e.g. threats to withhold supplies of goods, is a *civil* offence and an action can be brought against them by retailers, consumers who have suffered from this price-fixing, or by the Director General of Fair Trading.

Restrictive Trade Practices Act 1976. Under this Act, agreements by traders to restrict competition among themselves, e.g. by fixing prices, must be registered with the Office of Fair Trading. A registered agreement may be referred to the Restrictive Trade Practices Court to determine whether it is in the public interest. Any agreement found to be contrary to the public interest is prohibited.

The Act applies to both goods and services (with certain important exceptions such as law and medicine) and the Office of Fair Trading can bring a *civil* action in the Restrictive Practices Court against anyone who operates a restrictive agreement which has not been registered. A consumer who has been affected by an unregistered agreement can also bring a *civil* action for damages.

A possible way of avoiding the Act is for companies to merge, but the Monopolies and Mergers Commission (considered below) protects the public interest by investigating potentially undesirable mergers.

Sale of Goods Act 1979. The original 1893 Act was the first great landmark in consumer protection and as amended and re-enacted is still the foundation of all protection relating to the purchase of goods. The Act automatically implies certain conditions into every contract for the sale of goods when they are bought from someone who sells in the course of a business, namely: that the goods must be of "merchantable quality", i.e. new goods must not be broken, damaged and must work properly; "fit for their purpose", i.e. do what they are supposed to do; and must correspond to their description, whether on the good itself, its packaging or by any other sales description. Remember, these implied conditions cannot be excluded in a consumer sale.

Furthermore, the Consumer Transaction (Restrictions on Statements) Order 1976 (as amended), the first order prohibiting undesirable trade practices to be made under the Fair Trading Act 1973, makes it a *criminal* offence to purport to exclude these implied conditions by notice or other documents, e.g. a "no money refunded" notice. In addition, any statement on the goods, their container or in any document, relating to the consumer's rights or obligations where the goods are defective, not fit for a particular purpose or do not correspond with their description, must be accompanied by a clear and conspicuous notice informing the consumer that his statutory rights are not affected. The Order is necessary because it is open to an unscrupulous trader to purport to exclude his liability and rely on the ignorance of the law on the part of his customers to render a legally ineffective exclusion effective in practice.

The Act is part of the *civil* law and failure to comply with these implied conditions is a breach of contract entitling the buyer to return the good and receive the purchase price back. Although a repair, an exchange or a credit note may be acceptable alternatives to the consumer, he cannot, as you have seen, be compelled to accept these in lieu of a complete cash refund. In addition, a buyer of faulty goods can also claim damages for other loss, e.g. to property, personal injury and the cost of hiring a replacement.

Theft Act 1968. It is a *criminal* offence under the Theft Act 1968 to "obtain property by deception". Thus, for example, a car salesman who deliberately falsifies the distance recorded on a car's odometer has committed an offence. The Act is of general application rather than specifically designed to be part of the machinery of consumer protection.

Trade Descriptions Act 1968. It is a *criminal* offence under the Act for a trader to misdescribe goods, or to make false statements about services if he knew that they were false or if he did not care whether his statements were true or false. It also bans certain false or misleading indications as to the price of goods; for example, it is an offence to simply cross out the price on a price ticket and substitute a lower price unless the goods have been sold at the higher price for at least twenty-eight consecutive days in the last six months. The trader must make it quite clear if they have not.

Under the Act a trader can be fined a maximum of £400 on summary conviction and an unlimited amount and/or imprisonment after conviction on indictment. In addition, the local authority trading standards or consumer protection officers have the power to enter premises, seize and inspect goods if a trader is suspected of contravening the Act.

The Act does not apply to private sales and any descriptions of houses or land.

Unfair Contract Terms Act 1977. This Act, part of the *civil* law, is another landmark in consumer protection. It restricts the extent to which liability can be avoided for breach of contract and negligence. You have already seen that this Act is sufficiently wide in its scope to cover purported exclusions of liability under the Occupiers' Liability Act 1957 for death or personal injury arising from negligence in connection with the occupation of premises used for the business purposes of the occupier. In fact, with the exception of liability for breach of implied obligations in sales of goods and hire-purchase contracts, the Act regulates only *business liability*, i.e. liability arising from activities in the course of a business or from the occupation of business premises. However, "business" includes professions, and the activities of government departments and local or public authorities.

Basically, it is not possible to exclude or restrict liability for death or personal injury caused by negligence, and liability for other loss or damage caused by negligence can only be excluded or restricted in so far as the term or notice used satisfies a test of "reasonableness". Where one party deals as a consumer or deals on the other's written standard terms of business (this includes business organisations), *any* exclusion of liability for breach of contract, or any term allowing him to substantially vary his contractual obligations, is ineffective unless the "reasonableness" test is satisfied. The latter provision is particularly important in consumer dealings for it covers services as well as goods, the Sale of Goods Act 1979 already covering the most important aspects of contracts for the sale of goods.

The Act contains two other very important provisions protecting consumers. Firstly, manufacturers' guarantees can *never* exclude or restrict liability for loss or damage caused by goods which are faulty through negligence while in "consumer use". Secondly, in contracts (other than sale or hire-purchase) where ownership or possession of goods passes, liability in respect of the goods' correspondence with description or fitness for purpose cannot be excluded or restricted against a person dealing as consumer, e.g. where a consumer rents a TV or hires plumbers to install central heating.

It is worth noting that while the consumer is now quite comprehensively protected, and a relatively simple procedure exists in county court arbitration (*see* page 603) for the redress of his grievances, he must refer to at least two Acts and one Statutory Instrument to appreciate his rights and bargaining strength. These are the Sale of Goods Act 1979, the Unfair Contract Terms Act 1977 and the Consumer Transactions (Restrictions on Statements) Order 1976. One wonders whether the barriers, intentional or accidental, to the "litigant in person" will ever be totally raised.

Unsolicited Goods and Services Act 1971. The main way in which this Act affects the consumer is to make it a *criminal* offence, punishable by fine, for traders to demand payment for goods which they have sent to persons who did not order them. The teeth of the Act are in the *criminal* liability that it imposes. A person would not be legally bound to pay for the goods sent in any case because no contract exists: the essential ingredient of "agreement" is totally absent.

Furthermore, if unsolicited goods are sent to you, they become your property after six months, or thirty days if you write to the sender giving your name and address and stating that the goods were unsolicited, providing of course that you agree neither to keep them nor to send them back.

Weights and Measures Acts 1963 and 1979. The 1963 Act established a uniform system of weights and measures, provided for the control of weighing and measuring equipment used for trade purposes, provided protection against short weight and measure in commodities, and required for certain pre-packed items an indication of the quantity of the contents.

The 1979 Act introduced the "average contents" system and, where the Act applies, removes criminal liability from retailers who blamelessly sell short weight. The new system, another example of a response to an EEC directive, means that an offence arises only where a batch of packages falls below the stated weight on averaging their actual contents, or where more than a specified number of packages in a batch fall below a specified tolerance level. The Act imposes the duty of compliance with the system on packers and importers, not on retailers. However, where a retailer *knowingly* sells an "inadequate package", i.e. one where the shortfall is more than twice the permitted tolerance, he commits a criminal offence. In practice the consumer is very unlikely to suffer from the move to the average weight system.

Business practices, the consumers and the law

In a mixed economy such as ours, the best way to protect the interests of consumers is generally considered to be by the encouragement and maintenance of free and undistorted competition. However, you have seen in previous chapters that totally free competition is unattainable. Indeed, the growth of large business units in our economy and the creation of public corporations, particularly nationalised industries, distorts competition producing imperfect markets. Such distortion is always to the possible detriment of consumers and often and unfairly to the actual detriment of smaller business units.

Large business units and public corporations do in fact offer many important advantages to the economy, consumers and their employees. Indeed, competition is possibly harmful to public utilities, and in most countries postal and telephone services and the provision of gas and electricity and public transport enjoy government protection, and competitors are prevented from entering the market. However, successive governments have considered it to be necessary to use the law to curtail this latent economic might in the private sphere of the economy, with the paradoxical aim of preserving free competition in the market. Once again the common law has made only a very small contribution to the present legal framework and the relevant law is almost entirely statutory. The principal statutes are the Fair Trading Act 1973, the Restrictive Trade Practices Act 1976, the Resale Prices Act 1976 and the Competition Act 1980, all of which were mentioned in the previous section of this chapter. In addition, the competition rules of the EEC, based on Articles 85 and 86 of the Treaty of Rome 1957, embody the philosophy of competition more strictly than our own domestic law.

The main agency for implementing government policy on competition is the Office of Fair Trading. Under s.2 of the Fair Trading Act 1973 its Director General must keep under review commercial practices in the UK, and collect information about them so that he can discover monopoly situations and uncompetitive practices. Under the Restrictive Trade Practices Act 1976 he has a major role in the regulation of restrictive trading agreements.

Monopolies

At its simplest, a monopoly arises when one trading organisation supplies an entire market. This, however, is very rare (nationalised industries are an exception) and the Fair Trading Act 1973 defines a monopoly as being where one person, company or group of related companies supplies or acquires at least 25 per cent of the goods or services in question in the UK—a "scale monopoly situation". A "complex monopoly situation" exists if at least 25 per cent of the goods or services of a particular description are supplied in the UK as a whole by two or more persons, unconnected companies or groups of companies who intentionally or otherwise conduct their affairs in such a way that they prevent, distort or restrict competition in the supply of the goods or services, e.g. refusing to supply goods or services to particular customers. However, where an agreement registrable under the Restrictive Trade Practices Act 1976 exists between suppliers, a complex monopoly does not exist and the agreement must be dealt with under the 1976 Act.

"Complex monopoly situations" are far more common than "scale monopoly situations" for there are many cases where particular industries are dominated by a small number of suppliers, each of whom holds a very large share of the market, e.g. the motor industry (four major suppliers), detergents (two major suppliers).

The Director General of Fair Trading may refer what he considers to be a monopoly to the Monopolies and Mergers Commission for investigation.

The main inherent dangers of a monopoly, whether a pure

monopoly or the more usual "scale" or "complex" monopolies are restriction of output, price fixing, regulation of terms of supply and removal of consumer choice. Additionally, free competition may be stifled by preventing competitors entering the market, and a monopolist may use his monopsonic (monopsony is a situation where one buyer dominates the market) buying powers to dictate terms to his suppliers. The government uses the law to forbid or regulate these practices.

Restrictive trade practices

The Restrictive Trade Practices Act 1976 is concerned with any agreement or arrangement between suppliers of goods or services, including recommendations made by trade associations, which restrict competition. Examples include agreements between suppliers to charge the same prices, to divide up the market and to trade on the same terms of business. Such practices are unlawful and the object of the present Act is to ensure that only such agreements, arrangements and recommendations as are in the public interest are allowed to continue. To achieve this, full details of "registrable agreements" must be sent to the Office of Fair Trading for entry in a public register maintained by the Director General. The Director General then has the power to refer the practice to the Restrictive Practices Court to consider whether or not it is against the public interest. The proceedings are part of the *civil* law. There are a number of grounds (often called "gateways") on which the practice can be upheld as being in the public interest, e.g. where it is necessary to protect the consumer, e.g. certain patent medicines are only supplied to qualified pharmacists, or where removal of the restriction would prevent fair competition between producers, e.g. small businesses could be allowed to combine to prevent being driven out of the market by the business giants.

Under the Act the Director General may instigate a *civil* action for an injunction to restrain the continuance or repetition of the unlawful restrictive practice. A consumer directly affected by it may bring a *civil* action for damages.

The first Restrictive Trade Practices Act was passed in 1956 and at the end of 1980 3,873 agreements concerning the supply of goods had been registered (sixty-three in 1980). A further 3,211 agreements had been terminated since 1956 (eighteen in 1980) and 658 referred to the Court. In 1980 five organisations were found guilty of breaking previous undertakings to the Court and fines for contempt of £185,000 were imposed on four suppliers of concrete pipes and a fine of £50,000 was imposed on the British Steel Corporation.

Agreements relating to services became registrable in March 1976 and by the end of 1980 495 agreements had been terminated (thirty-two in 1980) and five have been brought before the Court (three in 1980).

Unfair trading practices
The powers given to the Director General of Fair Trading under the Competition Act 1980 to investigate and control the anti-competitive practices of single firms supplements the existing powers for investigation of monopolies and restrictive agreements among firms. The government's declared intention in the Act is to promote competition and efficiency in industry and commerce.

The Act is already beginning to bite. More than one company has agreed to alter its trading practices in accordance with the DGFT's suggestions rather than face an investigation by the Commission, and British Gas and British Rail have been the subject of preliminary investigations.

Although the Price Commission has now been abolished by the Act, the Secretary of State has power under the Act to investigate prices which he considers to be "of major public concern having regard to whether the supply, or acquisition, of the goods or services in question is of general economic importance, or the price is of special significance to consumers". There are no direct sanctions that can be taken in such a situation but it could be treated as an anti-competitive practice.

EEC rules on competition
Article 85 of the Treaty of Rome 1957 prohibits all agreements between business organisations, decisions by trade associations and concerted practices which may affect trade between *member states* and which have as their object or effect the prevention, restriction or distortion of competition within the Common Market. Article 85 would include fixing buying and/or selling prices or other terms of business, discriminating in favour of certain business organisations giving them a competitive advantage and sharing markets. If, for example, a manufacturer appointed a sole distributor of his products in each EEC country, and each distributor agreed not to export to other EEC countries, the "common market" would be divided into ten separate markets and competition among member states would be effectively distorted. Article 86 declares that the abuse of a dominant position in the market structure is incompatible with the EEC, e.g. imposing buying or selling prices or other trading conditions which are unfair, limit production, markets or technological development to the prejudice of consumers.

Practices infringing Articles 85 and 86 must be notified to the Commission of the EEC by the Director General of Fair Trading but if certain conditions are fulfilled the Commission may grant exemption.

The question of possible infringement of the Articles can be decided by domestic courts as well as by the Commission and the European Court of Justice.

Resale price maintenance

The enforcement of minimum selling prices by manufacturers or distributors of goods, either individually or collectively, is illegal under the Resale Prices Act 1976 unless held to be in the public interest by the Restrictive Practices Court. At present only minimum prices for books and proprietary medicines have the Court's sanction. Any person adversely affected, or the Director General of Fair Trading, may take *civil* proceedings against those who seek to reimpose minimum resale prices.

Resale price maintenance poses an economic dilemma to governments. On the one hand consumers benefit, and efficient organisations are rewarded, by allowing free pricing of commodities. On the other, consumers can suffer because many small businesses will be unable to compete with large multiple retailers in price cutting and may be forced to close down or face bankruptcy, thereby reducing retail service to the public. A good example at the present time is the decline of independent chemists since supermarkets have been allowed to sell patent medicines. Indeed, indiscriminate promotion of competition may have the effect of operating to the detriment of the very consumers it seeks to protect.

In practice, however, this effect is to some extent mitigated by "consumer loyalty" to local traders, for they can provide a level of personal service and convenience in return for slightly higher prices which large retailers cannot.

It is perhaps worth noting that it is often the less fortunate, those who are unable to travel to shopping centres or buy in bulk for example, who patronise the local "corner shop" which in turn may even begin to provide a kind of community service. This "class distinction" in consumerism will surely become even more marked with the continued development of out-of-town hypermarkets.

Mergers

The Fair Trading Act 1973 covers mergers involving the acquisition of gross assets of more than £15m., or where a "monopoly", i.e. 25 per cent or more of the relevant market in the UK or a substantial part of it, would be created or enhanced. Also included are situations where one company acquires the ability to control or materially influence another company without actually acquiring a controlling interest.

The Director General of Fair Trading is responsible for keeping a watchful eye on possible mergers within the Act, but his role is only to advise the Secretary of State as to whether a reference should be made to the Monopolies and Mergers Commission; he may not make a reference directly. This contrasts with his powers relating to monopolies. The Secretary of State has power under the 1973 Act to order that the merger shall not proceed or to regulate any identified adverse effects of a merger or proposed merger, e.g. the effect on labour relations.

In 1980, 182 mergers were within the Act, but only five actual references to the Commission were made. Each reference is considered on its own merits and on the criterion of the "public interest", the latter encompassing the maintenance and promotion of competition, consumer interests, effects on employment and, in some cases, the possibility of "asset stripping" or tax avoidance.

The Treaty of Rome makes no reference to mergers as such but the Commission of the EEC has sought to encourage mergers which lead to improved competition throughout the Community.

Advertising
Advertising is a multi-million pound industry. It is a perfectly acceptable way of bringing particular goods and services to the notice of consumers but it could be used as a device for persuading consumers to buy things they neither want, need nor can afford, by methods which are socially unacceptable. The power and effectiveness of advertising is recognised by the state and the practice is controlled by many criminal statutes, numerous voluntary codes of practice produced by trade associations, and an EEC Directive requiring all members states to ban unfair and misleading advertisements (*see* page 394).

Day-to-day control over all advertising, except that on radio and television, is exercised by the Advertising Standards Authority. The Authority draws up and enforces its own codes, ensuring that advertisements are: legal, decent, honest and truthful; consistent with principles of free competition; prepared with a sense of responsibility to consumers; and do not bring the advertising industry into disrepute. Radio and television advertising is controlled by a code drawn up by the Independent Broadcasting Authority.

The Trade Descriptions Act 1968 makes it a *criminal* offence for a trader to describe inaccurately the goods he is selling or the services he is offering, and any person induced to enter into a contract by a false advertising claim can rescind the contract and claim damages in a *civil* action under the Misrepresentation Act 1967. In addition the Director General of Fair Trading has a general responsibility under the Fair Trading Act 1973 to ensure that all trading practices, which includes advertising, do not adversely affect consumer interests, and local authorities are empowered under the town and country planning legislation to control the extent of outdoor advertising.

Administrative agencies of consumer protection
The Office of Fair Trading
You will have already gained a general idea about the working of the Office from the previous section of this chapter but, as its work is crucial to consumer protection, a more specific summary is necessary.

The Office was established in November 1973 following the passing of the Fair Trading Act earlier in that year. It describes its job as keeping watch on trading matters in the UK and protecting the consumer against unfair practices. It does not handle individual complaints from consumers (except about monopolies and restrictive and unfair trade practices) but acts as a central bureau for collecting and disseminating information, taking general action when necessary.

At its head is the Director General of Fair Trading who is responsible for the administration and enforcement of the laws designed to foster competition, protect consumers and regulate the credit industry. He can act independently of the government for he is neither a civil servant nor a politician. Ultimately, however, he has political masters. The Secretary of State for Trade has ministerial responsibility for the working of the Office of Fair Trading, Parliament makes the laws which he administers and enforces, and the Office is both a government agency and a quasi-governmental body financed wholly from public funds with clearly defined statutory powers and duties.

There are six main ways in which the Director General is active in protecting consumers.

(*a*) He collects information on business activities which are harmful or potentially harmful to consumers, which restrict or inhibit competition and which are against the public interest in general. He can refer such activities to the Consumer Protection Advisory Committee, Monopolies and Mergers Commission or Restrictive Practices Court as the case may be.

(*b*) He publishes information explaining to consumers their rights.

(*c*) He encourages trade associations to prepare and publish codes of practice which include explanations of how consumers can make complaints. These codes invariably raise standards of service.

(*d*) He takes action against organisations which commit "consumer offences" or infringe the competition laws. Usually the organisation involved is asked to give a written undertaking that it will cease the offence or restrictive practice, but a civil action for an injunction restraining a restrictive practice, or prosecution of organisations which persistently commit consumer offences, may be necessary.

(*e*) He licenses businesses which give credit or hire goods, as well as credit brokers, debt collectors and credit reference agencies. He is also responsible for the general regulation of the credit industry.

(*f*) He proposes new laws to put an end to unfair business activities by plugging loopholes in the existing law. The Consumer Protection Advisory Committee (a body appointed by the Secretary of State and operating independently of the Office) plays an important role in such proposals. It reports to the Secretary of State on the Director General's proposals after having had a particular matter referred to it by the Director General.

The Monopolies and Mergers Commission

The Commission is an independent body originally established by the Monopolies and Restrictive Practices (Inquiry and Control) Act 1948 but now under the umbrella of the Fair Trading Act 1973. Its membership includes industrialists, trade unionists and academics, and it is supported by a staff of civil servants including economists and accountants.

As its name suggests its function is to investigate monopolies or possible monopolies referred to it by the Director General of Fair Trading, and mergers referred to it by the Secretary of State for Trade on the advice of the Director General. Its role is then to assess whether such monopolies and mergers do or would operate against the public interest. The Secretary of State may make Statutory Orders to remedy the adverse effects identified by the Commission, although more usually the Director General is asked to obtain written undertakings from the business organisations involved to remedy such effects themselves.

Local authorities

Trading standards or consumer protection departments. These departments work very closely with the Office of Fair Trading in watching for unfair trade practices, and it is they that have the task of ensuring locally that consumer laws are obeyed and complaints from individual consumers investigated.

Environmental health departments. These departments deal with consumer complaints about health matters such as unfit food and drink, and dirty shops or restaurants.

The National Consumer Council

This independent Council was set up by the government in 1975. It does not deal directly with consumer complaints but seeks to further consumer interests by its representation on public and other bodies.

Consumer and Consultative Councils of nationalised industries

Nationalised industries are public corporations which often have a complete monopoly of their own particular economic activity. The apparent contradiction of their existence amidst extensive law promoting free competition can be explained by the enormous capital investment that they require and the crucial role that they play in the economy (*see* Chapter 6).

The control of nationalised industries has already been discussed, but the monopolies they have in basic social and economic resources nevertheless put the consumer in a uniquely weak position. For this reason it is generally accepted that it is appropriate to represent consumers in an advisory capacity in the policy-making of the nationalised industries with the aims of helping to prevent the misuse (perhaps quite unintentional) of monopoly power and of bridging the technological gap between the industry and its customers.

The creation of Consumer and Consultative Councils is the government's chosen method of protecting consumer interests in the activities of nationalised industries. They deal with all matters of consumer interest (including complaints), and the industries are bound to consult them before taking major decisions. The Consumer and Consultative Councils for coal, gas, electricity and transport industries and the Post Office are the responsibility of the Department of Trade, whose Secretary of State appoints their chairmen and members.

The work of the Councils does not meet with universal acclaim, and in particular their effectiveness is frequently doubted. Four main criticisms are made:

(*a*) that their close links with the industries affect their role as consumer champions;

(*b*) that the public is unaware of their existence and hence does not use their services;

(*c*) that they have inadequate resources to face the corporate might of the industry; and

(*d*) that the Secretary of State's power of appointing members prevents them being true "grassroots" representative bodies.

The European Consumer
The promotion of competition between member states is fundamental to the philosophy of the EEC, and the increasing remoteness of producers from consumers, partly fostered by this philosophy, means that there is a need for Community action on consumer protection.

In 1975 the Community adopted a programme for consumer information and protection embodying five basic consumer rights: the protection of health and safety; the right to protection of the consumers' economic interests; the right to redress; the right of information and education and the right to consumer protection. By the use of Directives to member states, the Commission of the EEC can implement the programme throughout the Community. Examples to date include bans on certain ingredients in foods and cosmetics, listing of dangerous substances which can only be marketed subject to specific conditions, and the introduction of "sell by" dates on food.

The Consumers' Consultative Committee, established in 1973, is the most important consumer protection body within the Community. It ensures that the Commission is aware of consumers' interests when taking policy decisions. The Committee consists of twenty-five members, ten of whom must be "persons particularly qualified in consumer affairs" and the remainder representatives of consumer associations.

CONCLUSION

This chapter has two distinct parts: the first outlines the essentials of a contract, and the second discusses the wider rules of trading practice within which business contracts are made. The chapter taken as a whole endeavours to show how the law is used to realise business objectives while at the same time protecting consumer interests by banning or regulating unacceptable business practices and reducing the inequality in bargaining power between producers or suppliers and their customers. Only the administrative safeguards provided by the main official administrative agencies of consumer protection have been covered. No attempt has been made to analyse the many voluntary codes of practice produced by trade associations, or the official and unofficial sources of consumer advice available, e.g. the Citizens Advice Bureau. Had this been done, you, as consumers (of this book) would probably have felt in need of protection from our product!

SELF-ASSESSMENT QUESTIONS

A. 1. Define the following: (*a*) "consideration"; (*b*) a "consumer"; (*c*) "scale" and "complex" monopolies; (*d*) a restrictive trade practice.

2. List the statutes protecting consumer interest which (*a*) impose criminal sanctions on traders and (*b*) give civil remedies to consumers.

B. 3. True or false?

(*a*) Acceptance of an offer must always be communicated to the offeror.

(*b*) All agreements are presumed to be legally binding.

(*c*) All contracts must be in writing.

(*d*) The Director General of Fair Trading can refer mergers direct to the Monopolies and Mergers Commission.

(*e*) A seller can never exclude his liability for breach of conditions implied into contracts for the sale of goods by the Sale of Goods Act 1979.

C. 4. In the light of legislation, evaluate the extent to which the consumer's position *vis-à-vis* business organisations has improved in the last ten years.

ASSIGNMENT

1. Prepare arguments for and against greater control being exercised over business practices by the government.

CHAPTER EIGHTEEN

The International Market Place

```
                    CHAPTER OBJECTIVES
        After studying this chapter you should be able to:
        *  explain the theory of comparative advantage;
        *  state the advantages of international trade;
        *  evaluate the arguments against free trade;
        *  list the main components of Britain's overseas trade;
        *  describe the distribution of Britain's trade;
        *  identify the most common types of export contracts;
        *  explain methods of payment in export sales;
        *  explain how the balance of payments balances;
        *  state the problems posed by multinational companies.
```

Many business organisations today operate in international markets. The bias of economic nationalism, however, often obscures the benefits of specialisation which appear self-evident within the economy. We therefore spend some considerable time explaining the theory of comparative advantage and how international trade leads to what J. S. Mill described as "a more efficient employment of the productive forces of the world". Later in the chapter we examine the components of Britain's trade and the balance of payments.

THE THEORY OF COMPARATIVE ADVANTAGE

Why trade?

Men and nations have traded since the time of the Phoenicians but for most of this time they provided for most of their needs out of the local economy. Trade was for such things as spices, wines and precious metals. By the nineteenth century Britain had embarked upon the course which would see her export her products all over the world in return for her basic food and raw materials. It was at this time that David Ricardo explained his *theory of comparative advantage*. This made it clear that, as individuals benefited through specialisation, so did nations.

We can first note that there are different conditions in different countries so that one country can produce a product more cheaply than another. For example, Britain can produce cars more cheaply than West Africa but West Africa can produce cocoa more cheaply than Britain. In these circumstances Britain is said to have an *absolute advantage* in cars and West Africa an absolute advantage in cocoa. If the West Africans want cars and Britain wants cocoa it is obviously to their mutual advantage to trade. But comparative advantage does not end there, for as Professor Samuelson says "it is not so immediately obvious, but it is no less true that international trade is mutually profitable even when one of the two can produce *every commodity* more cheaply".

Consider the example of a town which has only one doctor but the doctor is also the best typist in town. Should he be a doctor or a typist? Obviously his comparative advantage is greatest in the medical field and he should concentrate on that. If he employs a typist he will be better off because he can concentrate on supplying a rarer skill, the town will be better off and so will the typist he employs.

Comparative advantage: an example
To explain his theory Ricardo took an example using two countries, Britain and Portugal, and two commodities, wine and cloth. We

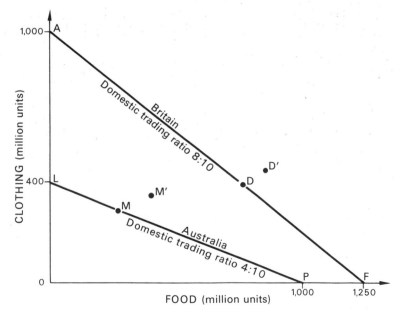

Fig. 79. *Production possibility curves before specialisation and trade, Britain and Australia.*

will follow his example using Britain and Australia as the countries and food and clothing as the commodities.

Figure 79 illustrates the situation in the two countries before there has been any specialisation or trade. This might have been the case in the early nineteenth century when distance and poor transport prevented effective trade. Britain can produce 1,000 million units of clothing or 1,250 million units of food or any combination of the two shown by the line AF. This *production possibility curve* shows the *domestic trading ratio*. It represents the *opportunity cost* of one commodity in terms of the other. Thus, if Britain gives up producing 10 units of food and transfers the factors of production to clothing manufacture, she is able to produce 8 more units of clothing; therefore the domestic trading ratio is 8 to 10. With its present supply of factors of production Britain can produce any combination of food and clothing on the line AF or within it. However, any point to the right, for example D′, is beyond its present capacity. Since there is no trade, Britain must produce both food and clothing and chooses point D on the curve. Here it is producing 400 million units of clothing and 750 million units of food. Australia appears to be worse off in both commodities, being able to produce only 400 million units of clothing or 1,000 million units of food. Therefore, it has a domestic trading ratio of 4 units of clothing to 10 of food. It chooses position M where it is producing 300 million units of clothing and 250 million units of food.

Remember in both cases that any move to the right of the existing production possibility curve is an improvement since it would mean that each country could consume both more food and more clothing. Let us imagine what happens as steamships, railways and refrigeration open up trade between the two countries. To the British food now appears cheap in Australia because, in Britain, they would have to give up 8 units of clothing to gain 10 of food whilst in Australia they only have to pay 4 units of clothing. Hence the British begin to buy food in Australia. Conversely, clothing appears cheap in Britain to the Australians since previously 10 units of food gained them only 4 units of clothing, whilst in Britain 10 units of food will buy 8 of clothing. Hence, the Australians begin to buy clothing in Britain.

Eventually we will have an *international trading ratio* for food and clothing which will be determined by the forces of demand and supply in the international markets. So long as the British pay less than 8 units of clothing for 10 of food they will be happy, and so long as the Australians obtain more than 4 units of clothing for 10 of food they will be happy. Hence the *international trading ratio* will be somewhere between the two. Let us assume that it settles at

6:10, so that instead of buying 8 units of clothing for 10 of food the British now only have to pay 6 whereas the Australians gain 6 units of clothing for 10 of food instead of 4 as they previously did. In order to benefit from trade let us assume that Australia devoted all its resources to food production, producing 1,000 million units, and trades for clothing, whilst Britain devotes 80 per cent of her resources to clothing production giving her an output of 800 million units of clothing and 250 million units of food.

The situation is summarised in Table XXX. Here we have assumed that Australia exports 600 million units of food which, at a trading ratio of 6:10, will buy her 360 million units of clothing. It can be seen that as a result of specialisation and trade both countries have benefited. Britain's consumption of food has risen from 750 million units to 850 million units (250 + 600) and her consumption of clothing has risen from 400 to 440 million units. In Australia the consumption of food has risen from 250 to 400 million units and consumption of clothing from 300 to 360 million units.

Figure 80 shows that the result of international trade might be likened to moving to a new production possibility curve to the right of the old one. Thus it would appear that by utilising comparative advantage where no absolute advantage existed, both the output of Australia and Britain, and therefore of the world, has been increased.

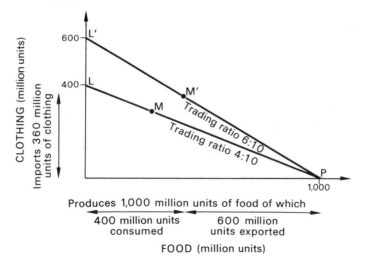

Fig. 80. *New possibilities: Australia. International trade enables Australia to move to a new production possibility curve to the right of the old one. At point M' Australia enjoys both more food and more clothing. A similar curve could be constructed for Britain.*

TABLE XXX. BRITAIN AND AUSTRALIA BEFORE AND AFTER TRADE

Country	Trading ratio clothing/food	Clothing output	Clothing consumption	Clothing exports (+) or imports (−)	Food output	Food consumption	Food exports (+) or imports (−)
Situation before specialisation and trade							
Britain	8:10	400	400	0	750	750	0
Australia	4:10	300	300	0	250	250	0
Situation after specialisation and trade							
Britain	6:10	800	440	+360	250	850	−600
Australia	6:10	0	360	−360	1000	400	+600
World gain from specialisation and trade							
Total	—	100	100	—	250	250	—

Does trade benefit everyone?

In the long run, yes; the living standards of a country will rise as the wages of those in industries with comparative advantage increase and more goods and services become available. However, we must also consider the fortunes of those in the industries without comparative advantage. In our example agriculture in Britain contracted as food was bought more cheaply in Australia. This was to the advantage of the average British consumer, but the contraction of agriculture involved farmers going bankrupt and agricultural labourers losing their jobs. This was indeed what happened in Britain in the late nineteenth century as Britain imported cheap food from Australia, America and Europe. Agriculture in Britain experienced the "Great Depression". In the long run, however, it was also to the advantage of those in agriculture since it was better to enjoy high wages in a factory than low wages on the farm.

Comparative advantage and exchange rates

Most international trade is not the swapping of one lot of goods for another but buying and selling through the medium of money and the exchange rate. To illustrate this let us assume that it costs the Australians $2 to produce a unit of food and $5 to produce a unit of clothing whilst in Britain it costs £1 to produce a unit of food and £1.25 to produce a unit of clothing. (This maintains the domestic trading ratios of 10:4 and 10:8.)

If the exchange rate is such that Australian goods are cheaper than domestically produced goods the British will buy them and vice versa. If the exchange rate were $1 = £1 no trade would take place since while the Australians would be willing to trade, the British would not, as the cost of imported goods is too high. Conversely, if the exchange rate were $5 = £1 then Britain would be willing to buy Australian goods but the Australians would not be willing to buy British.

When the exchange rate is $3 = £1 the British will buy Australian food and the Australians will buy British clothing. Trade is therefore possible. In our example trade is possible so long as the exchange rate lies between the limits £1 = $2 and £1 = $4 (*see* Fig. 81).

It is a mistake to think, however, that a country can improve its basic trading position by manipulating the exchange rate. An exchange rate set too high (overvalued) will bring about a balance of payments deficit, whilst if the rate is fixed too low (undervalued) consumers at home suffer although exporters may benefit. In addition, there will also be speculative pressure to revalue the currency (*see* Chapter 20).

Domestic price of food and clothing (assuming the same domestic trading ratios as in Fig. 79)	Import prices at various exchange rates		
	Exchange rate 1 $1 = £1	Exchange rate 2 $3 = £1	Exchange rate 3 $5 = £1
Price of food in Australia = $2	$1.00	$3.00	$5.00
Price of clothing in Australia = $5	$1.25	$3.75	$6.25
Price of food in Britain = £1	£2.00	£0.67	£0.40
Price of clothing in Britain = £1.25	£5.00	£1.67	£1.00

Import price higher than domestic price

Import price lower than domestic price but exports too expensive: no trade

Import price is lower than domestic price: trade will take place

Fig. 81. *Comparative advantage and exchange rates.*

International trade reflects the basic opportunity cost structure of different countries. This cannot be altered by changing the exchange rate.

BENEFITS OF INTERNATIONAL TRADE

Our example so far has examined two countries and two commodities. How does the theory work when it is placed in the real world?

Many commodities

The theory of comparative advantage will work no matter how many commodities are considered. In a way we have already considered many commodities in our example because food and clothing are generic terms which cover many products.

Many countries

The theory of comparative advantage will work better as more countries are brought into the example, for not only does international trade require a comparative advantage but it also depends upon countries requiring the goods which the other country produces. In Fig. 82 you can see that trade is possible between three countries but not between two. Britain wants Canada's exports but Canada does not want Britain's exports and so on. Multilateral trade allows for the international offsetting of debts from one country to another and so makes trade possible. In effect Britain pays for Canadian wheat with machinery exports to the West Indies. The greater the number of countries considered the greater are the opportunities for trade.

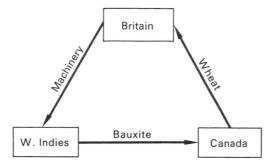

Fig. 82. *Multilateral trade.*

It is for this reason that economists usually favour multilateral trade agreements but oppose bilateral ones.

Higher incomes

Differences occur between wages and the incomes of other factors of production in different countries because their relative supply position is different. In our example land would be cheap in Australia because it is plentiful, whereas in England rents would be high because it is scarce. On the other hand wages would be low in Britain because labour is plentiful. If, however, Britain produces a product (clothing) which exploits that cheap labour and sells it to Australia, where it commands a higher price, this will increase the wage of workers in Britain. It is as though we had exported the labour to Australia.

International trade tends to lead to an equalisation of factor incomes in different countries. The rewards of low paid factors increase as those of high paid factors decrease. The equalisation of prices is, however, never complete, just as specialisation is never complete. You will note in our example that Britain did not specialise entirely but maintained a small agricultural industry.

Economies of scale: decreasing costs

As a country specialises in the production of a particular commodity it could benefit from economies of scale. In our example so far we have assumed a *constant cost case*. That is to say, every time Britain switched resources from food to clothing production it gained 8 units of food for 10 of clothing. It could be, however, that as Britain specialised in clothing production economies of scale reduced the cost of a unit of clothing.

This is illustrated in Fig. 83. Here the production possibility line is convex to the origin, illustrating decreasing costs, so that instead of producing B units of clothing it is possible to produce B′ with the same quantity of resources.

If an industry does experience decreasing costs, this will obviously increase the benefits of international trade. This was said to be one of the main reasons for Britain's joining the EEC. If industries in both countries could benefit from decreasing costs this would be a reason for specialising and trading even when no comparative advantage exists.

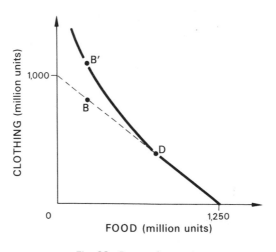

Fig. 83. *Decreasing costs.*

OBSTACLES TO INTERNATIONAL TRADE

Tariffs

If a country imposes customs duties on imports this has the effect of offsetting the comparative advantage and diminishing the benefits of international trade. Customs duties often have the effect of protecting inefficient home producers. This means that although the people employed in that industry may benefit, consumers generally are condemned to paying higher prices for goods.

Transport costs

Although a country may have a comparative advantage, this will be of little use if it is offset by high transport costs. It is for this reason that British farmers are able to continue producing milk for it is far too expensive to transport from those countries where it is produced more cheaply.

Resistance to change

In order for a country to benefit from comparative advantage it is necessary for it to contract those industries in which it is at a disadvantage and expand those in which it has advantage. This will involve wages, prices and employment falling in the declining industry. Naturally, there will be great resistance to this from those involved. This may prevent an economy from benefiting from comparative advantage.

It is not only labour which is immobile but also other factors. For example, it is very difficult to switch capital goods from one use to another. In addition to this the expanding industry may be in a different part of the country to the declining one. The briefest look at the British economy will show the great problem created by the decline of the old staple industries. This is compounded by the power of trade unions to resist change.

Increasing costs

Earlier in the chapter we considered the possibility that specialising in an industry might lead to decreasing costs. There is, on the other hand, the possibility that it would lead to *increasing costs*. This could come about as the expansion of an industry drove up the price of labour and other factors. It could also occur as an industry expanded into less and less appropriate factors (*see* page 66). This is illustrated in Fig. 84. Here, as output of clothing has been increased, increasing costs have decreased output to the level of B^2 instead of arriving at the expected point B^1. Since any industry will suffer from increasing costs if it is expanded sufficiently, this is another reason why international specialisation is seldom complete.

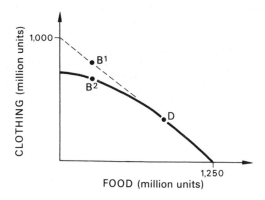

Fig. 84. *Increasing costs.*

Despite these qualifications to the law of comparative advantage, it is nevertheless apparent that the world benefits from international trade on a massive scale.

SHOULD WE HAVE CUSTOMS DUTIES?

Customs duties can be imposed either to raise revenue or to keep out foreign competition. In the latter case they can be described as *protective tariffs*. It is not possible for a customs duty to do both jobs simultaneously since if it keeps out imports there will be nothing to tax. If it were the government's intention to keep out competition it could also use *quotas*, i.e. a quantitative limit on the amount of imports, such as Britain has tried in recent years with Japanese cars.

Free trade has been advocated by economists since the time of Adam Smith, in addition to which the imposition of new duties is contrary to such agreements as GATT (*see* page 453). In the late 1970s, however, a vociferous lobby supported by many trade unions, began to advocate protection as a method of furthering Britain's economic development and protecting employment. Some of the arguments in favour of protection are listed below.

(*a*) *Cheap labour.* It is often argued that the economy must be protected from imports because they are produced with cheap "sweated" labour. This argument is basically unsound as it is contrary to the whole principle of comparative advantage. It would not only ensure that wages are kept low in the foreign country but it would protect inefficient practices at home, thus, in the long run, depressing our living standard.

(*b*) *Dumping*. This is when goods are sold or "dumped" on a foreign market at below their cost of production. This may be undertaken either by a foreign monopolist, using high profits at home to subsidise exports, or by foreign governments subsidising exports for political or strategic reasons. (For a full explanation of this *see* page 346.) It is quite legitimate for a country to protect the home market from this kind of unfair competition.

(*c*) *Infant industries*. It could be legitimate to protect a new industry from established foreign competition until it can compete on equal terms. However, such industries tend to become dependent on continued protection.

(*d*) *Unemployment*. Cheap imports may aggravate domestic unemployment and import duties could be a way of alleviating this in the short run. However, in the long run they cannot be justified as they will protect inefficiency and depress the living standards of the country.

(*e*) *Balance of payments*. It is often argued that import duties are one way of rectifying an adverse balance of payments. This is again only a short-term solution, especially as it may invite retaliation by other countries.

(*f*) *Self-sufficiency*. Two World Wars taught Britain the danger of being reliant on imports. For political or strategic reasons a country may not wish to be wholly dependent upon imports and so may protect a home industry even if it is inefficient. The EEC is committed to self-sufficiency in agriculture. Many countries maintain munition industries for strategic reasons.

(*g*) *Bargaining*. Even when a country can see no economic benefit from tariffs it may find it useful to have them as a bargaining gambit with other nations who have them.

THE TERMS OF TRADE

The "terms of trade" is a measure of the relative prices of exports and imports. It is calculated by taking an index of export prices and dividing it by an index of import prices. A change can occur in the terms of trade either as a result of a change in the relative costs of production or in the exchange rate.

For example, if we took 1975 (*see* Table XXXI) as a base year and discovered that in 1980 export prices were 190 whilst import prices were 169, then the index of the terms of trade would be:

$$\text{Terms of trade index} = \frac{\text{Index of export prices}}{\text{Index of import prices}} \times \frac{100}{1}$$

$$= \frac{190}{169} \times \frac{100}{1}$$

$$= 112$$

TABLE XXXI. EXPORT AND IMPORT UNIT VALUE INDEX NUMBERS (UK)

	1970	1971	1972	1973	1974	1975	1976	1977	1978	1979	1980
Exports (fob)	54	56	59	66	83	100	119	138	148	167	190
Imports (cif)	47	48	50	62	88	100	122	139	143	155	169
Terms of trade	115	117	118	106	94	100	98	99	103	108	112

Source: United Kingdom Balance of Payments, HMSO

This illustrates a favourable movement in the terms of trade, for we would now have to export only 88 per cent as much as in 1975 to sustain the same level of imports. This favourable movement in the terms of trade is somewhat deceptive because 1975, the base year of the index, was a particularly bad year for British export prices. In the late 1970s export prices were pushed up both by inflation and by an increase in the external value of the pound. In the early 1980s the terms of trade were beginning to swing against Britain again.

(For an explanation of an index number *see* McNamara, page 84.)

THE PATTERN OF BRITAIN'S OVERSEAS TRADE

The importance of trade

Of all the nations in the world few are as dependent as the UK upon foreign trade. The UK depends upon imports for half of its food requirements and for most of the raw materials needed by its industries. Equally, the continued well-being of the economy depends upon exporting a large proportion of the national product each year. In 1980 imports were equivalent to 23.9 per cent of the GDP whilst exports were 24.5 per cent. The growth of exports and imports is closely linked to the growth of GDP. It would appear that as we grow wealthier we become more international.

International trade is also a vital component of national income (*see* page 500). An adverse movement in trade has a depressing effect upon the level of income and employment in the economy. Britain suffers from the recurrent problem that as soon as the economy begins to expand it draws in increased imports of raw materials which are necessary to our manufacturing industries. This however causes a payments crisis which brings the expansion to a halt. In recent years a disturbing trend has been the tendency for the expanding economy to draw in manufactured goods which the domestic economy is failing to produce.

What is traded?

Table XXXII summarises the main categories of products which are traded. You will see that food, raw materials and semi-manufactured goods accounted for 61 per cent of imports but only 55.3 per cent of exports. The position is reversed for manufactured goods, which accounted for 46.7 per cent of exports but only 39 per cent of imports. Britain usually has a trade deficit but 1980 saw a trade surplus of £1,178m. This was due to the impact of North Sea oil and the depressed state of the economy, which restrained imports. The impact of North Sea oil also increased the percentage of raw materials in Britain's exports whilst decreasing their share in imports. As well as the earnings from export sales, Britain is usually in receipt of considerable "invisible earnings" from the sale of such things as insurance services.

TABLE XXXII. VALUE OF UK IMPORTS AND EXPORTS 1980

Commodity	Value of exports £ million	%	Value of imports £ million	%
Food and tobacco	3,241	6.8	5,619	12.2
Raw materials	1,467	3.1	3,413	7.4
Fuels	6,418	13.5	6,589	14.3
Semi-manufactured goods	14,152	29.9	12,523	27.1
Finished goods	20,727	43.8	16,862	36.4
Miscellaneous	1,384	2.9	1,205	2.6
	47,389	100.0	46.211	100.0

Source: United Kingdom Balance of Payments, HMSO

Exports
The competitiveness of Britain's exports has been badly affected by rates of inflation much higher than those of her trading partners. To some extent this was offset in the mid-1970s by the fall in the value of sterling. The recovery in sterling in the late 1970s had an adverse effect upon exports. This supposes that price is a major factor in determining the volume of export sales. It is possible to suggest, however, that other factors, such as poor marketing, inferior design, bad after-sales service, low quality and, perhaps most important of all, long delays and unreliable delivery, are at least as important as price disadvantage in impeding sales of British exports.

Imports
There was a huge growth in the value of imports in the early 1970s because of the rise in oil and other commodity prices. Britain was protected from the worst rigours of the 1978 oil-price rise because of her own earnings from North Sea oil. Depression of the home market also helped to restrict imports but, despite this, foreign manufacturers continued to capture an increasing share of the market for such products as automobiles and electronics.

TABLE XXXIII. BRITAIN'S TEN LEADING TRADING PARTNERS (BY VALUE) 1980 AND 1971

Country (in order of importance in Britain's trade)	International trade 1980				Trade 1971		
Position	Imports CIF £ million	%	Exports FOB £ million	%	Imports %	Exports %	Position
1. West Germany*	5,701	11.0	5,113	10.3	6.6	5.8	2
2. USA	6,044	11.7	4,668	9.4	11.1	11.9	1
3. France*	3,899	7.5	3,652	7.4	4.5	4.3	6
4. Netherlands*	3,407	6.6	3,845	7.8	5.2	4.5	5
5. Switzerland	2,615	5.1	3,076	6.2	2.3	2.5	13
6. Belgium/Luxembourg*	2,597	5.0	2,624	5.3	2.3	3.7	10
7. Ireland*	1,784	3.5	2,660	5.4	5.2	5.5	3
8. Italy*	2,311	4.5	1,899	3.8	2.9	2.7	12
9. Sweden	1,475	2.9	1,624	3.3	4.1	4.2	7
10. Saudi Arabia	1,927	3.7	1,050	2.1	1.8	0.4	32†
Total of these ten	£31,760	61.5	£30,211	61.0	46.0	45.5	
Total of all trade	£51,650	100.0	£49,511	100.0	£9,834	£9,176	

* Members of EEC.
† Saudi Arabia was twentieth in imports and forty-sixth in exports in 1971.

Source: Compiled from Economic Trends, CSO

Trading partners

In Table XXXIII you can see that over a half of Britain's overseas trade is with ten countries. Despite this one should not form the impression that Britain's pattern of trade is narrow, for the UK continues to have a more world-wide pattern of trade than any other nation except the USA. Traditionally Britain drew her imports of raw materials from the Commonwealth and Empire to whom in return she exported her manufactures. Since 1945 there has been a growing dependence on North America and Europe. This trend was quite apparent before Britain joined the EEC and, indeed, was one of the reasons why it was essential for Britain to join. Since joining the EEC Britain has become much more dependent upon European-produced food and less dependent upon Canadian and Australasian (for example Canada dropped from second trading partner in 1967 to fourteenth in 1980). There has also been a marked decrease in the percentage importance of trade with the USA.

The oil price rises of 1973 and 1978 increased the importance of the OPEC nations in Britain's trade, not only as a source of imports but also as a valuable market. This is well illustrated in Fig. 85 by the rise of Saudi Arabia as a trading partner. Considered together, Britain now usually has a positive balance of trade with the OPEC nations.

Figure 85 illustrates the proportions of British exports and imports going to different parts of the world. The majority of the growth in value of trade between 1970 and 1980 is accounted for by price rises. Whereas the *value* of exports had risen by 481 per cent in this time, the *volume* had only risen by only 41 per cent; similarly whilst the value of imports had risen by 465 per cent the volume of imports had risen by 61 per cent.

In Fig. 85 one can also see the growing importance of the EEC to Britain's trade. It is also noticeable that although the oil crisis caused the value of imports from OPEC countries to rise sharply it also brought about a growth in exports of much greater proportions. In 1970 OPEC countries accounted for 6 per cent of our exports; by 1980 they accounted for 10.2 per cent.

EXPORT SALES

It is possible to sell goods overseas by three main methods.

(*a*) By setting up a subsidiary business organisation overseas.

(*b*) By appointing agents overseas.

(*c*) By concluding an "exclusive sales" agreement with an

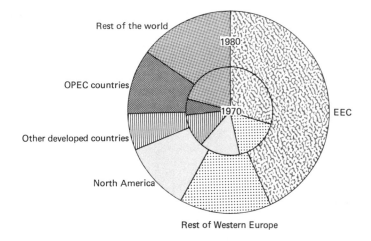

(a)

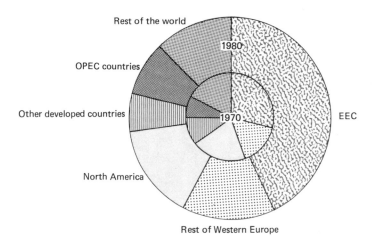

(b)

Fig. 85. *The destination and source of UK foreign trade.* (a) *Exporting. Total value of exports: 1970 = £8,150 m.; 1980 = £47,389 m.* (b) *Importing. Total value of imports: 1970 = £8,184 m.; 1980 = £46,211 m.*

importer based in each of the foreign countries to which the exporter hopes to sell. Such agreements must not infringe either domestic law or international agreements, e.g. Article 85 of the Treaty of Rome, relating to restrictive practices.

Types of contracts

A number of standardised contracts exist from which the exporter and importer may choose the one which best suits their requirements. The following are well-known and important terms in such contracts. They primarily indicate the price basis of the contract, although other important legal consequences follow, e.g. at what stage the *risk* of accidental loss of or damage to the goods passes from the seller to the buyer.

Ex works

Under this type of contract the exporter's obligation is to have the goods available at the agreed time and place. It is the buyer's duty to collect them and the price is normally payable on delivery. The seller must assist the buyer in obtaining any documents which are required in the transaction and available in the seller's country, e.g. an export licence.

FOR (free on rail)

At his own expense the seller is responsible for the packing and delivery of the goods to the nearest railhead or goods depot. If the contract is expressed to be *FOT* (free on truck) his obligations extend to loading the goods on to the railway truck. The price becomes payable when the goods are delivered to the railway authority; at the same time the *risk* passes to the buyer.

FAS (free alongside ship)

The seller's obligation extends one stage further. He must transport the goods at his own expense alongside a ship nominated by the buyer.

FOB (free on board)

Under an FOB contract the seller must pack, transport and place the goods on a ship nominated by the buyer. The buyer is responsible for the cost of the freight and insurance.

As soon as the goods pass over the ship's rail the *risk* passes to the buyer, although the Sale of Goods Act 1979 requires the seller to give the buyer sufficient notification of this to allow him time to insure them.

Ex ship

Here the seller must transport the goods at his own expense to a port named by the buyer. During transit the goods are the seller's responsibility and he must bear the *risk* of them being accidentally lost or damaged.

CIF (cost, insurance, freight)

The essential feature of CIF contracts is that they are performed by the delivery of the shipping documents, i.e. the bill of lading, the invoice and a certificate or policy of insurance. The goods are at the buyer's *risk* as soon as they are shipped and he is bound to pay the price when the documents are tendered to him, even though the goods may already have been lost. If this should have happened, he will be able to claim under the insurance policy.

The seller's obligations may be summarised as shipment of the contract goods within the agreed time, making the contract for their carriage, insuring the goods, and tendering the shipping documents to the buyer.

When the seller is responsible for the cost of the carriage but not the insurance, the goods are said to be sold CF (cost and freight). As with FOB contracts he must notify the buyer of the shipping so that the buyer may effect insurance cover.

FOB and CIF contracts are the most important contracts in export sales and, as Tables XXXII and XXXIII show, for UK statistical purposes imports are calculated on their CIF values and exports on the FOB values, i.e. their respective values at UK ports. Thus, a small proportion of an adverse balance of trade is accounted for by the cost of transporting goods from abroad.

Export documents

Bills of lading

Bills of lading are really three documents in one: a receipt for goods upon shipment; a contract for the carriage of goods; and a document of title enabling an exporter to transfer ownership or possession of the goods. They usually include a brief description of the goods, state the terms on which they are carried, the name of the carrying vessel and the port of destination. They are signed by the master of the ship or by some other person authorised by the shipowner. As they prove ownership, bills of lading are very important documents and the carrier will deliver the goods to the buyer against a signed copy.

If a bank is financing the export sale, the bill of lading is normally handed to the bank together with a bill of exchange or letter of credit, the seller's invoice and the certificate or policy of insurance.

Invoices
The seller's *commercial invoice* describes the goods, states their price and names the buyer; it will generally also include quantities, weights, packing details, etc., and a statement of the nature of the contract, e.g. FOB or CIF. Several copies are prepared, some for the buyer's use and some for the information of various authorities in his country, e.g. customs and bankers.

Consular invoices are mandatory when exporting to certain parts of the world, e.g. South America. They are specially printed invoices issued in the exporter's country by the consulate of the importing country. Their purpose is to corroborate the details of a particular shipment for the authorities in the importer's country.

A certificate of origin is a declaration by the exporter stating the country of origin of the goods shipped.

Insurance
Insurance cover against loss or damage during shipment is essential. In the case of regular exporters, it is now far more common to issue insurance certificates, based on the overall policy, than individual policies for each shipment. As you have seen, the terms of the contract determine whether it is the buyer or seller who must effect insurance cover (*see* also the ECGD below).

Methods of payment
Payment should be in sterling or in a foreign currency which is freely exchangeable for sterling.

Cash with order
This is the most desirable method of payment from the exporter's point of view. It is, however, rare and some form of credit for the importer is an accepted part of export sales.

Open account
This method is very simple; the documents of title are sent direct to the importer who then pays by his own cheque or by money transfer. However, it is only common where there is an established trading relationship between exporter and importer because the exporter takes a considerable financial risk. He loses control of the goods once they are despatched whilst the buyer may not pay for them, through either lack of funds or regulations restricting the transfer of money.

Bills for collection

Where the exporter is satisfied with the integrity of the importer the transaction may be completed on a collection basis. The exporter despatches the goods and sends the documents to his bank who will forward the documents to a bank in the importer's country (preferably the importer's bank or an overseas branch of the exporter's own bank) for collection by him.

Included with the shipping documents is a *bill of exchange*, i.e. a demand for the payment of a certain sum of money at a specified date, drawn by the exporter on the buyer, and settlement is made by the importer paying the bill of exchange. The bill must be paid according to its tenor, i.e. immediately if payable on demand ("sight bills"), or at a fixed or determinable future date (usually thirty, sixty or ninety days) after the bill is presented to the buyer for acceptance (i.e. after sight) or after the date on the bill itself. When the bill is not payable on demand the importer must *accept* the bill (by signing it) after which he is bound to make payment when the bill matures, i.e. on the date specified in the bill. The documents are then released to the importer and he is able to obtain possession of them from the master of the ship.

This method protects the exporter in so far as the documents of title are only released against payment or acceptance of the bill by the importer, although payment is neither immediate nor guaranteed in the latter case.

If the bill is payable after *sight*, the importer benefits from having a period of credit in which to pay for the goods.

Documentary credits

Documentary credits are a method of financing overseas trade by inserting in the contract of sale a provision that payment shall be made by a banker. In a *letter of credit* the banker in effect undertakes to pay the price for the goods upon delivery to him of the export documents. It is the surest and quickest method of obtaining payment.

The importer agrees with his bank (the issuing bank) to instruct a bank in the seller's country to make payment on the presentation of documents which conform *exactly* to the instructions and descriptions specified in the documentary credit.

Credits may be available for payment at sight (on demand), or for acceptance (at a fixed or determinable future date). In the latter case a bill of exchange will be drawn by the seller and accepted by the issuing bank. After payment or acceptance of the bill the documents are sent to the issuing Bank for processing and then to the importer to enable him to take possession of the goods on arrival.

Credits can either be *revocable* or *irrevocable*. The former are now rare because they can be cancelled or amended by the importer at any time without the prior knowledge of the exporter. The latter are the most widely used method of payment in export sales, for under them the issuing bank gives its irrevocable undertaking and guarantees payment if all the terms of the credit are met. Should the exporter require greater security than that afforded by the name of the issuing bank, the irrevocable credit can be confirmed (including the acceptance of the bill of exchange) by one of the leading UK banks (the advising Bank). This means that the letter of credit will be honoured irrespective of what might happen either to the importer or to the overseas issuing bank.

The Export Credit Guarantee Department (ECGD)

The ECGD is a government department which is of tremendous importance in export sales. It offers two main services; insurance and guarantees for bank finance.

ECGD insurance

ECGD insurance covers two broad categories of risk. These are:

(*a*) the creditworthiness of the importer;
(*b*) the political and economic risks of the country concerned.

It does not cover risks normally insured by commercial companies, e.g. fire and marine accidents.

Its success may be judged by the fact that in the last twenty years the average premium rates for short-term export insurance have more than halved whilst ECGD coverage of UK exports has nearly trebled.

ECGD guarantees

Most exporters selling on credit will need the help of banks to bridge the credit period. However, banks require security for the finance they provide and an exporter is usually able to obtain this at a preferential rate if the ECGD guarantees the advance.

Overall, the ECGD enables the exporter to conduct his business with greater security. He is able to adopt a more aggressive sales technique, selling to new customers and offering large amounts of credit on longer terms in order to match or defeat his competitors.

The export and import of goods is only one part of international commerce, there is also the sale of services and the movement of money and capital to consider. To do this we must consider the *balance of payments*.

THE BALANCE OF PAYMENTS

The balance of payments is an account of all the transactions of everyone living and working in the UK with the rest of the world. It is always recorded in £s. Whilst many different currencies are involved, these are converted into £s at the current exchange rate. If anyone normally resident in the UK sells goods or services to someone abroad this created an inflow (+) of money, whilst anyone in Britain buying goods or services from abroad causes an outflow (−) of money from the country. Not so obviously, if anyone in Britain invests abroad this will cause an outflow (−), whilst if a foreigner invests in Britain, e.g. an American company takes over a British company, then an inflow of currency (+) is created. When all these transactions are recorded we arrive at the balance of payments, as in Table XXXIV.

Items in the account
Current account
The current account has two components: visible trade, which is the export and import of goods (from which we get the *balance of trade*), and invisible trade, which is the sale and purchase of services. Invisible trade is vitally important to Britain. The balance of trade is often confused with the balance of payments. In Table XXXIV, you can see that the balance of trade is only a part of the balance of payments, albeit an important part. It is therefore possible to have a deficit on the balance of trade and surplus on the balance of payments. Britain is usually in deficit on the balance of trade (although this was not so in 1980) but makes it up with invisible earnings. It is regarded as very important to have a surplus on the balance of payments current account.

Investment and other capital transactions
This involves the movement of capital (money) rather than goods or services. That is to say, it is concerned with international loans (not currency loans) and investment. It includes such items as:

(*a*) government loans;
(*b*) overseas investment in the UK;
(*c*) UK investment overseas;
(*d*) borrowing and lending overseas by UK banks.

The balancing item
This amount is necessary to arrive at a correct balance and makes up for anything which has been left out, or for errors. It can be either positive or negative.

The balance for official financing (total currency flow)
This is the net flow of currency which results from all the country's
external transactions. It is the net result of the current balance, the

TABLE XXXIV. BALANCE OF PAYMENTS OF THE UNITED KINGDOM 1980

CURRENT ACCOUNT	£ million
Visible trade:	
Exports (FOB)	47,389
Imports (CIF)	46,211
Visible balance (Balance of trade)	+ 1,178
Invisibles:	
General government	− 791
Private sector:*	
Sea transport	+ 135
Civil aviation	+ 395
Travel	+ 208
Financial services	+ 1,595
Other	+ 2,646
Interest, profits and dividends	
General government	− 655
Private sector *	+ 617
Transfers	− 2,122
Invisible balance	+ 2,028
1. CURRENT BALANCE	+ 3,206
2. INVESTMENT AND OTHER CAPITAL TRANSACTIONS †	− 1,295
3. BALANCING ITEM	− 539
4. BALANCE FOR OFFICIAL FINANCING (made up as follows)	+ 1,372
Current balance	+ 3,206
Investment and capital transactions	− 1,295
Balancing item	− 539
OFFICIAL FINANCING (financed as follows)	
IMF	− 140
Other monetary authorities	nil
Foreign currency borrowing	− 941
Change in official reserve (drawings + /additions to−)	− 291
5. TOTAL OFFICIAL FINANCING	− 1,372

* Includes Public Corporations.
† Includes allocation of SDRs.

Source: United Kingdom Balance of Payments, HMSO

investment and other capital flows and the balancing item. This is the balance of the balance of payments. In Table XXXIV it is £1,372m, i.e. in 1980 there was an overall surplus of this amount.

Official financing
This is the borrowing or lending of currency by the government, and the running down or accumulation of the country's foreign currency reserves. This item is necessary to balance the total currency flow created by the overall deficit or surplus on the balance of payments.

How the balance is achieved

We often hear of balance of payments deficits but in fact the balance of payments *must always balance*. Since international trade is based on the exchange of goods and services it follows that we cannot continually sell less than we buy because other countries would quickly refuse to trade with us. The balance can be explained by considering the five headings (*see* Table XXXIV).

(*a*) Current account.
(*b*) Investment and capital flows.
(*c*) Balancing item.
(*d*) Balance for official financing (total currency flow).
(*e*) Official financing.

If there is an overall deficit on current account and investments this will have to be made up by the government's official financing, either running down reserves or borrowing (*see* Fig. 86). It also follows, however, that the government cannot continually run down reserves for they would become exhausted, nor can it continually borrow without paying back. It is equally true that a surplus must also be balanced out. This can be achieved by increasing the stocks of foreign currency, lending abroad or reducing one's overseas indebtedness. (Note that inflows of currency are shown as a ($-$) whilst an outflow is shown as a $+$.) Thus, in the long run, current flows must balance with capital and investment flows.

Cures for balance of payments problems

Balance of payments problems can arise out of either deficits or surpluses. Similarly, a balance of payments problem can be accompanied either by a high level of economic activity at home or a low level. For many years Britain was faced with recurrent balance of payments deficits accompanied by inflation. The late 1970s and early 1980s saw some handsome balance of payments surpluses but these were accompanied by such a low level of economic activity in

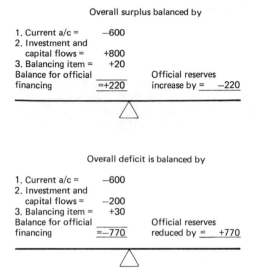

Overall surplus balanced by

1. Current a/c =	−600		
2. Investment and capital flows =	+800		
3. Balancing item =	+20		
Balance for official financing	=+220	Official reserves increase by =	−220

Overall deficit is balanced by

1. Current a/c =	−600		
2. Investment and capital flows =	−200		
3. Balancing item =	+30		
Balance for official financing	=−770	Official reserves reduced by =	+770

Fig. 86. *How the balance of payments balances. Increase in reserves shown as* −(*minus*), *decrease as* + (*plus*).

the domestic economy, i.e. heavy unemployment, that they seemed equally undesirable. There are many actions the government might take to combat a balance of payments problem; which is the correct one will depend upon the reasons for the problem.

Some of these measures are considered below.

Borrowing/increasing reserves
Faced with a deficit a government could borrow or run down its reserves; conversely, faced with a surplus it could lend or increase its reserves. This should only be done for a short-term disequilibrium—it is not a long-term solution. In 1976 Britain took a large loan from the IMF to meet its deficit.

Exchange control
A government could regulate its payments position by imposing restrictions on the exchange of its currency; this tends to annoy trading partners. Britain used this measure in 1967, but in 1979 all exchange controls were abolished.

Deflation
If a deficit is caused by inflation at home a "credit squeeze" or a tight fiscal policy might cure it. However, this is hardly the measure

to use if there is unemployment at home. This has been tried many times by British governments.

Devalue/revalue

A nation could try to cure a deficit by devaluation and a surplus by revaluation. This will only work if the demand for exports and imports is elastic. If the demands are inelastic these measures will exacerbate the situation. Britain devalued in 1949 and 1967 and the pound floated in 1972. West Germany revalued its currency in 1978.

Reflation

This would only be seen as a solution when there was a deficit on the balance of payments coupled with domestic unemployment. Britain has been prevented from doing this by the danger of worsening inflation.

Reduce expenditure abroad/overseas aid

A major world power such as Britain or the USA might reduce military expenditure overseas as a method of reducing a deficit. Conversely, the giving of overseas aid could reduce a surplus.

Restriction of imports

Reducing imports by tariffs might seem to be one way to get rid of a deficit. Britain tried an import surcharge in 1967, and in 1978 tried to put a quota on Japanese car imports. These measures invite retaliation and are not a long-term solution.

Change in investment

A country in deficit could sell off its overseas investments or receive investment from abroad. Conversely, a creditor nation could eliminate its surplus by investing overseas. Curiously Britain continues to be a net investor overseas despite (or perhaps because of) its problems.

Increasing productivity

For a nation continually in deficit a long-term and substantial increase in the productivity of its industries is the only solution to its problems.

MULTINATIONAL COMPANIES

We tend to think of the business organisation as a national entity, perhaps with interests overseas, whilst economies are in fact becoming dominated by large multinational companies. These pose special problems, for government, for law and economics. It is not just that such companies are large but that they are truly multinational. Something like 18 per cent of British industry is foreign owned but a glance at Table XXXV will show that Britain also owns vast overseas investments. In 1976, which was the worst year for the balance of payments, Britain nevertheless invested 1,874m. overseas. Amongst the many multinational companies operating in Britain are Ford, General Motors, Rank Xerox, IBM, Philips, Michelin, Alcan, Nestlé and Ciba-Geigy.

The existence of large multinational companies poses many problems.

(a) *Host and hostage.* A company may often pursue policies which are not in the best interest of its host state but equally it may find its assets held "hostage" to the particular demands of a country.

(b) *Taxation.* It is often difficult to stop companies avoiding tax by switching their revenues.

(c) *Legal.* The company may find itself having to comply with different regulations in different countries. However, it may in turn be able to avoid onerous regulations by having offices registered overseas, e.g. "flags of convenience".

(d) *Statistical.* One of the greatest problems posed by the multinational is one of information. Statistics are compiled in different ways in different countries and many of them take no account of the ultimate ownership of capital.

The conventional Marxist picture of *economic imperialism* is of companies investing overseas to exploit cheap labour. Whilst this

TABLE XXXV. THE TEN LARGEST MULTINATIONAL COMPANIES

Name of parent company	Based in	No. of states in which subsidiaries are located
1. Exxon	USA	25
2. General Motors	USA	21
3. Ford	USA	30
4. Royal Dutch/Shell	Neths/UK	44
5. General Electric	USA	32
6. IBM	USA	80
7. Mobil Oil	USA	60
8. Texaco	USA	30
9. British Petroleum	UK	52
10. Unilever	Neths/UK	31

may have been true once, there are now different geographical and technological trends. The tendency is for companies to move away from underdeveloped countries to high-consumption countries where industry is capital and skill intensive. Technology and market appear to win out over cheap labour. There are as yet no established economic theories to explain the behaviour of these businesses and no generally acceptable body of international law to regulate their behaviour. We do not know whether these large companies will become the basis of a more rational international behaviour or become a source of friction and conflict.

SELF-ASSESSMENT QUESTIONS

A. 1. Define: (*a*) domestic trading ratio; (*b*) multilateral trade; (*c*) terms of trade; (*d*) official financing; (*e*) a CIF contract; (*f*) a bill of exchange.

2. List the factors which extend and diminish comparative advantage.

3. List the seller's obligations under an FOB contract.

B. 4. True or false?

(*a*) A country must possess an absolute advantage in at least one commodity before trade is possible.

(*b*) Britain exported less in volume to the OPEC countries in 1970 than in 1980.

(*c*) In 1980 Britain had a positive balance of trade with Sweden.

(*d*) A rise in the price of exports would cause an adverse movement in the terms of trade.

(*e*) Running down the country's foreign currency reserves creates a debit $(-)$ on the balance of payments.

C. 5. True or false?

(*a*) If the index of import prices were 150.0 and the index of export prices were 120.0 then the terms of trade index would be 125.0.

(*b*) It is only worthwhile trading if the other country can sell you the goods more cheaply than you can produce them yourself.

(*c*) One of the chief obstacles to trade is economic nationalism.

(*d*) If tariffs are to be effective as a protectionist measure the demand for imports must be inelastic.

(*e*) General government spending abroad is shown in the balance of payments as an invisible import.

6. Construct a diagram similar to Fig. 80 to illustrate Britain's position after specialisation and trade.

7. To what extent does the EEC benefit from comparative advantage?

ASSIGNMENTS

1. List ten major foreign companies which operate in the UK which are not mentioned in the section on multinational companies.

2. Update the pie graphs in Fig. 85.

3. Prepare an information sheet outlining the full range of services of the ECGD.

4. Discover what other government services and agencies are available to help the exporter.

PART FIVE
THE ORGANISATION,
THE STATE
AND THE COMMUNITY

CHAPTER NINETEEN

How Britain is Governed

```
CHAPTER OBJECTIVES

After studying this chapter you should be able to:
* describe the four elements of central government;
* list the forms of local government;
* explain the rating system;
* define and describe the role of quasi-governmental
  bodies;
* state the functions of the Bank of England.
```

Throughout the book we have made reference to "the government". In this section we examine the influence of the government upon the organisation and the community. First of all we will examine the organisation of government.

CENTRAL GOVERNMENT

When we consider the central government we will find that it has four elements, the *legislature*, the *judiciary*, the *executive* and the *Civil Service*. The judiciary is considered in Chapter 25 and therefore in this chapter we will consider the other elements of government.

Parliament: the legislature

Parliament consists of the Queen, Lords and Commons and is the supreme legislative authority in the UK. To some extent this ancient and fundamental principle has been modified by our membership of the EEC (*see* page 461).

In practice the House of Commons is the most important part of the legislature, for it is the political party which controls the Commons which forms the government. Since the government can usually muster an overall majority in the Commons, and also controls the timetable, it has very considerable power over what is discussed.

Figure 87 traces the progress of a typical Bill through Parliament. Most Bills which run the full course and become law are government-sponsored and start off along the "Green Paper, White Paper" trail. There is only a small amount of time for *private*

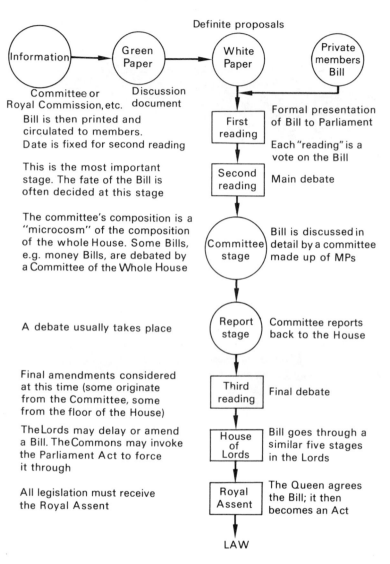

Fig. 87. *How a Bill becomes an Act.*

members' Bills and there is actually a lottery to decide who will be allowed to introduce one. Nevertheless, private members' Bills have often introduced important legislation, for example homosexual law reform.

Private members' Bills should not be confused with *private Bills*. The latter apply only to a group or section of the community or to a particular geographical area, e.g. British Rail "promoting" a new stretch of railway line. Such Bills are deposited in the private Bill Office and usually go through Parliament unopposed.

The amount of time it takes for a Bill to pass through Parliament varies enormously. The Prevention of Terrorism Act 1974 was introduced into Parliament on the morning of 27th November and received the Royal Assent at 9.40 a.m. two days later. On the other hand, the Scottish Devolution Bill had to be introduced in several separate sessions of Parliament before it was finally agreed in a much amended form. (In fact Scottish devolution was not achieved because it failed to gain the necessary percentage support in a referendum. Such was also the fate of devolution for Wales.) The speed with which a Bill passes through Parliament will be determined by whether or not it is opposed and the degree of urgency which the government places upon it.

The Prime Minister and the Cabinet

The Prime Minister, or First Lord of the Treasury, to give the official title, has many powers: appointing and dismissing ministers and determining the membership of Cabinet committees; deciding what the Cabinet will discuss and chairing the meeting; summarising the discussions of the Cabinet and sending "minutes" to ministers which are, in effect, directives. In addition to this the Prime Minister disposes a great deal of patronage in both government and non-government posts as well as the honours list, bishops in the Church of England and certain judicial posts. The Prime Minister can also ask the Monarch to dissolve Parliament. This is a very considerable power since he/she can choose the time which is considered the most favourable to the re-election of the government.

These many powers have led many people to suggest that we now have government by Prime Minister. The two foremost advocates of this point of view were the late Richard Crossman, in his *Introduction to Bagehot's The English Constitution*, and the late John Mackintosh in his book *The British Cabinet*. Whilst there may be much truth in this, Prime Ministers are still subject to serious constraints for they must secure the agreement of Parliament and must also command the loyalty of the Cabinet. In practice, Prime Ministers are particularly dependent upon the support of the *inner cabinet*, a small group of senior colleagues who are capable of commanding the support of the party and Parliament.

In recent years the *kitchen cabinet* has become more important. This is a small group of advisors on whose loyalty the Prime Minister can totally rely. They may be colleagues from Parliament or they may simply be advisors appointed by the Prime Minister. This begins to make Downing Street look more like the White House.

The word "cabinet" was originally a term of abuse used to describe the clique which advised Charles II. Today the composition of the Cabinet depends upon the preferences of the Prime Minister although it must, of course, include the most senior ministers such as the Chancellor of the Exchequer, the Foreign Secretary and the Minister of Defence. It will also include those responsible for the running of Parliament such as the Leader of the House of Commons. The Prime Minister and Cabinet constitute the *executive* branch of government for it is they who decide upon policies and implement them. The executive of the Labour government 1974–9 distinguished itself by becoming isolated both from Parliament and its own Party.

An important aspect of the Cabinet is the doctrine of *collective responsibility*. That is to say, the Cabinet should always appear to speak with one voice. If a member of the Cabinet is in serious disagreement with a policy then he should resign. On the other hand, the Cabinet takes responsibility for the actions of its members collectively, so that an attack upon one is an attack upon all. In recent years the disagreements of cabinet ministers have become more public, e.g. *The Crossman Diaries*, and this has called the doctrine of collective responsibility into question. The Thatcher Cabinet further eroded this doctrine when regular "leaks" of Cabinet discussions were made secretly to the press.

Government departments

The government of the country is divided between different departments of state: at the head of each is a *minister* or *secretary of state*. They are political figures and are termed *members of the government*. Most senior posts are filled by members of the House of Commons. The minister or secretary may, or may not be, a member of the Cabinet. Each minister is assisted by a *Parliamentary secretary*, whilst secretaries of state are assisted by *Parliamentary under-secretaries*. These people are known as *junior ministers* and receive a salary for their job. This is in contrast to Parliamentary *private* secretaries who receive no remuneration other than their salaries as MPs and usually undertake the task in hope of future advancement. There seems to have been a proliferation of secretaries of state recently as large composite ministries have appointed secretaries to be in charge of particular functions; examples of this are Defence and the Department of the Environment.

The three great departments of state, the Treasury, the Foreign and Commonwealth Office, and the Home Office, tend to remain the same, but the duties and titles of the other departments are often changed by the government of the day.

The Civil Service

The Civil Service is the *secretariat* which has to translate the policy of the government into action. Although legally civil servants are servants of the Crown, they are in practice employed by the separate departments of state and responsible to the minister in charge. If the government changes, civil servants do not. This gives continuity to the departments but it also tends to give a great deal of power to civil servants. It is perhaps another example of the growth of the "technostructure" (*see* page 87).

Each department usually has a *permanent secretary*. He is the minister's adviser and he is also responsible to the *Public Accounts Committee* of Parliament. Do not confuse the permanent secretary, who is professional administrator and civil servant, with the Parliamentary secretary, who is a political figure often without expertise in the work of his department. The permanent secretary and his deputies are often referred to as "mandarins" and are thought to wield enormous power. The administrative class of the Civil Service still tends to be made up of Oxbridge graduates.

Although the permanent heads of the Civil Service may have great power, it is the ministers who must accept the political and legal responsibility for the acts of the departments. Beneath the administrative class of civil servants are the thousands of other civil servants: executive class; clerical class; the professional, technical and scientific class; and the typing class, who carry out the work of the department. In addition to these there are civil servants in "industrial grades", such as those who work in the Royal Ordnance Factories. It is not usually the industrial grades we are thinking about when we speak of civil servants.

LOCAL GOVERNMENT

The structure of local government

Local authorities are responsible for a wide range of services from education to refuse collection. The forms of local government are diverse but they are all controlled by elected councillors who work on a voluntary basis.

The structure of local government has been revised in recent years. The present structure of local government in London came into being in 1965 following the London Government Act 1963. The London County Council was replaced by the Greater London Council which is larger and which is subdivided into the present thirty-two London boroughs and the City of London. Following the *Redcliffe–Maud Report 1969*, the Local Government Act 1972 created the present structure in the rest of England and Wales in 1974 and Scotland in 1975.

Excluding London, we now see a system whereby the country is divided into counties (regions in Scotland) which are in turn subdivided into districts. In the main urban areas of England there are six metropolitan counties and these are sub-divided into metropolitan districts. Administrative functions are divided between the two layers of authority. There is no common pattern of division throughout the authorities. One feature is that the London boroughs and the metropolitan districts are responsible for many more services than the ordinary county districts. Education, for example, is provided by the metropolitan district whilst elsewhere it is provided by the non-metropolitan county councils. In London there is a curious hybrid with the inner London boroughs banding together to form the *Inner London Education Authority*, whilst in outer London it is provided by the individual boroughs. Figure 88 summarises this organisation.

The *parish councils*, in some cases dating back to 1086, still continue in non-urban areas. Despite being criticised for the last 200 years they have proved the most durable unit of local government, although they possess few powers today.

To add to the confusion of local government some local authorities cling to titles such as borough, city or town councils. This is usually because they acquired this title by Royal Charter. It should be stated that these are merely courtesy titles and in the case of borough and city councils that are, in fact, district councils. Their Charter usually gives them the right to have a mayor or a lord mayor. Town councils are a curiosity; they are, in fact, parish councils which have been granted the right to call themselves town councils. Examples of this are Ely and Wells. Their chairman therefore becomes a city mayor.

Finance of local government
It is a common misconception that local government is financed by rates. Table LV on page 545 shows that only 36.5 per cent of local

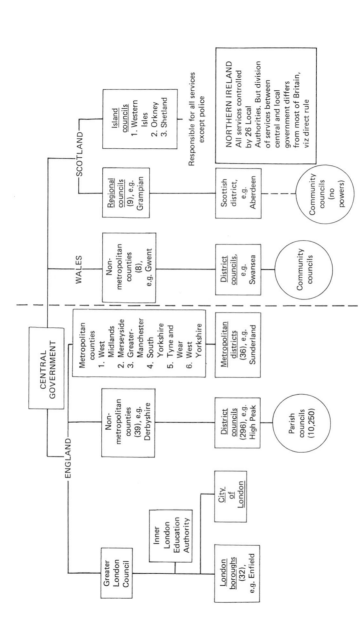

Fig. 88. The organisation of local government in the UK. There are ministers with special responsibility for Scotland and Wales. Northern Ireland is governed direct from Westminster. Authorities underlined collect the rates.

government revenues came from this source in 1981–2. The rating system is another curiosity; it is in fact a tax on the value of property. Each local authority has all the property in it valued by the *Inland Revenue*. The rateable value placed on a property is supposed to reflect the rentable value of the property. When added together this will give a total valuation for the local authority.

To calculate its rates the local authority will compare its expenditure plans with its revenues from non-rate sources, and the short-fall will have to be made up by rates. In Fig. 89 this is explained for the fictional authority of Becborough. Its revenue expenditure is £2 million whilst its non-rate income is £1.5 million. This means that £0.5 million must be collected in rates. If the total rateable value of Becborough is £0.75 million this means that each ratepayer must pay £0.66 for each pound of rateable value. For example, if someone had a house with a rateable value of £300 they would receive a rate demand for £200.

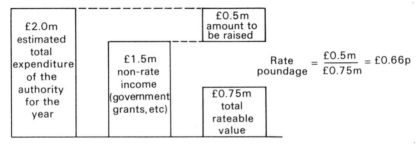

Fig. 89. *The rate poundage of Becborough.*

Rates are often criticised as being unfair because they are not related to the services the ratepayer receives from the authority. This is a difficult argument to maintain since few taxes are related to services received. Furthermore, it should be borne in mind that if rates were abolished some other way would have to be found to collect the £10,000 million p.a. which is raised in rates, e.g. it has been suggested that rates should be replaced by a local income tax.

In addition to *revenue spending* local authorities undertake *capital spending*, for example the building of council houses. This is mainly financed by borrowing.

Central government financial support for local authorities comes mainly in the form of the *rate support grant*. Pressure has been put on local government to curtail its spending since 1976. This pressure became acute under the Conservative government of 1979. This led to local authorities raising a greater proportion of their revenue as rates (*see* page 545). The reluctance, or inability, of local government to make the cuts demanded of it by the central government led to punitive measures being taken by the Secretary of State for the Environment. Such were the complexities of the financial arrangements which were introduced that many local authorities found them difficult to understand. In general it is fair to conclude that the independence of local authorities was considerably eroded in the early 1980s.

Other local authorities

Since 1974 the responsibility for water supply and sewage has been with regional water authorities in England and Wales, whereas in Scotland they are the responsibility of the regions. Also since 1974 health services have been controlled by regional and area health authorities. These organisations are better described as types of *quasi-governmental bodies.*

QUASI-GOVERNMENTAL BODIES

Any organisation which is neither a private business organisation nor an elected body but which fulfils an executive or administrative function designed to implement or further government policy can be described as a *quasi-governmental body.* In our complex society hundreds of such bodies exist because government departments cannot or do not wish to allocate directly their own resources to the organisation and control of certain specific activities within the economy.

Some *quasi-govenmental bodies* directly implement government policy, e.g. the Monopolies and Mergers Commission and the Office of Fair Trading. (Both of these have been previously considered.) Indeed, in so far as their commercial policy is to some extent determined by the government, nationalised industries and other public corporations can also be considered *quasi-governmental bodies.*

Others are concerned with matters which are generally considered to be outside the mainstream of government policy and decision-making. Such bodies are frequently referred to as *quangos*—quasi-autonomous non-governmental organisations. Quangos operate in the administrative "grey areas" between central government on the one hand and local government and organisations in the private sector of the economy on the other. Most are established by an Act of Parliament or by an Order made under an Act. Some, however, have been established by a minister's administrative act. Their chairmen are appointed by the minister responsible for their establishment and the Prime Minister has personal patronage of some.

The phrase "government at arm's length" has been used to describe their activities since they enjoy considerable autonomy from their parent department. Each was created following a policy decision to remove a specific governmental function from the direct control and responsibility of a minister. In consequence, the minister ceases to be answerable to Parliament for their day-to-day activities. Important examples of quangos include the BBC and the IBA under the Home Office; the Manpower Services Commission and the Industrial Training Boards under the Department of Employment, and the National Economic Development Office (NEDO) and the Review Board for Government Contracts under the Treasury.

In January 1980 a government White Paper listed 489 quangos with executive (decision-making) powers, e.g. the health authorities and the Arts Council, with a staff of 217,000 and a budget of £5.8 billion, and another 1,561 quangos with advisory responsibilities. At the time there had been a vogue for "quango-hunting" but the White Paper proposed the abolition of only 30 executive and 211 advisory bodies, at a saving of some £11 million. The White Paper called for greater controls on their spending, better information about them, and regular assessment of the need for each one, but it acknowledged the vital role they play in the running of the country. (In April 1981 their number had been reduced to 1785.)

Quangos undoubtedly serve very useful purposes. They are an excellent way of getting things done, allowing government departments to concentrate on broader policy issues. In their own policy-making they are free from the sensitivities of the political world and can maintain a long-term plan and exercise broader discretion than a government department ultimately dependent on public support. Above all, perhaps, they are free from direct political control in their day-to-day decision making.

However, three main criticisms are levelled against them. Firstly, there are simply too many of them; secondly, they give government ministers an undesirable power of patronage—"jobs for the boys" is the expression often used; and thirdly, they are not sufficiently accountable to Parliament, particularly in their spending.

THE BANK OF ENGLAND

A curious feature of central government is the Bank of England. Legally speaking it is a public corporation but it is in effect a major institution of government. It has assumed this legal form because it started life as a private company in 1694 and despite a close association with government throughout its life it was not taken into public ownership until 1946.

Its three main functions are the issue of notes, the implementation of monetary policy and the control of foreign exchange (these functions are fully reviewed in Chapter 22). Here we should note that, although it is a public corporation, the Bank of England is much more like a department of state with the Governor of the Bank of England as permanent secretary. On the other hand, although it is the Chancellor of the Exchequer who decides upon monetary policy, he does not head the Bank of England in the same way as, say, the Foreign Secretary heads the Foreign Office. The special nature of the Bank of England is further emphasised by its geographical isolation from government, being five kilometres from Westminster in the City of London.

CONCLUSION

Thus, we can see that the government of the UK is not vested solely in Westminster and the town hall, but in an amalgam of many diverse organisations and institutions. Many of these are not "democratic" bodies; the Bank of England, for example, is not a government department but exerts enormous influence over the economy, similarly, many other vital policy decisions are made by non-elected quasi-governmental bodies.

SELF-ASSESSMENT QUESTIONS

A. 1. Define: (*a*) a private Bill; (*b*) a parliamentary secretary; (*c*) a quango; (*d*) rate poundage.

2. List all the stages a Bill must go through before becoming law.

B. 3. True or false?

(*a*) Parliament consists of the House of Lords and the House of Commons.

(*b*) The Chancellor of the Exchequer is the First Lord of the Treasury.

(*c*) There are thirty-two London boroughs.

(*d*) Nationalised industries are quasi-governmental bodies.

(*e*) The Manpower Services Commission employs more people than the BBC.

C. 4. True or false?

(*a*) Cumbria is a non-metropolitan county.

(*b*) In Fig. 89, if the total rateable value of Becborough were £800,000 then the rate poundage would be £0.65.

(*c*) A committee of the House of Commons could be described as a microcosm of the House itself.

(*d*) The Bank of England is a government department.

(*e*) The Cabinet Office is situated at 10 Downing Street.

ASSIGNMENTS

1. Prepare a report on the activities of a quango.

2. Compile two lists to show which services are supplied by the respective local authorities in your area.

3. Prepare a diagram to show the major departments of state and their respective ministers.

CHAPTER TWENTY

International Organisations

CHAPTER OBJECTIVES

After studying this chapter you should be able to:
* list the important international organisations;
* state the objectives of the IMF;
* describe and explain the break-up of the IMF system;
* state the advantages and disadvantages of floating exchange rates;
* explain the structure of the EEC;
* analyse the functions of the European Court of Justice.

There are thousands of international organisations, ranging from Oxfam and the Save the Children Fund to the United Nations and the Common Market. In this chapter we consider some of these which have the most direct influence on the well-being of the economy. These are predominantly organisations concerned with international finance and trade.

THE WORLD IN 1945

The legacy of depression

Long before nations plunged into war in 1939, the old economic order had collapsed in ruin during the world depression which began in 1929. Although there were few international institutions concerned with trade, certainty was given to trade by the *gold standard*. The currency of a country which is on the gold standard is convertible into gold. To be on a *full* gold standard gold coins must be circulating freely in the economy as was the case in the UK up to 1914. This means that there is no need for special arrangements for international payments, since currency can always be exchanged for gold and the gold exported in settlement of a debt since gold is universally acceptable. When a nation has a deficit on its balance of payments then gold is exported to pay for it. Since the currency is tied to gold this has the effect of bringing about domestic deflation. As prices fall so exports become more attractive to foreigners and imports become more expensive to buy. This has the effect of eliminating the deficit. Conversely, if there were a surplus on a country's balance of payments then gold would flow into the country and cause inflation. The inflation would make the country's imports cheaper and its exports more expensive, thereby eliminating the payments surplus.

Britain had been forced to abandon the gold standard in 1931. After this time the exchange rate ($4.03 = £1) had been fixed by the government agreeing to buy or sell any amount of £s at the stated price. To try and ensure that the stated exchange rate was the correct one, the government established the *Exchange Equalisation Account* in 1932 which is run by the Bank of England. The Bank would buy £s when the rate was falling, thereby forcing it up again, and sell £s when the rate was rising, thus pushing it back down again.

The 1930s was a period of great instability in international trade with many countries devaluing to try to achieve a competitive advantage for their exports. In addition to this, states everywhere placed heavy import duties on goods. The effect of these measures was severely to restrict the volume of international trade and make it difficult for anyone to recover from the depression. For Britain this period marked the end of a century of free trade.

The new alignments

In August 1944, at Dumbarton Oaks, the Allies had begun to debate the new international order. This was to lead to the setting up of the *United Nations*, its Charter being signed in San Francisco in 1945. The United Nations is governed by the *General Assembly* which has representatives of all member nations and by the *Security Council* which has fifteen members. The "big five" (the USA, USSR, UK, France and China) powers each have a permanent member of the Security Council whilst the other ten are elected from other nations. Since each of the five permanent members has a *veto* on decisions it is impossible for the UN to take action with which one of the major powers disagrees.

The unity of the war was lost as the opposing economic and political systems of the allies divided into the eastern and western power blocs. The economic and political alignments became military alignments with the formation of the *North Atlantic Treaty Organisation* (NATO, 1949) and the *Warsaw Pact* (1955). The economic grouping of the communist bloc (COMECON) has tended to remain isolated from the international economic co-operation which has been achieved amongst other nations.

In addition to the communist and capitalist power blocs, the poorer nations of the world became aligned as the *third world* or *less developed countries* (LDCs). Since the oil crisis of 1973, the third world nations have tended to divide into two groups: those which have oil, the *OPEC* countries, and the *non-oil exporting de-*

veloping countries (NOEDCs). The failure of both the communists and the capitalists to help less developed countries has led to the LDCs being generally antagonistic to them.

The further oil price rises of 1978 made the plight of the NOEDCs even worse. The *Brandt Report* of 1980 urged greater help for poor countries but the depressed state of the World economy in the early 1980s led to aid being cut back rather than extended.

Bretton Woods

In July 1944 a conference took place at Bretton Woods in New Hampshire to try to establish the pattern of post-war international monetary transactions. The aim was to try to achieve freer convertibility, improve international liquidity and avoid the economic nationalism which had characterised the inter-war years. The conference was chaired by the Secretary of the American Treasury, Henry Morgenthau. The conference was dominated, however, by the great English economist John Maynard Keynes and the American Harry Dexter-White.

Keynes had the idea that an international unit of currency should be created. This he called *bancor*. It was to be a hypothetical unit of account against which all other currencies would be measured. This would be administered by a world bank which all countries would have an account. In effect this bank would perform the tasks of an ordinary bank, except its customers would be nations: cheques could be written out to settle bills; money would be created to finance trade and overdrafts could be given to those countries which required them. It was essential to the concept of the bank, however, that it be allowed to determine each country's exchange rate and adjust it to ensure that nations did not fall hopelessly into debt. The plan foundered because nations, none more so than the UK, were unwilling to allow an international institution to determine the value of their currency.

The result was that two compromise institutions were established in 1947: the International Monetary Fund (IMF) and the International Bank for Reconstruction and Development (IBRD). The latter is usually called, the World Bank, misleadingly, for it is the IMF which contains the remains of Keynes' idea for the bancor, not the IBRD.

THE IMF SYSTEM

It was the IMF system which dominated the pattern of international monetary payments from 1945–72. The objectives of the Fund were to achieve free convertibility of all currencies and to promote stability in international money markets. It has not achieved the first of these, but until the late 1960s there was comparative stability of exchange rates accompanied by economic prosperity for many of its members.

Quotas

Each of the 141 members of the IMF is required to contribute a quota to the fund. The size of the quota will depend upon the national income of the country concerned and upon its share of world trade. The quota used to be made up of 75 per cent of the country's own currency and 25 per cent in gold. In this way it was hoped that there would be enough of any foreign currency in the pool for any member to borrow should he get into balance of payments difficulties. The gold part of the quota has been abolished. In addition to its quota, members have an allocation of SDRs (*see* below).

Voting power in the IMF is related to the size of quota and in this way the USA and the other industrialised nations have managed to dominate the Fund for most of its life. The relative importance of countries has obviously changed since 1947 but member countries have resisted upward revisions of their quotas since it would involve contributing more to the Fund. Britain's quota was originally 14.9 per cent and it now stands at 7.2 per cent. The USA's quota is 20.8 per cent and that of the combined oil exporting nations 11 per cent. The total quotas have been revised upwards seven times since 1947 and an eighth review seems likely. All quotas are now expressed in SDRs.

Borrowing

Originally each member of the Fund could borrow a 25 per cent slice (tranche) of his quota in a foreign currency for up to five consecutive years, i.e. it was possible to borrow the equivalent of 125 per cent of one's quota. Today it is possible to borrow up to the equivalent of 450 per cent of one's quota over a three year period. This is not, however, an unconditional right to borrow, for the Fund may, and usually does, impose conditions of increasing severity upon a member as it increases its borrowing.

The methods of borrowing from the Fund have received several modifications.

Stand-by arrangements

Devised in 1952, this method has become the most usual form of assistance rendered by the Fund. Resources are made available to a member which he may draw on if he wishes. Attaining a stand-by facility is often enough to stabilise a member's balance of payments situation without him actually drawing upon the Fund. Stand-by facilities are similar to a bank overdraft. It is still necessary for a member to agree to conditions for each tranche.

General agreement to borrow (GAB)

In 1961 the ten leading members of the IMF agreed to make a pool of £6 billion available to each other. Although channelled through the IMF, the Group of Ten would decide itself whether or not to give assistance. Special arrangements have been brought in since the oil crisis and these are discussed below (*see* page 449).

Special drawing rights (SDRs)

In 1967 it was decided to *create* international liquidity for the first time. This was to be done by giving members an allocation of special drawing rights which could be used in settlement of an international debt if the creditor nation was willing to accept them. SDRs were first made available in 1970.

SDRs are the nearest equivalent so far to Keynes' idea of a bancor. Originally calculated as 1 SDR = $1, the value of SDRs is now calculated by combining the value of the five leading currencies in the following proportions: US dollar 42 per cent; Deutschmark 19 per cent; French franc 13 per cent; pound sterling 13 per cent; Japanese yen 13 per cent. This gives a value of approximately 1 SDR = $1.15.

The adjustable peg

The members of the IMF originally agreed to fix or "peg" the value of their currencies by defining them in terms of gold. This could be done directly or indirectly by defining the value of a currency in terms of one of the two reserve currencies, the dollar and the pound.

The pegged value of a currency was permitted to vary within a margin of 1 per cent. Thus if, for example, the exchange rate of the pound was £1 = $2.80 (1949–67) then its value could fluctuate within the limits:

$$£1 = \begin{matrix} \$2.78 \\ \$2.80 \\ \$2.82 \end{matrix}$$

Beyond these limits, adjustment of the pegged value of a currency required the permission of the Fund. The permission was to be virtually automatic for changes of up to 10 per cent, but more conditional beyond this.

Convertibility

It was the aim of the Fund that any currency should be freely convertible into any other. This would mean the abolition of all exchange controls, but not the controls on the movement of capital funds. The Fund was fairly successful in improving convertibility. The pound became freely convertible in 1958, and in 1979 all exchange control measures were abolished by the UK.

Discipline

A country which wants to borrow from the Fund is likely to have to agree to conditions before the loan is granted, e.g. the implementation of domestic deflation and credit control. In 1976, for example, Denis Healey had to provide the Fund with a "letter of intent" stating that limits to domestic credit expansion (DCE) (*see* page 531).

A country which is in continual balance of payments surplus could also cause severe embarrassment to the international scene. In such circumstances the Fund can, under Article Seven, declare as "scarce" the currency of the country in surplus. This scarce currency provision would then allow other members to take exchange control sanctions against that country. The provision has never been used, but its threat may have been instrumental in bringing about revaluations of the yen and the Deutschmark.

THE BREAK-UP OF THE IMF SYSTEM

Although the IMF is still extant, the system of fixed exchange rates which was the basis of the Bretton Woods Agreement has been swept away. This situation did not come about overnight.

The 1967 crisis

Although it was not realised at the time, the devaluation of the pound from £1 = $2.80 to £1 = $2.40, in November 1967, marked the beginning of the end for the adjustable peg system. The basis of economic power in the world had changed greatly since 1947 when the Fund was set up. At that time the economies of Germany and Japan lay in ruins, but no changes came about in the IMF system to take account of their subsequent recovery. Britain and America solidly refused to *devalue* their currencies whilst Germany and Japan refused to *revalue* theirs. In 1967 Britain could resist the pressures no longer and devalued. This precipitated world-wide instability. Speculators realised that gold was undervalued at $35 = 1 ounce (28.3 g) and there was, therefore, a great pressure on America to devalue. The final attempt to save the gold standard occurred in

1968 when a two-tier rate was established. This meant that the price of gold for monetary purposes was maintained at $35, whilst the price of gold for commercial purposes was allowed to float upwards.

The end of the gold standard (1971)

The announcement by President Nixon in August 1971 that America would no longer exchange dollars for gold at the official price ended the gold standard. This was brought about because of a massive deficit on the USA balance of payments. This was caused by the realignment of economic power in the world which had led to massive and continuing surpluses and the accumulation of vast reserves by Germany and Japan. The balance of payments crisis in the States was made worse by the following.

(a) *Inflation*, which made the price of gold ever more unrealistic.

(b) *Speculative pressure.* The vast USA deficit meant that there was a great amount of dollars in the world which could be used to speculate upon a rise in the price of gold.

(c) *The Vietnam war.* One of the consequences of the unpopularity of the war was that the government was not able to increase taxation to pay for it. The war was, therefore, partly financed by running up the deficit on the balance of payments.

(d) *The "Watergate" election.* President Nixon desperately needed to reflate the economy to win the election in the autumn of 1971. This was fatal for the external position of the dollar.

After the abandonment of the gold standard there were several attempts to repair the system of fixed exchange rates.

The snake in the tunnel

The Smithsonian Agreement (December 1971) patched up the system of fixed exchange rates for a while. Gold was now valued at $38 per ounce. This was a dollar devaluation of 8.9 per cent. The new rate for the pound was to be £1 = $2.60. This was a revaluation against the dollar but a devaluation against most other currencies. The extent to which the value of one currency could fluctuate against another was increased from 1 per cent to 2.25 per cent.

The establishment of a 2.25 per cent variation meant that the maximum possible variation between three currencies (cross parities) was 9 per cent. This amount of variation was unacceptable to the Common Market countries and therefore on 24 April 1972 they established a variation within European currencies of half that of the Smithsonian Agreement. The Smithsonian variation was said to provide the *tunnel* within which the smaller European *snake* moved. Britain joined the Snake on 1 June 1972 but left fifty-four days later when Anthony Barber announced that the pound was to "float".

Dirty floating

After Britain "floated" the pound in 1972 it was not long before most other currencies, including the USA, followed suit. Leaving the remnant of the European snake they moved around against all other currencies. When a country has a floating, or freely fluctuating, exchange rate, it means that it is determined by the forces of demand and supply in international markets. This is illustrated in Fig. 90. In this diagram all foreign currencies are considered together and are measured in terms of dollars. The supply of pounds (SS) in this market is the result of the British desire to import goods. Pounds are not acceptable to foreigners and they will demand payment in their own currency. The demand for pounds

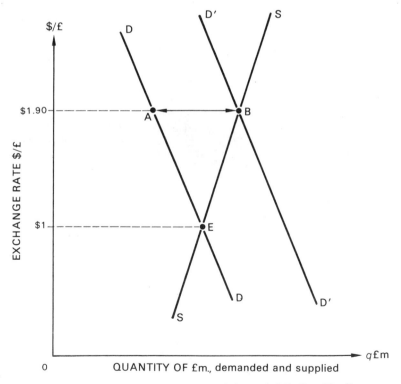

Fig. 90. *The determination of the price of the pound sterling. The figures used are for illustration only.*

comes from the desire of foreigners to buy British goods. To do this, however, they must obtain pounds and so they demand British currency by offering their own money. Where the demand and supply are equated is the equilibrium price (E) or the exchange rate. The exchange rate is thus determined by the interaction of import demand and export supply. It should be obvious from this why a failure to export goods can have a disastrous effect upon the exchange rate.

Although most exchange rates are nominally floating, virtually all governments intervene either openly or covertly to try and stabilise their exchange rate or to manipulate it to their advantage. In Fig. 90 the move to D'D' illustrates the exchange rate for the pound being driven up to $1.90 by the Bank of England buying pounds, thus increasing the demand for them and putting up their price. The distance AB represents the quantity of pounds which the Bank would have to buy to maintain the exchange rate at $1.90. When the government intervenes in this manner there is said to be *dirty floating*. *Clean floating* would occur if the government took no part but allowed the exchange rate to be fixed by the unrestricted forces of demand and supply. The movement from DD to D'D' could also be brought about by market forces. For example, in 1980 the effect of North Sea oil drove up the exchange rate as foreigners demanded pounds to buy our oil exports.

The oil crisis
As a result of the Yom Kippur war oil supplies were cut off. When they were resumed the OPEC countries contrived a fourfold rise in price. It is possible to argue that the resulting transfer of money from the developed countries to OPEC countries has brought about one of the most fundamental shifts in economic power of all time. It is estimated that this cost the oil importing countries an extra $100 billion per annum. Then in 1978 oil prices were doubled causing a liquidity problem even greater than that of 1973. This price rise was a major factor in the world depression. This hit the industrialised countries hard but was near disastrous for the NOEDCs. Since 1973 there have been many ways through which the OPEC funds have been recycled in attempts to maintain world trade.

(*a*) *The IMF.* As a temporary measure the OPEC countries lent money to the IMF which was in turn lent to members who had difficulties because of the oil crisis. The money was made available to members in the form of SDRs. The UK was the largest borrower, taking 1 billion SDRs. The *oil facility* was terminated in 1976 but several other special facilities had been established, for example:

(*i*) *The extended fund facility, 1974.* This was created to help members with special balance of payments problems.

(*ii*) *The Subsidy Account, 1975.* This was to help reduce the interest paid by the members most seriously affected by the oil crisis.

(*iii*) *The Gold Trust Fund.* This was established in 1976 to lend low-income developing countries part of the proceeds from the sale of one-sixth of the IMF's gold reserves.

(*iv*) *The first credit tranche.* This is borrowing to the equivalent of 25 per cent of the country's quota, and these days can be had on only the vaguest of conditions.

(*b*) *The Eurocurrency market.* The *Eurodollar* market arose originally from American dollars held in European banks, but it has since expanded to take in other currencies including the Japanese yen. Centred mainly in London, New York and Zurich, the Eurocurrency market is the biggest single mechanism by which money is recirculated. The market is now massive and represents a greater total of money than all the official reserves of all the countries in the world. This supply of "hot" money is a potential threat to the stability of any currency.

The 1973 OPEC surpluses diminished much faster than most people predicted, but the effect of the 1978 price rises seems set to last well into the 1980s.

Gold again?

The USA left the gold standard in 1971 because, at $35 per ounce, gold was clearly undervalued. Since that time its price has rapidly increased and has been above $600 per ounce on several occasions. The ups and downs in exchange rates and continuing high rates of domestic inflation have led many people to suggest that we should return to some form of gold standard. With gold now so expensive, the world's gold stock could effectively cover much more trade. However, the unmined gold stocks of the world are relatively small, so that if world trade is to continue to grow the price of gold would have to be continually increased to allow it to keep pace with the value of goods traded.

Britain: floating or sinking?

A floating exchange rate should bring about automatic rectification of any balance of payments disequilibrium. This comes about because a deficit on the balance of payments would cause the exchange rate to depreciate, thereby making exports cheaper and imports dearer so that the deficit is turned into a surplus. Conversely, a surplus would cause the exchange rate to appreciate, thus making imports cheaper and exports dearer. Advocates of floating exchange rates, or *managed flexibility* as dirty floating is politely called, claim several advantages for it.

(*a*) There is an absence of crisis meetings because imbalances sort themselves out.

(*b*) Because of (*a*) there are no disputes of the "You should devalue", "No, you should revalue" kind between nations in payments imbalance.

(*c*) Internal economic policy is freed from the constraints of the external payments position, e.g. the economy does not have to deflate to protect an unrealistic exchange rate.

Has this worked for the UK? When Britain floated in 1972 the exchange rate was £1 = $2.60; it reached an all-time low of £1 = $1.55 in October 1976, an effective devaluation of 40.4 per cent. Since this time it has climbed back up again. Now that the dollar is also depreciating, the exchange rate is quoted not only against the dollar but also as a weighted index against a "basket" of sixteen leading currencies. Taking the Smithsonian parities as 100, the value of Sterling in Autumn 1976 was 55. Thus, it had devalued by 45 per cent. However, the present index takes 1975 as the base year. This is illustrated in Table XXXVI. These figures show the plunge of the pound in 1976 and then its equally dramatic recovery.

TABLE XXXVI. STERLING EFFECTIVE EXCHANGE RATE (1975 = 100)

Year	Index
1971	127.9
1972	123.3
1973	111.8
1974	108.3
1975	100.0
1976	85.7
1977	81.2
1978	81.5
1979	87.3
1980	96.1
1981 (Feb.)	102.0

Source: Economic Trends

The massive drop in the late 1970s was not altogether unwelcome to the British government, who believed it would make exports competitive. The success or otherwise of this would depend upon the relative elasticities of demand for exports and imports. It should be remembered, however, that increasing the price of imports will also increase inflation. It is reckoned that a 4 per cent rise in import prices causes 1 per cent domestic inflation. The British government, however, seemed happy to settle for a rate of about $1.70, but no sooner was the rate stabilised around this level than the prospects of North Sea oil brought money flooding into London and the exchange rate soared, much to the displeasure of the government. It appeared that a pound that floated upward was almost as difficult to live with as a sinking one.

The autumn of 1981 saw the value of the pound drop from $2.35 to $1.80. It could be argued that whatever the advantages of a floating exchange rate may be, short-term fluctuations of such magnitude must have a damaging effect upon trade. One suggestion has been that Britain should join the EMS.

The European monetary system (EMS)
One of the objectives of the EEC is European monetary union (EMU). This has so far proved impossible, but on 13 March 1979 a step towards it was taken with the establishment of the European monetary system (EMS). This developed out of the old "snake" and is based on the same idea of limited fluctations. All the members of the EEC belong to it except the UK. Britain decided that, at a time when exchange rates were still highly volatile, it was not in its interests to join. EMS is based on a hypothetical unit of account called the European currency unit (ECU) (the calculation of the value of the ECU might be likened to that of the SDR), and the ECU is used as the basis for all EEC finances.

Members' currencies are allowed to fluctuate by plus or minus 2.25 per cent of the central rate established by the value of the ECU (the lire is allowed to fluctuate by 6 per cent). The importance of each currency in the ECU is related to the relative size of the member's economy. Thus Germany's currency was given an importance of 35 per cent but that of Luxembourg only 0.35 per cent. The value of the ECU moves up or down against other currencies as the whole basket appreciates or depreciates. The value of sterling is taken into account when determining the value of the ECU because Britain is an EEC member and it is hoped she will eventually join the EMS.

The EMS also envisages the establishment of a fully fledged European monetary fund but so far there is little progress towards this. It would appear, therefore, that EMS is still a long way from European monetary union.

OTHER INTERNATIONAL ORGANISATIONS

The IBRD (International Bank for Reconstruction and Development—"World Bank")

The IBRD was set up as a sister organisation to the IMF in 1946. Its aim was to make loans to help to redevelop war-shattered economies. The IMF, it will be remembered, does not make loans for capital projects but to help alleviate payments difficulties. The World Bank derives its funds from three sources.

(a) *Quotas.* Members make contributions in relation to their IMF quotas, 10 per cent of the quota being paid whilst the other 90 per cent acts as guarantee for the Bank's loans.

(b) *Bonds.* The World Bank sells bonds on the capital markets of the world.

(c) *Income.* A very small proportion of the Bank's funds comes from the Bank's earnings. As it progressed, the World Bank turned its attention from Europe to the poorer countries of the world. Today it is almost wholly concerned with helping LDCs. It is a valuable source of advice and information besides making loans.

The World Bank has also increased its operations by forming new organisations. These are:

(a) *the International Finance Corporation* (IFC, 1956) which was set up to enable the Bank to give loans to private companies as well as governments;

(b) *the International Development Association* (IDA, 1960) the object of which was to make loans for longer periods and on preferential terms to LDCs. The IDA has become known as the "soft loan window";

(c) *"the third window"*. In 1976 the IBRD announced its intention of making loans available to LDCs on even more favourable terms in order to try to relieve them of the enormous burden of debt interest. This has become known as "the third window".

Since 1968 the Bank's activities have become much more centred on LDCs but the IBRD remains hampered by lack of funds.

GATT (The General Agreement on Tariffs and Trade)

The twenty-three signatories of the Havana Charter 1948 had intended to set up a world-wide trading organisation (ITO). In the event, however, they could not reach an understanding and so instead came to a general agreement on tariffs and trade. The main parts of this agreement were as follows.

(*a*) *Tariffs.* All the signatories agreed not to increase tariffs beyond their existing level.

(*b*) *Quotas.* The signatories agreed to work towards the abolition of quotas.

(*c*) *"Most favoured nation".* Every signatory was a "most favoured nation", i.e., trading privileges could not be extended by one member to another without extending them to all. Existing systems of preferences, such as Commonwealth Preference were allowed to continue.

(*d*) *Trading blocs.* The establishment of common-market type agreements such as the EEC and EFTA were allowed, but were encouraged to be outward-looking rather than insular.

Several rounds of talks succeeded in reducing tariffs and virtually abolishing quotas. The most famous of these was the *Kennedy Round* of the 1960s. GATT members now account for about 80 per cent of international trade.

In recent years emphasis has shifted to the gap between the rich northern countries and the poor southern countries. This has become known as the north-south dialogue. This has mainly been conducted through the United Nations Conference on Trade and Development (UNCTAD). The poor countries are mainly producers of primary commodities, but they are unable to trade freely with the rich northern countries because they are discriminated against by protectionist policies such as those of the EEC. The poor countries insist that, if they are to progress, they must have freer access to markets and better prices for their products. So far little progress has been made.

OECD (The Organisation for Economic Co-operation and Development)

The OECD was originally called the *Organisation for European Economic Co-operation* and was set up in 1947 to administer the USA's *European Recovery Programme ("Marshall Aid")*. By 1960 it was considered that it had achieved its object and so it became the OECD with the object of turning its attention to the less developed countries of the world. The OECD now has twenty-one members which are most of the European countries, the USA and Canada, plus Japan, who joined in 1965. The methods of the OECD are to try to co-ordinate the economic policies of its members, to co-ordinate economic aid and to provide specialised services, one of the most important of which is information.

OPEC (the Organisation of Petroleum Exporting Countries)

The domination of the rich industrialised nations in world trade has done little to help the producers of primary products (mainly the poor countries), since it has prevented them from organising to obtain good prices for their products. The one exception to this is OPEC. It consists of a group of Arabian, African and South American countries who *export* oil. (America is still a great producer of oil but is a net importer.) The OPEC countries were able to combine successfully for three main reasons: geographically they are relatively concentrated; the demand for their product is highly inelastic; and they are united by a common political hostility to Israel. The 1973 fourfold increase in the price of oil must be one of the most successful coups of all time. They are not very worried that high prices will cause others to produce, e.g. North Sea oil, because their costs of production are so low.

The success of OPEC has encouraged other primary producers to try to form cartels. This has been attempted in coffee, bauxite, uranium, copper, tungsten and tin, so far with little success.

THE EUROPEAN ECONOMIC COMMUNITY

The setting-up of the Community

A plaque in Strasbourg marks the spot where Winston Churchill made a speech on European unity in 1945, but successive British governments turned their back on European co-operation. The origins of the EEC are to be found in the European Coal and Steel Community (ECSC) set up in 1952 by France, Italy and the Benelux countries. West Germany later joined the organisation, the object of which was to abolish trade restrictions on coal and steel between member countries and to co-ordinate production and price policies. The ECSC proved such a success that the members decided to investigate the possibility of the greater co-operation. The result of negotiations was that the Treaty of Rome was signed in 1957 and on the 1 January 1958 the EEC (usually called the "Common Market") came into existence. Britain had been invited to participate in both the ECSC and the EEC but had declined.

Britain eventually joined the EEC in 1972, together with Ireland and Denmark. The membership of the Common Market was increased to ten by the accession of Greece in 1981. Portugal and Spain have also applied for membership but have not, as yet, been admitted.

What is a common market?

The establishment of the EEC involved the setting-up of both a customs union and a common market.

(*a*) *Customs union.* The establishment of a customs union involves both the abolition of tariffs between members and the erection of a *common external tariff* to the rest of the world. If each country does not have the same external tariff then imports will simply flood into the member country with the lowest import duties and then spread out to the rest of the customs union. The general policy which the EEC used in arriving at its common external tariff was to take an arithmetic mean of the previous six duties. In some cases, e.g. the import of produce from France's tropical ex-colonies, the lowest duty was used, since this involved no disadvantage to members. Several of the old colonial states have special arrangements with the EEC.

When Britain joined it was particularly difficult for her to agree to the common external tariff because she formerly enjoyed duty-free imports from Australia, Canada and New Zealand. The products of these temperate countries were, however, in direct competition with those of European farmers and Britain was not allowed in until she had agreed to raise import duties against her Commonwealth partners.

(*b*) *Common market.* The EEC is known colloquially as the Common Market but this is only one aspect of it, although potentially the most important. It refers to the organisation of the economies of the members as if they were one country, i.e. the common prices and production policy of coal and steel would be extended to many other products. This implies the free movement of labour, capital and enterprise within the EEC. So far it is only in agriculture (the CAP, *see* page 293) that there has been a truly common policy. The achievement of European monetary union (EMU), however, would lead to a much greater integration of the economies.

The structure of the Community

The Treaty of Rome envisages that the EEC will eventually lead to European union. This, at present, seems distant, but the four main institutions of the EEC provide the four essential components of a state.

(*a*) The Council of Ministers (the executive or Cabinet).
(*b*) The European Commission (the secretariat or Civil Service).
(*c*) The European Parliament (the legislature).
(*d*) The European Court of Justice (the judiciary).

The first three of these institutions are examined in this part of the chapter, whilst the Court of Justice is examined in the next.

The Council of Ministers
This consists of ten members, one minister from each country, and it is the most important decision-making body of the EEC. Which minister it is will depend upon what matter is being discussed. If, for example, it was agriculture, then the agriculture minister of each country would attend. The Council takes the most important and political decisions and it also has the power to make new community law. Such law is known as *secondary legislation*, the *primary legislation* being that of the Treaty of Rome.

Since ministers are always busy with their responsibilities in their own countries they meet irregularly, and because of this a *Committee of Permanent Representatives* (Coreper) was formed. This consists of an ambassador from each of the ten countries. Coreper meets weekly and is able to take decisions on a lot of the proposals emanating from the Commission. In this way it leaves only the most important or controversial issues to be decided by the ministers themselves.

Before a decision can be arrived at in the Council it must have 70 per cent support, i.e. forty-five votes are necessary as Table XXXVII shows.

TABLE XXXVII. VOTING POWER OF THE COUNCIL OF MINISTERS

Country	No. of votes	Country	No. of votes
France	10	Netherlands	5
Italy	10	Greece	5
United Kingdom	10	Denmark	3
West Germany	10	Ireland	3
Belgium	5	Luxembourg	2
		TOTAL	63

However, to take important decisions on, for example, the entry of new members, unanimity is required. The Council usually tries to reach a decision without taking a vote.

The European Commission
The Commission itself consists of fourteen commissioners (two from each of the largest countries and one from the six others, *see* above), but behind the Commission is a staff of about 2,500 people, working at the EEC headquarters in the unlovely Berlaymont district of Brussels. The staff of the Commission are of mixed

nationalities and successive presidents are selected from different countries. Roy Jenkins was the first British president.

It is the job of the Commission to undertake the day-to-day administration of the EEC. They are supposed to do this in a European manner without national bias. It involves monitoring the activities of member states to see that they do not conflict with community policy. In addition to this, they implement community policies such as the CAP.

The Commission also tries to develop EEC policy. They mainly do this by formulating policies for economic co-ordination for consideration by the Council. It is proposals by the Commission on such things as food hygiene which provoke outbursts in the British Press about "the European sausage" or "the European chicken". Things such as the introduction of tachographs into lorry cabs have provoked great opposition from many people in Britain. The Commission's most important objective at the moment is the achievement of European monetary union (EMU). This has been strongly opposed by the British.

The European Parliament

The European Parliament meets in Strasbourg. Originally it consisted of MPs nominated by national parliaments. Thus, a member of the European Parliament would be doing two jobs. However, since 1979 members are elected directly to the European Parliament. The UK elects eighty-one MEPs out of a total of 434 (see Table XXXVIII). In the Parliament members are seated according to party allegiance, not according to nationality. Thus, for example, Labour MEPs sit with the SPD members from West Germany.

TABLE XXXVIII. COMPOSITION OF THE EUROPEAN PARLIAMENT 1981.
NUMBER OF MPS PER STATE

Country	No.			Country	No.
England	66 ⎫			Netherlands	25
Scotland	8 ⎬ UK	81*		Belgium	24
Wales	4			Greece	24
N. Ireland	3 ⎭			Denmark	16
France		81		Ireland	15
W. Germany		81		Luxembourg	6
Italy		81			
				TOTAL	434 seats

* Average size of UK constituency is 514,000 electors.

As yet the Parliament has little authority or power. Its main function is to monitor the activities of other community institutions. It is to be expected, however, that direct elections will increase its legitimacy and ultimately its power. To achieve *authority* the Parliament will have to gain the ability to initiate and enact legislation. To gain *power* the Parliament will have to obtain control of the EEC budget; at the moment it only has control over a part of the EECs administrative budget.

If European unity is to be achieved the development of the European Parliament is essential.

Britain and the EEC

In 1972 the British Parliament passed the European Communities Act and in 1973, Britain, together with Ireland and Denmark, joined the EEC. Norway, after a referendum, decided not to join. In 1974 the Labour government "renegotiated the conditions of entry" but this was largely a window-dressing exercise to assuage the anti-EEC members of the Labour Party. In joining the EEC Britain became part of a community of 259.7 million people (269.1 after the entry of Greece). The economic advantages which Britain gained were enormous and fundamental—those of increased *specialisation* and *comparative advantage* (*see* page 398), i.e. the potential market for British goods increased fivefold from 55 to 269 million. It would have been economically impossible for Britain to have stayed out of the EEC since British industry had long ago joined it by exporting its capital to Europe. The gains from the EEC are not, however, appreciated by the man in the street; he tends to see only the petty inconveniences of it. Opposition to the EEC still remains strong and in 1981 the Labour Party pledged itself to withdraw from the Common Market if it was returned to power. Similarly the government elected in Greece in 1981 declared its intention of leaving the EEC.

The common external tariff of the EEC, however, prevents us from benefiting from comparative advantage world-wide. The most obvious example of this is foodstuffs, where we are condemned to eat expensive European food whilst we could import it more cheaply from the Commonwealth. This diminution of comparative advantage is termed *trade diversion*. Complete economic unity is a long way off. Meanwhile the EEC aims at the harmonisation of the economies of members. Some of the implications of this for Britain are listed below.

(*a*) *Taxes.* It is EEC policy that there should not be big differences between the rates and methods of taxation. One of the reasons why VAT was introduced into the UK was to bring us into accord with the EEC. Differences in tax can be discriminatory. France, for example, claims that high excise duty on wine discriminates against French exports.

(b) *Social security.* It is Community policy that social security benefits and payments be similar and transferable. This will enable people to work more easily in different countries. Anyone who has travelled in the EEC will be aware that form E111 gives the right to free medical care anywhere in the Community.

(c) *Competition.* Community law is aimed at regulating competition throughout the EEC. An example of the operation of this was the case of the Distillers Company Ltd who, in 1977, were ordered to stop their practice of selling the same brand of whisky at different prices in the Community (*see* page 344).

(d) *Metrication.* Most of the Community members use similar weights and measures, but for Britain this has meant abandoning the old imperial and avoirdupois standards in favour of metric units, e.g. in 1981 petrol began to be sold in litres rather than gallons.

(e) *Free movement of labour.* It is a part of Community policy that its citizens should be free to work anywhere in the EEC. Generally, however, it is necessary to have obtained a job in the country to which one wishes to move before a work permit is granted.

(f) *Free movement of capital and enterprise.* There is supposed to be freedom for capital or enterprise to move anywhere in the Community, but this is in fact limited. For example, in 1978 Peugeot-Citroen was allowed to take over Chrysler UK but at the same time France forbade a Lucas take-over bid for a French electrical component company.

A comparison of the economies of the members of the EEC can be made by studying the figures in Table XXXIX. When the EEC was first formed the UK had a strong economy and felt confident staying outside the Community. As Britain's economy declined relative to that of the members of the EEC so Britain felt more and more constrained to join.

In joining the EEC, Britain was only following the trend of her own trade, the European market having occupied a larger and larger share of UK trade since the Second World War. Whilst the EEC may be beneficial to Britain, many Third World countries have described it as a "rich man's club". This is because the common external tariff seems to be designed to keep out many primary products (*see* page 454). The USA has also attacked the EEC's protective duties, but since the USA is one of the world's

TABLE XXXIX. THE ECONOMIES OF THE EEC MEMBERS COMPARED

	Greece	Belgium	Denmark	Germany	France	Ireland	Italy	Luxem-bourg	Nether-lands	United Kingdom
Population (millions, 1978)	9.4	9.8	5.1	61.3	53.3	3.3	56.7	0.4	13.9	55.9
Employment (per cent, 1979)										
Agriculture	30.8	3.2	8.3	6.2	8.8	21.0	14.8	6.1	4.8	2.6
Industry	30.0	36.7	30.2	44.9	36.3	31.9	37.7	44.7	32.7	39.9
Services	39.2	60.7	61.5	48.9	54.9	47.1	47.5	49.2	62.4	58.4
Gross domestic product										
Annual average growth 1973–8 (per cent) (a)	3.6	2.3	1.9	1.9	3.0	3.5	4.0	0.6	2.6	1.1
Per inhabitant, in 1978 (EUA)*	2,628	7,530	8,601	8,186	6,960	2,899	3,602	7,821	7,366	4,345
Standard of living										
Private consumption per head in 1978 (EUA)*	1,827	4,604	4,781	4,882	4,276	1,842	2,278	4,469	4,261	2,608
Cars per 1,000 inhabitants in 1978	80	302	276	346	333	195	291	428	295	258
Telephones per 1,000 inhabitants in 1978	266	322	569	404	372	172	301	539	453	447
Doctors per 1,000 inhabitants in 1977	2.2	2.2	2.0	2.0	1.6	1.2	2.2	1.3	1.7	1.5
Consumer price index (a)										
Average annual increase 1974–9 (per cent)	14.1	7.5	9.8	4.2	10.1	14.5	15.8	6.9	6.7	15.5

* EUA (European unit of account) = approx. £0.058 (at exchange rates current on 13 October 1980).
Reproduced by permission of the Commission of the European Communities.

Source: Eurostat, except (a): OECD 1980

most protectionist nations this is not to be taken seriously. The USSR, however, remains opposed to the EEC on political grounds because it does not wish to see a strong united Europe.

Community law

You have already seen in this chapter how the secondary legislation of the Community is made by the Council of Ministers but drafted by the Commission after consultation with and advice from the European Parliament. Remember, however, that, unlike our own Parliament, the European Parliament is not a legislative body; nor does it, at present, exert more than a modest degree of democratic control over the Commission and Council of Ministers. This relationship between national governments, Community institutions and Community law is shown in Fig. 91.

Community law consists of Community legislation and judgments in disputes concerning it referred to the European Court of Justice. It is mainly concerned with customs duties, agriculture, free movement of labour, services and capital, transport, restrictive trade practices and the regulation of coal, steel and nuclear energy industries.

Community legislation

There is a basic distinction between *primary* and *secondary* legislation, and a further distinction between legislation which is *directly applicable* to the population of each member state and legislation which requires *further action* by the member states for its implementation.

Primary legislation is Community law contained in the Articles of the main treaties. It takes precedence over domestic law, although domestic legislation may sometimes be required to implement it. Secondary legislation is the law made by the Council of Ministers and the Commission under the authority conferred on them by the Treaty of Rome. The Treaties themselves are not open to review by either the Court of Justice or domestic courts, although both may interpret them. Secondary legislation is open to review on the grounds that it is *ultra vires* (beyond the powers of) the Council of Ministers or the Commission, or because the proper procedures have not been followed.

Secondary legislation takes three forms.

Regulations. These apply directly to the population of the Community. They automatically form part of the law of member states and confer individual rights and duties which the national courts must recognise.

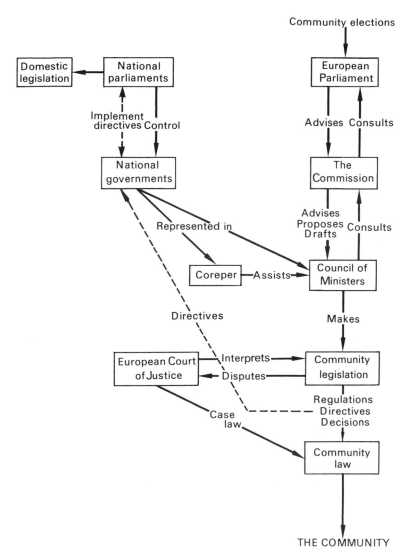

Fig. 91. *National governments, EEC institutions and EEC law.*

Directives. These are binding instructions to member states but they are not directly applicable. The member states must take appropriate steps to implement them. The Companies Act 1981, for example, implements the EEC's fourth directive on company accounts by reducing the amount of information required from small and medium-sized companies in accounts filed with the Registrar of Companies. The directive's aim is the harmonisation of company accounting throughout the Community. In Great Britain directives are normally implemented by statutory instrument.

Decisions. These are directly binding but they are addressed to specific individuals or organisations within the member states and not to the population generally.

Obtaining an interpretation of Community legislation. The European Court of Justice is the final arbiter on all questions of law arising from the Community Treaties, in particular questions of interpretation. Any court or tribunal of any member state can ask the Court for a "preliminary ruling" on a question which concerns the interpretation of the Treaties. Where such a ruling is considered necessary for a decision, and no appeal lies from the court or tribunal hearing the case, reference must be made to the Court of Justice. Hence, in Great Britain the High Court and Court of Appeal have a discretion whether to allow an appeal to be made to the Court of Justice, but the House of Lords (being the final appeal court in the UK) must allow such an appeal if requested to do so.

In *Bulmer* v. *Bollinger* (1974) the Court of Appeal laid down guidelines to help judges decide whether or not to refer a case to the Court of Justice. The English court must consider the delay involved; the danger of overloading the Court of Justice (all judges must sit to hear all cases); the expense to the parties involved; the importance of referring only problems of interpretation and not issues of fact or application of the Treaties; the practical advantages of deciding all but the most important and difficult questions of interpretation itself; and, to some extent, the wishes of the parties.

The actual case concerned an alleged contravention of Community law by the use of the word "champagne" to describe English cider and perry. Bollinger sought an injunction forbidding its use, maintaining that it should only be used to describe wine produced from grapes grown in the Champagne region of France. The Court of Appeal was unable to accept the argument that there could reasonably be confusion between "Champagne Cider", "Champagne Perry" ("Babycham") and "Champagne", and since each was made from a different fruit Community regulations had not been infringed.

Community case law.
Community case law consists of judgments of the European Court of Justice in disputes involving interpretation or breach of the Treaties, and the review of secondary legislation. Like Community legislation, it is binding on member states and their courts. Should our own case law conflict with it, Community case law will prevail.

The effect of Community law in the UK. You have seen that by the European Communities Act 1972 the UK acceded to the Treaties constituting the European Communities and, by so doing, a system of supra-national law, often binding upon organisations and individuals without further Parliamentary enactment, was introduced into this country. Law which was inconsistent with Community law was repealed by implication, e.g. laws relating to trade tariffs and custom duties, for the Act provides that all rights, powers, liabilities, obligations, restrictions, remedies and procedures under the European Treaties are to be given immediate effect in English law. As Lord Denning (the Master of the Rolls, head of the Civil Division of the Court of Appeal) put it: "The courts will graft the new law on to the old as a gardener does a shoot. The sap from our main stock will circulate through the shoot and make all one."

The supra-national structure of Community law clearly affects the principle of the *supremacy of Parliament*. This declares that within the UK only Parliament has the right to make law and that no one Parliament can bind its successors, i.e. any Act passed can be repealed. However, for three reasons this effect is not so drastic as it may seem. Firstly, Community law does not affect any of the matters which concern solely England and the people in it, i.e. domestic law is unaffected. Secondly, the supremacy of Parliament must be seen in political as well as legal terms. Thus, whilst the repeal of any Act, including the European Communities Act 1972, is legally possible, political considerations may make it impossible. Britain could hardly repeal the various Acts giving Commonwealth countries their independence, and it would be a politically extreme step, and very probably disastrous to the economy, to repeal the 1972 Act. Thirdly, Community law affects the sovereignty of all member states and not just the UK.

Business organisations and Community law. Almost by definition Community law directly affects business organisations rather more than it does individuals. There are many examples of this which could be mentioned but a few directly relevant to the *Organisation in its Environment* will serve as illustrations.

In the formation of *partnerships* the Treaty confers on citizens of member states the right to establish firms, subject to certain restrictions concerning professional qualifications, on the same footing as those laid down for nationals of the country in which it is desired to establish the firm. Furthermore, any general discrimination on grounds of nationality is expressly prohibited.

Certain aspects of English law were brought into line with Community law in the European Communities Act 1972 itself. Section 9 makes important alterations to *company law*, in particular, the application of the *ultra vires* doctrine to the objects clause of a registered company's memorandum of association (*see* page 32).

As you saw in Chapter 17 *Community competition law* directly affects business organisations by forbidding all agreements between business organisations which may adversely affect trade between member states.

The most important recent example of a change in UK law to conform to Community law is the change in certain companies' accounting duties made by the Companies Act 1981, passed to implement a Community directive. We mentioned this earlier in this chapter and the changes are outlined on page 37.

THE EUROPEAN COURT OF JUSTICE

Functions

By Article 164 of the Treaty of Rome, the role of the Court is to "ensure that the law is observed in the interpretation and implementation of the Treaty". It is the final arbiter on all questions involving *interpretation* of the Community Treaties and it deals with *disputes* between member states, between member states and the Commission (as "Community watchdog"), and between the Commission and business organisations, individuals or Community officials.

The Court also has *review powers*. These enable member states to question the legality of acts of the Council of Ministers and the Commission, e.g. a member state may ask the Court to investigate its complaint that the Commission has:

(*a*) acted outside the powers allocated to it;
(*b*) failed to follow proper procedures;
(*c*) misused its powers.

If the complaint is upheld the Commission's act will be annulled.

Composition

The Court of Justice comprises ten judges appointed by the governments of the member states, the president of the Court being elected by the judges from among their own number. Judges hold office for a renewable term of six years. Unlike the British practice, an academic lawyer or a lawyer in private practice can be appointed a judge of the Court. Their independence is protected by the fact that a judge can only be removed by a unanimous vote of his colleagues.

The judges are assisted by four advocates-general, an office modelled on the *commissaire du gouvernment* of France's *Conseil d'Etat* (Administrative Court) and without a British equivalent. An advocate-general will sum up at the end of each case; he will do this impartially, looking at the issues involved from the point of view of Community law. They are not members of the Court, and take no part in the judges' discussions or drafting of judgments. The judges do, however, pay great attention to the submissions in court of the advocates-general.

Practice and procedure

The Court's practice and procedure are based on a code of rules of procedure drawn up by the Court, and there are four main ways in which it differs from that of British appellate courts. Firstly, proceedings are inquisitorial as opposed to the adversary or contest system of procedure found in British courts. Basically, this means that the judges of the Court of Justice investigate the dispute, or question, themselves. British judges, on the other hand, are essentially "umpires" between two contesting parties. Secondly, the Court does not sit in divisions, and all cases brought before the Court are heard by all the judges. Thirdly, one collective judgment is made; dissenting judgments are not given. Fourthly, it is not bound by its previous decisions, although it will follow them where possible to achieve consistency.

There is no appeal from a decision of the European Court of Justice and the decision cannot be challenged by a national court when called upon to enforce it.

SELF-ASSESSMENT QUESTIONS

A. 1. Define: (*a*) gold standard; (*b*) tranche; (*c*) dirty floating; (*d*) common external tariff; (*e*) "secondary legislation" of the EEC.

2. List the reasons for the abandonment of the gold standard in 1971.

B. 3. True or false?

(a) A full gold standard is when gold coins circulate freely in the economy.

(b) COMECON is an institution of the EEC.

(c) The USA has the largest quota in the IMF.

(d) Eurodollars have been introduced as part of European Monetary Union (EMU).

(e) The European Parliament is a legislative body.

(f) The House of Lords is the final arbiter in disputes arising within this country over the interpretation of EEC legislation.

C. 4. True or false?

(a) Other things being equal, domestic inflation will cause the price of foreign currencies to rise.

(b) Devaluation should improve a country's balance of payments position if the demand for imports is inelastic.

(c) The EEC is the largest free trade area in the world.

(d) All members of the EEC are also members of NATO.

(e) Switzerland has applied for membership of the EEC.

5. Discover and describe one case which has come before the European Court of Justice.

6. What is meant by the problem of international liquidity and how does the IMF help to overcome it?

7. Compare and contrast Community legislation with our own domestic legislation.

ASSIGNMENTS

1. Compile a table or chart of Britain's fifteen most important trading partners showing the value of exports and imports in £m. Then express the importance of trade with the EEC as a percentage share of exports and imports.

2. Discuss the view that European unity would lead to the downfall of democracy.

CHAPTER TWENTY-ONE

The Components of National Income

CHAPTER OBJECTIVES

After studying this chapter you should be able to:
* list and define the main components of national income;
* define and calculate propensities to save and to consume;
* calculate the size of the multiplier;
* describe the operation of the accelerator;
* state the appropriate remedies for inflation and unemployment.

THE CIRCULAR FLOW OF INCOME

A Keynesian view of the economy

An organisation is one of hundreds of thousands which make up the *macro-economy*. In the same way that the organisation can be analysed in terms of cost structures, revenues and market behaviour, so the whole economy can be examined in terms of its various *components*. Much of our present understanding of the economy is based on the work of J. M. Keynes. His most famous work *The General Theory of Employment, Interest and Money* was published in 1936. The economic theories of the "classicists" had proved inadequate to deal with the Great Slump. Keynes believed that the economy was not self-regulating and that it was up to the government to intervene to ensure the economic welfare of society. This is so commonly accepted today that it is difficult to realise what a radical idea this was. Many people would argue that we have enjoyed economic prosperity since 1945 by adopting Keynesian ideas. The present difficulties which Western economies are suffering are partly because Keynes did not foresee the economic problems of today and we await someone whose vision is as profound as Keynes to explain these new problems.

Many Keynesian ideas are now regarded as common sense even by those economists who are not Keynesian. Today, many of these ideas are amalgamated with older concepts to form what is known as the *neo-classical synthesis*.

The macro-economy

When we examine the macro-economy we are no longer concerned with individual organisations but with broad aggregates. Therefore, it is not the demand for an organisation's product we consider, for example, but the total demand for all goods and services within the society. Similarly, we are not concerned with individuals' incomes but with the total of all incomes in the economy.

The level of national income is of critical importance to the well-being of the economy, for on this depends the level of employment. If, for example, there is a decline in national income then the result will be unemployment. What follows, in this chapter, might be regarded as "models" of the economy.

These are a simplified and formalised series of ideas and assumptions which help us to increase our understanding of the economy. There is no true model of the economy but a whole series of them which help to advance our understanding. As Professor Lipsey says in his book *An Introduction to Positive Economics*, "the student should beware of the essentialist belief that there is one true model and that debates between two theories should be settled according to which theory best approximates to the true model. Different theories and models may be best for different uses."

The quantity theory of money

In any economy goods and services are constantly being exchanged for money. At the same time organisations are buying the services of factors of production. Every time a person buys a commodity from someone else this creates income for the seller. It is impossible to spend money without creating income for someone else. Thus everyone's income is someone else's expenditure and vice versa. Exchange is carried out through the medium of money. However, the quantity of money in the economy is not simply the amount of money and coins, because each unit of currency may be used several times. The number of times that a pound note changes hands in a given period of time (a year) is referred to as the velocity of circulation (V).

This is perhaps best illustrated by taking a simple example. Imagine that there is an economy consisting of only three people A, B and C. They produce goods and services which they sell to each other for money. Each lot of goods that is sold is valued at £1 (*see* Fig. 92). Thus if A buys goods from B this creates income for B. This income is in turn spent by B in buying goods from C, thus creating income for C and so on. All these transactions could have been carried out using one pound note. The income generated is, however, £3. This is because income is a *flow* of money with respect to time, whilst the amount of money is a *stock*. An analogy might

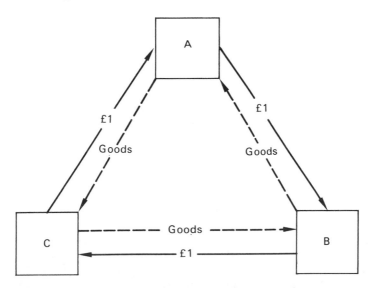

Fig. 92. *The counter-cyclical flow of goods and money between three individuals.*

be a central heating system. The quantity of water in the system is the stock, which is constantly being circulated around. The quantity of water passing through any particular part of the system is the flow. The stock may remain constant whilst the flow becomes greater or smaller as the system is speeded up or slowed down. Similarly, the amount of income in an economy does not solely depend upon the stock of money but also upon how quickly it is being used. The quantity of money is calculated as the stock of money (M) multiplied by the velocity of circulation (V).

$$\text{Quantity of money} = M \times V$$

In the above example this would be £1 $\times$ 3 = £3. Since everyone's income is someone else's expenditure this could also be looked at in another way. It is possible to take the *general price level* (P) of the goods, in our example £1, and multiply it by the number of transactions (T), in our example 3. This would give the same figure £3. So that we derive the formula:

$$M.V = P.T$$

This is known as the quantity equation of money. It was first developed by the American economist Irving Fisher in the 1930s. This is, however, two different descriptions of the same thing, so that it is not so much an equation as an identity.

$$M.V \equiv P.T$$

However, in a more sophisticated form the quantity theory has recently become widely used again. This is particularly associated with another American economist, Milton Friedman.

The quantity of money and inflation

If there were to be a rise in M then one result might be a rise in P. This is of particular interest today since a rise in P (the general price level) would be inflation and this is one of our most pressing economic problems. Inflation could also come about through a rise in V. It does not follow, however, that a rise in M or V will cause inflation. If, for example, there were unemployed resources in the economy then a rise in the quantity of money might cause an increase in the level of economic activity without any corresponding inflation.

Perhaps the most famous inflation of all time was the hyperinflation which hit Germany in 1923. This was brought about both by a phenomenal increase in M and V. The central bank had over a hundred printing plants working twenty-four hours a day to print the money whilst people were paid each half day and dashed out to spend their wages before they were devalued. Although the present problems of the British economy cannot be compared with those of pre-war Germany, it is certainly widely believed that some of our present inflation is due to a too rapid expansion of M (the stock of money).

Monetarists are those who believe that inflation is caused entirely by the expansion of the money stock. This belief is held because, it is maintained, V is constant (or at least highly predictable). Hence in recent years, there has been a great emphasis on controlling the money supply. (Definitions of the money stock are discussed in Chapter 22 and control of inflation in Chapter 23.)

The circular flow of income

As we go on to examine an economy in more detail, we might begin by identifying two main components—that is households and firms. Firms produce goods and services. Households buy them. These components are thus identified not by who they are but by what they do; that is to say, firms *produce* whilst households *consume*. Everyone in the economy belongs to a "household" since everyone must consume. The households also own the factors of production. Thus, in order to produce, the firms must buy *factor services* from households. This is illustrated in Fig. 93. Here you can see that goods and factor services flow one way round the diagram whilst money flows the other way so that the flow of goods and money are always *counter-cyclical* to one another. The money paid by households for goods purchased from the firms is termed

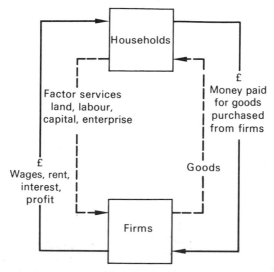

Fig. 93. *Flow of money and goods between households and firms.*

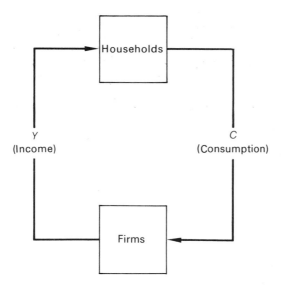

Fig. 94. *The circular flow of income.*

consumption (*C*) whilst payments for factor services such as wages, rent, interest and profit are collectively referred to as *income* (*Y*). Money flows from households to firms and from the firms back to households; this is referred to as the *circular flow of income*.

Since there is always a corresponding counter-cyclical flow of goods it is convenient to leave this out of a circular flow diagram and just include the money flows. It is possible, therefore, to construct a simple circular flow diagram showing the movement of money and using the abbreviations noted above. This is illustrated in Fig. 94.

INCOME CONSUMPTION AND SAVINGS

Savings

If the value of consumption (*C*) were equal to the value of income (*Y*) it would appear that there would be no tendency for the level of income to change. Households, however, do not spend all their income; a proportion is saved. Savings may be defined as money not spent. It is therefore money taken out of the circular flow and can be described as a leakage or withdrawal from the circular flow of income. Although most money saved is put into institutions such as banks and therefore becomes available for other people to spend, it does not follow that people will necessarily, or immediately, borrow it from the bank. So when we speak of savings we are talking of the function of not spending. This is illustrated in Fig. 95. Here you can see that saving leaves less money for consumption and therefore decreases the circular flow of income. In the diagram savings are represented as being carried out by households. Saving may, in fact, take place at any point in the circular flow. It is here reduced to one point in the system in the diagram for the sake of simplicity.

The prime determinant of savings is the level of income. As national income rises so does the level of savings. There may be variations in this from time to time but in general this is so. There are many reasons why people save, some of these are listed below.

(*a*) Deferred purchase—saving up for a holiday or car, etc.

(*b*) Contractual obligations—mortgage repayments, insurance premiums, etc.

(*c*) Precautionary motives—money put by for a rainy day.

(*d*) Thriftiness—some people, or societies, are much thriftier than others as a result of habit or custom.

(*e*) Age—people tend to save different proportions of their incomes at different times in their lives.

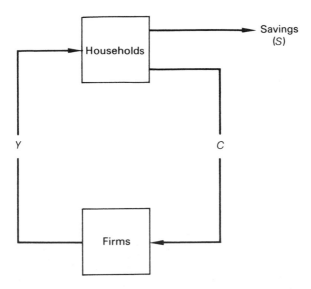

Fig. 95. *Savings are a withdrawal from the circular flow of income.*

The amount which people wish to save is also influenced by such things as taxation, the government's policy towards savings, the availability of credit and expectation of price changes.

The classical economists believed that savings were determined by the rate of interest. If the interest rate went up then people saved more to gain the higher rate of interest and vice versa. Today it can be seen that people will save whatever the rate of interest. In recent years saving has still taken place even when the rate of inflation was higher than the rate of interest. The rate of interest may be important however in deciding how people save, for example in choosing between banks and building societies, but the reasons for saving would appear to be primarily non-economic.

Hoarding

Although saving is money not spent, most saving is done through institutions so that the money is not lost to the economy but is available for other people to borrow. If, however, people *hoard* money, e.g. put it under a mattress or bury it in the ground, then it is lost to the economy until it reappears. If a lot of hoarding takes place this can have a detrimental effect on the economy. Fortunately hoarding is not a problem in the UK, although it is a problem in some Third World countries such as India.

Consumption and savings

If saving is money not spent it is clear that the determinants of savings and consumption are closely interrelated. It is therefore possible to conclude that consumption is also determined by income. As income increases so does consumption. The proportion of income devoted to consumption, however, decreases as income increases. Thus, although a greater amount is consumed at higher levels of income, this represents a smaller percentage of income. The reason for this is fairly obvious. When an economy is very poor virtually everything must be devoted to consumption. At very low income levels consumption can even exceed income and in such a situation there would be a negative saving (or dissaving). As income rises so more material wants can be satisfied and the economy can "afford" to save. To take an analogy with individual incomes, it is obvious that the rich are able to save more than the poor.

Propensities to save and to consume

If we take the amount saved and the amount consumed, and express them as proportions of income, we arrive at the propensities to consume and to save. In Fig. 96 you can see that of 100 units of income 10 are saved and 90 are consumed. Therefore the average propensity to consume (APC), which is the proportion of income

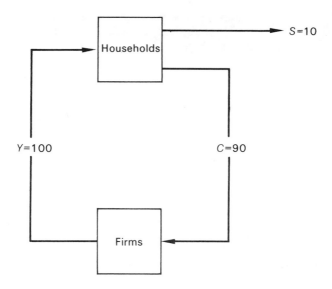

Fig. 96. *The average propensity to consume.*

devoted to consumption, is 9/10; this is expressed in the following manner:

$$APC = \frac{C}{Y}$$

The average propensity to save (APS) is the proportion of income which is devoted to saving and is expressed as

$$APS = \frac{S}{Y}$$

In our example above it is therefore 1/10. It follows that:

$$APC + APS = 1$$

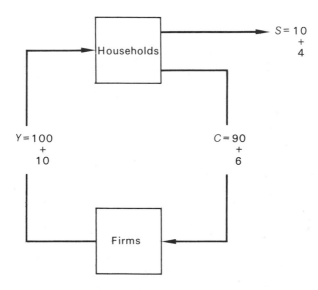

Fig. 97. *The marginal propensity to consume.*

This is always so since 1, here, represents the whole of income. If national income were to increase then a proportion of this increase would similarly be saved and the rest consumed. In Fig. 97 you can see that Y has been increased by 10 units, and of these 10 units 4 have been saved and 6 consumed. You will note that a smaller proportion of the additional income is consumed. This is because of the principle explained in the previous section; that is to say the proportion of income devoted to consumption will decline as income increases.

The marginal propensity to consume (MPC) is defined as the

proportion of any addition to income which is devoted to consumption. This is calculated as the increase in consumption divided by the increase in income.

$$\mathrm{MPC} = \frac{\Delta C}{\Delta Y}$$

In the above example this would be:

$$\mathrm{MPC} = \frac{6}{10}$$

The marginal propensity to save (MPS) is the proportion of any addition to income that is devoted to savings and is calculated as:

$$\mathrm{MPS} = \frac{\Delta S}{\Delta Y}$$

In the above example this would be:

$$\mathrm{MPS} = \frac{4}{10}$$

It also follows that

$$\mathrm{MPC} + \mathrm{MPS} = 1$$

because, here, 1 represents the whole of the addition to income. We would normally assume that the APC is greater than the MPC. This is because a greater portion of income is consumed at lower levels of income.

The consumption function

Table XL consists of some data relating to a hypothetical economy.

This shows the amount of income that is devoted to consumption at several levels of income. At point B dissaving has ceased and all of income is devoted to consumption. As income continues to rise so the proportion going to consumption declines. This is shown in column (5) which gives the APCs. In this example the MPC appears to be constant. As you can see, this is because every time income increases by £30 billion, consumption goes up by £20 billion. These figures can be plotted as a graph. National income graphs are rather special. Expenditure is plotted on the vertical axis and income on the horizontal axis, but in addition to this there is a 45° line. When the two axes are drawn to the same scale, then the 45° line will join all points where expenditure, as indicated on the vertical axis, is equal to income, as indicated on the horizontal axis. As you can see in Fig. 98, at point B consumption is £40 billion and income is £40 billion.

TABLE XL. INCOME DETERMINATION (ALL FIGURES £ BILLIONS)

	Levels of national income (Y) (1)	Planned consumption (C) (2)	Planned savings (S) (3)	Planned investment (I) (4)	Average propensity to consume (APC) (5)	Marginal propensity to consume (MPC) (6)
A	£10	£20	£ −10	£20	2.00	0.66
B	40	40	0	20	1.00	0.66
C	70	60	10	20	0.86	0.66
D	100	80	20	20	0.80	0.66
E	130	100	30	20	0.77	0.66
F	160	120	40	20	0.75	0.66

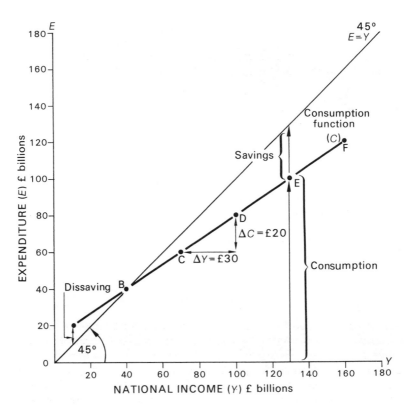

Fig. 98. *The consumption function.*

The graph constructed in Fig. 98 is called a *consumption function.* It shows the amount spent on consumption at all levels of income. To the left of point B the consumption function is above the 45° line, and this shows that consumption exceeds income and dissaving is taking place. To the right of point B the gap between the consumption function and the 45° line represents the amount of saving that is taking place. If you take any point on the graph and read off the two axes this will give you the APC. For example, at point D consumption is £80 billion and income £100 billion. If we arrange them according to the formula:

$$APC = \frac{C}{Y}$$

then we obtain:

$$APC = \frac{80}{100}$$

$$APC = 0.80$$

If we consider a movement between two points on the graph, for example from C to D, then we will obtain the MPC.

$$MPC = \frac{\Delta C}{\Delta Y}$$

$$MPC = \frac{20}{30}$$

$$MPC = 0.60$$

In this example the consumption function is a straight line. This has been done for simplicity. You will note however that when the consumption function is a straight line the MPC remains constant whilst the APC decreases from left to right (*see* McNamara, page 95).

One could also take the figures for savings and plot them on the graph to give a savings schedule (*see* Fig. 101).

INVESTMENT

In this section investment is investigated as a component of national income. In this context investment (I) may be regarded as any addition to the capital stock of the economy and it therefore consists of such things as building a new factory, acquiring new machinery, constructing a new road, indeed anything that adds to the physical stock of wealth. In everyday language the words savings and investment may appear very similar but in economics they are opposites. Savings is not spending and is mainly undertaken by individuals for non-economic motives, whereas investment is spending and is mainly undertaken by firms in the expectation of economic gain. Also, in saving a person is nearly always *lending* money whereas firms *borrow* money to invest. (Buying shares on the Stock Exchange is not investment, since all that is happening is that the ownership of the shares is passing from one person to another.)

Investment is an injection or an addition to the circular flow of income. It may be incorporated into our circular flow model as in Fig. 99. Here investment is represented as being undertaken by firms. You can see that it will have the effect of increasing the circular flow of income.

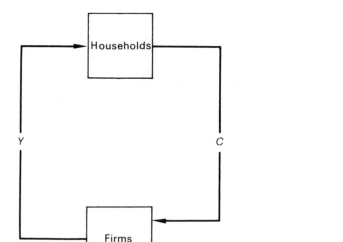

Fig. 99. *Investment is an injection into the circular flow of income.*

Gross and net investment

The capital stock of the country is constantly depreciating. This is due both to physical decay and to obsolescence. Therefore, in order that the economy remains at its present level of wealth a good deal of investment must take place simply to replace existing capital. This may be termed replacement investment. In order for an economy to grow, the capital stock of the country must be increased. Any addition to the capital stock is called net investment, thus:

Gross investment = Replacement investment + Net investment

The determinants of investment

When firms undertake investment they will almost certainly do so in the expectation of gain. Whether or not they expect to gain will depend upon their calculation of the cost of investing compared with the expected return. This is sometimes referred to as the marginal efficiency of capital (MEC). This will be influenced by several factors, one of which is the level of technology. If this is increasing it will make investment more worthwhile since it will increase the net productivity of capital (*see* page 245). Another factor is businessmen's expectations: if they believe prospects are good then this will encourage investment. One of the prime determinants of business optimism is the current state of income and consumption.

Profitability will also be influenced by the government's taxation policy towards both depreciation and profits. Although firms frequently finance investment from their own savings they must also calculate the return on their money if they placed it elsewhere. The cost of borrowing is obviously an important factor, but if businessmen are optimistic about the future they will tend to borrow even when interest rates are very high. Conversely, if businessmen are pessimistic about the future they will not borrow even if money is very cheap. This was well illustrated in the 1930s when the government tried to eliminate the slump by making money cheap. This did not encourage many people to invest and certainly did not get rid of the depression. The schemes that are most likely to be affected by the cost of borrowing are long-term schemes, because in these the interest payments will be a much greater proportion of the capital cost. To understand this you need only to consider taking a mortgage for twenty-five years. There is a relationship between the level of economic activity and the level of investment. This is called the "accelerator" and is dealt with later in the chapter.

The classical economists believed that investment was almost entirely determined by the rate of interest. If the rate of interest went up then the level of investment would decrease and vice versa. The failure of this argument was amply demonstrated during the 1930s. For much of this chapter we will make the simplifying assumption that investment is constant. In reality this is not so, but it allows one to consider the interrelationships of the components of national income more easily. It is an assumption that can be dropped later.

THE EQUILIBRIUM LEVEL OF NATIONAL INCOME

The significance of the equilibrium

We have now examined the main components of national income and we can therefore begin to discuss how they interrelate. Although there are withdrawals other than savings and injections other than investment we can, by examining these two, lay down the principles. We may then introduce the other injections and withdrawals at a later time. There is a tendency for the level of national income to reach an equilibrium, i.e. a level at which, other things being equal, it will remain stable. The equilibrium will be reached where the total of spending in the economy is equal to the total income. The significance of the equilibrium is that the level of employment depends upon the level of income. If the equilibrium is at too low a level of income then the result will be unemployment, whereas if the equilibrium level is too high there will be other unpleasant consequences such as inflation.

The equality of savings and investment

If the injections into the circular flow are greater than the withdrawals then, other things being equal, national income will rise. Conversely, if withdrawals are greater than injections, then national income will fall. If, as in Fig. 100, injections (I) are equal to withdrawals (S), then there is no tendency for the level of national income to change and it is in equilibrium.

We may summarise the situation like this.

(*a*) $I > S$ then national income will rise.
(*b*) $S > I$ then national income will fall.
(*c*) $S = I$ then national income is in equilibrium.

Thus, $S = I$ is the equilibrium condition for the economy. It would also follow that if there is a change in either S or I we will be returned to an equilibrium situation when $\Delta S = \Delta I$. Bearing in mind that the level of savings is directly determined by the level of income, the equilibrium of national income can be explained in the following way:

(*a*) if investment were greater than savings then national income would rise;
(*b*) if national income rises savings rise;
(*c*) this would continue until the increased savings equalled the original increased investment ($\Delta S = \Delta I$);
(*d*) the economy is returned to equilibrium at a *higher* level of income where once again $S = I$.

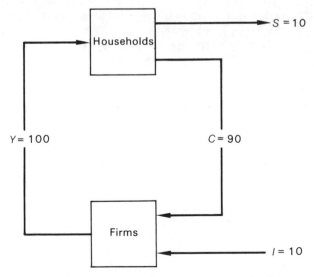

Fig. 100. *The circular flow in equilibrium: S = I.*

Conversely:

(*a*) if savings were greater than investment then national income would fall;

(*b*) if national income falls then savings fall;

(*c*) this would continue until savings were reduced to such a level that they once again equalled investment;

(*d*) the economy is returned to equilibrium at a *lower* level of income where once again $S = I$.

Thus, it can be seen that savings will always equal investment. This, however, is a *post factum* equilibrium. This means that although savings and investment may not equal each other at any particular time, they will when considered over a period of time.

The graphical analysis of national income

We have seen that savings and investment are dependent on quite different factors; savings tend to depend on the level of income whilst investment depends upon such things as the MEC. In this example the simplifying assumption has been made that investment is constant at £20 billion. This means that when it is plotted as a graph (*see* Fig. 101) it is a horizontal straight line (*I*). The consumption function utilises the data from Table XL and Fig. 98. If the amount of consumption is subtracted from the level of income the amount of savings is obtained. This can be plotted as a separate savings line (*S*). The savings line starts below the horizontal axis because at very low levels of income consumption exceeds income and therefore dissaving is taking place. Where the savings line crosses the horizontal axis (£40 billion) the whole of income is devoted to consumption so that we see the consumption function crossing the 45° line at the same level of income.

So far in this chapter we have assumed that there are two types of spending in the economy; spending on consumer goods (*C*) and spending on investment or producer goods (*I*). If these two are added together, they will give the total of spending on all types of goods and services in the economy. This is called aggregate demand or *aggregate monetary demand* (AMD). In the diagram above this is shown by the line $C + I$. The $C + I$ line is parallel to the consumption function since investment is constant. (Students often believe that the savings line is also parallel to the consumption function; this is not so as an examination of the diagram will verify.) As stated in the previous section of this chapter, the equilibrium level of national income is where the total of spending in the economy is equal to total income. Since the $C + I$ line represents total spending, the equilibrium level of income will therefore be where

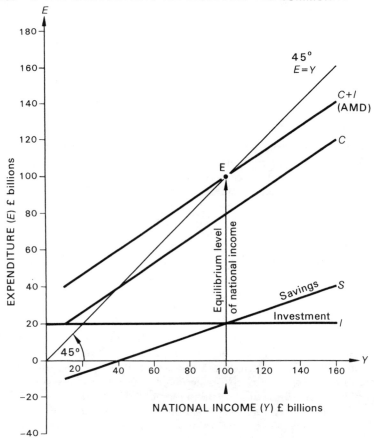

Fig. 101. *The equilibrium of national income.*

the $C + I$ line crosses the 45° line (£100 billion). You will see from the diagram that this is also the level of income at which savings equals investment. The diagram therefore demonstrates, once again, that the equilibrium level of national income is where $S = I$. Why this is so is demonstrated in Fig. 102. At point R the total withdrawals from the economy are equal to total injections ($S = I$) and the equilibrium level of national income is therefore D. If income were lower, for example B, then investment would be greater than savings and hence the tendency would be for national income to rise. On the other hand, if income were F then savings would be greater than investment and national income would therefore tend to fall.

It is worth reiterating that there is nothing necessarily desirable about the equilibrium level of national income. In Fig. 102 it could be

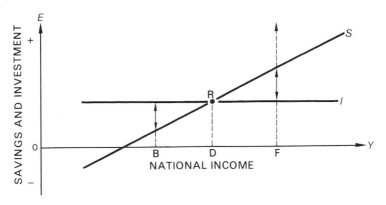

Fig. 102. *Savings equalling investment is the equilibrium condition for the economy.*

that the level of income which is necessary to maintain full employment is F but equilibrium level is lower than this, at D. There will therefore be unemployment. (This point is more fully developed on page 498.)

The paradox of thrift

Thriftiness is usually regarded as desirable. However, changes in the overall thriftiness of an economy can have some unusual consequences. If there is an autonomous increase in the level of savings, e.g. if for some reason households decide to devote a larger proportion of their incomes to savings but investment remains unchanged, then the savings line will move upwards. This is illustrated in Fig. 103. Here it can be seen that as the savings line shifts from S to S' so the equilibrium changes from R to R'. The effect of increased savings, therefore, is to *decrease* the equilibrium level of national income. This comes about because, if at a given level of income, people save more, they will automatically consume less. Therefore, there is less demand for goods and services. Since most incomes are derived, directly or indirectly, from the sale of goods and services, it follows that there will be less income. This is what brings about the paradox of thrift. The paradox can be further illustrated if we dispense with the assumption that investment is constant. We will now assume that investment is related to income. This is a fairly realistic assumption in that the production of more goods and services at a higher level of income will demand a greater capital stock and vice versa. The investment line now slopes upward from left to right. In Fig. 104, we again consider the effect of an upward shift in the savings line. Here the paradox is fully illustrated in that not only does increased saving bring about a lower level of

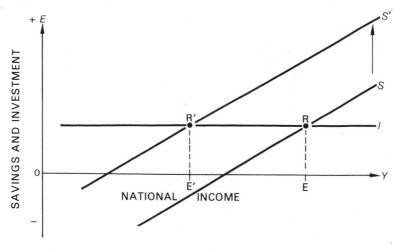

Fig. 103. *The paradox of thrift. Increased savings cause the equilibrium level of national income to fall.*

income and investment but it also leads ultimately to less being saved. This effect comes about because there is a lesser ability to save at the lower level of income.

The effect of increased thriftiness also depends upon the state of the economy. In times of inflation an increase in savings might reduce the inflationary pressure in the economy and therefore be a desirable thing. If, however, we have an economic depression with lots of unemployment an increase in thriftiness could be quite

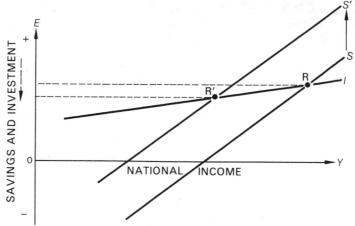

Fig. 104. *The paradox of thrift. Increased savings eventually lead to less being saved.*

disastrous, taking us into a vicious deflationary spiral. It would appear, therefore, that if we "tighten our belts" in times of economic depression, the depression is likely to be made even worse. This was well illustrated in the 1930s, the late 1970s and the early 1980s.

THE MULTIPLIER

In the previous section we considered the effect of a shift in the savings line. In Fig. 105 you can see the effect of an upward movement in the investment line. Here you can see that the equilibrium has moved from R to R' and that the equilibrium level of income has risen from D to E. You can also see that the rise in income D

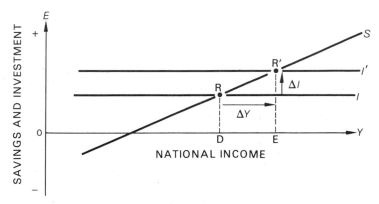

Fig. 105. *The multiplier effect.*

to E appears to be greater than the rise in investment I to I'. This is indeed so. If you turn back to Fig. 101 and imagine that investment were to increase by £10 billion, from £20 billion to £30 billion, you will see that the new equilibrium level of income would be £130 billion. In this case a rise in investment of £10 billion has caused an increase in income of £30 billion. This is known as the *multiplier effect*. If we measure the ratio of one to the other, that is the change in investment to the change in income, we obtain a figure known as the *multiplier* (K).

$$K = \frac{\Delta Y}{\Delta I}$$

$$K = \frac{30}{10}$$

$$K = 3$$

In this case the multiplier is 3. This means that every extra £1 of investment that is injected into the economy will eventually cause national income to rise by £3. This effect can also work downwards, so that if there were a decrease in investment this would cause a multiple decrease in national income.

The operation of the multiplier can be explained by taking a simple example. If a firm decides to construct a new building costing £1,000 then the income of the builders and suppliers of the raw materials will rise by £1,000. However, the process does not stop there. If we assume that the recipients of the £1,000 have a marginal propensity to consume 2/3 then they will spend £666.67 and save the rest. This spending causes extra income for another group of people. If we assume that they also have an MPC of 2/3 then they will spend £444.44 of the £666.67 and save the rest. This process will continue, with each new round of spending being 2/3 of the previous round. This a long chain of extra income, extra consumption and extra saving is set up.

	Additional income	*Additional savings*
1st Recipients	£1,000	£333.33
	+	+
2nd Recipients	£666.67	£222.22
	+	+
3rd Recipients	£444.44	£148.14
	+	+
4th Recipients	£296.30	£98.77
	+	+
5th Recipients	£197.53	£65.84
	+	+
. . .	. . .	. . .
Total	£2,999.99	£999.99
	or	or
	£3,000	£1,000

The process will come to a halt when the additions to savings total £1,000. This is because the change in savings is now equal to the change in investment and, therefore, the economy is returned to equilibrium because $S = I$ once again. At this point the additions to income total £3,000. Thus, £1,000 extra investment has created an extra £3,000 income, demonstrating that, in this case, the value of the multiplier is 3.

It would be rather cumbersome to work things out in this manner every time. Fortunately the figures above represent a well-known mathematical principle called an infinite geometric progression, which has the value of $1/(1 - r)$. In this case r represents the MPC. Thus, we can derive a formula for the multiplier, which is:

$$\text{the multiplier } (K) = \frac{1}{1 - \text{MPC}}$$

This can also be written as:

$$K = \frac{1}{MPS}$$

This is because MPC + MPS = 1. If the value of the MPC is 2/3, then:

$$K = \frac{1}{1 - 2/3}$$
$$= 3$$

THE ACCELERATOR

Induced and autonomous investment

So far in this chapter we have maintained that investment is determined by factors such as technological change, business expectations and the rate of interest. This investment is often termed *autonomous investment* because it is not determined by the working of the rest of the system in the way that, say, saving is determined by income. Indeed, for most of the chapter we have assumed that investment is constant. There is a theory, however, which maintains that new investment is determined by changes in the level of demand. Such investment is termed *induced investment* since it is induced by changes in the system. The relationship between the level of demand and the level of investment is called the *accelerator principle*. The level of aggregate demand in the economy may of course be equated with the level of income. The accelerator principle is that small changes in the *rate of change* of aggregate demand bring about much larger changes in the absolute level of investment demand. This is best explained by using a simple model of an economy.

A model of the accelerator

In this economy the initial capital stock is valued at £200m. When fully employed, this stock is just adequate to produce the £100m. of goods which constitute the aggregate demand in the economy for a year. That is to say, there is a capital–output ratio of 2 which means that a capital stock of £2 is necessary to produce a flow of output of £1. The capital in this economy has a life of five years and is replaced evenly so that a replacement investment of £40m. is needed to maintain the capital stock. This is illustrated in Year 1 in Table XLI.

TABLE XLI.   A MODEL OF THE ACCELERATOR
Capital–output ratio = 2
Capital is replaced over a five year period

Year (1)	Aggregate demand (2)	Capital stock required (3)	Investment		Total (6)
			Replacement (4)	Net (5)	
1	£100m.	£200m.	£40m.	—	£40m.
2	120	240	40	£40m.	80
3	130	260	40	20	60
4	140	280	40	20	60
5	120	240	—	—	—
6	120	240	40	—	40

In Year 2 demand rises by 20 per cent to £120m. To meet this demand the economy will need a capital stock of £240m. This is £40m. more than it has. Therefore in Year 2 the economy's demand for capital will be £40m. for replacement and an additional 40m. to meet the new demand. Thus, the total demand for capital is £80m. Between Year 1 and Year 2 a 20 per cent rise in aggregate demand has brought about a 100 per cent rise in investment demand. This is an illustration of the accelerator principle.

Now assume that in Year 3 demand rises to £130m. The capital stock required is now £260m. Therefore, there will be a demand for £20m. of extra capital, but the total demand for capital will have *fallen*. The capital demand is now £40m. for replacement and £20m. for the new capital. The £40m. of extra capital last year will not need replacing for a further five years. Therefore, although aggregate demand was still rising, capital demand has fallen. This is because when the *rate of increase* of aggregate demand falls the *absolute* level of induced investment will decline. This is further illustrated between Years 3 and 4 where the demand for capital is constant because the rate of increase is constant. Between Years 4 and 5 aggregate demand drops from £140m. to £120m. and the capital stock required, therefore, decreases from £280m. to £240m. There is therefore no need to replace the £40m. of capital stock which has worn out. Thus capital demand, both replacement and net, is eliminated. Finally, in Year 6 demand is stablised at £120m.;

it therefore becomes necessary to replace the £40m. of capital stock that will have worn out.

From this example it can be seen that the accelerator principle links the rate at which aggregate demand is changing to the absolute level of investment demand. It is because of this principle that the capital goods industries, such as shipbuilding, construction and iron and steel, tend to suffer from much more severe ups and downs in their fortunes than other sectors of the economy. For these industries it is often a case of "famine or feast".

A modified accelerator

From the example above it might be inferred that the capital goods sector of the economy is subject to massive reverses of fortunes. It should be remembered, however, that the accelerator principle only refers to induced investment. There is an addition to this autonomous investment. This is determined by other factors. Furthermore, we assumed that the capital stock of the country was fully employed and, therefore, that the additional demand could only be met by increasing investment. If there were unemployed capital in the economy, a rise in demand could be met by utilising the spare capacity. However, even if all the capital in the economy were fully employed, there are several factors which moderate the effect of the accelerator.

Firstly, businessmen learn from experience. This means that they are unlikely to double their capacity on the strength of one year's orders. Conversely, if demand is dropping, they might be willing to increase their inventories against a rise in demand in subsequent years. It may also be the case that the capital–output ratios are not as constant as suggested by our example. In the example it was assumed that £2 of capital was necessary to produce £1 of goods. If demand rose it might, however, be possible to obtain more output from the existing capital stock by varying the other factors of production. For example the workforce might undertake shift work or overtime to meet the extra demand.

Finally, the depreciation and replacement of capital might be a function of factors other than time. In our example it was assumed that the capital wore out after five years. If there was an increase in demand it might be possible to continue using old capital equipment after it was planned to scrap it. Often the period over which capital is depreciated is an accounting convenience and does not correspond to the physical life of the capital. Conversely, capital may become technologically obsolete long before it has physically depreciated.

The multiplier and the accelerator

Students frequently confuse the multiplier with the accelerator. From the above explanations of these two principles it can be seen that there is no direct relationship between them. Indeed, there is a great contrast between them in that for the accelerator to expand output it is necessary for the economy to be operating at or near capacity, whereas for the multiplier to affect output it is necessary that there be unemployed resources.

OTHER COMPONENTS OF NATIONAL INCOME

The economy we have been considering so far has been a closed economy with no government intervention, i.e. we have not considered the effects of the government and foreign trade upon national income. To obtain a full picture of the economy it is necessary to do so.

Government fiscal policy in income determination

The government's budget used to be regarded simply as a method of raising taxes to meet necessary expenditure. Since Keynes' analysis of national income we realise that the budget has other important effects. This is because taxation (T) is a withdrawal or leakage from the circular flow of income whilst government expenditure (G) is an injection or addition to the circular flow. Thus the effects of taxation and government spending are similar to those of savings and investment respectively. This is illustrated in Fig. 106.

If there is a *budget surplus*, i.e. taxation is greater than government spending, then, other things being equal, national income will fall. Conversely, if there is a *budget deficit*, i.e. government expenditure is greater than taxation, then the tendency is for national income to rise. Keynes realised that management of the government's budget could therefore be used to direct the economy. Directing the economy through government expenditure and taxes is referred to as *fiscal policy*.

The effect of government fiscal policy can be incorporated into the graphical analysis of national income. This is illustrated in Fig. 107. In the diagram you can see that in addition to consumption spending and investment spending we now add government spending (G). Thus total demand in the economy is now $C + I + G$. You should also note that there is a multiplier effect from government spending.

Other things being equal, if there were unemployment in the economy, the correct government policy would be to run a budget

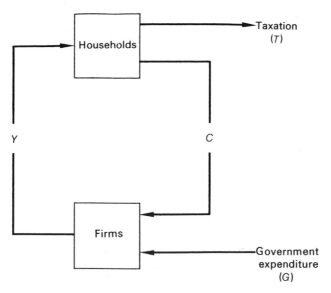

Fig. 106. *Fiscal policy in the circular flow of income.*

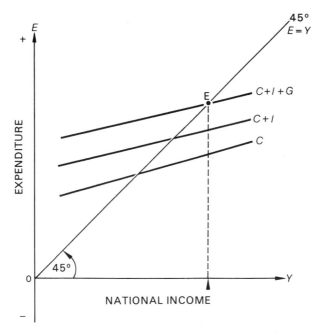

Fig. 107. *Government expenditure (G) as a component of aggregate demand.*

deficit, thereby increasing aggregate demand. Conversely, if there were too much spending in the economy, i.e. inflation, then the correct fiscal policy would be to run a budget surplus.

Foreign trade in income determination

Exports (X) may be regarded as an injection into the circular flow of income. This is because money will flow into the country in return for the goods exported, thereby creating additional income. Imports (M), on the other hand, are a leakage since we must send money out of the country to pay for them. If there is a *trade surplus*, i.e. exports are greater than imports, the tendency will be for national income to rise. A *trade deficit*, however, will decrease the level of national income. Hence the external trading position is crucial for the health of the economy.

We now have a complete picture of the components of national income. This is illustrated in Fig. 108. Aggregate demand for the economy is now $C + I + G + (X - M)$. Foreign trade may be incorporated into the graphical analysis of national income in a similar way to fiscal policy. There will therefore also be a multiplier effect from foreign trade.

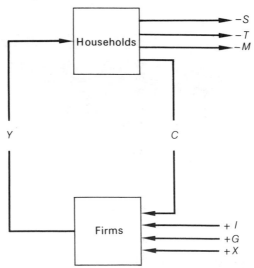

Fig. 108. *The components of national income.*

A combined multiplier for the economy

Earlier in this chapter we derived a formula for the multiplier:

$$K = 1/\text{MPS}$$

It is now apparent that savings is not the only leakage from the circular flow of income. A formula for the whole economy must also take account of taxation (T) and imports (M). If we total the leakages we would therefore obtain a formula:

$$K = \frac{1}{s + t + m}$$

where s is the marginal propensity to save, t is the marginal propensity to pay taxes and m is the marginal propensity to import. If, for example, $s = 0.15$, $t = 0.10$ and $m = 0.25$ then the value of the multiplier would be:

$$K = \frac{1}{0.15 + 0.10 + 0.25} = 2$$

Inflationary and deflationary gaps

At any particular time there is a level of national income, which, if attained would be sufficient to keep all resources in the economy

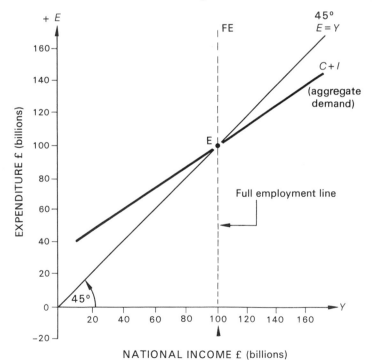

Fig. 109. *The aggregate demand line and the full employment line. The other components of national income have been omitted to simplify the diagram.*

fully employed. In Fig. 109 this is represented by the vertical line FE, the full employment line. In this diagram the equilibrium level of national income, £100 billion, corresponds with the full employment level. It has already been stressed, however, that the equilibrium level of national income is fortuitous.

If there is insufficient demand in the economy the equilibrium will occur at a lower level of income and to the left of the FE line. This is illustrated in Fig. 110(a). Here you can see that the equilibrium level of national income is £40 billion and there is therefore severe unemployment in the economy. The distance between the 45° line and the $C + I$ line at the full employment level of national income is referred to as a *deflationary gap*. In order for unemployment to be eliminated the $C + I$ line must be moved up by £20 billion. Why would extra spending of £20 billion raise national income by £60 billion? The answer is that in this case the multiplier is 3. In Fig. 110(b) the equilibrium level of national income appears to be to the right of the FE line at £160 billion. This is because people in the economy are trying to buy more goods and services than can be produced at full employment. There is "too much money chasing too few goods". The result of this is that excess demand forces up prices and there is inflation. The demand for goods and services has thus been met but only in money terms. The vertical distance between the $C + I$ line and the 45° line at the full employment level of income is referred to as an inflationary gap. In this example it would be necessary to lower the $C + I$ line by £20 billion to eliminate inflation. Again note that, because of the multiplier, cutting expenditure by £20 billion causes income to decline by £60 billion.

This is only one explanation of inflation—another explanation was mentioned earlier in the chapter. The origins of inflation are more fully discussed in Chapter 23.

NATIONAL INCOME ACCOUNTS

In this chapter we have considered the theory of how national income is determined. We now consider how the government measures national income. The figures are published annually every September by HMSO as the *National Income and Expenditure Accounts*, this publication usually being known as the "Blue Book". The figures are also to be found in the *Annual Abstract of Statistics* and the *Monthly Digest of Statistics*.

National income is measured in three different ways: as national income, national output and national expenditure. The idea of this is to give a measure of all the wealth produced, distributed and consumed in the economy over the period of a year. Since "every-

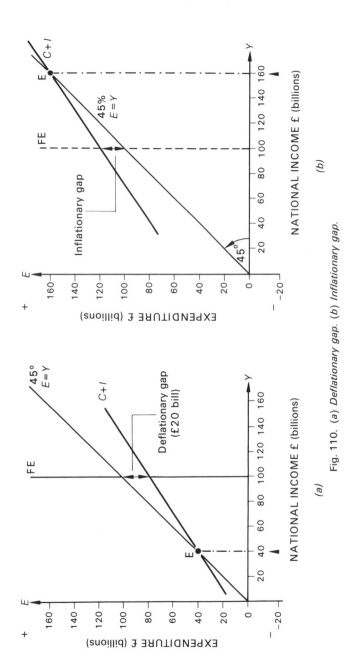

Fig. 110. (a) Deflationary gap. (b) Inflationary gap.

one's income is someone else's expenditure", it should be clear that the three are different ways of arriving at the same figure. Hence, we can arrive at the statement:

National income = National output = National expenditure

That is to say, National income is the total of the incomes of the inhabitants of the country, which should be equal to the value of all the goods and services in the economy (the production of which gives rise to incomes). This, in turn, should be equal to the value of all expenditure on goods and services, both consumer goods and capital (investment) goods.

National expenditure method

The national expenditure method of calculating national income is thought to be the most accurate. It is also the method which most closely corresponds with the way in which we have examined the components of national income. If you examine Fig. 111 and Table XLII together you will see this correspondence. Thus, if we consider items (1) to (7) we arrive at a total for the gross domestic product (GDP) in the same way that the total $C + I + G + (X - M)$.

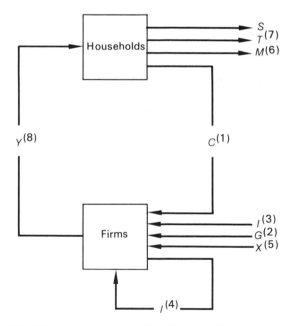

Fig. 111. *The components of national income. The numbered items correspond to items in Table XLII. See also Fig. 108.*

However, much of the investment that has taken place has been to cover depreciation, and therefore we must subtract *capital consumption*. After the minor adjustment for *net property income from abroad* we arrive at the figure for the national income (net national product). Thus we have demonstrated that national income $(Y) = C + I + G + (X - M)$.
We will consider some of the items in the account in more detail.

TABLE XLII. GROSS NATIONAL PRODUCT BY CATEGORY OF EXPENDITURE (EXPENDITURE METHOD) 1980

Category of expenditure	£ million
(1) Consumers expenditure (*C*)	135,403
(2) General government final consumption (*G*)	48,337
(3) Gross domestic fixed capital formation (*I*)	40,050
(4) Value of physical increase in stocks and work in progress (*I*)	−3,596
(5) Exports of goods and services (*X*)	63,198
(6) *less* Imports of goods and services (*M*)	−57,832
Gross domestic product (GDP) at market prices	225,560
Factor cost adjustments	
(7) *less* Taxes on expenditure (*T*)	37,287
Subsidies	5,215
Gross domestic product (GDP) at factor cost	193,488
Net property income from abroad	−38
Gross national product (GNP) at factor cost	193,450
less Capital consumption	−27,045
(8) National income (*Y*) (i.e. net national product [NNP])	166,405

Source: National Income and Expenditure, CSO

Consumers' expenditure
This includes all the consumers' expenditure on goods and services except for the purchase of new houses, which is included in "gross fixed capital formation".

General government final consumption
The main portion of this is the provision by the government of "public" and "merit" goods such as defence and education. Since these are not "sold" to consumers at an economic price they are, here, calculated at their cost of production.

Gross domestic fixed capital formation
Fixed capital formation is the major portion of *investment* in the economy. It is shown in Fig. 111 as being carried out by firms, but in fact investment is undertaken by firms, government and households and it includes such things as the construction of new factories, hospitals and houses.

The value of physical increases in stocks and work in progress
It is quite likely that the stocks of goods held by businesses at the end of the year will be different from that at the beginning. The difference in the value of these stocks is counted as part of investment in the economy. It is possible, however, for this figure to be positive or negative.

Exports and imports
Exports create income for persons in this country and are therefore added to national income, whereas imports create income for persons overseas and thus are subtracted from national income.

Foreign trade is extremely important to the UK and in 1980 32.7 per cent of our resources were taken up in producing goods and services for export. On the other hand we imported goods and services to the value of 30 per cent of our GDP.

Gross domestic product (GDP)
When we total all the above amounts we arrive at a figure known as the *gross domestic product at market prices*. This is the value of national income (net of foreign trade) in terms of money actually spent. This, however, is misleading since the price of many articles includes taxes or subsidies. To obtain the value of national income in terms of the resources used to produce it we must subtract the taxes on expenditure levied by the government and add on the amount of subsidies. When this has been done we arrive at a figure known as the *gross domestic product at factor cost*. This is the most commonly used measure of national income and you will see that it appears in all three modes of measurement.

Gross national product (GNP)
The GDP represents the extent to which resources (or factors) are used in the economy. National income can, however, be affected by rent, profits, interest and dividends paid to, or received from, overseas. This is shown in Table XLII as *net property income from abroad*. This figure may be either positive or negative. When this has been taken into account we arrive at the *gross national product at factor cost*.

Net national product (*NNP*)

The capital stock of the country such as roads, factories, machines, etc., gradually wears out. Part of the gross fixed capital formation is, therefore, to replace worn out capital and this is referred to as *capital consumption*. When this has been subtracted we arrive at a figure known as the *net national product*. The NNP gives the measure of national income in that it represents the most important determinant of the standard of living. The GDP, on the other hand, gives a measure of the extent to which resources are being utilised in the economy.

National income method

Table XLIII illustrates the second method by which national income is measured. Here you can see that income from all different sources is totalled to give the GDP.

The imputed charge for the consumption of non-trading capital is principally the imputed rent for owner-occupied houses. To arrive at the GDP an amount for stock appreciation must be deducted.

TABLE XLIII. GROSS NATIONAL PRODUCT BY CATEGORY OF INCOME
(INCOME METHOD) 1980

Category of income	£ million
Income from employment	137,083
Income from self-employment	18,394
Gross trading profits of companies	24,979
Gross trading surpluses of public corporations and government enterprises	6,185
Rent	13,231
Imputed charge for consumption of non-trading capital	2,138
less Stock appreciation	−6,477
Gross domestic product (GDP) (income based)	195,533
Residual error	−2,045
Gross domestic product (GDP) (expenditure based*)	193,488
Net property income from abroad	−38
Gross national product (GNP)	193,450
less Capital consumption	−27,045
National income (*Y*) (i.e. net national product [NNP])	166,405

* *see* Table XLII.

Source: National Income and Expenditure, CSO

Goods produced earlier in the year may appreciate in value whilst they are being stored; to include this increase would exaggerate their value (in terms of factor cost). This may be contrasted with item (4) in Table XLII where there was a *physical* increase in stocks, whilst here we are only faced with a change in the money value. When calculating national income by this method, the government must be careful not to include transfer payments. These are things such as old age pensions and unemployment benefits which are transfers of income from other sections of the community in return for which there is no corresponding production of goods or services.

When the GDP has been calculated by the income method it may be compared with the GDP obtained by the expenditure method. This will show the *residual error*, which is a measure of the statistical inaccuracy between the two methods. At £2,045 million it may seem like a large amount, but it is only 1.0 per cent of the GDP. By making the same adjustments as in Table XLII we can then arrive at the figures for GNP and NNP.

National output method
The final method by which national income is calculated is to total the contributions made by the various sectors (industries) of the economy. This is illustrated in Table XLIV, where, as you can see,

TABLE XLIV. GROSS DOMESTIC PRODUCT BY INDUSTRY
(OUTPUT METHOD) 1980

Industry	£ million
Agriculture, forestry and fishing	4,296
Petroleum and natural gas	7,649
Other mining and quarrying	3,222
Manufacturing	48,060
Construction	13,025
Gas, electricity and water	5,803
Transport	10,084
Communication	5,326
Distributive trades	19,328
Insurance, banking, finance and business services	18,288
Ownership of dwellings	11,996
Professional and scientific services	25,467
Miscellaneous services	18,734
Public administration and defence	13,987
Total	205,265
Adjustment for financial services	−9,732
Residual error	−2,045
Gross domestic product (GDP) at factor cost	193,488

Source: National Income and Expenditure, CSO

the largest contribution comes from the manufacturing sector. This is hardly surprising in a highly industrialised economy such as the UK. When calculating the GDP in this manner the government must be careful to avoid *double counting*. To do this only the value added by each business should be included. For example, the value of the steel in motor vehicles should not be included if it has already been counted in the steel industry. In Table XLIV the figures for the various sectors are shown before allowance has been made for the net interest payments on their borrowing. This is allowed for as the composite figure *adjustments for financial services*. After this and the *residual error* have been allowed for, then, we arrive at the GDP at factor cost. By then making adjustments for net property income from abroad and for capital consumption we can arrive at the GNP and the NNP.

CONCLUSION

Figure 112 attempts to summarise some of the main components of national income discussed in this chapter. The most important aspect is the level of income, because on this depends the whole well-being of the economy. As you can see from the diagram this is mainly determined by the interaction of savings and investment. Some of the factors which influence savings and investment are also shown in the diagram. The government and foreign trade have been omitted.

It has been emphasised from the beginning of the chapter that the economy is not self-regulating. Left to itself the equilibrium level of national income will not necessarily be that which is best for the welfare of society. Therefore it is up to the government to intervene in the economy to make sure that the level of aggregate demand is appropriate.

SELF-ASSESSMENT QUESTIONS

A. 1. Define: (*a*) savings; (*b*) APC; (*c*) induced investment; (*d*) fiscal policy.

B. 2. True or false?

(*a*) The higher the level of income the greater will be the proportion devoted to consumption.

(*b*) The APC is usually greater than the MPC.

(*c*) A budget deficit will increase the size of the national income.

(*d*) An increase in aggregate demand will have an accelerator effect upon investment if there is spare capacity in the economy.

(*e*) Aggregate demand $= C + I + G + M$.

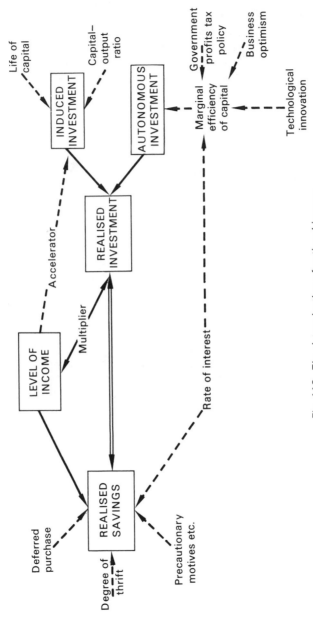

Fig. 112. *The determination of national income.*

C. 3. True or false?

(a) The quantity theory of money calculates the price level as $P = MV/T$.

(b) If MPS $= 2/10$ then the multiplier $= 10$.

(c) If investment increased by £1,000 and the MPC is 4/5 then, other things being equal, national income will rise by £4,000.

(d) If savings exceeds investment, taxation exceeds government expenditure and imports exceed exports then national income must fall.

(e) If there is a deflationary gap of £40m. and the MPC is 3/4 then increased investment of £10m. should eliminate it.

ASSIGNMENTS

1. The following data refers to personal disposable income and savings in the UK. (All figures in £ millions.)

Year	1971	1972	1973	1974	1975
Disposable income	£38,562	44,679	51,911	60,051	73,880
Saving	2,963	4,496	6,152	7,383	9,131

Year	1976	1977	1978	1979	1980
Disposable income	£84,832	96,360	113,761	136,852	160,821
Saving	9,880	10,359	14,814	20,135	25,418

Source: National Income and Expenditure, HMSO

(a) Update this information.

(b) Construct a table similar to Table XL and enter this information on it.

(c) Calculate consumption, the APC, and MPC and enter them in the table.

(d) With this information construct a consumption function similar to Fig. 98.

(e) How would you account for the observed variations in the size of the APC?

2. Reconstruct Table XLI assuming that the replacement period for capital is now not five years but ten years (columns (1)–(3) will be unchanged).

Financial Organisations

Banks are the most important of financial organisations. They provide several essential services to both the business organisation and the individual. Banking services sold overseas are also one of Britain's main export earners.

Banks act like *ledger clerks* for both individuals and businesses, providing a record of financial transactions. A bank statement is the closest the average individual gets to statement of his personal finances. Banks also constitute the most important channel for the settlement of debts. They are also a source of finance and a place where cash can be readily and easily deposited to gain interest. In addition to this, banks today provide many other services: tax advice, executor and trustee services, stockbroking, insurance, etc. However, if we look at the bank's place in the whole economy we will see that its most vital function is none of these; its function is in fact the creation of money. We will, therefore, first have a look at money and then go on to see how banks set about creating it.

MONEY

What is money?

Anything that is readily acceptable as a means of payment is money. Many different things have been used as money—cowrie shells, camels, cigarettes, pigs' teeth—but the most common form of money throughout most of man's history has been precious metals. Only one civilisation, the Incas, has flourished without some form of money. Today, bank notes, coins and bank deposits all form part of our money supply. Only notes and coins, however, are *legal tender* and yet they do not constitute the major part of the money supply.

A contrast between modern money and the old forms of money, for example gold or livestock, is that the old forms had *intrinsic value* whilst money today, almost exclusively, has only *exchange value*. Also, money is today created by governments or business organisations so that in examining these organisations we are also examining the creation of the money supply.

Listed below are some of the attributes that are necessary for something to function as money. From this it should be apparent not only why camels ceased to be used as money but also why such things as cigarettes function as money when paper money loses some of these important attributes.

Acceptability
The most important attribute of money is that it be readily acceptable. It does not, however, have to be universally acceptable.

Difficult to counterfeit
It is no good using something as money which people may readily forge.

Durability
Money should not wear out quickly. Unfortunately this is a problem with pound notes which are wearing out much more quickly now than they used to.

Stability of value
Inflation affects the acceptability of money. In 1923 it made it completely unacceptable in Germany.

Portability
It would not be very convenient to use coal as money as we would have to take a tonne of it to do the week's shopping.

Uniformity
Money should be uniform so that we may divide it into smaller amounts, e.g. the pound note into 100 pence. It should also not be the case that one form of money differs from another. For example, if gold coins circulated today everyone would be tempted to hold the gold thus pushing it out of circulation. This illustrates *Gresham's law*, "bad money drives out good".

What does money do?

Money is so much part of our lives today that we perhaps fail to recognise the jobs which it does.

(*a*) *A medium of exchange.* Its most vital function is to act as a medium of exchange, i.e., the means by which we swop one lot of real goods or services for another. For example a man exchanges his labour for food, clothing, etc., through the medium of money.

(*b*) *A unit of account.* All the many disparate commodities which make up the economy—suits of clothes, litres of oil, visits to the cinema—can all be reduced to a common unit of account and hence compared in value by giving them a price. Of course, one might argue that many things on which one places great value command little or no price.

However the accountant, the banker, the lawyer and the economist are interested only in exchange value, i.e. the price. Perhaps at this stage we might recall Oscar Wilde's famous comment: "What is a cynic? A man who knows the price of everything and the value of nothing."

(*c*) *A store of wealth.* If we did not have money and we wished to save we would have to stockpile the things which we thought we would need in the future. This would be most inconvenient and we might find our requirements changing. Money allows us a convenient means of saving up for any requirement.

(*d*) *A standard of deferred payment.* Money is the means by which we are able to settle debts in the future. Hence we can agree to work for so many pounds a year or the bank can agree to pay us *x* per cent interest on each pound we deposit with it.

It hardly needs saying that without the medium of money the economy would not have developed and would not continue to develop. It is important to note that bad management of the country's money supply can hinder the development of the economy since the functions which money carries out are essential to the economy's well-being.

Where does money come from?

Both paper money and modern banking practice originated from the activities of goldsmiths. Goldsmiths used to accept deposits of gold coin for safe-keeping and in return issue a receipt which was in effect a *promissory note*. As time went by these notes began to be passed around in settlement of debts, acting as bank notes do today. Goldsmiths also discovered that they need not keep all the gold they had on deposit in their vaults because at any particular time only a small percentage of their customers would want their gold back. Thus they discovered that they could lend out, say, 90 per cent of their gold deposits, keeping only 10 per cent to meet the demands of their depositors. This relationship of the cash kept to liabilities to pay is known as the *cash ratio*. Because he had put most of the gold he had accepted on deposit back into circulation and also circulated promissory notes for the amount of gold he had accepted the goldsmith could be said to have *created money*.

Some of the gold which the goldsmith had lent out would be used to pay bills and then the recipient would redeposit it with the same or another goldsmith. Then the process would be repeated, writing out more promissory notes and relending the gold. The limit to this process was that he always had to keep the equivalent of 10 per cent of his liabilities in gold. The banker, for this is what the goldsmith had become by this time, did not really create money, because he could not spend it. However, he could lend it out at interest and so he was said to have *created credit*.

The completion of this process occurred in the 1680s when Francis Childs became the first banker to print bank notes. Today this process of credit creation lies at the heart of our money supply. Originally the gold had intrinsic value and the paper money was issued on the faith in the bank. Any currency issued that was not backed by an equal amount of gold was called a *fiduciary issue*. Today, banks create credit in the form of cheque money against the security of Bank of England notes in the same manner that the old banks created bank notes on the security of gold. Today, however, it can be seen that the whole edifice of money rests on confidence in the banking system, since all bank notes are now fiduciary issue. The creation of credit is kept under control by the Bank of England, since it issues the bank notes and insists upon the banks maintaining specific ratios of assets to liabilities.

Changes in the value of money
One thing which could not happen whilst a bank note was backed by a specific quantity of gold was that its value could not change unless the value of gold changed. Today money has value only in so far as it can be exchanged for goods. Changes in the value of money affect adversely some of its most important functions.

The most common acceptable measure of the value of money is the *retail prices index* (RPI). In this the prices of some 3,500 goods are sampled and their importance *weighted* in eleven major categories. All these items are then combined to give one index number. Thus, if we start off in 1975 at 100 and in 1982 discover that the index is 265 this means that on average prices have gone up by 165 per cent or alternatively, that the pound in 1982 is only 37.8 per cent of its 1975 value.

HOW BANKS CREATE MONEY

A single bank system

Let us imagine there is only one bank, not a small bank, but a large bank with which every one in the country does business. This bank has initial deposits of £10,000 in cash so that its balance sheet would be:

Liabilities (£)		*Assets* (£)	
Deposits	10,000	Cash	10,000

The bank knows from experience, however, that only a tenth of this money will be demanded at any particular time and so it is able to lend out £9,000 at interest. The people who borrow this money use it to buy things. The shopkeepers, etc., who receive this money then put it into the bank and the bank finds that the £9,000 it lent out has been redeposited. This could be described as a *created deposit*. It is then able to repeat this process lending out nine-tenths of this £9,000 and retaining £900. The £8,100 it has lent out will find its way back to the bank again when it can again lend out nine-tenths of it and so on. This is illustrated in Fig. 113.

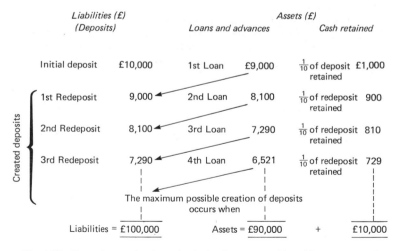

Fig. 113. *Deposit creation in a single bank system with a 10 per cent cash ratio.*

Thus, at the end of the process, with total cash of £10,000 in the system and a cash ratio of 10 per cent, the bank is able to make loans amounting to £90,000. Although so many more deposits have been created, you will see that everything balances out because the bank still has the necessary 1/10 of its assets in cash to meet its liabilities. You can also see that each horizontal line in Fig. 113 balances assets against liabilities and, therefore, at no stage are accounting principles infringed. The bank's balance sheet at the end of this process would appear:

Liabilities (£)		Assets (£)	
Initial deposits	10,000	Cash	10,000
Created deposits	90,000	Loans and advances	90,000
	£100,000		£100,000

N.B.: The bank itself cannot distinguish between initial deposits and created deposits. The limit to credit creation in this manner is the cash ratio—here it is 10 per cent. If it were 5 per cent created deposits could amount to £190,000 whereas if it were 20 per cent they could only be £40,000.

A multi-bank system

If we consider a system in which there are many banks, credit creation will go on in the same manner, except that money which is loaned out may find its way into a bank other than the one which made it. This is illustrated below where we assume that there are two banks in the system. Here each bank has raised the cash ratio to 12.5 per cent to guard against the possibility of losing potential deposits to the other bank. The initial £10,000 is divided equally between them and with a cash ratio of 12.5 per cent they are able to create deposits of seven times this amount.

Bank X

Liabilities (£)		Assets	
Initial deposits	5,000	Cash	5,000
Created deposits	35,000	Lo	35,000
	£40,000		

the bank must always be prepared to meet depositors demands for notes and coins.

The assets which a bank has will have differing maturity dates. For example, the bank might be able to turn a short-run loan to another bank into cash overnight, but a loan to a customer given over a five-year period will be much more difficult to liquify. The Bank of England has therefore laid down that banks should have *liquid assets* to cover their liabilities in proportions which are related to maturity dates of their liabilities. Thus much greater cover would be expected for short-run liabilities than for long-run ones. For example, liabilities with a maturity of over one year might require only 5 per cent liquid asset cover whilst short-run money market deposits might well require 100 per cent cover. Thus the liquid asset cover which a bank requires will depend upon the type of deposits it has accepted. It is therefore no longer possible to state it as a simple ratio; it will differ from bank to bank and from time to time. The clearing banks whose activities are relatively stable might well have a predictable ratio but this will differ from other members of the *monetary sector*.

Coins and notes

These are reserves of cash kept by the banks. Since 1971 there has been no requirement to keep a specific percentage. The amount of cash which a bank has to keep in hand will depend upon the type of business it does. All banks will naturally want to keep as small a proportion of their assets in cash as possible, because holdings of cash do not earn income.

Balances with the Bank of England

These are deposits of cash made by the banks at the Bank of England. They now take two forms, the non-operational accounts equivalent to 0.5 per cent of the banks' *eligible liabilities* and balances kept to operate the *clearing house* system. All cheques drawn by customers on their bank accounts go through the Clearing House at 10 Lombard Street. Here they are totalled so that at the end of each day the indebtedness of one bank to another can be settled by one transaction. This is done by the debtor bank transferring money from his Bank of England account to that own creditor bank. The five banks which operate this system then it as clearing banks. notes and

If we consider the balance sheet of the clears is becomes apparent that the proportion of balances with the Bank of England to per cent.

Market loans

The market referred to is the *London money market*, which is described in detail later in the chapter. The loans consist of money lent to other banks or to the discount houses. The money is usually lent *at call* (for one day at a time) or *short notice* (usually seven days). All banks must now agree to maintain an average of 6 per cent of their *eligible liabilities* in the form of secured loans to the discount market.

Certificates of deposit (CDs)

If a company agrees to deposit cash with a bank for, say, two years, it will receive a high rate of interest. However it may want its money back before then. It can have the best of both worlds by accepting a *certificate of deposit* which is *negotiable*, i.e. it can sell it on the money market if it wants its cash before the two years are up. CDs can be in sterling or in other currencies.

Local authority deposits

These are loans made through the money market to local authorities. Local authorities also issue bills and bonds in a similar manner to central government.

UK Treasury bills

These are Treasury bills (*see* page 522) which are bought by the banks from the discount houses, usually when they have only five or six weeks left to maturity.

Other bills

There are commercial *bills of exchange* issued by companies who wish to borrow money for a short period.

Special deposits

If the Bank of England wishes to control the banks' lending it may call upon them to make special deposits of cash with it. This would reduce bank lending in the multiple manner described on page 533. Usually the Bank of England calls for special deposits in amounts of 0.5 per cent or 1 per cent of the bank's assets. As you can see in Table XLV, at this particular time the Bank had not called for any al deposits.

Government stocks

These are bills, s to the British government other than Treasury bills. The ba   ays try to ensure that it has a *maturing portfolio*   e. that a quantity of these mature each week so that the bank has the option of liquidating its asset or re-investing.

Advances
These are bank loans and overdrafts to customers. Usually they earn a rate of interest at least 2 per cent higher than base rate and constitute the chief earning asset of the bank. In our example they constitute 44.6 per cent of assets. This is a typical ratio.

Liquidity

Until August 1981 banks were required to keep 12.5 per cent of their assets in the form of *reserve assets*. As explained above, this requirement has now been dropped and the liquidity required of a bank now depends upon the type of business it does. Banks must always maintain liquidity for *prudential* reasons and the assets which banks considered liquid before 1981 were around 33 per cent, i.e. considerably greater than the *reserve assets ratio*.

The new integrated approach to banks' liquidity does not closely define which assets are acceptable, as the old ratio did. However, the assets which the Bank of England considers as liquid are very similar to the old reserve assets. These are:

(*a*) balances with the Bank of England;
(*b*) money at call with the London money market;
(*c*) UK Treasury bills;
(*d*) local authority and bank bills eligible for rediscount at the Bank of England;
(*e*) British government stocks with less than one year to maturity.

THE REGULATION OF BANKING

Until recently there was little *statutory* regulation of banking in the UK. The Bank of England exercised control through *moral suasion* and through the operation of monetary policy. This has been partly changed by the introduction of the Banking Act 1979 but the Bank still tends to proceed by laying down guidelines which it expects the banks to follow. From 1971 to 1981 the Bank's guidelines were known as *competition and credit control*. The main change brought in by competition and credit control in 1971 was the dropping of the old *liquid assets ratio* of 28 per cent and its replacement by the 12.5 per cent *reserve assets ratio*. This brought about a massive expansion of bank credit which was one of the major causes of the high rates of inflation in the early and mid-1970s.

The 1970s saw great upheavals in the financial world. In 1973 there was the secondary banking crisis which forced the Bank of England to organise the "lifeboat" operation in order to save a number of fringe banks from collapse. Another factor was the oil crisis which vastly increased the amount of money in the money markets. Finally the 1970s saw a great influx of foreign banks into London. It is hardly surprising, therefore, that the government and the Bank of England have found it necessary to bring in new regulations for banks.

The Banking Act 1979

On 1 October 1979 two new Acts came into force, the Banking Act and the Credit Unions Act. The Banking Act gave the Bank of England statutory powers to supervise banks and other "deposit-taking institutions". There are three main parts to the Act.

(a) *Licensing of banks.* It became an offence for any institution to accept deposits unless it was licensed by the Bank of England. It also created two classes of deposit-taking institutions, *banks* and *licensed deposit takers* (LDTs). To be licensed as a bank an institution must have considerable funds and offer a wide range of banking services or a highly specialised banking service. In addition to this several other stringent criteria must be met. Deposit-taking institutions who do not offer a wide range of services may be allowed to operate as LDTs. The Bank has the power to revoke a licence or the recognition as a bank, demote a recognised institution to an LDT, or grant only a conditional licence. These powers brought the UK into line with the EEC banking directive that all member states must have a system of authorising banks by mid-December 1979.

(b) *The deposit protection scheme.* The aim of the scheme is to give protection to small depositors in the event of a bank failure. This part of the Act was a response to the secondary-banking crisis of 1973 and the "lifeboat" operation which had to be mounted to protect depositors. The scheme is similar to the Federal Deposit Insurance Corporation (FDIC) in the USA. The scheme is administered by the Deposit Protection Board which consists of representatives of the contributory institutions. The Governor of the Bank is chairman. The Board administers the Deposit Protection Fund, to which all banks and licensed institutions must contribute. No contributor's initial payment may be less than £5,000 or greater than £300,000. The size of each contribution is decided by the size of the institution's assets. No contributor is asked to contribute more than 0.3 per cent of its deposit base (unless that amounts to less than £5,000).

In the event of an institution becoming insolvent the Fund will pay the depositor an amount equal to three-quarters of his deposit, up to the maximum of the first £10,000 of any deposit. (The FDIC scheme repays all of the deposit up to the first $100,000.)

(c) *Banking names and advertisements*. Only recognised banks and certain other named institutions may use the title bank or banker. The other named institutions include the Bank of England, trustee savings banks and the National Savings Bank. Foreign institutions may use the name they operate under in their home territory provided that it is accompanied by an indication that the institution is formed under the law of that territory. The Bank also has powers to regulate the form and content of any advertisement inviting the making of deposits.

The reasons for passing the Act were the need to comply with EEC directives and also the desire to avoid another banking crisis like that of 1973. It is not clear, however, whether the Act is meant to insure consumers against bank failures or to prevent bank failures occurring. If the latter is the case there would be little need for the deposit protection scheme. Amongst other miscellaneous provisions the Act also requires the Bank of England to collect a much greater amount of information from both UK and overseas deposit-taking institutions.

Monetary control provisions 1981

New regulations came into force on 20 August 1981 and are set out in the Bank of England paper *Monetary control—provisions*. The main points of the provisions are as follows.

(a) Each institution in the *monetary sector* is required to keep 0.5 per cent of its *eligible liabilities* in a non-operational account at the Bank of England.

(b) A new "monetary sector" somewhat broader than the old "banking sector" has been defined. It includes:

(i) all recognised banks and LDTs (ninety-six in all);

(ii) National Girobank;

(iii) banks in the Channel Isles and Isle of Man;

(iv) the trustee savings banks (TSBs);

(v) the Banking Department of the Bank of England.

(c) Eligible liabilities are to be calculated in an integrated uniform manner for all institutions (*see* above, page 515).

(d) The special deposit scheme is retained.

(e) The list of institutions whose acceptances are eligible for discount at the Bank has been widened.

(*f*) The *reserve assets ratio* was abolished.

(*g*) The Bank of England discontinued the regular "posting" of the *minimum lending rate*. Instead it operates within an unstated band of interest rates. However, it retains the right to announce the rate at which it will operate if it thinks this necessary.

OTHER FINANCIAL ORGANISATIONS

Discount houses

The discount houses are a group of eleven financial organisations who make their income primarily from discounting Treasury bills. Treasury bills are sold every week by the Bank of England on behalf of the government. They are a method of borrowing and constitute part of the national debt. A Treasury bill is a promise by the government to pay a specific sum (£10,000) ninety-one days after the date they are issued. A discount house might offer to buy the bill for, say £9,750, in which case it has cost the government £250 to borrow £9,750 for ninety-one days. This is equivalent to an annual rate of interest of just over 10 per cent. The Treasury bill rate is, however, not a true interest rate; it is the rate of discount and is calculated in the following manner:

$$\left(\frac{250}{10,000} \times \frac{100}{1}\right) \times \frac{365}{91} = 10\%$$

The discount houses often resell these bills to the clearing banks before maturity. The nearer the bill is to maturity the closer the price will be to £10,000.

If interest rates are falling this will cause discount houses to tender at a higher price. Conversely, if interest rates rise the price the government can expect will obviously fall since the price of the bill and rate of interest are inversely proportionate to one another. The interest on a bill is therefore formed by its being sold at a "discount", and it is from this that the market takes its name.

TABLE XLVI. THE DISCOUNT HOUSES IN ORDER OF
ASSETS CONTROLLED

1. Gerrard & National Discount Co.
2. Unison Discount Co. of London
3. Cater Ryder & Co.
4. Alexanders Discount Co.
5. Smith St Aubyn & Co. (Holdings)
6. Joseph Toynbee & Co.
7. King and Shaxson
8. Clive Discount Holdings
9. Allen Harvey & Ross
10. Gillett Brothers Discount Co.
11. Seacombe, Marshall & Campion

The discount houses obtain most of their funds by borrowing money from the clearing banks at call or short notice. Thus they borrow at a slightly lower rate of interest than they charge the Government and in this manner they make their profits. The banks are pleased with this arrangement since it allows them to lend money for only twenty-four hours at a time instead of ninety-one days, thereby giving them an asset almost as liquid as cash but earning some interest. If a bank calls in its money from a discount house it is usually to settle an inter-bank debt. The discount house is then usually able to re-borrow the money from the creditor bank. In the event of all banks calling in money, the discount houses will be forced, in the last resort, to borrow from the Bank of England. The rate at which the Bank was willing to lend used to be announced every week and was termed the minimum lending rate (MLR). From August 1981 the Bank ceased to announce the rate at which it was willing to lend, but it still determines rates of interest through its actions in the money markets. The rate at which the Bank is willing to lend is always higher than the Treasury bill rate; thus the discount houses will lose money. It is this fear of losing money which ensures that market rates of interest move in sympathy with the Bank's interest rate, thereby allowing the Bank of England to control market rates.

Table XLVII represents interest rates at the end of October 1981. Here you can see that discount houses could borrow from the clearing banks at rates from 4 per cent upwards. This money they lend to the Government by buying Treasury bills. Here you see the discount rate for Treasury bills of 15.66 per cent. If they were forced to borrow from the Bank of England it would cost them over 16 per cent. Thus they would lose money.

Rates of interest for the ordinary customers borrowing from the bank would be from 18 per cent upwards.

TABLE XLVII. SELECTED INTEREST RATES AT 30 OCTOBER 1981

Clearing banks deposit rate	14.0%
Call money	4–19.0%
Discount market deposits (overnight)	14.5%
Eurodollars (3 months)	15.5%
Clearing banks base rate	15.5%
Treasury bill rate	15.66DR
Fine trade bills (3 months)	16.31%
Sterling certificates of deposit (3 months)	16.31%
Clearing bank loans (minimum rate)	18.0%

DR = discount rate

Source: The Financial Times

Merchant banks

Many institutions today claim the title merchant bank; indeed, some of the clearing banks have set up merchant banking subsidiaries. Usually, however, we limit the term to the seventeen members of the *Accepting Houses Committee*. This includes such institutions as Hambros, Schroders, Lazards and Rothschild's. Accepting is a process whereby the accepting house guarantees the redemption of a commercial bill of exchange in the case of default by the company which has issued the bill. For this they charge a commission. A bill which has been accepted by a London accepting house becomes a "fine" bill or a *first class bill of exchange*. This makes it much easier to sell on the money market, and it may make it eligible for rediscount at the Bank of England. In order to be able to guarantee bills in this way, accepting houses have to make it their business to know everyone else's business. A merchant banker may therefore specialise in certain areas of business or in certain areas of the world. (Companies from all over the world raise money on the London money market.) Hambros, for example, specialise in Scandinavian and Canadian companies.

In addition to accepting, merchant banks undertake many other functions. They might undertake to raise capital for their clients or even invest in the company themselves. They often act as agents in take-over bids and in the issue of new shares. In recent years many merchant banks have become involved in unit trusts and investment trusts.

Merchant banks do not involve themselves in high street banking activities.

Finance houses

These are the institutions which provide hire purchase finance. Before 1971 they were subject to general regulations on the amount of loans, size of deposits and repayment periods. In 1971 they became subject to controls similar to those on banks, except that they had to keep a 10 per cent reserve assets ratio. Although they attract deposits on the money market at rates of interest similar to those of other institutions, compared to banks they charge much higher rates of interest on loans to their customers.

Local authorities

Local authorities are comparative newcomers to the money market and they raise money both by the issue of bills and bonds. Local authority bills now form an important part of banks' liquidity.

The capital market and the money market

The money market used to describe the discount houses but now it is also used to describe the institutions concerned with the raising of *short-term money*. Today there are other participants in the money market. They include finance houses, local authorities and private individuals or companies who might want to place funds for a short period of time. It also involves the Euro-currency market (*see* Fig. 114, page 537).

The *capital market* refers to the people and institutions who are concerned with the raising and subscribing of capital for longer-run investment in companies. Some of the participants in this market are as follows.

Merchant banks
They act as issuing houses and arrange *underwriting* for new issues.

Insurance companies
The insurance companies have enormous funds at their disposal and a look at the ownership of many large companies would show that insurance companies have become the major institutional investor (*see* page 235).

Unit trusts
In recent years unit trusts have become a popular avenue for the funds of the small investor. He buys units in the trust which uses the money received to buy shares in a number of other companies, thus spreading the risk.

Investment trusts
These are joint stock companies whose business is investing in other companies. Shares are bought in them in the normal way, not as units on sale to the general public as with unit trusts. They therefore do not tend to attract small investors.

Government sponsored institutions
Two government sponsored organisations were created in 1945, the Industrial and Commercial Finance Corporation and the Finance Corporation for Industry. In 1973 a merger of the two corporations was proposed and in 1975 Finance for Industry Ltd (FFI) was formed. Its shareholders are the clearing banks (85 per cent) and the Bank of England. FFI has access to funds of £1,000 million and is intended to give medium-term assistance to industry. The government might also provide permanent capital to industry through a number of bodies such as the National Enterprise Board (*see* page 90).

Building societies

We do not usually regard the building societies as being participants in the money markets since they are obliged by law to devote the majority of their funds to making loans for house purchase. They do, however, have an influence on the market since they attract funds which might have been placed elsewhere. The clearing banks are concerned about the development of building societies as rivals in high street banking. In the early 1980s the clearing banks began to participate actively in the mortgage market concentrating on larger mortgages.

THE FUNCTIONS OF THE BANK OF ENGLAND

The Bank of England is the *central bank* of the UK. Most countries have central banks but not all are responsible for the issue of notes as the Bank of England is. In the USA, for example, notes are issued by the *US Treasury* whilst the *Federal Reserve Banks* together form the central bank. Central banks have many functions. The functions of the Bank of England were described briefly in Chapter

TABLE XLVIII. BALANCE SHEET OF THE BANK OF ENGLAND
AS AT 19 AUGUST 1981

Liabilities	£m.	Assets	£m.
	Issue Department		
Notes in circulation	10,663	Government securities	8,110
Notes in Banking		Other securities	2,565
Department	12		
	10,675		10,675
	Banking Department		
Capital	14	Government securities	527
Public deposits	33	Advances and other	
Special deposits	—	accounts	1,005
Bankers' deposits	557	Premises, equipment	
Reserves and other		and other	
accounts	1,559	securities	619
		Notes and coins	12
	2,163		2,163

19. These can be understood more fully if we examine the balance sheet of the Bank (Table XLVIII). The Bank has published a weekly return since the Bank Charter Act of 1844; this Act also divided the Bank into two departments. You can see in the balance sheet below that the *Issue Department* is solely responsible for the issue of notes, whilst the *Banking Department* carries out the other banking functions of the Bank.

Items in the balance sheet: Issue Department

Notes in circulation
This item illustrates the Bank's function as the *sole issuer of notes* in England. The Scottish banks were at this date responsible for the issue of £538 million of notes and the Northern Ireland banks for £60 million of notes. Beyond £4.3 million, all Scottish and Northern Irish notes must be fully backed by Bank of England notes. Therefore there is very little effect upon the volume of notes in circulation.

Notes in Banking Department
These are notes which have been created by the Issue Department and sold to the Banking Department where they are kept ready for distribution to the banks. You will see that this item appears on the assets side of the Banking Department as "notes and coins". Thus, since the two departments are separate, Bank of England notes are a liability to the Issue Department but an asset to the Banking Department.

Government securities
The main backing for the currency is British government securities. Thus one piece of government paper secures the other. The real backing of the currency comes from the fact that it is both readily acceptable and legal tender.

Other securities
These consist of securities other than those issued by the British government. It also includes the government debt dating back to 1694 and coins bought from the Royal Mint but not yet put into circulation.

The liabilities of the Banking Department

Capital
This represents the ownership of the Bank in the same way as the

capital of any other company. This was taken over by the government in 1946.

Public deposits
These are the British government's deposits at the Bank and represent the Bank's function as the *government's banker*. The figure is perhaps surprisingly small; this is because the government balances its revenue and expenditure through the sale and purchase of Treasury bills. This item also includes the dividend accounts of the commissioners of the national debt, for the Bank is also responsible for *servicing the national debt*.

Special deposits
The existence of this item illustrates the Bank's function as the *operator of government monetary policy*.

Bankers' deposits
These are the deposits of the main English banks. The main function of these deposits is to operate the clearing house system. This demonstrates the Bank's role as the *banker's bank*.

Reserves and other accounts
This item consists of undistributed profits and the accounts of other persons at the Bank. These fall into three categories: the bank's employees; private customers who had accounts at the bank in 1946; and other persons having a special need to bank with the Bank, such as foreign banks. This illustrates that the bank also functions as an *ordinary bank*.

The assets of the Banking Department

Government securities
Like the Issue Department, the main assets of the Banking Department are British government securities.

Advances and other accounts
These are loans which the Bank has made mainly to institutions such as discount houses. This illustrates the Bank's function as *lender of last resort*. By always being prepared to lend money, the Bank ensures that the major financial institutions never become insolvent.

Premises, equipment and other securities
As well as its well-known Threadneedle Street site the Bank also has branches, e.g. in Birmingham.

Notes and coins
The Bank is responsible for supplying the banks with the new bank notes and coins that they require.

Other functions of the Bank of England

There are several functions of the Bank of England which are not apparent in its balance sheet. Firstly, since 1946 it has had the responsibility for "disposing of the means of foreign payment in the national interest". That is to say all *foreign exchange transactions* in Britain are controlled by the Bank. In addition to this it operates the *Exchange Equalisation Account*. This is a fund, established in 1932, the purpose of which is to buy and sell currency on the foreign exchange market with the object of stabilising the exchange rate. The Bank also *sells stock* on behalf of the government. It advises the government on the issue of new securities, it converts and funds existing government debt, it publishes prospectuses for any new government issue and it deals with the applications for them and apportions the issue. The Bank is also responsible for giving the government more general advice on the monetary system. The Bank also publishes large quantities of statistical information on the monetary system, along with studies of various sectors of the economy. The effect of the Banking Act and the monetary control provisions has been to greatly widen the scope of the statistics which the Bank publishes.

Finally, an important function of the Bank is to *represent the government* in relations with foreign central banks and also in various institutions such as the Bank for International Settlements (BIS) and the International Monetary Fund (IMF).

MONETARY POLICY

What is monetary policy?

Monetary policy is the direction of the economy through the supply and price of money. However the supply of money is defined, bank deposits form the major part of it. Generally it is assumed that increasing the supply of money will stimulate the economy whilst restricting it will restrict the economy. Similarly, monetary policy is based on the premise that raising the price of money (the rate of interest) will discourage borrowing, and hence depress demand in the economy, whilst lowering the rate of interest will encourage borrowing, thereby stimulating the economy.

We might summarise the options as in Table XLIX.

Thus, it would seem that if we are faced with unemployment we need only adopt an "easy money, cheap money" policy to reflate

TABLE XLIX. MONETARY POLICIES

Name of Policy	Action	Effect
Tight money Dear money	Restrict money supply Raise interest rates	} Deflationary
Easy money Cheap money	Expand money supply Lower interest rates	} Reflationary

the economy. However, the economy may be faced with several problems simultaneously, for example unemployment *and* inflation. This means that monetary policy is usually used in conjunction with other things, such as fiscal policy.

The money supply

Earlier in this chapter we have defined money as anything that is readily acceptable in settlement of a debt. In Chapter 21 we looked at the theoretical concept of the quantity of money in circulation. At this point we examine the practical measurement of the money supply. Three measures are in common use at the moment: M1, M3 and domestic credit expansion (DCE). The M1 definition comprises notes and coins and all sight deposits of banks (that is any deposits which can be withdrawn without interest penalty, mainly current accounts). The M3 definition includes all deposit accounts, both private and public. A wider definition of M3 also includes UK residents deposits in other currencies. Although in general M3 is less liquid than M1, it gives a better measure of the total purchasing power available in the country and is the measure most commonly used by the Government.

Although the government tends to concentrate on the growth in M3, the IMF has insisted on using DCE as a measure of the change in the money supply. From this definition it is apparent that the PSBR plays a key role in credit expansion.

Before August 1981 figures for the money supply related to the *banking sector* but since then they include figures for the more broadly defined *monetary sector*. This led to an increase of 13 per cent, or £8 billion, in the M3 measure of the money supply. It could also be argued that there should be a measure which includes building society deposits. Such a measure was introduced in 1979 and is called private sector liquidity. There are two measures PSL1 and PSL2. The calculation of PSL2 is shown in Table LII. As you can see this measure of potential purchasing power in the economy

TABLE L. MONEY STOCK 15 JULY 1981

Money stock	£ millions	
Notes and coins in circulation	10,472	
UK private sector sterling sight deposits	21,833	
M1 money stock =		32,305
UK private sector sterling time deposits	39,033	
UK public sector sterling deposits	1,336	
M3 money stock (sterling) =		40,369
UK residents' deposits in other currencies	10,101	
		10,101
M3 money stock (total) =		82,775

TABLE LI. DOMESTIC CREDIT EXPANSION 17 JUNE TO 15 JULY 1981

Domestic credit expansion	£ millions
Public sector borrowing requirement (PSBR) (net)	+641
Bank lending in sterling to private sector	+1,536
Bank lending in sterling to overseas	+575
DCE	+2,752

Source: BEQB

suggests that liquidity is much more broadly based than does the M3 definition.

The weapons of monetary policy

Although monetary policy may be decided by the government, it is implemented by the Bank of England. The Bank has a variety of measures it can use to implement a policy. These are usually referred to as the weapons of monetary policy and they are mainly aimed at affecting the level of bank deposits and the rates of interest.

TABLE LII. COMPONENTS OF PRIVATE SECTOR LIQUIDITY 15 JULY 1981

		£ millions
Money		
Notes and coins in circulation	10,472	
Sterling bank deposits		
Sight	21,833	
Time*	32,010	
Certificates of deposit	5,607	
		69,922
Other money market instruments		4,434
Savings deposits and securities †		54,129
Certificates of tax deposit		1,074
PSL2		129,559

* Excludes deposits with original maturity of over two years.
† Mainly building society deposits and shares.

The issue of notes

Theoretically the Bank could influence the volume of money by printing more or less. In practice it is very difficult for the Bank not to supply the notes which banks are demanding, so that it is not too effective as a restricting mechanism. The reverse is not true, however, for expanding the issue of notes could expand the money supply. Indeed many people would argue that the over-printing of bank notes was one of the causes of inflation in the mid-1970s. Table LIII traces the growth of the fiduciary issue in the 1970s and early 1980s.

Liquidity ratios

For many years banks were obliged to keep a certain portion of their assets in a particular form. In 1981 the Bank of England abandoned the reserve assets ratio. The only requirement now is that banks should keep 0.5 per cent of their eligible liabilities with the Bank. It should not be thought, however, that this means that no control exists over banks' assets. As we have seen above (*see* page 521), although there is no stated ratio, banks are still required to order their assets in particular ways. Since the Bank of England is able to influence the supply of liquid assets it is therefore still able to influence bank lending. In addition to this the Bank has stated that it regards the funds which banks voluntarily retain with

TABLE LIII. THE GROWTH OF THE FIDUCIARY ISSUE

Years to mid-August	Fiduciary issue (£m.)	Percentage increase over preceding year
1972	4,052	—
1973	4,545	12.2
1974	5,109	12.4
1975	5,902	15.5
1976	6,674	13.1
1977	7,314	9.6
1978	8,512	16.4
1979	9,305	9.3
1980	9,798	5.3
1981	10,256	4.5

it for clearing purposes as "the fulcrum for money market management".

Interest rates
The Bank of England as the central bank guarantees the solvency of the financial system by always being willing to lend money. The way in which this is done is that the Bank rediscounts (buys) *Treasury bills* or other *first class bills of exchange*. However, the rate (of interest) at which it is willing to do this is always higher than the rate which the bill would earn if it ran to maturity. Thus it involves the borrower in a loss but, since the Bank is the only institution which guarantees to lend money, the rate at which it does so is extremely important and all other rates of interest tend to move in line with it. Until 1981 this rate used to be announced every week as the minimum lending rate (MLR). Now, however, the Bank of England works within a "band of interest rates" which are not announced. Nevertheless the clearing banks set their *base rate* at the rate at which the Bank of England is currently willing to lend.

Open-market operations
These are the sale or purchase of securities by the Bank on the open market with the intention of influencing the volume of money in circulation and the rate of interest. Selling bills or bonds should reduce the volume of money and increase interest rates, whilst the re-purchase of, or the reduction in sales of, government securities should increase the volume of money and decrease interest rates.
    Open-market operations affect the liquidity ratio of a bank and

can therefore bring about a multiple expansion or contraction of banks' deposits.

Let us consider a bank whose assets and liablilities are arranged in the following manner conforming with a 25 per cent ratio.

Bank X before open-market sales

Liabilities (£)			Assets (£)	
Deposits	100,000	25%	Liquid assets	25,000
		(ratio)	Securities	25,000
			Advances	50,000
	100,000			100,000

Let us now assume that the Bank of England *sells* £1,000 of securities to the general public. The public pays for these by drawing cheques on their banks. The Bank of England collects the money by deducting the £1,000 from the clearing bank's balance at the Bank. Thus after open market sales, the bank's balance sheet will be as follows.

Bank X after open-market sales

Liabilities (£)			Assets (£)	
Deposits	99,000	24.2%	Liquid assets	24,000
		(ratio)	Securities	25,000
			Advances	50,000
	99,000			99,000

The Bank of England's actions will have reduced the amount of money in circulation by the amount of sales, and may have increased the interest rate by depressing the price of securities. More importantly, however, it has disturbed the bank's liquidity ratio, reducing it to 24.2 per cent. It is the bank's actions in restoring its Liquidity ratio which brings about the most important effect of open-market operations.

Final Position of Bank X

Liabilities (£)			Assets (£)	
Deposits	96,000	25%	Liquid assets	24,000
		(ratio)	Securities	24,000
			Advances	48,000
	96,000			96,000

In order to restore its liquidity ratio it has had to reduce its deposits to £96,000. This it has done by selling off securities, thereby depressing their price and raising the rate of interest, and by reducing its advances, thus making money both harder to obtain and more expensive. Thus, £1,000 of open-market operations has reduced the volume of money in circulation by £4,000. The magnitude of the effect is the reciprocal of the liquidity ratio. The effect would work in reverse if the Bank of England were buying back securities.

Funding
This is the conversion of short-term government debt into longer-term government debt. This will not only reduce liquidity but also, if the Bank is replacing securities which could be counted as liquid assets by ones which cannot, it could bring about the multiple contraction of deposits described above.

Special deposits
The calling for special deposits will bring about a multiple contraction in bank lending and will also not be as expensive as either open market operations or funding.

Special directives
The Bank of England used to issue directives both on how much Banks should lend (quantitative) and to whom they should lend (qualitative). Since 1971 it has ceased to make quantitative directives and makes only qualitative ones.

Criticisms of monetary policy
The weapons of monetary policy might be criticised as either being ineffective or as having the wrong effect upon the economy.

(*a*) *Interest rates.* Raising the interest rate should discourage investment and consumption. Most investment decisions, however, are *non-marginal,* i.e. the entrepreneur will be anticipating a sufficiently great return on his investment so that small changes in the interest rate are unlikely to make a potentially profitable project unprofitable. If interest rates do affect investment schemes they are much more likely to affect long-run ones than short-run ones. This is because interest charges form a much greater percentage of the capital cost in the former schemes. This is the opposite to the desired effect, i.e. the government would like to leave long-run capital projects unaffected whilst cutting back on short-run consumer projects. One might draw an analogy with the individual consumer and ask which borrowing would be most influenced by a rise in the interest rate, borrowing to buy a car or to buy a house?

(b) *Liquid assets and the multiple contraction of deposits.* The efficacy of open-market operations will depend upon two factors.

(i) Who buys the securities which the Bank of England is selling. For open-market operations to work they must be purchased by the general public. If the securities are bought by the banks, they will have little effect upon the banks' liquidity, since most of them count as liquid assets.

(ii) How near the banks are to the liquidity ratio. For the multiple contraction of deposits to come about, the banks' liquid assets must be reduced below the appropriate level. If, however, the banks are operating well above this, as they often do, open-market operations will have to be massive before they are effective.

(c) *Funding.* This may indeed be effective in bringing about a multiple contraction of bank deposits, but it is expensive since the rate of interest the government must pay on long-term debt is much higher than on short-term.

(d) *Special deposits and directives.* Both these methods are simple, cheap, effective and quick-acting. The disadvantage they possess is that they may annoy the clearing banks. This factor is important since the willing co-operation of the banks is necessary for the effective implementation of monetary policy.

Thus, most of the weapons of monetary policy can be criticised. Some of this criticism is, however, due to monetary policy being asked to do jobs it was not designed to do.

In recent years governments have tried to use monetary policy as a method of directing the whole economy whereas, ideally, it should be used to regulate short-run movements in market conditions. The recent concentration on monetary policy has led to an emphasis on broad indicators such as M3. These have proved not only difficult to control but also difficult to define (*see* page 530). This has led to suggestions that monetary policy should be grounded on the *money base* (notes and coins in circulation and balances with the Bank of England). If this were to be adopted we would have a new measure of the money supply called M0. However, monetary policy will only be effective if used in conjunction with other means of control such as fiscal policy and prices and incomes policy.

SUMMARY

Figure 114 summarises the most important relationships in the money market. This is the market for short-run funds. There are

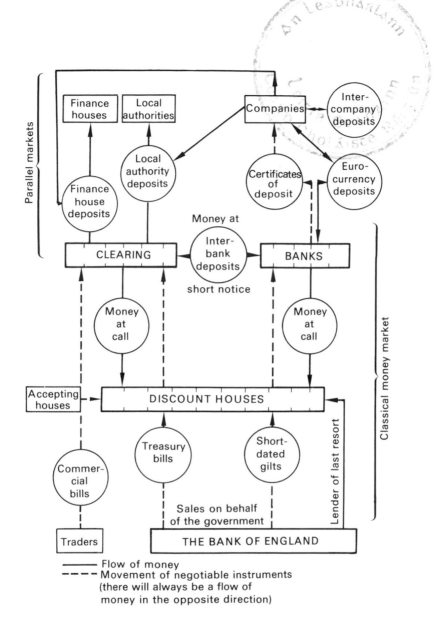

Fig. 114. *The main participants in the London money markets. The part labelled "classical money market" is often termed the money market, whilst the "parallel markets" are more recent developments.*

other participants and relationships in addition to those shown but these are most of the ones discussed in this chapter. We have not given much attention to companies as a source of finance or as demanders of liquid assets but you can see that they constitute an important part of the market.

Banks do not make their profits from this market nor does it involve the majority of their funds. This diagram concerns itself mainly with liquid assets. In addition to this, the vast majority of banks' assets are the loans and advances which they have made to customers.

SELF-ASSESSMENT QUESTIONS

A. 1. Define: (*a*) intrinsic value; (*b*) special deposits; (*c*) Treasury bill rate; (*d*) fiduciary issue.

2. List the functions of the Bank of England.

B. 3. True or false?

(*a*) Money is all those things which constitute legal tender.

(*b*) All banks are financial intermediaries.

(*c*) A certificate of deposit is a negotiable instrument.

(*d*) If the interest rates were increased this would be likely to cause a fall in price of Treasury Bills.

(*e*) The Exchange Equalisation Account exists to stabilise the exchange rate.

C. 4. True or false?

(*a*) Cheques and banknotes are both promissory notes.

(*b*) If the clearing banks (*see* Table XLV) sold some of their Treasury bills to the Bank of England this would reduce their liquidity.

(*c*) In Table XLV it would appear that the Bank of England has called for special deposits of 1 per cent.

(*d*) A 10 per cent rise in the money supply would cause inflation only if the growth in real goods and services were less than 10 per cent.

(*e*) Abrupt changes in monetary policy have formed part of the "stop–go" cycle of the British economy.

5. What would be the effect of a decreased liquidity preference on the rate of interest?

6. What advantages does a bank account offer the individual?

ASSIGNMENTS

1. Draw up a table to show the sources of borrowing of the central government.

2. Outline the procedures a bank manager might go through before giving a loan:

    (*a*) to an individual;

    (*b*) to a joint stock company.

3. Analyse the likely effect of the microprocessor revolution upon banking.

CHAPTER TWENTY-THREE

Directing the Economy

CHAPTER OBJECTIVES

After studying this chapter you should be able to:
* define fiscal and monetary policy;
* list and explain the main taxes;
* describe the pattern of government expenditure;
* analyse the shortcoming of fiscal policy;
* list and describe the causes and consequence of inflation.

THE GOVERNMENT AND THE ECONOMY

Methods of control

Adam Smith believed that the economy would run itself admirably if the government did not interfere and allowed the "invisible hand" of self-interest to guide the economy. Today everyone realises that the prime responsibility for the well-being of the economy rests upon the government's shoulders. The actions of the government now affect almost every aspect of the life of both individuals and organisations. The direction of the economy is not so much a legal process as an economic one, i.e. the government cannot pass a law to get rid of inflation or to decree that there must be economic growth. There are three main ways in which the government controls the economy.

Fiscal policy

This is the direction of the economy through taxation and government expenditure. In the UK the way in which the government spends money is obviously very important, since it is responsible for disposing of over 43 per cent of the *gross domestic product* (GDP). Even more important, however, is the relationship between taxation and government spending, i.e. whether the government is running a budget deficit or surplus (*see* page 494).

Monetary policy

This involves direction of the economy through the supply of and price of money. The government can try to influence the economy through varying the quantity of money in the economy and by raising or lowering interest rates (*see* Chapter 22).

Direct intervention
Both monetary and fiscal policy aim at *inducing* the economy to conform to the government's wishes. The government could, however, intervene directly to see that its wishes were carried out. Perhaps the most obvious example of this is a *prices and incomes policy*, the operation of which also illustrates that direct intervention in the economy is as difficult as trying to induce people and organisations to do the right thing.

The objectives of government policy
Even within one political party opinions differ on the correct objectives of policy, but it is possible to discern four general objectives which are the aim of every political party.

(*a*) *The control of unemployment.* Until recently British governments have been reasonably successful in achieving full employment. The rise in unemployment in the 1980s (3.0m. or 11.5 per cent in 1981) has made this once again an important objective of policy.

(*b*) *The control of inflation.* In 1975 prices increased by 26 per cent. All governments wish to avoid inflation of this magnitude.

(*c*) *A surplus on the current account of the balance of payments.* This has proved to be the most intractable problem of the post-war years. The revenues from North Sea oil returned us to surplus in the early 1980s but this will not continue if the rest of the economy is not well managed.

(*d*) *Economic growth.* The final object of all economic policies is a growth in the real national income of the country so that everyone may enjoy a better standard of living. The boom years of the 1950s and early 1960s gave way to stagnation and even to decline in the 1980s. Promoting economic growth should be the prime objective of every government.

There is no disagreement about these objectives of policy. The disagreement arises out of how to achieve them and which are the most important. Given just one problem, such as inflation, any government could solve it, but it must also try to achieve the other objectives at the same time. It is not just a question of priorities but also of conflict since curing one problem often aggravates another. For example, eliminating unemployment might well increase inflation.

FISCAL POLICY: RAISING MONEY

The most important aspect of fiscal policy is the relationship between the government's revenues and expenditure, i.e. whether it is running a budget deficit or surplus. Before considering this we must examine some of the items which make up the two sides of public finance. Table LIV shows the budget *estimate* of government income.

TABLE LIV. PUBLIC INCOME 1981–2

	£ billion
Direct taxes	
Income tax	28.2
Corporation tax	4.0
Capital gains tax	0.6
Capital transfer tax	0.4
Indirect taxes	
Customs and excise duty	
Alcohol	3.2
Tobacco	3.2
Hydrocarbon oils	4.8
Protective duties	1.0
Other (include car tax and vehicle excise)	4.1
VAT	12.6
North Sea taxes	5.9
National insurance and health contributions	16.4
National insurance surcharge	3.8
Local authority rates	10.3
Total taxes and national insurance contributions	98.5
Other income	7.9
Public sector borrowing requirement (PSBR)	10.6
Total	117.0

Source: Economic Progress Report

Direct taxes

Direct taxes are those which are levied on the income or earnings of an individual or an organisation. These are the most important revenue raisers for the government and can be considered under three headings.

Taxes on income
Before taxing an individual's personal income, allowances are made for such things as children and mortgage interest. The remaining taxable income is referred to as the *legal tax base*. For example, if a man had an income of £4,000 p.a. and allowances of £2,200 then his legal tax base would be £1,800. The *marginal rate of tax* is the amount of tax a person would pay on each successive unit of legal tax base. At present a person would pay 30 per cent on the tax base up to £12,800. At this figure tax rises to 40 per cent and continues to rise with income up to the maximum rate of 60 per cent. Such a tax is said to be *progressive* because it takes proportionately more off people with higher incomes.

Income from investments bears a surcharge of 15 per cent on investment income over £6,250. Thus, it would appear that it is possible for someone to pay 75 per cent of their income in tax. However, if one takes gross income and expresses the actual tax paid as a proportion of it we arrive at the *effective rate of tax*.

Corporation tax
This is a tax which is levied on the profits of companies. It starts at 40 per cent and rises to 52 per cent on profits over £225,000. It can be argued that corporation tax is a disincentive to enterprise, but on the other hand the possibility of offsetting the tax against capital expenditure has meant that many of the largest profit earners in the UK have paid little or no tax at all in recent years.

Taxes on capital
Capital as such is not taxed, although the Labour Party has suggested a wealth tax. Tax is paid when capital is sold or transferred. The most important taxes are *capital transfer tax*, which has replaced *estate duty*, and *capital gains tax*.

A disincentive to work?
It has been argued that direct taxes are a disincentive to work and effort. This is difficult to assess as far as companies are concerned, but when individuals are considered it will depend upon the person's *target level of income*. If a person is earning less than he would like (the target level) then increasing tax decreases his income and causes him to work harder or longer to make up his income. If a person is above his target level of income, increasing income taxes makes leisure appear cheaper to him and he will thus work less. It therefore tends to be those on very high incomes who find taxes a disincentive to effort. It follows that the high marginal rate of tax on higher incomes in Britian may be damaging British industry. On the other

hand, it has been argued that people receving very high salaries are more concerned with status than reward.

Direct taxes and inflation

Where progressive taxes are concerned, inflation will mean that the Chancellor takes a bigger and bigger proportion of a person's income as increased money wages raise him from a lower to a higher tax bracket. This tendency is known as *fiscal drag* and it is to offset this that the Chancellor frequently raises the tax threshold.

Indirect taxes

Indirect taxes are usually taxes on expenditure. They are so called because the tax is paid *indirectly*, the consumer pays the tax to the shopkeeper who in turn pays it to the government. For example, in the case of the duty on whisky it is the distiller who must pay the tax, this being referred to as the *impact* (*or formal incidence*) of the tax. The tax is then "shifted" down the chain of distribution until the *burden* (or *effective incidence*) of the tax falls upon the consumer. The determination of the incidence of tax is explained on page 318.

These are the following main forms of indirect tax in the UK.

(*a*) *Customs and excise duty.* Customs duty may be levied on goods coming into the country, but this only accounts for 1.3 per cent of government revenues. Excise duty is levied on a commodity no matter where it is produced. It is a *specific tax*, i.e. it is levied *per unit* of the commodity irrespective of its price. The main duties are shown in Table LIV.

(*b*) *VAT.* The most important of the indirect taxes, VAT was first introduced in 1973 when it replaced purchase tax. VAT is an *ad valorem* tax, i.e. it is levied on the selling price of the commodity. There are currently two rates of VAT: zero and 15 per cent. These rates were introduced in the first budget of the Conservative government of 1979 and replaced the system of four rates which existed previously.

Taxes on expenditure are generally said to be *regressive*, i.e. they take a large percentage of the incomes of the lower paid. To the government, however, they are cheap to collect and lack *announcement effect*, i.e. people are often unaware that they are paying tax or how much they are paying. For example, over £4 of the price of a bottle of whisky is excise duty.

Other indirect taxes include car tax, road fund, television licences and stamp duty.

National insurance, etc.

This used to be paid as a fixed price "stamp" with contributions from employer, employee and government. It is now levied as a percentage of the employee's income. Today the contributions are still tripartite but there is in addition the national insurance surcharge paid by employers, which has been the cause of much complaint.

Borrowing

If there is any shortfall between the government's expenditure and income this is made up by borrowing, i.e. the government increases the size of the national debt. If we consider the borrowing both by central and local government this gives us the *public sector borrowing requirement* (PSBR). This is where fiscal policy spills over into monetary policy, for a large PSBR would expand the banks' credit base, thereby pushing up the money supply. (This does not happen if foreign investors buy the government bonds; on the contrary, this restrains the money supply.)

Local authority revenues

The 1981–2 estimates are illustrated in Table LV. You will see how relatively unimportant rates are to local government. The finance of local government is explained in Chapter 19.

TABLE LV. LOCAL AUTHORITIES' INCOME 1981–2

Revenue	£ billion
Rates	10.3
Government grants (net)	13.6
Rent, dividends, interest	4.0
Other	−0.7
Total receipts	27.2
Borrowing from central government	0.9
Other borrowing	0.1
	28.2

Source: Economic Progress Report

Is there such a thing as a good tax?

No-one likes paying taxes, but if taxes are necessary then what makes one tax better than another? In the eighteenth century Adam

Smith laid down four *canons* (criteria) *of taxation*. Although taxes have changed a great deal the principles still remain good today.

(*a*) *Equitable*. A good tax should be based upon the ability to pay. Today, progressive income tax means that those with high incomes not only pay a large amount but also a greater proportion of their income in tax.

(*b*) *Economical*. A good tax should not be expensive to administer and the greatest possible proportion of it should accrue to the government as revenue. In general, indirect taxes are cheaper to collect than direct taxes, but they are not, however, so equitable.

(*c*) *Convenient*. This means that the method and frequency of the payment should be convenient to the taxpayer. The introduction of PAYE made income tax much easier to pay for most people.

(*d*) *Certainty*. The tax should be formulated so that the taxpayer is certain of how much he has to pay and when. This information is widely available today, but is often badly understood.

A good system of taxation should also be one which is readily adaptable to changing circumstances. A fiscal system might also be judged on the *welfare principle*, i.e. the extent to which the taxes are received back by the taxpayers as services, and on the principle of *least aggregate sacrifice*, i.e. that inconvenience to taxpayers is minimised. If sacrifice is minimised and welfare maximised, the fiscal system is running on the principle of *maximum social advantage*.

The objectives of taxation

(*a*) *To raise revenue*. The chief reason for taxation is to raise revenue for the government, but in addition to this there are many secondary purposes which a tax may serve.

(*b*) *Redistribution of income*. The government taxes those with high incomes heavily so that it may use this money to redistribute income towards the poorer section of society.

(*c*) *Discouraging consumption*. High rates of indirect tax might be placed on certain goods with the object of discouraging their consumption. This could be done, for example, to discourage imports. It is often argued that high excise duty on tobacco and alcohol serves to discourage consumption, but since the demand for these products is highly inelastic this cannot be so.

(*d*) *Influencing the location of industry*. Differences in the rate of tax and in tax reliefs in different parts of the country are used to persuade business organisations to locate in development areas.

The effect of taxation on the general level of demand for goods and services in the economy is considered below.

FISCAL POLICY: SPENDING MONEY

The provision of goods and services

As the government disposes of over 43 per cent of the GDP it is obvious that the most important effect of government expenditure is its influence on the general level of demand in the economy. The government, however, has other objectives. Governments, both central and local, provide *public goods*, perhaps the best example of this being defence. Armies are probably the oldest form of public expenditure. Today there are many other public goods paid for from taxation such as the police service, water supply and street lighting. These are commodities which have seldom been provided in any other way. Over the last century, however, governments have stepped in to provide such things as education and health services which were formerly sold to the public (*see* page 84).

Many goods and services are, of course, supplied by the nationalised industries, but these should not involve government expenditure since they should be self-supporting. On many occasions, however, the government has had to give financial assistance to nationalised industries.

The redistribution of income

We saw how it could be argued that the rich should pay more taxes. To complete the redistribution of income, government spending must benefit the poor. Those on low incomes benefit from the consumption of public goods in the same way as anyone else although they may have contributed little towards them. They may also benefit by way of *transfer payments* such as unemployment benefits and old-age pensions. They are called transfer payments because money is transferred from one section of the community to another without the recipient providing any corresponding product or service. Figure 115 illustrates the distribution of income and wealth. It can be seen from this that 20 per cent of the population enjoy 66 per cent of the wealth, whilst the poorest 20 per cent of the population only receives 8 per cent of the income. Thus, while the most blatant inequalities have been removed there still remain very large differences.

Prices support policies

If a government subsidises the cost of producing something it may do this either with the object of supplying it to the consumer at a lower price or in order to prevent the producer from going out of business. The old farming support programmes in the UK did both, for people enjoyed cheap food and farmers were maintained in

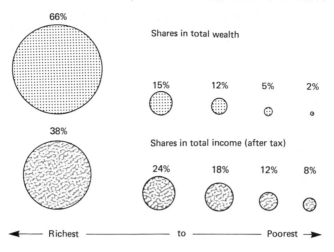

Fig. 115. *The distribution of income and wealth. Each circle represents the share of income or wealth enjoyed by each 20 per cent of the total population. Source: "What's going on", The Economist.*

business. The conflict between these objectives has become apparent since we joined the EEC, since the CAP supports agriculture by guaranteed high prices, to the disadvantage of the consumer. The government has not yet resolved this conflict and still continues to subsidise some food prices.

The pattern of government expenditure
Table LVI shows the different programmes on which the government planned to spend money in 1981–2. Not all the money is spent by central government. Education, for example, is nearly all provided by local authorities. Table LV, however, showed that local authorities receive most of their revenue from central government.

Debt interest
In 1981–2 the percentage of public expenditure going in debt interest was 10.9 per cent. There was a dramatic rise in the size of the national debt in the 1970s following the oil crisis and the "three day week". However, if we look at the nominal value of the national debt in 1982 and compare it with the national income, it represents the equivalent of twenty-seven weeks as compared with sixty-one weeks of the national income in 1962. This spectacular fall in its relative size is offset by the enormous increase in interest rates.

People often believe that increasing the size of the national debt is a bad thing, but all that happens is that wealth is transferred

TABLE LVI. COMBINED PUBLIC EXPENDITURE BY PROGRAMME 1981-2

Programme	£ billion
Social security	30.3
Education and science	14.1
National health service	13.4
Defence	12.3
Housing	5.5
Other environment services	4.9
Law and order	4.4
Transport	3.7
Industry	2.5
Employment	2.4
Nationalised industries	2.4
Overseas expenditure	2.0
Agriculture, fisheries, food and forestry	1.5
Energy	0.4
Trade	0.2
Other	4.2
Total public expenditure on programmes	104.2
Debt interest	12.8
Total public expenditure	117.0

from private control to public control. If the government uses the money wisely, increasing the debt may well benefit the community. In addition to this, inflation and growth of the economy will reduce the burden of interest and repayment. On the other hand interest payments are *regressive*, i.e. they transfer money from people with low incomes to the wealthy and, if the interest is paid overseas, they represent a real drain on the economy.

A balanced budget?

It was Keynes who first pointed out that the budget could be used as a method of directing the economy. The budget is a method of managing the level of aggregate demand in the economy. A budget deficit would mean that the level of aggregate demand was increased whilst, conversely, a budget surplus would reduce the level of aggregate demand. Theoretically a balanced budget should not affect the level of economic activity (*see* Chapter 21).

This ought to mean that if the government is faced with an inflationary situation it should run a budget surplus to restrain the level of demand and therefore take the heat out of the economy. This is unlikely to work by itself and the government would usually try to use it in conjunction with monetary policy. It should be the case that the government should be able to cure unemployment in the economy by running a budget deficit. There are, however, several types of unemployment.

(a) *Frictional.* People displaced by the normal working of the economy, for example people between jobs.

(b) *Seasonal.* People being made unemployed because their job depends upon the time of year. It is most significant in the construction industry.

(c) *Structural.* This is unemployment caused by a change in the structure of the economy, e.g. the decline of one industry and (hopefully) the rise of another. In Britain this has manifested itself as *regional unemployment.* This is because the declining *old staple industries* tend to be heavily concentrated in certain regions, notably the north of the country.

(d) *General or cyclical unemployment.* Originally taking its name from the trade cycle, this is unemployment associated with a general depression in the economy.

It is only the last of these types of unemployment which a budget deficit would cure. Running a deficit to cure structural unemployment tends to cause inflation by increasing demand in the already fully employed sectors of the economy. Structural unemployment is best dealt with by regional policy or by a policy aimed at a particular sector of the economy (*see* Chapter 10).

THE DIFFICULTIES OF FISCAL POLICY

Fiscal policy would seem to be a straightforward way of directing the economy. Certainly most governments since 1945 have relied on it as a major weapon of policy. In practice, however, its operation is subject to a number of difficulties.

The net effects of the budget

The effect of a budget will depend not only upon the amount of taxes and the amount of spending, but also upon who is taxed and on what the government spends money. If we imagined a very simple budget in which all the taxes were raised as capital transfer tax, whilst all the expenditure was on unemployment benefits, the amount paid could be less than the amount collected so that the budget was ostensibly in surplus. However, the money that has been collected in taxes is money that would not have been spent, i.e. people with high incomes would probably have saved a good deal of it. On the other hand we can be reasonably certain that all the unemployment benefit would be spent. Thus the government has moved the money from non-spenders to spenders, and, therefore, the effect on the economy would be that of deficit, although the budget was in an accounting surplus.

This would also work the other way round. If, for example, a government's budget were in deficit but its revenue had been raised mainly from taxes on expenditure, such as VAT, but the money thus raised was spent mainly on paying interest on the national debt, then the effect of the budget would be that of a surplus. This is because the government has, effectively, transferred money from spenders to non-spenders. Thus, when the government announces a deficit or surplus a much more careful examination of its plans will be necessary before we can decide what the net effect on the economy will be. Put into economists' language the effect of the budget will depend upon the *marginal propensity to consume* of those being taxed and of those receiving the government's expenditure. You will recall that there will also be a multiplier effect from any budget deficit or surplus (*see* Chapter 21).

The inflexibility of government finance

Adjusting the government's level of economic activity to suit changing circumstances is not as straightforward as it may seem. Much of the government's finance is inflexible. One of the reasons for this is that the major portion of almost any department's budget is wages and salaries, and it is not possible to play around with these to suit the short-run needs of the economy. In addition to this, for example, it would be impracticable to build a power station one year because more demand was needed, or conversely to stop the construction of a half-built motorway because less expenditure was needed. Much of the government's expenditure involves long-run planning.

Conflicts of policy

In devising its budgetary policy, the government must try to reconcile conflicting objectives of policy. In 1981, for example, the government might have liked to reflate the economy to try to cure unemployment but it was loth to do this in case it caused more inflation. The most famous conflict of different ends of policy is illustrated by the *Phillips curve* (*see* Fig. 116). By plotting figures for unemployment, inflation and wage rises in the British economy 1862–1958, Professor Phillips derived this relationship.

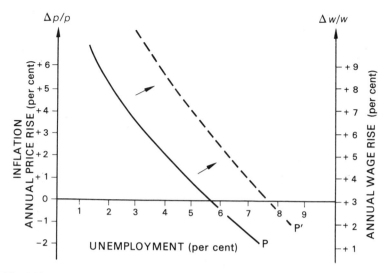

Fig. 116. *A Phillips curve. The Phillips curve is used as evidence for cost push inflation.*

Professor Phillips' research appeared to show that the nearer the economy was to full employment the greater would be the rate of inflation. When he wrote (1962) it seemed that if there were 5.5 per cent unemployment then inflation would be zero. It would appear in the 1980s that either this relationship has ceased to operate or that the Phillips curve has moved to the right (P—P') as indicated in the graph. This would mean that a much greater level of unemployment would be necessary to eliminate inflation. This would make the choices confronting the government even more formidable. The curve also demonstrated a connection between wage rates and inflation. This is evidence for cost push inflation and one of the reasons why successive governments have tried to restrain wage rises (*see* below).

Information

It is very difficult to assemble accurate information about the economy sufficiently quickly for it to be of use in the short-run management of the economy. There have been numerous occasions when, for example, the balance of payments has been declared to be in deficit in one quarter but a few months later, when more information is available, it has been discovered that the quarter was in fact in surplus. It is difficult, therefore, for a government to be sure about the accuracy of the information. Even if the figures are accurate, the government still has to decide what they mean. For example, if the balance of payments is suddenly in deficit, is this the beginning of a long-run trend or is it just a freak result for that month or quarter?

Time lag

One of the chief objectives of fiscal policy is stability, i.e. the government tries to avoid violent fluctuations in the level of economic activity. One way to do this is for the government to have a *counter-cyclical* policy, so that if, for example, the level of economic activity were low, government activity would be high, i.e. they would have a budget deficit. Conversely, if there were a high level of activity then the government would budget for a surplus.

Unfortunately it takes time for a government to appreciate the economic situation, then to formulate a policy and then to implement it. This may mean that the government's policy works at the wrong time. For example, if the government decided to reflate the economy during a recession, it could be that by the time the policy works the economy would have recovered anyway. The government's actions therefore have the effect of boosting the economy beyond that which is desirable. At this time the government decides to clamp down on the economy, but by the time the policy acts, the economy has naturally returned to recession. The government's

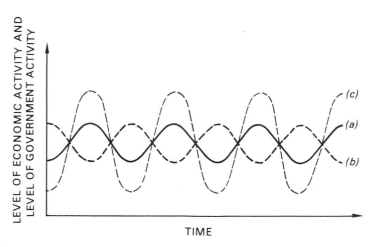

Fig. 117. *The time lag.* (a) *Fluctuations in the level of economic activity without government intervention.* (b) *Proposed pattern of government counter-cyclical activity.* (c) *Worsened fluctuations in the level of economic activity caused by government policy acting at the wrong time.*

action therefore makes the slump worse and so on. This pattern will be familiar to anyone who lived through the *stop–go* policies of the 1950s and 60s (*see* Fig. 117).

Thus, while fiscal policy appears at first sight to be an attractive way of running the economy it is subject to many shortcomings. As far as such things as information, time lags and inflexibility are concerned these may be offset by the use of *built-in stabilisers*. These are fiscal weapons which would automatically dampen the economy when it was overheating and boost it when it was in recession. Two such measures are progressive income tax and unemployment benefits. It would appear, however, that their effect is not great enough.

MONETARY POLICY

Monetary policy is the direction of the economy through the supply and price of money. The shortcomings of monetary policy were discussed in Chapter 22. It would appear that like fiscal policy there are problems involved in using monetary policy. Politically speaking, the use of monetary policy has been considered a right-wing method of directing the economy. Since 1974, and especially after Dennis Healey's "letter of intent" to the IMF in 1976, monetary policy has been mainly aimed at restricting the growth of the money supply. The Government tends to be most concerned with the M3 definition of the money supply, although the "letter of intent" said that DCE should not be greater than £6 billion during the year.

The 1975 Labour government's policy of restricting the money supply and cutting public spending was partially successful in reducing inflation and by the summer of 1978 the rate had dropped to 7.6 per cent. On the other hand wages continued to rise. It is an unfortunate fact that if wages continue to rise rapidly whilst the money supply does not, then there will not be enough money to meet the wages bill. The gap between wages and the money supply will be bridged by unemployment rising to reduce the wages bill. This was certainly true in the late 1970's.

In 1979 the Conservative government came to power, committed to an even more monetarist policy of restricting the money supply and cutting government expenditure. The government set targets for its *medium-term financial strategy*. However, other measures, like the abolition of the "corset" and of exchange controls, allowed the growth of the money supply to be very rapid and the *targets* were severely overshot. (The "corset" was the supplementary deposits scheme introduced in 1973 whereby banks had to make deposits of

cash at the Bank of England if they expanded their deposits too rapidly. The early 1980s, therefore, saw inflation once again at high levels and unemployment rising rapidly.) The government was unfortunate in having to try to impose this policy at time of world depression which undoubtedly made matters worse.

DIRECT INTERVENTION: INCOMES POLICY

Business organisations have always been used to government intervention in the economy in the form of taxes, the control of credit and the general framework of legislation. Since the Second World War, however, they have had to contend with periods of incomes policy when the government has sought to influence the price of their products and the wages they pay their employees. Almost always the object of incomes policy has been the control of inflation.

Inflation

Inflation is, quite simply, a rise in the general price level and therefore a fall in the value of money. Although there are several ways of measuring inflation the most common in the UK is the Retail Prices Index (*see* page 511). Inflation has several unpleasant consequences.

(*a*) *Effect on the balance of payments.* Inflation will make our exports dear to foreigners whilst imports become cheaper. Other things being equal, this will cause a deficit on the balance of payments. This will not happen, of course, if other countries are inflating at a more rapid rate than the UK. What is important, therefore, is the relative rate of inflation between countries. Unfortunately for the UK the rates of inflation of most of our trading partners have been less than our own.

(*b*) *Effect on savings.* Saving is rendered less attractive because at the end of the year the money saved will buy less goods. (Money put by for a rainy day only buys a smaller umbrella.) This could mean, therefore, that insufficient funds are released for investment, which would mean that the economy's development would be threatened. However, in recent years the high level of inflation has increased peoples' uncertainty about the future and thus caused them to increase their *precautionary* saving. This increase in the *propensity to save* has, unfortunately, had the effect of further reducing the level of *aggregate demand* in the economy and thus increased the level of unemployment.

(*c*) *Redistribution of income.* A fall in the value of money will remove purchasing power from those living on fixed incomes, such

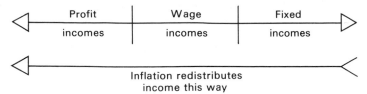

Fig. 118. *Inflation redistributes incomes.*

as pensioners, and redistribute it towards those who draw their living from prices. This is illustrated in Fig. 118. Wages are seen as being in the middle of the spectrum, their ability to keep up with or ahead of price rises will depend upon the wage-earners' bargaining power. This will tend to mean that those with strong unions, such as the miners, succeed in keeping pace with inflation whilst those with weak unions, such as shop workers, agricultural workers and bankers, lose out. Generally speaking, however, until recently, wage rates have kept ahead of inflation (*see* Fig. 119), at the expense of both fixed incomes and profits.

(*d*) *Instability.* A high rate of inflation might very possibly cause a crisis of confidence in the monetary system and a consequent breakdown of the economic order. Although we have so far avoided *hyperinflation* like that in Germany in 1923, we have experienced rates of inflation which have caused economic disruption. As inflation continues at a high rate and business organisations allow for it and predict it in their accounting systems, we stand in danger of building inflation into the economic system.

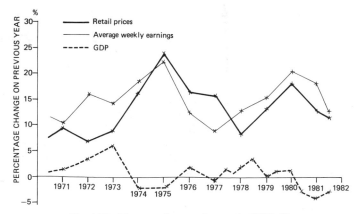

Fig. 119. *Wages, prices and growth, 1971–81.*

There are a couple of arguments to be made in favour of inflation. Firstly, a little inflation is conducive to growth. This is because it makes it easier to make profits. The business's costs are historic, i.e. it has hired the factors of production at an agreed price sometime in the past, whilst its revenues automatically increase with inflation. This, therefore, encourages investment. Secondly it would appear that eliminating inflation causes very high levels of unemployment.

The causes of inflation

There is no universal agreement amongst economists about the causes of inflation. To make matters more complicated, political viewpoints enter into the judgment. For example, right-wing opinion would blame inflation on greedy trade unions whilst the unions blame it on inept management. Three main causes of inflation are considered below.

Cost-push

This view of inflation maintains that inflation is a supply phenomenon with increased costs of production pushing up prices. Some of the factors which contribute to cost inflation are said to be the following.

(*a*) *Powerful trade unions* push up wage costs without any corresponding increase in productivity. This is one of the most widely held views of inflation. Although there is an undoubted connection between wage rates and inflation (*see* Fig. 119), the precise nature of it remains unclear.

(*b*) *Import prices* undoubtedly play a part in inflation. The rise in oil prices in the 1970s was an inflationary pressure which no government policy could combat.

(*c*) *The fall in the exchange rate* which followed the decision to float the pound in 1972 also contributed to inflation by adding to import prices. The pound devalued by over 40 per cent between 1972 and 1976 and it is estimated each 4 per cent fall in the exchange rate adds 1 per cent to domestic inflation. The pound recovered in the late 1970s to the level of its Smithsonian parity with the dollar, but then in 1981 its external value declined steeply again.

(*d*) *Mark-up pricing*, i.e. the method by which firms fix their prices on a unit cost plus profit basis (*see* page 347). This means that prices tend to go up automatically with rising costs whatever the state of demand in the economy.

Demand pull

Inflation occurs when people try to buy more goods and services than the economy is capable of producing, thus pulling up prices. This is the Keynesian view of inflation (*see* page 497). Evidence for it is said to be *wages drift*, i.e. the tendency of earnings to rise faster than wage rates. Thus a 10 per cent rise in wages may lead to a 14–15 per cent rise in earnings when overtime, bonuses, etc., are considered. This puts extra demand in the economy which will pull up prices. On many occasions the government has tried to restrain demand through fiscal and monetary policy as a way of combating inflation.

The money supply
At its simplest, the monetarist view of inflation maintains that inflation is caused by the government creating too much money. In Britain (1970–82) the average annual growth of GDP (in constant prices) has been less than 1.0 per cent. If the money supply is allowed to grow more than this it must, so the argument goes, cause inflation. The evidence for this is an observed tendency for any rise in the money supply to be followed by a rise in prices a year or so later. Certainly the 1970 Conservative government's large increase in the money supply (1971–3) was followed by massive inflation (*see* Fig. 119). It is, however, very difficult to discover the causal mechanism which links these two. In addition to this the money supply is difficult to define. Is it M3, PSL2 or DCE? Another problem is the control of the money supply. Although PSBR may be an important determinant, other factors, such as the velocity of circulation and banks' lending policies, enter into it which make it difficult to adjust the money supply with any accuracy.

What is an incomes policy?
The seeming inability of fiscal and monetary policies to deal with inflation has led successive governments to introduce incomes policies. An incomes policy tries to ensure that incomes do not rise faster than the increased wages costs can be absorbed by rising productivity. If incomes can be kept below this level there is the added bonus of extra resources which are free for investment. These simple aims have been very difficult to achieve.

Incomes policies are of two main types: *voluntary*, where the co-operation of employers and unions is sought; or *statutory*, where the government imposes its will by legislation. Just freezing wages or prices is not enough; the government must also take measures to alleviate the pressures which are causing inflation, otherwise price control is simply like breaking a thermometer to try to cure a temperature.

The "Jekyll and Hyde" syndrome

Sir Stafford Cripps, a Chancellor of the Exchequer in the 1945–51 Labour government, introduced the first incomes policy with his White Paper *Statement on Personal Incomes, Costs and Prices* in 1947. This was successful for a while but collapsed in the inflation of 1950–1. The Tories, when they came to power (1951), abandoned incomes policy in favour of fiscal and monetary measures. Incomes policy was not reintroduced until Selwyn Lloyd, the Conservative Chancellor, brought in the "pay pause" in 1961. In the years 1961 to 1978 there was some kind of incomes policy for twelve out of the seventeen years. A pattern may be discerned in this which the economist Michael Stewart has named the "Jekyll and Hyde" syndrome. Incomes policies, voluntary or statutory, are always unpopular, but Stewart says that governments have found it increasingly impossible to govern without them. The result of this is that, whatever platform the government is elected on, it adopts an incomes policy within a short time. The opposition then promises that if it is returned there will be no incomes policy. When the opposition comes to power, e.g. the Conservatives under Heath in 1970, it abolishes restraints and this results in inflation. The government is then forced to reintroduce an incomes policy (stage one, 1972). The party in opposition now declares its opposition to this, and when it in turn is returned to power (the Labour Party under Wilson in 1974) it abolishes restraints but a short while later (phase one, 1975) has to reintroduce them, and so on. This pattern was repeated again when the Conservative government was elected in 1979 on a policy of free collective bargaining. Although it continued to state that there was no incomes policy, the Government soon began to suggest norms for pay rises and to impose cash limits on nationalised industry pay settlements. Stewart's solution to this is somewhat Utopian in that he suggests that we agree that some issues are too important to be decided by party politics and that the two main parties agree on a long-term strategy for the economy. But even if all the political parties agreed, who is going to tell the unions?

WHATEVER HAPPENED TO GROWTH?

We have seen that there are four main objectives of government policy: stable prices, full employment, a sound balance of payments and economic growth. But the first three of these are only means to an end. The increased wealth and welfare of the economy is almost entirely dependent upon economic growth. It is no good having a large surplus in the balance of payments if the national income is declining, and it is no use curing inflation by depressing everyone's living standards. The UK's economic growth since the Second World War has been disappointing when compared with other European states and in the early 1980s it became positively depressing (*see* Fig. 119). Despite this, the last comprehensive plan for growth was Lord George-Brown's *National Plan* of 1964, unless one includes Edward Heath's ill-fated attempt at eliminating "lame ducks" in 1970.

North Sea oil may solve the UK's external problems but it will not put an end to the domestic malaise.

SELF-ASSESSMENT QUESTIONS

A. 1. Define: (*a*) fiscal policy; (*b*) PSBR; (*c*) cost-push inflation; (*d*) an *ad valorem* tax.

B. 2. List the taxes which are regressive.

3. True or false?

(*a*) Central government revenues come mainly from taxes whilst local government revenues come mainly from rates.

(*b*) The national insurance scheme is self-supporting.

(*c*) Income is more evenly distributed than wealth.

(*d*) A budget surplus will always have the effect of decreasing the level of aggregate demand.

(*e*) The government's borrowing has a deflationary effect upon the economy because it takes money out of circulation.

C. 4. True or false?

(*a*) Taxes on expenditure raise more revenue than income tax.

(*b*) The majority of the national debt is held by foreigners.

(*c*) Inflation will worsen the country's balance of payments if the elasticity of demand for its exports and imports is inelastic.

(*d*) Keynes' theory envisaged that inflation would not take place until the economy was fully employed.

(*e*) The government's borrowing has a deflationary effect upon the economy because it takes money out of circulation.

5. Analyse the reasons why inflation and unemployment (slumpflation) are occurring at the same time.

ASSIGNMENTS

1. Update Tables LIV and LVI.

2. Compile a table to go with Fig. 119 to show the national and international economic and political events during this period.

CHAPTER TWENTY-FOUR

The Nature and Functions of Law

CHAPTER OBJECTIVES

After studying this chapter you should be able to:
* discuss the nature of law;
* explain and discuss the role and functions of law with particular reference to business organisations and the government;
* define and distinguish between different types of legal rights and duties;
* explain the nature and forms of legal liability;
* outline the origin and sources of English law;
* discuss the role of legislation and outline the rules of statutory interpretation.

THE IDEA OF LAW

Any attempt to define and explain the "idea of law" in a book of this nature can do no more than give a very limited introduction to an important philosophical subject. Unlike scientific laws, *law* cannot be objectively defined, let alone proved. It is the product of man, not of nature, and it means different things to different people according to their time, culture and the social structure in which they live.

The greatest of the world's philosophers have considered the "idea of law", but no one definition has been universally accepted. There are, however, three main kinds of *jurisprudence* (legal theory): firstly *historical*, which studies the growth of law, particularly in connection with the development of the state; secondly *analytical*, which studies the concepts and structures of the law as they actually are (this is the approach which is usually favoured in this country); and thirdly *sociological*, which considers how the workings of the law affect society.

To a greater or lesser extent, all jurisprudence attempts to answer the following four questions:

(*a*) What is law?
(*b*) Why is law necessary?

(c) What is the purpose of law?

(d) How just is the law?

We will attempt to answer these questions, but you should always remember that different theories attempt to answer different questions. Some are concerned with the *form* of law, some with its *concept*, and other with law's *function*.

Similarly, methods of enquiry differ: an *inductive* approach produces definitions and answers from the observations of actual situations and legal phenomena, whilst a *deductive* approach involves formulating definitions and answers based on initial assumptions about the nature of law. In our own legal system the common law follows an inductive approach but legislation is often the result of a deductive process of law-making. Of greatest importance, perhaps, is the fact that all definitions of law are to a greater or lesser extent, consciously or subconsciously coloured by ideological factors—social, economic or political.

Our objective is not to attempt definitive answers to such questions, but to stimulate further thought, discussion and argument.

What is law?

Although there is no universally accepted definition of "law", we can usefully begin our discussion of this question by quoting three well-known jurists.

> The body of principles recognised and applied by the State in the administration of justice. ... In other words the law consists of rules recognised and acted upon by courts of justice. (Salmond)

> A law is a general rule of external human action enforced by a sovereign political authority. (Holland)

> A social process for settling disputes and securing an ordered existence in the community. (Paton)

In all three definitions two ideas are either expressly or impliedly involved. Firstly, that law is a *set of rules* by which human conduct within society is ordered and controlled. Secondly, reference to the *state* or other sovereign power within society (the state being basically defined in territorial terms). The first of these ideas is largely self-explanatory and uncontentious but reference to the state raises fundamental issues about the nature of our law.

Laws are certainly enforced by the state, but does the state impose its own corporate will on its members or is law essentially the will of the people recognised and adopted by the state? Clearly, an individual or business organisation is unlikely to volunteer money to the state to finance its activities, and taxation by law is therefore a necessary imposition. Apart from such examples, however, which is true? Perhaps the truth lies somewhere in between. Primitive law consists of basic social norms and customs which evolve spontaneously. In so far as modern law still reflects these basic social norms and customs, it comes from the people. However, factional interests very soon emerge in a society and in the past our law has been imposed blatantly to serve class or factional interests, for example those of landowners. Today it is used equally as boldly by governments to fulfil their policies and serve their political philosophy. To this extent law is imposed. You must decide for yourself the extent to which the imposition of law is for the benefit of society as a whole and the extent to which it is still used to further the interests of the ruling élite, whatever political party they may or may not belong to.

On the assumption that a great deal of our contempory law is imposed upon us by the government of the day, politics must be involved in its formulation, and any attempt to view law as a self-contained discipline is unrealistic. Indeed, *government* can be viewed as a composite of both the political and legal processes. Such matters as industrial and welfare law frequently raise issues of straight party politics. Furthermore, there is the view that we are governed by an "elected dictatorship" which, providing it can command a majority in the House of Commons, can quite lawfully use the political process and the supremacy of Parliamentary legislation to realise its political aims for up to five years without effective restraint. Consequently, it is argued that there should be a "bill of rights", which would be above the normal political processes and legislative repeal or amendment, allowing the courts to protect basic constitutional rights from dictatorial and arbitrary use of political power. Whilst it is true that politics and government are carried on within a framework of law, it is essential to remember that this framework is itself the product of the political process. Hence, we could say that it is the political process rather than law which actually rules us.

The concepts of morality and law are clearly closely linked. Virtually all serious crimes are immoral acts, e.g. murder and theft, and some essentially immoral acts are crimes, e.g. perjury (lying on oath) and libel may both be the subject of criminal proceedings; but a vast number of criminal acts committed each year, minor motoring offences in particular, are not usually considered immoral acts but are nevertheless punished. Conversely, many moral offences, adultery for example, go unpunished by the criminal law. The difference between them in legal terms is that law is enforced by the state whilst morals are not, except when law and morality coincide. However, the legal distinction between law and morality does raise an important socio-political issue about the purpose of law: should law be used to enforce morals?

Each of you will have your own views on this, but it is worth remembering that the law is inherently conservative and tends to reflect the views of an atypical élite from a previous generation, lagging behind contemporary social norms. Leading lawyers themselves tend to be conservative (with a small "c") by virtue of their socio-economic background and status, and often seem to be out of touch with the "real" world. In the celebrated *Lady Chatterley's Lover* Case in 1961, prosecuting counsel asked the jury, "Is this a book that you would ever wish your wife or your servants to read", and in the *Nasty Tales* Case in 1973, the judge asked whether it could be for the public good for hippies to go and live in communes. (Both cases were prosecutions for obscenity.)

Why do we need law?

All except anarchists would agree that the existence of law is necessary. A society presupposes order and it would seem that the natural order usually to be found in small primitive communities breaks down as the "forces of evil" (antisocial behaviour in general) become more powerful as the society becomes larger and more complex.

Whilst one could hardly maintain that a large organisation is an "evil force" within society, it is clear that controls on any powerful body or individual are necessary if the interests of the majority are to be protected. For example, experience has shown that the absence of health and safety, employment protection and monopoly legislation can have harmful socio-economic effects on a society.

What is the purpose of law?

Law's purpose is usually considered to be the general regulation and control of society, the criminal law in particular providing minimum standards of social behaviour. The legal system complements legal principle by providing means of resolving conflicts and dealing with those who infringe legally enforced social norms. However, on the assumption that it is only a small minority of individuals and organisations in society that the law has to positively control, law can equally well be considered as an *enabling medium* for the majority. For example, individuals are able to use and enjoy their land because the tort of nuisance restrains the few who would interfere with it, and companies could not exist or function as they do without the basic concept of juristic personality (*see* page 18) and the framework of commercial and industrial law in general.

Other more specific views of the purpose of law do, of course, exist, for it is the servant of economic and political forces and it is used by powerful pressure groups to achieve their objectives. Even Bentham's "greatest good for the greatest number" philosophy of "utilitarianism" and Pound's view of law as a process of "social engineering" (a sociological approach) must be seen in this context and not in isolation.

It is not within the scope of this book to argue the validity of different legal theories, but one well-known example will illustrate how economic and political ideology can determine theories of the nature and purpose of law. In classic Marxist philosophy, law is viewed as the institutionalisation of the prevailing ideology which the socio-economic élite of a society use to coerce the masses into obedience in order to preserve their privileged position. Thus, law's purpose is here seen in terms of achieving socio-economic and political objectives. This may be a rather too unsophisticated view of law's nature and purpose and it is certainly extreme, but many of you may often have considered that the government uses law to impose its will upon the individual, and that large organisations of all kinds are able to use the law to further their commercial (or other) interests at your expense.

It is clear from just this one example that it is difficult to discuss the ultimate purpose of law without asking fundamental questions about the nature of society as it is and as we might wish it to be. Such questions merit a book to themselves but we shall examine the specific functions and uses of law in relation to organisations and by the government, and the nature and sources of legal rights and duties and forms of legal liability in general later in this chapter.

Law and justice

The ultimate aim of all law should surely be to promote justice, but any attempt to define law in these terms meets two serious obstacles. Firstly, "justice" is a vague concept, meaning different things to different people; secondly, law must be considered within its socio-political context and, assuming that law exists to serve society, what may be justice with regard to one individual may not be useful to society. Theft, for example, is a serious crime and it is right that it should be punished. What, however, of the woman who steals food from a supermarket because she cannot afford to feed her family? Is justice served by her imprisonment? Law can at best hope to achieve the greatest good for the greatest number.

It is possible, however, to talk in more objective terms about the distinction between procedural justice and substantive justice. The former is concerned with the legal process and the latter, justice in particular cases. At one time the common law was concerned almost solely with procedure, and even today the complexity of the legal process seems to act as a positive deterrent to the ordinary man who seeks redress at law. It is probably not unfair to lay most of the blame for this at the door of lawyers themselves. A sociologist might further argue that lawyers have a vested interest in preserving the mystique of the law for by this they preserve their status in society.

Justice at law can be assessed in terms of *natural justice*, the assumption being that there exists a perfect code of rules to which human law should aspire. Two basic principles of natural justice are that a man must be allowed to speak in his own cause and that conflict resolution must be by an impartial judge. These are, of course, completely acceptable, but the weakness of natural justice as an objective criterion for comparison lies in its own human philo-sophical origins, unless, of course, you believe in divine intervention and guidance! Perhaps all that one can say is that some laws and some legal systems promote justice more than others.

ORGANISATIONS AND THE LAW

"Organisations and the law" is a basic theme of this book and the various aspects of the relationship have already been discussed in depth. Only a brief summary is necessary here. Law *regulates* the activities of organisations by providing a framework of rules governing their formation and dissolution; their use of resources and other activities; and their responsibility and accountability to providers of finance, employees, customers and the community in general. At the same time, however, this framework *enables* organ-isations to achieve their commercial and other objectives. For ex-ample, they are able to plan their activities and determine their responsibilities and liabilities according to known rules of law, and it is by making contracts that they acquire resources and sell their products and services.

GOVERNMENTS AND THE LAW

Any government that can maintain a majority in Parliament is vir-tually an "elected dictatorship" lasting up to five years. During this time the supremacy of parliamentary legislation gives a government almost totally unfettered power which it can use to try to achieve its social, economic and political objectives. In addition, it can sometimes curb the dissemination of information about its activities by invoking the Official Secrets Acts, and the Attorney-General (a minister in the government and its chief legal adviser) and the Director of Public Prosecutions (an officer working under the general supervision of the Attorney-General) will sometimes exercise a measure of control over the use of the judicial process, although both should fulfil their functions free from political influence and considerations. Certain criminal offences, e.g. under the official secrets legislation, can only be prosecuted by or with the consent of the Attorney-General or Director of Public Prosecutions and the Attorney-General exercises (albeit rarely) the Crown's prerogative power to stay criminal prosecutions on indictment by the entry of a *nolle prosequi*. In addition, the Attorney-General sometimes acts as a barrier between the individual and the courts in so far as there is a wide and growing range of laws which cannot be enforced without his consent. For example, there can by no prosecutions brought under the Race Relations Act 1976 or the Theatres Act 1968 (involving censorship) unless the Attorney-General agrees to associate himself with a private individual in the public interest. Similar consent is also necessary before actions to restrain a public nuisance or other interference with the public interest can be brought. These are known as *relator* actions and the Attorney-General has an absolute discretion whether or not to initiate such proceedings when requested to do so by an individual. He is accountable only to Parliament for his decision.

This is, of course, a rather too simple and somewhat cynical view of a government's use of law, but it is entirely valid in so far as it reflects both the important interrelationships between law, politics and the political process, and the weakness of legal controls over the executive (*see* page 432) under our present system of government. Nevertheless, the law continues to have an important regulatory function with regard to the exercise of executive power but, without a written constitution to protect the rights of the individual by placing limits on the power of the legislature and executive, "government according to the law" is theoretically open to whatever interpretation the government of the day wishes to put upon it. The courts may interpret legislation and review both quasi-judicial and administrative government decisions for possible illegality, but they cannot challenge government policy nor Parliament's power to legislate. Indeed it is possible (although unusual) for a statute to exclude all judicial review of government decision-making in matters covered by the particular statute. In other words, so long as a government does not exceed the power given to it by legislation (often its own), its activities and decisions are not open to judicial review and it is possible for even this power of review to be excluded.

Whether or not you feel that stronger legal curbs are necessary on the power of the executive, the law is the basic medium through which governments implement their policies. Acts of Parliament and delegated legislation directly give effect to government policies, whilst ministerial decisions (made under statutory authority) and the activities of quasi-governmental bodies (established by legislation) are indirect methods of using the law to implement policy. The quasi-governmental functions of the Monopolies and Mergers Commission and the Director General of Fair Trading are particularly important to trading organisations, whilst public corporations are both trading organisations and quasi-governmental bodies in so far as their economic activity is partly dictated by government policy.

THE ROLE OF LEGISLATION

The role of legislation and its use by governments merits further discussion. A government's ultimate objectives will always be the subject of political debate in the same way as the content of the legislation promoted by the government of the day will nearly always reflect its economic and political beliefs. However, all British governments use legislation for three main purposes.

(*a*) To maintain the fabric of society. In particular, it controls antisocial behaviour and protects an individual's basic social rights, e.g. to education, to welfare services and to freedom from discrimination. To a lesser extent it also protects some basic traditional "legal" rights of the individual, e.g. the Criminal Law Act 1977 supplements a residential occupier's common law right to possession of his property by making "squatting" a criminal offence in certain circumstances.

(*b*) To raise by taxation the necessary finance for its activities, thereby implementing its fiscal policies.

(*c*) To create or repeal, revise or reform the law. New principles can be introduced into the body of the law by legislation, e.g. the concept of "unfair dismissal" by the Employment Protection Act 1975, whilst bad, unpopular or unworkable law can be removed, e.g. the Trade Union and Labour Relations Act 1974 repealed the Industrial Relations Act 1971. Consolidating and codifying Acts are sometimes passed. The former re-enact a number of statutes on the same subject with little amendment but in a rationalised and therefore clarified form, e.g. the Employment Protection (Consolidation) Act 1978, which repealed and re-enacted the provisions of the Contracts of Employment Act 1972, much of the Employment

Protection Act 1975 and the Redundancy Payments Act 1965, and some of the Trade Union and Labour Relations Acts 1974 and 1976. The latter (codifying Acts) seek to rationalise both statute and case law on a given subject into one coherent code, although it is the expression rather than the content of the statute which usually differs substantially from the previous law. The Sale of Goods Act 1893 (now the Sale of Goods Act 1979) was a particularly good example of a codifying Act. The need to revise substantive rules of law ("lawyers' law") by statute may become apparent through the working of the doctrine of binding judicial precedent. This is particularly true following an unpopular (and perhaps politically unacceptable) decision of the House of Lords, e.g. the Trade Disputes Act 1965 overruled the House of Lords' decision in *Rookes* v. *Barnard* (1964). Since its creation in 1965, the Law Commission (*see* page 623) is the major influence on a government's use of legislation to revise substantive rules of law.

SOCIETY AND THE LAW

Within society in general, law is used as a method of organising, regulating and controlling activities in order to protect and preserve social norms. This it achieves:

(*a*) through a system of largely correlative (corresponding) legal rights and duties;

(*b*) by imposing criminal or civil liability and enforcing sanctions or remedies against those who infringe legally recognised social norms; and

(*c*) by providing methods of resolving conflict where the existence of a right or duty is disputed, or where conflicting rights must be reconciled. (Conflict resolution is discussed in depth in the next chapter.)

Rights and duties
Rights
A *right* can be said to be a legally protected interest, and a *duty* an obligation to respect such an interest. The obligation may involve either positive action or the avoidance of conduct which would infringe the right. In the strict sense, rights are protected by correlative duties, i.e. the existence of a particular right involves the existence of a corresponding duty, enforceable by the owner of the right, to respect that right. However, in a wider sense a right includes any legally recognised interest irrespective of the existence of a correlative duty. Thus the term embraces all legally conferred

benefits and advantages. For example, neither the right of a land-owner to walk on his land, nor the right of a person to make a will controlling the succession to his estate (property) involves the imposition of a duty upon anyone else.

Rights can be classified in various ways, e.g. into proprietary or personal rights, into rights *in rem* or rights *in personam*, and into public or private rights. There is of course overlap between the classifications.

Proprietary and personal rights. The distinction between proprietary and personal rights is based upon the object or subject-matter of the right. Proprietary rights are rights of property, either material property—personal possessions or land—or intangible property such as the goodwill of a business, trade-marks and debts. Personal rights are a matter of an individual's status or condition, e.g. the right to one's reputation, protected by the tort of defamation, is of general application, whilst the right to vote is restricted to persons over eighteen years of age and the right to social security payments is restricted to persons who satisfy certain socio-economic criteria.

Rights in rem and rights in personam. A right *in rem* corresponds to a duty imposed on persons in general, whilst a right *in personam* corresponds to a duty imposed on specific individuals. (We have already explained the origin of these terms on page 196.) The right of a freeholder to the occupation of his land is a right *in rem*, a right to the land itself which is enforceable against the "world at large". The owner of a trade-mark or registered design also has a right *in rem*. Conversely, the right of a creditor to be paid a debt is a right *in personam*, a right exerciseable only against the debtor himself. This distinction explains why a bank (or other lender) will usually take a legal mortgage over property when making a substantial advance to an organisation or individual. The contract of loan gives the bank a right *in personam* to recover the money from the borrower whilst the legal mortgage gives a right *in rem* to sell or otherwise deal with the property charged as security if the borrower cannot make repayment.

Duties

A *duty* may be *correlative* to a right or *absolute*, i.e. owed directly to the state in the interests of the members of society generally. The duty not to interfere with a landowner's right to possession of his land is an example of the former and the duty of an individual to refrain from breaking the criminal law is the primary example of the latter. In addition, many social-welfare and other public duties are absolute.

Any violation of a right or breach of a duty is a legal wrong which results in the state imposing some sanction against the wrongdoer and/or ordering the payment of compensation or the granting of some other form of legal redress to the injured party.

Public and private rights and duties
There is a basic distinction made between public and private law and hence between public and private rights. Basically, private law relates to rights and duties among individuals, e.g. those protected and enforced by the law of contract and the law of torts, while public law comprises those branches of law in which the state has a direct interest, mainly administrative, constitutional, criminal and revenue law. There is, of course, some incidental overlap: an individual may bring a private prosecution against another individual, e.g. for assault, and a public authority may be sued in contract and tort in much the same way as an individual.

Public rights and duties. Public rights and duties are mainly created and regulated by statute, although some basic principles of the criminal law and some traditional freedoms are still partly embodied in the common law. Statute imposes a wide range of public duties on an equally wide range of individuals and public bodies, e.g. an individual's duties to refrain from breaking the criminal law and to make a tax return, and the duties owed by public bodies to provide health care and education and to supply and maintain essential utility services such as electricity, gas and water.

Public rights range from an individual's right to various social security and welfare benefits, to the exercise of basic constitutional rights and freedoms, e.g. the right to vote and the freedoms of person, speech, association, worship and meeting and procession; and from the right of a local authority to make by-laws and compulsory purchase orders, to the right of the Attorney-General to refuse his consent to a *relator* action (*see* above).

Private rights and duties. Private rights and duties are derived from the common law rather than from statute and comprise the theoretical basis of the civil law, e.g. the law of contract protects rights and enforces obligations on the basis of the agreement reached between the individuals involved. Thus, each party has a right to expect the other to perform his contractual obligations, and each has a correlative duty to do so. It is the law of torts, however, which is the source of most important private rights and duties. You have already seen in Chapter 10 that a tort is a legal wrong against an individual which gives a right of action at civil law for damages, the purposes of the law of tort being to regulate and defend the rights and interests of individuals against certain types of wrongful conduct. It also decides in what cases compensation should be awarded for damage suffered by their infringement. The rights and interests protected and enforced by the law of contract differ in that their basis is the agreement between those involved and not a set of legal rules imposed on society in general as is the case in the law of torts.

For historical reasons each tort protects a particular private right or interest and does so by imposing a correlative private duty. This is probably best explained by a brief survey of the more important torts.

The tort of trespass to land protects an individual's possession of land by imposing a duty on others not to intentionally and directly interfere with it without lawful authority. By imposing similar duties, trespass to the person (assault, battery and false imprisonment) protects an individual's right to be free from intentional interference with his person or freedom of movement, and trespass to goods protects both an individual's right to possession of his goods and his interest in their physical condition. However, the tort of conversion, which also protects an individual's right to possession and control of his goods (but not their physical condition), is more usually relied upon where there is an intentional interference which amounts to an unjustifiable denial of title to them, e.g. by stealing goods or by selling goods without title to them.

The tort of nuisance protects a person's right to use or enjoy his land or some right over or in connection with the land of another, e.g. a right of way or fishing rights, free from interference. Nuisance and trespass to land differ in two main ways.

(*a*) Nuisance protects interests in land against indirect interference, e.g. by noise, vibrations and smells, or interference by pollution of a river in the case of fishing rights, and not direct interference.

(*b*) Damage must be proved for an action in nuisance to succeed whilst *all* forms of trespass are actionable *per se* (without proof of damage).

The tort of defamation protects the purely personal right of an individual to his reputation, whilst the tort of negligence protects an individual's right not to suffer injury to his person or property through the negligent act or omission of another. The correlative duty of reasonable care to "neighbours" (formulated in *Donoghue* v. *Stevenson* (1932)) is the best known and most important legal duty imposed by the law of torts.

The tort of passing-off protects proprietary rights in industrial property, e.g. the goodwill of a business and trademarks. As such, this particular tort has more relevance to business organisations than to ordinary individuals. Some rights and duties protected and imposed by the law of torts have a statutory origin, and these too affect organisations more than individuals, e.g. the "common duty of care" owed by an occupier of premises under the Occupiers' Liability Act 1957. Indeed some are specifically designed to apply to organisations, e.g. the duties imposed upon employers by the Health and Safety at Work, etc., Act 1974 and other legislation such as the Factories Act 1961, which the 1974 Act will eventually replace (*see* Chapter 10).

In a complex society, one function of law is to balance and re-concile conflicting rights. Hence it follows that virtually all rights, be they proprietary or personal, *in rem* or *in personam*, public or private, are qualified, not absolute, and therefore subject to some restriction. For example, the public right of freedom of speech is restricted by the private right to reputation and public duties relating to national security and obscenity. The right of a local authority to make by-laws is similarly not absolute for it is subject to a cor-relative duty not to exceed the powers given to it by statute—the *ultra vires* rule.

Private rights are similarly qualified. The rights of a landowner to possess and use his land are restricted by public duties imposed by planning legislation and by statutory public rights of compulsory purchase. Again, the right of an individual to his reputation is also restricted in several ways, e.g. Members of Parliament enjoy an absolute privilege (a right) to say whatever they like during Parliamentary debate even though it may be defamatory.

Different forms of legal liability

It is partly according to the type of legal liability involved that one workable distinction can be drawn between various types of legal wrongs. This is because a particular act or omission may constitute more than one type. For example, taking property belonging to another is both a crime (theft) and a tort (conversion), and negligent driving by a taxi-driver which causes injury to his passenger is a breach of contract in addition to being both a crime and a tort.

Workable distinctions can also be drawn on the basis of the dif-ferent functions, procedures and consequences involved in different branches of the law. Under the English legal system the basic dis-tinction affecting individuals and organisations alike is that between criminal and civil law. We will therefore discuss the nature and function of criminal and civil law and then, more specifically, criminal and civil liability. Having done this we will consider the different concepts of *faults*, *strict*, and *vicarious* liability, and their relevance to criminal and civil law.

Criminal and civil law

A crime is a breach of a public duty, a legal wrong which affects society in general. The state uses the criminal law to regulate the conduct of its citizens and to protect society. This it endeavours to do by prohibiting certain types of conduct and imposing sanctions upon those members of society that disregard the prohibition.

A civil wrong is a breach of a private duty which may arise from an agreement between individuals, as in the law of contract, or be imposed by a rule of law, as in the law of torts (the two areas of civil law with which we have been concerned in this book). Thus the *civil law* is concerned with protecting and enforcing legal rights and duties between individuals, and ordering the payment of compensation for damage suffered when they have been infringed or broken.

Since it is impossible to distinguish between crimes and civil wrongs (torts in particular) purely on the basis of the act or omission involved, various other criteria for distinction have been suggested.

(*a*) A functional distinction. This has already been drawn but you will no doubt have appreciated that the criminal law indirectly protects private rights by its deterrent effect.

(*b*) The consequences of a successfully brought action. A successfully brought prosecution results in conviction of the accused and the imposition of *sanctions* upon him, conventionally in the form of a fine or a term of imprisonment. A successfully brought civil action, however, usually results in the defendant paying damages to the plaintiff, although other remedies may be granted by the court, e.g. an order for the specific performance of a contract or for an injunction to restrain the commission of a tortious (wrongful) act.

(*c*) The different purpose of these sanctions and remedies. Criminal sanctions are intended to punish and reform the criminal and deter him and others from similar activities, thereby protecting society. Civil remedies are designed to compensate the individual for the damage he suffers as a result of the interference with his private rights. In an action for breach of contract an award of damages is generally intended to put the injured party into the financial position he could reasonably have expected to have enjoyed had the defendant fulfilled his obligations, e.g. the loss of profit on a cancelled order. In an action in tort, damages are designed to restore (as far as this is possible) the injured party to the position he enjoyed before his right was infringed. It is obvious, however, that money is poor compensation for many kinds of personal injury and even where business interests are injured, e.g. goodwill, it is often difficult to estimate the financial loss accurately.

However, civil proceedings may result in "punishment" and criminal proceedings in "compensation", but these are always ancillary to the primary purpose of the proceedings. In exceptional circumstances exemplary or punitive damages may be awarded in civil actions, e.g. for defamation. Here the award exceeds the plaintiff's actual loss and it is designed to satisfy his wounded pride and to act as deterrent to others. Under the Powers of Criminal Courts Act 1973 a criminal court may make a compensation order against a convicted criminal ordering him to pay compensation for personal injury, loss or damage resulting from his offence. In addition, the Crown Court can make a criminal bankruptcy order.

(d) There are different courts which deal with different infringements of the law. However, as you will see in the next chapter, most courts exercise both civil and criminal jurisdiction. Nevertheless, there are real differences in the form of trial, procedure and rules of evidence (although in this last matter the Civil Evidence Act 1968 provides that a criminal conviction is admissible evidence of the breach of public duty in a later civil action based upon the same facts). In particular the burden of proof differs. In a criminal case the prosecution must prove the accused's guilt "beyond reasonable doubt", whilst the plaintiff in a civil action must prove an infringement of his rights by the defendant "on the balance of probabilities", a lighter burden of proof.

(e) The role of the state. In effect, criminal proceedings are initiated and controlled by the state, whereas civil proceedings are initiated and controlled by individuals. Only the state can stop a criminal prosecution (by entering a *nolle prosequi*) once it has begun, whilst a civil dispute is often resolved by the parties before judgment. However, in so far as the stability of our society depends largely on the protection of private rights, the state has an interest in seeing that they are protected. Thus, it provides means of conflict resolution and enforces civil judgments.

Criminal liability
There are two distinct elements in criminal liability:

   (a) a specified act or omission (the *actus reus* or "guilty act"); and
   (b) a specific state of mind (the *mens rea* or "guilty mind").

For example, under the Theft Act 1968 the *actus reus* of theft is the appropriation of property belong to another, and the *mens rea* is a dishonest intention to permanently deprive the other of that property. Similarly, the *actus reus* of burglary is entering a building as a trespasser, and the *mens rea* is the intention to commit certain offences inside, e.g. theft. It follows that it is merely the *tort* of trespass and not the the crime of burglary to unlawfully enter a building without the required unlawful intention.

Both elements are necessary for criminal liability, for where punishment is involved the mere breach of a prohibition should not be a crime. You will see later, however, that there are a range of statutory criminal offences where a "guilty mind" as such is not required. These are crimes of strict liability.

The *actus reus* embraces not only the specific act or omission required for the offence but also the wider circumstances (if any) which may be specified in the definition, e.g. in theft the property taken must "belong to another" and therefore taking abandoned property cannot be theft, no matter how dishonest the intention.

It is common to translate *mens rea* as the "guilty mind", but this translation is somewhat misleading, since a person may quite possibly commit a crime without any sense of guilt, and even in the belief that his conduct is justified at law. It is more correct to explain the *mens rea* as one of four possible mental attitudes in relation to the *actus reus*. In order of culpability these are:

(*a*) *intention*—a person both foresees and desires the consequences of his act or omission;

(*b*) *recklessness*—a person foresees the probable consequences of his act but does not desire them, i.e. he takes a deliberate risk;

(*c*) *negligence*—a person does not foresee the consequences of his act that a reasonable and prudent man would have foreseen, and he does not, therefore, desire them;

(*d*) *blameless inadvertence*—a person neither foresees nor should have foreseen the consequences of his act.

The law must distinguish between these mental attitudes. Clearly, an intention to commit the *actus reus* should result in conviction and punishment, whilst blameless inadvertence should not, but to what extent should recklessness and negligence warrant punishment? As a generalisation, we can say that a reckless person is usually convicted and punished whilst a negligent person is not. Thus *mens rea* can be acceptably defined as intention or recklessness with respect to the circumstances and consequences of the *actus reus*.

Civil liability

We have already said a considerable amount about the nature of torts and breaches of contract, the *civil wrongs* with which business organisations are most likely to be involved, and you have seen that they are both infringements of private rights.

Civil liability clearly requires an act or omission but, because the essence of civil law is the protection of rights, it is neither realistic nor necessarily productive to attempt to list and define specific acts or omissions which infringe these rights. In contrast, the criminal law specifically defines the acts or omissions which it prohibits. In short, only acts or omissions within the definition of a particular crime can be prosecuted, whilst any act which unlawfully interferes with a private right gives grounds for an action at civil law.

The importance and relevance of mental attitudes in civil liability varies, but far less emphasis is generally placed upon it than is the case in criminal liability. This is because the purpose and consequences of a civil action is compensation of the injured party and not punishment of the wrongdoer. For example, whilst a breach of contract may have been *committed* intentionally, recklessly or negligently, the reason for awarding compensation to the plaintiff is the infringement of his private right by the breach itself. The wrongdoer's liability does not differ, whether he intended to break the contract, was negligent in his conduct or acted with blameless inadvertence.

In the law of torts mental attitudes are more important and most torts require *intention*, although *culpable inadvertence* (negligence) is the essence of negligence, the most important tort. However, whilst most people who commit torts other than negligence desire the consequence of their act or omission, *intention* as the required mental attitude usually has a more technical meaning and relates to the act or omission and not to its consequences. For example, a person who walks over another's land, believing reasonably but wrongly that he is entitled to do so (he may believe that he is following a public right of way), has committed trespass because he intended his actions, even though he did not intend to interfere with the other's right of possession.

If the law is going to protect private rights effectively, the mental attitude of the defendant towards the act or omission which infringed the plaintiff's right, must be a lesser consideration than the infringement itself.

Fault liability

Liability based upon *fault* is primarily associated with the tort of negligence, for here a person incurs civil liability for failure to exercise reasonable care in his activities. With a few important exceptions, e.g. manslaughter and causing death by dangerous driving, negligence is rarely the gist of a criminal offence and, therefore, person is rarely criminally liable if he is merely at "fault".

It is perfectly proper that anybody who is injured by the fault of another should be able to recover compensation from that person. However, fault liability has become widely and seriously questioned, particularly in relation to road traffic accidents, industrial injuries and injuries caused by defective products. The principle suffers from two important practical weaknesses. Firstly, it assumes that the person at fault has sufficient financial resources to compensate those that he has injured. Secondly, in reality compensation is frequently paid by an insurance company or by the employer of the person at fault. Taken together, these defects significantly reduce the validity of fault as a basis for civil liability. Indeed this strongly supports the argument for extending the principle of strict liability (discussed below) in combination with various techniques of compensation through insurance. This would relegate legal proof of fault to a position of secondary importance behind the social right to receive compensation for injury caused by another.

The report of the Royal Commission on Civil Liberty and Compensation for Personal Injury, 1978 Cmnd. 7054 (the Pearson Report) proposed that there should be an improved version of the existing state industrial injuries scheme to provide compensation to those who suffer injury involving motor vehicles on roads and other land to which the public has access. A conventional action in tort against the person at fault would still be necessary if the compensation paid under the state scheme was inadequate. The Report also recommended improvements in the industrial injuries scheme itself, and the imposition of strict liability in tort on producers of defective products which cause death or personal injury ("product liability" was discussed on page 376).

The partial replacement of fault liability by a scheme along the lines proposed by the Pearson Report raises important moral, social and economic questions. However, the future of such proposals may well depend on political factors; in particular the TUC will always use its considerable political influence to promote improvements in industrial accident compensation and this may be a spur to the introduction of the necessary legislation.

Strict liability

Where criminal or civil liability is *strict*, the wrongdoer's mental attitude is irrelevant, i.e. proof that he acted intentionally or was at fault in his conduct is unnecessary. He is liable merely because he has committed the *actus reus* of the particular criminal offence or has caused the plaintiff harm by breaking a legal duty owed to him.

The scope of strict liability in criminal law is limited because it is generally wrong in principle that a person who neither intended his action nor acted recklessly should be punished. However, many offences of strict liability have been created by statute because they are an effective means of social regulation; almost invariably they involve only a small degree of "wrong". Nevertheless, as you have seen, there is a legal presumption that *mens rea* is always necessary for criminal liability. Therefore, the statute must expressly or impliedly exclude it. Statutes creating road traffic offences and offences relating to the sale of food and drugs are good examples of this having been done.

In the law of contract a person commits a civil wrong merely by breaking his contractual obligations; therefore civil liability for breach of contract can be said to be strict. This applies even where a business organisation sells "unmerchantable goods" in breach of s.14 of the Sale of Goods Act 1979 without the slightest idea or opportunity to find out that the goods were unmerchantable.

Strict liability in tort is found where a particular activity is inherently dangerous to the community. The best-known (but probably least used) example is the rule in *Rylands* v. *Fletcher* (1868). This applies where a "dangerous thing" which a person has brought on to his land and which is not naturally there, e.g. water, gas or fire, escapes from the land and causes damage. The mere fact that damage occurs in such circumstances renders the occupier of the land liable in tort. However, liability is *strict* and not *absolute* and the occupier can plead certain defences, e.g. that the escape occurred through the unforeseeable "act of a stranger" or that the occupier was acting under statutory authority in the use of his land.

Quite clearly the rule cannot apply to every non-natural user of land, otherwise all industrial activity would be subject to it. Thus, strict liability is imposed on those who pursue activities which involve an unreasonable risk to the community or an extraordinary use of land. It is for the court to decide on the facts of the case whether an activity falls within the rule, and it is clear that a judge will balance the magnitude of the risk against the defendant's interest in the activity and its benefit to the community. The Law Commission's Report on *Civil Liability for Dangerous Things and Activities* (published in 1970) suggested that the general basis on which strict liability is imposed, and upon which the principle should be developed, is the concept of "special danger", i.e.

activities involving "a more than ordinary risk of accidents or a risk of more than ordinary damage if accidents in fact result." Whilst the rule in *Rylands* v. *Fletcher* (1868) cannot be allowed to interfere with necessary industrial activity, it is equally clear that the community must be protected from dangers inherent in the industrial use of certain materials. Consequently a number of statutes impose strict liability for damage caused by "environmental hazards". Examples are the Nuclear Installations Act 1965, dealing with nuclear incidents, the Merchant Shipping (Oil Pollution) Act 1971, dealing with escape or discharge of oil from a merchant ship, and the Control of Pollution Act 1974, dealing with unlawful deposits of poisonous, noxious or polluting waste. In addition, the Animals Act 1971 imposes strict liability on the keeper of a dangerous animal which causes damage.

Liability in the tort of nuisance is probably strict if the plaintiff only seeks an injunction, for here the defendant is merely forbidden from commencing or continuing a wrongful activity. (An action for damages in nuisance probably requires proof of fault.) More generally, liability for breach of a duty imposed by statute, e.g. under the Factory Acts, is usually strict on the grounds of public policy.

Vicarious liability

Liability is said to be *vicarious* where one person is liable for the actions of another. In so far as vicarious liability is independent of intention or fault, it is similar to strict liability.

Vicarious liability in tort often arises under a contract of insurance, but it is more usually associated with employment because the common law imposes liability on employers for the torts committed by their employees in the course of their employment. It follows that the principle of vicarious liability is directly relevant to most organisations.

It is important to distinguish between employees (servants) and independent contractors, for an employer is only liable for the tortious acts of an independent contractor in certain circumstances, e.g. where he expressly or impliedly authorises the tortious act, where the independent contractor creates a danger on the highway, where the rule in *Rylands* v. *Fletcher* (1868) applies, and where the employer delegated a duty imposed upon him by statute or common law to the independent contractor.

At law an employee (a servant) is employed under a contract *of* service whilst an independent contractor is employed under a contract *for* services. However, it is far easier to recognise than to define a contract of service and, therefore, it is difficult to satisfactorily distinguish between an employee and an independent contractor. For example, the "control" test, i.e. that a master (an employer) is able to tell the servant what to do and also how to do it whilst the independent contractor can only be told what to do, cannot be realistically applied today to most skilled employees. Other tests are somewhat involved and may still give an inconclusive result. The best general approach would now seem to be that an employee and his work are an integral part of the business whereas an independent contractor and his work, whilst playing a part in the business, are not integrated into it.

It is similarly difficult to define "course of employment". Whilst it certainly embraces an employee's negligence and mistakes, its scope must ultimately depend on the circumstances. The well known legal cliché that an employer is liable unless his employee is "on a frolic of his own" tends to restate the problem reversed and in rather more obscure language.

Vicarious liability in tort can be explained and justified in two main ways. Firstly, the employee's work benefits the employer and he should therefore answer for the damage which occasionally results from the employment. Secondly, an organisation (the employer) will almost certainly be better able to pay compensation than an individual (its employee). Indeed, employers will insure against the possibility of such liability.

In criminal law a person is not generally liable for the criminal acts of another. This is because criminal liability at common law requires intention or recklessness with respect to the *actus reus*. This a person clearly cannot have if he knew nothing of the other's action. Conversely, a person who authorises or commands another to commit a criminal offence will be liable as a *participant* in the crime.

There are, however, a considerable number of offences created by statute where the courts have held that the statute imposes criminal liability on one person for the acts of another. Such interpretations can be justified because they are necessary if the will of Parliament is to be implemented and the object of the legislation achieved. As in tort, vicarious liability in criminal law is almost solely concerned with employers and their employees.

Vicarious liability in criminal law would seem to arise in one of two circumstances. Firstly, where a person is under a statutory duty but delegates this to someone else, e.g. under the Licensing Acts, only the licensee can commit the offences. Secondly, where one person's acts are in law those of another, e.g. where an employee sells goods, the sale is deemed to be his employer's act for the purposes of such statutes as the Trade Descriptions Act 1968.

Organisations and legal liability

The civil liability of the members of a non-corporate organisation is the same as that of an ordinary individual. They are liable for breaches of contract and may be sued for their own tortious acts and those committed by their employees in the course of their employment. Special procedural rules apply in actions against both partnerships and trade unions, however, and complete immunity from legal liability is enjoyed by the latter, their officials and members for any tortious acts committed in furtherance of a trade dispute. In addition, there is a presumption that collective agreements made between trade unions and employers are not legally enforceable. The members of a non-corporate organisation are also in a similar position to private individuals as regards the criminal law. Nevertheless, a statute may sometimes provide for the criminal liability of an unincorporated organisation and proceedings are then taken against the organisation in its own name and not in that of its members.

Corporate organisations pose a theoretical problem in this context; as they have no physical existence and cannot be formed to pursue an unlawful activity they logically cannot commit an unlawful act or form any unlawful intention. However, such a theory put into practice would give a totally unacceptable result, and corporate organisations do incur both civil and criminal liability. They are liable for breaches of contract unless the corporation concerned is a registered company and the contract is *ultra vires*. However, this exception was significantly reduced in its scope by the European Communities Act 1972 s.9(1). The *ultra vires* doctrine does not apply to corporations created by charter or by Act of Parliament.

Since a corporation can only act through its directors and employees, both its criminal and civil liability must be vicarious. A corporation is vicariously liable for the tortious acts of its employees committed in the course of their employment in exactly the same way as any other employer. If any particular mental attitude is required this is supplied by the employee concerned and attributed to the corporation on the basis that it has a fundamental responsibility for his acts or omissions.

In criminal law a corporation's vicarious liability extends beyond that of an individual. This must be so if it is to be subject to the same public duty as that imposed on a natural person by the criminal law. The *ultra vires* rule is ignored and it commits the *actus reus* of an offence and has the required *mens rea* through the acts or omissions and mental attitudes of those persons who control and direct its activities: usually its directors. Their acts, omissions and mental attitudes are considered at law to be those of the company itself. It is, therefore, liable for its own acts and not for those of its servants. Despite this reasoning, however, its liability is still in reality *vicarious*.

It must be remembered that a corporation cannot be imprisoned, and therefore it can only be convicted of offences punishable by fine—in fact most offences are punishable in this way. There are, of course, certain offences which a corporation cannot possibly commit, e.g. rape.

Whilst corporate criminal liability both ensures that a crime does not go unpunished and acts as a more effective and public deterrent than punishment of its directors, the necessity for imposing criminal liability on the corporation, as well as on the individuals actually responsible, can be questioned. In particular, it is the blameless shareholders of a company or the customers of a public corporation who actually pay, although neither has any real control over those actually responsible.

THE ORIGIN AND SOURCES OF ENGLISH LAW

Law's origin in custom
Law has its origin in custom, a far cry from the sophisticated statutory law of today. A custom is nothing more than a group of people doing something in a particular way. It evolves spontaneously and becomes the accepted social norm followed by the members of the community to which it applies. Failure to observe social norms endangers society and breaches of the customary law would be punished. Today a lawyer would define a custom as usage recognised by law.

Originally, customs controlled the basic aspects of life necessary to preserve and protect a simple society. Custom would regulate marriage, the ban on incest being found in nearly all societies; provide a simple criminal law, e.g. "thou shalt not kill", "thou shalt not steal"; and, somewhat later, a method for determining property rights, particularly rights over land and its inheritance. Primogeniture (inheritance by the eldest son) is both an early example of the quest for status in society and recognition that it was not desirable to divide land into tiny units. Hence land passed from father to eldest son without division among others.

In the earliest communities, as with animal groups, customary rules would be enforced by the physically strongest. Gradually more sophisticated ideas of government and law-making would evolve. In many communities, rule by the eldest or group of eldest, or by a "wiseman" or "witchdoctor" of some kind, emerged. In time certain families might attain supreme power and the idea of "kingship" evolved. Perhaps the final stage in the evolution of law enforcement to date is to be found in a free and democratic system of government, although it is debatable whether a truly democratic system can ever be achieved.

The English legal system is unique in having followed the highly idealised process outlined above more closely than any other system. There has been very little external interference in our legal development; even the laws and legal system left by the Romans were almost totally destroyed during the Saxon dark ages which followed, and in contemporary times joining the EEC has had little effect on our purely domestic law.

The sources of English law

The term "source" has a number of different meanings in the context of English law.

The formal source

By this is meant the formal authority which gives a particular rule the force of law. Under the United Kingdom's constitution, the Queen in Parliament is the formal source of law and supreme power in the state. While legislation originates in Parliament, it must receive the Royal Assent before it is enforceable. In theory, the Sovereign could refuse her consent to a particular piece of legislation, but in practice it is highly unlikely that this would ever be done. In addition, the judges are the Sovereign's judges, deriving their authority from the Royal prerogative and making decisions in the Sovereign's name.

The legal sources

These may be defined as the ways in which ideas and principles become recognised as law. In chronological order, these are custom, case law and legislation. They are the sources of all public and private rights and duties.

Custom. Before the Norman conquest in 1066 there was no centralised English state, let alone a United Kingdom. The Normans began a process of creating a single nation under a centralised government but built upon the existing Saxon institutions. The *feudal system*, for example, predated the conquest but the Normans refined it into an efficient system of social, economic and political organisation and control, served by a developing *common law*.

From time to time the Norman kings would send tax officials and government administrators around the country to collect the

King's revenues and to look after his interests. Such officials must have inspired a good deal of awe in the native peasantry and it became common for these royal officials, who were not trained lawyers, to resolve local disputes and try those accused of crimes. It became the practice for their decisions to be based on the customs of the locality.

Over the years a body of customs emerged which were either to be found in all parts of the country or which the royal officials, or justices as they began to be called, thought should be applied everywhere. Such customs became known as *common customs* or *customs of the realm* (as opposed to local customs), and formed the basis of the common law which was enforced in the common law courts (the King's courts). The basic principles of contemporary criminal law can be traced back to such common customs, and some crimes, murder for example, are still common law offences, i.e. not defined by statute. Similarly, the basic principle of the law of torts and the law of contract are to be found in customs of the realm as refined by judicial decisions and the legal process.

Today, common customs have long since been absorbed into case law and statute and are only of historical interest. However, local customs (applying to a particular place, group of people, or both) which satisfy a number of legal requirements, are occasionally recognised as exceptions to the general law and enforced accordingly. A particularly well-known example was the custom of *Gavelkind* which was still found in Kent in the nineteenth century. Under it, land was inherited by all sons in equal shares and not by the eldest son alone. A recent celebrated example occurred in Windsor in 1975 when the customary use of a piece of land called Bachelor's Acre by local residents for lawful sports and pastimes was upheld by the Court of Appeal, preventing New Windsor Corporation using part of Bachelor's Acre as a car park.

Case law. As soon as Royal courts were established in England, common custom became the basis of their decisions. From the earliest times judges have always referred to the decisions in previous cases for guidance, but the present system of case law or *judicial precedent*, as it is technically called, dates from the later part of the nineteenth century and two events in particular. To base decisions on previous cases it is essential to have accurate records, and this was made possible in 1865 by the establishment of the Incorporated Society for Law Reporting. Similarly, it is necessary to have a rational court structure so that the avenues of appeal and the authority of each court are settled. The reorganisation of the court structure by the Judicature Acts 1873–5 brought this about.

The premise on which the system of case law is based is that previous decisions of a higher court are followed by lower courts. At the heart of the system is the concept of the *ratio decidendi* (the legal reason for deciding). This consists of three things: firstly, the judge's statement of the relevant facts, this being used for comparative purposes in later cases; secondly, an account of the way in which he reached his decision, e.g. which cases and statutes he referred to as "authority", i.e. the process of legal reasoning that he employed; and thirdly, the decision he made to resolve the dispute between the parties. The *ratio decidendi*, particularly the legal reasoning employed by the judge, becomes part of the common law and can be used as the basis on which to make later decisions.

The English legal system divides precedents (previous decisions) into those which have binding authority and those which are of only persuasive authority. The idea of being *bound* by previous decisions is a principle only found in countries which operate a system of law based upon our own, e.g. the Commonwealth countries.

Binding precedents are decisions of the House of Lords and the Court of Appeal which have not been overruled by a later case or by legislation. Such decisions must be followed whether the judge in the later case approves of them or not. This gives an important element of certainty to the system but may at times make it rather rigid and inflexible.

There are three kinds of persuasive precedents.

(*a*) Decisions of lower courts.

(*b*) Decisions of Commonwealth and American Courts, and the recommendations of the Privy Council.

(*c*) *Obiter dicta.* These are statements of law made by the judge when giving judgment which are not strictly relevant to the decision before him but which must be treated with respect in later cases. In some instances important principles have been introduced into the law through *obiter dicta.* The *obiter* statements made by the House of Lords in *Hedley Byrne & Co. Ltd* v. *Heller & Partners Ltd* (1963) are examples which directly affect business organisations. They established that in certain circumstances a person can be liable for making negligent statements which cause purely financial loss to a person who relies on them.

The operation of the system of judicial precedent is very closely tied to the court structure (*see* next chapter). Basically, higher courts bind lower courts. The House of Lords binds all other courts and, except in exceptional circumstances, is bound by its own previous decisions. Below this the Court of Appeal binds the High Court and County Court but is itself bound by the House of Lords and its own previous decisions. However, in all matters relating to the interpretation of the foundation treaties of the EEC, and subsidiary legislation made under them, *all* English courts must follow the decisions of the European Court of Justice.

Legislation. The common law—the system of judge-made law originating in custom—was designed to order a socially simple, economically underdeveloped and politically uneducated society. It existed largely to serve the interests and needs of the ruling élite (the nobility and landed gentry) from whose number almost all the judges were drawn. Consequently, the common law clearly reflected their interests in preserving property rights and the social *status quo*, for these were the bastions of their privileged position.

Such a system, reflecting interests and values perfectly typical of underdeveloped societies both before and since, could not survive the tremendous socio-economic upheaval brought about by the industrial revolution. The population dramatically increased, new towns grew up almost overnight and completely new problems of government associated with urban living and an industrialising society arose. A new type of law was needed: Parliamentary legislation.

Whilst there are a number of well-known statutes from earlier centuries, legislation only became an important source of law in the second half of the nineteenth century. In particular, the bulk of modern commercial law affecting business organisations today was codified into statutory form in this period, e.g. The Bills of Exchange Act 1882, the Factors Act 1889, The Partnership Act 1890 and The Sale of Goods Act 1893. Since the Second World War legislation has been totally dominant as the main source of law and the annual output of Acts and Orders made under their authority has reached staggering proportions. The structure of modern British society is now very heavily dependent on legislation.

Legislation takes two forms.

(*a*) *Acts of Parliament.* These may be defined as the will of a democratically elected assembly confirmed by the Sovereign. Acts of Parliament are the supreme form of law in this country and they can change, repeal or create law. Since the Bill of Rights 1688, the judges have recognised the supremacy of Parliament and, whilst they are able to interpret an Act when its meaning is ambiguous or obscure, they have no right to challenge the Act itself.

(*b*) *Delegated Legislation.* As the common law was too unwieldy and too unsophisticated to serve the rapidly changing socio-economic needs of the nineteenth century, so Acts of Parliament by themselves are inadequate to cope with modern society's demands on law. Governments have increasingly looked to delegated legislation as a means of implementing their policies. Delegated legislation is law made by a body to which Parliament has given limited powers of law-making. It follows that the *ultra vires* rule applies to such legislation and it may be challenged in court and declared void if it exceeds the power granted to the law-making body by Parliament.

In Chapter 10 you saw that the Health & Safety at Work, etc., Act 1974 enables the Secretary of State for Employment to make regulations altering, amending or repealing previous relevant legislation. These ministerial regulations and orders made under the authority of "parent" Acts are known as *statutory instruments*, and they are a type of delegated legislation. They are of crucial importance to the process of government for it is largely by statutory instruments that governmental policies are implemented. Parliament itself would certainly not be able to afford the time, and would probably lack the technical expertise and knowledge, to deal with the minutiae of policy implementation.

Parliament is ultimately able to control the use of statutory instruments by government ministers, since important regulations and orders may have to be submitted to both Houses for approval, and others are laid before Parliament and a resolution rejecting them may be passed within forty days. A great many are not laid before Parliament, however, but are subject to committee scrutiny in both Houses. Thus, Parliament should be informed if the minister exceeds the authority granted to him by the parent Act. Local authority by-laws are the other best known example of delegated legislation.

In addition to the two forms of domestic legislation, the United Kingdom is subject to the supra-national legislation of the European Communities. This has already been discussed in Chapter 20.

The interpretation of statutes. In a classic "David and Goliath" confrontation in *Daymond* v. *S.W. Water Authority* (1973), Mr Daymond achieved a notable victory for the individual consumer against a large public utility corporation. The House of Lords held that the Water Act 1973 did not give a water authority power to charge (in Daymond's case £4.89) an owner or occupier of premises not connected to the main drainage for sewerage and sewage disposal services, even though s.30 of the Act gave authorities "power to fix, and to demand, take and recover such charges for the services performed, facilities provided . . . as they think fit." Consequently, the statutory orders which prescribed the charges (an example of delegated legislation) made under the Act were *ultra vires*. Mr Daymond's property was not connected to main drainage and was 365 m away from a sewer. As a result of the decision, water authorities found themselves many millions of pounds worse off and as a result of this all owners and occupiers of premises connected to main drains had to pay more.

A somewhat unusual situation came before the court in *Bourne* v. *Norwich Crematorium Ltd* (1967). It had to be decided whether a crematorium was an "industrial building" within the meaning of the Income Tax Act 1952, because the company which operated it was entitled to a tax allowance if it was. An "industrial building" was defined by the Act as a building in use "for the purpose of a trade which consists of . . . the subjection of goods or materials to any process." The Court was unable to accept the argument that cremating human remains fell within the definition!

The Race Relations Act 1968, which made it unlawful ". . . for any person concerned with the provision to the public or a section of a public . . . of any goods, facilities or services to discriminate against a person seeking to obtain or use those goods, facilities or services by refusing or deliberately omitting to provide him with any of them . . .", had to be interpreted by the House of Lords in *Dockers Labour Club and Institute Ltd* v. *Race Relations Board* (1974). It was decided that refusing to serve a coloured associate member (there were about 1 million associate members of about 4,000 clubs) at the club's bar was not unlawful discrimination within the meaning of the Act because the club operated in the "private sphere" and the Act was designed to stop discrimination in the public sphere. The decision was correct at law but was politically and socially unacceptable, and the Race Relations Act 1976 repealed the 1968 Act, one of its provisions making it unlawful for clubs of twenty-five or more members to discriminate on racial grounds.

Parliament makes the law but the Courts enforce it, and it is sometimes necessary to ascertain the intention of Parliament before this can be done. The three cases above are all examples of statutes where this was necessary because particular words or phrases used in them were unclear or ambiguous when applied to the facts. However, it is essential to remember that:

(*a*) the courts cannot challenge Parliament's authority to legislate; and

(*b*) if the words of the statute are clear and unambiguous the need for judicial interpretation does not arise.

A thorough study of statutory interpretation uncovers a considerable diversity of rules, judicial attitudes and precedents; so much so that at times it seems that there are no real rules of interpretation. Nevertheless, a general summary should always be included in any consideration of legislation for, through their power of interpretation, the courts are able to affect the meaning and application of some statutes. In a few cases Parliament has seen fit to pass an amending act nullifying the judicial interpretation of the previous Act. This will be considered later, but the passing of the Race Relations Act 1976 is a good example.

It is presumed that an Act of Parliament does not bind the Crown and that it applies only to the UK. Similarly, it is presumed not to be retrospective nor to alter the common law. As you have seen, the common law is the fundamental law of the land and if Parliament wishes to alter it then it must do so in very clear terms. A well-known example of this is *Sweet* v. *Parsley* (1969). At common law *mens rea* (*see* page 576) is always required for criminal liability, but this is not always the case with offences created by statute. The defendant, a schoolteacher, was charged with being concerned in the management of premises used for the purpose of smoking cannabis contrary to the Dangerous Drugs Act 1965. The Act made no mention of *mens rea*. At the time of the offence the defendant had let the house that the police raided and was living a long way away, only visiting the house to collect the rent. The House of Lords allowed her appeal against conviction on the ground that where Parliament creates an offence without any reference to a *mens rea*, one will be presumed. Knowledge of the smoking of drugs was necessary for her to have committed an offence under the Act.

Conventionally there are said to be three basic judicial approaches to statutory interpretation: the "literal" rule, the "golden" rule and the "mischief" rule.

(*a*) *The literal rule.* The role of the judges is to ascertain the intention of Parliament from the Act itself. Thus, if the words of the statute are capable of only one meaning, this is the meaning the court will take and the statute will be enforced accordingly, even if the result is unlikely or harsh. The remedy for a harsh law lies in an amending act and not with the courts. However, in the great majority of cases a literal interpretation of the statute produces the desired result.

A somewhat harsh yet perfectly correct decision, based on a literal interpretation of the Agricultural Holdings Act 1948, occurred in *Newborough* v. *Jones* (1974). A notice to quit had been served on a tenant by pushing it under his door. Unfortunately, it was also pushed under the linoleum covering the floor, and remained there for some months undiscovered. The Act stated that a notice was "duly served if left at the tenant's proper address". Thus, the Act had been fully complied with and the notice was effective, even though the tenant was unaware of its service.

(b) *The golden rule.* This is said to be a modification of the literal rule and it is used either where a literal interpretation would produce a manifestly absurd or repugnant result providing, of course, a reasonable alternative interpretation is possible, or where the statute is capable of more than one literal meaning, i.e. it is ambiguous. In the latter situation the literal rule has no place and the golden rule is applied to effect the most reasonable of the alternative meanings possible. This latter use of the rule is more common than the former. If the converse was true, the court would be usurping Parliament's function and exceeding its allocated constitutional role as the interpreter and enforcer of legislation.

Both *Daymond's Case* and *Bourne's Case* are examples of the golden rule being applied.

(c) *The mischief rule.* This rule has a long history and dates from *Heydon's Case* (1584). It can be applied where the statute under consideration was passed to remedy a defect or "mischief" in the law, most commonly where the statute passed to do this is ambiguous. The rule is used to promote the interpretation which remedies the defect. Occasionally, however, it is applied in preference to the literal rule where an application of the latter would not remedy the defect in the law. However, in *Docker's Labour Club and Institute Ltd* v. *Race Relations Board* (1974), where the mischief in the law before the Race Relations Act 1968 was that there were inadequate means of controlling racial discrimination in public, the House of Lords allowed an appeal by the club against a declaration that it was guilty of unlawful discrimination, on the grounds that associate members of the appellant club were not "a section of the public" and so not within the "mischief" the 1968 Act was meant to remedy.

The mischief rule is notable for providing the sole exception to another basic principle of statutory interpretation: that the intention of Parliament is to be ascertained only from the words of the Act itself and not from external sources, e.g. Parliamentary debates or reports of Royal Commissions. When applying the mischief rule the court can look outside the statute to discover the defect in the law which the statute was designed to remedy, and hence interpret the statute to "suppress the mischief and advance the remedy".

You have already seen that the legislation of the European communities is somewhat different from our own. In particular, community legislation tends to enact broad principles rather than detailed provisions. Consequently, English courts must play a far more active role to affect the aims of Community legislation than they need or can do with our own domestic legislation. They must look to the intent and purpose of the legislation and not be concerned to examine the words in meticulous detail or argue about their precise grammatical sense. If there is a gap in the legislation they must fill it is they think the European legislators would have wished. This is in sharp contrast to domestic legislation where any gap must be filled by Parliament.

Thus, in following the European pattern far more use will be made of the golden and mischief rules than the literal rule. In addition, statements made on behalf of the Community, and Community publications which reflect the substance of and attitudes in the negotiations which led to the conclusion of the treaties (the *travaux préparatoires*), may be consulted to resolve any ambiguity or uncertainty in an enactment. This again is in sharp contrast with English principles of interpretation.

Organisations are affected no more and no less than any individual by legislation and its interpretation. However, *Daymond's Case* (1973) shows that a large organisation can suddenly find basic assumptions of its operation swept away or undermined by a single interpretation of a single statute. More generally, the interpretation and application of the various Companies Acts and detailed tax legislation can fundamentally affect organisations both large and small. Occasionally, judicial interpretation of statutes can have repercussions which directly affect important social and political issues, e.g. the *Dockers Labour Club Case*.

It is a fact that a very small number of men from a narrow and rather atypical socio-economic background, holding traditionally conservative views and appointed from the ranks of a small élite profession, have some power to affect the enacted will of a democratically elected Parliament. However, it is equally true to say that vigilance and positive intervention by the judiciary acts as a deterrent and safeguard against possible abuse of statutory power by the government or other public bodies.

The literary sources
These are the written records of the law. There are three main literary sources.

The statute books. These contain the Acts of Parliament. Two original copies of each Act are signed by the Sovereign or her representative, one being kept at the Public Records Office and the other in the House of Lords. However, for all practical purposes the Queen's Printer's copies are acceptable.

The law reports. These contain records of the facts, legal arguments and decisions in important court cases. Today, nearly all important cases are reported. However, the courts have never created a methodical system of producing reports and it has been left entirely in the hands of private organisations. Consequently, there is still an element of chance and individual preference as to whether a case is reported or not.

In 1865 the Incorporated Council of Law Reporting in England and Wales was founded and by convention since then its *Law Reports* are always cited in court when they contain a report of the required case. A few series of private reports are still published, of which the best known and most comprehensive are the *All England Reports*. (You are quite likely to have these in your college library.) In addition, *The Times* newspaper carries reports of the previous day's cases and these are sometimes cited in court when the decision is too recent to have been published in the more formal series.

Textbooks. Modern textbooks, no matter how well-respected, are not authority for legal rules until and unless a particular passage or passages have been accepted and adopted by the court as true statements of the law. This happens infrequently. Nevertheless, textbook writers influence successive generations of judges and lawyers and in this way they are an influence on the evolution of the law.

However, a few "classical texts" from the seventeenth century and earlier are accorded the status of legal sources of law because they contain the only reliable written record of the law as it was in the writer's time. Bracton's thirteenth-century treatise *De Legibus et Consuetudinibus Angliae*, the main literary source of the medieval common law, and Coke's *Institutes*, the contemporary authoritative work on early seventeenth-century law, are particularly good examples.

The historical sources
Custom. English law has its origin in custom and even today a local custom may very occasionally be established as an exception to the general law. To this extent custom is a legal source of English law. However, custom has long since ceased to be an important creative source, and it is far more realistic to classify custom as the major historical source of the common law. Its role in the evolution of the common law has already been discussed in this chapter.

Equity. English law is unique in having had two distinct systems of law operating side by side for at least four centuries, *common law* and *equity.* This duality of jurisdiction was ended by the merger of the administrations of the two systems under the Judicature Acts 1873–5.

All actions at common law were begun by a writ (a written command in the name of the Sovereign) and by the fourteenth century its procedure had become so rigid that no action could be brought unless one of a fixed number of writs fitted the plaintiff's claim. This inflexibility was the main reason for the evolution of equity. It became the practice for those with sufficient influence, money and determination to petition the King when the common law offered them no satisfaction in their claim. In time, petitions began to be heard by the Lord Chancellor instead of the King. Finally the Court of Chancery, presided over by the Lord Chancellor, was established to administer the rules of equity. The present Chancery Division of the High Court is a direct descendant of this early judicial function of the Lord Chancellor.

At first the Lord Chancellor decided disputes brought before him purely on the facts of each individual case, but gradually a body of case law emerged in the Court of Chancery which was applied almost as strictly as the common law in the common law courts.

Equity's growth in the late middle ages depended above all else on its recognition and protection of one particular interest in property, that of a beneficiary under a trust. A trust is an arrangement whereby legal title to property is given by one person to another (a trustee), with the latter promising to use the property for the benefit of a third person (the beneficiary).

Trusts (or "uses" as they were originally called) originated in the middle ages. Some of the earliest examples were the arrangements made by knights when they went to fight overseas and wished to ensure that their estates would be maintained and their families provided for, or when a person wished to provide for a monastic order which was forbidden to own property. As neither the knight's wife nor infant heir, in the former situation, nor the monks, in the latter, could, for different reasons, own a legal estate in land, a straightforward transfer of the legal estate was impossible and a trust had to be employed. Hence, legal title was vested in the trustee(s), but the benefit of the property was vested in the knight's family or monastery.

The common law only recognised the basic transaction—the transfer of legal title to the trustee(s)—and would not recognise nor protect the beneficiary's interest, e.g. where the trustee used the property for his own benefit. This was clearly unfair and the Lord Chancellor would intervene to compel the trustee, the legal owner of the property, to act according to his conscience and use the property for the benefit of the beneficiary, the owner in equity.

Trusts became increasingly common. They provided a way of avoiding some feudal payments and soon became a basic device for property settlements in landowning families. Today they enable people (or organisations) who are, for one reason or another, unable to hold legal ownership of property to enjoy the benefit of it. For example, a minor cannot hold a legal estate in land, but the land can be held in trust for him. (It is possible that you, or one of your fellow students, is a beneficiary under a family trust.) Similarly, since a partnership has no corporate existence, it cannot own property itself and the partnership property of a large firm is usually held by four of the partners (as trustees) on trust for the partners generally.

Equity ceased to be a separately administered system of law in 1875, and consequently it is best considered as a historical source of law. However, the principles of equity have still retained their identity in the modern system. A good example of equity's contemporary vigour is the *High Trees Case* (1947) (*see* page 365) and the subsequent evolution of the principle of promissory estoppel in contract law. The common law, even in full evolution, had serious deficiencies and equity always aimed at supplementing the common law to remedy these weaknesses. Promissory estoppel mitigates the rigidity of the common law's approach to *consideration*, holding a person to his promise when it would be inequitable for him to go back upon it, irrespective of whether consideration was given for it.

Perhaps the best practical example of equity's role is to be found in its remedies. If Mr X repeatedly trespasses on your property, the common law remedy of damages may achieve little. The amount received will probably be small and he may very well continue to trespass. The equitable remedy of an injunction, however, will, if awarded, order Mr X not to repeat his illegal interference. Should he do so he will be in contempt of court and ultimately liable to imprisonment.

The law merchant. This is a historical source of English law and its legacy directly affects business organisations. Much of our present law on the sale of goods and bills of exchange has its origin in the customs brought to England by foreign merchants in the days when England's economy was based almost entirely on agriculture and the production of raw materials, e.g. wool. These customs were based on the law of the Italian commercial cities in which Roman law was naturally a strong influence. From the seventeenth century onwards many of these customs became judicially incorporated into the common law and were eventually codified as the Bills of Exchange Act 1882 and the Sale of Goods Act 1893 in the burst of legislative law reform which took place at the end of the nineteenth century.

SELF-ASSESSMENT QUESTIONS

A. 1. Define: (a) a right *in personam*; (b) *actus reus* and *mens rea*; (c) strict and vicarious liability; (d) a crime; (e) *ratio decidendi* and *obiter dicta*.

2. State two basic principles of "natural justice".

3. List the main functions of legislation.

4. State the criteria on which crimes can be distinguished from civil wrongs.

B. 5. True or false?

(a) The criminal law protects private rights.

(b) Public duties are always imposed by statute.

(c) The tort of nuisance protects possession of land.

(d) An employer is never responsible for an independent contractor's acts.

(e) The Sale of Goods Act 1893 was a consolidating statute.

C. 6. True or false?

(a) "Negligence" involves greater culpability than "intention" in the law of torts.

(b) The state enforces morals.

(c) The breach of a public duty can infringe a private right.

(d) A tenant can bring an action for trespass to land against his landlord.

7. Compare and assess the following statements.

"If A is at fault and injures B, he (A) should compensate B."

"If B is injured by A, he (B) should be compensated."

ASSIGNMENTS

1. Collect and file according to subject, newspaper articles on "legal news" and cases, e.g. *The Times* law reports.

2. For one week, record the possible infringements of private rights that you become aware of and consider whether redress at law would be available.

CHAPTER TWENTY-FIVE

Conflict Resolving

CHAPTER OBJECTIVES

After studying this chapter you should be able to:
* explain judicial and quasi-judicial processes of conflict resolving;
* outline the jurisdiction of the superior courts and the most important inferior courts;
* explain the legal aid scheme;
* state the advantages and disadvantages of administrative tribunals as a means of conflict resolving, and account for their increasing use;
* explain the methods by which quasi-judicial and administrative decision making is supervised and controlled.

INTRODUCTION

It is a common misapprehension that trial by judge and jury is the typical conflict resolving process of the English legal system. This is, however, far from the truth. Of the 2,211,700 persons convicted of criminal offences in England and Wales in 1980, only about 74,000 were tried by judge and jury in a Crown Court, and about 50 per cent of these pleaded guilty! The remaining 2.14 million were tried by magistrates, most of these pleading guilty. In civil cases the use of the jury is extremely limited, for nearly all civil disputes *must* either be tried by a judge sitting alone, or be submitted to arbitration, or be resolved by an administrative tribunal.

The judicial process remains central to the trial of criminal cases, and the jury will no doubt continue to be used in certain civil disputes as well as in criminal trials where a person is accused of a serious offence. However, civil conflicts are increasingly being resolved by arbitration and administrative tribunals rather than by the formal judicial process. Administrative tribunals and formal arbitration bodies are quasi-judicial bodies. These may be defined as public bodies which have the power by law to establish facts and apply legal rules without being constituted as parts of the ordinary court system or following the strict rules of evidence and procedure which bind the courts.

To some extent the decline of the judicial process in civil disputes is inevitable. Quasi-judicial conflict resolving is far better suited to some increasingly important branches of the law, such as welfare and employment law, and could be usefully extended into other areas where wider discretionary powers would be an advantage. Welfare law is largely determined by socio-political policy, and whilst tribunals must reach their decisions judicially, i.e. according to the relevant law and procedure and not purely on policy, their composition and informal procedure make them far better able to deal with the often complicated combination of factual circumstances, policy and socio-legal problems involved.

Employment law and the judicial process have traditionally had a rather strained relationship, and the quasi-judicial conflict resolving system in this field—ACAS, industrial tribunals and the Employment Appeal Tribunal—appears to work much better. In the commercial world quasi-judicial processes are far from new and for centuries arbitration has been used to resolve conflicts between businessmen. Perhaps above all else it is the informality in procedure and the relevant expertise of the decison-makers involved that has brought quasi-judicial conflict resolving processes to a position of such prominence in the legal system.

The judicial process, whether with or without a jury, is better suited to the criminal law, where the full "majesty of the law" is probably an advantage, and to civil disputes involving questions of "pure law" where little discretion is needed, such as the construction of an Act of Parliament, conflicts involving an alleged breach of contract or the protection of an individual's legal rights. To some extent such purely legal issues (if there can ever be such a thing) can be considered in a "legal vacuum"; but even here *public policy* is being more openly considered in judicial decisions, e.g. in actions brought under the tort of negligence.

In addition to this natural process, it can be argued that lawyers themselves have been partly responsible for the increased use of alternatives to judicial conflict resolving. In so far as lawyers have created a mystique and procedures which leave "mere laymen" confused and trembling at the portals of justice, law all too often seems to presuppose the existence of lawyers—this is surely wrong. In particular, it usually follows that the poorer and less well-educated members of society are least able to cope with bemusing procedural technicalities. In consequence, they are most in need of expert advice and assistance. However, poverty and lack of education are often very effective barriers to obtaining proper assistance, although it is true to say that the modern legal aid scheme (*see* below) can to some extent raise these barriers.

Lawyers and the courts frequently seem isolated from both the problems of ordinary men and women and the actual day-to-day workings of the business world. Many lawyers are far more familiar with conveyancing than with anything else. However, welfare law may be equally, if not more, technical; for example, the entitlement to supplementary benefit is vital to satisfy many a family's material needs. Fortunately, in recent years there has been pressure to broaden the hitherto narrow, legalistic education and training of lawyers. It now often encompasses sociological perspectives and sometimes the study of welfare law. In addition, a few organisations willing and able to advise on such matters now exist, e.g. neighbourhood law centres. However, by themselves they can never hope to solve the problem; most lawyers will, unless forced to do otherwise, sell their services to the highest bidder.

If it was just a matter of money, one would expect business men to use lawyers and the judicial process whenever they encountered a legal problem or became involved in a legal dispute. However, businessmen will often prefer to take their legal problems to accountants rather than to lawyers because accountants are more likely to be in tune with the realities of the business world. Thus, whilst lawyers and judges may epitomise the "middle classes" and have at times alienated the "working classes" (particularly by their apparent hostility to trade unions), the isolation of the courts from social and economic conflict situations cannot be explained purely in "class terms". The judicial process appears to be its own prisoner, its prison being its own procedure and its gaoler its own isolation from social, economic and political realities.

We will now examine the work of the courts and the nature of the judicial process, and quasi-judicial conflict resolving by arbitration and administrative tribunals.

THE COURTS AND THE JUDICIAL PROCESS

Historically, the administration of justice is a prerogative of the Crown, but the Crown has long since ceased to play an active role in this function of the state. Nevertheless, all English courts derive their jurisdiction directly or indirectly from the Crown and the administration of justice is still formally undertaken in the Sovereign's name. For example, writs in civil actions are issued in the Queen's name and all criminal proceedings are taken on her behalf, the judges are "Her Majesty's Judges" and they sit in the "Queen's Courts".

Classifying the courts
English courts may be classified in various ways. One possible

classification is into those which have *criminal* and those which have *civil* jurisdiction. Unfortunately, this simple functional distinction is unsatisfactory; whilst some courts may have exclusively civil or exclusively criminal jurisdiction, most exercise both. A functional classification according to *original* (trial) or *appellate* jurisdiction is unsatisfactory for the same reason.

The one valid classification of practical importance is according to status and not jurisdiction. English courts may be divided into *superior* and *inferior* courts, the two characteristics of the latter being:

(*a*) that their jurisdiction is limited both by the value of the disputed subject-matter and geographically; and

(*b*) that they are subject to the supervisory jurisdiction of the High Court.

This latter characteristic is discussed with special reference to administrative tribunals later in this chapter.

The European Court of Justice, which has jurisdiction in this country in conflicts involving Community law, clearly does not fit into even this classification. Figure 120 shows the structure of the courts, including the European Court of Justice, in terms of their primary functions as criminal or civil, trial or appellate courts. (Refer to Fig. 120 as you read through the text.)

The work of the courts

The *superior* courts are the House of Lords, Court of Appeal, High Court, Crown Court, Employment Appeal Tribunal and the Restrictive Practices Court.

Appeal Courts

The House of Lords, the Court of Appeal (Civil and Criminal Divisions) and the Employment Appeal Tribunal have only appellate jurisdiction. In matters involving purely domestic law, the House of Lords is the final appeal court in the UK for both civil and criminal cases.

High Court

The High Court sits in three separate divisions, Queen's Bench, Chancery and Family, and has virtually unlimited original jurisdiction in civil matters. Trial is by a single judge, although a jury will sometimes sit in the Queen's Bench division to hear actions involving defamation or fraud.

Queen's Bench is the largest of the three divisions and deals mainly with disputes involving the law of contract or the law of

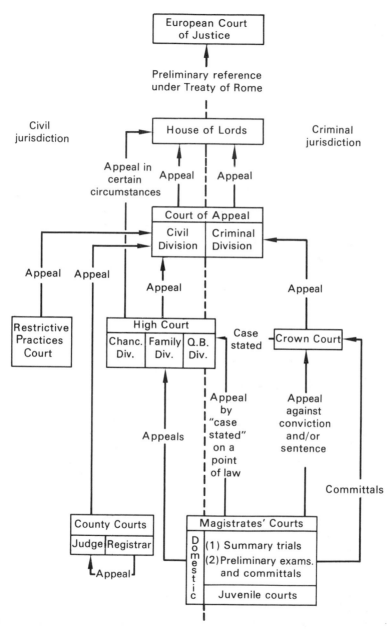

Fig. 120. *The principal civil and criminal courts and the system of appeals.*

torts. The division also exercises the criminal jurisdiction of the High Court. This latter jurisdiction is entirely appellate and consists of deciding points of law stated to it from magistrates' courts and from the Crown Court when it hears appeals against summary conviction or sentence. It also has minor appellate jurisdiction in some civil matters originally heard in the magistrates' courts or certain tribunals. In addition the division exercises the supervisory jurisdiction of the High Court over quasi-judicial decision making (*see* below) by the issue of the prerogative orders of certiorari, mandamus and prohibition.

In 1980, 200,989 proceedings were commenced in the Queen's Bench division. In 75,774 cases judgment was given without trial and there were only 11,376 hearings listed. In fact, only 2,278 disputes (1·1 per cent) had to be resolved by an actual trial.

The Chancery division exercises original civil jurisdiction in matters which were originally heard in the Court of Chancery (abolished in 1875), e.g. over trusts, the redemption and foreclosure of mortgages, specific performance of contracts concerning land and partnership actions. The division has statutory jurisdiction in company liquidation, bankruptcy, tax cases, town and country planning matters and probate disputes. In addition it has minor appellate jurisdiction, e.g. income tax appeals from the Commissioners of Inland Revenue.

The Family division has exclusive original jurisdiction over matrimonial disputes and conflicts involving children. It has limited appellate jurisdiction from the magistrates' courts and county courts in similar civil matters.

You can see from this outline of their jurisdiction that much of the work of the Queen's Bench and Chancery divisions of the High Court is of direct relevance to business organisations.

Crown Court
The Crown Court was created by the Courts Act 1971. It has exclusive original jurisdiction to try all indictable offences, i.e. offences, generally of a serious nature, where the trial *must* be by judge and jury, and jurisdiction to hear appeals against summary conviction or sentence from a magistrates' court. In addition, High Court judges may sit in the Crown Court to exercise the High Court's civil jurisdiction outside London.

Restrictive Practices Court
The Restrictive Practices Court was established by the Restrictive Trade Practices Act 1956 and exercises jurisdiction outside the scope of the ordinary civil and criminal law. Its functions are to

decide whether certain trade agreements and practices are caught by the Restrictive Trade Practices Act 1976 and, if so, whether they can be justified, and to hear actions concerning such practices and agreements. It also has jurisdiction in actions brought under the Resale Prices Act 1976. Having such jurisdiction, the Court has direct relevance to the activities of business organisations but in 1980 only six final orders were made. Restrictive trade agreements and practices are discussed in Chapter 17.

The most important of the inferior courts are the county and magistrates' courts. On the basis of the sheer number of cases with which they deal, they are undoubtedly the backbones of the administration of civil and criminal justice respectively.

County courts

The jurisdiction of the county courts is entirely civil and derived solely from statute. It is limited geographically, each court dealing with local disputes, and financial maxima are imposed by statute on the value of the disputed claims which they can hear. For example, at present the maximum claim in actions founded on contract and tort is £5,000, in equity matters, such as trusts, £30,000, and in extortionate credit agreements under the Consumer Credit Act the limit is also £5,000.

Although they may seem to operate as judicial debt-collecting agencies at times, they deal with a wide range of civil conflicts, including important socio-legal matters such as disputes between landlords and tenants under the Rent Act 1968 and undefended divorce petitions.

County courts are staffed by *circuit judges* and, whilst in theory a jury (of eight persons) can sometimes be called, trial is always by a single judge. Circuit judges are assisted by *registrars* who exercise both an administrative and a judicial function, the former of which is largely delegated to subordinates. Unless the parties object a registrar may try actions where the claim does not exceed £500 or any other actions with their consent. Appeal lies from the decision of the registrar to the judge.

In 1973 a system of county court arbitration was introduced and, after periodic amendments, most notably in April 1981, this system may be summarised as follows. Claims involving £500 or less, i.e. "small claims", are automatically referred to arbitration by the registrar as soon as a defence to the claim has been received. Normally, he himself will be the arbitrator but, if either of the parties ask, he can refer the dispute for arbitration by the judge or by an outside arbitrator. On the application of one of the parties the registrar has *discretion* to rescind the referral to arbitration where:

(a) a difficult question of law, or facts of exceptional complexity are involved: or

(b) fraud is alleged; or

(c) the parties are agreed that the dispute should be tried by the court; or

(d) the subject matter of the claim, the circumstances of the parties or the interests of any other person likely to be affected by the award make it unreasonable for the dispute to be resolved by arbitration.

County court arbitration hearings have the great advantages of informality, speed and cheapness. The strict rules of evidence (as used in the court) do not apply. In fact, the arbitrator is allowed to adopt any method of procedure which seems convenient and which will give each party a fair and equal opportunity to present his case. In particular, the arbitrator plays an active role in determining the relevant facts, testing the evidence and introducing relevant points of law—something of a compromise between the traditional adversarial procedure of English courts and an inquisitorial procedure. Perhaps of most importance is the "no-costs" rule. Neither side can recover the cost of solicitors' fees, although court fees, travelling expenses and other reasonable costs incurred in preparing the case can be awarded. In practice, the "no-costs" rule will keep solicitors out of the arbitration procedure; their presence in it should be, almost by definition, unnecessary anyway.

Such has been the success of county court arbitration, the county courts are now both fulfilling their original purpose as "small claims" courts as well as dealing with more difficult legal matters where the amounts involved are not that great. In particular, the county court arbitration procedure recognises that the fundamental problem with small claims is one of economics. To enable a consumer (most arbitration hearings concern consumer matters) to pursue his claim on relatively equal terms against organisations requires the system to exclude bought legal expertise and familiarity with legal procedures. While there is nothing to stop anybody employing a solicitor, the "no-costs" rule and the registrar's discretion over procedure go a long way towards ensuring equality between the parties. Nevertheless, there is pressure for a separate "small claims division", with its own separate code of procedure, within each county court in recognition that "small claims" require their own particular techniques of conflict resolving. This was the main conclusion of the National Consumer Council's 1979 publication *Simple Justice*, the other conclusions of which formed the basis of the changes in county court arbitration introduced in 1981.

In 1980, 1,933,444 proceedings were commenced in the county courts. However, in only 1.67 per cent (32,345) of these cases was judgment entered after trial, and only in a further 0.72 per cent (13,945) after arbitration. In the vast majority of cases, merely commencing proceedings was enough to achieve the plaintiff's objectives.

Magistrates' courts
Magistrates' courts have both criminal and civil jurisdiction, although the importance of the former far outweighs that of the latter. Magistrates have jurisdiction to try summary offences, i.e. those which do not have to be tried by jury, and certain other offences which may be tried either by judge and jury in the Crown Court or by summary procedure in a magistrates' court. In 1980, 1,756,300 persons were convicted in magistrates' courts of summary offences (of which 1,294,100 were convicted of motoring offences), and 448,000 persons were convicted of offences which may be tried either by a judge and jury or by summary procedure. Indeed, even this figure is not a true reflection of the importance of magistrates' courts, for a magistrate will have conducted a preliminary examination (*see* below) of the evidence before committing an accused person to stand trial at the Crown Court for an indictable offence.

From the above you can see that magistrates' courts have two quite separate functions in relation to criminal cases. Firstly, they conduct preliminary examinations of indictable offences in order to establish whether or not the prosecution has sufficient evidence to justify the accused being committed on bail or in custody to stand trial before judge and jury in the Crown Court. Secondly, they try a vast range of summary offences (all created by statute) and some hybrid offences, and offences committed by children and young persons under the age of seventeen years.

The civil jurisdiction of the magistrates' courts is very varied and includes the recovery of certain debts, e.g. unpaid income tax and rates, and the renewal and revocation of licences. Of greatest importance is its domestic civil jurisdiction. For example, it can make orders that one spouse need no longer live with the other and that the defendant must pay a reasonable weekly sum to the complainant as maintenance.

The judicial process
The judicial process consists of an independent adjudicator (a judge) making a reasoned decision according to known rules of law on the basis of the evidence available to both parties and offered to the court. Each party, usually through their legal representatives,

can test the evidence tendered by the other, and each may put forward factual or legal arguments. In conflicts where a jury sits with a judge, i.e. on the trial of indictable offences in the Crown Court and in some civil actions tried in the Queen's Bench division of the High Court, the judge decides disputed points of law and the jury determines questions of fact. If the plaintiff succeeds in his action, a civil jury will also determine the amount of damages (if any) that the defendant must pay him.

The process assumes that there is an applicable legal rule which will resolve the conflict, and that this can be discovered by a rigorous examination of *authority*, i.e. status and cases. In consequence, the judge can very seldom exercise completely unfettered discretion and in most cases he is bound to follow *precedent*.

By tradition, the English judicial process is an adversary and not an inquisitorial system (contrast the European Court of Justice). Hence, the court plays a passive role and the case is conducted by the parties (usually through their lawyers) with the judge as "umpire" to ensure that the procedural rules are observed and to adjudicate in the dispute at the end of the process.

The main advantages of the judicial process are:

(*a*) an independent adjudicator with an open mind;

(*b*) a clearly determined issue to be decided;

(*c*) a full and equal opportunity for both sides to present their case;

(*d*) the production of the best available evidence;

(*e*) the exclusion of all irrelevant material;

(*f*) the application of known legal rules to resolve the dispute; and

(*g*) a statement of reasons for the decison made.

Impressive though these advantages undoubtedly are, the process does have a number of disadvantages which can seriously detract from its benefits. Many would argue that the process resembles a gladiatorial combat where might—in the form of superior legal representation—can overcome right. Inherent in this particular criticism is the high cost of the process, perhaps its major detraction. A layman will usually find that the technicality of legal procedure and the formality of the process effectively bar his access to the courts unless he employs a professional lawyer, and yet the sheer expense which this involves may cause him to abandon all hope of redress at law. Even where legal representation and legal aid (discussed below) are readily available, considerable delay is inevitable before the conflict is resolved. In addition, the adversary system allows the parties to control the process and the truth may not be fully uncovered because the court is unable to enquire into the facts. Finally, it is argued by some that the isolation of judges from the "real world" makes it difficult for them to fully appreciate the background to many of the conflicts that they must resolve.

Legal aid

Legal aid is a scheme which pays or contributes to the cost of a litigant's legal fees. It is funded by the state and administered by the Law Society. The scheme is designed to enable a person unable to pay legal fees himself to obtain legal representation in court proceedings. To the parties involved it probably seems part and parcel of the judicial conflict-resolving process.

Legal aid in both criminal and civil cases is governed by the Legal Aid Act 1974. The Act, as periodically amended, determines an applicant's eligibility to legal aid and any contribution that he must make to the costs in the case.

Legal aid in civil court proceedings

Anybody who wishes to pursue a court action may make an application for legal aid to the appropriate local committee. Legal aid will be granted to the applicant if he fulfils two conditions.

(*a*) He must be in receipt of supplementary benefit or satisfy a means test. At present an applicant with a disposable income, i.e. gross income less rates, rent, mortgage repayments, tax, allowances for dependents, etc., of less than £1,850 a year and disposable capital of less than £1,310 will not be required to make a contribution to the costs of the case if legal aid is granted. Persons with a disposable income in excess of £4,440 are ineligible, and legal aid may be refused to a person with disposable capital of over £2,725. In between these maximum and minimum figures a successful applicant may be required to pay a proportion of the costs.

(*b*) The applicant must satisfy the local committee that he has reasonable grounds for taking or defending the action.

Two main criticisms are made of the present scheme. Firstly, with the exception of the Employment Appeal Tribunal and the Lands Tribunal, legal aid is not available in cases heard by administrative tribunals, even though the use of tribunals in conflict resolving is steadily increasing. It is never available for arbitration hearings. Secondly, too many people are excluded from the scheme on financial grounds; in particular, the means test is unfair to the prudent saver.

Legal aid in criminal court proceedings
An application for legal aid in criminal cases is made to the appropriate court and the applicant must include a "statement of means" with his application. Legal aid in criminal cases differs in two further ways from the civil scheme. Firstly, a criminal legal aid order is made before any possible contribution has been assessed. The need to expedite the trial of criminal cases explains this difference. Secondly, it is rarely refused, except on financial grounds, where the applicant is charged with a serious offence, and it must be granted on a murder charge. The grant of civil legal aid is far more discretionary.

After the conclusion of the case, the court may order the assisted person to make a contribution to his costs according to his financial commitments and resources.

ARBITRATION

Arbitration is a quasi-judicial process used in civil disputes where the parties involved agree to allow a third to resolve the dispute between them. It is an alternative to the judicial process and not a replacement for it. Most arbitration agreements are in writing and in these cases the process is regulated by one of a number of specific statutes, which provide for disputes arising out of their provisions to be settled by arbitration, or by the Arbitration Acts 1950 and 1975. (The latter Act gives effect in this country to the 1958 New York Convention on the Recognition and Enforcement of Foreign Arbitral Awards.)

Referring disputes to arbitration
A dispute can be referred to arbitration under the provisions of a specific statute or in accordance with a term contained in the contract between the parties in dispute. Since the middle ages the courts have recognised such contractual terms and enforced the arbitration awards made. Today, provision for disputes to be referred to arbitration is frequently found in partnership agreements, insurance and building contracts and in industrial relations.

It is not possible for an arbitration agreement to prevent access to the courts because such an agreement would be void on the grounds of public policy. However, a suitably worded provision (a "*Scott* v. *Avery* clause") will generally prevent one of the parties proceeding with court action until the dispute has first been referred to arbitration.

Arbitration procedure
Normally one arbitrator is appointed (often selected by a trade or

professional body), but each party may have the right to appoint an arbitrator of their own choice. Where this is so, an umpire must be selected whose function is to decide the dispute should the arbitrators fail to agree. A judge of the Commercial Court, part of the Queen's Bench division of the High Court, may sometimes sit as a sole arbitrator providing he can be released from his judicial duties.

The arbitration follows normal judicial procedure but by agreement it is possible to relax strict procedural rules and, in particular, to dispense with the rules of evidence. For example, whilst witnesses are often cross-examined and can be ordered to attend (by sub poena) by the High Court, evidence is frequently submitted by affidavit (a written statement made on oath).

The arbitrator's decision is in the form of an award. This may include the payment of money or costs and an order to perform the contract (specific performance). The award prevents the parties taking the issues decided to court, and unless the arbitration agreement provides for an appeal, e.g. to an appeal committee or tribunal, the arbitrator's decision on the facts is final.

The role of the court

The role of the court is to ensure that the arbitration process is conducted fairly, not to restrict its use. For example, it can revoke the authority of an arbitrator or umpire and set aside the award for delay or improper conduct, stay proceedings by an injunction and enforce the arbitration award in the same way as its own judgments, but it cannot hear appeals against the award (except where a judge of the Commercial Court sits as arbitrator). If this last rule were reversed, reference to arbitration would be pointless. However, the Arbitration Act 1979 provides that there may be an appeal to the High Court on a question of *law* providing both parties consent or the court gives permission. Where, however, the parties have entered into an agreement which excludes the right to appeal, this is binding upon them. In any event the court will give permission to appeal only if it considers that the determination of the question of law could substantially affect the rights of one or more of the parties. This procedure means that businessmen can ensure that their disputes are decided solely by the method of their choice, without any review by the courts on questions of law, and that costly and protracted delays by (unnecessary) references of points of law to the court are prevented.

An arbitrator acts in a quasi-judicial capacity and therefore no legal action can be taken against him for negligently conducting the arbitration. Negligence would, however, provide grounds for the High Court to set aside his award.

Advisory Conciliation and Arbitration Service (ACAS)

Arbitration has always been an important way of resolving conflicts in industrial relations and because its activities are directly relevant to business organisations, ACAS must be discussed further. Indeed, besides making arrangements for arbitration in industrial disputes, the Service plays a much wider role in industrial relations generally. Despite a few failures, e.g. the "Grunwick dispute", where ill will and the Service's lack of legal teeth were all too apparent, the Service has a very good success record.

The Employment Protection Act 1975 established ACAS as the successor to the Commission on Industrial Relations. This had been set up in 1969 but was abolished by the Trade Union and Labour Relations Act 1974.

The Service is run by a Council consisting of a chairman and nine members—three nominated by the CBI, three by the TUC and three independent members—with a staff of civil servants experienced in industrial relations. Its main functions are to provide:

(*a*) advice on industrial relations and the development of modern personnel practices;

(*b*) conciliation in industrial disputes;

(*c*) conciliation in certain disputes between individual employees and their employers, e.g. disputes under the Equal Pay Act 1970 and, in particular, cases of alleged unfair dismissal, thus avoiding the need to take the dispute to an industrial tribunal;

(*d*) help in improving collective bargaining.

By its very nature, industrial relations is a subject where a variety of issues may be involved in any one problem and the Service's functions are therefore closely integrated.

Arbitration arranged by ACAS can either be by a single arbitrator appointed by ACAS or by an *ad hoc* board of arbitration specially appointed to deal with a particular dispute. ACAS appoints an independent chairman, who acts as an umpire if required, with the other members nominated by the parties to the dispute. Unlike other forms of arbitration, an ACAS award is not legally binding. However, since the arbitration normally presupposes the parties' joint desire to resolve their conflict, such awards are normally implemented.

Advantages and disadvantages of arbitration

The advantages of arbitration can in some ways be considered to be the opposites of the disadvantages inherent in the judicial process. To the business world in general these advantages are most attractive.

Arbitration takes place in private and whilst counsel may appear for the parties the rules of evidence are relaxed and the process is relatively informal. In consequence, it is argued that disputes can be decided in a less emotionally charged and tense situation.

The resolution of many commercial disputes requires expert knowledge and a major advantage of the process is that a person with the necessary expertise can be appointed as arbitrator. In fact trade and professional associations maintain lists of suitably qualified persons. Many commercial arbitration agreements also leave the appointment of an arbitrator to the relevant trade or professional body.

Judged against a corresponding court action, the process of arbitration is cheap and speedy. In addition the date and time of the arbitration can be fixed to suit the parties. The one drawback in submitting a dispute to arbitration is that legal aid is unavailable. This can be unfair where there is a marked imbalance in the financial resources of the parties in dispute, particularly if the arbitration agreement is used to stop a claim being pursued in court where legal aid may have been available to the impecunious party.

ADMINISTRATIVE TRIBUNALS

Since the Second World War there has been a great increase in socio-legal problems, many of which the ordinary courts are ill-equipped to deal with. These problems are mainly associated with the tremendous expansion of social and welfare services. To resolve the inevitable conflicts which arise in such matters, increasing use has been made of administrative tribunals.

Administrative tribunals fall outside the ordinary court system and yet they have extensive powers of decision-making which directly affect the private rights of individuals. In fact the adjudication of civil disputes between the individual and the state by a court rather than by a tribunal is the exception rather than the rule, and the use of tribunals to resolve disputes between individuals is becoming steadily more common. Although they will usually have a legally qualified chairman, they are normally staffed by non-lawyers. They may have original or appellate jurisdiction.

Their functions and procedures are regulated by the Tribunals and Inquiries Act 1971. This makes provision for a statutory right of appeal on a point of law from a tribunal to the Queen's Bench division of the High Court, provides for considerable uniformity in standards and procedures, e.g. chairmen are selected by the appropriate government minister and appointed by the Lord Chancellor, and has established the Council on Tribunals to oversee the constitution and functioning of the most important administrative tribunals, including the work of the Director General of Fair Trading. The Council makes an annual report to the Lord Chancellor.

The work of administrative tribunals

There are some 2,000 individual tribunals dealing with a wide variety of socio-legal matters, their only common element being that they are all statutory bodies which exercise functions laid down by particular Acts of Parliament. For example, the lands tribunals deal with disputes over compensation paid to owners of land which has been compulsorily purchased by government departments or local authorities, and the Registered Designs Appeal Tribunal hears appeals from the Comptroller-General of Patents, Designs and Trade-marks. However, they play their most important roles in welfare and employment law. The national insurance tribunals decide disputed claims to unemployment and sickness benefits, and appeals against the withdrawal of supplementary benefit are heard by the supplementary benefits appeals tribunals. Industrial tribunals deal with a wide range of disputes arising from employment. In particular, they are used to resolve conflicts arising under the Employment Protection Act 1975. In most cases appeal lies to the Employment Appeal Tribunal.

The Employment Appeal Tribunal
The Employment Protection Act 1975 created the Employment Appeal Tribunal to hear appeals on points of law from industrial tribunals in disputed claims concerning redundancy, discrimination, including equal pay, and disputes under the Trade Union and Labour Relations Act 1974 (as now amended), the Employment Protection Act 1975 and the Employment Protection (Consolidation) Act 1978 (as now amended). It also hears appeals on points of both fact and law arising from proceedings before the trade union Certification Officer. In 1980, 671 appeals were made to the Tribunal.

In effect the Tribunal is the successor to the Industrial Relations Court (abolished in 1974) and in status, composition and some aspects of its jurisdiction it resembles its politically ill-conceived predecessor.

The Tribunal occupies a somewhat anomalous position in that it operates as a tribunal but has the status of a superior court. Its procedure is designed to be cheap and informal and the parties may appear in person or be represented by anyone they wish, e.g. a barrister or solicitor, or trade union or employers' association official. Strict rules of evidence need not be observed and costs are not normally awarded. However, the Tribunal can order the attendance and examination of witnesses, the production and inspection of documents and it can enforce its orders.

The Tribunal is staffed by judges from the Court of Appeal and High Court, nominated by the Lord Chancellor, including one from the Scottish Court of Session, and lay members with expertise in industrial relations sitting as representatives of either employers or workers. The Tribunal may sit anywhere in Great Britain and it must consist of one judge sitting with either two or four lay members (chosen to give equal representation to employers and workers), or one judge and one lay member where the parties consent. A decision of the Tribunal on a question of fact is final, but an appeal on a point of law can be made to the Court of Appeal or Court of Session.

As a superior court, the Employment Appeal Tribunal is not subject to the supervisory jurisdiction of the High Court (*see* below).

Advantages and disadvantages of administrative tribunals

Administrative tribunals are vital to the resolution of conflicts of a socio-legal nature. They are usually staffed by expert laymen and they are able to consider "policy" criteria far better than judges. They are relatively cheap, legal representation is unnecessary and costs are not usually awarded, a decision is reached relatively quickly, they are flexible in that they are not bound by a doctrine of binding precedent, and they are relatively informal.

However, the increasing use of administrative tribunals has its own disadvantages. Arguably, there are too many kinds of tribunals and they often have overlapping jurisdictions. More fundamentally, they are said to infringe the *rule of law* (which aims to protect the individual from arbitrary government) in that they are run by government departments with an interest in the dispute.

Though administrative tribunals are relatively informal when compared to the courts, most of the applicants to them are "working class" and tend to be very much out of their depth in any situation involving "officialdom". This being so, expert advice is often required in their applications but this is usually very hard to obtain. Legal aid is not available for such applications and even if it was, it could be argued that the involvement of lawyers would seriously detract from the significant advantages that administrative tribunals offer as a means of conflict resolution. Above all else, perhaps, they can never hope to solve the problems created by bad government.

Administrative decision-making

A statute frequently gives a minister the power to resolve disputes arising under its provisions, e.g. a disputed route for a new major road and the compulsory acquisition of land for it. These powers are necessary if government policy is to be implemented, for any independent quasi-judicial body might make decisions which would frustrate this. Such powers may be either original or appellate, and with or without a right of appeal. Similar powers are given to local authorities, e.g. in relation to the control of development under the Town and Country Planning Acts, public bodies and office-holders, e.g. the Monopolies and Mergers Commission and the Director General of Fair Trading.

Administrative decisions are made by an *administrative process*. This entails the collection of information and expert opinions, the preparation of analyses and summaries and the taking of a decision based upon them, the whole process rarely being open to public inspection. The administrative process is mainly used for matters that are to be decided on *policy*, i.e. decisions which can be based on any grounds or reasons which appear appropriate. In contrast, the judicial and quasi-judicial processes involve the application of given rules to resolve disputes. However, whenever an administrative decision presupposes the existence of a dispute and parties to it, the decision-maker is fulfilling a *quasi-judicial function* and his decision will be subject to judicial review accordingly (*see* below).

In some cases a minister is required to hold a public inquiry before making his decision. Such public inquiries are purely investigatory, and it can be argued that they are little more than public relations exercises which have very little effect on the actual decision-making process.

Control and supervison of quasi-judicial and administrative decision-making

Judicial control

Unless granted by statute there is no right of appeal to the ordinary courts against the *decisions* of administrative tribunals, for such a right would nullify most of the advantages that they possess as a means of resolving conflicts. However, it is essential that administrative justice should exist within a framework of effective legal controls and safeguards.

Judicial control takes two main forms:

(*a*) the supervisory jurisdiction of the High Court; and

(*b*) any statutory rights of appeal which exist from a tribunal to the High Court. Appeal must usually be on a point of law.

The supervisory jurisdiction of the High Court is exercised by a Divisional Court of the Queen's Bench division through the issue of the prerogative orders of *certiorari, prohibition* and *mandamus.* They can be used to challenge any decision which involves a *judicial element,* even though it is reached by an administrative rather than a judicial or quasi-judicial process. Consequently, they are available against ministers of the Crown and other administrative bodies besides inferior courts and administrative tribunals. They are now issued following an *application for judicial review,* a new procedure which encompasses applications for an injunction or declaration, the other remedies available in administrative law, and any consequential claim for damages. The leave of the High Court is required before an application for judicial review can be made.

Tribunals are kept within their jurisdiction by the orders of certiorari and prohibition. An order of *certiorari* brings a dispute, already resolved or still under the process of adjudication, before the High Court for the Court to consider whether the tribunal has acted in excess of its jurisdiction and whether the rules of natural justice have been broken. If such a transgression is found, the High Court will quash the decision made or remit the matter to the tribunal with a direction to reconsider and reach a decision in accordance with the findings of the court. It is also used to correct errors of law apparent on the record of the proceedings. It *cannot* be used to challenge the merits of the decision.

An order of *prohibition* is issued to prevent something from being done. It can be used to prevent inferior courts, tribunals, other public bodies and public office-holders exceeding their jurisdiction when exercising judicial or quasi-judicial powers.

Mandamus is an order to perform public duties or to exercise statutory powers. It may be issued against inferior courts, tribunals and public office-holders where they wrongfully refuse to deal with a dispute within their jurisdiction, or fail to fulfil other statutory duties.

In 1980, one hundred and twenty six prerogative orders were issued; thirty of mandamus, seven of prohibition and eighty-four of certiorari.

In addition, the courts will assume, in the absence of express provisions to the contrary, that any powers conferred by statute, whether quasi-judicial or purely administrative, must be exercised reasonably, without negligence, taking into account all relevant matters and following any conditions and procedures which may be specified. Thus, whilst a judicial element must be shown before the High Court can exercise its supervisory powers by prerogative order, purely administrative governmental decisions are also, to a limited extent, open to judicial review. However, in the final analysis the courts cannot nor should not control policy decisions to any greater extent. As Professor Jackson says in his book *The Machinery of Justice in England*, "It is quite as necessary to provide against being ruled by judges as it is to guard against being judged by ministers."

Administrative supervision
Responsibility for supervising parts of the machinery of government and administrative tribunals is shared between the Council on Tribunals and the Parliamentary Commissioner for Administration (the "Ombudsman").

The Council on Tribunals. The Council was established in 1958 to review the constitution and working of tribunals and inquiries. It must be consulted about procedural rules relating to them and it can make recommendations on its own initiative to the Lord Chancellor. Although its investigations rarely have any effect on decisions already made, substantiated complaints generally lead to improvements in procedure for the future. The raising of procedural standards is, therefore, the main function of the Council.

The Ombudsman. The office of Parliamentary Commissioner for Administration (the "Ombudsman") was established by statute in 1967. He is appointed by the Crown and investigates complaints of injustice caused by maladministration, in particular the failure of government departments to observe proper standards of administration where it falls short of actual illegality. He has no direct powers in relation to tribunals and cannot entertain complaints about the way they reach decisions, but he can investigate complaints of maladministration which prejudiced a case which went to a tribunal. In addition he can refer complaints concerning them to the Council on Tribunals of which he is a member.

The Ombudsman's jurisdiction is limited to complaints of maladministration in central government, excluding public corporations and the armed services, and he will only deal with complaints brought to him by Members of Parliament. Most of the relatively few complaints upheld (one hundred and ten in 1980) have been cases of unjustifiable delay.

He has no power to annul decisions which have been made but by making representations he may obtain forms of redress which no court could give. For example, he may be able to persuade a government department to reconsider a particular case, such as re-opening a planning inquiry, or possibly obtain an *ex gratia* payment where an administrative decision is irrevocable. In most cases investigation of a complaint has resulted in the proceedings at fault being improved.

Ombudsmen have also been appointed to investigate complaints of maladministration in the national health service and local government. In the latter case the complaints must be made through local councillors. This would seem to reduce the effectiveness of the supervision in that the complaints are essentially against the work or the responsibilities of the councillors themselves. In the year April to April, 1979–80, the three local government ombudsmen had 2,181 complaints referred to them.

CONCLUSION

In this chapter we have discussed judicial and quasi-judicial conflict resolving processes and, to a lesser extent, administrative decision-making. Whilst the discussion has been general, organisations are directly affected by these processes as much if not more than private individuals.

Arbitration, both in its traditional form and in its modern "official" role in the county courts and by ACAS, is without major critics. The judicial process of the courts, the quasi-judicial process of administrative tribunals, administrative decision-making and their interrelationship are, however, the subject of some controversy.

The distinction between courts and administrative tribunals is one of age rather than function, and the deficiencies apparent in the former when faced with the socio-legal conflicts of a complex industrial society led to the growth of the latter. Whilst it is wrong in principle to be either ruled by judges or judged by administrators, an element of discretion is sometimes essential in conflict resolving and a judicial element is sometimes necessary in administrative decision-making. The courts, bound by precedent, are rarely able to exercise any real discretion but most tribunals are able to consider "policy" alongside rules of law to some extent. In contrast, administrative decisions are based on policy rather than rules of law and, whilst any judicial element in such decisions is subject to judicial review, policy decision-making is, and indeed should be, ultimately controlled through the ballot box.

A valid distinction can be drawn between judicial and quasi-judicial conflict resolving by courts and tribunals, and administrative decision-making by the government or its agents. The former presupposes a dispute between two parties and the resolution of it, according to rules of law, by a third. The latter primarily involves policy decisions taken to achieve socio-economic or political objectives, although they may also involve a conflict between individuals and organisations, or between the government and individual or organisations. For reasons of principle and practice, administrative decision-making must remain separate from judicial and quasi-judicial conflict resolving processes. However, can the same be said for the latter? Tribunals can be considered a more modern form of court, differing from traditional courts more in procedure than function, and perhaps, therefore, moves may possibly be made towards a merger of the two systems in the future.

SELF-ASSESSMENT QUESTIONS

A. 1. Define the following: (*a*) summary and indictable offences; (*b*) quasi-judicial bodies; (*c*) arbitration; (*d*) the "rule of law".

2. List the advantages of (*a*) the judicial process and (*b*) administrative tribunals.

B. 3. True or false?

(*a*) The High Court has exclusive jurisdiction in all civil disputes.

(*b*) Only summary offences can be tried in the magistrates' courts.

(*c*) The House of Lords is the final court of appeal for all cases in the UK.

(*d*) The Ombudsman exercises direct control over administrative tribunals.

4. Distinguish between quasi-judicial and administrative decision-making.

C. 5. Explain the different circumstances in which business organisations may become involved with quasi-judicial bodies.

6. Examine the likely effects of making legal aid available in disputes referred to arbitration or heard by tribunals.

ASSIGNMENTS

1. Draft an information sheet fully explaining eligibility for legal aid.

2. Using the *Judicial Statistics* (HMSO), construct graphs or charts to show fluctuations in the number and/or types of actions commenced in the High Court and/or county courts.

CHAPTER TWENTY-SIX

How Government Policies are Formed

CHAPTER OBJECTIVES

After studying this chapter you should be able to:
* describe how policies are formed within government departments;
* explain the paradox of party difference;
* state the functions of the Law Commission;
* explain how pressure groups influence government policy-making;
* outline the reasons for the growth in the political power of trade unions;
* explain the importance of the media;
* identify external influences on government policy.

R. A. Butler defined politics as the "art of the possible". Therefore, when we examine the formulation of government policy, we will find that it is a combination of what the government would like to do, what it is persuaded to do and what is practicable. We will now consider the process of policy formation and the influences upon it.

POLICY FORMATION

Within government departments

The Treasury is usually considered the most important of the departments of state, the *primus inter pares*, as Professor Hood Phillips described it. The Treasury supervises and controls all public finance. It regulates taxation and controls government expenditure. This fiscal policy we often regard as the most important of its functions. As well as this supervision of the economy, it has to arrange the day to day financing of the public services. In addition to this it is also responsible for the establishment, that is to say the staffing, of all other departments. Most other departments try not to upset the Treasury, although they are often engaged in battles with it about their budgets.

There is no Department of Economics in Britain, i.e. no department responsible for the formulation of plans for the whole economy. Such a Department was formed in 1964 and was headed by

Lord George-Brown. Three years later it had been wound up and the residue of its functions transferred to the Treasury. Many people would argue that the Treasury is ill-suited for this role. By its very nature the Treasury is a watch-dog ministry, always trying to cut down on the other departments' expenditure. This is, of course, a vital task, but on the other hand it can be argued that we need a ministry to push for expansion and to act in the Cabinet as a lobby for growth. No individual minister at present can stand up to the Chancellor of the Exchequer other than the Prime Minister.

A government is, supposedly, elected to implement the policies it fought the election on. In practice they may be very vague and unformulated. Even when a government has a clear idea of what it wishes to do it is the Civil Service who have to formulate the detail of the legislation and implement it. How successful a minister is will to some extent depend upon the relationship between himself and his civil servants. It could be argued that civil servants have helped to prevent a lot of damage to the economy by protecting it from the vacillation of government policies. This continuity of policy is a good thing. On the other hand, a minister who is trying to implement a radical policy is almost bound to encounter opposition from the Civil Service whatever the merits of the policy. This is not helped by frequent changes of minister within a government and by the fact that most ministers are not experts in the area which they are supposed to govern.

We have, so far, supposed that a government has come to power with a policy formed by discussion and decision by its party conferences etc. However, there are often abrupt changes of direction in policy as a government encounters new or recurring problems. Under these circumstances policy is going to be determined at cabinet level, by the interplay of personalities within the cabinet, their party advisers and senior civil servants. The government, however, is also subject to pressures from outside, not least from its own party.

Political parties

If we assume that it is the political party in power which governs the country, then we could say that there are four possibilities for control of the party: Firstly, that it is controlled by the leader; secondly, by Members of Parliament of that party; thirdly, by party activists; or finally we could imagine that it is controlled by voters.

This picture may well be modified if there is a breakdown of the traditional two-party system as now seems quite likely. The domination of politics by the two major parties since the Second World War has given rise to what David Butler has termed the *paradox of*

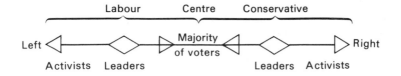

Fig. 121. *The paradox of party difference.*

party difference. He argued that party leaders are more extreme than electors but much less extreme than the activists in their own party (*see* Fig. 121). The democratisation of party structure in recent years has tended to make policies more extreme, as has the decline in party membership. Thus, party leaders are usually pulled towards the centre to please voters but to extremes to please their parties.

Whilst in opposition a political party will tend to become more extreme because it relies heavily on its party activists, and also, perhaps, because it does not have to implement its policies. It is also more difficult for the leader to keep the party in line. Once a party is in office much greater power is conferred upon the leadership because the leader is the bestower of government posts and patronage, and because the policy must be made acceptable to the electorate.

The same principle applies to MPs. Whilst out of office the party leadership is much more amenable to MPs' opinions, but once in power the leader is in an almost unassailable position. Thus, whilst a government is in power the decision-making ability tends to move from the party in general towards its leaders, centring upon the Prime Minister and the "inner Cabinet". This, Butler argued, brings it more to the consensus view of the voters. In opposition, power passes back the other way towards the party, but this takes the party away from the average voter. This could be seen as highly desirable for it seems to leave power with the middle of the road consensus. It could not be argued, however, that this was the case during the 1979 Conservative Thatcher administration. Certainly the Labour party became more extreme in opposition but the government stuck to its radical policies, alienating many within its own party as well as the electorate. This extremism on the part of both the traditional parties was a major factor in the rise of the SDP/Liberal alliance.

When we examine the economic policies of governments over recent years we see that they are subject to severe fluctuations. This, everyone admits, has a deleterious effect upon the economy. These fluctuations could be as a result of *adversary politics*, which is the tendency for one party to automatically assume the opposite point of view to the other. Over an issue like Northern Ireland both major parties agree that dispute would be a bad thing and both parties therefore support government policy. We do not seem to be able to agree that the management of the economy is a question of equal seriousness. Whatever one's politics it must be admitted that frequent changes in policy towards investment, inflation, employment and economic growth are the worst of both worlds (*see* also page 559). It could be argued that one way to avoid this would be to abolish the present "first past the post" method of elections to Parliament and replace it with some form of *proportional representation*. Both the Labour and Conservative parties, however, are resolutely opposed to this. If, as seems quite likely, there is no overall majority in a future Parliament, it could be that the SDP/Liberal alliance will insist upon proportional representation as their price for supporting one of the other parties. The possibility exists, however, that they may be strong enough to form their own government in which case proportional representation may seem less attractive to them.

Since 1951 the percentage of votes cast for the two major parties has declined from 96.8 per cent to 80.8 per cent in 1979. On the other hand the seats they control in Parliament have declined from 99 per cent to 94 per cent. However, by the end of 1981 twenty-two Labour MPs and one Conservative MP had defected to the SDP. Many people argued that this constituted the breaking of the mould of traditional politics and the start of a new era. It remains to be seen whether this is true but, on the basis of current trends, a hung Parliament is likely within the foreseeable future. This being the case, a change of the voting system to some form of proportional representation would possibly result. It is possible that this could lead us to some sort of consensus policy-making and the elimination of dangerous vacillations in policy. On the other hand it could lead to a permanent stalemate which would tend to place more power in the hands of bureaucrats rather than elected representatives.

The government and law reform

In 1974 Lord Scarman, the first Chairman of the Law Commission (from 1965 to 1972), warned in the *Hamlyn Lectures* at London University that our legal system fails to meet the challenge of today's society because it has not adjusted to the social, political and economic changes of the post-war world. In particular he questioned the ability of the *common law* system, moulded in very different times, to cope with modern socio-legal problems, e.g. "A law of torts, a land law, and a family law conceived on common law principles, however admirable in substance, cannot effectively protect the general public or the weak, the poor, the aged and the sick."

He chose five areas where he saw the present law as being particularly inadequate: human rights; matters arising from membership of the EEC; the environment; industrial relations; and constitutional devolution to the regions. Scarman's conclusion was that if the influence of law and the *rule of law* continues to decline, the administrative authorities will become dominant. Control over their decisions will be exercised by the government itself and not by the courts. The citizen would have no effective way to challenge governmental or administrative acts.

Amongst other cures for these consequences, Scarman proposed a new constitutional settlement, with provisions protecting it from administrative power and legislation by bare Parliamentary majority; a new supreme constitutional court; and immediate study of the possibility and problems of further statutory codification of the law. "Look to the new sources and fields of law and endeavour to retain the spirit of the old while abandoning habits of thought and action from a society that no longer exists." It is probably a truism to say that the law must adapt to meet the needs of a changing society for "if the law does not adapt and adjust, it will be rejected".

We cannot discuss such problems in depth in this book but it is clear that organisations either are directly or indirectly the cause of Scarman's worries, or directly or indirectly affected by the consequences that he foresees.

The power to change the law to resolve new socio-legal problems and more effectively protect and enforce existing rights and duties lies with Parliament, or more correctly, perhaps, with the government. Whilst judges may mould and modify particular aspects of the law, sometimes in effect "creating" new principles, e.g. the rule in *Rylands* v. *Fletcher* (1868) and the "neighbour" principle of *Donoghue* v. *Stevenson* (1932) they cannot nor should not openly affect fundamental changes either in principles or procedures.

Each government will undertake general law reform according to its own social, political and economic ideologies. This it will do by legislation, which it will then use to pursue its objectives. However, in those areas of law which are not openly political, the government now looks mainly to the Law Commission to propose reform. Examples of statutes mentioned in this book which were the direct result of Law Commission proposals are the Town and Country and Planning Act 1971 and the Unfair Contract Terms Act 1977.

The Law Commission was established by Act of Parliament in 1965 as a permanent full-time law reform agency. It consists of a chairman and four other commissioners who hold office for five years, and can be reappointed. It is charged to keep the law under review with the aim of systematic development and reform, including, in particular, codification, the elimination of anomalies, the repeal of obsolete enactments, consolidation and generally the simplification and modernisation of the law. To do this it has the authority to prepare programmes of consolidation and statute law revision, and to undertake the preparation of draft Bills. It may also advise government departments and other organisations at the instance of the government, and propose reform of any breach of the law.

There are, in addition to the Law Commission, several other standing bodies concerned with law reform, e.g. the Criminal Law Revision Committee which was responsible for the Theft Act 1968, and the Law Reform Committee which was responsible for the Occupiers' Liability Act 1957 and the Misrepresentation Act 1967. Both, however, are part-time bodies and the former is effectively moribund. Over the years there have also been innumerable departmental committees and royal commissions to look at particular aspects of law and the machinery of justice. However, of greater interest perhaps is the work and activities of the many "legal" *pressure groups* such as "Justice" (the British section of the International Commission of Jurists), "LAG" (the Legal Action Group), the Society of Labour Lawyers; and the Inns of Court Conservative and Unionist Association. In addition, the 1981 reform in the county court arbitration procedure was a direct result of pressure from the National Consumer Council.

Effective agencies of law reform exist and informed discussion takes place, but it should be remembered that:

(*a*) official law reform agencies are, and pressure groups tend to be, dominated by senior lawyers (part of the "establishment") who may not reflect the views of the "rank and file"; and

(*b*) effective reform depends upon the government's willingness to give Parliamentary time to the proposals.

INFLUENCES ON POLICY FORMATION

Pressure groups

Pressure (or interest) groups number many thousands and exist in all aspects of social, economic and political activity. Whilst their specific objectives and activities are probably incapable of definitive classification, they all exist to articulate ideas, interests and values, and by so doing hope to influence the government's decision and policy-making processes. They are a medium through which the government is made aware of the views of a section of the public or of organisations. Some, like the TUC and CBI, are of national importance and their activities can be seen to have a direct effect on the government and other organisations; others achieve temporary prominence and sometimes resounding individual success, e.g. the "anti-airport" groups in the Wing and Foulness areas. Most, however, pursue their own interests quietly and steadily, relatively unnoticed by the public.

Pressure groups may be distinguished from political parties in that they do not seek "office" in order to acquire political power, do not present a programme covering a wide range of political issues and may exist to exert their influence against non-governmental organisations. In addition, a major function of many, e.g. trade unions, is the provision of services for their members.

The role of pressure groups
Whilst Parliament is the real main formal institution for the representation of interests, MPs have become increasingly unable to represent and reconcile the ever more diverse and often conflicting interests present in modern society. The two major political parties are each traditionally identified with sectional interests, but these interests are often too general. Pressure groups provide continuous protection of far more specific interests which a government, constrained by wider political considerations and a maximum term of office, cannot. In particular, many pressure groups are a response to increasing government intervention in the economy, and they seek to influence government policy to their own advantage.

Types of pressure groups
Pressure groups are most easily classified on functional criteria.

Sectional groups. Such groups exist to promote the common economic interests of their members, e.g. trade unions and employers' associations are sectional groups. In addition, they will normally provide a range of services for their members.

Promotional groups. These are established to fight for particular causes, e.g. the various anti-airport or motorway groups and other environmentalist groups such as Friends of the Earth. Most are short-lived.

Other groups. Many other organisations, ranging from a local youth club to a large company, may find themselves fulfilling the functions of a pressure group through circumstances rather than choice. For example, they may be forced to promote their interest where limited resources are being allocated or where a local planning enquiry directly threatens them.

How pressure groups operate

The initial task of any pressure group is to *determine the interest* which it will promote and protect. It generally follows that the difficulty in doing this increases in proportion to the size of the group. Indeed, there may be directly conflicting interests to be resolved within a group. The CBI, for example, must reconcile its support for members in difficulty who may need government assistance, with its basic philosophy of free enterprise. So too must the TUC, e.g. excessive pay rises now may mean unemployment later.

A pressure group will partly determine the interests to promote by collecting information from its members. This in turn can be used to support its representations at a later date. The information will be collected in four main ways:

(*a*) *case studies*—these are particularly common in trade union activities;

(*b*) *specialist publications*, in particular their correspondence columns—publications such as the *British Medical Journal* of the British Medical Association are extremely influential;

(*c*) *surveys;* and

(*d*) *requests for information* from local and central government.

The second task is the *transmission* of their interest into the political or decision-making process. The target will depend upon the nature of the interest. Nationally it would be aimed at the EEC, the government and the central administration, Parliament, or the public. Locally it would be aimed at the council, or perhaps the management of a company, e.g. one involved in a pay or redundancy dispute with its employees.

Three main techniques exist for this transmission of ideas.

(*a*) *Propaganda.* This could take the form of public meetings, publicity exercises, advertising, etc. It will have three main objectives:

(*i*) to increase public awareness of and interest in the group;

(*ii*) to influence public opinion; and

(*iii*) to increase membership of the group itself.

The ultimate aim of all propaganda is to increase the political influence of the pressure group.

(*b*) *Representation*. This technique consists of direct communication with decision- and policy-makers. It is usually more effective than propaganda (which will tend to be used by groups without "contacts") and the relevant authorities are often receptive to representations which they consider could prevent problems or confrontations arising in the future.

Organised links exist between nationally important groups, such as trade unions and employers' associations, and government, Parliament and administration. Indeed, relatively obscure groups may be able to acquire such links either by direct retainers to MPs or buying the services of specialist public relations organisations. The extensive links between the Association of Metropolitan Authorities and central government and administration are a prime example of how such links may effectively promote group interests.

For pressure groups "recognised" and regularly consulted by government, achieving direct communication is not a great problem, but other groups can only do this through giving evidence before Royal Commissions and inquiries, and by lobbying Parliament and individual MPs (although the last technique is often more effective as a propaganda exercise). Undoubtedly, the most effective lobbying is done behind the scenes.

Whilst its structure and methods of operation are hard to define, the diverse but regular system of contacts among the government, administration, business organisations, trade unions and other well-organised pressure groups, is often termed the "Establishment".

(*c*) *Supply of information*. This technique increases public awareness of the group's interests and usually has a valuable propaganda function. In particular, a pressure group can seek to influence an MP's opinion by supplying information which he has insufficient time and resources to acquire himself.

Pressure groups are rarely successful if their interest is contrary to the wider political interest. Sometimes opposing pressure groups seem to counteract each other, the CBI and the TUC being the classic examples. The CBI urges the government to restore the profit incentive to the economy as the means of regenerating economic activity, and the TUC promotes policies designed to create more jobs and curb price rises. Such giants are well-matched, but in other areas of conflict the pressure group with the better organisation and finance will normally win.

As a socio-political phenomenon, pressure groups are of considerable importance. By acquiring political power and influence in policy and decision-making, they are able to affect the activities of both the government and other organisations. Although this effect may be difficult to quantify, the very fact that so many pressure groups exist and that so much time and money is put into their work is proof that a great many people believe their effect to be considerable.

The existence of powerful and successful pressure groups raises important questions about the nature and equality of representation in the UK. Should MPs be allowed to accept fees for acting on their behalf and should professional public relations organisations be able to use their Parliamentary contacts to further commerical interests by getting clauses inserted into a Bill already allocated Parliamentary time? Do government departments accept the advice of powerful pressure groups too uncritically, possibly at the expense of the wider public interest, and should they take such notice of the views of bodies which may be inherently undemocratic? Perhaps above all else, given that pressure groups cannot actually control policy and decision-making, the fact that so much representation goes on behind the scenes gives some cause for concern.

The political power of trade unions

A feature of politics since the mid-1960s has been the dramatic increase in trade union power, and consequently in their influence over political policy and decision making processes. The clash between the Conservative government and the miners in the winter of 1973–4 was the climax of this growth and, in the general election of February 1974, led to the election of a Labour government which was more sympathetic to union objectives. However, even the Labour government discovered that the need to gain the co-operation of the unions in economic policy gave the unions new and unprecedented influence over government policy and decision-making. For these reasons, the Conservative government, elected in 1979, tried to reduce the influence of trade unions.

Most major unions are affiliated to the Labour Party and it is within the Party that they exercise their *direct* political influence. Their political levies provide most of the Labour Party's funds (even though most union members are politically apathetic), and trade unions control the National Executive Council of the Labour Party and some 85 per cent of the votes at the Party Conference. However, neither the NEC nor the Party Conference control the Parliamentary Labour Party. The party leaders are elected by an electoral college consisting of the trade unions, the constituency parties and the MPs. There have also been attempts to make Party Conference decisions binding upon the Parliamentary Labour Party. Within Parliament unions sponsor about 40 per cent of Labour MPs and give financial assistance to many others, although they have not, as yet, sought to control their votes. Since 1972 direct links have existed between the Party and the TUC through the TUC–Labour Party Liaison Committee. The Trade Union and Labour Relations Act 1974 was a product of this link.

Since 1970, however, trade unions' recognition of their industrial power, and hence their *indirect* political power, has introduced a very important new element into union influence in political policy and decision-making. Increased industrial power has been the result of a combination of factors, e.g. the growth in trade union membership, the realisation that a few key workers can totally disrupt whole sections of the economy, increased willingness to strike for more pay because of fear of inflation, and the willingness of employers to concede large pay claims when faced with the possibility of long and damaging strikes, although very recently the fear of redundancy has tempered union militancy.

It is generally agreed that the 1970–4 Conservative government badly underestimated this increased industrial muscle and tried to impose legal restraints upon it by the Industrial Relations Act 1971. This became the focus for a trial of strength between government and unions which the unions won. Government concessions to the unions followed in order to gain their support for income policies. Eventually, however, the miners' strike directly challenged government policy and was largely responsible for the government's defeat in the general election of February 1974. The new Labour government chose to work openly with the unions of the basis of the "social contract". This theoretically meant lower wage demands in return for legislation and reforms supported by the unions, e.g. repeal of the Industrial Relations Act 1971 and the passing of the Employment Protection Act 1975. However, despite initial willingness and government "carrots", such as raising tax thresholds to help the poorly paid, trade unions since 1974 have become increasingly reluctant to co-operate with the government over pay policies. They want a return to "free collective bargaining".

The Labour government was for a time able to rely on public opinion and union fear of a Conservative victory at a general election to pursue policies, including wage restraint, but in the end the unions refused to accept further restraint. The resulting conflict became known as the "winter of discontent" and was a major factor in the defeat of the Labour government at the polls in June 1979. The incoming Conservative government sought no co-operation with the unions; rather it began to attack the privileges and influence they had acquired in the previous five years. The government skilfully avoided conflict with the more powerful unions, such as the miners, for the first two years of its office. In addition to this, unemployment escalating beyond three million dampened wage

demands, reduced trade-union membership and decreased the willingness to strike.

The media

When you watched the "news" or a current affairs programme on
TV last night, or listened to a news broadcast or read your newspaper this morning, you were receiving neatly packaged information likely to affect your views on contemporary political issues. It
follows that the *media*—the press, TV and radio—not only spreads
awareness of political issues by reporting them but also influences
policy and decision-making by manipulating public opinion.
Deliberate mis-reporting is unnecessary to achieve this; careful
selection of news and views is quite sufficient to influence public
opinion and promote certain causes. In turn the media can be used
as effective propaganda organs by policy and decision-makers
themselves.

In party political terms, radio and TV must by law endeavour to
remain neutral in their coverage of political events and issues.
Nevertheless, the BBC tends to be a mouthpiece for the "establishment" and commercial broadcasting companies must take into account the views of their advertisers. Some commercial broadcasting
companies make donations to Conservative Party funds.

Newspapers are often openly partisan. Amongst the "popular"
press, the *Daily Mail* and the *Sun* are Conservative while the *Daily
Mirror* usually supports Labour policy. The same is true of the
"quality" papers; the *Daily Telegraph* is openly right-wing, the
Guardian espouses Liberal policies and *The Times*, whilst being the
most objective, still tends to be conservative with a small "c".
Amongst the weeklies the *Spectator* is Conservative, the *New
Statesman* socialist and *The Economist* supports policies which
further the interests of "big business".

A wide range of extreme partisan publications also exist, e.g. the
Morning Star and *Socialist Worker*, but because they have small
circulations and usually preach to the converted, they tend to have
little impact on "opinion". In addition, there are many "fringe"
publications such as *New Left Review* and the *Leveller*.

Political partiality in reporting is not necessarily undesirable, but
there is a danger in the frequency with which it is reported as hard
fact. You should always remember this partiality when reading
political comment in newspapers.

The media's influence on public opinion is recognised and exploited by politicians, in part as a response to the potential power
of the media to undermine the politicians' own positions. Suitable
images for party leaders are projected via professional public rela-

tions organisations and the effect of news reports can be influenced through carefully calculated disclosures of information. The "lobby correspondent" system is one of the best ways of doing this. Under this system certain correspondents have free access to the Members' Lobby in Parliament and receive briefings from members of the government. Providing they do not quote their sources they can use this information in their reports. In turn, politicians gain much of their own information from the "quality" newspapers and weeklies. Thus, influence exists in both directions.

Perhaps the power of the media is best demonstrated by the extreme censorship it suffers in many undemocratic states, and how in any political coup control of the media is always one of the first objectives.

External influences

In the nineteenth century Great Britain "ruled the waves" and governments could formulate policies without taking much notice of influences outside the UK itself. Today the situation is very different: the UK is just one industrialised country among many, and the government and the other organisations are increasingly influenced by bodies external to the economy. Particularly good examples include the EEC, NATO, OPEC and the IMF (*see* Chapter 20).

THE ORGANISATION, THE STATE AND THE COMMUNITY

It has been our intention to show that the organisation is not a passive bystander, waiting to have government policy imposed upon it, but a cog in the machine which determines that policy. The primary factor which will influence the economic well-being of the business organisation is the general state of the economy. These days this is acknowledged to be the responsibility of the government. On the other hand, the health of the economy also depends upon the enterprise and the initiative of organisations.

Organisations are subject to much legislation which they may at first resent. An example of this may be the Health and Safety at Work, etc., Act 1974. However, we might compare this situation to that in the nineteenth century when factory owners warned the government that reducing the working day to ten hours would be the ruination of the country. We now realise that such legislation was essential and improved the economy rather than harmed it. Thus, in the long run it is hoped that any of the inconveniences of new legislation will be offset by its benefits.

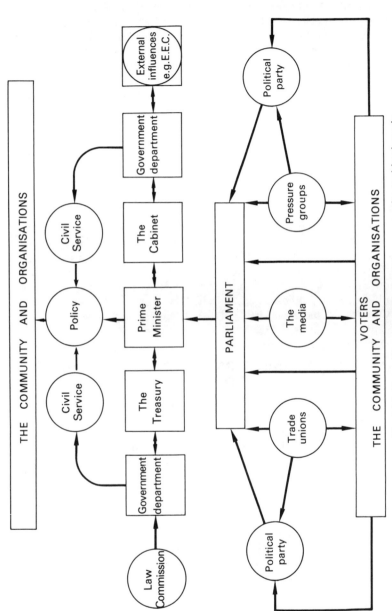

Fig. 122. *The policy machine: from the community and back again.*

In addition; business organisations receive much direct help and benefit from the government. Examples of this include the ECGD, the National Enterprise Board, regional development grants and ACAS. In a sense the government could be said to provide an organisational framework within which business organisations can operate.

This illustrates a basic argument of the book, which is that organisations cannot be viewed as individual economic phenomena nor studied in academically isolated disciplines. The market economy of Adam Smith is no longer, business organisations operate in a mixed economy which is not so much a compromise between, but rather a compound of, collectivism and capitalism, possessing its own separate character and properties. Within the mixed economy an amalgam of diverse social, economic and political forces determines government policy (*see* Fig. 122). Organisations are both the subject of government policy and a factor in its formation. In the words of Galbraith, organisations "influence government, influence the consumer. Only the textbooks hold otherwise."

SELF-ASSESSMENT QUESTIONS

A. 1. Define: (*a*) adversary politics; (*b*) consensus; (*c*) a lobby correspondent; (*d*) the media.

2. List the ways in which a pressure group transmits its ideas.

3. List the external institutions which influence government policy-making.

B. 4. True or false?

(*a*) The detail of government policy is formulated by the Civil Service.

(*b*) The "paradox of party difference" is that political parties always assume opposing viewpoints.

(*c*) The Law Commission is the only official law reform agency.

(*d*) Political parties and pressure groups fulfil the same functions.

(*e*) "Justice" is a pressure group.

(*f*) The trade union movement provides most of the Labour Party's funds.

ASSIGNMENTS

1. Construct a diagrammatic representation of the present composition of the House of Commons.

2. Discuss the argument that some decisions are too important to be decided by party politics.

3. Examine the different ways in which election to the House of Commons might take place if the present system was reformed.

4. Report on the activities of a local pressure group.

5. Compare and contrast different newspaper reports of the same political news story.

Index